# The Cornish Overseas

Philip Payton

# The Cornish Overseas

## A History of Cornwall's 'Great Emigration'

CORNWALL EDITIONS
FOWEY

To the memory of my mother
Hazel May Payton
1923–2004
And for my father
Tom Payton

CORNWALL EDITIONS LIMITED
8 Langurtho Road
Fowey  Cornwall  PL23 1EQ  UK
01726 832483
www.cornwalleditions.co.uk
Publisher: Ian Grant
This edition first published in 2005.

ISBN 1-904880-04-5

Art Director: Roger Bristow
Text editor: Luzette Strauss
Maps by Arka Cartographics
Index by Sue Lightfoot

The publishers thank Bob Crossley for permission to reproduce his painting
*Landscape* on the front cover of this book.

Typeset in 10/14 pt Minion Regular and Frutiger
Printed and bound in the United Kingdom

Papers used by Cornwall Editions are natural, recyclable products made from
wood grown in sustainable forests; the manufacturing processes conform to
the environmental regulations of the country of origin.

# CONTENTS

# ACKNOWLEDGEMENTS

In preparing this second edition of *The Cornish Overseas* I remain indebted to the countless individuals who helped me to prepare the first. Not least are the many people of Cornish descent at home and abroad who readily shared their own family histories, generously lent me material to be incorporated into my narrative and went out of their way to show me around the Cornish mining country of Australia and America. I am similarly indebted to those authors and publishers who allowed me to draw from their own work, as acknowledged here in detail in the notes and references to each chapter. If by chance any have been overlooked, correction will be made in subsequent editions of the book.

I owe the Cornwall Editions team a particular debt for their enthusiasm for a revised, paperback edition and for their encouragement and assistance in bringing the project to fruition. Ian Grant, especially, was a constant source of sage advice; his editorial and diplomatic skills combined to ensure that the text has been immeasurably polished and improved.

And, as ever, I owe a huge debt of gratitude to my family. My daughters – Brigid and Unity – accompanied me on visits to Moonta, Grass Valley and other sites of international Cornish significance. My mother – a Williams on both sides of her family – had long-lost relatives in South Africa, America, Mexico and New South Wales, and was herself a Cousin Jenny, living variously in Western Australia, New South Wales and South Australia. Alas, she did not live to see this second edition of a book of which she was so very proud – and of which she felt a part – but her ashes rest in the churchyard in Constantine. This is Williams country and the place of origin of a great many granite quarrymen, engineers, copper miners and agriculturalists and their families who went overseas in the 19th and early 20th centuries. My father, a merchant seaman in the Second World War and its aftermath, had sailed in the wake of that earlier generation of emigrants to America, Australia and New Zealand. In the 1950s he became a 'Ten Pound Pom' – as we all did. My sister Jackie was born in Perth, Western Australia, a child of the diaspora.

# ACKNOWLEDGEMENTS

My wife Deidre, part of the Irish diaspora, has empathised with the global dispersal of the Cornish, deploying pan-Celtic sympathy to adopt Cornwall as her other home and venturing enthusiastically with me into the arid expanses of Nevada and outback New South Wales in search of traces of Cornishry.

Philip Payton
Bodmin, 2004

# INTRODUCTION

ornwall is one of the great emigration regions of Europe.[1] First and foremost a maritime land, with links to a greater world beyond these islands stretching back even into prehistoric times, Cornwall has experienced at least two great waves of emigration in its long history. The first is shrouded in mystery, that still unexplained Dark Age exodus from south-western Britain which – somewhere between the 4th and 6th centuries AD – took hundreds, possibly thousands of settlers to the Armorican peninsula, present-day Brittany. Although its origins are obscure, the results of this emigration are everywhere apparent – not only in the common placenames and saints' dedications that are evidence of the long historical entwinement of Cornwall and Brittany but in the expressions of present-day pan-Celtic sentiment which range from the twinning of Cornish and Breton towns to the formal regional accord between Cornwall County Council and the Département of Finistère.

The second wave of mass Cornish emigration, that wholesale scattering of so-called Cousin Jacks and Jennies known to modern scholars as the 'Great Emigration', is a far more recent phenomenon – running for little more than a century from 1815 until the First World War and after – but it has been truly global in its impact and may have consequences which even now are not fully played-out, let alone fully understood. Cornish historians have long recognised the international significance of the Great Emigration. A.L. Rowse considered that 'the story of the Cornish emigration is the biggest and most significant of Cornish themes',[2] a claim that he put to the test in *The Cornish in America*, published in 1969. A.C. Todd and John Rowe – those two other founding fathers of Cornish emigration history – also helped to pioneer the study of the Cornish abroad, pointing the way for later writers who would take the story beyond the United States and Mexico to encompass Australia, South Africa, South America and elsewhere. Yet it is only very recently that we have been able to construct an overview of the Great Emigration in its entirety, to pull together the numerous strands of an extraordinarily complex and intriguing phenomenon. The result is this present volume: *The Cornish Overseas*.[3]

Cornwall's Great Emigration is best explained against the background – and as part – of a wider European emigration which ran from 1815 until the Depression years of the 1930s. This emigration created the ethnic and cultural complexity of the

'New World' in its widest geographical and political sense and facilitated the construction of the increasingly industrial international economy and the international labour market which supported it. But the Great Emigration was also distinctive. As well as its sheer volume, absolute as well as relative, it had particular characteristics which often set Cornwall apart from otherwise comparable European emigration regions and which ensured that emigration would exercise a profound influence over the making of modern Cornwall. Even today, Cornwall lives under the shadow of its Great Emigration, while the growing visibility of overseas Cornish communities is vivid testament to an enduring (if re-defining) Cornish ethnic identity located amidst the multicultural societies of America, Australia and elsewhere.

In 1815 Europe had emerged from the long struggle of the French revolutionary and Napoleonic wars into a 'new world order' which promised peace, security and stability. The Congress of Vienna, set up by the victorious powers, Britain, Prussia, Austria and Russia, reviewed and settled the political boundaries and structures of Europe, ushering in a period of conservative dominance which resisted further revolutionary impulses. Between 1815 and 1848 Europe enjoyed an unprecedented period of peace, with no armed conflict between its principal powers and relatively few major internal upheavals – notwithstanding the achievement of Belgian independence in 1830 and the mild 'revolution' in Paris that year. On the wider canvas, British sea power underwrote this new world order through the global exercise of maritime hegemony, the *Pax Britannica*. And yet this time of peace did not bring the happy release and new-found prosperity that many people, not least in Britain, had sought so earnestly. Instead, the new peace disguised an underlying discontent, a mood of repression which in Britain would lead to the Great Reform Act of 1832 and which elsewhere in Europe erupted in the renewed revolutions of 1848.

It was within this complex and paradoxical period that the great wave of modern European emigration was born, peace and the veneer of stability providing the conditions in which the first stirrings of mass emigration might be managed, the general air of discontent furnishing at least some of the motives which drove men and women from the Old World to the New World. To this was added the enticement of the New World – the prospects of civil and religious liberty, of social and economic mobility and opportunity in newly independent countries (such as the United States and, later, those of Latin America), or in virgin colonial territories. The extraordinary doggerel of 'The Emigrant's Farewell', dating from 1838, captures something of this spirit, the quest for freedom:

From Liverpool as I before have stated
We sail'd a motley set we surely were
With coals and iron was our vessel freighted
Scotch Irish Welsh and English were there
Going out to see if emigration
Was a recipe against starvation

There were ploughboys weavers blacksmiths tailors
Irish peasants and Welsh mountaineers
Together with a family of nailors
Scotch from the lowlands and some highland seers
Butchers bakers carpenters and joiners
There were also a lot of Cornish miners

Farmers grown tired of taxes tithes and rent
Paying unto an aristocracy
Were going out their minds all fully bent
To be landowners in the states democracy
Where good land can for something less be had
Than what In England's yearly paid for bad.[4]

Thereafter, despite – or perhaps, because of – the renewed European strife of the 1850s and 1860s, when the great powers once again took up arms against each other, the European emigration ran strongly – interrupted by the First World War from 1914–18 and dwindling to a halt in the economic doldrums of the inter-war years when the depressed New World no longer thirsted for new labour. Dudley Baines has estimated that perhaps as many as 66 million people left Europe for overseas destinations in the period 1815 to 1939, between 44 and 52 million having left the continent by the outbreak of war in 1914.[5] Some 10 million had emigrated from Britain by that year, with a further seven million from neighbouring Ireland, then an integral part of the United Kingdom. At least a third of these arrived in the United States of America; the rest headed overwhelmingly for the British territories of Australia, Canada, New Zealand and South Africa.

For much of the 19th century it was northern and western Europe – Britain, Ireland, Germany, to a lesser extent Scandinavia – which provided the lion's share of these emigrants, particularly to the United States, with the mass emigration from southern and eastern Europe not featuring strongly until after 1875. The evidence suggests that in the earlier period there was a tendency for people to emigrate in families, to try to build life anew as a family group in the United States, or – more often than not in the British context – to respond to prescriptive free or assisted passage schemes which sought deliberately to recreate family structures overseas and to maintain as far as possible the balance of ages and sexes in the new colonies. By the 1870s, however, this pattern was beginning to change, with emigrants – especially young adult males – leaving increasingly as individuals. Improved communications, not least the introduction of steamships, encouraged this changing pattern and the enhanced mobility that it implied, with males travelling singly or with friends: sometimes to a succession of different destinations, and often with one or more return visits to the Old World. In this way, European emigration became all the more complex, introducing a truly international experience for some emigrants (who, for example, might spend their lives journeying between America, Australia and South Africa) and emphasising the phenomenon of 'return migration', individual migrants returning temporarily or permanently to their native homes. Perhaps as many as a quarter of all European emigrants eventually went home to the lands of their birth.

Conventionally, emigration has been explained as an interplay of 'push' and 'pull' factors, the 'push' being those which drove or persuaded people to leave their homelands, the 'pull' being those which enticed them to new destinations abroad. Of course, such an explanation assumes a degree of free will and access to both information and resources, an ability to make rational choices and then to act upon them. Some historians, however, have argued that 19th-century European labour was essentially 'unfree', and that in the global expansion of the international capitalist economy, emigrants were merely pawns directed by market forces to those parts of the world where their skills or labour were in demand at any one particular time. The truth, perhaps, lies somewhere between the traditional 'push-pull' model and the 'market forces' approach, and it is unlikely to be found in broad-sweep generalisation but rather through the painstaking collection and comparisons of individual and community experiences.

Comparisons between the experiences of different emigration regions are also instructive, and it is useful to compare Cornwall with other parts of Celtic Britain and Ireland. The increasing political integration and industrial development of the British Isles in the 18th and 19th centuries had led not to a growing homogeneity but rather to new markers of territorial 'difference' and diversity. The nature of industrialisation was itself uneven and diverse, reflecting wider inequalities in the economic and political construction of the United Kingdom, while the types of industrial activity that emerged varied markedly from region to region. South Wales was coal; Ulster, linen and shipbuilding; Lancashire, cotton; Yorkshire, wool; Clydeside and Tyneside both shipbuilding; and so on. As the Welsh historian Dai Smith put it, 'there was an explosion into industrial pre-eminence of regions as regions'.[6]

This identification of industry with place had the effect of reinforcing and re-inventing national and regional identities. This was especially so for Cornwall, where a residual sense of ethnic 'difference' was reinvigorated now by Cornish pride in the highly specialised and extremely advanced industrial activity that underpinned Cornish mining and engineering. Significantly, although many Cornish emigrants in the century were farmers or agricultural labourers, it was the miners and their families that remained noticeably 'Cornish' overseas. It was on the new mining frontiers of America, Australia and South Africa that pride in Cornish industrial prowess gave birth to the 'myth' of Cousin Jack, the belief – encouraged by the Cornish themselves – that the Cornish were innately and uniquely equipped as skilled hard-rock miners, especially when compared with competing ethnic groups. And yet, while insisting upon their 'difference', the Cornish could also claim that – unlike many other ethnic groups (including sometimes the Irish) – they were perfectly attuned to the 'Anglo-Saxon' norms of American or colonial life, able to contribute to, rather than threaten, the fledgling English-speaking and largely Protestant societies of which they were now a part.

The Welsh overseas provide an interesting comparison, for while Welsh emigrants were also drawn from a wide variety of occupations, it was those from industrial backgrounds – the coal miners, iron, steel and tinplate workers, and slate quarrymen – who were again most visible in their new host societies. Moreover, the Welsh also emphasised their industrial credentials, like the Cornish asserting their superiority over competing ethnic groups. Similarly, the Welsh were also at pains to demonstrate their social and cultural alignment with the norms of the new societies, in destinations such as Scranton in the anthracite-mining district of Pennsylvania or Ballarat in the Victorian gold-fields in Australia, projecting images of themselves and their Welshness as models of American or colonial citizenship. The Welsh saw themselves as descendants of 'Ancient Britons' – as indeed did the Cornish – and thought themselves more 'British' than the English. Their separate language marked them as 'different', but this was a difference that emphasised their aboriginal Britishness and thus their innate suitability as settlers in the New World societies.[7]

If there are strong parallels between the Cornish and Welsh experiences overseas, then there are also important comparisons to be drawn between emigration from Cornwall and that from Scotland. T.M. Devine, the Scottish historian, has drawn attention to what he has termed the 'paradox of Scottish emigration'.[8] He argued that although a dynamic, industrialising economy able to absorb labour (including from neighbouring Ireland) and to create a great many new jobs, 19th-century Scotland was nonetheless one of the principal emigration regions of Europe. Moreover, those emigrants who left Scotland in their droves were not only the dispossessed from the Highlands and Islands – fleeing famine and later the Clearances – but also large numbers of skilled workers from Lowland urban areas. The paradox is resolved, or at least explained, by the fact that these urban workers possessed exactly the industrial skills that were in great demand in the New World: where rates of pay were considerably higher than they were in Scotland.

In this Scottish explanation we also glimpse an important aspect of the Cornish experience: for highly skilled Cornish hard-rock miners were being enticed by high wages to places such as Latin America long before the copper and tin industries at home were in decline. Likewise, the decision of many Cornish to emigrate was eased by a 'culture of mobility' that had been created in Cornwall before 1815. This mirrored a similar culture that had emerged in Scotland over the same period, one which made later emigration socially acceptable – even normal – and constructed lasting overseas contacts and conduits for subsequent generations of emigrants. A further comparison is that emigrant Scots, (especially the Lowlanders) – like the Cornish and the Welsh – deployed ethnic identity to assert their particular suitability to the rigours of life on the American or colonial frontier. They stressed thrift, hardiness, determination: their Protestant work ethic. In time, in Caledonian societies across the globe, Lowlanders even affected Highland dress and manners – perhaps even a smattering of recently-learnt Gaelic – to reinforce, re-invent or perpetuate this superior New World distinctiveness: despite the traditional Lowland disdain for Highland culture at home.

Irish comparisons are more complex. Historians such as Patrick O'Farrell – in *The Irish in Australia* – have shown that the Irish were at least as distinctive and as important as the Cornish, Welsh and Scots in the growth of New World countries.[9] However, they were overwhelmingly Catholic – seen by many as a threat in English-speaking, largely Protestant societies – and their reputation as political subversives ensured that they were eyed with suspicion wherever they went in the 'Anglo-Saxon' world. Moreover, a great many Irish emigrants were from the rural poor, with fewer skills to bring to their host societies and thus fewer opportunities to deploy ethnic identity as a positive economic or social device. Often, there was no love lost between the Irish and their Celtic cousins – or, for that matter, the English themselves. So, despite their veneer of 'Anglo-Saxon' homogeneity, these New World societies were from the beginning decidedly pluralistic, with the potential for deep-seated religious, ideological or ethnic conflict between different groups with different beliefs, values and aspirations. Not all ethnic groups found it as easy as the Cornish did to conform to the norms of the new societies. But also, as we shall see later in this book, not all were prepared to allow Cornish claims to superior status to go unchallenged: conflict in the workplace between the Cornish and the Irish was to become commonplace on the mining frontiers of America and Australia.

And yet, despite their differences, the Cornish and Irish had in common – along with the Highlanders and Islanders – their traumatic experience of the 'Hungry Forties'. Both peoples suffered acutely during the potato blight of the 1840s. A million Irish emigrated and a million more died at home of starvation. In Cornwall, there was widespread hunger and want, and if people were not actually dying in the streets as they were in Ireland, this was because emigration had already become an efficient mechanism for the removal of 'surplus' population. But the 1840s were also important for Cornwall in another respect. As Bernard Deacon has argued, this was 'the decade when Cornwall decisively moved from a proto-industrial to an industrial society'.[10] However, this mid-century modernisation was all too soon arrested by the crises of the 1860s and the 1870s and the inability of the Cornish economy to diversify in the face of the crash of Cornish copper in 1866 and the subsequent faltering of Cornish tin. The Cornish experience was thus unique, a somehow 'intermediate' position between that of Ireland and of the North of England.

To understand Cornwall's 'intermediate' position, we need to appreciate those contrasting experiences of Ireland and the North of England. The 1830s and 1840s were a time of economic dislocation and unrest in Britain and Ireland as a whole and acute depression hit the economically and, after 1832, politically important north of England in 1847, also the height of the Irish potato famine. However, while Ireland was unable to recover economically from the disaster of the mid-1840s, the British manufacturing heartland of the north of England soon emerged from the dark days of the 'Hungry Forties' into the bright sunlight of mid-Victorian prosperity. The recovery of the north was marked in the Great Exhibition of 1851 – the dawn of a new era of industrial resurgence – but for Ireland 1851 was the seventh consecutive year of famine and shortage. This was a major landmark in the growing economic and political disparity between Britain and Ireland.[11]

In Cornwall, hit as it was by both the potato blight and the economic downturn of the 1840s, recovery at the end of the decade and into the early 1850s seemed to be impressive, apparently mirroring the rise of the northern industrial economy and contrasting strongly with the inability of Ireland to recover. And yet, as we know, Cornwall's taste of new-found prosperity was brief, the crises of the mining industry in the 1860s and 1870s accompanied by the first signs of de-industrialisation as the over-specialised Cornish economy failed to diversify in the face of fundamental structural change. It was this failure which prompted what A.K. Hamilton Jenkin called 'The Exodus of the Seventies', the wholesale emigration of Cornish miners, often with their families, in the decade and more after the debacle of 1866, when the bottom fell out of the international copper market. According to Hamilton Jenkin, 'During this period, the short space of a few years witnessed the breaking-up of a tradition of centuries' as a wave of emigrant Cornish folk, 'answering the call of necessity, was seeking new fields of action overseas'.[12] It was, says Gill Burke, an experience which 'dissolved old networks of custom, tradition and reciprocity'[13] in Cornwall.

However, the real, fundamental changes to Cornish society had occurred two or three decades before in the 1840s. Nowhere was this more noticeable than in the sphere of emigration, where by the 1840s an internationalised mining economy – and with it an attendant global labour market – had already emerged, a process in which Cornish mine labour was already playing a significant role. Put another way, the history of Cornwall's 'Great Emigration' is not confined to that paroxysm of departure in the 1870s, it is altogether more complex in nature, with the movement of Cornish people overseas observable as far back as 1815 and beyond.

An all-embracing 'emigration culture' had been developing apace in Cornwall in the years after 1815, a culture which left no institution or community untouched and which both legitimised emigration – as part of Cornwall's Methodist self-help, improvement ethos – and increasingly portrayed emigration as the rational choice for those seeking to escape hard times or to embrace new opportunities. At the same time, a similarly ubiquitous 'emigration trade' had grown up in Cornwall after 1815. By the 1840s this emigration trade encompassed not only the widespread movement of populations from one place to another but also the myriad pattern of socio-economic activity that arose in response to this movement. Government officials, shipping agents, shipbuilders, local provisioners, newspapers, printers, publicans, learned societies, coaching operators, clergymen, solicitors and a host of other public and business interests became directly involved in the increasingly complex mechanics of this burgeoning trade.[14]

The construction of this emigration culture and its attendant emigration trade was assisted by a pre-existing 'culture of mobility' in which the Cornish were already accustomed to move from place to place. As we shall see in Chapter 1, long before the birth of the new era of European emigration after 1815 the Cornish had settled abroad in numbers in America and Australia. They were also accustomed to movement within Cornwall itself, the miners in particular moving from one locality to another as new mines were opened or as the relative fortunes of different mines and different areas waxed and waned. In the 18th century, the population of Cornwall had gravitated towards the expanding, industrialising districts of Gwennap and Camborne-Redruth. But from 1810 the Cornish copper industry began to look outwards from the core of this 'central mining district' – eastwards to the coastal area of mid-Cornwall around St Austell, St Blazey and Fowey, and westwards to St Just-in-Penwith at the very tip of Cornwall. Then in 1836 came the spectacular discoveries of copper in the vicinity of Caradon Hill in East Cornwall, leading swiftly to the development of the new mining country around St Cleer and Linkinhorne, and in the 1840s the focus of activity moved even further east to Callington and Gunnislake, on the Cornish side of the Tamar, and across the border to the neighbourhood of Tavistock. Each of these developments was matched by a corresponding movement of scores of Cornish miners, often with their families, from one part of Cornwall to another.

Behind the statistics lie the experiences of real people. For example, John Strike was living in Lucas Row, St Cleer in 1851. He had been born in Sithney in west Cornwall in 1803, his wife Elizabeth in the neighbouring parish of Crowan. Their son John was born in Breage in 1834, evidence that they had moved a short distance in the first years of their marriage, but the birth of two daughters, in 1841 and 1845 at St Blazey, showed that they had followed the eastward drift of the copper mining industry. Later, they had moved still further east to St Cleer, residing there at the time of the 1851 census. A similar case was that of John Thomas, resident in St Cleer in 1851, who was born in St Agnes in 1801 and who had been in St Austell between 1829 and 1840.[15] Significantly, this internal migration was often a prelude to emigration abroad. In 1848, for example, the *West Briton* noted the impending departure of miners from St Cleer, bound for Australia. In 1911 the *Burra Record* newspaper in Australia sketched the career of one John Vivian. Born in St Austell in 1809, Vivian had joined the Bible Christian denomination while domiciled in Tavistock and had later lived at both Ashburton (also in Devon) and Liskeard before emigrating to South Australia in 1845 to work at the Burra Burra copper mine.[16]

Additionally, this culture of mobility had also been reflected in early movement to other parts of Britain. Before the end of the 18th century, Cornish copper miners could be found in Anglesey, while the short-lived threat that Anglesey posed to the Cornish copper industry led Boulton (of Boulton and Watt fame) to argue that Cornish miners should seek alternative employment in the Coombe Martin silver mines in Devon or in coal mines up-country. In the mid-18th century Cornishmen had been brought into Devon to revive the Dartmoor tin industry and by the 1790s Dartmoor tinners hailed from places as diverse as Wendron, Redruth, St Agnes, Gwennap and Warleggan. In the early 1800s Cornish miners were an important component of the workforce of the expanding Mary Tavy mines, near Tavistock, while the 1851 census showed that of the 76 tin miners in the parish of Lydford, some 21 were Cornish-born. By then, as A.K. Hamilton Jenkin demonstrated in *The Mines of Devon*, Cornish captains and Cornish miners had already played a major role in the development of Devon's copper deposits as well as those of lead, silver and iron – a fact echoed in the resoundingly Cornish ring of many Devon mines' names: Wheal Anna Maria, Wheal Friendship, Wheal Emma, Wheal Albert, Wheal Betsy, even Devon Burra Burra.[17]

By the early 19th century the Cornish were in Shropshire. They were also in Somerset. In 1836 Phelps noted in *History and Antiquities of Somersetshire* that the Cornish had been involved in the Mendip lead and copper industries since the turn of the century, 'about forty years since a company was formed to mine for copper on the hill [Loxton], and some miners from Cornwall were employed for a time'.[18] Earlier, in 1794, the *Gentleman's Magazine* had complained that at Loxton 'the sparry incrustations in one of the chambers ... [were] much defaced by Cornish miners who, in trying for copper a few years ago, broke off the finest pieces to send to their friends'.[19] In the mid-19th century the Cornish were still in the Mendip Hills, with Nicholas Ennor acquiring the rights in 1852 of the Priddy Minery, the tell-tale Cornish-style engine houses and stacks in the locality evidence of a Cornish technological impact. The Cornish were likewise prominent in the Derbyshire lead mines, where in the 1740s Cornish and Welsh miners were said to have introduced the art of 'buddling' (ore washing) to the Peak District and where in 1846 the Cornish were brought in to work the ailing Magpie mine at Sheldon.[20]

In the lead districts of Wales, too, the Cornish made an early and lasting impact.[21] As early as 1731 the Cornish had been responsible for re-opening the

Old Darren mine, near Aberystwyth, while Cornish captains had supervised the development in the late 18th century of workings at Rhandirmwyn on Lord Cawdor's land in Carmarthenshire. In 1813 the Halkyn mines in Denbighshire were under the management of a Cornishman, one Absolom Moore, and an upsurge of lead mining after the peace of 1815 led to a major influx of Cornish into north-east Wales. In 1826 the Pen-y-fron mine boasted Cornishmen in all its key positions and in 1828 one Holywell company paid for John Rodda and his family to come from Cornwall to run the Brynford Hall mine. In the 1820s the Cornish were active in the Penrhyn-du mines in Caernarvonshire and by the mid-19th century they were busy in the Towy Valley east of Carmarthen and in the Llanidloes district of Montgomeryshire. In 1851 there were 343 Cornish and Devon born people in Cardiganshire's mining districts and in 1871 the mid-Wales mining counties contained some 523 Cornish-born. But by then hundreds of other Cornish had found work in the coal mines of south Wales and the north of England, in the copper mines of Ireland, in the coal and iron mines of Scotland. Not for nothing had the Cornishman acquired an early reputation as the 'rambling miner' – a sobriquet preserved today in the name of a public house in the old Cornish mining village of Chacewater:

> Oh! I'm a miner stout and bold,
> Long time I've worked down underground
> To raise both tin and copper too
> For the honour of our miners.
> Now brother miners I bid you adieu
> I'll go no more to work with you
> But scour the country through and through
> And still be a rambling miner.[22]

The Cornish labour market was already internationalised by the 1840s, the modern, industrial skills of the Cornish workforce increasingly sought after on the international stage. Indeed, Baines considers that, even without the catastrophes of the 1860s and 1870s, Cornwall was destined to become a significant emigration region. He notes that, in marked contrast to every English and Welsh county, the Cornish were, despite their early impact in Wales and England, more likely to emigrate overseas than to other parts of the United Kingdom.[23] Mark Brayshay considers that 'In some ways their [Cornish] attitudes are suggestive of an "island" mentality similar to that displayed by true island dwellers such as the Hebrideans',[24] an attitude of mind also detected by Rowse: 'At home people knew what was going on in South Africa often rather better than what was happening "up the country": the journey across the seas to another continent was more familiar than going very far "up the country", say as far as London'.[25] Similarly, Claude Berry noted the telling if apocryphal story of the young St Just girl who was asked if she had ever been to Land's End, some five miles down the coast. The girl replied, 'Aw, no ... We St Just people don't travel much, only to South Africa'.[26] As Berry observed, 'Up to comparatively recent times it was by sea, and not to England, that Cornish people usually went when they left their native county. Hundreds, if not thousands, of people ... who ... emigrated from our little ports in the 19th century to Canada, or the United States, had never set foot in England; while large numbers who did cross the River Tamar went that way only to embark immediately at English ports for Australia, South Africa, or the Americas'.[27]

But the 'island mentality' of cultural and geographical isolation is only part of the explanation, for the attraction of overseas destinations was increasingly a function of sophisticated information flows and networks, which in turn prompted streams of chain emigration from particular loca-lities. Like the Scots, the Cornish were increasingly aware of international job opportunities and wage differentials, with Cornwall itself becoming a kind of clearing house for news and advice from the rapidly growing Cornish communities abroad. As early as the 1830s and 1840s, potential emigrants in Cornwall had access to detailed, com-parative information on overseas destinations, enabling informed choices to be made. As the international mining economy developed apace, so the Cornish recognised that overseas – rather than British – destinations offered the brightest prospects. As Burke noted: 'In the early 1870s ... a Cornish miner stood to gain more by working in a metal mine overseas than in a coal-mine in Britain'.[28] By then, of course, the Cornish international network had reached formidable pro-portions, the lynch-pin of a burgeoning international Cornish identity which lasted to the First World War and beyond.

A.L. Rowse's memories of the pre-1914 years are for us an important window on that culture:

> There were all the letters going to and fro between Cornwall and Cape Town and Durban; the weekly newspapers sent out to keep them in touch with doings at home, the South African

papers and journals and illustrated books that came back.(One of the first papers which I read regularly for a time, later on when I was a schoolboy, was the *Cape Times*, which Charlie Courtenay sent to his wife and which she used to lend me). One of our few books, I remember, was a book of views – Table Mountain, the long main street of Cape Town, the beaches of Durban, the Drakensberg, the tall new buildings of Johannesburg, the rickshaws, the natives. Then there were the photographs sent back: groups of Cornish miners with their native boys.[29]

In common with other emigrant ethnic groups, the Cornish used their international network not only as a source of information and advice but as a means of smoothing the way in a new country for the newly arrived from Cornwall, taking him (or her) into the home, introducing friends, finding lodgings, organising a job, offering financial assistance, even providing protection from other competing ethnic groups. Here the myth of 'Cousin Jack' was all-important, the Cornish deploying separate ethnic identity to 'stick together' in the manner described above and to assert their superiority as miners and as frontiersmen.[30] As time went on – and like those Caledonian and Cambrian societies that sprang up across the globe – Cornish Associations emerged throughout the New World to celebrate Cornish achievement, to nurture Cornish sentiment and to protect Cornish interests.

Craft tradition and trade unionism could also on occasions fulfill these roles. The predominantly Cornish miners' union that emerged at Moonta and Wallaroo in Australia in the latter part of the century took a keen interest in the welfare of immigrants and potential immigrants, while – like the Aberdeen granite-cutters – Cornish quarrymen and stonemasons from Constantine and elsewhere in Cornwall became intimately involved in the Granite Cutters' National Union (GCNU) in North America. As Horst Rossler concluded: 'Thus craft tradition, union membership, and ethnic background combined to earn the Constantine and other Cornish granite stonemasons a privileged position in an atmosphere in which immigrant labour was often viewed with hostility'.[31]

Moreover, through the GCNU and its equivalent in Cornwall, the Operative Stone Masons' Society, the Cornish stonemasons constructed a sophisticated information flow which promoted both seasonal return migration between Cornwall and overseas destinations – principally, but not exclusively, America – and migration between and within continents. Of a sample of 17 Constantine union men researched by Rossler, six had been abroad once, four had been abroad twice and three had gone overseas three times. Four had gone abroad four times or more. Constantine men like Francis Williams, Alfred Waters and John Sampson Jenkin had spent the greater part their lives travelling between and within Australia, the United States and South Africa, interspersed with visits back home to Cornwall when times were lean overseas.

Rossler considers that 'A dynamic sense of Cornish ethnic identity was fuelled by the frequent travellings between the New World and the Old, cementing the links between those in the United States and those who had stayed behind'.[32] In 1888 George H. Spargo, the Cornish secretary of the Westerly (Rhode Island) branch of the GCNU wrote in the union journal: "A great number of boys have left within a few days for a trip across the ocean to see their friends, the old home, and spend the winter. We are sorry to miss them at the banker [the work face], in the different organizations they may be identified with, and also, but not at least, in our churches .... I suppose some of them will be taking a wife."[33]

The close-knit world of the stonemasons may have been something of a special case but international mobility was also a feature of other Cornish emigrants, notably the miners. Again, the complicated experiences of countless individuals bears witness to this process. Thomas Gregor, for many years a captain in the copper mines of Cornwall, was later a copper miner in America, then Cuba and finally in South Australia where he found lucrative employment as a mining consultant. George Verco, another captain, born in Marazion, worked briefly in the neighbourhood of Bodmin before going to the lead mines of Wisconsin, then making his way to Ireland and from there emigrating to Australia in 1845. William Henry Moyle was engaged to assist in the erection of two Cornish engines on the banks of Lake Superior in the Keweenaw copper-mining district of Upper Michigan in 1857. Two years later he was hard at work in the Kapunda mines in South Australia. John Riccardo Stephens, born in St Agnes in 1827, went first to New Brunswick in Canada and to Jamaica in the West Indies before arriving in Australia in 1853. Henry Crougey was born near Carn Marth in March 1825 and as a youth sang in the Wesleyan choir at Carharrack. At the age of 21 he married Ann Bray of Twelveheads and a little over a year later the couple emigrated to Chile where Henry worked as a miner for over 12 years. From Chile they went briefly to California and from there to South Australia where Henry toiled in the Burra Burra mine until its closure in

1877. From there they went to the goldmines of Ballarat and Clunes in Victoria before returning to South Australia, where Henry was employed in the Moonta Mine on Yorke Peninsula. In later life, Henry suffered greatly from 'miner's complaint' (disease of the lungs) and he died of the illness at his daughter's home in Broken Hill in New South Wales in 1910.[34]

Charles Simmons, from Menheniot, had mined variously at Peak Downs (Queensland), Broken Hill and Kalgoorlie (Western Australia) before leaving Moonta for South Africa some time before 1905. Charles Pyatt – 'Camborne Charlie' – was born in Cornwall in 1860 and had emigrated to Australia in 1883 to work at the Wallaroo Mines. He soon moved on to Moonta, Broken Hill and Western Australia. Then, leaving his family safely behind in Moonta, he went to try his luck in South Africa, returning to Australia some time before his death in 1910. James Collingwood Coad, a Cornish-Australian born at Moonta, spent many years at the Bloemfontein mines in the Orange Free State in South Africa, and Nicholas Nicholls, another 'Moontaite', died at Boksburg in the Transvaal in 1912. Captain James Datson was a senior manager at the Moonta Mine but in July 1862 he visited the South Island of New Zealand following the gold discoveries on the Molyneux River. He and his brother spent several months prospecting at Tuapeka, Wakatipu and on the Shotover River before returning to Australia at the end of 1864.[35]

Ambrose Grose had an extraordinarily mobile life. He was christened at Constantine on 11 February 1866, the son of William Grose, from Roche, who had himself enjoyed a varied career in Devon as manager of the Haytor Granite Quarries and as captain of both the Sharkham iron mine near Brixham and the Atlas iron mine near Haytor. Ambrose started work in the 1880s as a traction-engine driver for Holman's of Camborne. From there he went to the Atlas mine in Devon but by the 1890s he was in Michigan, working for the Buffalo Mining Company and other local concerns. His wife, Jessica Bonney, meanwhile, had been left back in Cornwall at St Just-in-Penwith, where their son William had been born in 1886. From Michigan, Ambrose Grose made his way to the Balghat Nundadrug Gold Mine in Mysore, India, and from there to the Gold Coast (modern Ghana) where in June-July 1898 he was captain of the Wassau mine at Adjah Bippo. But fever took its toll and he returned to Britain to recuperate and to seek gentler climes. He then became captain of the Hexworthy tin mine on Dartmoor before moving to Owlacombe, near Ashburton, in 1903. Ambrose's son William, like father and grandfather before him, was also a wandering Cousin Jack, working first of all for an engineering foundry at Buckfastleigh in

Devon, then for Holman's of Camborne and eventually emigrating to the United States in 1921. He was still alive in the early 1990s.[36]

Of course, the Cornish were well aware of the existence of this international mobility and the network that both underpinned it and which it helped to perpetuate. For example, newspaper reports in the Moonta *People's Weekly* brought news of Cornish folk in America as well as in Cornwall itself. One newspaper in Cornwall was interested enough in the exploits of Moonta-born Cousin Jacks to record that James and Albert Retallick – 'Australians, but of Cornish descent – their mother being a native of Redruth'[37] – were the acclaimed champion stopers [miners] of the Knight's Deep mine and probably of all South Africa. Significantly, this report was later reprinted from the original Cornish source in the *People's Weekly*. Indeed, Australian newspapers from time to time carried articles reflecting upon the international nature of the Cornish experience, noting that the Cornish 'go to Lake Superior or Nevada, ... to the Brazils, or across to Africa and then to Kimberley ... [to] Spain or Norway, or any part of Europe, or ... to the Australian colonies'.[38] At other times newspapers merely reported the phenomenon: 'Mrs T. Penrose and family left here [Moonta] on Wednesday morning, en route for America. They will join Mr Penrose at Salt Lake City, their future home'.[39]

On the mining frontier of North America, Masonic and other Lodges often behaved as surrogate Cornish Associations or trade union branches, providing solidarity and security in an otherwise volatile environment and furthering the interests of the Cornish whenever possible. As Sharron Schwartz has observed, Masonic societies were a prominent feature of life in 19th-century Cornwall, and 'The continuance of the Masonic tradition abroad, particularly in the USA, must have served the Cousin Jacks well with its expressed aims of social philanthropy and welfare, which would also have strengthened the kin network and provided a degree of security'.[40] Significantly, one of the first buildings erected in the overwhelmingly Cornish town of Gold Hill on the famous Comstock Lode in Nevada was the Masonic Lodge, while the majority of Cornish burials in public cemeteries in the United States will be found today in the sections reserved for Freemasons or Oddfellows. Schwartz notes an exemplar: 'Carn Marth miner Joseph Kemp, buried at the Glenwood Cemetery in Park City, Utah, has Masonic insignia on his headstone'.[41]

Similarly, Cornish mine captains often engaged in a kind of extended nepotism designed to reserve or secure the best jobs for the Cornish. Even into the 1920s and 1930s such practices were commonplace in the gold mining town of Grass Valley in California, preferential treatment extending to both second or third generation American-born Cousin Jacks and the trickle of emigrants that still found its way from Cornwall. In the Depression years, thousands of unemployed Americans headed West in the hope of finding better opportunities, not a few making their way to Grass Valley where they aimed to land one of the much sought after $5 or $6 a day jobs in the gold mines. Back in Cornwall, young William Corin (still alive in Grass Valley in 1997) was one of the five children his mother struggled to bring up after the death of her husband from 'miner's complaint' at the age of 32. When he was 14, William went to work in South Crofty tin mine, situated between Camborne and Redruth, but he later decided to try his luck in Canada. His mother borrowed £12 for his passage to Timmins, Ontario, where he found employment – like other Cornishmen in those years – in the Hollinger mines.

But soon William Corin was looking for better opportunities and in 1929 he was drawn, again like many other Cornish at that time, to the great manufacturing city of Detroit across the border in the United States. From there he hitch-hiked across America to Los Angeles, joining a tramp steamer which took him to San Francisco. In nearby Oakland a fellow Cornishman lent him a few dollars to pay for the trip inland to Grass Valley. Arriving there late at night he slept in a pear orchard. Next day, as he walked into town, a stranger called out from the verandah of a nearby house: 'Are you a Cousin Jack?'. Corin replied 'I sure am!', to which the friendly response was 'Come pardner, come on in and have dinner with us'. Three days later, with 150 unemployed men from Back East queued at the mine office in search of work, William Corin – armed with a letter of introduction from his new-found friend (a Camborne man, it transpired) – went underground to earn his living as a Cornish miner.[42]

By the period between the First and Second World Wars, however, the myth of Cousin Jack which underwrote such behaviour was no longer sustained by the reality of Cornish prowess, the huge structural changes that had overcome Cornwall since the latter part of the century making claims of Cornish superiority seem increasingly hollow. The widespread deployment overseas of an assertive Cornish identity was only credible for as long Cornwall itself was credible as the root source of that identity. Even in South Australia, where Moonta had become 'the Hub of the Universe', replacing Cornwall as the focus of Cousin Jack identity and loyalty, all-consuming structural change after the First World War had brought an abrupt end to the Yorke Peninsula copper mining industry and scattered the local population in a process not unlike that experienced in Cornwall itself. In Australia and New Zealand, in North America, even in South Africa, the once mighty Cornish Associations were all in swift decline by the eve of the Second World War, the Cornish Association of South Australia in 1930 lamenting the fact that 'the younger generation had no interest in the old Land [Cornwall] or its traditions, having been born here with different surroundings'.[43] It was not until half a century later, in the very different climate of the 1980s and 1990s with their burgeoning 'globalisation' and the consequent worldwide explosion of ethnic identities, that in the increasingly multicultural societies of Australia and America (and, to a degree, South Africa) the Cornish could again become visible and vociferous on the international stage.[44]

In Cornwall itself, the fading of industrial prowess had ushered in a new period, an era of socio-economic 'paralysis' and 'making-do' in which the hitherto confident, outgoing Cornish identity was replaced by a new introspection. Central to this was the 'dependency culture' that had emerged by the end of the century, an informal welfare system in which large proportions of the Cornish population, especially in the old mining districts, were increasingly dependent upon the efforts of their émigrés in distant parts, particularly South Africa. In 1879 the *West Briton* had recognised the changing nature of emigration, with fewer families leaving Cornwall as permanent emigrants but with more individuals, usually male, departing as itinerant workers in the world's mining districts. 'Thousands of people are supported [by these itinerant migrants]', claimed the newspaper, for the Cornish miner 'leaves the women, the children, and the old people behind – not on the parish, be it said to his honour.'[45] By the end of the century the situation had become even more stark, so much so that in January 1902 the *Cornubian* newspaper could claim that 'We are living on South Africa.'[46] In 1905 it was estimated that there were some 7000 Cornish miners on the Rand in South Africa, earning perhaps £300 per annum each. As Richard Dawe noted, if the cost of living accounted for perhaps half their wages, then perhaps as much as £1,000,000 could have been coming home to Cornwall from South Africa alone.

It was, of course, the women left behind who were largely the recipients of these all-important remittances, and it fell to them to manage the household budgets, and much else, in the often extended absences of their menfolk. In this way, the Great Emigration had huge effects upon Cornwall itself as well as upon the new lands in which the Cornish settled and it was an indicator too of the singular role performed by women in this vast panorama. All too often overlooked in the male-oriented narrative of the Great Emigration, with its emphasis on masculine occupations and masculine culture (everything from hard-rock mining to male-voice choirs), Cornish women – the 'Cousin Jennies' – were a vital part of the story at home and abroad.

Shyrle Pedlar Hacker, the daughter of a miner whose 'family fished off the rocky coast of Penzance on ... [the]Cornish coast',[47] recalled what it was like as a young girl to be stranded with her mother in a small wooden cabin in the Divide mining district of Nevada in the cruel winter of 1916. Dad had gone down the mountain to buy stores when the blizzard struck, cutting them off for days:

> On the first day of the big storm we ran out of kerosene for the lamps and oil burner. On the third day the wood pile was empty. Mother said we would go to bed and tell stories. She tried to make it sound like fun, but something in her eyes and voice told me she was frightened. Were we going to die? I thought of the frozen birds and rabbits we usually kept in our snow cupboard and wondered if it hurt to freeze before you died.[48]

Women, perhaps more than the men, were given to quiet stoicism, of enduring stress and pain without murmur. At least this is the perception of popular literature, as in the fictional story *Not Only in Stone* – set in Wallaroo Mines in South Australia – where Mary Elizabeth 'Polly' Thomas, a Cornishwoman, is confronted with the deteriorating health of her copper-mining husband Nathan and 'courageously assumes the responsibility of raising four children by herself. A simple but stout-hearted woman, she stands fast in the face of many tragic setbacks'.[49] Such a view has an echo in recent academic analyses, emphasising the community of women in the face of adversity. Lyn Bryant notes that:

> The role of women in Cornish families again shows both similarities with other regions and important differences. In mining areas generally women tend to stay in close contact with their female kin and exchange help both at times of crisis and in the everyday problems involved in childcare. High male death rates occasioned by dangerous work, such as mining, also tend to pull the women of the family together in self-help groups. Such kinship links have also been shown to be particularly important when husbands are absent through work or their presence in the home is "unreliable". Relationships with kin, then, would have been doubly important for many Cornish women.[50]

In late and early 20th-century Cornwall such a community of women, it might be argued, kept the otherwise disintegrating fabric of Cornish society together – at least in the depressed working-class mining districts such as Gunnislake, Redruth, Camborne, St Austell, St Day, St Agnes, St Just – and gave backbone to the culture of 'making-do'. As the *Cornubian* observed in 1892 of one mining village near Redruth, 'If the women and children emigrated to the same extent as the men, it would be "Good Night" to Lanner'.[51]

Certainly, the women supported their communities against the backdrop of sustained population loss which was as catastrophic as any in Europe. A.C. Todd estimated that 'Cornwall lost more than a third of its population'[52] during the Great Emigration, and Bernard Deacon has shown that at least 240,000 Cornish had gone overseas in the years 1840–1900 with a further 220,000–230,000 leaving Cornwall for England and Wales during the same period.[53] The population of Breage and Germoe had fallen by 27 per cent between 1841 and 1851, that of Tywardreath fell by 29 per cent between 1861 and 1871 and that of St Just-in-Penwith by 27 per cent between 1861 and 1871. The parish of Perranzabuloe lost 22 per cent of its population between 1871 and 1881, and St Cleer lost 25 per cent during the same decade and a further 22 per cent between 1891 and 1901. Between 1861 and 1900 Cornwall as a whole lost no less than 10.5 per cent of its male population overseas and 7.0 per cent to other counties, far and away a greater loss than that of any English or Welsh county, with a corresponding loss of 5.3 per cent of the female population overseas and 7.1 per cent to other counties.

More shocking still are the stark statistics which show how Cornwall was robbed of the younger, more energetic and better trained elements of its population. Between 1861 and 1900, 44.8 per cent of the Cornish male population aged 15 to 24 had left for overseas, with a further 29.7 per cent leaving for other counties. Over the same period and in the same age group, 26.2 per cent of Cornish females went overseas while 35.5 per cent departed for other parts of Britain. As the historian Dudley Baines concluded, reflecting upon these extraordinary figures and providing his telling assessment of Cornwall's place in emigration history, as a proportion of population loss: 'This is not as high as from the famous regions of Italy .... but it must be remembered that mass emigration from Italy lasted not much more than twenty years. Cornwall was probably an emigration region comparable with any in Europe.'[54] It is for this reason alone, even if we disregard all other imperatives, that Cornwall's Great Emigration demands our continuing attention. It is the greatest saga in Cornish history and at the beginning of this new millennium it explains much about the current condition of Cornwall and the Cornish – at home and overseas.

# CHAPTER ONE

# A CULTURE OF MOBILITY

In Cornwall the emergence of large scale emigration after 1815 was facilitated in part by a 'culture of mobility' that was already an ingrained feature of Cornish life. By the 18th century the Cornish were already a familiar feature of the mining landscape of much of England and Wales, from Somerset and Devon to Derbyshire and Denbighshire. But the same culture of mobility had had an earlier and wider aspect – in the colonisation of America and, latterly, Australia and in Cornwall's time-honoured seafaring tradition which was much enhanced by Cornish participation in Britain's commercial and naval expansion. Cornwall was geographically well placed to participate in both the development of North American fisheries (notably Newfoundland) and the settlement of the American continent itself.[1] In 1583 Humphrey Gilbert marshalled his fleet in Cawsand Bay for his expedition to Newfoundland and in that year one Captain Amadas, of an old Launceston family, was sent by Sir Walter Raleigh on an exploratory voyage to America.

There was also a Cornish element in the early and ill-fated Roanoke colony of 1585-86, perhaps not surprisingly so, given that it was organised by Raleigh – then Lord Lieutenant of Cornwall – and planted by Sir Richard Grenville of Stowe in north Cornwall. Among those early settlers were a Master Kendall of Lostwithiel and a Master Prideaux from Padstow, together with Anthony Rous (or Rouse or Rowse) of Halton on the Cornish bank of the Tamar.[2] John Arundell of Trerice sailed with the colonists and shortly after their arrival at Roanoke Island, off Virginia, was sent home to Cornwall to announce the successful establishment of the first settlers. Included in their number was the cartographer and artist John White, thought to have originated from Truro, who produced a series of maps and watercolours to illustrate various aspects of the new land, his subjects ranging from the exotic local fauna to the appearance and lifestyle of the Native Americans, the 'Indians' as they were then known. His depictions of these 'Indians' were to be of enduring importance, not only as documentary evidence for us of the first contacts between the Cornish and the indigenous populations of America but because his characterisations of Native Americans have informed our – Cornish, British and European – perceptions and indeed stereotypes of the native inhabitants of the dense eastern woodlands of North America. Our images of the Hurons, Mohawks and Delawares and of the mighty chief Pontiac and of Chingachgook – the last of J. Fenimore Cooper's Mohicans – are largely the creation of John White's imaginative illustrations, exemplified in his famous painting of a chief of the Pamlico people.[3]

But the colony failed. The settlers were increasingly dispirited, not least because Grenville's promise to keep them supplied with provisions appeared to have been forgotten, and when Francis Drake passed that way his offer to evacuate them was readily accepted. Shortly after a provision ship did arrive but, finding the colony deserted, it sailed immediately for home. Two weeks later Grenville himself arrived and, disappointed to find his plantation abandoned, left a garrison of 15 men with enough supplies for a couple of years – long enough to organise the refounding of the colony. In 1587 100 men and 15 women arrived as new settlers, their task to search for the 15 at Roanoke and then to plant their new settlement on Chesapeake Bay. Their leader was none other than John White, now governor of this new colony. The scene that greeted them at Roanoke was a grim one: the bleached skeleton of one of the 15, the fort razed, the houses abandoned. On nearby Croatoan Island they learned from friendly Native Americans that the Roanoke garrison had been surprised and overwhelmed by 'hostiles', as those Native Americans who resisted European invasion were soon to be known universally. While all this was being contemplated, John White's daughter Eleanor gave birth to a baby girl, Virginia, probably the first Cornish child born in America.[4]

This colony also perished. Leaving the settlers still based on Roanoke Island, John White had returned home to collect further provisions but it was 1588 – Armada year – and attentions were directed elsewhere. Eventually, two small ships were allocated for his return voyage to Roanoke but they were swiftly intercepted by marauding Spanish and came running home to Bideford. It was not until 1590 that he managed to cross the Atlantic in three ships. Landing at Roanoke, he found the sign CRO – an agreed message to indicate that the colonists had gone to Croatoan Island – but all around was evidence of another attack by Native Americans. As well as smashed guns, White found:

> five chests that had been carefully hidden of the planters, and of the same chest three were of my own, and about the place many of my things spoiled and broken and my books torn from the covers, the frames of some of my pictures and maps rotten and spoiled with rain, and my armour almost eaten through with rust.[5]

Extraordinarily, John White never did go to Croatoan Island to see if any of the settlers had survived. Instead, with storm clouds gathering and the weather ready to deteriorate, he forlornly set sail for home and he never did learn the fate of his daughter and her little girl. The failure of Roanoke put an end to the colonisation of America for more than a decade. But then, with the receding Spanish threat, thoughts again turned to the New World, the enticement being not so much the mythical tales of fabulous wealth in the elusive Eldorado but rather the promise of an independent and honest life away from the disabilities of home. As Alistair Cooke noted wryly: 'It is hard to imagine a Scot, a Lancashire man, or even a native of barren Cornwall believing in chamber pots made of gold. But life was bleak for the common man, and he must have been greatly taken with these hints of a country with no recruiting sergeants and bailiffs, no spies, magistrates, tithe gatherers, or other such badgering types.'[6]

The Cornish were prominent among those who petitioned James I in 1606 for a licence to plant a new colony in America. In fact, two companies emerged to undertake the business of colonisation – the London (later Virginia) Company, which planted the colony of that name, and the Plymouth Company which settled New England. Among the early 17th-century adventurers who put up the money for the Virginia Company were Cornish gentry such as William Godolphin, Robert Killigrew, John Borlase, William Roscarrock, Peter and John Arundell, Edward Carne, and Richard Connock. There was also a Cornish contingent among the first settlers, notably one Thomas Spilman from Truro who survived both a Native American massacre of 1622 and the subsequent period of starvation. Of the 10,000 souls who had gone out by 1622, only 2000 remained alive a few years later. Spilman was among them, although he too soon succumbed to illness and disease at the sadly early age of 21. Other Cornish there included Richard and Elizabeth Arundell, who arrived in 1620 as personal servants of the governor, Sir George Yardley, and John Treherne and John Penrice who settled in Charles City and Elizabeth City in 1622 and 1623 respectively. Additionally, there was by the late 1630s what A.L. Rowse called 'a small clutch of Cornish settlers'[7] at Lynnhaven on the lower James river: folk with names such as Pearce, Bolitho, Trevethan, Harris and Cock who owned sizeable properties in the neighbourhood of Henrico.

Meanwhile, the Plymouth Company had also attracted the attention of Cornishmen. Robert Trelawny, the well-known Plymouth-based merchant, was anxious to develop trade with New England. In 1631 he obtained a grant of property for Cape Elizabeth (Maine) and neighbouring Richmond's Isle – the surrounding seas there rich in sturgeon, bass, salmon and cod. In 1635 his younger brother Edward went out from St Germans to manage the emerging Cape Elizabeth business and those who travelled with him were distinguished by their Cornish names. Prominent among these were Mellin, Jose and Bonython, while the surnames Hunkin, Edgcombe, Treworgey, Herle, Freethy and Jope were especially redolent of East Cornwall, the country around Trelawny's native St Germans. Other tell-tale Cornish surnames in early Maine and New Hampshire included Carkeet, Carveath, Curnow, Kitto, Lander and Polgreen. And among the other Cornish settlers who found a new home in 17th-century New England were individuals such as Sampson Angier (sic) of Lezant, Arthur Gill of Saltash, Hercules and Mark Hunking, also of Saltash, Paul Mitchell and John Odiorne (sic), both from Sheviock, Samuel Penhallow of St Mabyn, Benjamin Stevens of Landrake and John Libby from Fowey. Again, the East Cornwall connection is apparent, not surprisingly so given both the importance of the Trelawny family in the New England venture and the close proximity of Plymouth, the focus of the plantation company. Such was the strength of this influence that by 1665 the colony of Maine even had its own County of Cornwall.[8]

The mid-17th century was a time of political and religious conflict and Civil War in the British Isles, a complex period in which, as we now know, issues of ethnic, regional and national identity were inextricably entwined in the constitutional and other grievances that were being fought over. There was a Cornish angle to all this, the Cornish overwhelmingly siding with the Royalists in a fierce display of Cornish particularism which echoed the rebellions of 1497 and 1549 and resisted the intrusion of the Parliamentarians in Cornish affairs.[9] There was, however, as Anne Duffin has argued,[10] a powerful minority of Parliamentarian sympathisers among the Puritan lesser gentry of south-east Cornwall; many of whom would have had business connections with Plymouth (itself a Puritan hotbed, though Robert Trelawny was a Royalist) and thus with the colonisation of America. It is no surprise then, to find that there are echoes of the Civil War in Cornwall in the events of mid-17th century America, with Cornish Royalism challenged by the vociferous ideological fervour of the Puritans and yet with those same Puritan ranks sporting more than a smattering of Cornish – mainly from East Cornwall.

Among the Cornish Royalists was the Bonython family in Maine. Richard Bonython, born in 1580, was over 50 years of age when he arrived in America, a senior figure who stoutly defended the reputation of the Anglican Church against its Puritan critics. His son John, a volatile individual with a reputation to match, inherited his father's loathing of the Puritans and in 1652 was one of those who resisted the annexation of Maine by the Puritan enthusiasts of Massachusetts, an act which was itself undone at the Restoration of 1660. Ironically, John Bonython eventually fled to Massachusetts in 1675, in the face of Native American hostilities, where he became the butt of the unflattering rhyme:

> Here lies Bonython,
> The Sagamore of Saco:
> He lived a rogue and died a knave,
> And went to Hobbowocko [the Devil].[11]

Massachusetts, with its strong ideological commitment to Puritanism, had been settled largely from East Anglia and the east Midlands of England – good Puritan country – but there was also a sprinkling of Cornish. Prominent among these was Hugh Peters, born in Fowey in 1598. Peters was of Flemish descent but his mother was a Treffry (a member of the notable Fowey family of that name) and his grandmother was a Penhale, another old Cornish family. But Peters was a Puritan with firm Parliamentarian sympathies, an allegiance which led eventually to his execution as a regicide (he was one of Cromwell's confidantes), condemned as the 'most vilified man in the whole Civil War period'.[12] In Massachusetts, however, his reputation was anything but that. Ordained in 1621 he went to New England in 1635 to escape the attentions of Archbishop Laud who was robustly defending the church from Puritan influences. In Massachusetts, Peters was appointed pastor of the church at Salem where, as the late John Keast noted in *The Story of Fowey*, Peters became active in politics and religious affairs and prominent in commercial undertakings.[13] In particular, he raised funds for a public fishing company and encouraged trade with the West Indies. He helped establish the settlement of Marblehead, known originally as Foy (the phonetic and archaic spelling of his hometown, Fowey), and he encouraged Cornish fishermen to emigrate and settle there. He also pioneered the development of shipbuilding. As one contemporary account explained, 'Mr Peter (sic), being a man of very public spirit and singular activity for all occasions, procured some to join for building a ship at Salem of 300 tons, and the inhabitants of Boston, stirred up by his example, set upon building another at Boston of 150 tons.'[14]

Peters also played a leading role in the establishment of Harvard College. His biographer, R.P. Stearns, has observed that as a promoter of the public good

Hugh Peters was unsurpassed in New England at the time.[15] Additionally, Peters' religious and political beliefs prompted him to raise funds for the parliamentary cause. His brother Thomas, also a Puritan pastor, had been driven from his living at Mylor in Cornwall to New England; and he returned home to become the leading chaplain of Oliver Cromwell's Roundhead 'New Model Army' – with his own official apartments in Whitehall. Significantly, he supported Cromwell's policy of religious toleration for other Protestant sects, something that was not approved of in hard-line Massachusetts and which in the years that led up to his death prompted an unfortunate rift between Peters and the colony he had done so much to nurture.

The Restoration proved Peters' undoing, executed as he was for his alleged complicity in the death of Charles I, but the disappearance of the Cromwellian regime also had the effect of precipitating a new wave of Dissenter emigration to the American colonies. Puritans, who resented what they saw as the re-emergence of 'Papist' tendencies in the Anglican church, and 'Quakers' (members of the Society of Friends) who sought religious toleration in new communities of their own making. Many Quakers crossed the Atlantic to settle in the hitherto unoccupied (by Europeans) country of the Delaware Valley, in what was to become west New Jersey. There was a sprinkling of Cornish among these newcomers – names such as Trenoweth, Rescarrick, Tregidgo, Penquite, Trelease, Chenoweth – and one of the promoters of Quaker settlement in west New Jersey was Edward Billing, a member of the well-known Billing family of Hengar in St Tudy whose daughter was the famous Loveday Hambly, a stalwart of Quakerism in Cornwall.

Pennsylvania first attracted Cornish settlers in the 1680s, the decade of William Penn's original land grant for a refuge for Quakers wishing to escape religious intolerance at home and anxious to seize the opportunities for commerce and trade offered by new settlements abroad. Among their number was Lawrence Growden, a pewterer from St Merryn (in the same stretch of north Cornwall as Billing's St Tudy) who along with his brother Joseph purchased a huge tract of some 10,000 acres in the virgin colony. They sailed from Fowey with 45 other emigrants, arriving in Pennsylvania in January 1684. Growden named his property Trevose, today a suburb of Philadelphia. Other Cornish settlers attracted by the promise of freedom and economic opportunity in William Penn's new colony included the Rawles from St Juliot, another of those prominent North Cornwall Quaker families. Francis Rawle joined forces with James Fox of St Germans (yet another Quaker) to purchase

5000 acres in what is now Montgomery County, where they settled in 1686.

In 1692 Peter Grubb arrived from Stoke Climsland in East Cornwall to take up land near Wilmington on the Delaware. Later, he stumbled across rich iron deposits in the neighbourhood of Lebanon, at the foot of the Appalachian Mountains in south-eastern Pennsylvania, perhaps the first major contribution by a Cornishman to the development of metalliferous mining in North America. Certainly, his son, also called Peter, recognised the significance of the find and before long the Cornwall Mines were in production in an iron-rich district soon known as the Cornwall Ore Banks. This, in turn, stimulated the development of iron founding. The younger Grubb had erected his first bloomery c.1735, and in 1742 his Cornwall Furnace was opened. The village that grew up around the furnace was inevitably dubbed Cornwall, an early industrial town which represented a remarkably early technological transfer from Britain where the process of industrialisation was still at an embryonic stage, even in precocious Cornwall. When relations between the American colonists and the authorities in distant London began to break down, Pennsylvania, with its culture of Quaker self-help and independence, was generally behind the call for freedom. The younger Grubb's sons, Curtis and Peter, who had inherited the furnace from their father, in 1776 declared their support for the Revolution and – it is said – their Cornwall Furnace produced 42 cannons and countless shot for use against the British.[16]

It is tempting to suggest that mixed up in this revolutionary allegiance was something of a Cornish inheritance, though we should not forget that prominent families such as the Bonythons and Rawles were committed Loyalists, anxious to preserve allegiance to the British Crown. But if there was an inheritance sympathetic to the Revolution, then it was rooted especially in the parishes of North and south-east Cornwall, one which not only echoed Quaker and even earlier Puritan influences but which anticipated the Nonconformist rural radicalism that was to emerge in Cornwall – particularly north Cornwall – after 1815. For example, we may note among the 18th-century arrivals in Philadelphia the influential business couple Thomas and Mary Williams, who had emigrated from Bristol but were Cornish in origin, exemplars of that self-made Quaker tradition which so suited the ethos of America and yet which was in its own way very Cornish. Thomas came from Trevarrick, St Austell, his wife Mary from Treganeeves, Menheniot: Loveday Hambly's old home and a 'spiritual centre for the Cornish Friends'.[17]

Rowse considered that 'the exodus of so many Quakers for Pennsylvania left the Society of Friends much depleted in Cornwall, where in the beginning it had been strong',[18] but in transferring their numerical strength to the colony they had created something of a Cornish community. Certainly, Methodist arrivals from Cornwall in the late 18th century seemed to adapt effortlessly to the state's Quaker culture. Paul Burrell, from Illogan, arrived in Philadelphia in 1783 where, he wrote in his autobiography, 'we met with our friends and Mr John Nancarrow that went from Market-jew [Marazion] about ten years before. And he got me lodgings and board to an old gentleman Quaker where I was greatly cared for.' The Methodists were thin on the ground. There was but one chapel 'and Mr Asbury the only preacher that was there and most of the society was the negroes so simple, so free and so artless that if I was to tarry here these people would be my people'. The Quakers were much stronger, however, and Burrell found them to his liking, comparing their meetings 'as to a Methodist love-feast, and full of love, and full of heaven, and full of God'.[19]

Following the Revolutionary War and the achievement of independence, Cornish Quakers continued to be attracted to America by the prospect of religious freedom and economic opportunity. Significant among these was Josiah Fox, a shipbuilder who had learned his trade in Plymouth dock constructing warships for the Royal Navy, a member of the celebrated Fox family of Falmouth which contributed so much to the arts, sciences and commerce of Cornwall in the late 18th and early 19th centuries. On completion of his apprenticeship at Plymouth, Fox made a number of voyages aboard his family's ship, the *Crown*, visiting shipyards in England and at Cadiz, Venice, even Archangel. In 1793 he arrived in Philadelphia, then elevated as capital of the United States of America, where a Cornish relative already resident in the city recommended him for a position in the War Department. His connection with the engines of war, not to mention his marriage to a non-Quaker, strained his relations with the Society of Friends – with its pacifist leanings – but he was anxious to play his part in th creation of a new United States Navy and in the defence of his newly adopted country. He established the dockyard at Norfolk, Virginia, where he built the famous frigate *Chesapeake*. He also played a key role in the construction of other ships for the United States Navy, including the *United States, Constitution, President, Constellation* and *Congress*, and in so doing he helped the fledgling nation-state to give the Royal Navy more than a run for its money in the War of 1812.

There may well have been a Cornish sympathy for American independence, and a Cornish role in its achievement and protection. But equally there was strong Cornish participation in the great British maritime expansion of the period. For part of the culture of mobility was not only this long-established movement to America but also the voyaging, often extensive, undertaken by Cornish sailors in the service of exploration, commerce or war. Again, it is possible to peer back to the early modern period and beyond for evidence of these trends, not least to the activities of Sir Richard Grenville and the other Cornish 'sea-dogs' of the Elizabethan era. But the phenomenon is most closely observed in the post-1707 period when the Act of Union had created a 'Great Britain' whose *raison d'être*, as Linda Colley has argued in her seminal work *Britons: Forging the Nation 1707–1837*, was commerce, industry and empire. A new 'British' identity had emerged, underpinned by Protestantism and forged in war, an identity which did not imply the integration or homogenisation of disparate cultures within the island but which did allow constituent peoples – such as the Cornish, or the Lowland Scots – to deploy separate identity in support of (or to exploit) the new 'Britishness'.[20]

The Falmouth Packet Service itself, which had been set up as long ago as 1688–89, was a vehicle for this expanding Britishness, with Falmouth the focus of the Post Office's maritime connections with Spain, Portugal, the Mediterranean, the West Indies, Canada, the United States, Mexico and Central and South America. Falmouth's transatlantic links were also fostered by local commercial activity, Cornish businessmen following where the Post Office had led. Falmouth had developed swiftly in the latter part of the 17th century, the entrepreneurial zeal of local Quakers – notably the Fox family – making the most of opportunities for overseas trade. At neighbouring Penryn, the Enys family was likewise active, the surviving Letter Books of Valentine Enys an important window on the Atlantic operations of a successful Cornish merchant in the period 1704–1719.[21] His trading contacts ranged as far as Jamaica and America and he imported wine from the Canaries. He traded in pilchards, cloth, timber and tin, and – like many other Cornishmen of his day – he was not above a little smuggling.

Falmouth and environs were also a focus for the Royal Navy, not least for Admiral Edward Boscawen, Lord Falmouth, born at Tregothnan in 1711. Often criticised by his detractors (and teased by his wife) for giving preference to Cornishmen in his ships – 'a little Navy of your own making'[22] – Boscawen was conscious of his Cornish identity and was indeed prepared to favour his fellow Cornishmen, particularly at times of acute manning crises when the Royal Navy was in dire need of recruits. Thus it was that many Cornishmen sailed with Boscawen – 'Old Dreadnought' or 'Wry-necked Dick' as he was known to his men – to participate in such actions as the interception of the French Fleet off Newfoundland in 1755, the attack (with Wolfe) on

Louisburg in 1758 and the destruction of the French in Lagos Bay in 1759.

In much the same way, Edward Pellew (later Viscount Exmouth) recruited extensively among his fellow Cornish for the ships of the semi-independent frigate squadron that he commanded at Falmouth in the early French Revolutionary wars. When the *Nymphe* was commissioned in 1793, she had 104 Cornishmen in her ship's company, while the frigates *Arethusa* and *Indefatigable* also enjoyed widespread reputations as 'Cornish ships', not only at Falmouth but throughout the Royal Navy.

The names of many of these roving Cornish sailors have disappeared from view and we are left, by and large, with the noteworthy as our examples – such men as Charles Penrose, born in Penryn in 1759, who served in the Royal Navy in the West Indies during the 1790s in the wars with France and went on to become Commodore of Gibraltar, or the remarkable Trevenen family which earned a reputation as sailors, adventurers, travellers.[23] James Trevenen, born at Rosewarne, Camborne in 1760 joined the Royal Navy as a Midshipman. He sailed with Captain James Cook in his last voyage in the *Resolution* and was present at Cook's violent death in Hawaii. Not achieving the promotion he believed he deserved, Trevenen, now a Lieutenant, offered his services to the Russians in 1787. Appointed Captain, he settled his family in St Petersburg and fought against the Swedes. Knighted by Catherine the Great, he was subsequently wounded in the action in Viborg Bay in 1790 and died of his wounds. His nephew, the Rev. John Trevenen, born in Helston in 1781, was, by contrast, a man of the cloth but he too was a wanderer, travelling as far afield as Peru in 1811 where he kept both sketchbook and notebook, illustrating and describing his journey to Lima and the Andes. Later in the century, Henry Wilberforce Trevenen, born in 1840, perpetuated this South American connection by living for several years in Buenos Aires, his two sons deciding to settle permanently in Argentina. Other Trevenens settled in Hawaii, and still others made their way to the vastness of Alberta, Canada. The Trevenen family experience was at once both extraordinary in its diversity and yet typical of Cornish mobility.

Samuel Wallis, one of Boscawen's protégés, born in Lanteglos-by-Camelford, was responsible for the European 'discovery' of Easter Island and Tahiti in 1767. The latter find was thought to be of inestimable value because it afforded a well-located and clearly identifiable island from which to take observations for the transit of the planet Venus, a phenomenon which would allow the calculation of the distance between the earth and the sun. When

Wallis had first arrived off Tahiti in his ship the *Dolphin* he had been given a rough reception, a force of some 500 canoes and 4000 men attempting to prevent his landing and even trying to board his ship. Wallis was forced to open fire on the Tahitians to avoid being overwhelmed. Subsequently, however, in a subtle display of diplomacy and patience, reciprocated by the Tahitians and in the gracious behaviour of their Queen Obarea, these opening hostilities were smoothed over and soon forgotten. This was the prelude to a five-week stay in which the by now tired and ailing Wallis and his crew could recuperate from their arduous journey to the south seas and prepare for the long voyage home. When Cook arrived at Tahiti (for the purpose of conducting the Venus observations) in the *Endeavour* in June 1769 with Lieutenant Zachary Hicks, a Cornishman, as his second-in-command, he found the Tahitians entirely welcoming. So too did his men, having been continuously at sea for some eight months – with no fresh food and no contact with women – Tahiti seemed like paradise. Not only were there provisions aplenty but the voluptuous Tahitian women proved more than ready – whether willing or bribed – to respond to the sailors' advances.[24]

However, it fell to the Cornishman Hicks, as First Lieutenant, to maintain good order and Naval discipline. Thus, when one of the Tahitians stole (probably for a joke) the ship's all-important quadrant, an instrument indispensable for astronomical observations (and irreplaceable in Tahiti), it was Hicks' difficult duty to disturb the harmonious atmosphere by taking one of the chiefs hostage. The chief was soon released, the quadrant having been returned, but the conditional nature of the relationship between invader and invaded had been revealed. A few weeks later, on 9 July 1769, as the *Endeavour* prepared to set sail, two Marines absconded. Cook was told – in an interesting foretaste of what Bligh would experience some years later – that 'they were gone to the mountains and that they had each got a wife and would not return.'[25] Cook took Tahitian hostages (including Queen Obarea) to ensure Tahitian compliance in the search for the deserters but it fell to Zachary Hicks to locate and arrest the two men and to bring them back to the ship.

It was not until July 1771 that the *Endeavour* eventually arrived home, having examined New Zealand and explored the eastern coast of Australia in the meantime. Cook spent six months charting the coastline of New Zealand's two main islands before heading off on 1 April 1770 into the unknown ocean in the guessed-at direction of New Holland (as Australia was then known). It was at first light on 19 April that Lieutenant Zachary Hicks spotted land ahead, the southeastern-most tip of Australia which Cook duly named Point Hicks. Cook hugged the coast until he found a suitable harbour, a place they soon dubbed Botany Bay in commemoration of the astonishing flora and fauna that so delighted Joseph Banks, the expedition's botanist. Hicks went ashore with the two jolly boats dispatched from *Endeavour* – it is said that he was the first of the party to set foot on Australian soil – but it took the firing of several shots to disperse the potentially hostile reception that the Aborigines ashore had been planning. As in Wallis' arrival in Tahiti, the European entry had been marked by violence – or at least the threat of violence – and the use of superior technology to press advantage. A week later, the Union flag having been raised ashore, the *Endeavour* continued its exploration along the eastern coast of the continent and from there the long voyage back to Britain. It proved a difficult journey, the crew sticken with dysentery and malaria, and among the several who succumbed was Lieutenant Zachary Hicks, buried at sea.

In the wake of Cook came William Bligh, born in St Tudy in 1754. As an up-and-coming young navigator, Bligh had sailed with Cook as master of the *Resolution* in 1776, visiting Tahiti and learning about the southern oceans. Later, when, at the instigation of Sir Joseph Banks, it was decided to collect specimens of the breadfruit tree from Tahiti to see whether it would be possible to transplant them in the West Indies, where they might provide food for the African slaves, Bligh was the obvious choice to lead the expedition. In addition to his experiences in Cook's third voyage in the *Resolution*, he had also served in the West Indies trade between 1783 and 1787 and knew the slave islands well. Bligh sailed from Britain in the *Bounty* in November 1787 and after an especially difficult rounding of the stormy Cape Horn arrived in Tahiti 11 months later. He was forced to wait on the island for nearly five months for the breadfruit seedlings to mature sufficiently to be potted for the voyage to the West Indies and in that time a slackening of discipline and the crew's growing fondness for the island's apparently languorous lifestyle combined to present Bligh with his intractable problem. He duly sailed from Tahiti but when the *Bounty* reached the Friendly Islands the crew staged their famous mutiny, the sailors determined to return to the relationships they had formed ashore in the recent months. Bligh and 18 loyal crewmen were put into an open boat and it is extraordinary testament to Bligh's capacity as a navigator that he not only managed the 3618 miles from Tonga to Timor but was able to chart part of north-eastern Australia en route. The mutineers and their women, meanwhile, found refuge on remote and inhospitable Pitcairn Island.[26]

In 1791 Bligh made his second voyage to Tahiti in support of the breadfruit experiment, this time in the *Providence*, and he also charted part of south-eastern Van Diemen's Land (Tasmania), together with Fiji and the Torres Straits. Later, in 1806, Bligh became governor of New South Wales, the fledgling Australian colony proclaimed less than two decades earlier in 1788 when Captain Arthur Phillip arrived at Botany Bay with the First Fleet and its convict cargo. Here Bligh suffered the indignity of a second mutiny, one which historians have blamed traditionally on the deficiencies of his leadership. Manning Clark, the great Australian historian, considered the *Bounty* mutiny directly attributable to Bligh's 'rages and cruel discipline', and wrote that:

> When William Bligh was welcomed ashore at Sydney Cove [New South Wales] with great ceremony and rejoicing, he was almost 52 years old. In stature he was short. His form erred on the side of the corpulent, but not from over-indulgence in food or drink, for he was by nature temperate in all the passions of the flesh. In his soul, however, he harboured a deep and ungovernable rage which was to unleash a great upheaval among the men and women he had been sent to govern.[27]

Recent research, however, has painted a somewhat different picture. In this revised view, Bligh was the victim of an unscrupulous *coup d'état* by the New South Wales Corps, the local military force which dominated colonial life and resented the restraints placed upon its self-seeking activities by a succession of Naval governors, of which Bligh was the last. The officers of this 'Rum Corps', as it was known, had cornered much of the economy of New South Wales, not least through its control of the supply of rum. Bligh complained that 'the thirst after spirits was so strong that [the settlers] sacrificed everything to the purchase of them, and the prices were raised by that monopoly to so high a degree that it was the ruin of many of those poor people'.[28] The 'Rum Song', thought to date back to those penal days – when Pinchgut was a barren rock in Sydney Harbour, the 'Norfolk Dumpling' 100 lashes, and the 'Newgate hornpipe' a hanged-man's dangling death throes – confirms the all-important role of rum in that early colonial society:

> Cut yer name across me backbone,
> Stretch me skin across a drum,
> Iron me up to Pinchgut Island

From today till Kingdom Come!
I will eat your Norfolk Dumpling
Like a juicy Spanish plum,
Even dance the Newgate hornpipe,
If you'll only give me rum![29]

So successful was the Rum Corps in its manipulation of the New South Wales economy that by 1799 it owned 32 per cent of cattle in Australia, 40 per cent of goats and 77 per cent of sheep. According to Australian writer Robert Hughes, the Rum Corps officers were 'Grasping, haughty, jealous of their privileges and prerogatives, [they] were on top and meant to stay there.'[30] The confrontation with Bligh came to a head on 26 January 1808, 20 years to the day since European settlement had commenced in Australia, when he was deposed as governor by the Rum Corps. New South Wales was then ruled by a military junta for two years. The British government, anxious to avoid any whiff of colonial rebellion – the loss of America was still felt keenly – turned a blind eye and none of those responsible for the coup was ever punished severely. It was left to Lachlan Macquarie, governor from 1810 until 1821, to straighten out New South Wales and break the power of the Rum Corps once and for all. On Macquarie's appointment, Bligh returned from his exile in Van Diemen's Land and shortly after he left Australia for good. On his return to Britain in 1811 he was promoted Rear Admiral and, in 1814, Vice-Admiral of the Blue.

Bligh's predecessor as governor of New South Wales had been Philip Gidley King, another Cornishman, born in Launceston in 1758. He joined the Royal Navy as a Midshipman in 1770, and sailed with the First Fleet as First Lieutenant in Captain Phillips' ship, the *Sirius*. On the fleet's arrival at Botany Bay on 18 January 1788, King was one of those who went ashore looking for water. He had his first encounter with the Aborigines, offering them beads and mirrors, recording that these 'trembling' natives 'seemed quite astonished at the figure we cut in being cloathed (sic). I think it is very easy to conceive the ridiculous figure we must appear to these poor creatures, who were perfectly naked.'[31] Botany Bay itself proved a disappointment, a poor anchorage surrounded by marshy land unsuitable for settlement or cultivation. It is said that it was King who recommended the alternative location at Port Jackson,[32] the stupendous natural harbour only a few miles to the north, and it was on 26 January that the colony was formally proclaimed at this new site. Lieutenant Ralph Clark, an officer of Marines, enthused about this new home, contrasting it with the River Tamar in Cornwall, 'I cannot compair (sic) any think (sic) to come nearer to it than about 3 miles above Saltash on the Wair.'[33]

But for all this enthusiasm, the foundation of the new settlement was not easy. To the intrinsic difficulty of managing convicts was added the harshness and strangeness of climate and environment, together with the huge problems of establishing agriculture and the basic components of economic and social life. Moreover, the French were showing more than a passing interest in the region and, anticipating a scramble for control of the southern Pacific, Phillip decided upon the speedy settlement of the strategically placed Norfolk Island. He dispatched the auxiliary ship *Supply*, tender to the *Sirius*, with 22 people under the command of Philip Gidley King to colonise the island, allowing them six months' rations and instructing them to commence cultivation immediately. Norfolk Island soon acquired its reputation as 'the worst place in the English-speaking world'[34] (it was abandoned as a convict settlement in 1806), and King struggled from the beginning to make anything of this new colony. His aspirations were high-minded but unattainable, as the caustic pen of Manning Clark reminds us: 'He wanted to dispense with corporal punishment; within six weeks he had a boy of 15 flogged with 100 lashes for stealing rum. He was appalled by the sexual promiscuity and the drunkenness; within two years he had fathered two illegitimate children, and had begun to drink heavily.'[35]

King was intent upon the cultivation of flax as the island's primary produce, to establish it as the colony's *raison d'être*, perhaps even as a source of fledgling prosperity. But the Admiralty had neglected to send flax workers with the First Fleet, and – perhaps a measure of the desperation felt by him – King remembered that the Maoris of New Zealand were – as Joseph Banks had attested – accomplished linen weavers. King contrived to kidnap two Maoris from the Bay of Islands in New Zealand but their efforts contributed little to the settlement's paltry output and after six months they were repatriated. Meanwhile, Phillips had dispatched the ships of the First Fleet on their return voyage to Britain, retaining only the *Sirius* and *Supply* for local use. In March 1790, alarmed at the continuing pressures on the dwindling stores and provisions at Sydney Cove, Phillip had sent a further group of convicts aboard the *Sirius* to supplement those already established on Norfolk Island. But disaster struck, the ship being wrecked on the island's treacherous coast. All lives were saved, but such stores as there were, were lost. King was returned to Britain for a period of recuperation, his place taken temporarily by Nicolas Nepean, from Saltash, brother of Evan Nepean, the under secretary of state in the Colonial Office. But by November 1791 King was back on Norfolk Island, together with his new wife – Anna Coombe of Hatherleigh in North Devon. King remained as lieutenant-governor of the Island for five harrowing and extraordinarily difficult years in which he was confronted with the seething resentment of the Irish convicts – many of whom were political prisoners – and threatened with subversion and mutiny by his discontented garrison in this failing colony.

In 1800 Philip Gidley King became governor of New South Wales, and by now his earlier idealism and altruism had hardened into cynicism and suspicion. He failed to confront the hegemony of the Rum Corps and in his dealings with the Aborigines his former belief that these people could be successfully accommodated as citizens of the Crown was replaced by a new anxiety that these 'savages' were a threat to the peace and progress of the European settlers, and should be treated accordingly. To this was added his Protestant hostility to the 'Papist' practices of the (numerous) Irish convicts, practices which were, he thought, both an affront and a threat to the political establishment of the colony. As Manning Clark observed: 'So in two of the major questions of the day, the relations between the Europeans and the Aborigines, and the relations between the Protestant ascendancy and Irish Catholicism, evil stalked the land, and New South Wales added its drops to the never-ending tears of humanity.'[36] However, King had not lost his gift for strategic thinking and in 1803 he ordered the occupation of Van Diemen's Land as a convict settlement. He explained his reasons to Evan Nepean, writing:

> My reasons for making this settlement are: the necessity there appears to be of preventing the French gaining a footing on the East side of these Islands; To divide the Convicts; To secure another place of procuring timber, with any other natural production that may be discovered and found useful; The advantage that may be expected by raising Grain; and to promote Seal Fishery.[37]

Among King's lasting impact upon the colonisation of Van Diemen's Land was the founding of Launceston (named after his hometown though today pronounced Lawn-cess-ton rather than the Cornish dialect form, Lanson) and the quaintly titled district of Cornwall-shire, together with the naming of the River Tamar. At first convicts were transferred to Van Diemen's Land from Norfolk Island but before long others began to arrive directly from Britain and Ireland. The penal camps soon acquired a reputation for harsh conditions and brutal treatment, not least for the so-called 'secondary' convicts – those who had committed additional crimes during the voyage out or once ashore in the colonies. Moreover, the treatment of the Aborigines was nothing short of genocidal, the population diminishing from 20,000 to a mere 2000 by 1830 and disappearing altogether not long after.

The picture that we have of early convict Australia, the land of Philip Gidley King and William Bligh, is one of unrelieved gloom and wretchedness, a veritable hell on earth. The Cornish were numbered not only in the ranks of these governors, those who had fought against the odds to create a semblance of order and decency, but also among the governed– those 'undesirables' whom society at home had decided to unload in the new penal colonies half a world away. There were Cornish convicts in the First Fleet itself, 19 tried in Cornwall (11 at Launceston and eight at Bodmin), together with two Cornish-born tried at Plymouth and Exeter respectively. They sailed in the convict transports *Charlotte* and *Scarborough*, the former having been sent down to Plymouth to collect inmates from the local prison hulks before embarking upon the long voyage to Australia. The *Scarborough* carried 208 convicts all told, the prisoners confined almost permanently to the squalid 'tween decks (where the head room was but 4 ft 5 in: 1.35 m) in the conditions of heavy security described by Philip Gidley King:

> [There were] very strong and thick bulkheads, filled with nails and run across from side to side 'tween decks abaft to the mainmast, with loopholes to fire between the decks in case of irregularities. The hatches are well secured down by cross-bars, bolts and locks, and are likewise rail'd round from deck to deck with oak stanchions. There is also a barricade of planks about three feet high, armed with prongs of iron Centinels (sic) are placed at the different hatchways, and a guard always under arms on the quarterdeck of each transport in order to prevent any improper behaviour of the convicts.[38]

Twelve Cornish convicts were transported in the Second Fleet of 1790 (six had been tried at Launceston, five at Bodmin and one at Truro), sailing together in the disease-ridden *Neptune*. Six of these poor souls died at sea and were committed to the deep without even a glimpse of New South Wales. In 1791 the ships *Atlantic*, *Mary Ann* and *Salamander* of the Third Fleet carried 16 Cornish prisoners, who had been convicted variously at Launceston, Bodmin, Lostwithiel and Truro. In all, some 600 convicts were transported from Cornwall to the Australian penal colonies between 1787 and 1852, of whom 78 per cent were male. It sounds a considerable number but in fact it was only 0.4 per cent of all transported convicts and, interestingly, less than half the Cornish proportion of the population of Britain at that time.[39] Put another way, the Cornish were on average less likely than other inhabitants of these islands to be transported as convicts to Australia, a testament perhaps to the 'civilising' impact of the Wesleys upon late 18th- and 19th-century Cornish society but also, maybe, evidence of a growing ideological opposition within Cornwall to the practice of convict transportation.

Certainly, Cornish society was aware of the contrasting but equally telling experiences of two of its early transportees: Mary Bryant and James Ruse. The story of Mary Bryant (née Broad) is something of an epic and has survived in the folk memory of both Cornwall and Australia, most recently in the form of an acclaimed and highly readable biography *To Brave Every Danger* by Judith Cook.[40] Mary was born in Fowey, a sailor's daughter, and was sentenced to seven years' transportation for stealing a cloak. She sailed with the First Fleet in the *Charlotte*, and during the voyage she gave birth to a baby girl, christened Charlotte in memory of the ship. On arrival in New South Wales she married another of the *Charlotte's* Cornish convicts, a 31-year-old fisherman called William Bryant, the father of Mary's second child, Emanuel, born in April 1790. William Bryant was a smuggler and in 1784 had been convicted for resisting arrest by excise men. He had already served three years in the prison hulks before being selected for transportation. As a fisherman he possessed skills that were vital in the infant colony, and he was put in charge of the fishing boats that worked Port Jackson. However, as Robert Hughes has remarked, 'the black-market opportunities were too good for a Cornish smuggler to resist'.[41] He was caught selling some of his catch, instead of delivering it all to the government store, for which misdemeanor he received one hundred lashes.

William Bryant decided to escape and when in October 1790 an East Indiaman, the *Waaksamheyd*, put into Port Jackson he managed to persuade its obliging Dutch crew to sell him a compass, quadrant, muskets, charts and provisions. The Bryants bided their time and on 28 March 1791 they decided to make their move, taking their two children and seven other convicts, and dashed for the open sea in the governor's own six-oar cutter which they had stolen. The plan was to head for Timor, over 3000 miles away in the Dutch East Indies. At first the going was easy but the winds soon blew them far out to sea. One of the convicts, James Martin, later describing: 'a heavy Gale of Wind and Current, expecting every moment to go to the Bottom, next morn saw no land, the sea running Mountains high I will leave you to consider what distress we must be in, the Woman [Mary] and the two little Babies was in a bad condition we had nothing to Eat except a little raw rice.'[42]

Turtle meat proved their salvation, discovered on one of the many small islands of the Great Barrier Reef, and thus fortified they were able to turn westwards at Cape York – the northernmost tip of Australia – and venture into the thousand miles of ocean which would take them to Timor. They arrived at Koepang, in Timor, on 5 June 1791 and managed to pass themselves off to the Dutch authorities as shipwreck survivors. The idea was that they would then await a passing ship able to repatriate them to Britain. But William fell out with his wife Mary and in an inexplicable, but perhaps drink-induced, pique spilled the beans. As James Martin recalled, 'Wm Bryant had words with his wife, went and informed against himself Wife and children and all of us, [upon] which we was immediately taken Prisoners and was put, into the Castle [at Koepang] [where] we was strictly examined.'[43]

Captain Edward Edwards, who had been chasing the *Bounty* mutineers in his frigate the *Pandora*, had had the misfortune to be wrecked and had also made the long voyage to Koepang. On arrival in Timor he promptly took charge of the Bryants and their accomplices, placing them aboard the East Indiaman *Rembang* with a view to taking them to the Dutch colonial capital Batavia in Java for removal to Britain or Australia. Batavia was renowned for its unwholesome, disease-infected environment, and it was there that William Bryant and his young son Emanuel died of fever just before Christmas 1791. Mary and the surviving convicts were sent back to Cape York Peninsula, in Australia, there joining a British warship on its return journey to the United Kingdom. Mary's three-year old daughter Charlotte died on 5 May 1792 and was buried at sea. Mary survived the long voyage home and on arrival in London was committed to Newgate gaol with the prospect – as an escaped felon – of a further sentence to transportation.

However, the already romantic story of the 'Girl from Botany Bay' had by now caught the attention of London society, or at least that of James Boswell who began to lobby on her behalf. Boswell wrote to Dundas, the Home Secretary, and to Evan Nepean, urging clemency for Mary Bryant and recommending a pardon. In May 1793 Mary received her pardon and went home to Cornwall. The sentimental Boswell settled an annuity of £10 upon her. Boswell's critics, who sensed his weakness for working-class girls, made fun of his championship of Mary's cause, one William Parsons penning a fictional 'Heroic Epistle from Mary Broad in Cornwall to James Boswell, Esq., in London' in which Mary – marooned in her Cornish fastness – is pining for the company of the great man and benefactor:

> Was it for this I braved the ocean's roar,
> And plied those thousand leagues the lab'ring oar?
> Oh, rather had I stayed, the willing prey
> Of grief and famine in the direful bay!
> Or perished, whelmed in the Atlantic tide!
> Or, home returned, in air suspended died![44]

However, there is nothing to suggest that Boswell was motivated by anything other than pity for Mary Bryant's suffering and admiration for her stoicism and endurance in the face of catastrophe, and it may be that in Cornwall others shared this view. Certainly, the experiences of another early Cornish convict, James Ruse, did much to encourage a growing belief that transportation was no way to deal with either the problem of criminality at home or the settlement and development of colonies overseas. James Ruse was born at Lawhitton, near Launceston, in 1760, where he grew up to become an agricultural labourer.[45] In July 1782 he was taken to Bodmin Gaol and committed for trial at Bodmin Assizes on the charge of having burgled the house of one Thomas Olive and stolen two silver watches (valued at £5) and other items to the value of ten shillings. Ruse was duly found guilty and sentenced to death by hanging, a routine outcome in those days of draconian punishment in which crimes against property were every bit as serious as assault or murder, but for reasons that are not clear this was commuted to transportation for seven years. He went first to the prison hulk *Dunkirk*, anchored at Plymouth, and from there joined the transport *Scarborough* in the First Fleet.

James Ruse always claimed that he was the first person ashore in New South Wales (he carried Captain John Hunter from a jolly boat to the beach) and in his eagerness to be remembered as the founding colonist we see something of the spirit that he continually displayed in his new home. From the beginning he was prepared to seize all opportunities that came his way, and, with this positive attitude and his knowledge of husbandry, he soon caught the attention of his keepers. He was put to work at the government farm at Rose Hill, working alongside a hundred other convicts, many of whom had little knowledge of or interest in agriculture. He performed well and when his sentence expired in August 1789 he was given a trial grant of one-and-a-half acres. Phillip recorded:

> In order to know in what time a man might be able to cultivate a sufficient quantity of ground to supply himself, I last November ordered a hut to be built in a good position, an acre of ground to be cleared, and once turned up. It was put into the possession of a very industrious man [James Ruse], who was told that if he behaved himself well he should have thirty acres. Others may prove more intelligent, though they cannot well be more industrious.[46]

The trial was a success and Ruse was given his 30 acres, at Parramatta, which he named Experiment Farm. He was illiterate and unable to record this progress himself but he was sufficiently aware of the significance of his work to dictate a short autobiographical note to one Watkin Tench, a Captain of Marines. In the very first description of independent, self-help agriculture in Australia, James Ruse explained:

> I was bred a husbandman, near Launceston, in Cornwall. I cleared my land as well as I could, with the help afforded me. My land is prepared thus: having burnt the fallen timber off the ground, I dug in the ashes, and then hoed it up, never doing more than eight or perhaps nine, rods a day, by which means, it was not like the government farm, just scratched over, but properly done; then I clod-moulded it, and dug in the grass and weeds: – this I think almost equal to ploughing. I then let it lie as long as I could, exposed to air and sun; and just before I sowed my seed, turned it all up afresh. When I shall have reaped my crop, I purpose (sic) to hoe it again, and harrow it fine, and then sow it with turnip seed, which will mellow and prepare it for next year. My straw, I mean to bury in pits, and throw in with it every thing which I think will rot and turn to manure.[47]

In September 1790 Ruse had married a 19-year old convict, one Elizabeth, who had arrived in the Second Fleet. She too earned a reputation for 'industrious-ness', and was the first woman convict to be emancipated, her sentence having been cut by two years for good behaviour. Her husband was full of praise for his new wife, though rather less enthusiastic about the quality of the land upon which they both toiled and the society in which they were forced to live:

> I have no person to help me, at present, but my wife, whom I
> married in this country: she is industrious. The governor, for
> some time, gave me the help of a convict man, but he is taken
> away. Both my wife and myself receive our provisions regular-
> ly at the store, like all other people. My opinion of the soil of
> my farm is, that it is middling, neither good or bad. I will be
> bound to make it do with the aid of manure. The greatest
> check upon me is the dishonesty of the convicts, who, in spite
> of all my vigilance, rob me almost every night.[48]

By December 1791 Ruse had taken his wife and child 'off the store', making them totally self-sufficient and independent of government assistance. Although a severe drought drove him from the land in 1793, he was back in business with a new 30-acre grant in 1794 and soon other farmers were follow-ing his example by starting up at Parramatta. Severe flooding at the turn of the century drove many from their properties, though James Ruse survived the dif-ficult times. His wife Elizabeth continued to run the farm while he went to sea as a mariner to earn extra cash. By 1819 James and Elizabeth Ruse had some 200 acres to their names and during their long career they opened up 13 grants or purchases of virgin land, clearing in total some 400 acres. Elizabeth, who had borne eight surviving children during those arduous years, died at the age of 65 in 1836. James followed her 18 months later, aged 78. The inscription on his gravestone, with its painful illiteracy but honest sentiment, tells his story simply but with fitting pride:

> My Mother Reread Me Tenderley
> With me She Took Much Paines
> And when I arived in This Coelney
> I sowd the Forst Grain and Now
> With My Hevenly Father I hope
> For Ever To Remain.[49]

Today James Ruse is honoured as 'the father of Australian agriculture',[50] but in his own time the lessons of his experience seemed more complex and confused. On the one hand, here was a fine example of a man 'made good', and of a couple who had mended their ways and exhibited all the best qualities of thrift and self-improvement. And yet, on the other hand, James and Elizabeth were forced to exist in the midst of sin and wickedness, it was argued, when a more enlightened colonial policy might have seen the new lands as not merely the dumping ground for the dross from home but rather as a precious resource where good yeomen stock from Britain and Ireland might prosper for the good of all. Such arguments were rehearsed in radical circles throughout the United Kingdom, particularly in the years after 1815, and even *The Times* opined that, 'We have no right to cast out among other nations, or on naked shores, either our crime or our poverty. This is not the way in which a great and wealthy people, a mother of nations, ought to colonize.'[51] But the arguments had a particular resonance in early 19th-century Methodist Cornwall, with its emerging Nonconformist-Radical political tradition and an already well-established culture of mobility with the Cornish active in the opening-up of America, Australia and elsewhere.

The Bible Christian denomination, a breakaway Methodist sect founded in the parishes of Week St Mary and Launcells in North Cornwall in 1815, combined grass-roots religious fervour with political and social commitment to advocate emigration as a mechanism of 'improvement'. For the Bible Christians, the religious, civil and economic freedoms of the United States of America were especially attractive. British colonial policy, however, was to be criticised heavily if it rested upon the shameless expediency of convict transportation. But it was to be applauded when it embraced the radical notion of 'systematic colonisation', as it did in 1836 when industrious artisans, good yeomen farmers and other deserving emigrants were offered free passages to South Australia's newly proclaimed 'Paradise of Dissent'.

For the political classes in Cornwall, similar criteria were seen to be important and similar perspectives were offered. Sir William Molesworth of Pencarrow (the 'Radical Aristocrat', [52] as Alison Adburgham has dubbed him) argued in parliament that transportation corrupted most of those who experienced it and rehabilitated none, and when his Molesworth Committee reported to the House in 1838 it was careful to catalogue in great detail the depravity of the Australian penal colonies. Molesworth also advocated 'systematic colonisation', and was enthusiastically supportive of radical plans to colonise New Zealand on such principles in the late 1830s. His own brother

Francis had been persuaded to join the emigrant throng and Sir William urged others to follow his example, to leave the overcrowded United Kingdom with its frustratingly limited opportunities and to put their energies to greater use in the abundantly promising new lands overseas:

> All occupations here are over-stocked; in every branch of industry, in every description of trade, in all professions competition is excessive. "Go then" I said "imitate the example of your ancestors, and make for yourself a career in a new world of your own creation, and be assured that in seeking in this manner to advance your own interests, you will confer a great and lasting benefit upon your natural country". And this advice which I have given to him, I give to all persons who find this island too thickly populated.[53]

This, then, was the radical ideology of emigration as it was articulated after 1815, advocated here by a Cornishman with a passionate commitment to the cause of colonisation and a fervent belief that emigration was to the benefit of all. He proposed the abolition of transportation and the creation in its stead of free colonies based upon equality of opportunity, civil liberty and religious tolerance. It was, as we shall see, a message that struck many chords in Molesworth's native Cornwall in the years after the Napoleonic Wars.

# CHAPTER TWO

# THE RAGE FOR
# EMIGRATION

In the autumn of 1810 relations between the United States of America and Great Britain were at a low ebb. Still locked in a deadly struggle with revolutionary France, Britain feared the republican and democratic energy of recently independent America, not least the cavalier audacity with which American merchant vessels regularly ran the British blockade of French ports. And yet there was none of this animosity when the American schooner *Packet of Boston* sailed from Penzance, Cornwall, on 28 September of that year, bound for New York. Instead, the 'Stars and Stripes' were roundly cheered by onlookers as the sailing ship slipped from the quayside and made its way into the open waters of Mount's Bay with its cargo of mixed goods and passengers. As one contemporary observer put it, this unusual outburst of exuberance demonstrated a Cornish 'cordiality towards the Americans'.[1]

Among the passengers aboard the schooner was one James Martin Hosking, then already 50 years of age. He was a Cornish farmer from near Castle-an-Dinas in the parish of Ludgvan who 'was not unsympathetic to the aims of either the American or the French revolutions'.[2] Indeed, Hosking had decided to journey to the United States to see for himself the opportunities that might lie there for Cornish folk who, tired of what he saw as the restrictions and disabilities of the Old Country, could build life anew in a land of civil and religious freedom, of social and economic mobility. Following a stormy passage of some seven weeks at sea, he at last reached Martha's Vineyard, an island off mainland Massachusetts, where he was instantly impressed by what he saw of American society. From there he went on to New York and then to Washington DC, travelling up the Potomac river where he was delighted to note 'the happiness of the farmers in this place, which flowed in the abundance of the necessities of life, their wants few and easily supplied; no cares about rent, all being peace, plenty, and happiness around them'.[3] But the political climate was already deteriorating, and James Hosking was only just able to make it home to Cornwall before the outbreak of open hostilities between Britain and the

United States in 1812. The burning of Washington DC, the battle of New Orleans and the other events of the War of 1812 may have been a temporary distraction for potential Cornish emigrants anxious to know the prospects of life abroad. But the message that Hosking and others like him had brought from America – that there was for the ordinary people of Cornwall the opportunity of a freer, more secure existence overseas – had gained common currency by the time James Hosking died in 1823.

The final defeat of France in 1815 had allowed the development of a more stable relationship between Britain and the United States, as well as confirming British global maritime hegemony and, through the Congress of Vienna, constructing a new, conservative compact in continental Europe designed to 'keep the peace'. One of the consequences of this new world order was the creation of the conditions in which the first stirrings of mass emigration from Europe might be managed. In Cornwall, peace with the United States combined with post-Napoleonic discontent to revive and perpetuate the previously well-established pattern of emigration to America. The Tory *Royal Cornwall Gazette* (deadly rival of the Radical *West Briton*) expressed its disapproval of this trend, voicing hostility to the United States and its pretensions as the land of freedom and opportunity as well as pouring scorn on those malcontents (as it saw them) who were seduced by such propaganda:

> The rage for emigration to the United States will be checked for neither the deluders nor the deluded can so easily pretend that they are departing to a land flowing with milk and honey ... can such things be in this modern Utopia ... this happy region which ignorance and sedition are so apt to compare with England, and sigh at the comparison?[4]

Such criticism cut little ice with popular opinion in Cornwall. In May 1818 some 50 eager emigrants set sail for America from the Cornish port of Charlestown. The *Western Luminary* newspaper thought the emigrants 'the wandering victims of political discontent',[5] but while political discontent may well have been a primary motive for leaving these shores these people were in their own estimation neither 'wandering' nor 'victims'. Their choice of America as destination was hardly incidental, while the decision to go was for them the rational exercise of free will. The *Royal Cornwall Gazette* was not impressed, complaining again in May 1819 when:

A vessel sailed last week from Charlestown for America with upwards of 60 passengers, principally farmers and husbandmen from the vicinity of St Austell. From all that we have heard of these wholesale emigrations we have every reason to believe that most of them are instigated by interested parties who dexterously avail themselves of the discontent excited in the minds of the ignorant by a certain class of our public writers.[6]

Leaving aside the journalistic swipe at its competitors (the *West Briton* was to emerge as a significant champion of emigration and radical causes), the criticism of 'interested parties' was evidence of an emerging 'emigration trade' in Cornwall, business interests which saw advantage in becoming involved in this growing area of commerce. For example, when in June 1820 a party of emigrants sailed from Fowey to join the Guernsey schooner *Phoenix* bound for Baltimore, the applications for passage had been handled by Messrs Pomery & Walkom, drapers of St Austell, who were busy diversifying at a time when business generally was dull.[7] Cornish shipping and legal interests were also keen to become involved in this potentially lucrative trade, as in March 1837 when it was advertised that the vessel *Caroline* of Gweek (a small harbour on a creek of the Helford River) was due to sail shortly for Philadelphia. Described as an A1, copper-fastened fast sailing ship of 400 tons burthen, the *Caroline* was commanded by John Broad (a Cornishman), with enquiring passengers requested to contact the Gweek offices of the Penzance solicitors, Messrs Cornish & Borlase, for details.[8]

Of course, economic depression, particularly in the agricultural sector, was itself a determinant of emigration. In 1822 a 'County meeting' of Cornish landowners and tenants was held at Bodmin, at which there was a demand for a reduction in taxes, tithes and rents. The poor harvest of 1829 drove many from the land and in April 1832 the *West Briton* wrote that, 'The rage for emigration that now prevails in the north of this county is wholly unprecedented in Cornwall; in different parishes from 200 to 300 persons each, have either departed or are preparing to leave.'[9] A decade later things had not changed, the *West Briton* again noting the strong flow of emigrants from North Cornwall, 'The spirit of emigration continues active in the neighbourhood of Stratton. High rents, heavy rates, and obnoxious taxes are driving some of the best of our agriculturalists to climes where these demons of robbery and ruin are unknown.'[10]

Inextricably entwined within these economic considerations were questions of political and religious ideology, the critical tone of the *West Briton*'s reporting reflecting a growing radicalism in Cornwall which was impatient for reform after the period of post-Napoleonic repression. The already profound impact of Nonconformity (given renewed impetus by the foundation of the radical Bible Christian denomination in North Cornwall in 1815) was given fuller expression by this radicalism. It began to question institutions of church and state, articulating the growing demand for religious freedom, social and economic mobility, and civil liberty. The Great Reform Act of 1832, with its widening of the franchise, was for many only a step in the right direction with many of the key issues left unaddressed or unresolved. Emigration was one response to this dissatisfaction, to suppose that further reform at home was unlikely or impossible. People sought instead the desired freedoms in new countries overseas – typically, in the United States, or even in British territories, especially after 1836 in South Australia's 'Paradise of Dissent', the very first British possession to break the link between church and state.

On occasions, the political motivation behind an individual's emigration could be explicit. Down on the Lizard peninsula in West Cornwall Samuel James, a solid yeoman farmer typical of his class, articulated his opposition to the political establishment and thus his reasons for deciding to leave Cornwall. Foremost among these considerations was the need 'To escape the heavy charges of supporting certain useless institutions'. To this was added the desire 'To escape from supporting a State religion ... [and] To live under free and useful institutions'.[11] Taking stock of these concerns, Samuel James sailed in the *Orient* from Falmouth for New York in April 1842, together with 188 other Cornish people from Redruth, Camborne, Helston, and their hinterlands.[12] The overt ideological language of James' testimony, not least the deep resentment at having to pay tithes to an Anglican Church to which he did not otherwise subscribe, would have been echoed across Nonconformist Cornwall, especially in the Bible Christian heartland north-east of Padstow. Indeed, as the *West Briton* had intimated, it was in that part of Cornwall that the Great Emigration first began to exhibit its mass characteristics.

Founded by dissident Methodists in the North Cornish border parishes of Week St Mary and Launcells in 1815, the Bible Christian sect spread its influence throughout Cornwall but its core was the 'debatable land' of the wild North Cornwall–North Devon border country, the district stretching eastwards across the Tamar (at that point but a trickle) towards Bideford and Holsworthy. As Margaret James-Korany has observed: 'In a sense, the remote extremities of north-western Devon were part of a "Greater Cornwall"', this

Cornish-Devon frontier country 'a geographically and in certain respects socio-culturally homogeneous area, a relatively poor and isolated district'.[13] In the midst of this bleak and somewhat forbidding landscape was the parish of Morwenstow, the most northerly part of Cornwall and from 1834 to 1875 the living of the Rev. Robert Stephen Hawker, the celebrated High Churchman in whose literary outpourings we may discern some of the earliest evidence of Cornish Anglo-Catholic and Celtic revivalism. Hawker enjoyed an ambivalent relationship with his Bible Christian parishioners, or 'Bryanites' as they were known after their founder – William O'Bryan (or Bryant) from Gunwen in the parish of Luxulyan. Hawker considered the Bible Christians a serious threat to orthodox religion and conventional morality.[14] As he expressed it:

> I've no respect for Calvin's Face,
> Nor Whitfield's locks of gray,
> John Wesley's Picture hath no Place,
> Where I kneel down to pray![15]

And yet, Hawker supported the poorer tenant farmers and agricultural labourers, by and large the Bible Christian folk, against the richer landowners and he also opposed the horrors of the Workhouse:

> The poor have hands, and feet and eyes
> Flesh, and a feeling mind:
> They breathe the breath of mortal sighs
> They are of human kind.[16]

It is against this paradoxical background that we can best consider Hawker's well-known 'The Cornish Emigrant's Song'. It provides a fascinating insight into the radical ideology of emigration in early/mid 19th–century Cornwall, not least in terms of how it was understood at the time by its conservative critics – including Parson Hawker:

> Oh! the eastern winds are blowing;
> The breezes seem to say,
> 'We are going, we are going,
> To North Americay.

'There the merry bees are humming
Around the poor man's hive;
Parson Kingdon is not coming
To take away their tithe.

'There the yellow corn is growing
Free as the king's highway;
So, we're going, we are going
To North Americay.

'Uncle Rab shall be churchwarden,
And Dick shall be the squire,
And Jem, that lived at Norton,
Shall be leader of the quire;

'And I will be the preacher,
And preach three times a day
To every living creature
In North Americay'.[17]

The themes of plenty and freedom are obvious enough, as is the happy release
from the payment of church tithes. More complex are the social aspirations of
Uncle Rab, Dick, Jem and the unidentified 'I'. Uncle Rab and Jem have ideas that
are above their station, while Dick and 'I' are positively subversive. Dick seeks to
usurp the position of his traditional superior, while the enthusiastic but ill-qual-
ified 'I' arrogates to himself an evangelical calling to preach to all and sundry in
the vastness of America. Significantly, it is left to the reader to reach these critical
conclusions. Hawker offers no overt criticism himself, though there is in the wistful mood of this poem the suggestion of sad delusion, not only that such social
advancement is in reality unattainable but also that emigration is not the simple
panacea the poor imagine it to be. He is, perhaps, echoing the attitude of the
*Royal Cornwall Gazette*, though we see here not patronising contempt but rather
a sympathetic regret for the naiveties of the uncomplicated poor.

Hawker's view of the Bible Christians may have been coloured by the
temporary rift that had occurred in the movement between 1827 and 1829, a
few years before his arrival in Morwenstow, caused by increasing criticism of
William O'Bryan's possessive and authoritarian style of leadership. Some

circuits (notably Kilkhampton in North Cornwall) remained resolutely behind O'Bryan, but O'Bryan himself reacted by going off on a one-man evangelical mission to America, the first of his 13 crossings of the Atlantic.[18] However, the movement that emerged from this controversy had been hardened by the experience – by the 1830s most members had returned to the fold – and the strategic vision of missionary duty that it constructed was hardly the naive and simple yearning that Hawker's poetry might suggest. Moreover, the appeal of emigration (and indeed of the Bible Christians) was not just to the innocent poor but to a politically aware and economically astute class of small yeoman farmers (like Samuel James) anxious to make an informed and rational choice about its future.

Additionally, the Bible Christians – and other evangelical Nonconformist churches in emigration regions such as the Highlands and Islands of Scotland – when confronted with the phenomenon of emigration deployed a sophisticated sense of kinship in moulding their responses. This was not only kinship in the 'blood-relative' meaning of the word but also in the wider 'spiritual' sense of 'a particular group or community with a distinctive set of cultural or social values and an assumed common origin or ancestry'.[19] Thus when individuals or families within this spiritual kinship community were offered the chance to emigrate, the potential for maintenance (or loss) of such kinship overseas was foremost amongst the pressing issues to be considered. When the continuity of kinship was thought to be important, as so often it was, then this might well prompt the parallel emigration of other individuals and families with a view to reconstructing their communities anew in the distant lands. This, indeed, may help to explain the extensive emigration from North Cornwall –where such a spiritual kinship community may be said to have existed amongst the Bible Christians – in the early and mid-19th century. It also sheds light upon the creation of Bible Christian communities overseas and the enthusiasm with which the Bible Christian Missionary Society recruited trained preachers for its work abroad.

In the United States, for example, there seems to have been an influential Bible Christian element in the clusters of related Cornish farming families that settled in the Beach Lake and Wayne County region of Pennsylvania in the 1830s, 1840s and 1850s. Grace Spettigue, from Bude, was one such emigrant, a letter from her parents, Thomas and Susanna Venner, in North Cornwall dated 4 April 1842 showing that emigration from that district was in full swing: 'Richard and Mary are thinken if they can get money sufficient to take them there in the same vessel that you sailed in she is going to sail May 12 an land to Quebec because the price is so high to New York it will be a great tryel but there is no living here .... There are thousands going to America.'[20] Other families – many related in the 'blood' sense and still others from within the wider 'kinship' community – came from the neighbourhoods of Bude, Jacobstowe and St Minver (with a further sprinkling from further south around Liskeard and St Pinnock), including the Olvers (who had arrived in 1829) and the Tamblyns, Penwardens, Bullocks, Hams, Bellamys, Trevertons, Hicks, Daveys, Sprys and Orchards.

In Wisconsin, a similar cluster of Cornish families was observable, not just the familiar Cornish mining communities of Mineral Point and Linden in the south-western lead region (see Chapter 4) but instead the farming settlements in the rural south-east of the state. These have been the subject of extensive investigation by Jean Jolliffe, who has identified a wave of emigrants from North Cornish parishes such as Jacobstowe, Warbstow, Poundstock, Trevalga, Stratton, St Gennys, Egloskerry, Blisland, North Petherwin, Launceston, Boyton, Laneast, Tremaine, Tresmeer, Treneglos and North Tamerton. These folk, first arriving in the 1840s, settled primarily in the Palmyra/Eagle/Little Prairie area of south-eastern Wisconsin, with a sprinkling in Yorkville in Racine County, and by the 1850s they had erected a string of modest Bible Christian chapels – Siloam, Zion, Pleasant Valley, Little Prairie – across this open agricultural country.[21]

For many, the process of kinship reconstruction had started even before they had set foot in Wisconsin. In April 1850 the *Belle*, a barque of some 283 tons, sailed from Padstow for Quebec with 201 Cornish emigrants bound for North America. Among their number was George Davey, a Bible Christian local preacher from Egloshayle in North Cornwall, who was shortly to settle in Ottawa Township, just north of Palmyra in Wisconsin. Davey kept a diary of the 49-day voyage across the Atlantic which, as well as charting the day-to-day occurrences of this eventful journey, recorded his own efforts to bring together like-minded people for religious worship and fellowship.[22] There are various mentions of prayer meetings, together with 'our first class meeting when 18 attended. Brother W. Trewyn took the lead'. There was also his attempt,

> to ascertain how many [Bible] Christian Members on board. Found them to be as follows. Mr John Langdon, Mary Langdon, Henry Brokenshire, Elizabeth Brokenshire, George Davey, William Trewyn, Ann Trewyn, William Trebilcock, Mary Trebilcock, James Jewell, William Chapman, Matthew Biddick,

Peternell [sic] Biddick, John Williams, Mary Williams, Hannah Biddick, Richard Biddick, Ann Biddick, Mary Biddick, Charles Williams, Richard Rundell, Grace Brenton, Jane Kellow, Jane Brenton, Elizabeth Ivey, Stephen Ivey, Catherine Ivey, Mary Ivey, Elizabeth Howe [Rowe?], William Gilbert.[23]

The Biddicks and Rundells were already related by blood and marriage, coming from the districts of St Breock and St Issey, as were the Brentons and Iveys from St Merryn, with the Brokenshires hailing from Colbiggan in the parish of Roche. The remaining family names were also typical of Cornwall. To their number were added others who had come to light during the voyage as a result of Davey's efforts: 'two names more as members of the [Bible] Christian Church, Thomas Rowe and Ann Rowe making altogather [sic] 32, twenty-five members, seven new converts, several more appear concerned'.

Davey's evangelical endeavours no doubt accounted in part for the conversions and the 'concerned'. But the *Belle's* encounter with the notorious ice floes of the North Atlantic also concentrated more than a few minds. As Davey recorded:

4th [May] Aroused this morning between the hours of one and two with the crashing of ice against the sides of the ship. Everyone aboard appeared concerned, some much alarmed .... The thrilling voice of the captain and the trampling of sailors on deck added to the shrieks of the females made it indeed a very solemn time. But Bless the Lord for his supporting grace in time of need .... We shortly returned below, exhorted those around us to prepare for the worst, and gave ourselves to the Lord in prayer, felt refreshed and comforted. Soon hastened on deck again .... It was indeed the most splendid and yet affecting sight I ever saw. Such a mighty space of water, a great part of which was entirely covered with flakes of ice .... Some of them resembled the rocks on Roughter [sic] hurled one on the other .... Left the deck for prayer meeting a little before six o'clock, at which time our situation never appeared more difficult .... Sorrow and sadness depicted in every countenance. Commenced our prayer meeting. A most gracious influence rested on us, believers were comforted and enabled to rejoice in God. Every one was interested and concerned. Several appeared in great distress and cried to God for mercy ... did not go on deck until meeting was over, when, to my great surprise, found we were altogether clear of ice .... We were all constrained to say "What hath God wrought?" Heart felt gratitude now prevails throughout the ship, ascribing all the praise to Him who said in his word "call upon Me in this day of trouble and I will deliver thee".[24]

Intriguingly, Richard Rundell – one of Davey's Bible Christian colleagues – also kept a journal of the *Belle's* voyage. He too commented on the ice – 'She struck it with tremendous force; if she had not been strong we would have sunk to the bottom' – but he was also concerned to describe the construction of religious life on board: 'April 21 Sunday. Fine wether [sic]. Preaching in the afternoon, Trebilcock from Wadebridge. Although prevented from attending chapel, we feel Christ precious in our floating bethel. Preaching in the evening'.[25]

Safely in Wisconsin, these people did not forget their experiences and, with the Bible Christian church the focus of their social and cultural as well as religious lives, they began the settlement of Jefferson, Walworth and Waukesha counties. In the farming country around the town of Eagle, Waukesha County, Cornish families such as the Burdens, Corys, Leans, Rundles and Wiltons gradually acquired land. So too did the Bray, Hicks, Hooper, Sleep, Piper, Northey, Pethick and other families in the districts of Palmyra and Sullivan in Jefferson County – and likewise the Bluets, Dymonds and Strikes around the town of Troy in Walworth County. At first these communities were served by itinerant ministers sent by the Canadian conference but soon they had preachers chosen from their own kind, men such as the Rev. Samuel Jollife from Tremaine in North Cornwall and the Rev. Samuel 'Elder' Lugg from Martin-in-Meneage on the Lizard. Obituaries in the *Palmyra Enterprise* news-paper, carefully collected by Jean Jolliffe, give chapter and verse to these early Wisconsin settlers, with affectionate pen-portraits of individuals such as William Uglow, from Jacobstowe, who 'was one of the pioneer men of the community – men who came here to make fields from the forest, to help make a thriving farming community out of what a few years before was a wilder-ness'. There was William Dymond, from Launceston, known for 'His manli-ness, his honesty, his thrift', and the kindly Amos Bray: 'Brother Bray was a good man. Uniting with the Bible Christian denomination .... He found not a few on his arrival [in Wisconsin] and entered at once into Christian fellowship with them to maintain and support the church that he loved.'[26]

Across in Racine County, where the Rev. Samuel Lugg had dwelt before his move to Palmyra, settlement was pioneered by John Foxwell from Mullion. In contrast to the North Cornish flavour of the Palmyra/Eagle/Little Prairie area, this stretch of country was linked closely to the Lizard peninsula. Sailing from Falmouth in 1840, Foxwell had made the long journey to Wisconsin by way of Quebec, the St Lawrence and the Great Lakes. He built a log cabin in the neighbourhood of Yorkville and sent home to Cornwall for his relatives – his sister Susan and her husband Thomas Moyle (from Constantine) and their small baby, together with his elderly widowed mother. They sailed in the *Orient*, along with Samuel James of Trelan, St Keverne (the radical critic of church and state noted above) who had married Foxwell's other sister, Anna Maria. Many of the Redruth and Camborne mining folk embarked in the ship, destined originally for the lead country of south-western Wisconsin, made it no further than Racine County where, perhaps wisely, they decided to go on the land instead. The Goldsworthys farmed 120 acres at Yorkville, while the Luggs from Ruan Minor set to with a will to clear the prairie for agricultural purposes.[27]

Samuel Skewes, born in 1811, had farmed in Cornwall at Tresodden and Chybarles in the parish of Ruan Major before emigrating to Yorkville via Quebec and the Lakes in 1842. Effortlessly, he settled into the reassuring and mutually supportive religious community of the so-called Wesleyan Methodist Association of Yorkeville, though in a letter written some years later in 1857 to one William Lugg, a kinsman in Geelong, Victoria (Australia), we see that religious conviction did not always protect the Cornish emigrant from the self-doubt and the sense of loss or error that sometimes afflicted the lonely frontiersman far from the land of his birth:

> 15 years ago I was tossed on the broad Atlantic. I believed I was going in the path that providence had pointed out. So I went, nothing doubting. We were 21 passengers besides a young man from the east of Cornwall and out of that number six have already gone the way of all the earth. John Lory died from the kick of a horse. Mary Carter wife of T. H. Foxwell died of consumption. Alice Dale died of consumption. Charles Hosking, T.H. Foxwell's boy went to California and died there. Old Mrs Dale died of consumption or something similar. Poor Catherine [Skewes' wife] died in peace after a lingering disease

of a consumptive kind of three years standing. And now
Edward Dale has died.[28]

However, there was little or no place for such cautionary reflection in the
continuing clamour for emigration. In addition to the relentless movement to the
United States there was growing pressure for Cornish participation in the settlement of British territories, particularly the Canadian and Australasian colonies.
As early as July 1819 the *Royal Cornwall Gazette*, disapproving as it was of the
cause of emigration and hostile to the United States, considered that if people
must go overseas, then they should at least choose British destinations: 'We
recommend an attentive perusal of the terms held out in an official circular to
persons disposed to join the British colony about to be established in Southern
Africa.'[29] This was Cape Colony, a Dutch territory that had been acquired by
Britain during the Napoleonic Wars. Its strategic importance to British interests
hardly needed emphasis, and settlement was seen as one means of making its
possession more secure.

Nevertheless, fewer than 12 Cornish families – mainly from the Falmouth
and Penryn district – took advantage of the offer of assisted passages to the
Cape.[30] Their leader was Benjamin Osler, from Falmouth, and they arrived in
the Cape in early 1820, the *West Briton* suggesting optimistically that the
colonists 'speak in the highest terms of the country and the attention paid to
them by the Government'.[31] They settled at a spot Osler named Pendennis,
some 12 miles south of Bathurst, but it was clear from the first that they were
ill-equipped for the project they had been set. Without proper finance and with
little agricultural experience, the settlement soon disintegrated and within two
years Osler and his wife and five younger children had returned to Cornwall.
Others stayed on under the leadership of one John Dale but they too drifted
away from Pendennis: William Mallett to Uitenhage, Stephen Sawle Osler and
his sister Susannah and her husband to Simon's Town, Joseph Richards to
Grahamstown. This inauspicious start can hardly have recommended the Cape
to aspiring Cornish emigrants, although Richard Lander – the Cornish
explorer who with his brother John in 1830–31 gained lasting fame through his
charting of the River Niger in West Africa – had visited the Cape in 1823 and
thought it delightful. He declared that: 'This beautiful country has written itself
on my heart and if I was to die today I am confident that the words South Africa
would be found on my heart strings.'[32]

However, the Cape's failure to catch the attention of Cornwall at this time was perhaps not so much a result of uncertainty as to the new colony's merits but due rather to the lack of propaganda sufficiently persuasive to offer credible and plausible alternatives to America. But within a few years all this had changed, the emergence of a vigorous government colonial settlement policy establishing in Cornwall what might be termed a 'formal' or 'official' emigration trade, the progress of which was recorded in great detail in the so-called Parliamentary *Blue Books* with their 'General Reports of the Colonial Land and Emigration Commissioners' and their miscellaneous colonial government reports and correspondence. This trade, in turn, was wedded swiftly to the already established Cornish emigration culture, in particular persuading Bible Christians and other Methodist-inspired seekers of political, religious and economic freedom that their aspirations might indeed be met in British colonies. And, for all its resonance for many as a symbol of oppression in the United Kingdom, the Union Flag overseas at least promised stability, security and citizenship. As the *Western Luminary* observed in June 1830, announcing the sale of some 80,000 acres in lots of 100 acres or less for intending emigrants to Prince Edward Island, the territory was a 'British Colony, where English Laws and English Custom prevail, only one Month's sail from England.'[33]

Indeed, in the promotion of British colonies, Canada had something of a head start. Unlike Australia, it did not suffer the stigma of convict transportation and Quebec was already well-known in Cornwall as the familiar destination for those entering the United States by the tortuous 'back door' of the St Lawrence and the Lakes. Moreover, there was a long tradition of maritime contact with the eastern seaboard of Canada, particularly Prince Edward Island. As early as 1819 and 1820 the *Royal Cornwall Gazette* and the *West Briton* had noted the regular departure for Prince Edward Island of emigrant ships such as the *Wellington* and the *John* (the latter wrecked tragically on the Manacles reef, off the Lizard, in 1855 with the loss of almost 200 Cornish emigrant lives) while in July 1825 the *Western Luminary* opined that 'Emigration to the Canadas appears to be increasing at a very rapid rate'.[34] By the late 1820s and early 1830s the sailings for Canada from Cornish ports were so commonplace as to be almost hectic. In 1828 the *John*, sailing from Charlestown, was bound for Halifax, Nova Scotia. In 1832 the *Alchemyst*, then lying in Restronguet Creek, was for St Johns, New Brunswick; the *Springflower*, lying at Malpas, for Quebec; the *Endymion* for Quebec from Penzance; the *Phoebe* for Quebec from Hayle; the *Caroline* from St Ives, also for Quebec. A decade and more later, the pace had not diminished, the *West Briton* in April 1844 recording that:

> Our Camelford correspondent informs us that the rage for emigration continues, scores of men, women and children having passed through the town, on Tuesday last, from the north of the county, with waggon loads of luggage, on their way to Mopus [sic, Malpas] to embark in the *Clio* for Quebec; and great numbers are preparing to start from Padstow for the same destination.[35]

Yet another decade later, the *West Briton* could still note that, 'There is at present a very great emigration from this district [Stratton] to Australia, America', suggesting that parishes in North Cornwall were losing between 50 and 100 people each.[36]

An early arrival in Prince Edward Island was James Yeo, from Kilkhampton in North Cornwall, one of the 10,000 emigrants from that area and contiguous North Devon who settled in North America in the half-century or so after the Napoleonic Wars.[37] A particular North Cornwall/North Devon variant of the emigration trade emerged in the years after 1815, one which saw emigrants for the Canadian colonies setting forth across the Atlantic from ports such as Padstow and Bideford, the ships returning later to those harbours laden with North American timber. Between 1809 and 1811 imports into Britain of oak timber and plank from 'British North America' (the Canadian colonies) had gone up from 6000 loads to some 24,500, with softwood imports increasing even more dramatically. The oak came from the Ottawa valley, from Vermont and New York State and flowed out through Quebec and the St Lawrence. Softwood came mainly from New Brunswick and Nova Scotia. James Yeo, who arrived in Prince Edward Island perhaps as early as 1819, became intimately involved in this transatlantic trade: to the extent of building ships in Prince Edward Island of that abundantly available and almost ridiculously cheap timber to sail back and forth between Canada and Cornwall, bringing the Cornish in their droves to British North America. In the words of the contemporary song:

> And now my boys we're outward bound,
> Young girls go a-weeping;
> We're outward bound to Quebec Town
> Across the Western Ocean.[38]

**67**

James Yeo had first made his name in a carrying business that he had set up at Kilkhampton, offering a weekly service to Stratton and Bideford. He caught the attention of Thomas Burnard, a wealthy Bideford merchant, who sent him across to Prince Edward Island to run his lumber business at New Bideford and Port Hill. Soon Yeo was working for himself and in 1829 he acquired his first sailing ship, the 35-foot schooner *Mary Ann*. The years 1826–30 were formative ones for Prince Edward Island, with Charlottetown emerging as its administrative and economic centre. Significant areas were cleared of timber and under cultivation, producing a variety of crops from potatoes to oats – some of which was exported to both the United States and Great Britain – while ships built at the island were already trading with London and Liverpool and transporting passengers for British North America from ports such as Falmouth, Plymouth, Cardiff and Bideford. Island ships such as the *Collina* and the *Calypso*, with passage fares as little as £3, soon began to service the huge demand for emigration from North Cornwall and neighbouring areas of North Devon. Between 1830 and 1841 some 2250 souls sailed from Bideford to North America, at least 850 for Prince Edward Island, the majority of these labourers, craftsmen and small farmers from the northern border country of Cornwall and Devon. As Basil Greenhill and Ann Giffard concluded in their study of the locality, by the 1830s 'one person in every hundred, more in some areas, in the Taw and Torridge valley countries and the wild country over into Cornwall went to the Island or to New York or Boston or St Andrews or Quebec.'[39]

In the spring and summer of 1830 the *North Devon Journal* advertised ships such as the *Collina, Calypso, Sappho* and *Euphemia* as 'conveniently fitted up for Families and will take out passengers on moderate terms to Prince Edward Island, Cape Breton, Nova Scotia or New Brunswick.' When the *Collina* arrived at the Island in late May the Charlottetown *Royal Gazette* reported 'seventy four passengers, men, women and children ... a good many of whom seem in comfortable circumstances. The men consist of Farmers, Labourers and Mechanics, and are chiefly from the Counties of Devon and Cornwall.'[40] In April 1831 the *North Devon Journal* noted approvingly that many emigrants were:

> respectable farmers and their families who carry with them considerable property, thus transferring their property, their talents and, their influence to another land .... And such is the prevailing rage for emigration, that a female who had given

birth to a child but three days before, would not be persuaded by the most urgent entreaties of her friends to remain behind for another season.[41]

James Yeo was by this time fully engaged in this symbiotic trade, shipping lumber to Plymouth in 1831 and Penzance in 1832, his vessels returning to the Island laden with emigrants. In the spring of 1842 100 people from the vicinity of Kilkhampton, his home parish, emigrated in his ship the *British Lady*. By now a prominent as well as successful colonist, he entered the Island Assembly in 1839, serving for some 29 years and earning a reputation as a canny operator as well as for quaint but pithy turns of phrase which he used to good effect in parliamentary debates: 'one scabby sheep infects the whole flock', 'we cannot expect figs to be produced from planting thorns', 'let every tub stand on its own feet'.[42]

Using the *Blue Books* as her source, Margaret James-Korany has attempted to quantify emigration from Cornwall to Canada in this period.[43] The task is made difficult because the many who slipped away from tiny ports such as Helford and Boscastle probably escaped the official statistics, while many others who were counted sailed from Plymouth and Bideford alongside emigrants from Devon and elsewhere. Also, as we know, many of those who journeyed from Cornwall to Quebec were in fact using Canada as a back door to the United States, and are more properly considered emigrants to that country. Moreover, the *Blue Book* statistics are themselves inconsistent and incomplete. In the period 1825–30 they include emigrants to the whole of British North America, Canada 'proper' plus the so-called Maritime Provinces of Prince Edward Island, Nova Scotia, New Brunswick and Newfoundland. For 1831 to 1860 they include only the Province of Canada itself and not the maritime colonies. But despite these problems, James-Korany has identified some 42,000 emigrants who left the principal ports of Cornwall – Padstow, Fowey, Truro, Falmouth, Penzance, St Ives – together with Plymouth and Bideford for Canada in the thirty years between 1831 and 1860. The peak year was 1832 – the year of the Great Reform Act – with a further surge during the potato famine of the 1840s. The majority of these emigrants, she infers, were Cornish folk bound for Canada or for the United States through Quebec.

From Padstow alone, some 6200 emigrants sailed to Canada between 1831 and 1860. Indeed, in 1841 Padstow was the third most important departure point for Canada, surpassed only by Liverpool and London. Ships such as the *Clio*, *Economist* and *Springflower* were familiar sights in Padstow harbour during this period, the latter-named vessel earning an enduring place in Padstow lore as result of its extraordinary experience in 1842. Carrying some 40 emigrants bound for Canada, the *Springflower* ran into heavy gales some 1400 miles out into the Atlantic and sustained considerable damage. Although halfway to her destination, she turned her back to the prevailing wind and, partially dismasted, she limped home to Padstow where she was met 'with sympathy and respect'.[44] She was a Padstow ship, registered there in 1827, and she served as an emigrant vessel – taking passengers to British North America and to the United States – until well into the 1840s.

The *Clio*, built at Grenville, Nova Scotia in 1838, was another Padstow-registered ship and she crossed from her home port to Quebec at least a dozen times in the 1840s, with other sailings from Malpas and Truro. A crew list from an 1842 voyage has survived and it shows that the *Clio* was entirely locally manned. The Master was Thomas Brown of Tintagel, his Mate one Frederick Jenkins of Crantock, the 17 other sailors including individuals such as Richard Philp (second mate) of Portquin, Nicholas Bunt (seaman) of Port Isaac, William Tremayne (steward) of Sticker, and William George (apprentice) of St Teath. These Cornishmen, an integral part of Cornwall's by now increasingly sophisticated and complex emigration trade, were as familiar with the ports and harbours of North America's eastern seaboard as they were with the coves and villages of their native land.[45] The Master of the Padstow brig *Dew Drop* was also a Tintagel man, Michael Wade, who in July 1836 sailed from Boscastle with emigrants for Quebec. The *John &Mary*, owned by the Padstow ship-builder John Tredwen, was engaged in the classic export of emigrants and import of timber that made the Atlantic trade so lucrative in North Cornwall, as were the *Alchemyst* (built in Prince Edward Island but registered in Padstow) and the Nova Scotian *Voluna* which was owned in Padstow.[46] Together, these and other ships were the glue that held together the strong social, economic, cultural and kinship bonds between Cornwall, particularly North Cornwall, and maritime Canada.

The *Blue Books* are again significant for the glimpses that they provide of the human dimension of these bonds, the emigrants themselves. For example, they record the comments of A.C. Buchanan, the chief immigration officer for Canada, based in Quebec in the 1840s. Thus in May 184, 'In the *Clio* from Padstow were 146 very respectable people; they are all going to settle in the Township of Whitby and near Port Hope in Upper Canada [Ontario].' In September the *Clio*, making its second transatlantic crossing of the year, arrived with 58 emigrants from Cornwall – 24 males, 10 females and 24 children. In a comment which reveals the mechanisms by which 'kinship communities' were built abroad, Buchanan recorded that:

> The passengers in the *Clio* from Padstow ... are chiefly mechanics and farmers; a few of the former remain in Montreal for employment, the remainder are going to the townships of Aspadel [sic] and Darlington in the Newcastle District and Whitby in the Home District; they all possess sufficient means to enable them to settle on their own lands, and have friends and relations already settled in that part of the country.[47]

Again, as in Wisconsin, the Bible Christians were an important part of this process. In 1831 Francis Metherall was appointed an 'overseas missionary', and he sailed for Prince Edward Island with his wife and two children. As he wrote later, 'I travelled on foot the first three winters that I was on this mission; but I found it very great slavery. I have often suffered, and one time was likely to lose my life in a storm.'[48] In 1833 help arrived in the form of Philip James, another overseas missionary, and by 1836 there were 106 Bible Christian members on the Island. By 1865 the number had risen to 566. In Upper Canada, the expansion of the Bible Christians was led by John Hicks Eynon and his wife Elizabeth Dart (a celebrated local preacher from Poundstock), who sailed from Padstow in May 1833. They settled in Coburg, some 70 miles east of Toronto, which was to become the centre of Bible Christian activity in Canada. From 88 individuals in 1833, the membership of the Coburg circuit had expanded to 1207 by 1850. This expansion was marked by the characteristic cycles of 'revival', a preacher in 1840 describing how in one revivalist meeting he was 'suddenly stopped by the descent of a heavenly influence, which struck several to the ground ... some wept, some shouted, and others lay on the floor as if insensible'.[49] By 1850, 14 Bible Christian missionaries were at work in Canada, with a further two in Ohio and Wisconsin. In 1854 the Bible Christians in Canada were given permission to set up their own conference. Thirty years later when, in 1884, it merged with other denominations to form the Methodist Church of Canada, it brought with it 79 ministers, 7398 members, and 281 chapels. Thomas Greenway, born in Kilkhampton in 1838, became premier of the Province of Manitoba four years later in 1888 – a product of Bible Christian endeavour in Canada and testament to Cornish ambition born of self-help and the religious imperative of self-improvement.[50]

One of Coburg's early settlers was Peter Davey, originally from St Cleer, who in about 1830 left Treverbyn in the parish of St Neot for Upper Canada. Writing to a friend in Cornwall at the end of 1831, Davey emphasised the appeal of political and religious freedom, and of the opportunity for social and economic advancement for those who were genuinely committed to self-improvement:

> Soon after my arrival, I bought a lot of land (200 acres) for which I gave £275; the wood will nearly pay for the land and clearing. We can make 6/3d per cord for wood and 6 dollars per hundred bushels of coals [charcoals] .... Everything grows well; the soil is rich and will bear crops without manure. Cucumbers, pumkins and water-melons grow, in natural soil here .... Wheat, Indian corn [maize?], pease [sic] and potatoes also produce a fine crop ... the country is improving fast. I shall have forty acres of wheat next year, and having no rent to pay, no poor rates, no tithes, no Church rates, no land tax and only about five shillings a year to Government, I may fairly hope to do well: but it is useless for idlers or drunkards to come here, as they will be sure to starve. Industrious labourers can support themselves and their families well; wages are from 3/9d to 5s a day. Tell Mallett and Keast if they could get here their families would soon cease to be a trouble to them.[51]

Close to Davey's property was the village of Camborne, named after Camborne in Cornwall by William Hore and his wife Elizabeth – the latter born in Luxulyan, O'Bryan's parish – who emigrated to Upper Canada in about 1830 with their two-year-old son.[52] They acquired 106 acres of dense white pine, which they cleared for agricultural purposes, also constructing a water-powered saw mill with which – as resourceful frontier folk – they created a useful side-line in pail and tub manufacture. The Hores were among the original three or four families which encouraged the appointment of Bible Christian missionaries to Canada – it was with William and Elizabeth that John Hicks Eynon and Elizabeth Dart first stayed on their arrival in Ontario. Other Cornish settlers in the Camborne district included one Ben Barker, said to have been a tin miner and a fisherman back in Cornwall, the influential Roseveares (who owned some 1300 acres around Camborne) and the Sowdens and the Cocks, these families coalescing together through the medium of the Bible Christian chapel to construct a society – rather like that in south-eastern Wisconsin – based upon a keen sense of spiritual kinship.

In contrast to close, accessible and convict-free Canada (marred only by the short-lived 'mutiny' of French-speakers in Lower Canada in 1837), the Australian colonies seemed altogether more distant and dangerous. The experiences of Cornish convicts in Australia had alerted public opinion in Cornwall to the shortcomings of those colonies, while eminent Cornishmen such as Bligh, King and Nepean (see Chapter 1) had had direct experience of the unenviable task of trying to run such places as New South Wales, Norfolk Island and Van Diemen's Land. Religious opinion in Methodist Cornwall, particularly amongst the Bible Christians, was hostile to the principle of convict transportation, as were the radical political classes under the influence of men such as Sir William Molesworth of Pencarrow. In these circumstances, it was difficult to engender enthusiasm for emigration to the Australian penal colonies. Nevertheless, strenuous attempts were made to attract Cornish emigrants to Van Diemen's Land, New South Wales and, after its foundation in 1829, Swan River Colony – later Western Australia.

In March 1828, for example, the *West Briton* carried an advertisement announcing the forthcoming sailing of the *Henry Wellesley* for Van Diemen's Land and New South Wales, with advice to intending emigrants to seek further information from the Rev. W. Lawry of St Austell or the agents, W. Broad & Sons of Falmouth. As criticism of transportation mounted, policies were introduced to try to create more 'normal' societies in the penal colonies. In March 1839 a notice in the *West Briton* entitled 'Emigration to Sydney, New South Wales' informed readers that a Mr T.H. Edwards of Helston could provide details of free passage to that colony, with the next ship for Australia due to sail from Plymouth on 8 April. Similarly, the *West Briton* reported in April 1839 that 'A line of First Class Packet-ships sail punctually every month ... from London and Plymouth, for Sydney. These ships are from 500 to 800 tons each, with ... very superior accommodation for the conveyance of Cabin, Intermediate, Steerage Passengers.'[53] Mr Edwards of Helston was again named as agent, with other emigration agents appointed strategically in different parts of Cornwall: William Broad in Falmouth, Charles S. Edsall in Truro, John Oliver in St Teath, George Jennings in Liskeard and James Lynn in St Austell.

But even compared to the often stormy North Atlantic crossing, the long voyage to New South Wales was particularly lonely and frightening, especially the rounding of the Cape of Good Hope and the huge seas encountered in the 'Roaring Forties'. When the *Florentia* sailed from Plymouth for Sydney in August 1838, she carried 85 passengers of whom at least 12 were Cornish – bound mainly for the Bathurst and Cornish Settlement districts of New South Wales – including George and Jane Hawke of St Eval, William Rowe of Bodmin (described as a house carpenter and joiner) and his family, 26-year-old Edward Nicholls (a farm overseer of Treglossack, St Keverne) and others from areas such as Truro and St Columb Major. When the ship was off the Cape of Good Hope, a storm blew up:

> as quick as thought there was a general cry to 'hold on' when she gave a terrific lurch to larboard and fairly buried herself in the waves, the water rushing in at the ports – over the bulwarks & in every direction – the cuddy door was forced open & in an instant was knee deep in water the chairs actually floating about and & everything in the greatest possible confusion – the scene at this time beggars description, what with the cries & fainting of the women, the scurry of men, jumping on the table, anything to get out of the way, the laughter of the sailors, the rushing backwards & forwards of the immense body of water in the cabin – the howling of the wind & sea, altogether formed such a scene as cannot easily be imagined.[54]

Discipline among the emigrants could also be difficult to maintain on the long and often boring journey, particularly when personality clashes developed in the cramped confines of the 'tween decks. When the *Fitzjames* sailed from Plymouth for Sydney in early 1857 she carried some 429 emigrants of whom 85 were Cornish: 33 adults and 28 children, plus seven single females and 17 single males. They came from all over Cornwall, from Truro; from the district around Camborne, Redruth, Illogan and St Agnes; from mid-Cornwall at St Austell, Mevagissey, St Enoder, Newlyn East and St Columb Major; from eastern parishes such as St Neot, Cardinham, Duloe, Lanreath, St Veep and Calstock; from the areas around Breage and Mabe, Mawnan and Penryn; from the far-west at Penzance and St Just-in-Penwith.[55] The seven single Cornish women were part of a much larger party of 96 young single women, a formidable group which, according to the matron appointed to look after the females, indulged in immodest behaviour, quarrelling and malicious gossiping, as well as provoking a near riot when demanding additional water supplies over and above the daily ration. The women were 'in their fury like Tiger and Hyenas, tearing down the woodwork ... and yelling horribly'.[56] Especially irksome was a lazy Cornish woman, Grace Hocking, who was reported to the ship's surgeon for staying in bed after breakfast: 'I told her she must get up before 7 o'clock or I should get the bed taken from her, or get some water used for her for a shower bath. She replied this way – if you were to do this you should never breathe again. Can she really mean this? Her general conduct answers yes I fear so.'[57]

Nonetheless, despite such experiences and reports, emigration to New South Wales did, with the passage of the years, become more acceptable, even attractive. Certainly, some 4000 Cornish men and women arrived in the colony as assisted emigrants between 1837 and 1877. Of these, 413 men were described as miners, 755 were labourers (agricultural and otherwise), and 436 were tradesmen or in other occupations. Among the women were skilled occupations such as milliner, nurse, tailoress, needlewoman, teacher, safety-fuse maker.[58] Complementing this drive to recruit for an increasingly 'rehabilitated' New South Wales, Isaac Latimer – the Truro-based emigration agent – announced in December 1840 a new government-sponsored scheme for free passage to the notorious Van Diemen's Land. This strategy met with some success, the *West Briton* noting in May 1843 that the *Orleans* had arrived in Hobart Town from Cornwall in July of the previous year with a party of what it called 'Government emigrants' (i.e. recipients of free passages). Encouragingly, it added that 'The emigrants met with immediate employment at excellent wages'. A couple of months later, the same newspaper noted the impending departure of a 'large number of Cornish emigrants' for the same destination.[59] And then, ten years on, it was announced that convict transportation would come at last to an end and on 1 January 1856 Van Diemen's Land became Tasmania – no longer a by-word for vice and hopelessness but evocative instead of a gentle land of flowing rivers, airy mountains and lush forests with a temperate climate that contrasted favourably with the harsher environment of continental Australia.

By then the 'official' emigration trade had become deeply entrenched in Cornwall, with a network of government-sponsored emigration agents and a (generally) supportive press, especially the *West Briton*, working hard to both explain colonial settlement policy and to act as a source of practical information and as a conduit for applications for free or assisted passages. At the same time, Cornwall's emigration culture had become all-pervasive, the Cornish Methodist ethos increasingly in tune with government colonial policy as the latter moved towards the abolition of transportation and as it promoted settlement schemes likely to appeal to the ideology of self-help and mutual improvement.

The Poor Law Amendment Act of 1834 added a potentially new dimension to the 'official' emigration trade, although curiously Cornwall was slow to make use of the new opportunities for parish-assisted emigration. Cornish parishes might have begun to exploit the system as early as 1836 or 1837, but in fact pauper emigration was hardly measurable until 1841–42 when ten parishes in Cornwall used the scheme to assist some 69 emigrants. After 1843, the system was rarely employed and in the entire period 1836–47 only 260 pauper emigrants were sent overseas (mainly from the north and east, places such as St Columb Major, Altarnun and St Germans) – 123 to Canada, 70 to Australia, and 67 to New Zealand.[60] Margaret James-Korany has suggested that the lack of a large landowner/philanthropist class – coupled with the existence of a fiercely independent self-help Nonconformist ideology – might account for this reluctance or inability in Cornwall to resort extensively to pauper emigration. However, it should also be noted that in this period 'pauperism', as it was understood by the 1834 Act, was much less a problem in Cornwall than it was elsewhere in southern Britain. Devon and Somerset had higher levels than Cornwall, while Dorset and Wiltshire had amongst the highest incidences of pauperism in Great Britain.[61]

A far more intriguing phenomenon, a telling insight into how the culture of emigration had become ingrained in Cornish society, was the extent to which potential Cornish emigrants applying for free or assisted passage schemes were able, allowed, encouraged and even assisted to lie about their status or to at least misrepresent or exaggerate their occupational skills or other attributes, such as age. There were often deliberate and premeditated efforts to abuse the emigration regulations – calculated attempts to gain financial assistance or to qualify in other respects – while officials, agents and referees in Cornwall would often collude in such misuse. In condoning a liberal interpretation of assisted passage criteria, these officials were not simply corrupt but were identifying emigration as an 'improving' cause so important to Cornwall that the bending of the rules – and even the occasional falsehood – were more than justified.[62] But in New South Wales, even though the free settlers had the opportunity through that colony's Bounty scheme to nominate suitable emigrants from Britain, there were continual complaints about the quality of emigrants arriving in the colony, particularly, with regard to occupational skills and moral 'respectability'. The inference was that intending emigrants had routinely pulled the wool over the eyes of the selecting agents.

It was impossible for the Immigration Boards some 12,000 miles distant from Britain – which interviewed immigrants on arrival in Sydney – to verify with certainty each person's name, age, place of birth, occupation, religion, state of health and other details: including the names of relatives already in the colony.

But some of those who had lied were caught during interrogation, while the suspicions of officials were often noted down. Moreover, Patricia Lay has identified in illuminating detail numerous case studies which show the extent to which Cornish emigrants to New South Wales were prepared to stretch the truth or misrepresent their credentials. For example, in the *William Metcalfe* in 1844, which carried 241 emigrants of whom 43 were Cornish, Joseph Evans described himself as an agricultural labourer – one of the occupational categories most sought after in the Australian colonies – although just a few years before in the 1841 census he had been recorded as a carrier in Penzance. He told immigration officials in Sydney that he was bound for Hobart Town (Van Diemen's Land) and that he had no relatives in Australia. In fact, he made straight for Tumbarumba in southern New South Wales to join his brother on a large pastoral property. Similarly, to gain an assisted passage John Phillips had stated that he was merely a farm labourer. In reality he was in 1841 a gardener at Penzance, prosperous enough to employ a servant. In the *Harbinger* in 1849 there were 77 Cornish – mostly from the Gwennap district with a sprinkling from Redruth, Helston, St Keverne and St Erth – amongst its 288 'government emigrants'. James Collins was one of their number. A copper miner from Gwennap parish, he thought it safer to claim that he was a farm labourer, an occupation that would qualify him automatically for assistance. Similarly, in the *Lady Ann* in 1854 William Carah of Crowan considered it better to insist that he was a 21-year-old farm labourer rather than the 15-year-old son of a copper miner that he really was. James Pool from Phillack said that he was a farm labourer aged 19 but in fact he was a mason (from a family of masons) and only 17.[63]

The fact that early and mid-19th-century emigrants in Cornwall were able to make such intricate adjustments to their personal details to suit the often prescriptive requirements of the regulations demonstrates the extent to which the emigration trade and its attendant culture had become a commonplace element of every-day life. In one sense intellectually demanding – with the need to assimilate large amounts of technical detail which was likely to change from one year to the next – the 'official' emigration trade was actually well understood by an increasingly well-informed Cornish public. For intending emigrants in Cornwall, the myriad regulations were not so much a confusing and daunting obstacle with which to wrestle but rather an opportunity to be carefully exploited.

The 'official' emigration trade in this earlier period reached its ideological apogee with the so-called 'systematic colonisation' schemes propounded by Edward Gibbon Wakefield and his group of friends and colleagues drawn from the utilitarian and radical circles associated with liberal thinkers such as Jeremy Bentham. Wakefield, as a utilitarian, believed in 'the greatest happiness for the greatest number', and he felt that this aim could be achieved, not through the redistribution of existing wealth, but rather by harnessing hitherto latent resources of land, labour and capital to create new wealth in societies based upon equality of opportunity. And this is precisely what his 'systematic colonisation' was designed to achieve. Briefly, the broad structure of the scheme was this: land in a colony (or colonies) would be sold at a fixed minimum price or above, with sales strictly regulated to prevent disorganisation (such as had occurred in New South Wales and Swan River Colony), the proceeds of which would then be used to finance emigration. The resultant emigrants would be selected carefully to ensure that they were 'respectable', of good character, energetic, and also to create the right balance of ages, sexes and occupational skills. The volume and pace of emigration would be related closely to the amount of land being made available, and the settlements themselves would expand in contiguous blocks to prevent the over-dispersion of colonists (another failing of Swan River). Finally, there would be a considerable degree of local self-government.

Wakefield had founded his 'National Colonisation Society' in 1830 as a vehicle for these aims and between 1830 and 1833 he published numerous articles and pamphlets on the theme. His lobbying was remarkably successful and in 1834 he secured parliamentary sanction for a plan to establish South Australia on the principle of 'systematic colonisation'.[64] The colony was proclaimed by Captain John Hindmarsh, who had arrived in the wake of the first colonists, at Glenelg – a few miles from the site selected to become the city of Adelaide – on 28 December 1836. Although the practical difficulties of settlement and the severe financial crisis in the early 1840s combined to force a partial abandonment of 'systematic colonisation', the Wakefieldian heritage remained of vital importance to South Australia and its political and cultural identity. As late as 1880 it was still hailed as 'A Model Colony', while its utilitarian and Nonconformist flavour – to which the Cornish were to contribute in no small measure – earned it a second and equally apt description – 'Paradise of Dissent'.[65] In the late 1830s, as the handful of early colonists struggled to establish the new settlement, ideological supporters of Wakefield and the South Australian project mounted a propaganda campaign designed to 'sell' the particular advantages of the new colony. One such activist was John Stephens, the son of a Cornish miner-turned-Methodist minister, who came from an old Cornish family rooted in Helston and Tregoney.[66] His publicity work on behalf of South Australia culminated in the appearance in London in

1839 of his book, *The Land of Promise*. As he explained to his readers: 'Land, capital, and labour, are the three grand elements of wealth, and the art of colonization consists of transferring capital and labour from countries where they are in excessive proportion to the quantity of fertile land, to countries where there is plenty of fertile land, but neither capital nor labour.'[67]

To illustrate that South Australia was indeed a 'fertile land' – for some had dismissed it as an arid desert – Stephens gave glowing reports of lush countryside and the life-sustaining waters of the mighty River Murray, 'All the authenticated accounts that we have seen, agree to the fertility of the soil, and most settlers speak quite rapturously on the subject, comparing it to the richest parts of our own country'. As he observed, 'in South Australia at least, the climate of Paradise appears to have survived the fall'.[68] Addressing his comments to the respectable working people and energetic middle classes that he hoped would soon populate the new colony, he emphasised that South Australia did not experience the degradation and lawlessness of the penal colonies (the colony was to be entirely convict-free) and that (an important observation in the aftermath of the French-speakers' 'mutiny' in Lower Canada in 1837) the colony was – unlike Canada – also free from the threat of Popery. Indeed, he noted the conditions of religious liberty that had been established in South Australia and was careful to point out that the Wesleyan, Baptist and independent denominations were already thriving in the colony. His conclusion was that:

> The superiority of South Australia, not only over the British colonies in North America, and Africa, and Asia, but also over New South Wales, Swan River, King George's Sound, and Van Diemen's Land, themselves, appear to be established on testimony that cannot be disputed. Persons who have had experience of all the other colonies in question agree in awarding the palm of decided excellence to the new settlement.[69]

It was almost as though Stephens' comments had been tailored with Cornwall in mind (perhaps they were): his brother Samuel was 'the first adult colonist to put foot on South Australian soil'[70] when he landed at Nepean Bay, Kangaroo Island, from the *Duke of York* on 27 July 1836 and he was followed shortly by literally hundreds of other Cornish in the late 1830s and 1840. A veritable recruitment campaign was waged in Cornwall during those years. In March 1839 Isaac Latimer of Rosewin Row, Truro, was appointed by the

Colonisation Commissioners for South Australia to act as agent in Cornwall. A reporter on the staff of the *West Briton*, Latimer was an ardent supporter of 'improving' causes, always anxious to promote education, self-help and self-improvement, as in December 1839 when he delivered lectures on the art of printing to the 'St Austell Useful Knowledge Society' and the 'Truro Institution'.[71] Together with his colleagues – A.B. Duckham at Falmouth, G. Jennings in Penzance, John Geake at Launceston, and J.B. Wilcocks across the border in Plymouth – Latimer preached tirelessly to the lower classes of Cornish society, seeking 'Every kind of laborer [sic] and artizan [who] may, if married, of good character, and within the age prescribed by the Commissioners, obtain a free passage to this flourishing colony'.[72]

As well as placing newspaper advertisements, Latimer and the other agents also made great use of public meetings as a device to reach their prospective clients, lecturing to large audiences up and down Cornwall in places such as St Austell, Bodmin and Chacewater. In August 1839, for example, it was said of Latimer's meeting at the Market House, St Austell, that 'The place was extremely crowded, by persons from a great distance'.[73] In addition to explaining the 'improving' benefits of emigration and detailing the particulars of free passage – even to the extent of carefully elucidating Wakefield's 'systematic colonisation' – such meetings were also an opportunity to read impressive testimonials from those who had already gone out from Cornwall to South Australia. Thus, at the Market House, 'Many letters of the most pleasing nature were read, which had been received from Cornish emigrants, who all spoke in most flattering terms of the province, and invited their friends to come over and join them.'[74] But sometimes audiences remained unconvinced and in 1839 a particular cause of concern for many would-be emigrants was the charge for children made to adults who had otherwise secured free passage to South Australia. As Latimer admitted:

> there are hundreds of families, said an intelligent labouring man to me on Monday last at St Austell, across the water (alluding to the parishes of Fowey, Tywardreath, Lanteglos and their neighbourhood) who would be glad to emigrate, who would do anything to pay for their children, but who could not remove from their parish if it cost them a shilling.[75]

Latimer took up the issue with his Commissioners, and by the December was able to announce that henceforth children of emigrants would receive free passage, so long as they were under one, or seven years old and over at the time of embarkation.

As noted above, letters written home to Cornwall were powerful propaganda tools in the cause of the 'official' emigration trade. Sometimes they might be read aloud at public meetings, others might find their ways into the correspondence columns of local newspapers (especially the 'improving' *West Briton*) or to journals such as the *South Australian News* and the *South Australian Record*, which were published by the Commissioners to promote emigration to the colony. In the latter newspaper in September 1839 appeared the missive of one Thomas Sleep of Falmouth who had written home from Australia to explain that 'none of us desire to return to the bondage which holds our fellow countrymen', while in 1840 John Holman had written from the colony to his father in South Petherwin: 'I am freer than when I was in England ... we would not be back to South Petherwin for £500'. Another Cornishman in South Australia, John Oats, whose letter appeared in the *South Australian News*, wrote to doubting relatives in Cornwall in exasperated tones, 'if you mind to bind yourself in the chains of slavery all the days of your life, you had better stay where you are.'[76]

Occasionally, such letters were reproduced in handbills and posters, such as that published in Falmouth on 24 June 1839 by A.B. Duckham. Addressed to tradesmen and labourers, the main text of the poster was a long and wordy letter from a Cornish settler in South Australia, one Marmaduke Laurimer. The account Laurimer gave of the colony was seemingly candid but also subtle and ultimately very persuasive. It began by admitting shortcomings:

> I should have written before, but it takes some time for a person to be in a new colony to know its ins and outs. In the first place, no farming has yet been done in the colony; not an acre of corn planted; nothing but a few sections of 80 acres each, has been ditched; the colonists were not in possession of their country lands before last May; they have lived on their means the while ... shoes are dear, earthenware very dear .... Cornish ploughs would be broken to pieces in our soil.[77]

However, the tone soon changed to one of praise, optimism and enthusiasm, the letter giving a reassuring picture of South Australia while addressing itself frankly to common fears about the climate, the obligations of free emigrants in the colony and the disposition of the Aborigines. It was also careful to hint at the potential mineral wealth of the province. The capital city, Adelaide:

> which only 2 years ago was a desert, is rising rapidly, some of the buildings would grace London itself; there is no colony in history has risen so fast as South Australia. Work, I expect, will be very brisk near winter; the ground then, is soft: plenty of heavy rains fall in the winter, and there is neither frost nor snow ... it is a fine climate, and very healthy ... an Emigrant is free the moment he lands, he is allowed a home to live in for six months, with 14 days rations; his luggage is brought from the ship to Adelaide, free of expense, to his very door .... I was out the other day with three others, unarmed, and met two natives .... I walked up to them and shook hands, they were pleased as you like .... I tell you this to show how friendly they are with us .... I saw a piece of silver ore about 28lbs weight, last week, that was picked up by a young man of the name of James Nichols, who was a shipmate of mine; on the mountains he traced the load [sic] for a mile, and picked up about thirty pieces as big as a hens egg, all of which he showed me.[78]

Similarly, other letters employed to facilitate the 'official' emigration trade dwelt upon such issues as wages and prices in the colony, conditions on-board ship, colonial social life and the prospects for economic development. For example, in November 1839 Mrs E.J. Willoughby from Newlyn wrote home from Adelaide to her father in St Clement, near Truro, explaining that in the year she had been in the colony she had set-up shop with a turnover of £150 a week. She employed a shop assistant on £50 per annum, together with a personal maidservant at £18 a year: 'She is a Cornish girl, from near Launceston'. Her advice to relatives was for them to join her in South Australia, for 'if you are steady and careful, you could soon make your fortune'.[79] Not surprisingly, her letter soon found its way into the pages of the *West Briton*. In the same way, in 1838 a letter from William, Joseph and James Pedlar to their brother Thomas at Perranarworthal was soon published in the *South Australian Record*:

> It is with much pleasure that I am able to inform you that, after a very pleasant passage of sixteen weeks, we arrived safely here;

with the appearance of the country and my future prospects I have no reason to be dissatisfied. The price of provisions is as follows: fresh meat 1s per lb; tea 4s per lb; coffee, 2s per lb. Taking things as they are, I can maintain my wife and four children very comfortably for £1 10s per week. Wages for labourers are from 6s to 7s per day; contractors for work, 8s to 12s per day; masons and carpenters, 10s to 12s per day; sawyers, 15s to 20s per day. I am engaged to shoemaking at £2 14s per week. The climate is excellent, especially for those of an asthmatic affection; therefore, the only thing that makes us uncomfortable is the absence of our families.[80]

Thomas Scown, a builder from Launceston, had emigrated to South Australia in 1838 in the *Katherine Stewart Forbes*, a ship that in the years ahead was to appear regularly on the Australian run. Scown wrote approvingly to his brother that 'This vessel is a most noble ship for strength, accommodation and fast sailing ... we gave our captain, doctor, and mates, and ship's crew, three cheers each when we were asked by the Emigration Agent what causes of complaint we had during our voyage. To you this must be cheering'. Scown also stressed that the demand for labour in the colony was high, with Cornishmen especially sought after: 'We have not only given general satisfaction, but other mechanics are surprised at these Cornish operatives. Londoners, in South Australia, are already put by by Cornish men'.[81] Samuel Bray, from Falmouth, commented on the importance of the Methodist church as a vehicle for cultural life and social relationships within the colony, 'We have a chapel as large as Budock Chapel, and about one hundred in society. They held their quarterly meeting on 27 March; we were invited to take tea with them; we went, and enjoyed ourselves very much.'[82]

The cumulative effect of all this correspondence, skillfully woven together and exploited by the emigration agents and other propagandists, was to create in Cornwall not only an enthusiasm for emigration to South Australia but also a sense of anticipation and expectation, the community always eager to hear about the exploits of its émigrés half a world away. Perhaps for this reason, more negative reports from abroad were played down in the supportive press, accounts of some of the more traumatic experiences endured by Cornish emigrants remaining unpublished. For example, in 1839 the *West Briton* had carried a fulsome advertisement for the emigrant ship *Java*, bound for South Australia. She was 'a fine first-class teak-built ship .... This splendid ship's accommodations are unusually spacious and lofty .... She will carry an experienced Surgeon'.[83] However, the account of the *Java*'s subsequent journey, compiled by a Cornish emigrant, one George Richards, told a different story. There was 'no nourishing food on board for the sick ... the intermediate cabins are insufferably hot ... great complaints about the provisions'. The ship was infested with cockroaches 'which destroy the clothes', while there was 'beef thrown overboard, pork stinking'. Crossing the Equator turned into a barbarous brawl ('A French gent was served so bad that he ran into the Cabin and struck the Captain which put an end to such a foolish custom'), while fever took a terrible toll. There was the gruesome spectacle of a coffin thrown over the side bursting open as it hit the sea, while 'Girl to Bastian of Crowan died aged 11 years'. Richards' own daughter also succumbed: 'Dear little Caroline died this morning about 5am committed to the deep 12 o'clock about 4000 miles West of Australia, for 12 days she made use of nothing but cold water. 3 days before her death when she could eat something we had nothing to give her but Red Herring or Salt Pork which was poison for her complaint.'[84]

However, such dreadful experiences were not widely reported. Latimer concentrated unswervingly on the positive with an insistence that 'NO CONVICT SHALL EVER BE TRANSPORTED THITHER' and, despite his own role as an agent for Van Diemen's Land, trumpeted loudly that 'the vice and demoralisation of Australia, has reference only to the penal settlements of New South Wales, Van Diemen's Land, and Norfolk Island ... the morality of South Australia is secured in every way that can be thought of'.[85] It was a message that went down well in Cornwall and in the period 1836–1840 almost 1000 applications for free passage to the colony were lodged in Cornwall: 10 per cent of all applications in Britain and Ireland.[86] Even in 1836, before Hindmarsh had made his historic declaration at Glenelg, applications had been received from five Cornish families. Down in the far west, in St Levan parish, James Bennetts, a 30-year-old carpenter carefully submitted his application, pointing out to the commissioners that he was keen to purchase land in South Australia if his application were successful. His kinsman, Pascoe Grenfell, a joiner and wheelwright from nearby Madron, also made an application for free passage. John Richards of adjoining Sancreed parish also applied, as did another John Richards, a labourer from Falmouth. At the other end of Cornwall, James Harmer – a farm labourer from Warleggan, a rural parish on the southern slopes of Bodmin Moor – submitted an application, though we know he was not successful for we find him applying again in 1839.

By 1837 this trickle had turned to something of a flood, some 79 applications being received from adult males (often in their capacities as heads of households), with a further 23 from single or widowed women. Again, the greatest interest in South Australia was exhibited in the more heavily populated, western parts of Cornwall, with Gwennap and Penryn heading the list and Falmouth running a close third. But information concerning South Australia was by now finding its way into every corner of Cornwall, with applications coming from a diversity of sources: from Stithians in the wild country between Penryn and Redruth to Lewannick in the east. Twenty-six male applicants were described as labourers, and they came from all across Cornwall – William Batten from Altarnun, Richard Cornelius from Redruth Highway, James Pedlar from Tywardreath, William Thomas from Treskirby near St Day. Others were in skilled trades: for example, eight carpenters, seven masons, six shoemakers and six miners. Again, there was a fair geographic spread – William Carne was a carpenter and joiner from Helston Road, Penryn; J. Paul was a boot and shoe maker from Bodinnick-by-Fowey; and James Bennetts was a miner from Pool. Most of these 1837 applicants were accepted, sailing in the ships *Red Admiral*, *Trusty*, *Lady Emma*, and *Katherine Stewart Forbes*.

In 1838, as the programme of lectures began to take effect, there were more than 170 applications for free passage to South Australia lodged in Cornwall, from localities as diverse and far apart as Tresmeer, Perranarworthal, and Towednack. Labourers still constituted the major occupational group, although there were many applicants from a great variety of other occupations. There was a maltster from Ruan High Lanes, a blacksmith from St Dominick, a harness maker from Calstock, a female domestic servant from Pillaton, a roper from Torpoint, a thatcher from Hayle Foundry. It was not until the following year, 1839, that Cornwall's principal occupation – mining – began to achieve any kind of prominence, at a time when the total number of applications had doubled to reach almost 360, with still further Cornish parishes contributing their share of applicants: from St Keverne on the Lizard to Jacobstowe in the far north. Some 45 applications were from miners: from Gwennap, Camelford, Creed, Kenwyn, Luxulyan, Perranzabuloe. Agriculturalists came from across Cornwall, from St Goran and Gerrans to Landrake and North Petherwin. In 1840, the miners achieved numerical dominance for the first time, their 132 applications hardly matched by the 27 agricultural labourers and 12 blacksmiths out of a total of about 300 Cornish applications. Gwennap could only muster one miner-applicant, the vast majority coming from the adjoining districts of Camborne,

Illogan, Perranzabuloe, Redruth, and St Agnes. Many of the Camborne appli-
cants came from Tolcarne Street, Trelowarren Street and Pengegon; the Redruth
applicants were mainly miners living at North Country and Redruth Highway.
Further afield in the locality there were others: Isaac Barkla, miner of Mengoose,
St Agnes; James Barrett, miner, of Nancekuke Downs; John Climas of Rosewarne
Downs; Sukey and Jane Fletcher, balmaidens (female mine workers) of Wheal
Butson, St Agnes; William Menadue, miner and labourer of Mithian.

However, despite this enthusiastic response, the infant colony of South
Australia was hit by a financial crisis in the early 1840s, with emigration to the
colony reduced sharply as a result. Some 14,000 colonists had arrived between
1836 and 1840, perhaps as many as 1400 of these from Cornwall, but the intake
was cut back in 1841, with only 145 persons arriving in 1842 and a full flow of
colonists not restored until 1844. For those who had the misfortune to arrive
at the height of the financial crisis and its attendant economic depression,
Adelaide and the colony of South Australia appeared much changed. James
Sawle, from Truro, was one of the unlucky ones. 'It is necessary that the public
should know what to expect on the voyage', he wrote, for 'hundreds have found
a watery grave through the unkindness of those under whose care they have
been placed'. One arrived in Adelaide, 'exhausted with hunger and fatigue,
your dear children crying with hunger and cold', to find that 'We are subject to
diseases, painful and distressing; I could name many who have found a grave
in Australia.' As to reports of an abundant demand for labour, 'this is not true
... it is truly distressing to be out of employ in this place ... trade is at a standstill. Do not let any of my neighbours be deceived by false representations.'[87]

In fact, the South Australian depression and the consequent lull in
emigration to that colony proved only temporary, the discovery of copper there in
1844–45 more than rekindling Cornish interest (see Chapter 5), but for the
moment Cornish attention had already been diverted to the second of Wakefield's
'systematic colonisation' projects: New Zealand. Wakefield had formed his New
Zealand Company in 1838, two years before New Zealand was officially proclaimed a British colony, and the Company and its various offshoots (such as the
New Plymouth Company) was responsible for five foundation settlements:
Wellington, Nelson, Otago, Canterbury, and the so-called 'cinderella' town of New
Plymouth. As noted in Chapter 1, Sir William Molesworth's brother Francis had
been drawn to the new project, sailing in the ship *Oriental* in September 1839 and
settling in Wellington. Among those Cornish accompanying Francis was James
Bryant, one of the gardeners at Pencarrow, who collected exotic plants and

specimen trees to send back to Sir William, an early example of a habit which would result in the establishment of some astonishing gardens in Cornwall, the mild Cornish climate allowing the remarkable transplantation of species from Asia and the Antipodes. Alas, Francis Molesworth was seriously injured by a falling tree in New Zealand when working on a forestry project and he returned to Britain where he later died of his injuries: he is remembered in Wellington in Molesworth Street and in the Pencarrow Lighthouse at the harbour's entrance, along with the extensive Molesworth pastoral property in South Island.[88]

Other Cornish folk, perhaps as many as 40, including John Goldsworthy from St Blazey and his wife Elizabeth Richards, were also in Molesworth's party. They settled along the Hutt River in a string of cottages, some 14 all told, which they called 'Cornish Row'. It proved an unsatisfactory location, ravaged by fire, floods and even an earthquake, the resentful Maoris all the while lurking menacingly in the background, and in February 1841 they were evacuated by ship to Auckland.[89] Sir William, meanwhile, had taken the lead in the establishment of a [New] Plymouth Company to undertake the colonisation of New Plymouth on 'systematic' principles, his co-directors drawn from amongst the worthies of Cornwall: Lord Eliot, Sir Charles Lemon, E.W.W. Pendarves, Edward St Aubyn, and Sir Hussey Vivian. In March 1840 the *West Briton* stated that this company was 'the best medium of Investment and Emigration for the Counties of Devon and Cornwall', and in July of that year it was announced that the New Plymouth project was ready to receive applications for free passage to New Zealand. In the same month a second of the New Zealand schemes was unveiled, with the ubiquitous Isaac Latimer appointed as emigration agent.[90]

The New Plymouth project has been characterised by today's historians as unrealistically utopian, a naive attempt to build an idealised society in the southern ocean, and P.A.J. McNicholas' recent study of the settlement indicates its swift descent from high-minded vision to a state of weakness and insecurity and warlike confrontation with the indigenous Maori population. As McNicholas has concluded, 'As the colonial elite's paranoia over the decline in the liberal vision intensified, their perception of Maori resistance to land sales adopted all the assumptions and prejudices of the dominant ideology of popular liberalism'.[91] In other words, behind the lingering rhetoric of radicalism was the reality of ethnic conflict as the European settlers, Cornish amongst them (including one Henry King who had previously operated a company transporting lime on the Bude Canal), felt increasingly threatened by the Maoris.

William Woon, born in Truro in 1804, a Wesleyan missionary in the South Seas – he served in the Friendly Islands (Tonga) – had set foot on New Zealand as early as January 1831. He returned there as a missionary in 1837, before formal colonisation had commenced, and was horrified by 'the most revolting acts of war and cannibalism' perpetrated by the Maoris, especially when he realised that they had 'been on our premises with baskets of human flesh after killing their enemies'.[92] But although Woon shared the widespread fear of Maori resistance to European invasion, he came to feel a certain regret, even guilt for what he saw as the inevitable demise of the Maori people. When he had first come to New Zealand, he wrote in 1852, the Maoris were 'killing and devouring one another' but now all that had changed:

> how has the savage become tamed? The lion become a lamb? Was it through the wisdom and policy of governers, or by the force of arms? No. The gospel has effected these changes. Now thousands of the natives are united in the Church and Wesleyan Missions... I am sorry to state, however, that the New Zealands [Maoris] are in decline. Notwithstanding the philanthropic measures of our good Governor Grey, in the establishment of schools, founding hospitals, &c., to preserve the race they are dwindling in numbers. I cannot see how this country is to be an exception to New South Wales, Van Diemen's Land, North America, &c., where the aborigines have disappeared in consequence of colonizing measures. The Europeans are rapidly increasing, and in a few years the country will team [sic] with a European population.[93]

The [New] Plymouth Company, however, had only succeeded in attracting some 300 colonists to New Plymouth and even by 1846 the settlement was hardly more than a large village. Richard Grylls, a carpenter from Cornwall whose skills were much in demand in the fledgling township, wrote home in 1843 to Thomas Adams of Laneast and his wife Tabitha Knill Grylls (the parents of John Couch Adams, the astronomer), putting a brave face on things as he struggled to express himself in writing. The Maori threat had receded – 'the Nativs are a very sivle tribe and a great many of them converted to God' – and carpenters were making anything up to 48s a week, while 'I have purchest a pice of Land I gave 15 pounds for it about half a Howrs walk from Town on Devon street a plesent place.' But the pain of separation at such a huge distance from home was acute: 'My Dear when you received this letter I hope you will reply Amedently ... Give our kind love to John and Thomas George and all the little ons Mr Dear Give our love to Johnn and Salley and all the Fameley'.[94] 'Systematic colonisation', meanwhile, had been largely abandoned, proving as difficult in its application in New Zealand as it had been in South Australia, another dent in the colony's radical façade.

Although not as false a start as that in Cape Colony 20 years before, this was a lacklustre beginning in New Zealand. But for Cornwall, it hardly mattered. In the years since 1815 a vast network of emigration flows and contacts had been constructed and it was inevitable that some of these would be seen as more enduring and more successful than others. Thousands had already left Cornish shores in the search of freedom and opportunity, not a few taking advantage of free or assisted passages to British territories, others making their way to the United States of America. Many of these emigrants had come from agricultural districts such as North Cornwall and the Lizard, and in emigrating to new lands more than a few sought to recreate the religious and cultural kinship communities that they had known at home.

In Cornwall itself, an emigration trade – much of it 'official' in nature, with a network of government-sponsored agents – and a parallel emigration culture had become significant elements of Cornish life, equipping Cornish society for the traumas that it would encounter later in the century. However, as we shall see in Chapter 3, this 'rage for emigration' had been accompanied by a second and equally important phenomenon: the first stirrings – in Latin America – of a process that would lead to the rapid construction of an international mining economy and with it an international mining labour market. From the first, the Cornish were involved as key players.

# CHAPTER THREE

# BONANZAS AND
# BUGBEARS –
# LATIN AMERICA

The United States, together with the colonies of British North America and Australasia, as was seen in Chapter 2, emerged as the principal destination for Cornish emigrants in the years of discontent after 1815. The thousands who left Cornwall in those two or three decades were often small farmers and agricultural labourers, along with their families, taking advantage of cheap fares to the eastern seaboard of North America or of free or assisted passages to places such as New South Wales and South Australia. Much of this emigration was from rural, farming districts such as the Bible Christian heartland of North Cornwall or the remote Lizard peninsula and much of it was 'political' in that many of its participants sought freedom and opportunity abroad. At the same time, however, there was a parallel emigration of Cornish miners, beginning even before the end of the Napoleonic wars, which drew Cornish know-how, Cornish skills and Cornish technology to the emerging world of Latin America.

Taking their cue from the United States' successful assertion of independence from Great Britain, the European settlers in Latin America attempted to throw off Spanish rule in like manner. From 1810 until 1824 a succession of independence movements sought to drive Spain from its American possessions. Spanish rule ended in Mexico in 1821 but Peru was the focus of Spanish resistance, not achieving independence until 1824, and in the scramble by both sides to marshal resources for the long struggle, attention was turned to re-working the ancient Peruvian silver mines. At about the same time that James Hosking was planning his important journey to the United States in 1810 (see Chapter 2), a gentleman of Swiss origins – one Francisco Uville – was discussing with local Peruvian businessmen the possibility of unwatering the

*Central and South America*

long-abandoned mines at Cerro de Pasco.

In 1811 Uville travelled to Britain to seek the advice of the mine engineering firm, Boulton and Watt. He was told that its low-pressure pumping engines would not work efficiently at the high altitude of the Peruvian mines (some 14,000 feet above sea level) and that their components would not be small enough or light enough to transport over the difficult, mountainous terrain. However, Uville was able to purchase a working model of a high-pressure steam engine designed by Richard Trevithick, the Cornish-born mine engineer and inventor. Uville returned to Peru, finding to his delight that Trevithick's model worked perfectly in the heights of Cerro de Pasco. Suitably encouraged, he returned to Britain and in May 1813 met Trevithick in Cornwall to discuss his project.[1]

Richard Trevithick responded enthusiastically to Uville's suggestions and wasted no time in designing and building the components for four pumping engines (along with associated pitwork), four winding engines, a portable rolling mill engine, four spare boilers and other equipment. Uville sailed for South America in September 1814, taking with him Trevithick's mining machinery and four Cornishmen charged with its erection and maintenance. Some of the equipment worked well enough but there was a succession of problems, persuading Trevithick that he should travel to Peru to oversee operations himself. He set sail from Penzance in the South Sea whaler *Asp* in October 1816 and once in Peru made his way to Cerro de Pasco. However, Trevithick soon found himself embroiled in petty jealousies and squabbles and he left Cerro de Pasco to tour other parts of Peru, inspecting mines, advising on Cornish mining methods and even opening a copper and silver mine in the province of Caxatambo. But he was soon caught up in the wars of independence, serving for a time in the army of Simon Bolivar. The arrival of the Spanish army in Caxatambo caused Trevithick to abandon his workings there, and he made his way back to Cerro de Pasco where – following Uville's death in 1818 – he took charge of the mines. But again the war caught up with him, a skirmish at Cerro de Pasco leaving much of his machinery smashed. Abandoning Peru altogether, Trevithick set out through Ecuador en route to Bogota in Colombia but was persuaded instead to make for Costa Rica, acquiring valuable silver and gold-mining rights along the way. He decided to return to Britain to raise capital to develop these important deposits, completing the dangerous crossing of the Isthmus of Nicaragua on foot (he narrowly avoided drowning) and (so we are told) later surviving an alligator attack while heading for Cartagena in Colombia. It was not until October 1827, 11 years after he had left Cornwall, that he arrived back in Falmouth.

Although Richard Trevithick never returned to South America (he died almost penniless a few years later in 1833) his experiences there alerted the Cornish mining world to the possibilities of newly emergent Latin America. For what Trevithick had witnessed, and had himself helped to pioneer, was not only the first inklings of a new 'informal' British imperialism in Latin America which was to replace the erstwhile Spanish colonial presence, but also some of the first movements in a process which over the next century would produce an international mining economy – and with it an international mining work-force. Rather like the journey of James Hosking to the United States, Trevithick's adventures in Latin America sent powerful messages to Cornwall and the Cornish as they emerged into what was in 1815 the post-Napoleonic new world order. Put another way, the Great Emigration as it first developed in the years after 1815 was driven not only by the quest for political, religious and economic freedom but also by the temptations of the newly visible, newly available opportunities of Latin America. At the same time, the 'official' emigration trade of British and colonial government policy and officially appointed emigration agents was complemented in Cornwall by an 'unofficial' or 'informal' trade in which business interests managed their own emigration schemes, often hiring local agents to act on their behalf and sometimes relying on the construction of local 'Cousin Jack' information networks.

Much of what would later characterise the emigration of Cornish miners is first observed in Latin America. Even in the earliest days, and in stark contrast then to the emigration of entire families to the United States, Canada or Australia, the men – sometimes married, sometimes single – often went off on their own in response to recruiting drives by particular mining companies. Contracts were usually for a fixed and often relatively short period of time. If they were not extended or renewed, then the miners would find themselves on the move again, perhaps hoping for work in a neighbouring mine, or just as likely shifting to another part of the country or continent. Mobility was thus inherent within the system, encouraging the Cornish miner to always look ahead for new or better opportunities. It is said that among the first 'Forty-Niners' on the gold-fields of California in 1849 were Cousin Jacks heading northwards from Mexico,[2] and there is evidence of a two-way movement not only within the Americas but also between Latin America and more distant destinations such as Australia and South Africa. At the same time, this inherent mobility encouraged a degree of return migration, establishing the outline of a pattern which would reach its apogee in the relationship between Cornwall and South Africa at the end of the century. Sometimes miners would return to Cornwall for good from Latin America, but they were equally as likely to go back to Mexico or Chile or Peru for a further sojourn, or perhaps to move on to pastures new in other parts of the world. Needless to say, some died in Latin America, never to be reunited with their families in Cornwall, while others decided to settle out there: persuading or requiring their families to join them.

Of course, with menfolk overseas, it was left to the women to manage budgets, families, properties, smallholdings and much else, establishing a pattern with which Cornwall would become increasingly familiar as the century wore on. In the mining areas, many of the women would have worked – certainly before marriage and sometimes afterwards – as balmaidens, employed at surface in breaking and grading the ore. This had given them a sense of independence and the self-confidence to act on their own initiative, together with the experience of managing a personal income. Male critics complained that such work 'begets a want of modesty and delicacy' which 'render them wholly unfit to perform and attend to those domestic duties which should constitute the comfort and charm of every home', with hard physical work 'quite improper to the female frame' and wages spent indulging in 'rivalry of dress ... the pendant earings and showy bead necklaces ... a fine bonnet or shawl.'[3] But, despite these objections, there can be little doubt that such experiences equipped the women to be effective managers in the absence of husbands, fathers, brothers, sons. Money sent home from overseas helped, and indeed for many families was the vital component of their income. Here again the early incidence of remittances from Latin America was a prelude to the 'dependency culture' that had grown up by the end of the century, with Cornwall reliant so pathetically on South Africa. And just as South African money was later responsible for the erection of grand Methodist chapels and fine rows of superior housing in an otherwise decaying economy, so earlier in the century Latin American money had been put to good use in Cornwall. It is said, for example, that funds sent home from Chile were responsible for the fine facade of Lanner Wesleyan chapel.[4]

Alongside the remittances was the steady stream of return migrants, miners who had done well from their Latin American contracts and were keen to come home to Cornwall. Some were fired with the entrepreneurial zeal of the New World, helping Cornwall to devise coping strategies as – in the years after 1860 – it was faced with huge structural difficulties as the mining industry collapsed. Some put their money into Malayan tin or other foreign mining ventures, living comfortably off the proceeds and using surpluses to invest in new economic activities in Cornwall. But many others came home for a quiet life, content to run a smallholding, public house or corner shop. In the 1850s, according to George Henwood in the *Mining Journal*, the village of Chacewater:

appears to be a colony of miners who have worked in mines in various parts of the world. Scarcely a family is to be found one member at least of whom has not been out either to Mexico, California, Brazil, New Zealand, Australia, Africa, Spain .... The Portuguese and Spanish is well and very generally spoken by them when conversing on the subject of their foreign experience. It is not only amusing but highly instructive to listen to the details of their trials by field and flood. From these it is to be gathered that the first who went out to Cuba to work the copper mines suffered far greater loss by death than later emigrants to that country .... Many have returned a second time, and some remained in the country for fifteen years and upwards. Nearly all secured a little competency, to enable them to get into some way of business, a public-house or beer-shop being the principal and favourite speculation. Some few have realised sufficient to maintain themselves in a state of independence.[5]

Although it was the silver and gold of Latin America that first caught the Cornish imagination, it was copper – in Cuba and in Chile – that was to have the greatest impact upon Cornwall. Having fought off the challenge of Anglesey's Parys mountain, whose copper deposits were all but worked out by the turn of the 19th century, Cornwall's near-monopoly was successively challenged by Cuba, then Chile, and later the United States and South Australia, a process of progressive internationalisation of the copper market which culminated for Cornwall in the great crash of 1866. Although there was something inexorable, if not inevitable, about this phenomenon, the rise of Latin American copper had caused alarm in Cornwall as early as the 1840s. Paradoxically, while Free Trade was to become the shibboleth of Cornish Nonconformist Liberalism, the attempts by Sir Robert Peel's government in this period to reduce tariffs on the import of foreign ores were the source of much worry. In 1842 John Basset of Illogan, a much respected commentator on Cornish mining affairs, reported the general unease felt in Cornwall at that time:

in Cornwall the work [in copper mines] is done entirely by Cornishmen, and on the failure of a large mine, from 1000 to 3000 men are thrown on the parish, who cannot be absorbed in agricultural pursuits, or easily transferred to our manufacturing districts ... the scale of duties will be such under the new Tariff as must of necessity lead to the destruction of our Cornish Mines, and the consequent throwing out of employment the numerous hands hitherto employed in their production ... the Cornish Mines must be abandoned in consequence of the reduced duty.[6]

In the end, the Cornish copper mines were indeed each one abandoned, a result of changes and developments in the international copper market of which the reductions in tariff were but one element. But in the hard times of the 1840s, when the general depression of the British economy was complemented in Cornwall by the distressing failure of the potato crop, the Free Trade policy seemed to have much to answer for. In May 1849 the Tory *Royal Cornwall Gazette*, suspicious of Peelite and Liberal commitment to Free Trade, observed that: 'On Tuesday seven miners left Hayle in the *Cornwall* steamer for Bristol to sail thence for Chili [sic]. Four men were from Redruth, two from Crowan and one from Gwinear. Two of them shed tears on leaving and declared that they were literally starved out of Cornwall by the evil effects of Free Trade.'[7]

The ironic fact of men having to emigrate to and assist the production of the very country (Chile) whose output had apparently forced them into starvation at home, stands as a telling exemplar for much of the Cornish experience in the 19th century. It raises again (see Introduction) the issues of 'push' and 'pull' in determining emigration, and the extent to which individuals such as the miners described above left of their own free will or were 'coerced' by market forces. But it also illuminates that very Cornish paradox, that the 'crown of Cornish accomplishment' – the Great Emigration – was also a symptom, indeed a cause, of Cornwall's own decline. In the case of Latin America, the paradox is especially vivid, the high enthusiasm and excitement of the early bonanza years, with their promise of adventure and opportunity, giving way to the situation described by one newspaper in September 1845 in which 'The copper of Chili and Cuba is at present the great bugbear of Cornwall'.[8] The means by which that 'bugbear' had emerged had also more than a touch of irony, being largely the result of the speculative boom in 1823 in which three British companies – the Anglo-Chilean, the Chilean, and the Chilean-Peruvian – had moved decisively (which the help of Cornish agents already on the ground in Chile) to exploit the opportunities with which they had been presented. Among the directors of the Chilean Mining Association were George C. Fox and Alfred Fox, members of the well-known and commercially successful Fox family of Falmouth, and John Williams and William Williams, the mining magnates of Truro and Scorrier. To their interests was added that of another Cornishman, Pasco Grenfell, a partner in the Cuban Cobre mines and a director of the Colombian Mining Association at it launch in 1824. Although the 1823 boom itself was short-lived, the full potential of Latin America was now understood, and the stage was set for the long-term and widespread extraction of copper there.[9]

It is against the background of these ironies and paradoxes, then, with the glimpses of a complex and bitter-sweet relationship between Cornwall and the new lands of silver, gold and copper, that we can begin to throw light on the Cornish experience in Latin America. In Mexico, the Cornish connection was linked inextricably to the activities of John Taylor, the Norfolk-born mining entrepreneur who was already intimately involved in the Cornish industry.[10] Like other British capitalists, he had been encouraged by Mexico's new-found independence to investigate the possibilities for investment there, particularly in the old silver mining area of Real del Monte. Taylor contracted with John Rule of Camborne, then a captain at the celebrated United Mines in Gwennap, to undertake a technical inspection of the abandoned Mexican silver-lead mines, many of which had suffered at the hands of marauding armies during the recent war of independence. Rule reported favourably, and part of his brief was to recruit like-minded Cornishmen to join him in Mexico. Inevitably, he sought those he had known personally or by reputation (a networking mechanism that was an essential element of many of the 'informal' emigration schemes that were soon to emerge), recruiting Cousin Jacks to work as miners, carpenters, sumpmen, engineers, wheelwrights, foundry-men and mill-men. Among them were the captains James Morcam, John Dailey, and Garby, together with three miners of the names of Glasson, Penberthy and Allen.[11]

Captain Garby, who arrived in Mexico during 1824, echoed John Rule's sanguine estimate of the mines' worth, writing to a friend in Cornwall that he had 'no doubt of the profitable manner in which the Mexican mines can be worked by British capital and miners',[12] an observation which found its way into the pages of the Cornish press, further fuel for the informal network. Thereafter, the *West Briton* and other local papers were peppered with recruiting advertisements for Mexican ventures. Thus, for example, in March 1838: 'Wanted to go to Mexico immediately, 2 pitmen, 4 engine-men and 5 sumpmen. Apply to Mr Thomas Lean, Marazion.' And in September 1846: 'Wanted for Mexico, an engineer competent to prepare drawings of engine work, also a smith and a carpenter;

both well accustomed to mine work. Apply Edwin O. Tregelles, Falmouth.'[13]

As well as engaging John Rule, Taylor had enlisted the services of one Captain James Vetch, a Scotsman and a former Royal Engineer who had fought alongside Wellington in the Peninsular War. While Rule was to be entrusted with the task of technical inspection and surveying, Vetch was given a wider logistical and administrative brief aimed at managing Real del Monte and other Taylor-owned ventures in the vicinity. Rule and Vetch had sailed together from Liverpool on 24 March 1824, travelling via New York to Tampico on the Gulf of Mexico, arriving finally at Real del Monte on 11 June. Rule was to spend an entire year surveying the wreckage he found there, working hard to make the mine serviceable and safe.

Meanwhile, the first contingents of Cornish recruits were already on their way. As the *West Briton* reported:

> We understand that two Mexican mining companies have engaged some of the most active and best practical miners in this country, to proceed across the Atlantic to superintend the working of the mines in that country. These persons consist principally of young men, who are to act as mine captains, draughtsmen and accountants. Some of the ablest working miners are also engaged to act as superintendents of pitches [underground extractive areas]. The salaries we hear are liberal, and the engagements are for three years. A vessel will touch at Falmouth for the second party, the first, we believe, is on its way to its destination.[14]

In February 1825 the *Western Luminary* noted 'Great numbers of miners' waiting at Falmouth for sailings to Mexico, adding that 'Several captains, we understand, have lately accepted situations in the Mexican Mines at salaries from £700 to £1000 per annum'.[15] A little over a month later, the *West Briton* observed that:

> The Gentlemen Agents [mine captains] and the Miners, forming the second party destined for the Real del Monte Mines, embarked at Falmouth on Wednesday last on board the *Melpomene* which sailed soon after. During the embarkation a band of music played airs and the hardy adventurers were saluted with the firing of cannon.[16]

The *Melpomene* was accompanied by three other vessels, the *Courier, General Phipps* and *Sarah*, and in addition to their human cargo of perhaps as many as 350 Cornish miners and mechanics they carried nine Cornish beam engines together with Cornish boilers, Cornish shovels, hammers, drills, capstans, iron bars, wagons and a host of other accessories supplied by Harvey & Co. of Hayle, equipment necessary for serious deep mining.[17] Other Cousin Jacks sailed for Mexico in the *Cambria*, and it was due largely to the courage and strength of the embarked Cornish miners, notably two eminent Cornish wrestlers named Warren and Carkeek, that 547 passengers were rescued from the *Kent*, an East Indiaman which the *Cambria* had encountered on fire and sinking in the Bay of Biscay. The subsequent kindness of the Cornish in offering provisions, clothing and bedding to the survivors was noted by the ship's captain in his report to the owners, an echo perhaps of the 'superior' quality of the recruits recognised the year before by the *West Briton*.[18]

So far so good, or so it seemed, but in fact difficulties were already beginning to make themselves apparent. To begin with, relations between Rule and Vetch were strained. Although Vetch was able to get along with some of his Cornish colleagues, particularly Captain Trenear, agent at John Taylor's Bolanos Company mine in the Veta Grande district of Zacatecas, he distrusted Rule and resented the independence and individualism of the Cousin Jack miners. Vetch expected military-style obedience and deference and when these qualities were not forthcoming he regretted bitterly that the Cornish were not 'steady and submissive characters' but were instead (in contrast to the *West Briton*'s estimation) 'of the lowest class ... the most difficult we have to manage ... and the most ungrateful'.[19] Vetch wrote to John Taylor, emphasising that 'I must express disappointment with the miners sent out from Cornwall'. The younger men 'disgrace the streets with their drunken brawls at night and will not work until goaded to it', while among the more experienced miners Captain Robartes was useless because 'he is too old'.[20] All this was implicit criticism of John Rule's ability and judgment in the recruitment of miners for Real del Monte, and the conflict between Rule and Vetch came to a head when the latter began to question Rule's competence as a practical miner. Pleading sickness, Rule escaped from his contract and returned to Cornwall, an angry man.[21] Others were sent thither, notably the dismissed Emmanuel Jenkins 'whose drunken habits are a disgrace to the Company'.[22]

Vetch's labour management problems were exacerbated by his inability to deal with the Mexican miners who worked under the Cornish, failing as he did to persuade them to adopt new methods in the light of the new technologies that he was attempting to apply. But those new technologies were not without their own difficulties, especially as the machinery in the *Melpomene* and her accompanying ships had been, to all intents, abandoned at Veracruz. The ships had arrived later than had been expected, the onset of the rainy season making the going all the more tiresome, while the ousted Spanish – who still held the fortress of San Juan de Uloa – resisted Cornish attempts to discharge their cargo. When unloading was achieved, many of the lighters simply overturned in the surf, depositing their precious engineering components into the sea, while the machinery that did make it ashore sunk several feet into the soft beach sand. Far worse than these reverses was the impact of the new climate and its diseases upon the recently arrived Cornish in Mexico, more than a few afflicted by the dreadful *vomito*. Similar to yellow fever, *vomito* debilitated many first-time visitors to Latin America. Of the 45 Cornish miners in the *Melpomene* party, no fewer than 15 died of the disease.

This desperate situation called for desperate measures, and Vetch organised a huge expeditionary force of some 120 Mexicans, 550 mules and 50 wagons to rescue the equipment from the beach at Veracruz. Rusting machinery was salvaged from the shallows and the sands, and prepared for the long and difficult journey to Real del Monte. Meanwhile, three of the surviving Cornishmen had been declared unfit for the rigours of Mexican life and were sent back to Cornwall. The *West Briton* gave a touching account of the home-coming of the two who made it safely:

> The town of Redruth was enlivened on Tuesday last, by the appearance of two miners who had left for Mexico about eighteen months before; but who have returned on account of ill health. They entered the town in a post-chaise, and were heartily welcomed …. They left Mexico in company with another miner named Teague, who died on passage …. On Wednesday, one of the emigrants named Warren (brother to the celebrated wrestler of that name, who suffered so severely by assisting the sufferers from the *Kent*, East Indiaman) astonished the natives by appearing in the streets in the dress usually worn by the Mexican miners.[23]

Back in Mexico, the rescue party took a whole year to traverse the difficult country to Real del Monte, encountering and eventually overcoming the trials of swamps, floods, ravines and mountains. At the mine itself, the Cornish set to to complete the refurbishment commenced by John Rule and to construct the engine houses, miners' cottages and other necessary accommodations. Contemplating the huge task of restoring these old mine workings, some wondered if it might not have made more sense to have started afresh and from scratch at another site. In February 1826 the *Western Luminary* commented on the 'unfavourable accounts' in letters sent home from Mexico, the consensus of opinion being that instead of lavishing money on old workings, new prospecting for new deposits should have been undertaken. There was also news of German miners in Mexico, the Germans in characteristically efficient manner having already established a printing press and German-language newspaper: a sophisticated innovation that caused wonder among the Cornish miners who observed it.[24]

Despite the criticisms, Vetch remained optimistic, estimating in September 1826 that the simultaneous working of the Santa Brigida and Biscaina lodes would give Taylor a return of £1,500,000. Personnel problems continued to dog him, however, not least the drift away from Real del Monte of disillusioned Cornish, alongside those he had dismissed already like Captain Job Jenkins and M. Geach. Suspicious as he was of the Cousin Jack network that Rule had been able to tap so well, Vetch was forced to resort to it to recruit new workers. In this way, he sought to entice to Mexico Henry Tregonning (formerly of United Mines, but then working at Perran Great St George) and John Painter and Thomas Simmons, both of Poldice Mine. He even asked his employees to recommend friends and relatives back in Cornwall, the classic mechanism of the Cousin Jack network. When a blacksmith from Lelant named Glasson suggested that his father and brother could usefully join him in Mexico, Vetch rejected the former as too old though welcoming the brother as 'the Glassons seem good lads'.[25] However, he remained deeply suspicious of the myth of Cousin Jack, with its tendency to exaggerate the worth of Cornish workers and its air of ethnic exclusivity. As he wrote to Taylor:

> I can easily perceive that character and recommendations in Cornwall are often acts of courting, and a personal acquaintance of your agents with the individual would be far more valuable than 50 such recommendations from other quarters. Of this the pitman Treweek is a powerful example. No man brought so many recommendations and none so unworthy of them. His conduct on board ship did him no credit. He appears a stupid man, is very

lazy and disobedient, dissatisfied, insolent to his superiors and has endeavoured to impose his own refractory conduct onto others. You will have observed that I was nearly on the point of dismissing him shortly after his arrival. That measure I was obliged to put into execution the other day. Mr Simmons remarks on the ridiculous notions with which a great number of the Company's agents ... come out here with, respecting their importance – this is perfectly true, is very lamentable and requires some time to reduce them to their true dimensions.[26]

If the Cornish were still causing difficulties, then so too were the Mexicans. Vetch had intended to introduce the Cornish tribute system of remuneration, in which part of the entrepreneurial function was performed by the miner himself and where the miner was paid according to the value of the ore won, but the Mexicans resisted it. Although tribute rewarded those prepared to work long and hard, the Mexicans preferred their traditional *partido* in which they were paid overtime in (often the best) ore.[27] Such were these problems that, despite the huge expenditure and Herculean efforts, not to mention the appalling loss of life, the first consignment of silver was not actually dispatched from Real del Monte until September 1827. By then, however, Vetch had been replaced by Charles Tindal who had arrived in the spring of that year, a man of tact and altogether a different personality. His first task was to stop the drift of deserting Cornishmen (he persuaded John Rowe, a key man at Bolanos, to stay by offering him a salary increase of £500 a year), and he restored the morale of the Mexican workers by approving *partido*. However, longer term problems were caused by the political instability that beset Mexico, with its revolutions and counter-revolutions, and in 1830 four Cornishmen en route from Mexico City to Real del Monte – part of an escort accompanying a wagon loaded with provisions and money – were severely wounded by bandits who made off with the booty. In the end, despite his flexible and willing attitude, Tindal really never did grip the problems of Real del Monte. He resigned in July 1832, to be replaced by none other than Captain John Rule, the man who had fallen out with Vetch six years before.

As A.C. Todd stated, 'With John Rule there entered the administration a freshness, vigour and determination to prove that, where the soldier and the administrator had failed, the practical mining man would succeed.'[28] He moved to put the mines on a more secure financial footing, took a keen interest in the political and military affairs of the country with an eye to protecting the company's position, and took the precaution of arming his Cornish workforce in case the civil war came too close for comfort. In Rule's correspondence of 1833, dealing with this armament policy, are the names of some of his often otherwise 'invisible' Cornish miners and mechanics: Henry and Richard Artha, Stephen Bennett, James Berriman, James Bullock, Thomas Bawden, John and James Chynoweth, Joseph Grose, James Hosking, John Job, William Jeffery, John and James Michell, John Martin, James Pascoe, Edward Prideaux, Cyrus Paul, William Rule, Thomas Straffan, Joseph Teague, John Tresidder, Simon Uren.[29]

Rule undertook excellent developmental work underground but profit still proved elusive. The wars of Antonio Lopez de Santa Anna, the Mexican dictator bent on establishing his military rule in the region (including the breakaway territory of Texas), had again made the simplest of tasks difficult to achieve. Rule also encountered difficulty with the Mexican miners – again over *partido* but this time as to whether its payment was appropriate (Rule thought not) when the Mexicans were engaged in the driving of levels (tunnels) rather than the actual winning of ore. In 1833 cholera swept the Sierra Madre uplands in which the silver mines were located, killing nine of the Cornish at Bolanos and adding to Rule's problems. The scale of this tragedy is apparent in John Taylor's own report of the incident:

> At the beginning of August [1833] Bolanos was visited by the Cholera which raged there with the greatest violence, and produced the most distressing effects. Not only were the numbers of deaths very great in proportion, but the alarm caused so many to leave the place that the Mines were nearly deserted, and for some time the Works were at a stand. The steam engines could only be worked occasionally, as all but one of the men who were competent to superintend it [sic] were attacked by the disorder, and the Underground Agents were so reduced by illness that they were obliged to seek a better climate for a time, in order to recover. We have since lost Captain [Thomas] Rich [from St Hilary], by death, who was at the Head of this Department, and Captain Manuel has been obliged to leave the service of the company and return to England.[30]

With his record of only qualified success, Rule left for extended leave in Britain in May 1834. In his absence, the management was put in the hands of his brother

William and one Roderick Mackenzie. Another Scotsman, like Vetch before him, Mackenzie did not always see eye to eye with the Cornish. Simon Uren was dismissed for using obscenities when speaking to superior officers, but William Rule and Captain Hosking promptly re-instated him. Henry Tonkins was dismissed for disobedience, Captain John Trenoweth was admonished for irregularities in his expenses claims, and Titus Geach was warned for taking liberties with Mexican women: 'Unless it comes from your own relation, Mr Francis, with whom Mr Taylor may communicate on the subject, I think that your wife may never hear of what I have written.'[31] And when John Rule returned to Mexico in March 1835 he was disappointed to find that progress had not been as great as he had hoped. The sinking of the all-important Dolores Shaft (designed to reach a rich ore body that had had to be abandoned two years before) had been delayed by unusually hard rock, and Rule warned that further outlays would be required before the mines showed a profit. He tried to economise, and one of his measures was the abolition of 'subsist', an advance of wages paid in anticipation of the successful completion of tribute contracts, a practice commonplace in Cornwall but (Rule thought) hardly necessary in Mexico where salaries were high. This hit some of the Cornishmen hard but for others, those who had worked well and had demonstrated loyalty to the company, there was preferment and promotion: James Pascoe became a grass (surface) captain and Captain Chynoweth was elevated to underground captain. There was also some investment, new machinery being brought out from Cornwall (including a 54-inch engine built at Hayle Copperhouse), along with new recruits.

It was not, however, until the political situation began to stabilise that John Taylor's Mexican mines began to settle into anything like a more secure existence. Santa Anna's defeat in Texas had led, in turn, to his fall from grace in Mexico, ushering in in 1837 the new (or rather restored) government of Anastasio Bustamente who had been in exile in Britain and was, in consequence, pro-British. Alongside this welcome turn for the better the usual irritations continued to vex Rule, such as the case of Captain Barratt whom he had had to dismiss for attempting to take 'improper liberties' with the wife of Captain Grose.[32] This latter case reminds us that, more than ten years after the arrival of the first Cornish in Mexico, the Cornish communities consisted now not only of the individual 'birds of passage' – single men, and others who had left their wives and families in Cornwall – but women and children too. Although these family groupings were still very much the exception rather than the rule, their very existence indicated that the Cornish in Mexico had become well and truly established, Latin America by now already a significant element of the Cornish diaspora. But with the creation of an ethnic community came the potential for ethnic conflict. Although Cornish-Mexican relations had been generally good, their cultural differences – especially in the realms of mining practice – and the unequal power relationship between the two groups could lead to difficulties. On one occasion Tobias Mannell, a Cornish carpenter, was goaded (or so he said) to breaking point by the insults of a Mexican labourer. Mannell hurled his axe at the man, and although the Mexican was only slightly injured his fellow countrymen sprang to his defence, turning their wrath on Mannell and other Cornishmen in the vicinity. George Mannell, Tobias' brother, managed to escape unhurt from the unsheathed knives and raining stones, as did Jon Whatburn, but John Vial was severely cut on the face and Job Sallis was wounded in the back.

John Rule, anxious not to be diverted from the increasingly desperate task of making the mines pay, urged the Cornish to bite their tongues and turn the other cheek, recognising that ultimately he had more control over the behaviour of his own countrymen than over the often perplexing Mexicans. Although he might already have begun to make a profit if he had concentrated on exploiting even the indifferent ore bodies located thus far, Rule insisted that more developmental work and investment was necessary if Real del Monte was to have a long-term future, and it was on this activity that he expended his efforts. In 1841 he acquired a 30-inch pumping engine from Harvey & Co. of Hayle and recruited further workers from Cornwall – men such as Andrew Stevens, John Kinsman, James Blight, Digory Morcam, William Blarney and Thomas Trewhella. And, aided by the decision of the Mexican government to relinquish its duty on the export of silver, it seemed as though Real del Monte might at last start to pay its way. Comforted by this thought and reflecting upon his long battle to refurbish and then develop the mines to modern Cornish standards, John Rule must have considered that his work was complete, his objectives achieved, for by the end of 1842 he had decided to retire. He returned to Cornwall, settling in Penzance where he became active in the affairs of the Royal Geological Society of Cornwall, donating Mexican mineral specimens to its collection, writing and lecturing on Mexico, and eventually becoming vice-president of the Society. The place of Mexico in the iconography of the Great Emigration was assured.

John was succeeded at Real del Monte by his brother, William Rule. Sadly, the long hoped for upturn in fortunes had, despite all the expectations that had preceded John Rule's retirement, failed to materialise. By 1848, the year in which

Mexico lost California, Texas and the huge area west of the Mississippi, the company seemed on the point of collapse and the decision was made to suspend operations. William Rule relinquished his position shortly after and in the following year some of the Cornish hurried northwards when news came of the Californian gold strikes. Meanwhile, Rule had been replaced by one John Hitchcock Buchan. Buchan persuaded the increasingly frustrated directors to sell Real del Monte to Mexican business interests and then, remarkably, set about making the mine pay for his new masters in a way that had eluded the Rules in the days of John Taylor. He abandoned the capital-intensive search for high-grade ore and instead worked the easily accessible low-grade material, both cutting costs and earning revenue. Even so, it was some time before the Real del Monte was truly profitable, one shareholder complaining to the *Mining Journal* as late as March 1868 that 'Ever since I have been a shareholder in this company in Real del Monte, I have been constantly annoyed and persecuted with letters "Private and Confidential" and in reference to its not only gloomy prospects, but absolute and certain ruin.'[33] However, taking his cue perhaps from those Cousin Jacks who had argued more than 20 years before that new deposits should be sought rather than old ones re-worked, Buchan surveyed the Pachuca district on the other side of the mountain to Real del Monte, leading to the discovery of the fabulously rich Rosario bonanza which was developed vigorously in subsequent decades. By November 1874 one R. Tredinnick, a Cornishman, could write in the *Mining Journal* that there were 500 mines in Mexico and that 'The mineral produce of Mexico is remarkable even when compared to the richest countries of the world. The silver coinage is about 20 million dollars – £4,000,000 sterling.'[34]

At once Pachuca became the focus of Cornish attention. Cornish engines were erected there in 1853 and again in 1863, and in 1873 a huge 85-inch engine was provided by Harvey & Co. As late as August 1908 we find the Cornish engineering firm, Holmans of Camborne, providing the La Blanca mine, Pachuca, with one horizontal duplex compound hoisting engine, two Lancashire boilers, steel headgear and other material at a cost of £5489.[35] Meanwhile, despite the growing attractions of competing destinations from California to South Australia, Cornish miners continued to arrive in Mexico. John Gundry from Helston (son of the famous Cornish wrestler, Tom Gundry) went out to run the Santa Gertrudis mine at Pachuca for Frank 'Francisco' Rule. Francisco Rule, no relation, apparently, to the earlier generation of Cornish captains in Mexico, had arrived around 1858 and became manager of many Pachuca workings, discovering the Santa Gertrudis deposits and forming the companies that produced the

Maravillas, Santa Anna and La Blanca mines. An energetic and flamboyant fig-
ure, he all but dominated Mexican mining by 1900. He was a personal friend of
the president, a benefactor of the poor, known in Mexico and Cornwall as 'the
Silver King'. Among the Cornish community that he created around him were
individuals such as Thomas and Jacoliah Honey from Wheal Busy, near
Chacewater, and Matthew Trezise and Jane Curtis from neighbouring St Day.
Also from Chacewater was Richard Honey, born in 1839, who married Emma
Jane Phillips of Stithians and emigrated to Pachuca in 1862. He started his own
iron mine at Ixmicilpan, transporting the ore to Pachuca for smelting, and in
time came to own a string of mines and foundries. He also invested in railroads
and became president of three Mexican banks. John Williams Goldsworthy, born
in Redruth on 15 June 1852, emigrated to Pachuca with his family in the late
1870s. They all returned to Cornwall in the mid-1890s, but not before John had
made a contribution to the economic and civic life of Pachuca sufficiently distinguished for him to be presented on his departure with a gold, chiming pocket
watch by the governor.[36]

Although the focus of attention had now fixed firmly upon Pachuca, the
Cornish remained in strength at Real del Monte. Lists of employees of the Real
del Monte Mining Company have survived, affording surprising details of the
Cornish who worked there.[37] A fascinating feature of these returns is the
adoption of Hispanic forms of Christian names, the surnames remaining
thoroughly Cornish. Thus we learn that in March 1859 Juan Boskean is aged 34,
is of normal stature, and has black hair and a regular beard. His colleague
Nataniel Faull is 30, short, with chestnut-brown hair and no beard. The
Safety/Identification Lists for the whole of 1859 contain some 190 named individuals. One of the names is French, five seem very English and are unlikely to
be Cornish, while the remainder are either exclusively or typically Cornish.
Names such as Jory, Rosevear, Trevethan, Sandry, Curnow, Penberthy, Kessell
and Rapson are clearly Cornish and, given the context, it is extremely likely that
the bearers of names like Bennett, Thomas, Richards, Hodge, Holman,
Stoneman, Noble and Kinsman were also Cousin Jacks. Again, the details are
intriguing. Francis Blackwell (born on 27 January 1802 at Crowan, and married
to Jenifer Champion) is 57 years of age, has blue eyes, chestnut hair and a regular beard. Carlos Grose is 21 and has blue eyes, blond hair and no beard.
Guillo Beckerleg is 46, with brown eyes, chestnut hair and a regular beard. In
December 1866, some 41 names are recorded. Again, they seem overwhelmingly Cornish. There is no doubting Thomas Pascoe, Ricardo Cambellack,

Emillermo Tregoning or Jaime Skewis. We also know that Guillermo Dudley is Cornish and we can safely assume from the company that they keep that so too are the likes of Carlos Richards and Enrique Williams.

The other great surviving clue to the identity of the ordinary Cornish at Real del Monte and Pachuca are the headstone inscriptions in the so-called English Cemetery, which have been carefully and lovingly recorded by Terry Dudley.[38] They are also an insight into the hard and tragic lives endured by many of the Cornish emigrants. There is Isaac Edward Richards, from Breage, who was killed in the Santa Gertrudis mine in 1896 aged 26 years. There is Isaac Prout who was assassinated on the road from Real del Monte to Pachuca on 31 July 1864 aged 31 years. His headstone recalls the words of Psalm 102 v.25, 'They weakened my strength in the way/They have shortened my days'. Sometimes whole families seemed afflicted by such shortened days, as the Pengilly grave testifies:

> Sacred to the memory of
> THOMAS PENGILLY
> Beloved husband of
> ELIZABETH PENGILLY
> who died at Pachuca
> November 22 1893
> aged 48 years

and also of:

> Their dearly beloved son
> THOMAS ALVINO
> WHO DIED AT PACHUCA
> March 12th 1888
> aged 4 years 3 months.

Even sadder, perhaps, is the headstone of 'John the son of/ MARY RULE/ Died January 2nd 1871 aged 1 year and 6 months'. Did poor Mary have a husband, one wonders; who was the father of her ill-fated child?

For many, hardship and tragedy were intensified by the separation from loved ones at home in Cornwall. The strain could be financial as well as emotional and in the earlier days at least the paternalistic Real del Monte company was at pains to organise its own 'homepay' arrangements, requiring employees with dependents back in Cornwall to allocate a proportion of their wages to be sent home by the company. Thus on 16 March 1867, for example, the company arranged for an amount of £4619 to be transferred to Cornwall as remittances. Some £633 of this went to Redruth, to be administered by Messrs Williams & Co. of that town. Individual payments varied from the meagre to the generous, from the £6 James Job sent Margaret Curnow and the £11 forwarded by Samuel Knight for William Knight, to the £32 sent home by James Kinsman to Grace Kinsman.[39] For the 'birds of passage', of course, the separation experienced in Mexico was but one chapter in a series of separations, many Cornish marriages and other relationships of necessity being conducted at huge distances with infrequent opportunities for intimate contact. Pity the many who could not read or write, or for whom letters sent from obscure parts of the world went astray or were delayed for months on end.

But even the literate and the educated could not be protected from the 'tyranny of distance'.[40] Consider for a moment the career of William John Oates, born in 1859, whose wanderings took him to Mexico and elsewhere in Latin America, as well as a good many other places besides.[41] He worked as a youth at Wheal Unity Wood, near Chacewater, but his first 'real' job was at a silver mine at Arequipa, Peru, run by his uncle: the well-known William Oates. From there he moved across to Bolivia, working in the Huanchacha and other mines, before returning to Cornwall in 1887 to marry Mary Crothers. Soon after the birth of his daughter in 1888 he departed for Uruguay, journeying inland from Montevideo to the Corrales district where he became captain of the Hermanos Goldfields Mining Co. Ltd. His wife joined him in South America in 1889 but by 1891 they were back in Cornwall. Within the year William was off on his own again, travelling to Peru where in the October he found work at the Mineria de Portara workings. He soon moved on, becoming captain of the Calyoma Silver Mining Co., again in Peru, before returning home to Cornwall in October 1894. By June of the following year he was on his way back to Peru once more, having secured a two-year contract at the Acari Mines, accompanied this time by his brother Henry Martin Oates and his brother-in-law George Crothers. Back in Cornwall again in 1897, he was swiftly snapped-up to report on several gold-mining properties in the Ural Mountains in Russia, moving on quickly to Southern Rhodesia where he was engaged to report on mineral deposits in Matabeleland in the latter months of 1898. In April 1902 he contracted with the Chiapos Mining Co. to go to its Santa Fe silver mines in Tabasco, Mexico and was yet again on his way back to Latin America. The Santa Fe was reputed to be one of the richest properties in Mexico but in reality it was all but worked out and when the lode soon began to fail Oates returned to Cornwall. Thereafter, his wanderings took him briefly to County Cork, back to Peru for the fourth and last time, on to a gold-mine in Malaya and even to Argentina. He retired eventually to Newquay and finally Lostwithiel, dying there in 1935.

Such hectic careers, often spanning several decades of two centuries and encompassing three or four continents, make exhausting reading – even in outline – and in detail they are all the more extraordinary. Like William John Oates, for James Skewis (born in 1826) a sojourn in Mexico was but one component of a complex international working life and we see in his journals and letters the intimate thoughts and experiences of a world-travelled Cornishman.[42] From Vyvyan's Row in Camborne, where the Skewis family lived, Edward Skewis – James' father – set out for North America in 1848, to be followed in the next year by the rest of the family. They landed at New Orleans where James was astonished by the inhuman cruelty of the slave trade. Remarking that 'We soon found out that the white folks were not pleased for us to be free with these poor, helpless negroes', James Skewis expressed his feelings – as he so often did – in verse:

> The child was sold from mother
> The husband from the wife
> We never saw such barbarity
> Before in all our life.[43]

The Skewis family made its way by steam boat up the Mississippi to Galena, Illinois, a mining town, staying there overnight in a hotel owned by a Camborne man, one of the Rablings. From there they travelled on to Shullsburg, Wisconsin, their intended home, where they 'bought a lead mine for fifty dollars'. But no sooner had they settled than they were off, like many of Wisconsin's Cornish miners, to the Californian rush. The route was not across the unknown expanses and mountains of the West but by sea, necessitating a long drawn-out journey via New Orleans, Cuba, Panama and Mexico. James travelled with his brother Henry and five other companions. Their first taste of Mexico was Acapulco, with which James Skewis seemed well pleased, writing that 'We went ashore and had a comfortable time' and that 'I should imagine there was not a more secure harbour in the world than that of Acapulco.' Once in California, James explored the gold country of the Sierra Nevada and the Mother Lode and then travelled back to San Francisco with vague thoughts of entering the carrying business. However, he fell in with a group of miners determined to try their luck on the newly discovered Victorian gold-fields in Australia, so he decided to join them too. Having crossed the Pacific, James and his cousin Will Skewis landed at Melbourne, making their way through the gold-fields to such spots as Bendigo, Castlemaine, Creswick and Ballarat. From there they agreed to visit Cornwall, landing at Penzance in the spring of 1855. To the surprise of many, James Skewis announced his engagement to – and swiftly married – Jane Thomas Rabling, a member of the relatively well-to-do Rabling family of Camborne that had made its money in Mexico, where Jane's father and grandfather were both still working as mine captains. Together, the newly weds set off for the United States.

James and Jane had intended to settle down on a farm near Shullsburg and raise a family. The children came along – Anita in 1856, William James in 1858 and Francis Harry in 1860 – but farming was not a great success. Consequently, in 1861, they decided upon Mexico. They travelled south with two other Cornishmen making their way from the States to Pachuca: Harry Oates and Joseph Rule. James Skewis recorded:

> We arrived in Mexico without accident. The Port of landing was Veracruz. At certain seasons of the year yellow fever pre-vailed. At that time there were no finished roads by rail ... we were drawn by mules on the old road to Mexico [City] .... Every day we had to pass a long plain, then would have to go up another flight of high mountains, and the descent to the great plain of the city of Mexico. After a brief stop in the city we made for Pachuca arriving the same day. We were received at the house of the wife's father William Rabling, also brother William Rabling and sister Elizabeth Rabling.[44]

In all James Skewis and family – two more children were born in Pachuca – spent seven years in Mexico, James rising to the rank of grass captain, but in 1868 they decided to return to the United States. James explained:

> By this time there had been many changes in the Mexican gov-ernment ... in 1867 he [the Emperor Maximillian] was shot, and

many were sad at the event. While there were many encounters with soldiers, about two or three miles from us sixty Austrians were going to Real del Monte to relieve a force there. They were [way]laid by three or four thousand Mexican troops, and all were killed with the exception of two who made a break over the mountains, bullets flying-all around them. We were near enough at other times to hear the bullets rattling on the top of the houses near us, and many a poor fellow lost his life. Sad indeed it is to live in the midst of revolutions.[45]

Back in Shullsburg, where James divided his time between mining and farming, three more children were born and in 1876 the family moved to Iowa where they built a farm on virgin territory. For James, however, there was the constant pull of Mexico, to which he returned time and again, even in 1908 when he was 82 years old! For James Skewis, 'Mexico as a mining country is second to none .... By present indications Mexico will become a powerful nation. Everything is being fostered to that end, and many of the old customs one by one are done away with. As the light comes, darkness through ignorance disappears.'[46] In this reflection we see something of James' personal philosophy, of his typically Cornish Methodist commitment to 'improvement' and 'progress', an optimism which had given him the courage and strength to rise above difficulties in his life's quest. It was ultimately a religious conviction, like that which drove so many Cornish emigrants in the 19th century: 'There is no day of my existence on which I forgot to give thanks to that Eternal Power, who, out of unconscious past, called me into the present of this world; a world so lovely in its natural beauty that we can imagine nothing lovlier save Heaven.'[47]

The life experiences of William John Oates and James Skewis show, among other things, the developing role of Mexico in the grander panorama of Cornwall's Great Emigration: from one of the very earliest destinations for Cornish personnel and Cornish technology in the years after 1815 to its position at the turn of the 20th century as typically but one leaf in a Cornish individual's portfolio which might range as far as Australia, Malaya, Russia or Southern Africa, as well as other parts of Latin and North America. Of the enduring Cornish impact in Mexico there is no doubt. It is said that in 1903 the Mexican national football team was composed entirely of Cornishmen, and just after the First World War a Cornish Association of Mexico City was founded. By all accounts, its events were grand affairs, especially the annual picnic excursion to

Xochimilco, with its famed floating gardens, on 23 June each year, the birthday of the then Duke of Cornwall. The British Ambassador attended, 'Trelawny' was sung, and a pasty luncheon was provided for upwards of 200 guests.

In 1949 C.C. James listed those families he knew which, until very recently at least, had had connections with relatives resident at Pachuca, families such as the Carnes, Iveys, Maynes, Retallacks and Dunstans of Camborne and Troon, the Cornish and Waters families of Redruth, the Gidleys, Odgers and Phillips of Gwennap, the Northeys and Skinfields of Chacewater and Blackwater, the Bunts of Penzance, the Crowles of Perranwell, the Earles of Falmouth, the Hearles and Porters of Truro.[48] Even in 1968, A.C. Todd encountered:

> the doyen today of all matters Cornish in the City of Mexico .... Eduardo Northey who, at the Christmas of 1968, was living with ... his frail but spirited ninety-five year old mother .... Now, after an English education and a lifetime among the Mexicans, he wonders whether he is Mexican or Cornish .... His mother, however, harboured no such doubts; she clearly recalled her Cornish descent from the same family of Honey as the railroad industrialist and banker; her marriage to Paul Northey; her strict Methodist upbringing; and an uncle who worked the pumps of the Dolores shaft at Real del Monte .... One of her friends is Mrs Isabelita Jenkins, who relates with enthusiasm how she, a Rogers from Redruth, made the long journey to Mexico to marry.[49]

If Mexico has a special place in the collective Cornish memory of the Great Emigration, then so too had Cuba. This time, however, long years of trial and tribulation were not tempered by the warm glow of affection born of eventual success. Instead, Cuba stood as a memorial to all the harshness and disabilities that foreign climes could visit upon the emigrant Cornish and in time it would be remembered also as one of those overseas rivals which first mounted the international challenge to Cornwall's copper kingdom. That said, in the earliest days Cuba was every bit as attractive a destination as Mexico, if only for the reason that extremely competitive rates of pay were offered, while seductive handbills and posters circulated in the mining districts of Cornwall hinted at wealth and opportunity for the adventurous. The principal magnet was the Cobre Mine, a copper working which lay in the valley of the Rio del Cobre in the Sierra Maestre mountains, some 12 miles north-west of Santiago Bay.[50]

The Cobre Mine was active from the mid-1830s, and in the period 1836–39 the Cornwall-based agent for the Cobre Mining Association which sought to develop the property was Alfred Jenkin of Trewirgie House, Redruth. His own records indicate that between August 1836 and April 1838 he was successful in engaging 136 Cornish miners and mechanics to go to Cuba.[51] As well as selecting suitable emigrants and arranging for their medical examinations, Jenkin organised the shipping of mining machinery from Cornwall to Cuba, together with other materials such as safety fuses and even clothing for the West African slaves who were forcibly employed in the Cuban mines. Although Jenkin was the most visible of the recruiters, others were active in Cornwall on behalf of Cuban mining interests (such as the San Jose and San Jago mines), notably an American named Smith who engaged at least 50 Cornish miners for Havana on the instructions of the New York-based Cuba Mining Company. Michael Williams of Scorrier was also active, contributing another 15 or so to the Cornish workforce out there in the mid-1830s. The Cousin Jack network was important in locating suitable recruits and on occasions the usual advertisements appeared in the Cornish newspapers. In November 1839, for instance, a notice in the *West Briton* invited potential applicants for the position of captain at 'an extensive copper mine in Cuba' to make enquiries at the offices of H. Sims at Scorrier. Later, in January 1842, the *West Briton* carried an advertisement for a mining engineer to superintend the workings of a copper mine some eight to ten miles from Havana, the Cuban capital. Pay was £350 per annum plus a free passage to Cuba.[52] The press also reported on the departure of recruits, the *Royal Cornwall Gazette* in February 1851 noting the sailing from Hayle for Cuba of some 25 miners from the districts of Illogan, Redruth and Gwennap: 'Most of them are engaged at £8 per month but some few are going out on speculation'.[53]

Alfred Jenkin, recruiting in the 1830s, sought young, fit, sober, single men as miners and mechanics for the Cobre Mine. He offered £100 per annum plus free accommodation, supplying each successful applicant with a Bible plus £10 for an outfit and a further £10 as an advance on wages. In 1836 he wrote of these recruits, 'I have selected them from a considerable number of applicants and trust they will give satisfaction to their employers – they are mostly young men.'[54] The majority of them were from the mining parishes around Camborne, Illogan and Redruth, and they were dispatched from the nearby industrial ports of Portreath and Hayle (and occasionally Falmouth) where they travelled across the Bristol Channel to Swansea to join Cuba-bound ships. Mirroring the experiences of Mexico some years before, the Cornish were much affected by the climate and environment which greeted them on arrival in Cuba. The humid heat was exhausting and to its debilitating effects were added the ravages of yellow fever, typhoid, smallpox, malaria and other life-threatening diseases. Michael Tangye tells the story of the batch of 24 miners which sailed from Portreath on 15 June 1837:

> within six months many were seriously ill with Yellow Fever and nine were dead – John Clemo, John Harry, William Gribble, William Tangye, Martin Andrew, William Bishop, Jonathon Harry, William Blight and William Carpenter. Many, discharged with illness, succumbed on the dreadful [return] voyage from Cuba to Swansea. James Whitburn Junior, a devoted Wesleyan, died thus on the *Tom Gringle*. His mother went to Portreath to meet him, but received only his clothing![55]

To this sorry list Alfred Jenkin added the name of Jeremiah Hampton (another death), together with those of James Rule and John Pearce, two further Cornishmen who were sent home from Cuba with notes confirming their discharge on medical grounds. William Curnow, from Ludgvan, died in Cuba in 1837. His clothes were sold by public auction – not the heartless act it first appears because this was the traditional mechanism by which miners could raise money to send home to an otherwise destitute family. On this occasion 32 dollars and five cents went back to Cornwall. Alfred Jenkin admitted that these reverses were bad publicity which would have a deleterious affect on recruiting – 'The sickness and deaths ... will, I expect, cause some shyness in the minds of our miners as to going there'[56] – and for those already out in Cuba solace was sought in the bottle and in religion. Poor William Morcom drank himself to death in 1838, while some Cousin Jacks at the Cobre Mine made a nuisance of themselves by habitually drinking too much. Others, however, exhibited a remarkable religious faith, often dropping their tools spontaneously to join together in hymns and prayer. As Michael Tangye has remarked, some of these men may well have been converted by John Wesley himself, giving their conviction a freshness and immediacy which the mine company found difficult to understand. At any rate, the directors complained to Jenkin about these religious habits but Jenkin resisted such criticism, particularly when it was levelled at the popular local preacher William Whitburn: 'I have known Will Whitburn for seven years – his wife was a servant in our family'.[57] As Jenkin explained, Methodism was strong among the labouring classes of Cornwall, and the holding of prayer meetings and the singing of hymns underground was not at all unusual. William Whitburn (whose son James had died on the *Tom Gringle*) was, for his part, scathing about the Cubans. He returned home to Gwennap in the autumn of 1839 and was asked to address the Redruth Institution on the subject of the Cobre Mine. In his talk he condemned 'the pride, indolence and ignorance of the Cubans' and explained that among the natives 'morality and intellectual intelligence are at a fearfully low ebb'. Worse still was the practice of slavery, anathema to all Cornish Methodists, which in Cuba existed 'in its worst form'.[58]

Whitburn's attitude was complex, a whiff of ethno-religious conflict fuelled by an unwavering ideology which condemned human wickedness and confronted human failings – from the evil of slavery to the sin of indolence – advocating instead thrift, self-help and mutual improvement. To this was added the all too routine contempt of the coloniser for the colonised, apparent even in territories where Britain was not the formal imperial power but where the Cornish, like the Scots or the Irish or the Welsh, could be just as firm as the English in the exertion of European cultural hegemony. In Whitburn's defence, however, we should also recognise that it was Cuba that had taken his son away from him, a loss that would have made intensely personal the sense of malevolence that he had experienced in that place. The unsavoury picture of Cuba admitted by Jenkin and made explicit by Whitburn created a dilemma for many Cornish people, making it all the more difficult for them to weigh up the advantages and disadvantages of Cuba as a potential destination. Of course, there were rival destinations to tempt the Cornish miner, but they were not always available, competition for them could be stiff and wage rates might not be so high as in Cuba. The anguish, disagreement, perhaps even conflict, that such debates must have caused within many a Cornish family is intimated in the letter sent home in September 1839 from the Cobre Mine by William Tyacke Toll to his wife Charlotte in Germoe Churchtown. In the 1830s Toll had been landlord of the 'Dolphin Inn' in Germoe and in the 1840s he had begun farming at Trethewy. All had not gone well, however, and he was forced by circumstances to seek work overseas. Struggling to convey his regret that he had left without Charlotte's sanction, William's loneliness and heavy guilt show through in almost every phrase. He had no choice but to go, he says, and life in Cuba is difficult:

> Dear wife and children I hope you
> Are satisfied as to my going away if I had a
> Stopd at home what should wee have a don

**116**

By this time I know I left without your consent
Give my kind lov to Mr Treloar and tell him that
Wm Toll would lick to liv in England and will
Com home as soon as posabel if hee will let
The land that I can liv my deer Charlote
It is not all pleasuer in this cuntrey my
Worck is not hard but I have a great deal to
Mind and Everey one is very kind to mee
Except The Spanyards with I have a great deal to do with
Richard Nichols is very well at present and so is
Stephen Williams I have now seen them both
My deer Charlot I must conclude I hope
You will give my lov to oall enqueering friends
I remain for Ever your loving husband
William Toll.[59]

William Toll was home in Cornwall by 1851 but his dream of letting land from Mr Treloar was not to be. Soon he was off again and within two years he was on the gold-fields of Victoria in Australia, and it was there, on the Ovens River diggings, that he died in 1854 aged 49. One can only guess at the distress suffered by his family back in Cornwall, those who had not wanted him to leave in the first place, but in a pleasant irony which shows us just how quickly the culture of emigration had permeated Cornish society, his daughter Honnor married another wandering Cousin Jack, Captain John Pope of Trescowe in the parish of Breage. John Pope had been manager of the West Godolphin mine in Breage but had already been out in Mexico. He later made a name for himself in Swaziland, before moving on to other parts of Southern Africa. Honnor joined him in South Africa, dying in Johannesburg in 1910. Their three sons, William, John and Joseph, each became mine captains – in the Eastern Transvaal, on the Rand and in Swaziland – and other members of the extended Pope family turned up mining in places as disparate as the Counties Cork and Wicklow in Ireland, Ebbw Vale in South Wales, the Cliff Mine in Michigan, Kapunda in South Australia, Ballarat and Bendigo in Victoria and Broken Hill in New South Wales. As ever, the impression we gain is of how quickly the international network developed as the Great Emigration grew apace and, particularly, of the early role of Latin America in this global process.

The place of Cuba in this early activity was mirrored in that of the British

Virgin Islands, also in the Caribbean.[60] In the 18th century the Spanish had discovered and worked copper on the island of Gorda, part of the Virgin group, but
the workings had been long since abandoned. In 1835, however, as interest in the
region was rekindled, a syndicate was formed in London – the Virgin Gorda
Mining Company – to rework the deposits. A shaft was sunk in 1838 and an
engine was shipped out from the Perran Foundry in Cornwall. The workers –
some 31 men and six women from the St Austell district, plus over 160 locals –
were placed under the management of one Captain Joel Hitchins. However, the
mine was abandoned in 1842 and was not re-opened until 1859, with Captain H.
Clemes, another Cornishman, as manager. Work continued until 1862, when the
mine was again abandoned at a time when international copper prices were
beginning to falter. Today, the ruined engine house and stack stand sentinel
above the waters of Hansom Bay, not unlike those at Trewavas Head and
Botallack in Cornwall, while the remains of the engine's beam – with the legend
'Perran Foundry 1836' clearly visible – lie at the water's edge.

The collapse of the Gorda project was followed by what were in effect the last
days of Cornish emigration to Cuba, the violent civil disturbances there after
1868 persuading many Cousin Jacks that they were better placed moving to
other parts of Latin America. However, by then the Cuban mines were already in
decline. The peak years had been 1841–50, when some 56,000 tons of fine
copper had been produced, but this had fallen to 47,500 tons by 1851–60 and to
25,600 tons in the decade 1861–70. Although these figures were by no means
insignificant, mounting as they did an important challenge to Cornish hegemony in the supply of copper to the voracious British economy, they were from
the first surpassed by the awe-inspiring statistics of Chile: 65,000 tons of refined
copper in the years 1831–40, rising to an astonishing 447,400 tons by the decade
1861–70, the years when Cornish production reached only 116,300 tons and
collapsed almost entirely shortly thereafter.[61] Indeed, by 1880 Chile had moved
to first place among the world's copper producers.

Richard Trevithick himself had drawn attention to the potential of Chile as a
copper producer and, as noted above, Cornish commercial interests had participated in early British investment in the country's mining industry. This, in turn,
was encouraged by the Swansea smelting interests, which in the 1820s hoped to
replace Russia as the principal supplier of copper to France and continental
Europe, but which were hampered by the fact that Cornish production was hardly enough to satisfy British domestic demand. By attracting the new-found
Chilean copper to Swansea for smelting, it was thought, the requisite volume nec-

essary to penetrate the European markets might be marshalled. As Culver and Reinhart have observed, 'This interest in Chilean mines was a part of a generalised infatuation with mining investment in Latin America, and while the [initial] boom everywhere collapsed in 1827, it did establish that Chile had ... high quality copper'.[62] Indeed, Chilean ores were to average an impressive 10 to 15 per cent copper in the period up to the 1880s, with some mines – such as the exceptionally rich Cerro Blanco – producing ores at an astounding 35 to 40 per cent copper.[63]

By 1831 Chilean and Cuban copper ore was arriving at Swansea for smelting in sufficient quantities to ensure the sought after British predominance in European markets. Not surprisingly, the Swansea smelting interests also added their powerful voice to those in Britain clamouring ever more loudly for free trade, in the hope that the unrestricted entry of cheap Latin American copper ore into the United Kingdom would facilitate an ever more profitable servicing of the growing domestic demand for refined copper. As noted above, such a strategy began to cause alarm in Cornwall, with the *Mining Journal* – always a strong advocate of Cornish mining interests – using its editorial space to attack the 'monopolistic' activities of the Swansea Smelters Association. In 1842 a compromise position was reached, whereby customs duty on Chilean copper for domestic use was reduced by more than a half but copper ore imported for processing for subsequent re-export was, for the first time, subject to such duty. At the time, the compromise seemed to be fair to both parties: Cornish and Swansea. In the longer term, however, it did (as those in Cornwall had feared) open up Cornish production to Chilean and other overseas competition. The Swansea smelters, too, soon encountered the downside of the agreement, for the duty on ore for re-export had the effect of encouraging the smelting of copper ore overseas. The duty was removed in 1847 but by then it was too late, the international copper industry having become irreversibly decentralised, with Chile establishing its own smelting facilities and with several new, important producers entering the international market.[64] The bonanzas that British interests – Cornish and Swansea among them – had clamoured to exploit had already become the bugbear that they were soon to dread. Indeed, one might observe that Cornish capitalism had contained within itself the seeds of its own destruction, with the enthusiastic activities of the Fox, Williams, Grenfell and other interests opening up Cornish mining ultimately to overwhelming overseas competition, and yet doing little to diversify Cornish industry in the face of the changes that they themselves had helped to create.

Nonetheless, the supremacy of Chile as copper producer was relatively short-lived. At first, the United States – anxious to develop its own indigenous copper production industry – had imported large quantities of Chilean copper ore to meet the demand of its recently constructed smelters. However, as we shall see, the United States itself rapidly became a major copper producer: first with its mines in Michigan and then in Montana, Arizona and elsewhere. In the 1860s, when the price of copper fell on the international market, the United States took steps to reform and stimulate its own copper industry, and in the 1880s – as copper prices fell further and as the international market was faced with over-production – the United States began to achieve what Chile had long feared: American penetration of the British market. The Chilean industry tried to respond by adopting a capital-intensive, high-growth policy but it was already too late. The Chileans had been content for too long to use traditional methods to extract the rich, abundant and easily accessible reserves, and had failed to develop a self- sustaining technology that might overcome the challenges of declining ore grades and geologically complex ore bodies.[65] In 1880 the *Chilean Times* recalled with wry and ironic amusement those who had, all those years before, greeted with bewilderment the activities of the Cornish miners who – rather like John Rule in Mexico – had tried to develop a heavily capitalised, Cornish-style industry in Chile while copper ore was there more or less for the taking: 'steam power had not even been dreamed of then, and even whims, or horse-power drawing machines, were looked upon as costly and probably unsuccessful innovations, recently introduced by Cornish Mining Captains: what might answer very well in *Inglaterra* they thought might not answer in Chile at all.'[66]

The Cornish had been in Chile from the first. The firm of J.& J.H. Gill of Tavistock was recruiting in East Cornwall and West Devon for the Chilian [sic] and Peruvian Mining Co. as early as January 1825, while recruiting meetings were also being held at that time in hotels in Truro and Redruth.[67] In July of the same year the *West Briton* noted that the *Auriga* had sailed from Falmouth for Valparaíso, in Chile, with some 40 Cornish and Welsh miners engaged by that company.[68] A little over six months later, in February 1826, the *Western Luminary* published a letter from Valparaíso which claimed that 'This country is overrun with miners and miners' followers.'[69] J.R. Polglase has counted some 35 Cornish individuals at the Coquimbo mines, north of Valparaíso, who were mentioned in the pages of the *West Briton* between 1859 and 1908. They sport the tell-tale Cornish names – Pelmear, Richards, Reynolds, Williams, Buzza, Gurney, Halse, Leggo, and so on – but they are only the tip of the iceberg. So too are the 37 at Tocopilla (originally in Bolivia but annexed by Chile) who appeared in the *West Briton* between 1860 and 1912 – with names such as Nicholls, Combellack,

Carne, Gerrans, Annear, and Lean. The Checo mines at Copiapó attracted Cornish miners, such as one W. Tregallas, as did the neighbouring Dulcinea Mine and probably the majority of the 17 significant copper producers active in Chile during the 19th century. The Chilean mines also acquired Cornish mining implements, such as the whim pulleys and whim kibbles (buckets) produced by Harvey & Co. of Hayle in 1850, or the 40 sets of miners' tools, four horse whims, a dozen winze kibbles, ten dozen picks, and other items provided by Harvey's for Captain Trebilcock in Chile in 1849.[70]

Individual biographies have survived. In the Introduction we glimpsed the typically international career of Henry Crougey, born near Carn Marth, who after 12 years as a copper miner in Chile moved on, like many others, to the gold-fields of California, then crossing to Australia where he toiled in the copper and gold-mines of South Australia and Victoria before ending his days in Broken Hill in New South Wales. Similar in its extent was the working life of Captain John Brokenshire, from Roche, who as a young man had managed mines at Brixham (Devon) and in Ireland and in North Wales before going on to Chile, Bolivia and Peru in Latin America. Returning to Cornwall, he then left with his son and with his colleague Thomas Parkyn of Roche, 'the well-known explorer and mining expert', for the Australian colonies. Having prospected in various parts of the continent, they moved on to Coolgardie in the gold-fields of Western Australia where, sadly, Brokenshire was killed in a mining accident. When inspecting a winze (an underground shaft connecting two or more levels) he was caught in a premature explosion, 'when extricated he was found to be terribly injured. Medical aid was promptly rendered, but proved no avail, Capt. Brokenshire dying about three hours after the explosion'.[71] Equally sad was the career of William Scoble, born in Gwennap in 1830 of strict Bible Christian parents. He became a local preacher in Camborne and, following his marriage in 1853, went twice to the United States before venturing to Coquimbo in Chile, where he arrived in January 1859. From there he moved up the coast to a copper mine at Copiapó, where he found nine Cornishmen and 50 'natives' at work. After nine years in this demanding environment, the Cornish miners – Methodists all – were 'leading such dissipated lives' amidst 'the fruits of iniquity',[72] a great shock for the young Scoble who was ill-prepared for such wanton examples of backsliding and immorality. Scoble remained at Copiapó for three years, returning to Cornwall in June 1861, living on his savings until his death in 1864 at the early age of 34 years.

In August 1893 an article in the *West Briton* described the Iquique railway works in Northern Chile, part of the territory that had been annexed from Bolivia in 1883. It transpired that not only was the chief of the locomotive department a Cornishman, but so too were the traffic manager, the station master, the chief carpenter, the manager of the blacksmiths' department, and the superintendent of the foundry. The report added, 'There are also Cornishmen managers of silver mines in the locality; in fact, it seems to me that a mine [in Chile] without a Cornishman employed in some capacity is similar to a man going to church without his hat on'.[73] In Cornwall itself, the existence of Chili Road – spelt in the traditional 19th-century manner that the Cornish understood, and situated in Illogan Highway in the midst of the Camborne-Redruth mining district – was a workaday but fitting memorial to the intimate, curiously love-hate relationship that existed between Cornwall and Chile.

In neighbouring Bolivia, there was a similar relationship, prompting the old Cornish Methodist jibe against atheism, 'There do be some people that do say when we die we do go to Bolivian'.[74] In March 1825 the *Western Luminary* had observed the departure of the schooner *Lynx* from Plymouth with Captain Joseph Malachy embarked: the agent and resident director of the Bolivar Mining Association which had been formed to work the Aroa copper mines in the Province of Venezuela (then part of Colombia). Prospects were good, the newspaper thought, for 'The Aroa mines have been but partially and defectively worked by the old Spanish Govt., about 40 of the natives only being employed at one time and even then yielded 300 tons of refined copper annually'.[75] As noted above, individuals such as William Henry Oates from Chacewater spent parts of their complex Latin American and international careers in countries such as Bolivia and Venezuela, as they did in adjoining Peru where Oates, his uncle and his brother-in-law all spent time as miners. Richard Trevithick had established an early Cornish interest in Peru, one which endured despite the huge enthusiasm for other destinations such as Mexico, Cuba and Chile, the *West Briton* noting in January 1852 that emigration to Peru remained a feature of Cornish life.[76] In Colombia itself, away to the north-west, the same was true, and again that country often featured in the international portfolios of successful Cornish mine captains, such as that of Henry Roach, one-time employee of the Tresavean mine at Lanner in Cornwall, who had worked in Colombia before going on to become captain of the far-famed Burra Burra copper mine in South Australia.

In the excitement of the 1820s, Colombia featured alongside other Latin American destinations in the pages of the Cornish press. In January 1826 the *West Briton* noted the impending departure of the brig *Lavinia* from

Falmouth for Santa Martha and Cartagena de Colombia, inviting interested persons to apply to William Broad & Sons of Falmouth. In the April the same newspaper informed readers that:

> A letter has been received from the party of miners who left this county for Colombia about 12 months since. Four of their number died on the passage; the remainder were 53 days ascending the river Magdalena which passage they describe as dangerous from the number of alligators with which it abounds and by which one of the native boatmen who plunged into the water to recover his oar and a dog that was brought from Cornwall, whilst walking on the bank, were seized and devoured. The party suffered much from heat and the mosquitoes before they reached the mines ... they represent the mines as being promising'.[77]

In the following November the *West Briton* conveyed news of the safe arrival at Cartagena of four vessels chartered by the Colombian Mining Company, adding that 'We regret to learn that in consequence of a delay in conveying miners up the river several deaths had taken place'.[78] In February 1827 the *Western Luminary* reported the progress made by these early arrivals, 'The last accounts from Colombia state the Cornish miners are going on steadily at Mariquita and have begun breaking good ore.'[79] By 1827, their contracts over already, some of the early arrivals were returning to Cornwall for a respite from the land of alligators, heat and mosquitoes – in April of that year, for instance, the *West Briton* noted that 13 miners had recently come home from Colombia. A year later the *Western Luminary* explained that 'several miners lately returned to Cornwall from Colombia and Mexico speak in most favourable terms of the abundance and quality of the copper ore found in Colombia but the accounts from the Mexican mines are less promising.'[80]

Notwithstanding the up-beat reports from Colombia in those early years, its production of copper never did match that of Cuba or Chile, while its gold output was from the beginning overshadowed by that of neighbouring Brazil. Unlike those other areas of Latin America considered thus far, Brazil had been colonised by the Portuguese and was, therefore, Portuguese- rather than Spanish-speaking. However, despite that distinction, the experience of Brazil had much in common with other areas of Latin America. The country had gained its independence from Portugal after the Napoleonic Wars, and, as elsewhere, this had opened the way for the intrusion of British capital intent on modernising a long-established but (from a British perspective) under-capitalised and technologically rudimentary mining industry. Long before the gold rushes of California and Australia, Brazil had become established as a gold producer with the region of Minas Gerais emerging as the focus for this activity. Mining methods ranged from the simply alluvial to the more complex hydraulic, with its diverting of streams and cutting of trenches, but there was little deep shaft mining. The workforce was composed largely of slaves while foreigners were allowed neither to work in the mines nor to own them. However, independence in 1822 changed all that. An intensive period of British investment lasted until the 1830s, followed by a second wave of high activity in the 1860s and a less hectic, more protracted cycle of investment in the last quarter of the 19th century and on into the 20th.

The deep lodes of Minas Gerais, hitherto untouched by alluvial and hydraulic mining, could only be exploited by the introduction of underground mining – and then only on such a scale as to make it economically viable. As Marshall C. Eakin has observed, this, in turn, could only happen 'when the mining techniques of the Europeans (especially the Cornish) became readily available to Brazilians.'[81] The mechanism for this was the injection of British capital and the introduction of Cornish miners consequent upon the formation of the Imperial Brazilian Mining Association, founded in London in 1824 with an initial nominal capital stock of £350,000. Significantly, Michael Williams of Scorrier was one of the directors of this substantial new venture. The association was intent upon re-equipping and re-working the old mine of Gongo Soco, situated some 200 miles north of Rio de Janeiro, and to that effect a core of Cornish mine captains was hastily recruited. As ever, they are distinguished by their surnames – Trebilcock, Blamey, Martyn, Pengelly Luke, Hitchens, Treloar, Tregoning, Bennets, Prideaux, Hambly Harris, Bray, Collins and Williams.[82] The usual advertisements appeared in the Cornish press, such as that in the *West Briton* in October 1826 which announced: 'Wanted, to go to Brazil. A mining engineer who has some practical knowledge of pitwork, water engines etc. a carpenter capable of erecting water wheels and a good mining smith. Applications to be made to Mr John Pearce of Scorrier, near Truro.'[83] A year later and John Pearce was advertising for two further mine captains, while in June 1828 applications were invited to Messrs Banfield & Lake of Falmouth for 'An experienced mining captain and a few able miners to proceed to the Brazils in the service of the National Imperial Brazilian Mining Association.'[84] A month later, the *West Briton* announced:

> The *Swallow* packet sailed from Falmouth yesterday for Rio de Janeiro and Buenos Ayres [sic] by which went passengers, Mr Oxenford [the first foreigner to gain a mining concession in Brazil] and the head of a new Mining Establishment about to be formed under the auspices of that gentleman in the province of Minas Geraes [sic] .... A mining captain and a select body of experienced miners, we understand, are to follow in the next packet.[85]

The wave of recruiting continued into the 1830s, an advertisement in the *West Briton* in September 1831 calling for 50 miners and three blacksmiths for Gongo Soco, potential applicants being advised to make enquiries at Wheal Damsel count house, Gwennap. In June 1835 John Pearce was after a mine carpenter for Brazil capable of erecting water engine wheels, stamping mills, and making drawings. In February of the following year W. & A.C. Carne were advertising for 'Two active intelligent men for a mining establishment at Brazil as first and second captains.'[86] In August 1844 the *West Briton* drew attention to the forthcoming sailing of the schooner *Sarah* from Falmouth for Rio de Janeiro, 'This is an eligible opportunity for Miners and others wishing to proceed to the Brazils.'[87] By the 1840s the mine at Gongo Soco employed some 200 Europeans – the majority of them Cornish – together with more than 500 slaves (to whom the Cornish from time to time objected) and 200 free Brazilians. As Eakin has observed:

> The company introduced the deep shaft-mining techniques of Cornwall, and the latest milling procedures of the era. The cost of fuel and the difficulties of transport prohibited the use of steam engines, but the abundance of water more than made up for the excessive costs of steam power. Water was utilised to power stamping mills, arrastras, and amalgamation equipment. In European mining this technology was not novel; its application on a rational, large-scale and systematic basis in Brazilian gold mining was.[88]

Of other British mining companies formed in the 1830s, far and away the most important was the St John d'el Rey, which became the most successful British gold-mining company in Latin America in the 19th and early 20th centuries, its Morro Velho property in the central Minas Gerais proving astonishingly rich. The first manager was one Captain Thomas Treloar, a deeply religious Cornishman who on being asked by the directors to give an estimate of the mine's prospects replied: 'The Good Lord did not give me eyes to see through the rocks, and I am consequently unable to give you the information you desire'.[89] Nonetheless, Captain Treloar was sufficiently optimistic to recommend the extensive recruitment of miners and mechanics from Cornwall – more than 800 men offered themselves for the 53 available positions. Gongo Soco and many other mines faded from the scene once the 1820s boom and its 1830s aftermath had been spent, but St John d'el Rey endured, benefiting from the next round of activity in the 1860s.

Morro Velho was situated near the small town of Nova Lima, some 200 miles north of Rio de Janeiro, and by the late 1840s had already become something of a Cornish community.[90] Despite the end of the boom, St John d'el Rey was still recruiting Cornish workers, and one of those brought out in 1848 was William Pascoe from Helston. He was engaged for a period of six years, the first three at £9 per month and the second three at £10 per month, at least double the amount he might expect to earn in Cornwall. He sent £3 per month 'homepay' back to his wife, Ann, in Cornwall, and he eventually made arrangements for his family to join him at Morro Velho, which they did in 1854. William, who as a mine carpenter was responsible for constructing headframes, stamps, waterwheels, launders and separating tables, was eagerly re-engaged by the company in 1854 for a further three years. Although considered a first-rate worker he was, like many of his countrymen in Latin America, considered a little too fond of the bottle. Among his Cornish colleagues at Morro Velho were William Daniell (carpenter), Captain Martin Raby (reduction department), Thomas Hodge (under mine captain), Joel Treweek (smith), James Jory (smith), John Gregor (carpenter), Samuel Clemence (smith), Joseph Tonkin (mine office clerk), William Hooper (reduction department), James C. Polmear (fitter), Richard Hodge (under mine captain), Henry Davey Cocking (foreman smith), William Cocking (carpenter), Samuel P Jory (smith), and Captain Joseph Eslick (under mine captain).

Renewing his contract several times over, William Pascoe stayed at Morro Velho until 1870, when he returned to Cornwall with his wife, two sons and grandson. A year later he was back in Brazil, with his two boys. His elder son, also named William, had married a local Cornish girl, Caroline Gregor –

daughter of John Gregor the mine carpenter – but she died in 1867, and so in 1870 William junior married another Cousin Jenny, 17-year old Emma Jane Verran who had been born at Morro Velho. In 1886 there was a serious run of ground in Morro Velho. Some ten miners lost their lives, and work was curtailed at the mine. William and his Brazilian-raised family 'returned' to Cornwall, settling in Helston. But with the restoration of workings in 1887 he was persuaded to go back to Brazil to take up his old job. By 1895 he was earning £20 per month but on 4 November 1900, after a short illness, he died and was buried in the so-called English Cemetery on the hill next to the mine. Other members of the Pascoe and Verran families stayed on at Morro Velho until the 1920s, then drifting back to Cornwall or moving on to other mining camps. But by then others were arriving fresh from Cornwall, the fearful hardship of the years 1921–22 in Cornwall coinciding with the latest recruitment drive by the St John d'el Rey Mining Company. In August 1922 the *West Briton* recorded that, 'Twenty five miners from Redruth and district left the town yesterday morning for Brazil, where they have been engaged to work the St John del Rey Gold Mining Company's famous property at Morro Velho. The company at present employs a considerable number of Cornishmen'.[91] Among those Cornish arriving in Brazil at about this time was William Reginald Trethewey, born in Callington in 1890, a mining engineer who had emigrated to Canada in the early 1900s and had made his way to Morro Velho by way of the United States and Central America. His daughter, Joy Brealy, lived at Morro Velho from 1934 until the family left for Britain in 1946. She remembered other Cornishmen who worked at the mine in those days – Archibald and Kingwell Ould, Percy Crocker, and others called Blight, Uren and Davey.

The survival of Brazil's Cornish connection well into the 20th century is a further reminder of the significant part played by Latin America in Cornwall's Great Emigration. J.R. Polglase has estimated that, even leaving aside the significant destination of Mexico, Cornish emigration to South America in the 19th century may have numbered at least 14,000 souls.[92] Nicaragua, Venezuela, British Guyana – visited in 1901 by Francis Oats,[93] the celebrated Cornish captain in South Africa – and other Latin American destinations also featured in this important dimension of the Cornish diaspora. But the enduring significance was neither the geographical spread achieved by the Cornish nor the numbers of individuals involved. Rather, as Sharron Schwartz has demonstrated convincingly in her recent study 'Cornish Migration to Latin America', the singular role played by the Cornish miners in facilitating the penetration by

British capital of newly independent Latin America after 1815 had laid the foundations for the rapid development of an international mining economy and its parallel labour market, together with the first signs of what would become a truly international Cornish identity.[94]

# CHAPTER FOUR

# FROM FAMINE TO

# FRONTIER –

# THE HUNGRY FORTIES AND

# THE FIRST AMERICAN

# MINING BOOM

I n the two or three decades after 1815 the characteristics of Cornwall's Great Emigration had become firmly established. An 'emigration culture' had become pervasive, and an 'emigration trade' had emerged to manage – and make money from – the wholesale movement of Cornish people overseas. That movement itself was broadly of two types. First of all, there was the often politically driven emigration of families from agricultural parts of Cornwall to the United States and to emerging British colonies in Canada, Australia and New Zealand. To this was added the growing movement from Cornwall to Latin America, a movement more often than not of individuals (rather than families), skilled workers from the mining areas of Cornwall who accompanied the shifting attention of British capitalism to the Spanish and Portuguese-speaking expanses of the Americas. This movement, in turn, heralded the construction of an international mining economy and an attendant labour market in which the Cornish assumed a central role. At the same time, the 'formal' emigration trade which managed and regulated emigration to British colonies, was complemented by an 'informal' trade in which a complex network of contacts recruited Cornish workers – often in an extremely *ad hoc* manner – for mining ventures overseas. This Cousin Jack network was to become increasingly significant, deployed as it was with increasing strength as Germans, Irish, Finns, Italians and

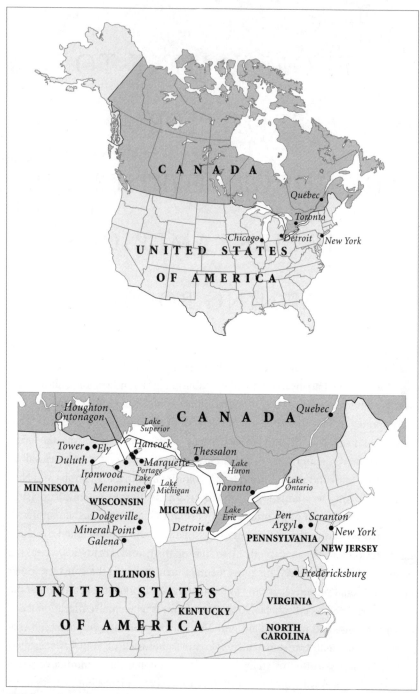

*Southern Canada and the north-eastern states of the USA*

other ethnic groups sought to join – and compete with – the Cornish in the international mining labour market.

By the 1840s, then, emigration had become an inescapable fact of Cornish life, while the Cornish had already made a significant contribution to the new movement of European people across the world. The 1840s themselves were a time of economic dislocation in much of Britain and Ireland, and Cornwall shared in the tragedy of the potato famine which ravaged Ireland and the Highlands and Islands of Scotland.[1] The importance of the potato in pre-famine Ireland is generally understood. Less clear is the fact that by the mid-19th century the potato was also a staple food of the Cornish poor.[2] Thus, when the previously unknown fungus *phytophthora infestans* struck the potato crops of these islands for the first time in 1845, Cornwall was one of the worst affected areas. As in Ireland and the Highlands, one consequence was the widespread departure of hungry people for overseas. But, in contrast to many of those who fled Ireland and the Highlands to escape starvation, Cornish emigrants were often skilled workers whose trades were much sought after overseas – especially on the continually expanding mining frontiers. Thus the 'push' of the Hungry Forties and its aftermath in Cornwall was matched by the 'pull' of the continuing overseas demand for Cornish labour – not only from established destinations like Latin America but from new bonanzas such as the copper mining districts of 'the Lakes' in the United States and Kapunda and Burra Burra in South Australia (see Chapter 5). In other words, the principal effect of the Hungry Forties in Cornwall was to give still further impetus to the Great Emigration, perpetuating the supply of Cornish labour to meet the increasing demand for it from abroad.

Although much energy was devoted in the 1990s to marking the potato famine in Ireland and, to a lesser extent, in the Highlands and Islands of Scotland,[3] Cornwall generally has not sought to commemorate its own disaster of 1845–47. Moreover, the scale of that disaster has generally not been appreciated.[4] If people in the 1840s were not expiring in their thousands as they were in Ireland, this was because the scale of emigration in Cornwall was sufficient to stave off the worst excesses of starvation. In the Penwith peninsula of far-western Cornwall, the potato had by 1801 become established as a major element of the diet of the mining communities of Marazion, St Just and St Ives,[5] local farmers learning (ironically, from the Irish experience) that potatoes were a useful preparatory crop for barley on heath or bog land. As early as 1758 Borlase had insisted that the potato was 'a more useful root'[6] than the turnip, as indeed it was when hitherto uncultivated croft country was being hurriedly utilised to meet the demand for food from the then rapidly expanding mining populations. When the potato crop failed, it was those very populations that felt the pinch. In July 1846, the *West Briton* noted that: 'A correspondent from Lelant informs us that the blight among the potatoe (sic) crops, which occasioned such a sensation last year, has again made its appearance in that neighbourhood; and, according to various reports, he fears it has become extensive ... thus cutting off from the farmer and poor labourer their hopes of the next year's potatoe crop.'[7]

In 1847 William Allen, an emigration agent at Penzance, explained that 'there is great excitement in this county and neighbourhood. Many persons in the Penzance district are preparing to emigrate to South Australia, and among them a fair proportion of first rate miners'.[8] In distant Adelaide the *South Australian Register* echoed his analysis, adding that 'Mr Allen says business was dull in Cornwall, and as the potato crop in his neighbourhood participated in the general failure, much distress was felt and anticipated'.[9] For the first time the population of parts of Cornwall, which had grown so strongly in recent decades and had continued to expand despite increasing emigration, registered a decline in absolute terms. In 1849 J.R. Leifchild, a contemporary observer of Cornish mining affairs, estimated that nearly five per cent of the Penzance Poor Law Union area (encompassing West Penwith) had recently emigrated to Australia and New Zealand, to say nothing of the Americas or other destinations. As Leifchild concluded, 'Emigration has tended to keep down the Cornish population.'[10] Indeed, the parishes of Breage and Germoe were to lose some 27 per cent of their people between 1841 and 1851. Elsewhere in Cornwall, the failure of the potato crop was also significant. The population of Stratton Hundred in North Cornwall, already the cradle of Cornish emigration, diminished absolutely by some ten per cent during the 1840s.[11] The Rev. R.S. Hawker, vicar of Morwenstow in that district, wrote of the local labouring population, 'How they exist is a mystery to me, especially after the potato blight.' The potato, he said, was once: 'the principal staff of Cornish life. When I first came here, December 1834, 30 years ago, every labourer had his pig and his potato patch. But of late years both these comforts have disappeared together and the privations of the people have been in consequence extreme.'[12] Potatoes had been the staple diet; ownership of a pig had indicated a degree of economic self-sufficiency – even modest prosperity – in happier times.

The loss of the potato from the working people's diet was also lamented by

George Henwood, another keen observer of Cornish mining, who in the 1850s wrote with regret that, 'Until within the last ten years, Cornwall was celebrated for the excellence of its potatoes; these were also cheap and abundant'.[13] For those who actually experienced this loss, the deprivation was acute. Although many turned to emigration, the immediate response to hunger was often violence. The Cornish tinners had acquired an unenviable reputation for rioting and lawlessness, and on past occasions had resorted to direct action to achieve 'fair prices' for corn, to prevent the export of wheat and barley, or to demand the distribution of bread to the poor.

Sometimes the mere threat of force was enough. In February 1831, for example, the *West Briton* recorded that:

> On Tuesday last, about eight o'clock, a party of 3000 miners collected from the parishes of Breage, Gwennap, Crowan, Wendron, &c. passed through Helston in complete order, having selected eight men for their leaders, for the avowed purpose of preventing further shipments of corn at Helford. Near Mawgan, they were met by H. Grylls, Esq. on his way to Bosahan, who intreated them to return, but they would not. One of the leaders said, "if you, sir, will go with us, we will not do you any mischief, but if you do not, perhaps we shall be unruly". Finding all his endeavours to induce them useless, Mr Grylls and Mr Black, accompanied them to Geer, where were deposited about 150 bushels of barley, which the proprietor promised should be sent to Helston market on Saturday.[14]

At the height of the Hungry Forties, such events were almost commonplace. Despite the repeal of the Corn Laws, bad harvests had doubled the price of corn, exacerbating the shortage and distress occasioned by the failure of the potato crop. To these high prices was added the fact that wheat and barley were still being exported routinely from Cornish ports, not so much a calculated affront to the hungry poor of Cornwall but rather testament to an unyielding ideology which insisted that nothing should stand in the way of free trade and market forces. After the hard winter of 1846–47, bands of miners laid siege to Cornish towns such as Callington, Launceston, Wadebridge, St Austell, Redruth, Helston and Penzance to prevent the export of corn and to force 'fair prices'. In May 1847 a small army of quarrymen, miners, tin-streamers and china clay workers from all over mid-Cornwall marched on Wadebridge:

the owners of the corn in the cellars proceeded to ship it on board a vessel ... when information was received that a large body of men from the Delabole quarries was approaching ... and soon after about four hundred men entered the town, and proceeded at once to the Quay ... [as] a great proportion of the men were really in want of food, the magistrates and others purchased all the bread procurable in the town, and distributed it them, each receiving a part of a loaf on his passing over the bridge on his way home. Most of them had crossed the bridge when a rumour was spread that a party of the preceding day were again at hand. This rumour was soon realised, and between three and four hundred men entered the town, each armed with a bludgeon, and marched on the Quay, cheering as they proceeded. The quarrymen, or most of them, then returned, and mixed with the others (streamers, china clay men, and tinners from Roche, Luxulyan, St Austell, &c.), and when assembled together they presented a most formidable appearance, and created great consternation.[15]

Thomas Oliver, a former miner who in 1914 published his reminiscences, recalled what it was like to have been a boy during the Hungry Forties:

One Saturday I went with my mother to Helston market, and it was pay-day for the miners. I shall never forget what I saw on that Saturday afternoon. Coinage Hall Street was thronged with miners from the bottom to the Market House on the top of the street, all armed with shovel handles and pick handles. I saw the soldiers march with great difficulty up the street; they were about sixty or seventy in number, very young men. They were pressed so tightly by the miners that they could scarcely move along. I saw a gentleman on the Market House steps reading: my mother told me it was the Riot Act. I could not hear what was being said because of the tumult. I was told that the commanding officer ordered his men to fire a volley in the air, but they refused, and no wonder. If they had fired, every man of them would have been killed or disarmed. I saw a great quantity of bread distributed among the hungry crowd.[16]

Oliver also described the general condition of Cornwall in the 1840s:

> Everything was very dear and the working people were half starved .... For our breakfast we had barley gruel, which consisted of about three quarts of water and a halfpenny-worth of skimmed milk thickened with barley flour .... We lived about half a mile from the mine, and I had to go home to dinner. I ... was sometimes so feeble that I could scarcely crawl along. For dinner we had sometimes a barley pasty with a bit or two of fat pork ... and for supper a barley cake or stewed potatoes or turnips with a barley cover.[17]

It was against this background, then, of continuing discontent and near-starvation that Cornish emigration continued throughout the mid-1840s and beyond. Significantly, the Hungry Forties coincided with the rapid development of hard-rock mining in the United States of America. The already emerging international mining economy was thus provided with an important new focus of activity, while those seeking to abandon Cornwall in search of a more secure living had another potential destination to add to their portfolio of choices. As the works of A.C. Todd, A.L. Rowse, and John Rowe have shown at length, Cornish folk did indeed rise to the challenges offered by North America's 'first mining frontier', making their ways in large numbers to destinations in Wisconsin, Illinois, Michigan and later Minnesota – a movement that was still discernible in the late 1860s as the American Civil War drew to a close and as Cornwall was overtaken by the crash of its own copper industry.[18]

Independence from Britain and, especially, the war of 1812 had encouraged a drive for national self-sufficiency in the United States, not least in the production of strategic metals such as lead, iron and copper to underpin America's incipient industrialisation. Copper had already been worked in modest amounts in Connecticut, New Jersey, Maryland and Kentucky, with the Cornish as ever lending a hand,[19] and in North Carolina the Cousin Jacks had been mining as early as 1835. In July of that year a local clergyman noted in his diary that he had 'attended the funeral of a deceased miner, by name Trewartha, and about twenty-five years of age. He had come out from Cornwall ... but a few weeks previous, and went to his grave unwept by a single relative or friend.'[20] Lead was scarcer than copper and more valuable, and it was this metal that first drew the Cornish in numbers from the eastern

States to the unfolding frontier. Perhaps first (and certainly prominent) among these was Francis Clymo (or Clyma) from the parish of Perranzabuloe who had emigrated to Maryland in 1818 at the age of 27.[21] From Maryland he shifted to Virginia, prospecting for copper, and then moved on to Kentucky, arriving at Galena in the north-western corner of Illinois in 1827, where he was soon joined by his wife Frances Maynard of St Ewe.

Galena was on the southern fringe of what was to become the celebrated Wisconsin – or Upper Mississippi – lead mining region and the discovery there of mineral deposits led to the systematic dispossession of the Winnebago 'Indians' as newly arrived prospectors grabbed their land. This calculated ethnic cleansing of the Native Americans was graced with the title the Black Hawk War, and among those who fought in it was Francis Clymo. So too did Edward James, from Camborne, who arrived in Mineral Point, Wisconsin, in 1830 and immediately became embroiled in the conflict. Also embroiled was Francis Vivian, born in Camborne in 1801, who turned up at Mineral Point in 1832, fought in the Black Hawk War, went lead mining, then opened up a general store, and finally moved through farming to a life in politics. Of course, these early Cornish frontiersmen were just a handful among the motley band of prospectors and adventurers who arrived to provoke and endure the violence of far-flung Illinois and Wisconsin. However, as the American historian Albert Louis Copeland observed in his now famous essay 'The Cornish in South-West Wisconsin' of 1898, 'there was no real mining done by the Americans, before the Cornish came'.[22] The battle of Bad Axe effectively ended the Black Hawk War, opening the way for unimpeded mineral development, and the ensuing demand for skilled hard-rock miners prompted the arrival of the Cornish in large numbers – many from the older mining districts back east such as Maryland and Kentucky but increasingly from hungry Cornwall itself, especially the district around Camborne, Redruth, Illogan, St Day, Kenwyn, St Allen, St Agnes and Perranzabuloe. As John Rowe observed, by 1850 there were perhaps 6000 Cornish people in the three Wisconsin counties of Grant, Iowa, and Lafayette, and possibly two or three thousand more in the neighbouring counties of Jo Daviess, Illinois and Dubuque, Iowa.[23]

Certain districts became especially associated with the Cornish, such as Platteville in Grant county – settled by no fewer than 52 related families from Perranzabuloe – and the country around Shullsburg in neighbouring Lafayette county. Dodgeville, in southern Iowa county, also sported more than a smattering of Cousin Jacks and Jennies. But it was in Linden and (especially)

Mineral Point that the Cornish most enduringly left their mark. In Mineral Point, Cornish architectural influence is reflected to this day in the solid lime-stone cottages in Shakerag Street (so called, it is said, after Cousin Jenny's habit of signalling to her man in the open-cast workings on the opposite hill when his meal was ready), notably in three beautifully restored Cornish-style houses: 'Trelawney', 'Polperro', and 'Pendarvis'.[24] Nearby Linden was nicknamed 'Pard Town' after the Cornish practice of calling one's colleague (typically, in a tribute or tutwork gang or 'pare') 'Pard' or 'Pardner': another expression of Cornish identity, of the clannishness that underpinned the myth of Cousin Jack.[25] Intriguingly, in an echo of the Linden experience, the district about St Just-in-Penwith in West Cornwall was still known as 'Pard Country' as late as the 1970s, an indication of the longevity of that clannish spirit and evidence of continuing cultural links between contemporary Cornwall and that first American mining frontier.[26]

But, however strong the cultural bonds, there was always room for misunderstanding and error. For example, Judge Oscar Hallam grew up amidst the Cornish at Dodgeville but, as Rowse observed, not even he could get all the names right. Hallam recalled:

> There were Treseder and Trezona the grocers, Trogilius [i.e. Tregilgas] the butcher, Treloar the stone-mason, Trelaway [?] down by the lime kiln, Tredinick the painter, Treweek the jew-eller, Tregonning and Tremain farmers, and there were Trepenny [?], Trevelyan, Trevillian, Trevethan and Tremont, whose occupations I never knew. Then there was the Methodist local preacher, John Penberthy, the Penhallegons and the Pengelly brothers, who ran on opposing tickets for sheriff. One was elected: it helped the livery business. Then there was Penrose the butcher and Penhall whom I never knew. Then there were Polkinghorns and Kinghorns, not to speak of Edyveans and Eddashanks.[27]

Despite his difficulties with Cornish-language surnames, Hallam's evidence suggests the creation of Cornish communities in which the Cornish settled into a variety of occupations, a view echoed in Todd's analysis where he notes that, 'Over and over again in Wisconsin the pattern of the miner-turned-farmer repeats itself'.[28] Henry Prideaux, a miner from Camborne, was clearing land for farming around Dodgeville as early as 1838, with the Native Americans still fighting to retain their land, while Samuel Treloar from Roseworthy, near Camborne, soon forsook mining at Linden for a life of farming in that district. So too did Marmaduke Trebilcock, from Ludgvan, who gave up mining at Shullsburg to take on 80 acres of virgin land. In 1850 John Rule of Mineral Point, another Cornishman, owned 200 acres (which, in the previous season, had produced over a thousand bushels of cereal crops), together with seven horses, two cows, four bullocks, and two pigs. Philip Allen, also a Cousin Jack, had arrived in Mineral Point in 1842 at the age of 26; he went back to Cornwall to marry Elizabeth James and returned to Wisconsin with his bride to become a prominent storekeeper. Simon, William and John Lanyon, brothers from St Allen, were blacksmiths at Linden and at Mineral Point, their trade as useful to the burgeoning agricultural industry as it was to mining.

Such diversification helps to explain why, despite the dispersals caused by the Californian goldrush and (later) the Civil War, the Cornish remained a significant element of the lead region population in Wisconsin – in 1898 Copeland could insist that were still some 10,000 people of Cornish birth or descent in the district. Indeed, of the many who went to the Californian goldrush, not a few returned to Wisconsin, the lucky ones with enough funds to buy land and start farming. For those who remained in mining, there was certainly greater economic security than there had been back in Cornwall, the relatively high earnings of the 1840s offering a comfortable standard of living in stark contrast to the poverty, privations and uncertainties of life at home. Of course, life on the frontier had its own particular dangers, initially in the conflict with the Winnebago and always through the threat posed – especially to the very young and the very old – by outbreaks of disease. In May 1849, for example, an engineer by the name of Nicholas Phillips, son-in-law of Richard Wearne from Hayle, by then a resident of Mineral Point, died of cholera at Galena while journeying from Cornwall to Wisconsin. In 1851, 136 people died in a cholera epidemic at Dodgeville. A decade or so later death visited many Cornish families in Wisconsin in the form of losses on the battlefields of the Civil War. The Wisconsin Volunteer Infantry, the 'Miners' Guard' as it was known, was about one-third Cornish in its composition and fought and suffered for the Union at bloodbaths such as Bull Run, Antietam, Fredericksburg and the terrible victory of Gettysburg in 1863.

As ever, the Cornish turned to their Methodist faith for succour and support, their chapels providing religious sustenance and social cohesion in times of danger and upheaval. Indeed, a Methodist chapel had been organised at Mineral

Point as early as 1834, its founding members sporting tell-tale Cornish names such as Kendall, Phillips, Remfrey and Thomas. In Shullsburg Methodist church, names in the memorial book and stained-glass window echo the former presence of Cornish congregations: Rowe, Trebilcock, Tangye, Kittoe, Rule, Skewes, Stephens, Berryman, Odgers, Tregonning, Sincock, Trewartha, Trestrail, Tregloan, Hancock, George, Oates, Richards.[29] For those who had remained in Cornwall, faith also offered hope and reassurance when contemplating the pain and distance of separation from loved ones abroad. In July 1871 'William an Martha Painter' of Hayle Mills, near St Day, wrote to their children in Wisconsin: 'My dear Son an daughter we fel very thankful for the Lickness [photograph?] the are very hansum in our Eyes we should be very glad if we Could kis them and you likewise .... [I] Suppose I should never See you no more in time But i hope to see you all in heaven My Dears I have writin to you with tears in my eyes.'[30]

As the years passed, for many the hurt became less, the new generations born in Wisconsin only dimly aware of kinfolk back in the Old Country and unquestioningly sure that America was 'home'. And yet, as Donald S. Rickard wrote in 1960, as he constructed his Cornish grandfather's biography from letter-books bequeathed from those earlier lead mining days:

> When my brother Eric and I were little boys and our schoolmates boasted of being German or Irish or Yankee, we felt we had to be something too. We dared timidly to echo, at recess time one day, my father's assertion that we Rickards were Cornish. This statement was met by some derision and some curiosity which we were unable to satisfy, for we had no idea what Cornish was .... Gradually we learned more about this tribe, our tribe, but never were able to find anyone very interested or willing to be aware of its importance.[31]

Nonetheless, the Cornish had made a major impact in Wisconsin. John Rowe has argued that it was the presence of the Cornish, with their sophisticated hard-rock mining techniques, that in the late 1830s, 1840s and 1850s facilitated the rapid economic development of Wisconsin, transforming the territory from so-called wild 'Indian country' into a fully fledged State of the Union.[32] Moreover, the Cornish in Wisconsin also participated in the rush to California (as will be seen in Chapter 6), and played a significant role in developing that other mineral frontier of the 1840s: 'the Lakes' copper country of Upper

Michigan. As early as 1778, it is said, Cornish miners had been sent from Redruth to prospect for copper deposits along Lake Superior, but it was not until the summer of 1844 that serious attention was paid to that district by the newly formed Lake Superior Copper Mining Company. This company engaged an initial party of some 20 or so Cornish miners to begin the work. Some were recruited from Wisconsin, where the Cornish had already proved their worth. Others came from the Bruce iron mines near Thesalon on the shores of Lake Huron in Ontario, Canada, which were shortly to develop their own copper deposits and remained – until their closure in 1876 – a source of Cornish labour for the rapidly expanding Michigan mines.[33]

Indeed, extensive discoveries had been made in Michigan by the initial party of Cornish miners and those who came in their wake, leading shortly to the widespread exploitation of the Keweenaw Peninsula, that portion of land jutting out from the Upper Peninsula of Michigan into Lake Superior. Like Cornwall itself, Keweenaw is geographically remote and self-contained, its limits clear and defined. The Ontonagon River acts as its base in the west, and half way along its extent is Portage Lake, with the twin towns of Houghton and Hancock on either side. Further south are the iron ranges of Gogebic, Menominee and Marquette, stretching from the town of Ironwood in the north-western tip of Michigan to Iron Mountain on the Menominee River and Marquette in the country between Lakes Superior and Michigan. In the earliest mining days, the Keweenaw and the adjoining copper-mining counties of Houghton and Ontonagon were almost inaccessible, the overland route restricted to 'Indian trails' and the maritime journey on the Lakes themselves. The latter was often a perilous undertaking: as in August 1865 when the steamship *Pewabic* collided within another vessel on Lake Huron and, as the *West Briton* recorded, 'there were some ten to fourteen Cornish miners lost'.[34]

The region was first surveyed by Dr Douglas Houghton, a young scientist who had been recently appointed state geologist. His enthusiastic report to the Michigan State Legislature in 1841 drew important comparisons between the Lakes and Cornwall, 'In the main, the resemblance between the character and contents of the copper veins of Cornwall and Michigan, so far as can be determined, is close; the veinstones are essentially the same.'[35] Such an assessment promised success on at least the scale that Cornwall had known (in 1841 Gwennap parish had been within living memory 'the richest square mile on earth') but it also hinted that the Cornish could with little difficulty bring their expertise to bear upon mineral deposits whose characteristics they would recognise instantly. Of course, the Cornish were more than happy to accept such a suggestion, reinforcing as it did the myth of Cousin Jack, the insistence that the Cornish were inherently superior miners who possessed innate qualities of skill and tenacity. Echoing this belief more than a century later in 1945, James Fisher mused upon the impact of 'Michigan's Cornish People':

> Though in most cases not possessed of any great degree of book-learning, the natural shrewdness and almost instinctive knowledge of mining affairs, inherited from generations of those who had preceded them in the same calling, made the Cornish leaders in their work and in their community .... No mining community in the world can boast of a more loyal group of former employees than the Central [mine] in Keweenaw County.[36]

Such was Cornish self-belief that when a 'Yankee' (one Edwin J. Hulbert, son of a Detroit businessman and a graduate of the University of Michigan) discovered the rich Calumet conglomerate lode earlier workings undertaken by the native Chippewa (Ojibwa) people, the Cousin Jacks insisted that they had got there first – attributing the find to one Richard Tregaskis. The reality, in fact, was that when Hulbert had shown specimens to Cornish miners in the locality, they retorted dismissively that conglomerate ('pudding stone') was occasionally found in Cornwall but never in payable quantities. 'Pudding stone be a brave and handsome ore, but there bain't enough of it in the whole world to keep one man in baccy.'[37] When proved wrong, the Cornish nonchalantly put it about that they had known of the deposit and its worth all along, thanks to the keen eye of Cousin Richard Tregaskis. And yet, the Cornish as a group *did* in the 1840s and 1850s possess more experience of deep hard-rock mining than any other nationality. The mining companies set up to exploit the Upper Michigan discoveries certainly recognised this, and noting how Cornish miners had been brought in to work the anthracite coal deposits of Pennsylvania, decided that they too should recruit directly from Cornwall, as indeed they did.

By 1844 there were two copper mining companies operating on the Keweenaw, with a stamp mill erected at Eagle River to crush and dress the ore. Two years later and a dozen ventures were in business, the result of a 'copper rush' which – notwithstanding the awful problems of communications and supply – had caught the frenzied attention of investors in New York and London. A thousand immigrants had poured on to the peninsula by the end of 1844 and in 1845 some 25,000 lb of copper ore had been produced in Michigan – a modest but credible enough amount, though dwarfed by later production figures such as the 14,000,000 lb of 1865. Hundreds of new claims were now appearing, most with little chance of success, but the better organised companies were already making headway. In the summer of 1844, for example, it was reported from the Lake Superior Mining Company's operation at Eagle River that 'one vein of copper, eleven feet wide and one mile long ... will repay all the outlay of the company. The Cornish miners there have sunk four shafts on the banks of the river, intending to work the mines under the river.'[38] This seemingly audacious intention excited comment but for Cornish miners who had driven workings out under the furious Atlantic at home, it was merely routine. So too was the fact – incredible to the lay observer – that 'One shaft is already sixty feet, another forty, another thirty feet deep – all done by hand power.'[39] This same hand power had also extracted $30,000 worth of copper from the exploration shaft at the Eagle River Mine, and it was on the back of such feats that the reputation of the Cornish miner was made legendary. The fact that this particular mine failed two or three years later was neither here nor there.

As in Latin America, mining companies contracted with local agents in Cornwall to recruit and dispatch suitable migrants. In 1846 the Boston and Lake Superior Mining Association arranged for the well-known Falmouth merchants, G.C. and R.W. Fox, already experienced in the selection of Cornish miners for overseas, to send out Captain Henry Clemo (or Clema, sometimes even Climes) and nine other Cousin Jacks. In an intriguing echo of the difficulties that arose between James Vetch and his Cornish workforce at Real del Monte in Mexico (see Chapter 3), Captain Clemo was soon at loggerheads with Daniel Webster, the mine's general manager. Webster was alarmed by the independent disposition of the Cornish miners and resented Captain Clemo's complaints about everything from the quality of the food to the standard and condition of the mining tools. Irritation moved to mutual antagonism when Clemo dismissed a prospector hired by Webster. As Rowe has remarked, 'Webster was acting as business manager on the location, but Clemo, in all likelihood, looked on him as a mine purser who, in Cornwall, would only deal with financial accounts, leaving complete powers of "hiring and firing" to the "Captain".'[40]

No doubt such conflict was replicated at other workings on the Keweenaw and the wider Upper Michigan, exacerbated by the failure of many workings to meet their initial expectations and by the rigours of life on the frontier, especially in the astonishingly hard winters on the Lakes. And in a further echo of the Mexican experience, Cornish captains like Henry Clemo – drawing upon their experience in the very different conditions of Cornwall – were insistent that mines could only achieve long-term stability and viability through the early installation of heavy equipment for pumping, winding and stamping. Even when the Cornish Vivians established a foundry in Pittsburgh capable of building the largest Cornish engines, the cost of bringing such equipment to the Lakes was huge. For all their skill, flair, self-belief and reputation, the Cornish were already exhibiting a professional conservatism that later in the century would leave them increasingly open to criticism from a new generation of college-trained American mining engineers. That said, the Cornish were by no means opposed to innovation when they could see its practical value, such as the speedy intro-duction on the Upper Peninsula of machine drills (at a time when hand drills were still *de rigeur* at home) to sink shafts more quickly. After all, the Cornish had been hardly conservative in their desire to emigrate and had already shown great flexibility and enterprise in making their way to America's mining frontier. It was their lack of schooling rather than an innate conservatism that sometimes made them fearful of change or of ideas that were not Cornish, and which made them seem quaint and untutored in the eyes of educated 'foreigners'.[41]

Go-ahead Germans were especially critical of the supposed 'rule of thumb', unscientific approach of many Cornish miners, not least the impatient Cousin Jack recklessness in blasting the huge masses of copper encountered underground. In the 1850s one Johann G. Kohl visited the Minesota (sic) Mine, where a Cousin Jack named William Harris was underground captain. Kohl was horrified by what he saw as the excessive use of explosives – up to four kegs of black powder stuffed into deep drill holes – to try to dislodge the copper masses. When one such mass was only partially shifted, 'They left it hanging there with no fear that it would pull loose of its own weight, until they were ready to cut it with the use of tools.'[42] Cool disregard for personal safety was one thing, and perhaps rightly castigated, but sometimes criticism of the Cornish took on a more unsavoury character, the clannishness and air of superiority that the Cornish cultivated infuriating those who saw themselves as a cut above the rough and ready Cousin Jacks. In 1863–64, for example, during the Civil War, one Henri A. Hobart arrived at Cliff on the Upper Peninsula to work as a school master. At first he warmed to the 150 Cornish children in his care, but it was not long before he was sick of this 'most God-forsaken place' with its 'Cornish twaddle and nonsense'. The young Cornish miners were full of 'self conceit and pride and affectation ... as ignorant as jackasses', while 'It is true there are young girls and Cornish girls, but I cannot appreciate their excellent pasty qualities. When I hear a young lady of 180 lbs saying, Now here, he ain't good for noffing for such a brave one as she, Thee art a nice man etc ... I am sick'. There was further racist abuse from Hobart for the 'crowd of whisky soaked Beer Bellys [that] are the blue-eyed set of Cornish', together with the familiar criticism of Cousin Jack conservatism: 'The Fourth was celebrated in this place in the Cornish way. There must be no change – whatever was done by preceding generations must be done today .... They are like hogs in every sense of the word.'[43]

The above suggests at least the potential for ethnic conflict on the Lakes, a potential exacerbated with the passing of years as an ever greater mix of nationalities, notably varieties of Scandinavians, arrived on the Upper Peninsula. Antagonism between the Cornish and the Irish, both ethnic groups with much to gain and to lose on the mining frontier, a rivalry spiced with religious conflict and with political overtones imported from the Old Country, was certainly a feature of the Michigan mining camps. In 1857, in one memorable incident, a Cousin Jack named John Terrell was almost sliced in two by an Irish axeman who cut him down outside Dan Ryan's saloon in the Keweenaw community of Cliff.[44] Terrell was killed instantly but, despite the hue and cry raised by the enraged Cousin Jacks, Ryan was never brought to justice, not even the rough justice of the frontier.

For the moment, however, the Cornish were in the ascendancy, their legend still so much bigger than the sniping criticisms of educated class snobs and ethnic rivals, and they delighted in offering gratuitous advice to those mine companies who needed – they thought – to be shown the errors of their ways. One such outfit was the Nebraska Mine Company which in 1859 was taken to task for listening too often 'to outsiders',[45] while in the same year even the mighty Minesota Mine was castigated by Cornish observers for being slow to adopt the Cornish tribute and tutwork system of employment. Another Cornishman, writing in the *Mining Journal* in 1861, complained that in the mid-1850s at the Cliff Mine 'a new manager was appointed who knew little or nothing about mining', a state of affairs which led the mine into (temporary) difficulties but which also indicated – it was contended – that 'Too often it is the case that the difference between a sound practical man and one of no practice is lightly admitted.'[46] In fact, the Cornish had found their way into managerial positions in most of the mines, both large and small, and T.A. Richard, the celebrated mining historian of Cornish stock, estimated that almost every underground captain on the Lakes was a Cornishman.[47] The Cliff Mine and the Minesota Mine – together with the twin concerns of Calumet and Hecla – were the biggest enterprises on the Upper Peninsula by the 1850s, and their skilled workforce was predominantly Cornish. In 1866 a Methodist minister at Houghton exclaimed that 'Cornwall has emptied her army of miners among these hills'.[48] It was hardly an exaggeration, as the innumerable surviving biographical sketches of Cornish folk attest.

Josiah Hall, for instance, born in Devon of Cornish parents, was at various times captain in the Cliff, Pewabic, Central, and Calumet and Hecla mines. John Hoar, born in Cornwall in 1817, went first of all to Ireland and to Germany, arriving on the Keweenaw in 1846. Following a brief interlude as a coal miner in Pennsylvania, he was soon back on the Upper Peninsula where he formed a partnership with his brother Richard (who had emigrated to Canada in 1854), purchasing the steamship *Ivanhoe* and organising the Overland Transportation Co. whose task it was to manage the export of copper ore from the region. Another Cousin Jack, Richard Edwards, born in 1809, had emigrated to Brooklyn in 1849 but by 1850 was already on the Upper Peninsula where he was captain of the Eagle River mines. By 1850 he was manager of the Albion Mines at Houghton, and later he invested successfully in the Calumet mine, on the proceeds of which he started farming in the locality. His eldest son Joe had been captain at the Consols Mines in North Carolina in 1860, but with the outbreak of the Civil War headed west – to the famous Cornish towns of Grass Valley and Virginia City in California and Nevada – before moving eastwards again to South Dakota and eventually settling at Houghton. Another son, James, was a civil engineer and was responsible for building the important bridge linking Houghton and Hancock.[49]

We should also mention Captain Henry Buzza (or Buzzo), a regular contributor to the *Mining Journal* (sometimes under the *nom de plume* 'A Cornish Captain'), who had mined in Ireland, New Jersey and Pennsylvania before becoming manager of the Ridge Mine in 1850. There was Captain Richard Uren, secretary and treasurer of the Lake Superior Native Copper Works, and William Harris from Illogan (the underground captain at the Minesota noted above) who had arrived on the Upper Peninsula from the Bruce iron and copper mines in Ontario in 1850. A popular figure in the community, Harris went on to serve in the Michigan Legislature from 1871 until 1875. Thomas B. Dunstan, a Cornish miner from Camborne, became lawyer, judge, state legislator and senator, and finally Lieutenant-Governor of Michigan. William Lean, of a similar legal turn of mind, after five years training at Ontonagon also went on to become a local judge. At the mighty Hecla mine Captain William Stephens was in charge; at the Calumet his opposite number was the well-known Captain William Daniel, another Cousin Jack. Captain Thomas Daniell, yet another Cornishman, was a practical miner whose shrewd knowledge of geology led to the discovery of the Tamarrack mine, destined to become one of the area's principal producers and – ultimately – to merge with the Calumet and Hecla mines. His successor at the Tamarrack was William Parnall, a noted Cornish wrestler.[50]

If we expand our view to encompass the iron ranges further south, then still further Cornish come within our field of vision. First discovered in the 1840s, the Gobegic range was not developed until much later, while the Menominee finds were not made until at least the 1860s and 1870s. However, by the 1880s the town of Iron Mountain had a population of 5000 strong, the Cornish – many of whom had worked previously on the Keweenaw – as ever found in key positions as skilled workers and captains. William Bray, who had mined variously in Vermont, North and South Carolina, Illinois and the Lakes, made his way to Iron Mountain to become manager of the Hewett mine. William Bice was captain of the Ludington, and Thomas Rundle was at the Chapin: a mine discovered by one John Wicks from Tywardreath. William Trestrail was inspector of mines for Dickinson County in the Menominee range. His father, originally a stonemason from Redruth, had been in Cuba before travelling to the Upper Peninsula. Like many others, Trestrail senior sojourned briefly in California before returning to work in the Hecla, then moving south to take up a position in the Chapin – where he died at the age of 46. His son William had left Cornwall to join him in California, travelling with his father to Hecla and then to Iron Mountain. Thereafter, William branched out on his own, mining gold in the Dakotas and Colorado before returning to the Chapin mine and eventually being appointed inspector of mines.

At Ironwood, in the Gobegic range, one notable Cornish captain was Thomas Stevens, manager of the Pabst mine and originally from Leedstown. His was the classic Cousin Jack background – his father had worked in the celebrated Godolphin mine in Cornwall, his father-in-law had been killed in an underground accident in Cuba – and A.L. Rowse has told the story of his extraordinary career:

> Of five children, three came to America, one went to South Africa. Young Tom worked at a mine from eight and a half, and

at nineteen went to work at Abercarn in Monmouthshire – the most dangerous mine in' South Wales from ever-present fire damp. Tom realized the danger in which he worked and, after a few months, emigrated. Three years later the entire working force was killed in one of the worst explosions in mining history – 282 miners, including two of Tom's uncles and two cousins. He went to Scranton, Pennsylvania, then back to Cleator Moor [in the North of England] for eleven years. He returned to the United States to work in Alabama and Massachusetts, until 1888 when he came to Iron Mountain [sic, Rowse means Ironwood]. He worked thirteen years as miner, shift boss, timber foreman – the usual steps up the ladder – until he was made a captain in 1902.[51]

The movement of Cornish folk from the Upper Peninsula to the iron ranges was mirrored in a similar move to the land as those who had done well on tribute and tutwork contracts (or had returned from California with cash to spare) emulated the miners-turned-farmers of Wisconsin or turned to other occupations such as lumbering and storekeeping. However, prospects were more limited in the poor soil and harsh conditions of Keweenaw, Houghton and Ontonagon counties, and – as John Rowe has explained – agricultural activities were generally restricted to horse and oxen breeding and the production of milk and dairy produce: together, ironically, with the growing of potatoes.[52] At a time when the potato had disappeared almost overnight from the Cornish diet at home, with disastrous consequences, its introduction on the Upper Peninsula was welcomed as a major contribution to meeting the expanding demand for staple foods. As early as June 1849 the *West Briton* had noted the planting of potatoes in Michigan,[53] and by 1864 the region was producing over 60,000 bushels per year – an important counter to the difficulties and expense of bringing in food supplies from outside, especially in the worst of the winter months. For the Cousin Jennies, the miners' wives, this was a crucial improvement on conditions in post-1840s Cornwall, notwithstanding the constant need to save every scrap of bacon, pork and other provisions to endure the long freeze.

But when times were good, then so too was the living, as Angus Murdoch remembered nostalgically in 1943 in his wonderfully evocative book *Boom Copper: The Story of the First U.S. Mining Boom*:

So lusty a worker and so great a talker and singer as the Cornishman naturally gave a good deal of attention to food. Sunday breakfast was the peak of the Cousin Jack's dietary week, and then his good Cousin Jennie spread the table with favorite Cornish dishes. The meal started with mush, drowned in the inimitable Cornish scalded cream. Seedy buns or heavy cake abounded, and were accompanied by potatoes in their jackets and a heaping platter of salt codfish, creamed and steaming-hot. After church, if the [tribute or tutwork] 'contract' had gone well, the family ate the favorite of all good Britons, rare roast of beef. And with the left-over the Cousin Jennie made that typically Cornish dish, the pasty.[54]

Murdoch's picture of contentment and plenty, even if a little too cosy and contrived, presents a striking contrast to the Cornwall of the 1840s and the later decades of distress. We should remember that sentimentality would have done much to colour his recollections after the passage of so many years. And yet, we must take Murdoch seriously, for elsewhere in *Boom Copper* he was a faithful recorder of the Cornish and their habits. Consider, for example, his estimation of Cornish religion:

the Cornish preferred hell-fire and brimstone Methodism to the formalized religion of the Church of England. No chanting and ceremonial rites for the Cousin Jack. Whenever original ideas of the hereafter occurred, he liked to stand right up in church and air them. He was highly articulate, if uneducated, and took turns with fellow Wesleyans in preaching the weekly sermons. In fact, Methodist churches had no regular preachers during the early days on the range; competition, it was felt, made for livelier sermons.[55]

Similarly:

The Cornishmen sang on their way to work and blended their song into a chorus as the man car took them down the shaft. It must have been quite an experience to hear the strains of 'Rock of Ages' gradually fade as the singers were lowered underground. And the singing at a Central Mine funeral could move a man with a heart of stone ... as the cortege left the church the men began the dolorous words of 'Nearer, My God, to Thee' and continued through the verses until they reached the grave. Until you have heard Cornish singers, their rich, natural baritones echoing from the bluff back of Central, and seen them stand bowed before an open grave in a mine cemetery, you can't know how truly beautiful and dignified the burial service can be.[56]

Cornish carols were sung at Christmas and a fierce rivalry existed between the several choirs, played out each year in the annual choir competition held at the First Methodist Church of Calumet. A similarly competitive spirit existed within the ranks of Cornish wrestlers, Murdoch recording that 'no holiday was complete without a bout or two of Cousin Jack huskies tossing one another around a ring with the Cornish-invented "flying mare"'. As he explained: 'The opponents wore stout, canvas jackets, buckled at the back ... it was a matter of strength, each wrestler striving to grab hold of the other's jacket and toss him to the mat'.[57] The Cornish were also experts in the hand-drill contests held every Fourth of July at Calumet, 'Nowadays, not many can beat a drill "either hand afore" – that is, swing a sledge fast and true from the right or from the left'. In earlier times, however, the Cornish had been masters of the task, in one contest at Calumet at the turn of the century the achievement of an impressive $9^1/4$ inch hole in ten minutes by one 'foreign' team being dismissed by Cornish observers as 'somewhat amateurish'.[58]

Angus Murdoch's yarns were matched in fiction by the novel *The Long Winter Ends* by Newton G. Thomas, first published in 1941 but fortuitously reprinted in 1998 thanks to the Wayne State University Press.[59] Thomas was a Cornish miner, born at Stoke Climsland in the east of Cornwall, who emigrated to the Lakes as the local mines around Kit Hill and Hingston Down began to close. This too is the experience of the book's hero, Jim Holman (the novel has more than a hint of autobiographical inspiration), who takes the advice of a miner who has returned from Michigan's Upper Peninsula to tell those facing an uncertain future in Cornwall that they would be better off on the Lakes. Jim, like many others, heeds the advice and heads for the Keweenaw, the decision to go taking on an almost mystical quality, the fulfilment of a pre-ordained destiny which made inevitable the global wanderings of Cornish folk.

Fatalistic rather than triumphalist, this is nonetheless the essence of the myth of Cousin Jack:

> Another mine. That was a part of their history; it was written in their marrow. Another mine and another until in some dark gut of the earth they found a place for their skill. Every Cornish miner answered the question, met the emergency .... Mining was his trade. For generations his ancestors had picked and pried, mauled and shoveled, blasted their way by candlelight in the Cornish pits. They knew ground and how to break it, to timber it, to channel its water and dispose of it. They knew the whimsy of the veins and followed them as if by scent. In the narrow ways they cut to obtain the precious dirt, they acquired a skill with their simple tools that has been equalled by no others. Given a hammer and a few drills these men would make passage through anything that steel would dent and powder break .... Their pride in their tools and their own skill never abated. When the small bits of their drills were insufficient and their shoulder muscles inadequate for the tonnages demanded from the thick veins of the Peninsula and together gave way to air-driven machines, they still persisted that a man was no miner if he had no skill with a hammer and drill. Wherever they went, they found that their methods had preceded them; wherever they went the copy of their work made them feel at home. In mines everywhere their terms were established. What would these men do? They would go to another mine and would mine.[60]

Again, the familiar characteristics of the Cornish are readily observable in Thomas' book. 'You'd think Cornwall was a chip off the 'oly Land an' all the Cousin Jacks pious', was one opinion, though Cornish ethnicity did have its darker side – such as when the Cousin Jacks were too clannish to attend the funeral of a fellow miner because he was Finnish. Essentially, *The Long Winter Ends* is about the adaptability and tenacity of the Cornish, exemplified in the experience of Jim Holman, who grabbed the opportunities of America, on the one hand becoming archetypal Americans and yet, on the other, ensuring that 'The flavour of Cornwall will last in the [Upper] Peninsula a long w'ile hafter the Cornishman be extinc.'[61] This paradoxical experience is sensed by William H.

Mulligan in his perceptive introduction to the 1998 edition of the book. He writes: 'The Cornish are an extreme case of the phenomenon identified by Charlotte Erickson in her *Invisible Immigrants: The Adaption of English and Scottish Immigrants in 19th Century America* (1972). As English-speaking Protestants with economically valuable skills as underground miners, the Cornish were able to enter into American society with few difficulties.'[62]
And yet, as Mulligan adds:

> On the Michigan mining frontier, the Cornish were not invisible immigrants and played a major role in the development of the mining industry and its early communities ... Because of their expertise, the Cornish defined the language of American mining and established its earliest industrial organization ... In the tiny early mining communities of the Keweenaw and Marquette range, they clung to their traditions in the mines and in the Methodist chapels they established. They were no longer in Cornwall, however, and everything in their environment conspired to challenge their old ways. Ultimately, they faced the challenge of becoming Americans.[63]

This was the challenge that confronted both the fictional Jim Holman and his creator Newton G. Thomas who, after a brief spell in the iron mines in Norway, Michigan, went on to become a school master and university professor. It was the same challenge that was met by Alfred Nicholls, a Cornish miner whose as yet unpublished autobiography tells the story of his emigration from Cornwall, where he had worked as an ore-dresser at Wheal Peevor, near Redruth, to the Upper Peninsula. His poignant departure is typical enough but nonetheless moving for that:

> I sometimes wonder if many of us have given serious thought to the heartaches of a mother who sees her grown boys leave the fireside in successive years, possibly never to return. Never shall I forget that parting from a mother's love that knows no bounds. She could not go to the station, the strain was too great. If ever I realized her unbounded affection, her tenderest devotion, it was when I left her embrace. My father died about one year previous to that day, and she looked upon me as her

support and counselor. I promised to be a true and faithful son to her through her remaining years. 'I don't worry about that', she said, 'I am sure of your kindness. It is your leaving that breaks my heart'.[64]

Arriving on the Keweenaw, Alfred Nicholls lodged, in the normal Cousin Jack way, with his brother Dick who put in a good word for him at the Central Mine and found him work underground. At first, Alfred was surprised by what he found: 'I was not very favourably impressed with America .... Such tiny log houses, no streets, no shops, no social activities. Not much of anything except work. Well, I was accustomed to that'.[65] Distressed to find that he was teased as a 'greenhorn' by the other miners, Alfred's sense of alienation and discomfort was gradually ameliorated through his contact with the Upper Peninsula's lively musical scene (he had been wrong about the lack of social activities) and, especially, through a growing desire to become 'American'.

As he recalled:

Music was an important asset in my life. My reputation in musical circles had, evidently, preceded my coming into the community. Within a few days I was asked to become a member of the choir, composed of ten voices and a small reed organ. Our weekly rehearsals were held in the choir leader's house. An attractive young woman, by the name of Eliza Carter Chinn [a Cousin Jenny], was one of the sopranos. Winter was approaching and after rehearsal, on one occasion, the lady of the house suggested I accompany this young soprano home – the road being rough and stony, the evening dark, and cows roaming as fancy suggested. I was anxious to become American; to acquire their customs, to acquaint myself with such duties of etiquette as are becoming to young men. The proposal to accompany her home had been suggested, and the only thing, the courteous thing, was to say it would become a pleasure indeed to do so. The young woman offered no objection and into the darkness we followed a path that led to her door. Suffice to say, that was the beginning of a friendship that led to courtship, courtship to matrimony, and matrimony begat unto us children, one daughter and five sons.[66]

This rite of passage, a first step to learning the American way and indeed to putting down roots in America, may have had an ulterior motive (sex), but later steps were forced upon Alfred Nicholls in the most dramatic manner. As he put it, after several years of marital bliss, 'Then came a day when the heavens darkened! In a moment, like some terrible thought fashioned in a dream, my life became one of unutterable sadness and depression. The austere hand of adversity came into our home, and my days and nights were of unfathomable blackness.'[67] Put briefly, Alfred had suffered an accident underground, one that had badly fractured his left arm at the elbow. To prevent a stiff joint, the arm was bound tightly – too tightly, for when the bandages were removed the arm had swollen horribly, resulting in the loss of both feeling and movement. His left forearm and hand were useless. Precluded from work in the mine, the club and doctor fund paid him a dollar a day for a year, after which he received help – in the Cousin Jack way – from his Masonic lodge. A visit to a specialist in the mining town of Osceola, 22 miles from Central, brought the grim news that Alfred would never use his arm again. Struggling with his now deeply assailed Christian convictions, Alfred stumbled the two miles to neighbouring Calumet, where he stayed the night in a boarding house full of Cousin Jacks. They 'were of my kith and kin. They enjoyed themselves playing games, and told Cornish stories. Laughter, jokes, and the spirit of merriment pervaded the entire little company .... I had eyes that saw not; ears that heard not. In my state of mind their laughter was vanity, vexatious, torturous.'[68]

Alfred's spirits were lifted, his faith restored, by the company of a one-armed, lame and blind Cornish miner who accompanied him on the stagecoach back to Central. This Cousin Jack had been grievously injured in a premature explosion in the Phoenix Mine, near Central, and when told of Alfred's own disability exclaimed: 'Well, my son, I don't know you, have never seen you, but if I were as well off as you physically, I would ask for nothing more. My joys would be complete.'[69] Such a story might have been heard in a hundred Bible Christian or Wesleyan chapels in Cornwall or on the Lakes, the allegorical text of any number of earnest local preachers. But the tale did not end merely with hope restored, for Alfred Nicholls went on – largely through the loyal insistence of his wife Eliza that he was not a 'blockhead' – to go to college where, eventually, he qualified as a teacher. This rise from disabled miner to member of the professional classes was not without its trials and tribulations, but it was a transformation almost unheard of in the Old Country, a tribute to the egalitarianism and economic opportunities of the United States – as indeed it was to Alfred Nicholls himself who in a very real sense had risen to the challenge of 'becoming American'.

Told with an engaging old-fashioned eloquence, Alfred Nicholl's story appears singular in content but in fact it was not. He possessed a literary gift that allowed him to articulate his thoughts on paper, an ability perhaps not shared by the great many other Cornish on this American frontier who – also suffering misfortune of one sort or another – nevertheless 'made good' under American conditions. For all their clannish willingness to play the Cousin Jack card, to deploy ethnic identity to gain favour or protect privilege, the Cornish were also well placed – and motivated – to make the most of American opportunities. This was, one might add, also reflected in the readiness with which the Cornish were keen to take out American citizenship and in the willingness with which many were prepared to fight for the Union in the Civil War.

By the 1860s, the decade of the Civil War, there were some 20,000 settlers in the Upper Michigan mining counties of Keweenaw, Houghton and Ontonagon, of whom at least 3000 were Cornish. In the iron ranges there was a small but growing Cornish presence, especially in the towns of Ironwood and Iron Mountain. Of course, the Civil War brought disruption and dislocation to the Lakes but the victory of the North, and with it the safeguarding of the Union, precipitated a short boom of increased demand for copper and for mining labour, the resultant scarcities prompting high copper prices and high wages. This renewed prosperity was fleeting, however, the declining international copper prices of the late 1860s catching up with American producers as surely as they had caught up with Cornwall in the awful crash of 1866 (see Chapter 8). Although the Upper Peninsula mines were ultimately in a far better position than those of Cornwall to weather the vicissitudes of the 1860s, in the short term their position seemed every bit as parlous, and one sharp lesson was the need for care and economy in the management of mines, particularly with regard to investment and developmental work. In earlier days, especially in the larger, richer and more productive mines, there had been little thought given to efficiency or conservation of either effort or reserves. In effect, many mines had been managed badly, or at least extravagantly, because they had been developed swiftly in boom times when the pickings were easy and the demand for a quick return irresistible. In the end, the fortunes of the Keweenaw and surrounding copper country were restored only through the new life breathed into the Calumet and Hecla mines by the discovery of new conglomerate reserves at depth, and through the skillful application of the latest technology to achieve the maximum exploitation of these new resources.

The rise of Calumet and Hecla – soon amalgamated into one vast company –

as an industrial giant was indicative of the changing nature of mining on the Upper Peninsula, the smaller, more intimate workings having long since disappeared or been incorporated into larger concerns. The surviving mines had become big, heavily capitalised, sternly paternalistic – even authoritarian – organisations, their workforces increasingly 'proletarian' in terms of their distance from the sources of management and decision-making. The Cornish, with an individualism and independence born of their tribute and tutwork system, resented being treated like pawns, especially over issues like the length of the working day or wage rates. During the spring and summer of 1872 there was the first sign of trouble, two Cousin Jacks, Grose (a Methodist class leader) and Vivian, emerging as ringleaders in a strike that lasted for a month. The demand for an eight-hour day was heard first at Calumet and Hecla, and from there the strike spread to the Pewabic, Quincy and other mines. Grose and Vivian were arrested on two occasions, and on the latter a thousand miners demonstrated peaceably for their release. There was little or no violence – though one Cousin Jenny was reported to have killed a horse belonging to the local sheriff – and it is significant that the Cornish had persuaded the Irish to claim common cause on this occasion: the only workers to ignore the strike call being newly arrived Scandinavians happy to accept existing conditions.[70] Also significant, perhaps, was that 1872 had – following a brief outburst of activity in 1866 – seen the re-emergence of labour trouble in the Cornish mines at home, the (short-lived) tin boom of that year precipitating calls for an end to the notorious 'five week month'. Focused on the Camborne-Illogan-Redruth mining district, the strikes in Cornwall stretched as far east as St Blazey and the Caradon area, and westwards to St Just-in-Penwith, creating a heady atmosphere which may well have been communicated to – and influenced – Cornish workforces overseas.

Be that as it may, the 1872 strike on the Upper Peninsula seemed to herald a new industrial culture. Despite Cornish leadership and participation in the strike action, there were Cornishmen among the captains and bosses who perforce took the management's side, the growing divide between capital and labour serving to dent if not undermine ethnic solidarity. As time went on, the Cornish would find themselves caught even more acutely in the tensions between management and workforce. As Murdoch explained, 'As more and more immigrants appeared on the copper range, the Cousin Jack advanced in caste. He became shift boss, mining captain, or mine superintendent. His skill was too great to waste on mere labor, and thereafter other nationalities beat hand drills and trammed the rock.'[71] In 1878 William Tonkin, a Cornishman, had been appointed Captain of the Atlantic Mine, south of Portage Lake. Copper prices rose during the early 1880s, precipitating higher wages and a scarcity of labour. Tonkin complained, 'I have never since the [Civil] "war times" had so much trouble to set contracts and get men to do a fair day's work .... When men are scarce they will do as they please, but when plenty, as they are told.'[72] He introduced the Rand 'widow-maker' drills (so-called because of the silicosis caused by the dust they created) in the summer of 1880, remarking cautiously that 'I shall have to let the men get acquainted with the machines before I can set their contracts.'[73]

Fluctuating copper prices meant fluctuating contracts, a complication made more complex by the ever-increasing mixture of nationalities with their different habits and expectations. An exasperated Tonkin wrote in 1883:

> There are some Finlanders and Swedes travelling around, but they work a few days and leave. I had six a few days ago on the Railroad heaving snow; two of them worked two days and left and four worked three days and left. I hired, February first, 6 Swede miners and gave them a drill, and they broke 40 fathoms in that month. Another party of 6 Swedes started March first, and I am afraid by what they have done so far that they will not pay their cost and board. I have tried to reduce the contract price a little, but the Cornish miners will not stand it yet.[74]

By the turn of the 20th century, the increasingly 'Americanised' Cornish – with their socio-economic mobility that had either brought promotion within the mines or led them into new professions – were even further distanced from the multi-ethnic, multilingual workforces of Finns, Swedes, Italians, Croats and others. This, inevitably, was reflected in the changing nature of industrial relations on the Upper Peninsula. Thus, as A.L. Rowse observed, 'The big copper strike of 1914 was of unskilled miners – Finns, Slavs, Italians; the Cornish were skilled workers, foremen, bosses, mining captains, to whom the unskilled objected.'[75] By then, however, the Upper Peninsula had long since ceased to be the focus of Cornish activity in the American mining industry. Many had moved to the neighbouring state of Minnesota, for example, working in the iron mines – especially those in the neighbourhood of Ely – while others had drifted to the industrial magnet of Detroit where they found work in the expanding automobile industry.

Iron had been found in the early 1880s in the remote country of northern Minnesota, the dense evergreen forests and the many hundreds of lakes bordering the Canadian province of Ontario. Hitherto the preserve of the Chippewa (Ojibway) Native Americans and the occasional white trapper – not to mention the profusion of brown bear, moose and wolves – the north of that state was even then very much a *terra incognita*, almost impenetrable in the impossibly hard depths of winter. After the Civil War, a trail – known later as the Vermillion Trail – had been pushed northwards into this country in the hope of finding gold. There was no gold but, as later prospectors discovered, there were huge iron deposits. In 1883 the Minnesota Mining Company, formed for the purpose, decided to exploit these reserves. To this end it engaged Captain Elisha Morcom, superintendent of the Qinnesec Mine in the Menominee Range in Michigan, to survey the company's newly acquired properties on the Vermillion Range. A Cousin Jack of considerable experience, Morcom had been born in the parish of Kenwyn in 1835, at the age of 19 emigrating to Michigan with his uncle William Grose. In 1863, aged 28, he became a mining captain at Rockland, Michigan, in 1868 marrying one Elizabeth Anne Wicks, the daughter of another Cornish mine captain. By the 1880s, with his extensive background in both copper and iron mining, he was one of the most senior and respected Cornish captains on the Lakes.[76]

Elisha Morcom spent the summer of 1883 in the vicinity of what would become the settlements of Tower and Soudan in northern Minnesota, surveying the mine sites and making them ready for the arrival of men and machinery. He returned to Michigan in the autumn to recruit miners and mechanics for the new ventures, signing up some 300 volunteers (many Cornish among them) who accompanied him to the Vermillion Range in the spring of 1884. The mines were developed on a successful footing, Morcom himself becoming a pillar of this newly created frontier society, not least as mayor of the township of Tower. Captain John Pengilly was another Cousin Jack on the Vermillion Ranges in the 1880s. Under the auspices of the Minnesota Mining Company, he ventured northwards from Tower in September 1886 in a canoe with a few chosen colleagues to examine a new discovery at what would become the Chandler Mine near the township-to-be of Ely. Close by, on the banks of Lake Shagawa, was also established the important Pioneer mine.

Ely, with its iron mines and Post Office and Methodist and Lutheran churches, was destined to become the communal centre for this area of northern Minnesota, a focus for the Cousin Jacks and Jennies and, subsequently, for the many Finns and other Scandinavians who made this remote lakeland spot their home. Captain Pengilly was elected Ely's first 'village president', later becoming its first mayor when it had assumed the status of city. It is said that

Samuel Ely Polkinghorne was the first European child born at Ely, a son of Captain Richard Polkinghorne (who was born in Cornwall in 1844), and we are told – in a poignant vignette which is a fleeting clue to the hardships of pioneer life in the northern forests of the United States – that poor Mrs Polkinghorne (we know her by no other name) was unable to produce milk for her baby. In desperation her friend, Mrs Johns, another Cousin Jenny, walked to Tower, purchased a cow and drove it back to Ely so that the new-born Samuel might have the nourishment he needed to live and thrive.

By chance the tale of resourceful and kindly Mrs Johns has survived. Generally women were invisible when performing their routine duties of childbirth and domestic chores, at best seen as supporting adjuncts of their menfolk. By and large women were the subject of comment only when they resorted to the exotic or the disapproved-of. Thus:

> Some of the women also liked their drinks and other vices. Ely had women who chewed tobacco and snuff, who smoked a pipe, and of course there were those who liked a snort. Mrs Kent [a Cornish name], the wife of the part-owner and general manager of the Chandler Mine, had one-half gallon of brandy delivered to her each week by a saloon keeper.[77]

As ever, Cornish wrestling was one of the favourite Fourth of July events, and Cornish pasties became a staple element of the diets of Cornish and non-Cornish alike: the Cornish 'gift to all nationalities on the Iron [Vermillion] Range'.[78] At Ely was preserved one of the many sentimental rhyming pasty recipes that were prevalent in late 19th-century Cornwall:

> I dearly love a pasty
> A' ot and leaky one
> With mayt, turmit and taty
> H'ony on and parsley in un
> The crus' be made with suet
> Shaped like a 'alf moon Crinkly
> B'edges freshly baked
> 'ees always gone too soon.[79]

The usual Cousin Jack yarns were also prevalent at Ely, not least those that surrounded the exploits of Captain Charles 'Charlie' Trezona. Fires were a constant threat to the largely timber built towns of frontier America, especially in the summer months when buildings were tinder dry but also during the freezing winters when fires burned around the clock in domestic hearths. In the late winter of 1905 a blaze threatened to sweep through Ely. Discovered at 5 am on the morning of 5 March in a four-storey timber-framed hotel, the fire was burning out of control by 9.30 am, the local fire brigade helpless to intervene through loss of water pressure. Then came Captain Trezona to the rescue, his men laying a pipeline from the Pioneer Mine to the township more than a mile away and successfully tackling the flames. Charlie Trezona was the hero of the hour, but only the year before local miners had threatened to lynch him. A strike by seamen on the Great Lakes had paralysed much local commerce, with pay to the Ely miners stopped until business was resumed. Captain Pengilly resigned his position in disgust, and at the Chandler Mine the miners refused to let anyone go underground, then setting off in angry mood to accost Captain Trezona. Charlie Trezona managed to escape by hand-car down the local railroad to Tower, the next day catching a train to Duluth. Cooly, he remained there until the miners and Ely businessmen – uncertain what to do next – asked him to return to re-open the mines. Thereafter, Trezona remained in command until his death in 1931, an almost legendary figure whose Cornishness underwrote and gave meaning to the mystique he cultivated.

However, the events of the preceding 50 years and more had opened a vast new mining frontier in North America, part of the ever-widening international mining economy in which the Cornish played their part. Within this continental diaspora, the Cornish took with them an American frontier version of their Cousin Jack – and Cousin Jenny – ethnic identity, one moulded in Wisconsin, honed on the Lakes and given expression in a score of Western mining camps from Grass Valley and Virginia City to Leadville, Nevadaville and Butte. John H. Forster, who in Michigan had worked alongside the Cornish in 1862, breaking up the extraordinary 'pudding stone' that had been piled up at surface, caught the mood of this identity, articulating it for his American readers:

> The Cornishman, or 'Cousin Jack', is a native of the duchy of
> Cornwall .... I suppose that a residence of a thousand years or more
> in the insular kingdom entitles him to the protection of the Queen,
> but he has (unadulterated) no Anglo-Saxon blood in his veins ....
> The Cornishman of the present day, like his father, is of a roving

disposition. His footsteps may be traced around the globe. There is no prominent mining field in the world wherein you will not find 'Cousin Jack'. He is in Alaska, California, the Rocky Mountains, Mexico, Central and South America, in Australia, India and Lake Superior. He is a first rate miner and possesses a certain sturdiness of frame and disposition that commends him to the observer. He works hard, eats well and fights bravely. He is, numerically, very strong in our northern mines, and, being, as a rule, steady, conservative and skilful, he finds ready employment. He likes mining; esteems his vocation among the most honorable, if not aristocratic. He despises the duties of an ordinary day laborer. In short, he is a born miner and nothing else.[80]

In fact, as we know, the Cousin Jacks were very much more than this, many having turned their hands successfully to farming or even having entered the professions, the opportunities of America seemingly tailor-made for the hard-working Cornish with their Nonconformist drive for self-improvement. But, as Mulligan has acknowledged, this is the nub of the Cornish paradox, for equipped as they were to be the 'invisible immigrants' *par excellence* of American society, they nonetheless remained distinctively different when it was in their interests to do so. And, of course, it was the 'visible' rather than 'invisible' Cornish that caught the eye and drew the comment of observers like Forster, perpetuating on the American mining frontier the Cousin Jack stereotype of which the Cornish themselves were so fond. For them 'getting on' was all important, and many emigrant Cornish would have shared the Nonconformist work-ethic opinions of George Cocking, who had toiled in the Pednandrea mine at Redruth before mining in various parts of America and becoming eventually an ordained minister in the Methodist Episcopal Church of the United States. His 'highest aim', he said, was:

> to encourage the thousands of young people who like myself, have been cast forth, with the stern truth staring them in the face that, if they are to be successful in this life, *they must pave the way from the pit to the throne*; or, if the emergency demands it, HAMMER SUCCESS OUT OF THE ROCK.[81]

# CHAPTER FIVE

# SOUTH AUSTRALIA'S
# COPPER KINGDOM

The lead mining region of Wisconsin and Illinois, together with the burgeoning copper country of the Lakes and (later) the iron of Minnesota, had proved significant destinations for the Cornish, providing important sources of employment at a time when economic downturn in Cornwall had combined with the potato blight to perpetuate the Great Emigration. To these destinations, crucial as they were, was added a further focus of Cornish emigration in the 1840s – the rapidly emerging copper kingdom of South Australia, a major new element of the fast developing international mining economy. The foundation of South Australia in 1836 had occurred in the midst of the so-called Reforming Thirties, the decade when the clamour for socio-economic opportunity and civil and religious liberty in Britain had grown ever louder, and when the new colony's commitment to 'systematic colonisation' and its reputation as a 'Paradise of Dissent' had matched the spirit of the times, not least in Nonconformist Cornwall. In the subsequent decade, the 1840s, South Australia also seemed uniquely attuned to the needs of Cornwall, for the rapid expansion of the colony's copper mining industry served as a powerful attraction for many of those in Cornwall seeking to escape the Hungry Forties.

Although South Australia's financial crisis in the early 1840s had led to a brief curtailment of emigration to the colony, the bumper harvest of 1842 revealed a fundamental labour shortage. Moreover, the discovery of silver-lead in the Adelaide Hills at Glen Osmond in February 1841 by two miners, Hutchins and Thomas, 'we believe two emigrants from Cornwall' and 'persons in the humbler walks of life ... practical and experimental miners'[1] (as the local press described them), ushered in a period of mining frenzy that was to last until the Victorian gold rush in 1851. In fact, the first traces of mineral wealth had been spotted as early as 1838 by James Nicholls, a Cornishman, who had collected a large number of silver-lead samples from the Adelaide Hills and had at one point been able to trace the lode for a mile – this presumably being at Glen Osmond where, 'The

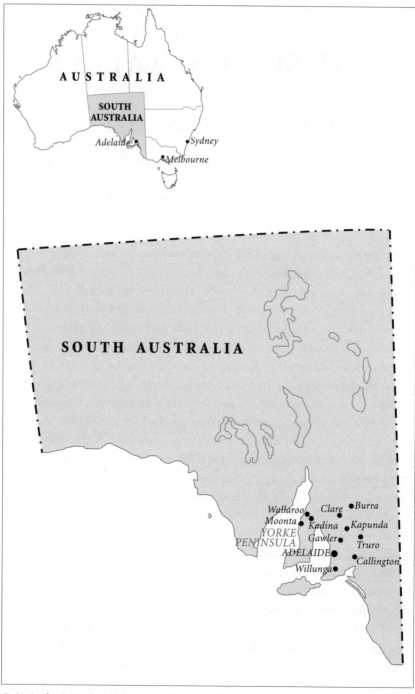

*Principal mining locations in South Australia*

first undoubted indication of the existence of silver-lead ore was made in 1838, on a section belonging to Mr Osmond Gilles, at the foot of the hills near Adelaide.[2] At the time, no effort had been made to develop the find, but with the onset of financial troubles a year or two later, attention was turned (not least by South Australia's already large Cornish community) to the colony's mineral potential, resulting in the Hutchins and Thomas discovery.

By April 1841 Australia's very first metalliferous mine, Wheal Gawler (named after the colony's governor) was in production, with six miners employed on the Cornish system of tribute and tutwork and balmaidens recruited to wash and dress the ore (the only recorded instance of women being employed to work on South Australian mines).[3] By 1843 a second mine, Wheal Watkins, was opened on an adjoining section, to be followed in 1846 by the Glen Osmond Union, managed by a Cornishman, one J.B.Pascoe. Other mines were worked intermittently in the district over the years – Wheal Hardy, Wheal Augusta, Mount Osmond – and the workforce was overwhelmingly Cornish: Captain Stephen Lean, George Prout, Stephen Carthew from Redruth, William Odgers, William Trethowan, and others named Trewartha, Knuckey, Thomas, Veal and Eade. The use of the Cornish prefix 'Wheal' (a working) was significant, indicating as it did the central role that Cornish personnel, terminology, technology and practices were to play in the development of the South Australian mining industry. Nowhere outside Cornwall itself was mining so overwhelmingly Cornish. Wheal Friendship, Wheal Fortune and Wheal Virgin, all South Australian mines, were names entirely reminiscent of Cornwall, and as early as 1848 the *West Briton* noted the extensive use of the prefix in the colony.[4] Other South Australian mine names were equally as evocative of Cornwall and the Cornish: Callington, Crinnis, Ding Dong, United Hills, Carn Brea, Bottallock (sic), Trevue, Tresevean (sic), Truro, New Cornwall, Old Cornwall, Duke of Cornwall, Benalack's Mine, Ivey's Claim, Kirkeek's Treasure, Toy's Find, Paull's Consolidated, Hooper's Luck, Jago and Harris' Prospect, Phillips' Copper Show, Hicks' Shaft and very many more.

Employment in most South Australian mines was according to tribute and tutwork contracts (in the former a miner or group of miners was remunerated according to the value of the ore won, in the latter payment was dependent upon the volume of ground dug), mine companies were organised on the Cornish cost-book system, and an independent legal system – with its own warden and warden's court (not unlike the Stannaries in Cornwall) – was set up to regulate the mining industry. Indeed, on one occasion in 1868 Cornish enthusiasts were moved to petition the Adelaide parliament for the creation of a fully fledged Stannary system in South Australia, a move which would have enhanced the legal and constitutional independence of the colony's mining districts.[5] The language and culture of South Australian mining was entirely Cornish, so that mine refuse was 'atal' (or 'attle'), a 'costeen' an exploratory trench, an 'adit' a drainage tunnel, a 'vugg' an underground cavity, a 'kibble' a shaft bucket, a 'whim' a winding device. A good vein ('lode') of ore was a 'keen-ly lode' or 'champion lode', and a lucky strike of exceptional ore was a 'sturt'. Clay-slate was 'killas', 'elvan' was hard, close-grained rock, and 'prill' was high-grade ore. Pyrites was 'mundic', mine depths were measured in fathoms, and a changing room was a 'dry'. The term 'Cornish' was itself used on innumerable occasions: Cornish captains, Cornish boilers, Cornish engines, Cornish stamps, Cornish picks, Cornish shovels, Cornish wheelbarrows. The Cornish miners themselves were, as ever, Cousin Jacks, their womenfolk Cousin Jennies.

The silver-lead finds in the Adelaide Hills had created a stir but far more exciting was the discovery of copper in South Australia, first of all at Kapunda, some 50 miles north of Adelaide in what was then isolated pastoral country. Francis Dutton later famously described how, when rounding-up stray sheep in the district, he came across what he first thought to be 'beauti-ful green moss'[6] but which on closer inspection proved to be malachite. He and his colleague, Charles Bagot, quietly acquired the mineralised land and arranged for a sample of the ore to be sent to Swansea: where it assayed at an extraordinary 21.5 per cent copper and sold for £21 per ton. Bagot later recalled how: 'This result of our first trial was encouraging, and induced us at once to prepare for opening the mine in a regular and permanent manner. To effect this I agreed with Robert Nicholls, a Cornish miner, for a twelve month to work on tribute. He forthwith began, and in a little time turned out a fine pile of good ore.'[7]

At first, the Kapunda mine was developed as two distinct workings – Wheal Dutton and Wheal Charles – and soon it was found necessary to recruit further supplies of miners as the enterprise expanded into a consider-able complex. Francis Dutton wrote:

> Amongst the general population of the colony were some few
> Cornish miners who were quietly following pastoral and agri-
> cultural pursuits; when we gave notice of intending to com-
> mence working the mine, the pickaxe was quickly resumed by
> them, and we gave them a liberal 'tribute' for the first year (3s

6d per £1) to set the thing going. These men were highly successful, and raised a considerable quantity of rich ore.[8]

By 1846 a sizeable community had grown up around the Kapunda mine, its
flavour overwhelmingly Cornish. William Trevena, from Redruth, was reputed-
ly the first person to build a house at Kapunda, and he was joined by numerous
other Cousin Jacks: John Dunstan who arrived in the colony in 1847 at the age
of 21 and worked in the Kapunda mine for 20 years; Stephen Carthew who
travelled to Kapunda from Glen Osmond and who in later years went on to
Moonta, the Victorian gold-fields and Broken Hill; Ralph Kestel, from
Portreath, who spent a year at the mine as an ore-dresser before going on to the
Burra. There was Thomas Axford from Chacewater, Henry Waters from
Penzance, Henry Bastian from Truro, Henry James Truscott from St Austell and
many more.[9] With this experienced core of Cornish miners, development work
at the mine proceeded apace, and from 1848 until the temporary halt in
operations caused by the Victorian gold rush in March 1852, production
averaged some 2500 tons of fine copper per annum. In 1847 a second-hand
30-inch beam engine was ordered from Cornwall. It arrived at the end of 1848,
certainly the first engine to be acquired anywhere in Australia. The purchase of
second-hand engines from Cornwall was a practice encouraged by the *South
Australian Register*, which in 1850 explained, 'We know that there were many
engines of abandoned mines in Cornwall for sale .... The old engine of the
Hallenbeagle, with 70 in cylinder and 200 horses' power, with two good boilers,
all in excellent repair, was for sale for £600 in September 1848.'[10] In January
1851 a second Cornish engine was acquired by the Kapunda mine, while
stamps, winding gear and even a smelter had also been erected.

The discovery and successful development of the Kapunda mine spawned a
number of copy-cat ventures in the same locality, each hoping for the same luck
and fortune, workings such as the South Kapunda, run by Captain Henry
Francis, and the North Kapunda and Wheal Gundry, both managed by a
Captain Gundry, while the attention of the Adelaide Hills prospectors turned
from silver-lead to copper. The Montacute mine, some ten miles north-east of
Adelaide, was in operation by early 1844 when 32 tons of copper were extracted under the watchful Cornish eye of Captain Tyrell. Abandoned in 1847, the
mine was operational again in 1848 under the management of Captain
Morcom, another Cousin Jack. Again, the workforce was largely Cornish: men
such as John Robins, J.Harris from Liskeard, and William Gummow, born in

Padstow in 1821. Gummow had driven beam engines at Wheal Rock and Perran Great St George before emigrating to South Australia in 1847. He worked at the Kanmantoo copper mine before going across to the Montacute, moving on later to the Burra. There was also Thomas Roberts, who in Cornwall had worked in the small Greenwith mine near Truro and who having arrived in South Australia in 1844 was engaged to work in the Montacute.[11] Other mines in the locality were the North Montacute, the Mukurta, and the claims of the Adelaide Mining Company, Francis Dutton insisting that the development of mines in the Adelaide Hills 'will undoubtedly be furthered by their engaging, as soon as possible, the assistance of practical Cornish mining captains, as the proprietors of the Kapunda mine have done.'[12]

While all this was going on, another major discovery of copper had occurred at Burra Burra in the then wild outback country almost 100 miles north of Adelaide. In June 1845 two shepherds had made separate finds of copper ore – the tell-tale greens and blues of malachite and azurite – on the banks of the Burra Burra Creek. Independently, they traded the secret of the locations to two rival commercial groups in Adelaide, the 'Nobs' and the 'Snobs'. These two groups competed for possession of the land in question but, to raise the £20,000 necessary for the 20,000-acre survey insisted upon by Governor Grey, they were forced to combine their efforts. Having purchased the property, the two groups divided the land: the 'Snobs' (the South Australian Mining Association) drawing the section that was to become the Burra Burra mine, the 'Nobs' acquiring what was to be the Princess Royal. The Princess Royal mine was initially very successful. It was worked through 1847 and 1848 by miners on tribute under the management of two Cornish captains, Messrs. Bath and Richards, but by 1851 the company's resources were all but expended. The mine was abandoned and the property sold as a sheep run. The South Australian Mining Association (SAMA), by contrast, had struck a veritable bonanza.

On 24 September 1845 Thomas Roberts, the SAMA prospector who had worked at the Montacute mine, was sent up to Burra Burra – or 'the Burra' as it was soon known – in charge of nine other Cornish miners. On their arrival the miners opened the first sett, which they called Great Wheal Grey (in honour of the Governor), and by October they were raising 60 tons of copper ore per week – mostly malachite and azurite – which assayed at an incredible 71.25 per cent copper. It was immediately obvious that this mine, the 'Monster' as it was dubbed in the press, was not only the richest find in the colony to date but was potentially of international significance as a copper producer. A contemporary verse, composed in those heady days of 1845, conveys something of the frenzied atmosphere that pervaded South Australia after the Burra discovery:

> Have you not heard of the Monster Mine?
> There's never a man to be got to dine,
> There's never a clerk who will pen a line,
> At my behest or thine.
> They are all gone to the houseless North
> To gaze on the Monster Mine.[13]

From the first, there was a determination to procure Cornish miners to work the Burra, the positive experiences at Kapunda giving credence to Cornish claims that Cousin Jacks were the best qualified miners and mechanics. A party of German miners that arrived at the Burra looking for work was summarily turned away, in contrast to enquiring Cornishmen who, having been 'recommended as good miners',[14] were eagerly snapped-up. In time, as the demand for miners began to outstrip supply, Germans were engaged but, from the evidence of their names – Lean, Teague, Pedlar, Edwards, Gregor, Thomas, Cundy, and so on – it is clear that most of the early Burra miners were Cornish. The captains, too, were exclusively Cornish. Henry Roach, from Redruth, had worked in Cornwall at the Tresavean mine and had visited Colombia before going to South Australia to become general superintendent of the Burra Burra mine in January 1847, a position he was to retain until his retirement in 1868. A visitor to the Burra in April 1848 wrote that he encountered 'A Captain Tre-something, and a Captain Pen-something',[15] for Roach was careful to recommend for employment as his assistants only men with a thorough Cornish background.

In June 1847 Captain Matthew Bryant was engaged as second captain, and in March 1848 Richard Goldsworthy, from Bodmin, became third captain. William Mitchell was appointed to the fourth position in 1849, and in the same year Samuel Osborne became chief ore-dresser. His immediate superior, the 'grass captain', Samuel Penglaze, had been appointed the previous year. Philip Santo, from Saltash, was employed as clerk of the works in September 1849. Peter Spargo, another Cousin Jack, was chief engineer from 1848 to 1851, when he was replaced by John Congdon, from the Caradon mines in East Cornwall. A Mr Boswarva was put in charge of administrative duties, while two Cornish masons, Ambrose Harris and Thomas Paynter, were entrusted with the building of engine houses and chimney stacks. Among the miners themselves, there were characters·

such as John Snell, the celebrated pitman (underground pump mechanic) of Morphett's Shaft, and James Datson, a tributer who went on to become one of South Australia's most successful mine agents. In 1848, of 63 tributers listed in SAMA's returns, 47 bore either exclusively or typically Cornish surnames. In 1860–61, of the 198 tributers listed, 135 had Cornish names – William Trevorrow, Henry Bosanco, Thomas Andrewartha, Thomas Yelland, James Tremewan, and many more, while only two – Henry Pelz and Charles Eisler – were clearly German. William Whita sounded German but his surname was probably a variant of 'Whetter', the well-known mid-Cornwall name. Many of those with 'English' surnames such as Hill, Bishop and Buckingham (names common enough in Cornwall) were also Cornish.[16] And as well as dominating the ranks of captains, managers and tributers, the Cornish settled into a variety of other occupations around the mine – men like James Grylls from St Buryan, James Thomas from Ludgvan, Henry Pinch from St Mabyn and William Escott from St Ives, who all worked variously as teamsters and dray operators. By November 1849 there were no fewer than 782 men employed directly at the mine. Probably well over half, and possibly very many more, were Cornish.

As at Kapunda, the Cornish facilitated the rapid development of the Burra mine, working according to the familiar tribute and tutwork system. At the end of the first financial year of the mine's operation, March 1846, 3000 tons of copper ore had been raised at very little cost and in the first six years of production some 80,000 tons were shipped to the United Kingdom, yielding a profit of £438,552. The firm of John Williams & Son of Truro and Scorrier was appointed SAMA's Cornish agent early in 1847 and it arranged for the sale of Burra ore at the Swansea ticketings. Meanwhile, a number of settlements had sprung up around the Burra, the *South Australian Register* declaring in April 1846 that 'we shortly expect to find our mining villages vieing with those of Cornwall and Devon.'[17] The SAMA township was named Kooringa, though the directors had earlier thought to call it Truro, and of the several other Burra 'suburbs' three were graced with names of Cornish towns: Redruth, Copperhouse, and Lostwithiel. The miners frequented the 'Cornish Arms', the 'Redruth Arms' and the 'Ancient Briton', and at Redruth lived in streets named after places at home in Cornwall – St Dye (reflecting the Cornish pronunciation of St Day), Truro, St Just, Mevagissey, Lelant, Ludgvan, Illogan, Tregony, Morvah, Sancreed, Crowan, Helston.

The Burra being, quite literally, so far off the beaten track, transport was always a problem in those early days, especially in the winter months when the track northwards to the Burra was 'strewed with laden drays bogged up to their axles'.[18] Water, however, was an even more pressing problem, and as the mine became ever deeper so it was increasingly difficult to keep the underground workings 'in fork' (dry). Accordingly, in August 1847 Henry Ayers, the SAMA secretary, wrote to John Bibby & Sons, SAMA's agent in Liverpool:

> The Directors wish you to procure for them as soon as possible a second hand steam engine as used in the mines of Cornwall. It is to have a fifty inch cylinder with eight or nine feet stroke and seventy fathoms of pitwork complete, including ten inch plunger lift, matching pieces, seatings, buckets, windboxes, strapping plates, castings for balance bob, pulleys for shears, centres for capstan, lathe, and <u>two new boilers</u> which had better be shipped in parts and put together here, and also any other articles of great bulk where practicable as our mine is nearly a hundred miles inland and the only means of cartage is by Bullock Drays.[19]

Ayers added that, if it was impossible to obtain a second-hand engine to such specifications, then the agent should approach Cornish foundries for tenders for the construction of a new one. He also asked that Captain Robert Roach of Tresavean, an uncle of Henry Roach, be allowed to inspect the pitwork (pump rods and pipes) before it was dispatched to South Australia and, almost as an afterthought, mentioned that the 'Directors also require you to forward us a crushing machine such as are in common use in Cornwall.'[20] The plans for the engine house, stack and boiler house were sent out direct from Cornwall, and, as a second-hand engine proved to be unobtainable, a new one was constructed by the Perran Foundry. Not long after, in early 1849, Ayers wrote to Richard Hallett & Sons, SAMA's London agents, asking them to obtain tenders from the Hayle and Perran foundries for a 30-inch whim (winding) engine, together with winding gear and chains, further requesting that the relevant foundry 'cast the name "Burra Burra Mines" on the engine bob' and that 'the boilers ... be of the usual Cornish construction as they consume less fuel.'[21] Five months later, in the August, Ayers was again writing to Hallett, this time asking for a 30-inch stamps engine (to be used in ore-crushing), stipulating that it be 'as near as can be made a duplicate of the Winding Engine ordered in mine of the 28th April last'[22] so that the same set of engine-house plans would suffice for both. In the December, Ayers wrote to Hallett yet again, telling him to procure from any

Cornish foundry a vast amount of mining machinery and materials, ranging from pitwork to iron nails. As before, Captain Roach of Tresavean was to inspect the pitwork before it was dispatched.

During 1849 and the early months of 1850, it became apparent that, with the Burra mine becoming ever deeper, the existing pumping arrangements would not be sufficient to keep the workings 'in fork' for much longer. Thus a further order was placed through Hallett, this time for a giant 80-inch pump engine. Ayers stressed that the engine would have to arrive by March 1851 at the latest, before the winter rains, and as an incentive offered a bonus of ten per cent on the contract price if the engine could be in London, ready to be shipped, by 20 November 1850. Any loss of time, he said, would lead to 'an event I dread to contemplate'.[23] But by March 1851 not even the plans for the engine-house had arrived, and Ayers was fearful that further delay: 'will be attended with most disastrous consequences to the interests of this Company, and to a great number of our workmen, as we have too much reason to apprehend that our present appliances will be inadequate in keeping our water in fork during the coming winter, and the stoppage of our operations would then be inevitable.'[24] Hallett had visited Cornwall personally to acquire the plans and had dispatched them from Falmouth on 17 December 1850. But they arrived in the colony too late to be of any use during 1851. Fortunately, the existing pumps were able to keep the water in check throughout the Antipodean winter. The new engine itself, built at Perran Foundry and christened 'Schneider's' by SAMA (after one of the directors), finally arrived and was erected during 1852. It was started, amidst great celebrations, on 16 September, and the hero of the day was the chief engineer, John Congdon, who had supervised its erection. The South Australian Mining Association rewarded him with a gift of £50 and a substantial pay rise to £4 4s per week, a measure of the intense gratitude and relief felt by the directors.

The arrival and installation of a massive 80-inch Cornish engine was a momentous event but the acquisition of spare parts, supplies and stores direct from Cornwall had by now become a routine occurrence. In May 1851, for example, SAMA ordered three copies of copper ore tables published by F. Symons of Redruth, along with three copies of another 'small work common in Cornwall, being Tables for ascertaining the quantity of water contained in ores.'[25] Numerous miscellaneous items, from turpentine to iron bars and emery paper and chemicals, were supplied by J.C. Lanyon Jun. of Redruth, crucibles were obtained from the Calenick smelting works, near Truro.

The Cornish impact at the Burra mine, then, had involved not only the appointment of Cornishmen to key positions and the engagement of Cousin Jacks as the backbone of the skilled workforce but also the acquisition of machinery and materials direct from Cornwall. It would be some years yet before South Australia was in a position to construct its own heavy equipment or to provide the full range of supplies, and until such industrial self-sufficiency was achieved, the myth of Cousin Jack – which had persuaded SAMA almost without question of the superiority of Cornish miners – could also insist that Cornwall was the natural source for all mining necessities.

Meanwhile, the amazing success of the Burra Burra mine had created an atmosphere of 'coppermania' in the colony, an excitement which would prevail until Victorian gold stole the limelight in the early 1850s. Notwithstanding the disappointing results at the Princess Royal, prospectors were eager to try the country near the Burra. A Bon Accord mine was opened close to the Burra property in 1846 but met with little success, while in 1849 Captain James Trewartha was engaged to report on a copper strike on Emu Plains, to the south of the Burra. By 1850 a shaft had been sunk and, following a favourable report by Captain Bath, the Emu Flats Mine was soon at work under the management of Captain Berriman (yet another Cornishman). SAMA later acquired the claim (renaming it the Stanley Mine) and let it out on tribute to one Joseph Trevean who worked the property until he disappeared to join the Victorian gold rush. Nearby was the Karkulto mine, worked by men such as William Bennetts from Camborne, heralded in its day as a second Burra Burra but which, despite lavish investment and the installation of a Cornish pump engine, failed to live up to its initial promise. In the Adelaide Hills, 'coppermania' resulted in the opening of yet further mines. Wheal Acraman was worked from 1848 until 1851 by Captain Long, and nearby were the Riversedge Mine and Wheal Boone. To the south of Adelaide, copper was found at Hallet's Cove, where the Worthing Mining Co. arranged to bring out from Cornwall Captain Alfred Phillips (a Redruth man), together with five other miners and mining machinery.[26]

Thirty miles north-east of Adelaide was another clutch of copper workings, at Tungkillo, where the Reedy Creek, Great Wheal Orford and Wheal Rothschild mines attracted a considerable body of Cornish miners – men such as Henry Adams from Tuckingmill, James Spry from Launceston, and John and Edward Dunstan from Wendron. Development at the Reedy Creek was especially impressive, and in 1849 Harvey & Co. of Hayle built two engines for the mine, of 36 inches and 48 inches respectively. Some 20 or so miles south of

Tungkillo lay a tract of mineralised country running through Mount Barker to Callington. The Kanmantoo mine was started in 1846 and nearby was the Paringa. The latter was formed into the Britannia Mining Company in 1849, a concern which opened a string of small mines in the locality – the Tresevean, the Menkoo, Wheal Rose, Wheal Fanny, Wheal Prosper (worked in 1851 by Captain Lean), Wheal Fortune, the Preamimma, Wheal Harmony and Wheal Emma. Wheal Emma was commenced in April–June 1850 under Captain Mitchell – who had been especially brought out from Cornwall for the purpose – and in the same area was the Callington (or Bremer) mine which had been started in 1849. In the same year Wheal Maria was being worked by Captain Simmons (another Cousin Jack), and nearby was Wheal Margaret.

The *South Australian Register* thought the Mount Barker-Callington district 'the Cornwall of Australia',[27] for in addition to the plethora of Cornish-sounding mine names were settlements called Callington, St Ives and Kelynack, while the miners themselves were overwhelmingly Cornish: men like Captain Absolom Tonkin, born in St Blazey in 1829, who arrived in the colony in 1847 and worked in the Paringa, Kanmantoo, Tresevean, and Callington mines before opening a general store in Callington township. Arthur Bray, from St Just-in-Penwith, was another Callington miner, and so too was his father-in-law, Captain William Penhall – 'well known in the Mount Barker and Callington districts'[28] as one newspaper put it – who had arrived in the colony from St Austell in 1847. Thomas Cornelius, from Redruth, was captain of the Paringa at its opening, and Richard Rodda, from Penrice, near St Austell, was likewise manager of the Kanmantoo in its early days.

Captain Rodda also ran Wheal Maria for a time. But he was especially known for his work in the Barossa Valley. He arrived in South Australia in 1846 to work the mineral deposits on the lands of George Fife Angas, one of South Australia's founding fathers, and laid out the mining village of Penrice at the northern end of the Barossa. By 1847 he had two promising setts already in production – the Greenock Creek Mine and the Lyndoch Valley – and in 1850 he opened Wheal Friendship. He was later responsible for a North Rhine mine and for the Crinnis: 'named after the celebrated Crinnis Mine of Cornwall'.[29] Also on Angas' property was Wheal Barton, situated at the northern extremity of the Barossa district near Truro, a mining village 'named after the Cornish glory'.[30] The captain, however, was not Rodda but John Rowe, another of South Australia's early Cornish mining personalities who became involved in the early (and largely unsuccessful) attempts to develop smelting in the colony.

Despite all this activity, the Victorian gold rush brought a decade of feverish mineral development to a close in South Australia. By December 1851, the smaller mines were already closing (many of them never to reopen), and even Kapunda and the Burra were feeling the pinch, their key workers having left in droves to try their luck on the gold-fields of the neighbouring colony. In March 1851 there had been 1042 men working at the Burra mine. This figure declined to 380 by March 1852, to 157 by the following September, and was soon less than 100 – only a handful of these being underground miners. Ore raised fell from 23,000 tons in the year ended September 1851 to a low of 2000 for the year ended September 1853. In November 1852, Henry Ayers, the SAMA secretary, wrote that 'the operations of this company are in great measure suspended from the want of the necessary labour',[31] and the deeper levels of the mine were allowed to fill with water, the pump engineers and engine drivers having all gone to Victoria. Although, as we shall see in Chapter 8, the South Australian copper mining industry was soon to resurge with a vengeance, the downturn in the early 1850s occasioned by the Victorian gold rush marked the end of an extraordinary era. As well as creating Australia's very first metalliferous mining industry, this period had witnessed the initial phase of mass emigration from Cornwall to South Australia and the transplantation in that colony of Cornish culture.

The discovery, first of silver-lead and then of copper, in South Australia had created widespread interest in Cornwall. When Francis Dutton had visited Britain in 1845 to promote his Kapunda mine, one 'mining gentleman' ridiculed Dutton's view that South Australia might come to challenge the Cornish industry. 'Pooh! Pooh! my dear sir', exclaimed the gentleman, 'all the ore you will ever produce from South Australia will be but a drop in a bucket of water.'[32] Dutton's only comment was 'Time will show.' In fact, others did share his opinion of South Australian potential. As early as July 1845 the *South Australian Gazette and Colonial Register* had predicted that, with the rise of the colony's mines, 'many of the Cornwall ... mines, at present worked at an enormous expense, compared to the value of the ore, must be abandoned',[33] and in February 1846 a correspondent in the *Perth Inquirer* (published in Swan River Colony: Western Australia) wrote that 'I am sure that all the inferior copper mines of Cornwall will in a few years be rendered useless.'[34] Back in Britain, the *Devonport Telegraph and Plymouth Chronicle* in 1846 feared that 'it is certain that the very rich ores from South Australia will operate most prejudicially upon the mining interests of Cornwall',[35] for colonial producers could send their ore to the Swansea smelters as cheaply as could their Cornish rivals. As

Seymour Tremenheere explained to the Royal Geological Society of Cornwall, South Australia was also a wool-exporting colony, so that:

> the wool-ships on account of the lightness of the cargo are obliged to take in a large quantity of ballast, and they are therefore glad to take the lead and copper ore at a merely nominal rate of freight; at the time in question about eight or ten shillings per ton. That circumstance was considered as bringing their mines, as it were, actually into Europe, or at all events as placing them upon an equal footing with European mines.[36]

As South Australian copper increased in output, the *South Australian Register* observed grimly that – with this increase due to the efforts of Cornish miners and the application of Cornish technology – it was now a case of 'Cornwall against Cornwall'.[37] Oddly enough, despite the fact that Cornwall was already deeply worried about the impact of Cuba and Chile (as was mentioned in Chapter 3), the Cornish did not always see it that way. As John Rowe observed, 'Few if any in Cornwall begrudged the success of Australian copper' because the South Australian mines were 'regarded as nothing more or less than extension of Cornish mining enterprise to the Antipodes'.[38] Moreover, with Cornish emigrants forming a significant proportion of the South Australian population, and with Cornish cultural influence observable in a range of behaviour from religion and politics to sport and music, South Australia was already seen by many as an Antipodean extension of the land of Cornwall.

That said, it was clear that a vicious circle was by now in the making, the expansion of the South Australian mining industry further challenging Cornwall's already dented supremacy. The growing demand for Cornish labour in the colony had been matched by an expanding supply of Cousin Jacks anxious to better themselves at Kapunda or Burra Burra, their arrival in South Australia further facilitating mining development. Thus the vicious circle was perpetuated. A brief respite was provided by the Victorian gold rush, when South Australian output was curtailed through want of labour. J.R. Leifchild – using his own metaphor – noted wryly that, 'The scales may be said to be suspended over Australia and Cornwall, and the fall in one produces a corresponding rise in the other.'[39] Certainly, South Australia's difficulties in the first half of the 1850s were reflected in better days for the Cornish economy, but the vicious circle was set in motion once more by the resurgence of the colony's copper industry in the latter part of the decade. Not only did Cornish miners return in increasing numbers to Kapunda and the Burra from Victoria but the discovery of vast new deposits on northern Yorke Peninsula in 1859–60 – in a district soon acknowledged across the world as 'Australia's Little Cornwall' – added dramatically to the world production of copper on the eve of falling prices and financial instability. As the Kapunda *Northern Star* was to put it, South Australia was by then 'out-Cornwalling Cornwall altogether'.[40]

By then, of course, literally thousands of Cornish people had arrived in the colony. The early discoveries of silver-lead and copper had caught the attention of potential emigrants in Cornwall. South Australia had emerged already as a popular home for Cornish emigrants and now Cornish miners (and their families) were offered another plausible – and reassuringly British – alternative to the decidedly dangerous destinations of Latin America. Extracts from South Australian newspapers were enthusiastically reprinted in the Cornish press and extravagant claims were made for even fledgling properties in the colony. Thus the Glen Osmond silver-lead mines were 'more than equal to the celebrated East Wheal Rose of Cornwall',[41] while the *South Australian News* (published in Britain to promote emigration to the colony) argued (correctly, as it turned out) that – after the temporary economic setback of the early 1840s – South Australia was on the edge of a mining boom:

> The extent and value of the mineral treasures of South Australia, and the facility and economy with which they can be raised and exported are, we believe, unexampled, and the investment of English capital in working its mines ... will have a most important bearing on the future of its agricultural and pastoral properties, and giving profitable employment to its farmers and merchants in providing food and other necessities for a population daily becoming more numerous and important, by the emigration of labour, not needed or not remunerated at home.[42]

One Adelaide paper, the *South Australian Gazette and Colonial Register*, noted in September 1845 that 'The greatest excitement has been produced in Cornwall' by the mineral finds. It was proud that the colony was 'a British Province, with mines worked by Cornish hands', and looked forward to 'the capitalists of Cornwall transferring their energies to the more rich and generous mines of South Australia'.[43] The South Australian Mining Association echoed these sentiments,

as early as January 1846 urging the Colonial Secretary to make special arrangements for the procurement of Cornish miners. This rhetoric was reflected in the
numbers of Cornish folk actually arriving in the colony. In 1845 most ships arriving at Port Adelaide carried contingents of Cornish emigrants. The *Isabella
Watson*, for example, arrived from Plymouth in April 1845, carrying nearly 120
passengers of whom 30 were Cornish. The surgeon's return for the *Rajah* in 1846
indicated that 30 out of the 55 passengers listed were Cornish. A number, including Uriah Scoble, Peter Spargo and John Trenowith, were listed as having been
recruited to work at the Burra.[44] Others had come out to work at the Reedy Creek
mine and in June 1846 it was said that another 500 emigrants – mainly Cornish
miners and their families – were to sail from Plymouth for Port Adelaide over the
next few months. On 5 October the *Kingston* put into Falmouth to pick up 66 passengers, of whom 44 were Cornish miners selected by SAMA. In 1847 the South
Australian Company wrote to the *West Briton*, requesting further supplies of
Cornish miners for the colony.[45]

In November 1846 a group of journalists was invited to inspect the *Princess
Royal*, bound for South Australia, then lying at Plymouth. The reporters noted
that the passengers on board were 'chiefly from Cornwall', and further observed
that: "South Australia, owing to its having been colonized chiefly from the West of
England, has more of this class of men [Cornish miners], than, perhaps any other
colony in our possession, and it would seem to be more than mere chance that
drew them into a land which is now found to be abundant in mineral treasures."[46]
When the *Princess Royal* finally dropped anchor at Port Adelaide, the *South
Australian Register's* correspondent echoed the words of his British counterparts, observing that the emigrants were 'chiefly from the mining districts of
Devon and Cornwall'.[47] The passengers on the *Britannia* and *Hooghly*, two
other arrivals during 1846, were also mainly Cornish, being the party of miners arranged by Captain Richard Rodda to work the copper deposits on the
land owned by George Fife Angas in the Barossa Valley. Rodda, like many a
Cornish miner engaged according to the 'informal' recruiting arrangements
that now existed across Cornwall, arrived in the colony with a letter of
introduction in which Angas drew 'attention [to] Capt. Richard Rodda who had
gone to South Australia with some miners to work the copper lodes in my
lands'. The port authorities, said Angas, should 'afford the Captain the aid he
requires in the landing of his party and goods'.[48]

Meanwhile, during 1846 specimens of the dazzling Burra Burra ore were sent
to J.B. Wilcocks, the South Australian emigration agent stationed at the Barbican,

Plymouth. In February 1847 the *Devonport Telegraph* reported excitedly: 'We have seen at the offices of Mr Wilcocks, the agent for HM Colonial Land and Emigration Commissioners, more specimen copper ores from South Australia; and as far as our judgment enables us to form an opinion, we should say that the richness of the specimens exceed even those from the far-famed mines of South America.'[49] Appointed in the late 1830s, J.B. Wilcocks was agent at Plymouth for some 30 years. His skill as a selector of emigrants and as an administrator was widely recognised and he played a central role in the selection of Cornish emigrants for South Australia at a time when movement from Cornwall to the colony was at its height. He took great pride in his work and was at all times methodical and meticulous. Thus the miners dispatched in the *David Malcolm* in 1846 were 'as fine a body of people as ever left England'.[50] John B. Tregea was 'A very superior miner', while James Rundle was 'A good wheelwright, miner, carpenter and excellent character', and William Spargo was 'an excellent captain'.[51]

If 1846 had been a busy year for Wilcocks, then so too was 1847. In the January it was reported that the *Theresa*, in Plymouth Sound, carried: 'upwards of 230 emigrants, for the very prosperous colony of South Australia, her destination being Adelaide, and ... most of those on board were from this [Devon] or the neighbouring county, Cornwall ... they consist principally of miners and agricultural labourers and female servants.'[52] The *China*, which sailed in the October, carried a large body of Cornish miners selected by Wilcocks. In the following year, 1848, Colonel Carlyon of Tregrehan, St Austell, wrote to Captain Richard Rodda, explaining that there were 'many still emigrating from this neighbourhood to Australia.'[53] Others came from the East Cornwall mining villages around St Cleer, while it was claimed that as many as 600 folk had left the far-western district of St Just-in-Penwith for South Australia. To these were added emigrants from the non-mining districts. In 1850 alone, 50 persons left the parish of Mawgan-in-Meneage to go to South Australia and in the period 1841–51 the population of the Meneage area dropped by some five per cent – another part of Cornwall to experience absolute population decline.

This exodus was reflected in the arrivals at Port Adelaide. During 1849 a whole stream of ships arrived in the colony from Plymouth. The *William Money*, for example, carried 366 passengers of whom half were Cornish, as was a similar proportion of the 266 emigrants in the *Pakenham*. The *Prince Regent* carried 60 Cornish settlers, the *Eliza* 42, the *Himalaya* 53, and so on. As ever, these arrivals wrote home to friends and relatives in Cornwall with news of the colony. 'Oh! Richard, it would make your mouth water to see the Burra Burra Mine',[54] enthused one Cornish miner, while in 1846 Thomas Davey implored his fiancée Elizabeth to join him in the colony:

> I am working at the Burra Burra copper mine, and my wages is from £3 to £4 a week, and I hope I shall have the pleasure of seeing you out at South Australia, and your sister Mary: whether Mary comes out or not I hope you will, and I am sorry you did not come out with me, for if you had it would have been much better for you. I am still single and I shall remain so until you come. Miners get more wages than they do in Cornwall in two months.[55]

In 1850 the average wage of a miner in Cornwall was about £3 per month. As Davey had observed, at the Burra at least this amount could be earned in a week. Peter Medler [Medland] wrote in similar vein from the Glen Osmond mines:

> We are all doing well, and I am still working in the mines on silver and lead ore, about 3 miles from house, and getting 30s to £2 per week. Brother and sister, and neighbours, we wish to let you know what a rich and splendid province this is. There are mines in the province that are worth all Cornwall ... hundreds and hundreds of tons of pure copper on the surface ... In a short time miners' wages will be £3 or £4 per week ... we should be glad to see all the miners in Biscovey and Turnpikegate [St Blazey Gate] out here, to have £3 or £4 per week, in such a flourishing country where there is everything to nourish and cherish you.[56]

From Kapunda, the message was the same, John Oats writing to his brother in Cornwall:

> Here is the place to live! the dogs have got more beef and mutton than ever we could get in England; if you could but see how we are living you would not stop home a day. The gettings, when we arrived on tutwork, were 10s per day, but I got a great deal more than that on tribute ... An industrious man need not work all his days here, for he can get paid well for his labor and live cheap. Me and Caroline can live on £1 0s per week, and you all know that I like a good living.[57]

Such letters arrived in Cornwall at the height of the Hungry Forties, many finding their way into local newspapers. Tales of vast mineral wealth, high wages and easy living must have sounded fabulous to their recipients at home. But the key message was that articulated by one Cornishman who in 1845 wrote from the colony to friends in Launceston, 'there is no cry in our streets for bread'.[58] And yet, the task of persuading friends, relatives and neighbours to join the colonists was not always straightforward. Samuel Robins, from Penryn, who had arrived in South Australia as early as 1838, wrote home in exasperated tones to his sister in October 1846:

> You remind me of my promise to return in ten years; I was young and foolish when I uttered that speech, and I hope you will not expect me to leave a country like this .... I cannot help thinking how inconsistent you write; you give me a wretched account of things at home, and expect me to leave a country which is flourishing fast .... It is a pity you make remarks about this country, when you know nothing of it. A handsome expression to tell me I am bringing up my children unnamed savages. Penryn is nothing to Adelaide – we can buy everything we want, from a needle to an anchor, we have schools, chapels, and other institutions that are needful – Unnamed savages!! What next shall we hear from home? You think this place is a wilderness – you are as much mistaken as though you were to say Plymouth is in France.[59]

For the doubters among his constituencies in Cornwall and Devon, J.B. Wilcocks had a favourite saying: 'The difference between England and Australia is this: – That in England we have more mouths than meat while in Australia there is more meat than mouths.'[60] He was, of course, correct – at least as far as Cornwall was concerned – and the inescapable logic of his argument accounted for the continuing exodus from Cornwall. In 1846 one Robert Dare wrote home to his parents in Britain, explaining that 'The principal part that come out here are Cornwall miners'.[61] Even more telling, perhaps, was the September 1849 issue of the *South Australian News*, one of those newspapers published in London to promote emigration, which carried a short story supposedly reflecting life in the colony, in which the fictional characters were given Cornish surnames such as Trefusis and Vivian.[62]

The relative strength of the Cornish community in South Australia was reflected in the emergence of the short-lived but influential 'Cornwall and Devon Society' in December 1850. Its secretary was the enigmatic Plymothian, John Bentham Neales, who liked to boast that from his initial investment of £250 in the Burra mine he had received a dividend of £1000 after only one year, and there were two treasurers: one a Cornishman, the other a Devonian. The committee members were drawn from the ranks of Cornish mine captains in the colony and from a sprinkling of Adelaide businessmen. Most South Australian mines seem to have been represented in the society – Henry Roach from Burra Burra, Captain Gundry from North Kapunda, Captain Lean from Wheal Prosper, Captain Long at Wheal Acraman, Captain Paul at Wheal Margaret, and so on. The aims of the Society were to: "encourage Emigration direct from the Counties [Cornwall and Devon], devise the best means by which that desirable end can be accomplished, to watch over the interests of Devon and Cornish colonists, and generally to promote harmony and good feeling among them."[63]

The inclusion of Devon in what appears to have been a Cornish-dominated society may have reflected the influence of its secretary, Neales, but was, far more likely, recognition of the increasing significance of the Tamar Valley mines to Cornwall's mining economy, many of these properties located on the Devon bank of the river. Be that as it may, the Cornwall and Devon Society is of particular interest because it represents an early attempt to give institutional and political expression to the 'myth of Cornish Jack'. It operated unashamedly as a pressure group, lobbying government officials, constructing information networks with opinion leaders back in Cornwall, and arguing for the creation of Cornish ethnic communities in South Australia. The Society corresponded directly with mine captains in Cornwall to publicise 'the highly remunerative employment that awaited the skill and enterprise of Cornish miners'[64] and in early 1851 it submitted a memorial to Governor Young, complaining that too few Cornish miners were being recruited for the colony. It also insisted that miners should be sought exclusively from Cornwall and the adjacent mining districts of Devon, for 'early association and knowledge of each other's habits and character are calculated to preserve the best moral restraint on the conduct of all'.[65] Finally, the Society demanded that more emigrant ships should sail directly from Cornish ports. The governor replied to all this by stating that between June 1850 and May 1851, one-seventh of colonists dispatched to South Australia from Britain and Ireland were Cornish miners. He added that Plymouth was more suitable than any Cornish harbour as a departure point for emigrants, as it was central to both Cornwall and Devon as well as being reasonably accessible from other parts of the United Kingdom.

Despite its initial impact and vigour, the Cornwall and Devon Society seems to have fallen victim – like many institutions and initiatives in South Australia – to the conditions created by the Victorian gold rush, when so many of the colony's Cornish settlers went off to neighbouring Victoria. However, the Burra mine, then easily the largest and most influential business concern in South Australia, reacted to the sudden threat of labour shortage by continuing to cultivate the links with Cornwall that the Society had advocated. Here the continuing relationship with J.B. Wilcocks was crucial. On a number of occasions in 1850 Henry Ayers, the SAMA secretary, had insisted in correspondence with government officials in the colony that 'very extensive Immigration'[66] be maintained, and throughout 1850 and 1851 Wilcocks had sent out a steady stream of Cornish miners. In the *Stag*, for example, which arrived at Port Adelaide from Plymouth in June 1850, there were 32 emigrants from Cornwall, some – like John Grigg, Joseph Hooper, and William Harris – having been engaged specifically to work in the Burra mine. The *Ascendant*, which arrived in January 1851, carried 50 Cornish passengers, the *Omega* 131, the *Sultana* 59, and so on.

However, as the colony's Cornish population began to disappear at an alarming rate to the neighbouring colony of Victoria, Henry Ayers recognised that the rate of immigration from Cornwall would have to be redoubled if the Burra mine was to stand any chance of remaining in production. Accordingly, in November 1852 Ayers wrote to Wilcocks:

> We have for many years past experienced the benefit of your judicious selection of Cornish and Devonshire Miners for this Colony and we hope you may be able to furnish us with as many "good men and true" as heretofore. We could find employment for a thousand hands consisting of Miners, Smiths, Engineers, Carpenters and others employed at Copper Mines – at wages varying from £6 to £10 per month. Such wages as these should be sufficient inducement to the thousands in your district who cannot in the best of times expect to make more than a third of this.[67]

The shortage of labour in the South Australian market continued to worsen, and only a month later Ayers was again writing to Wilcocks, complaining that 'We are thirsting for labour ... [and] looking forward with great anxiety to extensive emigration from your Port, in which, I trust we may not be disappointed.'[68] During 1852 and 1853 ships sporting large numbers of Cornish emigrants continued to arrive at Port Adelaide but, as Ayers had feared, they were not yet enough to make good the losses to Victoria. Indeed, many of these newcomers were themselves seduced by news of the Victorian diggings, making their way to the gold-fields in the neighbouring colony almost as soon as they had arrived in South Australia. By 1854 the labour situation had not improved significantly, and again Ayers was writing to Wilcocks, this time offering him a personal bounty of £2 per head for up to 500 Cornish miners. Ayers suggested that Wilcocks might wish to use some of this money to appoint sub-agents in the different parts of Cornwall, and as a further inducement the SAMA directors sent Wilcocks another £500 'to be disbursed by him in small sums among intending Emigrants from the Mining population of Cornwall.'[69] Although the Cornish economy had by now recovered from the worst days of the 1840s, Wilcocks was able to respond magnificently to Ayers' demands, sending over 1600 Cornish emigrants, mainly miners and their families, to South Australia during 1854 and 1855, furnishing every male colonist with a letter of introduction to prospective employers in the colony.

By now locked firmly into the Cousin Jack network and the intricacies of Cornwall's emigration trade and culture, the South Australian Mining Association let it be known that it was prepared to give financial assistance to those needing to purchase 'the necessary outfit'[70] for the voyage, or for those for whom travelling expenses to Plymouth from the mining districts of Cornwall were otherwise prohibitive. SAMA sent Wilcocks copies of the Adelaide *Observer* to keep him up to date with developments in the colony, and to facilitate Wilcocks' work Ayers continued to lobby the Colonial Secretary, explaining that it was necessary 'to select and dispatch to this Province a considerable number of Miners and others accustomed to work in Copper Mines.'[71] Generally, SAMA was well pleased with Wilcocks' work. Although Ayers was not entirely happy with the miners who arrived in the *William Prowse* (the first of the vessels sent out after the bounty offer) because he considered them too young and inexperienced, he was delighted with those on the *Nile* and subsequent ships: 'very superior [miners who] ... will meet with immediate employment'.[72]

Towards the end of 1855, the Victorian gold-fields experienced a new surge of popularity, and Ayers was once again pleading for more miners. He also wrote to the Colonial Secretary, railing against the increasing practice of dispatching colonists from Southampton rather than Plymouth: 'the cost of joining a ship at

Southampton, is far greater than the majority of Emigrants from Devon and Cornwall can afford to pay'.[73] Ayers was also furious about the way in which some emigrants abused the assisted passage scheme by making for Victoria as soon as they had landed at Port Adelaide. He collected the names of the miscreants – Andrew and Philadelphi Stevens, Humphrey and Mary Johns, Richard Roe, William Martin, and other surnames common in Cornwall – and sent them to the Colonial Secretary, the implication being that some action should be taken against such offenders.

In his attempts to secure a steady flow of Cornish miners, Henry Ayers also made use of the 'nomination' scheme which was experimented with from time to time in the 1850s, inviting miners at the Burra to nominate friends and relatives in Cornwall. As early as May 1850, Ayers was sending lists of nominees to the Colonial Secretary, and in some instances SAMA itself was prepared to bear the cost of emigrants from Cornwall. This was the cause of some debate within the colony, some observers objecting to what they saw as a discriminatory practice, one correspondent in the *South Australian Register* asking if it was 'becoming to make this offer of assistance to *Cornish* alone?'[74] Ayers, in characteristic fashion, ignored such criticism and continued to give special treatment to Cornwall and the Cornish. In March 1856, for example, he authorised J.B. Wilcocks to send out from Probus – at SAMA's expense – the wife and family of William Kent, the chief timberman at the Burra. Kent missed his family and had hinted that he might return home to Cornwall. Ayers thought 'it would be very inconvenient for him to leave',[75] and so the payment was arranged. On other occasions, when those nominated were too old to qualify for an entirely free passage, SAMA undertook to pay the remaining part of the fee. In 1850, for example, William Richards of Herodsfoot and Mary Goldsworthy of Tywardreath were both over 50 years of age, and so SAMA was required to pay £11 each towards their passages. As it happened, William Richards died on the eve of his departure from Cornwall, and soon Ayers was writing to the Colonial Secretary, asking for his money back!

The nomination system had obvious advantages in that, by mobilising the Burra miners, it was possible to organise lists of potential emigrants from Cornwall at almost a moment's notice. However, there was little or no quality control, and Wilcocks wrote of those miners dispatched in the *Lady Ann* in 1857 that 'a more miserable lot of people never before left the shores of England'.[76] Ayers found these emigrants 'more favourable than I had expected' but had to agree 'that you [Wilcocks] would have been severely censured ... had you selected such people'.[77] The nomination system, Ayers admitted, did have its faults. But by then the case was increasingly academic, for in 1858 an anti-immigration campaign – spurred on by partial failures of the wool and wheat crops – was gaining the sympathetic attention of the Adelaide Parliament. In 1859 only six shiploads of emigrants arrived in South Australia, and by 1861 immigration had ceased, albeit temporarily.

When immigration was resumed a year or so later, Cornish miners and their families again arrived in South Australia in their thousands. But this time, as we shall see in Chapter 7, this movement was in response to new and extremely rich strikes of copper at Wallaroo and Moonta on Yorke Peninsula – 'Australia's Little Cornwall' as it was shortly to become. Although both Kapunda and Burra Burra had survived the rigours of the gold rush, they were eclipsed by the Yorke Peninsula discoveries, both succumbing to the international fall in copper prices and falling silent by the end of the 1870s. The *Burra Record* newspaper felt that the setback was only temporary but it was truly the end of an era.[78] Although new engines were purchased from Cornwall and new initiatives taken, by February 1867 the Burra had been losing £100 a day, its best miners drifting northwards to Yorke Peninsula, with poor Captain Sanders (who had replaced Henry Roach) asking his brother in Cornwall 'to make a selection of good Cornish Miners'[79] and accosting Cousin Jacks as they landed at the port. In July 1876 it was noted that Sanders had 'secured nine Cornish miners from [the] late arrival in Adelaide'.[80]

In the 30 or so years of their existence, the Kapunda and Burra Burra mines had been responsible for the large-scale immigration of Cornish people into the colony, and for the creation of Cornish communities in the mining districts as well as a wider Cornish impact in South Australian society. The existence of a Cornwall and Devon Society had demonstrated a degree of Cornish ethnic consciousness in the colony, together with a willingness to deploy that identity for political and socio-economic ends. The early prominence of the Cornish in South Australia was reflected in the staging of grand CORNWALL V DEVON-SHIRE wrestling matches in Adelaide in the late 1840s and early 1850s (William Hodge was the Cornish champion, John Hoskin his Devon rival), with seating for 2000 spectators.

At Kapunda, where all the early miners were Cornish, the usual Cornish customs were observed. The Duke of Cornwall's birthday was a public holiday and the Cousin Jennies baked the traditional Cornish fare. In 1929 one old resident recalled that '[my] earliest recollections of Kapunda go back three quarters of a century ... a plate of Saffron Cake fresh from the oven, and the vivid yellow colour of which I can still often, through the lapse of so long a time, plainly visualise'.[81] The Kapunda Mines Brass Band was an entirely Cornish affair, or nearly so, the *Northern Star* newspaper noting in January 1861 that the bandsmen were 'all Cousin Jacks with the exception of one, and he's a foreigner'.[82] First published in 1860, the *Northern Star* became a vehicle for Cornish sentiment. It carried regular 'News from Cornwall' items and published letters and stories in Cornish dialect. Humorous tales addressed to 'Cussan Josey, Rosemurgy, Ashton, three miles this side of Germoe, Breage, Cornwall' or 'From Cousin Molly Jones of Kapunda to Cousin Betty Hicks, Gwendern [Wendron], Cornwall', described the 'Keepunder Bal' and were full of colourful expressions such as 'put to Bodmin' [i.e gaol or asylum] and 'scat me chacks laffin'.[83]

Although the mine was abandoned by 1879, the Cornish element in the community remained significant, for in that year Kapunda responded enthusiastically to appeals for help from the destitute in Cornwall. At a public meeting in the May, reports of distress from Marazion, Penzance, Helston and Truro were read out, and the Mayor, J. Rowett, from St Austell, thanked 'God his father brought him from Cornwall when he was young.' Henry Wheare, who had emigrated from Marazion in 1847, felt that 'South Australians should support the Cornish miners in their distress, for to the energy of some of them in opening up the mines, the colony owed its prosperity'.[84] Intriguingly, we see in some of the responses to these statements the signs of friction, of ethnic jealousies and suspicions. Speaking from the floor, one Kapunda resident considered that if there was to be a relief effort, it 'must not be considered a Methodist movement', while another said, 'He should be sorry to see it made altogether a Cornish question.'[85]

The Irish, more than any other, were wary of the Cornish. They had first arrived in Kapunda in numbers in 1854 in response to the labour shortage occasioned by the departure of many of the Cornish for Victoria, and they were immediately seen by the Cousin Jacks as ethnic rivals in the hitherto Cornish-dominated workplace – a rivalry sharpened by religious antagonism in which the predominantly Methodist Cornish were suspicious of Irish Roman Catholicism. In May 1862 a number of miners claimed that their ores were being unfairly assayed and anonymous threatening letters were sent to the mine captain. A public meeting was held to discuss the issue. The Cornish put their weight firmly behind their captain, implying that the Irish were responsible for the intimidating poison-pen letters, and with the situation becoming a little ugly, several speakers found it politic to express 'their opinion that the writer was neither a Cornishman or an Irishman' in an effort to diffuse the situation.[86] Violence did break out in the elections to the Adelaide Parliament in 1893 when Patrick McMahon Glynn – the hero of the Irish community – was surprisingly defeated. Glynn blamed his defeat on religious bigotry and one eyewitness recalled that 'The bone of contention was the Irish vote.'[87] In the fighting that followed, the two most badly beaten by the enraged mob bore Cornish names – James Rowe and W. Pengelly. When Michael Davitt, the Irish Land League agitator, visited the district in the 1890s he felt as though 'Kapunda was somewhere in Connaught instead of being fourteen thousand miles away.'[88]

At the Burra, the great majority of the mine workers were Cornishmen (as Henry Ayers noted in 1854) but among the other ethnic groups were the Welsh (reflected in the Burra suburb of Llwchyrr), the English, the Scots, the Germans, even the Chileans (muleteers), along with the Irish. As at Kapunda, the Irish were fiercely nationalistic, deploying their claims to a Celtic heritage as both non-British and anti-British, and – again as at Kapunda – their presence was resented for religious reasons and because they were perceived as a threat to 'Cornish jobs'. Conflict between the Cornish and the Irish was never far from the surface, as in August 1867 when two groups of workers – one Irish, the other Cornish – were entrusted with the construction of a stone hedge. As the *South Australian Register* reported, 'On the morning in question, one of the Irishmen laid in wait for a Cornishman and attacked him. A fight ensued between the two parties in which the Cornishmen got the worst.'[89] In the same way, in the elections of 1851, the Burra Cornish opposed the local Irish-born candidate (G.S. Kingston) and his 'sons of Tipperary', championing instead their own candidate with the cry: 'Mildren for ever, and down with the Greens.'[90] In opposing Irish claims to Celticity, the Cornish insisted that they were 'the sons of ancient Britons',[91] more British than the English and progenitors of Britain's Imperial greatness, the Rev. Charles Colwell, from Cornwall, telling Wesleyan chapel goers at Kooringa in March 1859 that the Cornish were 'the real descendants of the Celts.'[92]

As the years passed, expressions of Cornish ethnicity became less pugnacious and more sentimental, less a struggle to defend identity and uphold privileges and more a medium for romantic reflection. This changing mood was captured in the poetry of the ethereal 'Cousin Silvia'. Nonetheless she sought to define the Burra (in particular its suburb of Redruth) as a Cornish town, affirming the distinctive nationality of the Cornish people:

Twas Grannie who lived near the old Burra Mine,
And we often went up on a Sunday to dine
At Redruth, where Grannie lived. Grannie would tell
Us stories of Cornwall when she was a 'gel',
Oh, not in the world was a country so fine
As Cornwall.[93]

In another of her poems, 'Lucky Find, 1845', Cousin Silvia drew an intentionally romantic link between Cornwall and the Burra, insinuating a connection between the 'magical' qualities of Madron Well (in Cornwall) and the 'miraculous' discovery of the Burra mine. In the first verse:

The boys and girls of old Penzance,
Truro, Redruth, and Newlyn –
Threw pebbles in the Madron Well
Asking its depths their fates to tell:
'What luck, blue deeps of Madron?

In subsequent stanzas, the fate of each of the pebble-casters is revealed briefly but one is singled out for particular attention, the 'discoverer' of the Burra bonanza:

Twas here he found the copper-ore
Outcroppings: 'Now, by Madron!
Eighteen Hundred Forty-five
Brings luck to man and boy alive:
The Mine is worth a fortune!'

And, oh, ye emerald Malachites!
Ye azure deeps of Madron!
A harvest of five million pounds
Was taken from those Burra mounds –
What luck! What chance! What fortune![94]

The Burra did not get its own newspaper until 1876, the year before the mine closed, but when the *Northern Mail* (soon renamed the *Burra News* and then the *Burra Record*) first appeared, it carried numerous Cornish items. There were the various dialect stories, similar to those published at Kapunda, and in May 1879 the paper led the campaign to respond to the call for help from Cornwall. At Redruth Wesleyan Chapel, a special sermon was preached on destitution in Cornwall, and a Cornish Relief Fund was set up in Kooringa. As at Kapunda, the Duke of Cornwall's birthday was observed as a general holiday, while brass bands were popular. Cornish wrestling was especially popular, one report from the Burra in 1848 noting that wrestling was 'the favourite amusement of Cornwall'[95] and describing how up to 1000 people would gather at the Burra to watch the matches. Contests were 'conducted in the real Cornish style',[96] not only in those heady early days but also in January 1863 when it was reported (disapprovingly!) that the miners had spent their Christmas 'lounging round the taverns, playing skittles and wrestling.'[97] St Piran's Day, 5 March, was also marked appropriately, at least in the earliest days, the *South Australian* noting in 1848 that 'Monday the 6th March was a great day amongst the Cornish people at the Burra',[98] (Sunday 5th, of course, being the Sabbath), celebrated with wrestling bouts and feasting. Midsummer bonfires were also popular at the Burra, as they were in Cornwall, held on the traditional date, 24 June (St John's Eve), even though this was in the midst of the Antipodean winter. According to the *South Australian Register* in June 1863, Midsummer at the Burra is 'a red-letter day in Cousin John's calendar ... celebrated by diverse juveniles who lighted up numerous bonefires [sic]'.[99]

At Callington, another of South Australia's mining towns, Midsummer's Eve was also observed by the Cornish. In 1859 the Callington mine owners chose 24 June as the occasion for starting and christening their new 60-inch Cornish pump engine, thus combining two traditional Cornish activities. They celebrated the event by holding a great dinner in the nearby 'Tavistock Hotel', an echo of the famous count-house dinners of Cornwall. There had been a similar dinner at the starting of Schneider's engine at the Burra in 1852, and in June 1850 there was a great feast at the Reedy Creek mine at Tungkillo, 'Tables were arranged in the timber yard at the mine, for 120 persons, who partook a Bullock, which was roasted whole, outside the yard, and at 2 O'Clock they all assembled to prepare for the Christening of the Engine.'[100] These dinners remained a feature of South Australian mining culture for many years, at least until 1882 when an enormous feast was held in the 'Blinman Hotel' to celebrate the reopening of the [Wheal] Blinman mine in the Far North of the colony. Such tales of feasting and plenty would again have struck those at home as wildly extravagant. Even the most lavish count-house dinner might have seemed modest in comparison, especially in the dark days of the Hungry Forties when any kind of nourishment was hard to come by. In 1847, by contrast, as starvation drove many from their homes in Cornwall, one Johnson Frederick Haywood recorded in his diary the abundant supply of cheap meat at the Burra, 'Of Beef and Mutton, the primest joints sold at 1d per lb, and wages were so high at tutwork or tribute that a Miner rarely came away from the Butcher's Store with less than 20 lbs of meat on his shoulder.'[101]

At Kapunda, to high wages and cheap meat was added the provision of sound housing (in contrast to the damp hovels of Cornwall), much of it constructed by the mining company itself. Writing in 1846, Francis Dutton noted that:

> several rows of substantial cottages, on a uniform plan, are already erected, a hill of clay slate on the property affording excellent building stone, which being tinged more or less with copper, give the walls of the cottages a pretty mottled appearance. The miners having their families now living with them, are happy and contented, and are not continually wanting to go to town [Adelaide] as they formerly did .... A chapel, which will also serve as a schoolhouse, is by this time completed.[102]

At the Burra, SAMA also provided similar accommodation but many Cornish families, keen to avoid rent and anxious not to become too beholden to the Association, adopted the extraordinary habit of excavating dug-out houses in the steep banks of the Burra Burra Creek. In April 1848 the *South Australian News* recorded that 'Many of these [dugouts] ... are fitted up in the neatest style imaginable and form cool and comfortable habitations. They extend for about three miles on both sides of the creek, and contain a population of 400 to 500 persons.'[103] When the Rev. James Rowe, a Bible Christian minister from Cornwall, arrived at the Burra in 1850 it seemed to him that 'the banks swarmed with people like a rabbit warren from Redruth to the cemetery [at Kooringa].'[104] Inevitably, practical jokers took advantage of the unusual construction of the dugouts. As Haywood observed, there was 'usually placed an empty flour barrel to show pedestrians the danger of walking into a chimney or the fire at the foot, there was however no prevention to a passerby dropping a brick or a stone, or log, into the iron pot boiling or stewing below, and thus the jokers indulged themselves.'[105] In 1851 it was estimated that some 2600 people were living in the dugouts. A horrified visitor observed that 'infantile diseases are greatly prevalent' and thought that, with the ever-present threat of flooding, habitation of the dugouts 'equals the madness of living under Mount

Vesuvius.'[106] In fact, severe flooding in June of that year caused 'Much loss and ruin',[107] with one miner killed in his collapsed dugout and scores of families made homeless, temporary accommodation being provided for the unfortunate in chapels, stables, and the hospital.

The unsanitary and dangerous environment of the dugout community is a sharp reminder that, despite the escape from hunger and poverty in Cornwall, conditions in the Australian mining camps could be every bit as unsavoury and debilitating as those at home. In 1847, for example, Allan Thomson, SAMA's 'bal surgeon' (mine doctor), had written to Henry Ayers complaining that fever was widespread as a result of the 'Slaughter Houses & C., Stock Yards, and Piggeries attached to the different stores, together with the chamber filth thrown out of the cottages, and that deposit in the creeks.'[108] Ayers himself complained in 1850 about pigs and dogs running wild in the cemetery, and in May 1855 three Cornish miners – John Julien, Robert Roach, and John Bowden – were fined for allowing their pigs to wander at will amongst the cottages. Typhus fever remained a constant threat, and even in 1872 Kooringa was said to be 'the shabbiest town in the Australias', its cottages 'the most squalid in the British Empire.'[109] In other respects, the Burra communities – especially in the early days – exhibited a roughness and brutality which reflected the worst of the 'lawless tinner' reputation at home. In October 1846 one report alleged that at the Burra 'drunkenness exists ... to a frightful degree. Wages are so high that the men have the means of gratifying their worst passions',[110] an opinion echoed by Haywood who recorded in his diary in 1847 that in one of the Burra's 13 public houses:

> the toughest characters congregated, breaking windows, singing and fighting, and ... the landlord used a cricket bat to clear his house at night – on pay nights, Saturday, fights would be coming off all the afternoon and evening, and [the] ring formed and kept by two policemen, who were powerless to do anything but see fair play – on Sunday mornings also there were often 8 to 10 matches (pugilistic) come off at the back of the Inn, the house being closed on that day.[111]

Two years later, in August 1849, another report alleged that 'the brutalising amusements called prize fights are rife at Kooringa and its neighbourhood',[112] but by then local inhabitants were taking steps to improve conditions in the neighbourhood. During 1849 a party of Cornish miners submitted a petition to the Colonial Secretary, drawing attention to lawlessness and immorality at the Burra and demanding action. Foremost amongst its signatories were Thomas Ninnes, from Towednack, and Samuel Bray, from Falmouth, both Methodist activists in the locality. Although, as in Cornwall itself, we should beware of uncritical embrace of Methodist claims to have 'transformed' the Burra, it is clear that the increasing organisation and activity of the several Methodist denominations did address conditions there and at other South Australian mining camps. As early as 1849 one observer claimed a 'visible improvement in the state of society at the Burra',[113] while at the end of the year another could make the startling claim that 'The almost total absence of crime among a population of nearly 5000 inhabitants, speaks volumes for the morality of the people.'[114]

Certainly, the Methodists were well-placed to exploit the conditions associated with the colonising process. As the frontiers of the colony were pushed ever onwards, so the Methodist denominations could expand their spheres of influence. They did not need fixed buildings or paid clergy to initiate their work or to survive, lay (local) preachers providing the impetus for expansion. Where no chapel existed they would hold services and class meetings in their own homes and they were prepared to ride many miles through hazardous country to bring the Word to the remotest spots. Although centrally controlled, Methodism allowed for considerable freedom of action at local levels and this combined with the Methodist commitment to self-help, individual improvement, thrift and sheer hard work to generate all kinds of local fund-raising and 'improving' activities such as tea-treats, lectures, bazaars, outings, and picnics. Amongst other things, this enabled Methodist societies throughout South Australia to finance and build their own chapels.

As ever, the Bible Christians were especially adept at such activity. James Blatchford, a Cornish miner born at Stoke Climsland in 1808, had been converted from a sinful life of 'drinking and smoking ... rollicking humour ... dancing and wrestling'[115] at the age of 26, and in 1847 emigrated to South Australia with his wife, Charity Jury. He found work at the Burra mine, and at first he and Charity attended Primitive Methodist services at Kooringa. However, they soon met John Stephens – another Bible Christian from Cornwall – and initiated prayer meetings at his house. Shortly, they were joined by other like-minded Cousin Jacks and Jennies – Thomas and John Pellew, John Halse, Mary Richards from Marazion, John Vivian from St Austell – and SAMA was persuaded to donate a plot of land on which to build their chapel. They raised the funds and constructed the building themselves, Charity sewing the calico for the ceiling. The chapel was big enough for 200 people and after it was opened a Sunday school and choir were formed. All this had been achieved before the first ordained Bible Christian minister had set foot upon South Australian soil and at home the Bible Christian Conference at Shebbear (North Devon) was so impressed by this progress – and the call from the colony for trained guidance – that it decided to send out two ministers. As the Bible Christian Missionary Society put it, this 'appeared as a Providential call, which it was thought it was our bounden duty at all hazards to obey'.[116]

The two who volunteered for South Australia were James Rowe and James Way. Way was a Devon man but the Rev. James Rowe was Cornish, born at Penzance in October 1824. Together with their colleagues at Shebbear, 'standing in a circle on the platform, [they] joined hands in solemn covenant that they would remain one in heart when oceans rolled between them. Fervent ejaculatory prayer and loud shouts of praise continually ascended to heaven. The weeping, the rejoicing were general'.[117] Arriving in the colony at the end of 1850, James Rowe made his way to the 'North Mines' (as Kapunda and the Burra were known collectively):

> things were primitive and strange to us. We travelled to the Burra in a spring cart, staying at night, by the way, in a rough bush pub. The heat was almost unbearable and sleep impossible ... [but] The loving welcome and subsequent hearty co-operation of the splendid men and women, among whom we had come to labour, made up for it all. The names of Blatchford, Halse, Pellew, Richards, Ould, and others remain a joy to me to this day.[118]

Rowe remained at the Burra for a month, then returning briefly to Adelaide before setting off on a tour of the scattered Bible Christian communities in the so-called North of the colony:

> At the end of a month I journeyed to Adelaide on foot, visiting and preaching at Kapunda, Lyndoch, and other places en route. The weather was excessively hot, and I suffered much from exposure and thirst. On my return journey I fell ill at Kapunda, and for weeks my life was despaired of, and it was two years before I fully regained my strength.[119]

During 1852 the Rev. Samuel Keen, another Devonian, was sent out to join Rowe and Way, and between the three of them the foundations were laid for the growth of the Bible Christian denomination in South Australia. Within ten years the Bible Christians had more than 1000 members in the colony and had erected 37 chapels. South Australia had become established at the centre of Bible Christian activity in the Antipodes, in much the same way that Cornwall was its focus in the United Kingdom.

The Primitive Methodists, too, were active at the Burra in those early days. In September 1849 they opened their chapel at Kooringa, the names of the local preachers – Rowe, Symons, Hayes, Berryman, Prior, Scoble, Moyle, Nicholls – suggesting an overwhelming Cornish influence. The Wesleyans were similarly energetic, and again the names of their class leaders at Kooringa illustrate a strong Cornish involvement – Chapman, Moyses, Whitford, Jeffery, Trehair, Bray. By 1847 the Adelaide Circuit had been divided into three – Adelaide itself, Willunga (where a strong Cornish presence had grown up around the local slate quarries), and the North Mines (Kapunda and the Burra). In the same year the Rev. Daniel J. Draper wrote to the *Wesleyan Methodist Magazine*:

> I have ... the pleasure to inform you that a new Wesleyan Methodist chapel has been opened at the famed Burra Burra Mine, one hundred miles north of Adelaide. The proprietors leased me an acre of land for ninety-nine years, and I laid the foundation stone of the chapel in March last. Since that time ... the cause has improved through the labours of Local Preachers and the zeal and piety of the members ... Many of them are from Cornwall, a considerable number of whom were members of our society at home.[120]

In 1848, the following year, Draper wrote to the Wesleyan Conference in Britain, urging that it send further missionaries to the colony to minister to 'the numbers of persons who come from our societies and congregations in Cornwall, and are like sheep without a shepherd.'[121] The 'Scotch Baptists' (as the evangelical Church of Christ was known) were also active at the Burra, where Philip Santo, the clerk of the works, persuaded the SAMA to donate land for a chapel. One Scotch Baptist, Joseph Verco, son of James Crabb Verco from Liskeard and Ann Cooke of Harrowbarrow, years later recalled the atmosphere of those early Church of Christ meetings:

> Mr Santo was ... liked by the [Verco] boys because his sermons were shorter and simpler and much more pathetic. He often shed tears which would run down his cheeks and have to be caught in his pocket handkerchief. Mr James C. Verco was also an occasional preacher. He wrote out his sermon in full and read it verbatim to his audience, and not infrequently it ended with the mournful strain of the unconverted, 'The harvest is passing, the summer is ending, and I am not saved'.[122]

Despite all this activity, the progress of nonconformity in early South Australia was not always smooth. To begin with, in the 1840s the possibility of state aid to religious denominations was raised on several occasions, a spectre for the non-conformists which appeared to threaten their much-prized freedom and independence. The *South Australian Register*, under the editorship of John Stephens, a Methodist of Cornish descent, led the campaign against state aid. Stephens' brother Edward, along with another Cornishman, the Rev. James Sawle, headed the proactively aggressive 'Society for the Preservation of Religious Freedom in the Province', arguing fiercely for the maintenance of religious independence and opposition to state interference. So successful was their campaign, that not only was the notion of state aid defeated but when responsible government was granted in 1857 there was no mention at all of a relationship between church (or churches) and state. As the *Primitive Methodist Quarterly Review* reflected in 1890, 'Civil and religious equality have been definitely established. They [South Australians] have no House of Lords, no state-endowed church, and no system of sectarian education subsidised by the state.'[123]

But if the Cornish had played a commendable role in the defence of religious freedom, then in the second of the challenges to confront non-conformity they were clearly part of the problem. This was the Victorian gold rush which both eroded the strength of local congregations, as the Cornish left in droves for the neighbouring colony, and posed a spiritual threat through the new obsession with gold and worldly wealth. As copper miners working for concerns such as the Burra and the Kapunda, the Cornish hoped for a fair wage for a fair day's work. But the prospect of striking it rich at the diggings prompted a new mood of avarice and opportunistic individualism. The Rev. James Rowe recalled that 'we had good congregations and much blessings at the Burra and Kapunda ... but the discovery of gold in Victoria the year after the beginning of our work shattered everything.'[124] The Primitive Methodists complained that the gold rush had 'exerted a withering influence on many of our societies and congregations',[125] while the Wesleyans regretted that, 'The amount of worldliness is extreme; and our best people are lamenting the deadness which is induced by so much care respecting gold, as well as by the spiritual privations suffered by those who go to seek it.'[126]

However, it was not all bad news. Not only did those successful on the goldfields remember to send back funds to support their faltering chapels and societies, but when the diggers returned, as many did, there were remarkable 'Revivals' at Kapunda and the Burra. The Rev. James Rowe enthused over 'that splendid work of God known as the great Burra Revival',[127] and in 1854 could note that 'The cause here has recovered from the shock it received from the discovery of the Victorian Gold Fields.'[128] In the same year the Wesleyans experienced 'conversions, the recovery of back-sliders, and the prosperous state of the Sunday-schools',[129] while the Primitive Methodists in 1855 could report that 'the mission has been recovering from the severe shock it sustained ... more members from Cornwall have gone there.'[130]

The diary of the Rev. John G. Wright, the Primitive Methodist minister at Kooringa during the 1850s, is an authentic and exciting testimonial from those heady days:

> This has been a day of days. In the morning I was called to visit a poor man who had been for days under conviction of sin. When I entered the house he fell on his knees with horrific groans. For one hour he was in the greater agony. 'I cannot live, I cannot live. I will not let thee go. I will believe.' Soon he found Christ and began to sing 'I never shall forget the day, When Jesus washed my sins away'.[131]

And again:

> Attended a prayer meeting at Kooringa. A man by the name of F. Cock was brought to God. He had been notorious for crime, had took his wife by the hair of the head and swung her round the room. When made happy he ran round the house praising God. A poor man by the name of Jenkin had not long before got his jaw broken, he got so happy he praised the Lord shouting 'I will praise the Lord, I will praise the Lord though I have a broken chack [cheek]'.[132]

The Sunday schools, in particular, were the pride of Burra Burra, and in their activities we have a valuable insight into the religious (and thus cultural) education of Cornish children in colonial South Australia almost a century and a half ago. At the Kooringa Bible Christian Sunday School Anniversary in June 1859, for example, the youngsters were encouraged to perform recitations of pieces they had prepared in previous weeks. Thus young Absalom Tonkin warned listeners to 'Prepare to Meet Thy God' while Susannah Trevithick recited 'A Prayer.' 'Jesus Wept' was the piece chosen by Elias Nankivell, while Edward Fellows and William Stephens together performed 'Two Miners – A Dialogue.' In the following year, John Varcoe talked about 'The Old Negro's Religion', while T. Trembath tackled 'Sacred Mountains' and Elizabeth Hoskins attempted 'The Young Master.' The prizes awarded are equally revealing. In 1859 Stephen Davey was presented with *Historical Tales for Young Protestants* and Elizabeth Curnow received a copy of the *Dairyman's Daughter*. Richard Hawkin was given a backnumber of the *Bible Christian Magazine* and both William Prideaux and Francis Rowe acquired backnumbers of the *Child's Magazine*. In 1861 Richard Andrewartha and John Hawke were each given copies of *Burn's Youthful Piety* and Julia Hocking received *Jamaica Enslaved and Free*. Mary Coombe was presented with *Australia and Its Settlement*.[133]

In later years the cause of Burra Methodism was strengthened by the arrival of important personalities from Cornwall who brought with them news of the latest religious debates back home together with strong personal opinions which helped local activists to discuss and form their own ideas. One such arrival was the Rev. Joseph Hancock, born in Camborne in 1822, together with his wife Charlotte Pascoe, from Higher Menadue, Luxulyan. Hancock succeeded James Way as Bible Christian minister at the Burra in 1862, his son-in-law, John Harry from Kilkhampton, also becoming a Methodist minister of note in South Australia, serving as inspector of schools in the early 1900s. In the debates that attended the moves towards Methodist Union in South Australia at the end of the 19th century, these Burra and Kapunda Cornish played a significant role, variously arguing the cases for and against the several denominations, including the Bible Christians, Primitive Methodists and Wesleyans, coming together to form one united Methodist Church in South Australia. Those in favour argued that there was nothing to be gained from maintaining rival sects and that the cause of Methodism would be better served if they joined together and pooled their resources.

The Rev. James Rowe, whose opinion was much respected in the colony, emerged as an important advocate of Union, and in 1894 the Bible Christians and

Primitive Methodists voted in support of amalgamation. In 1896 a general Methodist referendum, encompassing all the different denominations in the colony, declared in favour of union, and a united Methodist Conference was held in Adelaide in 1899. The Bible Christian Conference at High Street Chapel, Penzance, in 1900 was the last attended by representatives from South Australia, because formal union between the several Methodist denominations in the colony had been achieved on 1 January of that year. At Kapunda the joyful Methodist minister declared, 'not only would the union be a great and useful factor in the colonies, but to the town of Kapunda. Let their motto be that good old Cornish one – 'One and All' – and let them work together for the cause of God.'[134]

From the successful defence of religious freedom in the 1840s and 1850s to the achievement of Methodist Union in 1900, the Cornish had played a significant role in the advancement and protection of South Australia's 'Paradise of Dissent.' This, amongst other things, had given a radical, political edge to their religious activity, mirroring the Nonconformist radical tradition that had by now emerged in Cornwall itself and demonstrating the transplantation of that tradition in South Australia. As we shall see in Chapter 7, this process reached its apogee in the emergence of the miners' trade unions and in the United Labor Party at Wallaroo and Moonta in the years after 1864, but an early manifestation was the extraordinary miners' strike at the Burra in 1848. As Mel Davies, Australia's mining historian, has observed, it is only recently that the full significance of this strike has been recognised.[135] As well as flying in the face of deeply entrenched conventional wisdoms, articulated by Cornish historians such as A.K. Hamilton Jenkin and D.B. Barton, that have insisted that notions of collective action came late to the Cornish miners at home and abroad, the strike was important in that it was the first major industrial dispute in South Australia. Moreover, the almost hysterical response to the strike by SAMA and the colonial establishment indicated both the fear of proletarian rebellion – 1848 was, after all, the year of European revolution – and the fearsome reputation of the 'lawless tinner'. Despite the improving impact of Methodism, Cornish miners still enjoyed their reputation for riot and violence and it is very likely that among the Cousin Jacks at the Burra in 1848 were individuals who only a year or two before were in the crowds that had forced 'fair prices' for corn at Helston or Wadebridge.

The Burra strike was actually about two separate issues – the assaying of ores, and wages. Initially, it was discovered that assays of ore samples provided by the tributers had consistently overestimated their copper content, resulting in the over-remuneration of the miners in question and suggesting the existence of fraud on the grand scale. Thomas Burr, the SAMA superintendent ultimately responsible for managing such sampling, was dismissed but refused to go quietly. A deputation of SAMA officials, including Henry Ayers, made its way to Kooringa on 13 September 1848 to force Burr's resignation, only to find that the Cornish miners had struck in his support. An urgent note was dispatched to the governor in Adelaide, containing alarming news:

> of acts of the most violent character and actual force having taken men up from the shafts tied together and carried them off the mine ... [warrants had been obtained] against two of the ring leaders but the police prevented from making the capture by a mob of about one hundred and sixty men. The total number of men now in revolt is about three hundred. The men have virtual possession of the Mine and have prevented the ore from being carted away. The only work permitted to go on is the Whim at the Water Shaft which they threaten to stop ... unless means are taken to stop this ... the Mine will be ruined .... This being the first time that anything like this has occurred in the Province the Deputation feel that it is necessary to act with energy and decision or otherwise we should be entirely in the hands of the people.[136]

The *South Australian* newspaper proclaimed 'Revolution at the Burra Burra Mines',[137] and 26 armed police troopers were immediately dispatched to the Burra. When they arrived they found that Ayers had exaggerated the extent of the crisis, not least because several Methodist local preachers had taken charge of the strikers, organising a committee and drawing up a list of grievances. The committee won the support of the radical *South Australian Register*, whose editor, John Stephens, was an ardent Methodist and of Cornish descent, but the directors refused to meet the committee to discuss the grievances, declaring that as tributers were individual contractors they (the directors) would only negotiate with individual miners. With the mood turning ugly, the commissioner of police intervened, organising a meeting between the directors and the tributers' representatives who – as well as raising the assay question – also complained about compulsory deductions for the Club & Doctor Fund and the high charges for tools, fuses, powder, and candles. By and large, the miners got their way, not least with regard to the assay question where new procedures suggested by the tributers were accepted by the directors.

However, no sooner had this agreement been reached than Ayers announced a general cut in wages for labourers, carters, blacksmiths, sawyers, mechanics, and other grass workers. In response, these surface workers went out on strike and the tributers and tutworkers – acting in sympathy – refused to bid for their contracts. John Stephens used the pages of the *South Australian Register* and the Adelaide *Observer* to publicise the workers' case, but this time the directors were in no mood to compromise. The strike was broken finally by desperate miners persuaded to return to work, while SAMA drew up a list of 'obnoxious persons' who would be barred from employment in the future and given notice to quit the association's cottages. Two days before Christmas, Ayers wrote that Joe Trevean, A. Penna, Thos Cocking, M. Rogers, and F. Polkinghorne were to be offered the chance to return to work on tribute or tutwork. Messrs Bosance, Robins, Hoskins and Stephens, however, were told to vacate their premises immediately.

Significantly, some of the striking Cornish miners had already left for New Zealand, where copper deposits on Kawau Island were being opened up in the mid-1840s. Situated in the Hauraki Gulf, some 40 miles from Auckland, the Kawau mine was developed in 1844 by the Aberdeen Ore Company which brought out Captain James Ninnes from Cornwall to supervise operations. Ninnes and his party of Cornish miners and mechanics arrived in New Zealand in January 1846, and by the time the Burra strike broke out work was already well-advanced. The links between the Burra and Kawau appear to have been close, the flow of workers between the two extending beyond the immediate crisis of 1848. In the early 1850s, for example, James Snell from Roche, who had already spent time in Canada, left the Burra to try his luck on the Victorian gold-fields, moving on to Kawau Island a few years later with his wife, Mary Roberts, where he became underground captain.

For those who had gone to Kawau in 1848, demand for their specialist skills had been the key to their escape from the wrath of SAMA. Or, put another way, the ease with which they moved from one location to another demonstrated that the inherent mobility of the Cornish miner was an important weapon in confronting the bosses. Put simply, if the Cornish did not like the pay and conditions that they were offered in one location, then they could always move on. Additionally, attempts by SAMA to recruit blackleg labour from the ranks of Cornish miners newly arrived at Port Adelaide were generally unsuccessful, evidence of an ethnic solidarity amongst the Cousin Jacks which would be an important factor in industrial disputes in the colony in later years. Thus although Ayers and the directors were able to present the outcome of the strike as a victory for the employers, in fact their position was not as unassailable as they had imagined. In the end, the potential strength of the miners remained unrealised, not through the resistance of SAMA, but because the miners were unable to perpetuate their organisation in the years after 1848. The Victorian gold rush in 1851 destroyed any lingering sense of unity, and it was not until more than a decade later that the colony's Cornish miners were again to resort to collective action.

The Victorian gold rush, as we have seen, played a generally disruptive role in the development of South Australia's copper mining industry. It occurred in the aftermath of the Californian Rush of 1849 and that to New South Wales in 1850 and offered an important new destination for emigrant Cousin Jacks and Jennies. In the preceding years the copper of Cuba, Chile, Michigan and South Australia had dominated the emergence of the international mining industry and its labour market. But the rushes of 1849–51 marked a radical departure from this pattern, emphasising as they did the increasing importance of gold production and creating dislocation (or at least new directions) in the international labour market. For the Cornish, the gold rushes were of considerable significance, increasing the choice of potential destinations for those considering emigration from Cornwall, as well as diverting those already abroad in places such as Mexico or South Australia to the new diggings of California, New South Wales, and Victoria.

# CHAPTER SIX

# GOLD!

# THE CALIFORNIAN RUSH

In the Cornish imagination – and in much of the Western world – gold and California are virtually synonymous. The discovery of the yellow metal in that embryonic state in 1848 so unsettled the minds of men and women – so it is said – that the course of North American history was altered radically as many thousands of people from across the globe rushed to become 'Forty-niners'. In essence, this characterisation is true enough, even if it disguises the emergence of Brazil as an early gold producer in the modern international economy. But it does obscure part of the wider story. To begin with, gold had already been wrought with some success in the United States before 1848–49, while California was even before that date a mining region: quicksilver having been discovered in the cinnabar hills of New Almaden, south of San Francisco, in 1845. Moreover, the Californian gold rush was a prelude to a series of further 'rushes' during the 1850s and into the 1860s and beyond, a remarkable catalyst in the continued development and diversification of the international mining economy which much affected Australia, New Zealand and, later, other areas such as South Africa.

Gold had already been worked in the southern Appalachians in Georgia, North Carolina and Virginia.[1] In February 1835, for example, the *West Briton* advertised on behalf of the Union Gold Mines in Virginia for an engineer 'competent to erect some steam engines',[2] together with three engine-men, one foreman blacksmith, one foreman mason, one pit-man, and nine sumpmen. As ever, the Cousin Jack network of local knowledge and contacts was important, prospective applicants for the posts being advised to contact William Petherick of Redmoor Mine, Callington, or William West of Fowey Consols. The Vancluse, another Virginian gold-mine, situated on a branch of the Rappahannock River some 17 miles from Fredericksburg, had been in operation since as early as 1832. Initially an alluvial working, the mine – with the help of Cornish miners – had followed the lodes underground to a depth of at least 100 feet by 1848. In

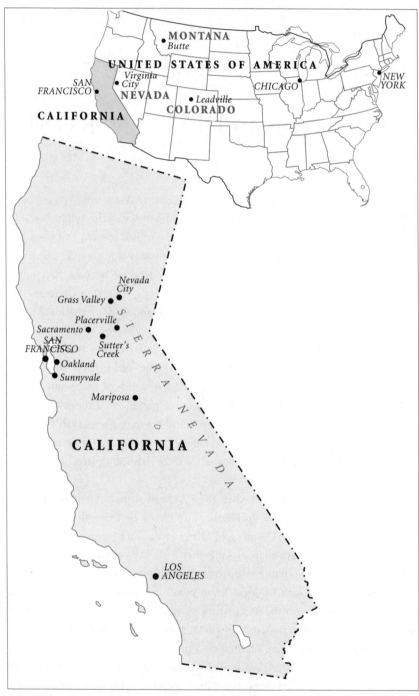

*Mining locations and principal cities in California*

March of that year a cautious assessment of the mine's prospects appeared in the pages of the *West Briton*:

> On the whole the mine is certainly a very extraordinary one, well worth visiting, and cannot fail, if properly managed, of yielding a very large profit .... In fact, the quantity of 'vein stuff' (all of which ... is more or less impregnated with gold) seems inexhaustible. I went to the spot prejudiced against the whole concern, and believing it to be like so many other gold mines I have read about in ancient and modern travels, but came away altogether changed in opinion, and satisfied that, with careful management, and an improved method of cleaning and smelting, even a gold mine may be a good speculation.[3]

The gold-mine as a 'good speculation' was a temptation that would soon inspire many a 'Forty-niner' in the Far West of America but California's first introduction to mineral wealth was through the quicksilver of New Almaden. Extracted by roasting cinnabar ore, quicksilver – mercury – was increasingly sought for a variety of scientific and industrial purposes, including (fortuitously, as it turned out) as a component of the amalgam used in the reduction of gold. Worked for many generations by Native Americans seeking the rich, deep-red colouring of the cinnabar for their ceremonial body adornment, New Almaden was 'discovered' by a Mexican soldier, one Captain Andres Castillero, in the autumn of 1845.[4] It is not clear when the first Cornish arrived at New Almaden but it is likely that they were amongst the party of miners and other workers who turned up there with equipment and machinery from Mexico two years later in 1847. In February 1848 California and the whole of the South West were acquired from Mexico by the United States for $15,000,000. As A.L. Rowse noted, 'within seven years New Almaden had produced as much'[5] in value from the quicksilver it had won. That said, development of the mine was hampered by a series of lawsuits regarding its ownership, a situation that was not resolved until 1863 when the workings were taken over by the Quicksilver Mining Company. This American concern had difficulty in managing its large Mexican workforce and took steps to increase the number of Cornish miners at New Almaden. Six years earlier, the previous regime had admitted that 'We are gradually getting rid of these Mexican miners and substituting Cornish miners in their stead'[6], a policy adopted by the new owners with increased vigour and determination.

By the 1870s the workforce at New Almaden consisted of 115 Mexicans and other Latin Americans, 90 American-born (some, no doubt, of Cornish descent), and 172 from Great Britain of whom the majority was Cornish.[7] As ever, the Cornish came from a variety of places, some directly from Cornwall itself but many others from across America and the wider world. Arthur Berryman, for example, had arrived in Pennsylvania from Cornwall in 1854 to work as a coal miner. In 1855–57 he was digging for gold in California, and from here he journeyed to South America where he spent seven years mining in Chile, Bolivia and Peru. From there he returned to California, toiling for 12 years in the New Almaden and neighbouring New Idria quicksilver mines. In 1876 he visited the gold-fields of British Columbia but he was soon back in quicksilver country, working in the mine at Guadalupe, near New Almaden, until 1882. Later, in 1887, he retired from mining to run the Los Gatos Hotel, a staging inn on the road from San Jose to Santa Cruz. Equally active and peripatetic was Richard Bailey Harper, born in Redruth in 1847, the son of a mining engineer who had travelled extensively in England, Scotland, Wales and Spain (where he died) in his pursuit of his occupation. Richard had emigrated from Cornwall to California in 1863, working first in the gold-mines at Grass Valley and then moving across the Sierra Nevada mountains to Virginia City where he found employment in Nevada's famous Comstock Lode. From there it was back to California, working for six or seven years at New Almaden, then on to Mariposa and Grass Valley in the gold-fields, and then yet again to the silver mines of Nevada, before returning eventually to the cinnabar hills where he became 'the fortunate discoverer of the North Almaden quicksilver mines.'[8] Later, in the 1870s, he was off again, this time to Mexico in search of new quicksilver deposits in the Chihuahua district. In the end, he returned to California, first of all managing the Santa Teresa quicksilver mine near San Jose and then retiring to a spot near New Almaden.

Others included William L. Pearce, who as a boy had worked underground in the Balleswidden mine near St Just-in-Penwith and who in 1848 had emigrated to the United States where he found employment first of all in the Connecticut copper mines. From there it was on to the familiar Cornish lead-mining country of Wisconsin and then to the gold-fields of British Columbia, arriving eventually at New Almaden where he worked for some 15 years. James Varcoe, from Tywardreath, was another of the district's enormously experienced Cornish miners, another wandering Cousin Jack who had mined in New Jersey, Michigan, Grass Valley, and Virginia City before arriving at New

Almaden. Most famous of all, perhaps, was Captain James Harry, born in Breage in 1833, who followed his five brothers to America at the age of 33, taking his wife Emma Carlyon first to Grass Valley and then, two years later, to New Almaden. He rose inexorably from tutworkman to timberman, pumpman, shaft-boss and captain, eventually becoming general superintendent of the New Almaden mine in 1881. By 1885, it is said, he had no fewer than 300 Cousin Jacks working for him – John Eddy, Alf Tregonning, Thomas Trevarthen, Charles Tonkin, John Bowden, Richard Jacka, George Reseigh, William Bunney, William Doidge, Percy Dunstan, William Gilbert, John Rowe, Thomas Pryor, Thomas Odgers, and very many more.[9] Although the mine declined quickly in the opening decade of the 20th century, its fortunes revived during the First World War. The Depression years led, in turn, to its virtual abandonment, although in the Second World War quicksilver was again sought after as a strategic metal, leading to a vigorous reworking which lasted until 1946. This longevity was matched by the lingering presence of the Cornish at New Almaden well into the 20th century; folk such as Charles Berryman who moved down from the iron country of the Marquette Range in Michigan and John George from Perranarworthal who had mined in Missouri and Nevada before making his way to California.

Adjoining the mine site at New Almaden were the twin settlements of Spanishtown and Cornish Camp (or Englishtown as it was sometimes known), the former inhabited by the Mexicans and other Hispanics, the latter the preserve of the Cornish. One eyewitness report in 1876 drew an intriguing picture of the two townships:

> The Mexicans have the gift of harmoniousness; they seem always to fit their surroundings, and their dingy little camp has made itself at home on the barren hills, over which it is scattered; but the charm of the Cornish camp lies partly in vivid incongruity between its small, clamorous activities, and the repose of the vast, silent nature about it ... Many trees in the camp, standing at the meeting of the ways, bear upon their trunk certain excrescences in the shape of oblong boxes. To the New England mind they would at once suggest the daily paper; but the Cornish sustain life on something more substantial than 'bread and newspapers'. The meat-wagon, on its morning rounds, leaves Tyrrel his leg o' mutton, Tregoning his soup-

bone, and Trengove his two-bit's worth of steak, in the boxes bearing these names respectively. Such is the honesty of Cornish camp, that trees bearing soup-bones, leg-of-mutton and steaks, are never plucked of their fruit, save by the rightful owners.[10]

In 1880 another commentator observed what she saw as the entirely beneficial fusion of Cornish Methodist morality with the benign paternalism of the Quicksilver Mining Company:

This is New Almaden, the prettiest, neatest, cleanest, and most cheerful mining village we have ever visited ... Looking down from Mine Hill into the valley below we see by the character of the houses that there are two divisions in the little burg, one allotted to the Mexican miners, the other to the English speaking, which are mostly Cornish. Strolling about the town we are struck with the cleanliness and neatness of the place and with the absence of saloons and dance halls such as characterize and mar our western mining towns. There is an air of cheerfulness and sobriety among the people also and ... from nearly every house we hear music and singing in which the Cornish so much delight, while a band is playing in a substantial city clubroom hall and reading room and nearly every cottage has an organ or piano. The secret of all this is that the town and all connected with it is in the hands and under the control of the company, and it is their aim, whilst keeping out things of immoral and hurtful nature, to supply their people with healthful recreation and elevating amusements. Such is New Almaden.[11]

This alliance of Nonconformist self-improvement ideology and company intervention was also evident in an 1886 description of the Helping Hand Hall in New Almaden, published in the *San Jose Daily Mercury*:

The manager of the mine [Captain Harry] conceived the idea that by fitting up a nice, cozy and in every respect comfortable hall where all kinds of popular games could be indulged in and have attached to it a reading room and kitchen, that by so doing a great public want would be met that the social sphere would be enlarged in usefulness and our community become better natured and consequently more happy and contented. Our rules and regulations are very simple. Everybody ... who pays $1 a month to the Miner's Fund are members and entitled to all privileges and can come to the hall when open, play games, read or make a cup of tea, coffee or chocolate at less than cost. No gambling or drinking of spirituous liquors is allowed. Smoking is allowed in the main hall but no games; no talking or smoking is allowed in the reading room. We have a library of 450 volumes.[12]

Recently, Gage McKinney in his *A High and Holy Place* has shed more light on the Methodist culture of Cornish Camp, illuminating the history of the local Methodist Church itself but also bringing to life the many who toiled in its cause both within its walls and beyond in the wider New Almaden community. He writes of the pastors, such as Cornishman J. Lewis Trefren, who provided spiritual leadership and guidance but he also focuses on the ordinary people, the local preachers, class leaders, Sunday school teachers, musicians and others who gave Cornish Methodism at New Almaden its particular strengths and qualities. Significantly, McKinney devotes an entire chapter to the women, the 'Madonnas of the trail' in American parlance, who shared in the hardships of their menfolks' lives but were expected to provide unwavering domestic security and support. As one stoic and no doubt long-suffering pastor's wife recalled:

> In old times husbands went where all the tribes do gather, not knowing what would befall them there. And wives waited for the reading of the appointments [to far-flung Methodist circuits] while getting ready to move .... Dark side of itinerant life this moving is! Yet tired feet and aching hearts never allow a dark side where love and loyalty hold sway.[13]

This was just as well, for the huge task facing Cornish Methodism in California went far beyond the relatively peaceable and ordered flock of New Almaden to encompass the altogether more difficult and fast-changing gold-mining communities of the Sierra Nevada and the Mother Lode country. As Rodman Wilson Paul observed in 1963 in his seminal study of the far-western mining frontier, 'If the word "frontier" connotes sparceness [sic] of population, richness of untapped natural resources, isolation, hardship, and danger, then the region of the Sierra Nevada of California was a true mining frontier during much of the decade that began in 1848.'[14] The world-famous first discovery of Californian gold was made at Sutter's Mill on the American River, a tributary of the Sacramento River, on 24 January 1848. San Francisco became the jumping-off point for the subsequent rush inland, with several thousand anxious miners heading north to California from Mexico, Peru and Chile by the close of 1848, Cornish amongst them. These early arrivals were joined by a further wave from other parts of the Americas (including Cousin Jacks from Wisconsin and the Lakes) during the early part of 1849. The contemporary painter and writer, J.D. Borthwick, noted that in 1852 in Placerville he met a knot of Cornish miners who had been attracted to California from 'from mines in Mexico and South America and from the lead mines in Wisconsin.'[15] Before long others were arriving directly from Cornwall, from elsewhere in Europe and even from Australia. In 1848 the European population of California stood at about 14,000. The figure was approaching 100,000 by the close of 1849, and perhaps as many as 250,000 by the end of 1852. The numbers of actual miners in California may have been as high as 5000 at the end of 1848, rising to some 100,000 by 1852. The Census of 1860 reported 82,573 men in California self-describing as miners.

From the Lakes of Upper Michigan came Cousin Jacks like Josiah Phillips, originally from Porthtowan, who also mined in Nevada and later invented the prize-winning 'Wee Pet' assaying machine so useful in the analysis of ore on the western frontier. In Wisconsin there was at least as much excitement, with many miners at Mineral Point, Linden, Shullsburg and in the adjoining lead-mining area of Illinois heading west to California, a few by the hazardous and little-known overland route but many more via the sea and Nicaragua. By and large it was the menfolk who left, leaving wives and families back home, with the intention of returning once they had 'made their fortune.' Many, indeed, did return to Wisconsin (having met with varying degrees of success on the gold-fields) but perhaps as many as a 1000 Wisconsin Cornish settled in California for good, eventually sending for their families to join them. Yet for others, their Californian sojourn was but the first episode of a western frontier odyssey that drew them on to new areas as new discoveries were made – to destinations such as Nevada's Virginia City or perhaps further afield in Montana, Colorado, Arizona or the Dakotas.

Henry Roberts, from Jo Daviess County in Illinois, took the Nicaragua route to California, landing at San Francisco and making his way to

Placerville in the Mother Lode country where he mined for gold for three years before returning to Illinois wealthy enough to build a brick hotel in the settlement of Scales Mound. James Bennett, from Dodgeville in Wisconsin, travelled to California with his wife in 1854. They stayed there for five years, returning to Wisconsin to buy a farm of 160 acres. Later, in 1865, Bennett was off on his travels again, this time to Colorado and from there to Utah and the gold-fields of Montana before returning home to increase his farm to some 280 acres. John Penberthy, whose father had died in Canada, leaving a widow and seven children in Dodgeville, borrowed money from his friend, James Roberts, to purchase his fare to California. Richard Wearne and his companion, William Jacka, both Cornishmen, started out on the overland route with a yoke of oxen but Jacka had lost heart by the time they reached Omaha and turned back. Wearne pressed on, arriving safely in California where he mined for three years. After another four years in British Columbia he returned at last to Mineral Point, marrying a Cornish girl and settling down. The Skewis brothers from Shullsburg – Edward, Henry and the literary James – made their way to the Californian gold-fields in the early 1850s. Like the 'Forty-niners' before them, they made for the alluvial diggings, using separating devices such as the ubiquitous 'Long Tom' to locate the tiny crumbs of gold. As James explained:

> Thousands of men with tools in hand,
> Travelling all o'er the land,
> This they did with greatest pleasure
> Searching for the hidden treasure.
> And fixed their Toms close by their side
> And washed a piece about eight feet wide.
> And at the close of every day
> Took their little scales to weigh
> The gold they had taken from the pit,
> By this they knew how much they got.
> And thus they would work from day to day,
> As long as they could make it pay.[16]

Working the alluvial deposits brought its rewards, especially for those first on the diggings and who found they had easy pickings, but – as the Skewis brothers well knew – the real wealth would be hidden at depth in the quartz rock. This was where the knowledge and skill of the Cornish hard-rock miner came into its own:

> More gold to find was our intent
> We picked and shovelled the dirt away,
> To get to bedrock without delay.
> 'Twas there the gold was mostly found,
> Twelve ounces only made a pound.
> The rocks glistened with the shining stuff,
> And hard we worked hoping to have enough
> That at some future time we might retire,
> With all the gold we might require.[17]

Meanwhile, back in Cornwall, the *West Briton* had announced as early as January 1849 that 'The gold of California is no foible. Midas lives. The greatest ass in the United States may if he will abandon his thistles, touch nothing but gold.'[18] A few weeks later and a correspondent in the same newspaper reported from Sutter's Mill, the site of the first discovery, that 'there are now about 2000 persons engaged and the roads leading to the mines are thronged with people and waggons.'[19] In the summer of 1851 another Cornishman, one Edward Dale, wrote home to his wife in St Agnes to explain that he had made $100 on his very first day at the diggings, while 'yesterday I got four ounces of the prettiest gold I ever saw.'[20] In the September the *Royal Cornwall Gazette* commented that a 'splendid lump of Californian gold' weighing at least fourteen ounces and worth nearly £55 had been brought the previous week to Mr Pascoe, a jeweller in Penzance: 'It was of the purest quality.'[21] More cautionary was the tale in the newspaper's columns in the November. 'A few days since', it was reported, 'a man named Welsh, a Cornish miner, arrived in London from California with £540 in gold besides other valuables in securities.' Not unnaturally, he was 'Desirous of visiting his native place' (Cornwall) and made for Euston Square. But while waiting for his train, 'he fell in with several ladies by whom he was conducted to a house and drugged.'[22] Such foolishness mirrored life on the hectic, bewildering gold-fields of California, one John Roberts writing from near Sonora to his brother Thomas in Camborne to complain – with Methodist indignation – that 'Sunday is the day for the exhibition of circuses, bull-fights, horse-races, concerts, fandangoes, for drunkeness and all sorts of excentiousness. Scarcely a Sunday passes but some man is killed and sometimes two or three.'[23]

Indeed, it was in these heady early days that the Californian gold-mining camps acquired their racy if often unsavoury reputations (at least in Cornish Methodist eyes), as in the Mother Lode town of Placerville – or Hangtown, as it was more popularly known:

> Hangtown gals are plump and rosy,
> Hair in ringlets mighty cosy;
> Painted cheeks and gassy bonnets;
> Touch them and they'll sting like hornets.[24]

In these early days most diggers – professional miners and amateurs alike – were working alone or (more usually) in small syndicates to try their luck on the apparently limitless gold-fields. As early as January 1849, the *West Briton* had noted the establishment of one such syndicate. This was the Cornwall Association for Streaming of Gold in California, set up rather grandly under the Cornish cost-book system with John Wood of St Austell as its secretary. It was actively seeking Cornish recruits, for 'If ever there was a call for the skilled labour of Cornwall ... this gold district demands it.'[25] As a contributor to the *West Briton* declared in June 1851 in a classic assertion of the Cousin Jack myth, the Cornish were of course 'the most accomplished of all miners. The Californians cannot do without Cornishmen.'[26]

However, notwithstanding the superior knowledge of the Cornish, mining methods initially were primitive, especially the winning of 'placer' deposits along the Mother Lode (that stretch of country from around Grass Valley in the north down to Mariposa), although the ready supply of quicksilver facilitated the development of advanced refinement techniques as early as 1849. 'Long Toms', similar to earlier separation cradles but now stationary and elongated, a forerunner of the practice of sluicing, were quickly developed as an aid to alluvial working, allowing the separation of gold particles from stream-bed detritus. Towards the end of 1851 John Roberts, from Camborne, informed his brother Thomas back in Cornwall that 'Everyone is digging and working like men fighting for prizes. I have never worked so hard in my life.' He and his partner had 'bought two mules, two carts, with the privilege of a stream to wash with and a "long tom" for seven hundred dollars.'[27] Despite this initial expense, they had already cleared a surplus of $300. Communications were rudimentary at first, pack trains of mules or horses, together with wagon trains, linking the larger towns like Placerville and Sonora, and opening up the multiplicity of smaller camps with their strange but evocative names such as Brandy City, Red Dog, You Bet, Rough and Ready, Poverty Bar, and Whisky Diggings. Often these camps had particular ethnic affiliations, creating a complex community of interlocking but nevertheless differentiated groupings. Thus Hispanics or Chinese tended to stick together in their own camps, as did Americans from specific localities such as Missouri or Arkansas, while 'Still others grew up around a nucleus of Irishmen, or Cornishmen, or Englishmen.'[28]

This, in turn, was reflected in the rough justice of the early communities of the gold-fields, the absence of established law and order allowing, even encouraging, the miners to institute and execute their own legal codes. As Paul noted: 'The Cornishmen and Germans were ... familiar with well-developed codes grounded on many generations of experience. From these old and tested codes, as explained by those who knew them, the Californian miners drew their precedents, and for some years the resulting practices were adequate for the relatively simple needs of the day.'[29] Needless to say, these practices reflected in part the inheritance of the Stannary system in Cornwall, the independent Cornish legal code which, in its Californian manifestations, allowed the creation of 'districts' (like the individual 'Stannaries' in Cornwall) and defined the territories in which the miners' codes might operate. A presiding officer was duly elected for each district, a code of 'laws' drafted and adopted, and a 'recorder' chosen to keep a careful list of all mining claims. To deal with the inevitable disputes, 'judges' were elected and 'miners' juries' (which on occasion might constitute an entire camp) were formed to try serious cases such as robbery or murder. In the absence of proper gaols, at least in the early days, 'guilty' verdicts might mean whipping, branding, banishment, or even execution.

James Skewis encountered one such occurrence at Deer Creek, recording it for posterity:

> An incident happened one day there, just after dinner. Moyle [a Cornish name] and his partner, who worked a mile or so above us, came to us and enquired if we had seen a man pass by. We said that one just went along. They said the fellow had robbed them of a bag of gold, and asked if we would go with them to recover it. We went with all the men we could gather up, and went to a little town at that time called Newtown, and we found the man in a saloon. He had just taken a glass of beer.[30]

Skewis, Moyle and the others arrested the man, accusing him of theft, a charge that he denied vehemently. He declared that they might search him, which they duly did, discovering the bag of gold that had been taken. The landlord of the saloon took possession of the bag until Moyle could positively identify it, which he did, and then 'There was a Miners' Court established, a judge appointed, and two of the best talented men to defend each side.' The prisoner was found 'guilty' but there was a difference of opinion over the sentence. Some favoured execution but in the end Moyle, a powerful man, was given the satisfaction of administering two dozen lashes, to be followed by the branding of the letter 'R' on the prisoner's face:

> So the iron was shaped into the letter 'R', and the thief tied to a tree and stripped to the bare back. A rough whip was made for the flogging and he got it severely. His back was a mass of torn flesh, then the iron was applied to his face, but it was too hot to leave any readable letter. He was loose with these words "if caught again to be hanged by the neck until dead". I have since heard that he continued robbing and was finally arrested by the civil authorities, and hanged in the same county Nevada, California.[31]

It was many years before Nevada County, situated in the foothills of the high Sierra Nevada in California, lost its reputation as the wild frontier but in fact 'civilisation' intruded early in the form of embryonic townships, notably Grass Valley and Nevada City. Here, alongside the inevitable saloons, emerged chapels, churches and schools, together with the provision of all kinds of goods and services to meet the needs of the rapidly expanding populations of the gold-fields. Grass Valley was named, simply enough, after the lush, luxuriant grass that grew there, while Nevada City, founded on the site of the Deer Creek diggings where Skewis and Moyle had had their encounter with the thief, took its name from the surrounding mountains and the Spanish word for 'snow'. Of the two townships, Grass Valley was most especially associated with the Cornish. Even though many of its wandering Cousin Jacks had been enticed across the border to Washoe County in the neighbouring Nevada State, following the discovery there of the famous Comstock lode silver deposits in 1857, the 1860 Federal Census identified no fewer than 470 'English' miners among a total population of 3940 in Grass Valley. A decade later and the population of Cornish miners had risen to well beyond a thousand, and in the closing decades of the 19th century the Cousin Jacks and Jennys fairly dominated the town's social, cultural and economic life as they continued to arrive from across North America and from Cornwall itself to facilitate the deep quartz mining that had progressively replaced the earlier 'placer' activity. As Ralph Mann has noted in his social history of Grass Valley and Nevada City, 'The expansion of quartz mining [from the 1860s] meant the continued influx of Cornish miners into Grass Valley. The two were inseparable and mutually dependent; mining techniques advocated by Cornish miners helped the industry to develop and created a need for more Cornish miners'.[32]

According to Mann, it was Grass Valley's early embrace of quartz mining that accounted for its decidedly 'Cornish' flavour when compared with the more cosmopolitan, multi-ethnic character of neighbouring Nevada City: 'In Grass Valley ... the Cornish deeply influenced the town's identity.' This was because, 'Deep-shaft quartz mining was carried out by the Cornish ... In 1870, Grass Valley was largely a quartz town ... Nevada City was part quartz and part placer.'[33] A trawl through the files of the local newspaper, the *Grass Valley Union*, reveals the tell-tale Cornish surnames in abundance, not only the familiar patronymics such as Martin, Matthews, Mitchell or Richards, Rickards and Roberts but those that are resoundingly Cornish. There are Angove and Argall, and Bennallack, Borlace and Bosanko. There's Chegwidden, Craddock and Curnow, and Glasson, Gluyas and Goldsworthy, together with Penaluna, Penberthy, Penhall, Rodda, Rowett and Rule. There's Scadden, Scobel and Searle, and inevitably any number of the archetypal 'Tre-' prefixed names – Trebilcox, Tregidgo, Tregloan, Tregown, Tregonning, Treloar, Tremaine, Tremewan, Trenberth, Tregarthen, Tresidder, Treverton, Trevillion, Trevithick, Trevorrow, Trewhella, Trezona, Trezise. More subtly, there are names whose contexts suggest their Cornishness, among them Batters, Deacon, Heather, Hooper, Montgomery, Quick, Whiting and Wills.[34]

Newspapers such as the *Nevada Gazette*, *Nevada Journal* and *Nevada Democrat* also shed led light on the Cornish presence in Grass Valley and Nevada City, detailing as they do births, deaths and marriages. As ever, the pain of personal tragedy is conveyed across the years. In October 1869, for example, poor little Lillie Bennallack, aged five years and six months, died at Grass Valley – her father, Mark, had been killed the previous year when he fell down a shaft at the Eureka Mine where he was underground captain. On 4 March 1864 Nicholas Oates, nearly seven years old, died of scarlet fever at Nevada City. A week later his three-year old brother, William, succumbed to the same disease, no doubt to the immense distress of his parents, Samuel and Harriet Oates. Both distressing and depressing is the catalogue of children lost to another unlucky couple, Henry Scadden and Mary Yendel. Henry junior died in 1857 at Grass Valley, to be followed by William in 1858, Samuel in 1864, Amanda in 1865, Jacob in 1867, and Ellen in 1869. Mining accidents, inevitably, took their toll. William Gribble, a Cornishman, had only just arrived in Grass Valley from Brazil when he was killed underground in October 1868. In April in the same year, Josiah Mitchell lost his life in an accident in the New York Hill Mine in Grass Valley – it is said that his wife, who had been in poor health for some time, died of shock when she heard the terrible news. Happier events were marriages which brought Cornish couples together, strengthening on the Sierra Nevada the sense of Cornish kinship and solidarity, as in February 1867 when Mahala Carbis was joined in holy matrimony to Richard Rowe, or when in May 1869 Lemniah Champion married Joseph Harry, or when Mary Anna Kitto and William George 'tied the knot' in July 1869. Paradoxically, this bonding of Cornish couples did not suppress the desire to 'become American', the newspapers recording a steady stream of naturalisations – Thomas Crase in June 1867, John Rundle in October 1868, Sampson Bolitho in July 1869, Joseph Polglase and William Prisk in August 1869, and so on.[35]

Many biographical sketches have survived of these early Cornish immigrants. James Williams, for example, arrived in Grass Valley in 1862 and worked in several of the major mines – the Eureka, the New York Hill, the North Star, and the famous Empire Mine. He married Mary Cheynouth (sic – probably Chynoweth, a Cornish name), with whom he had four children. Another Cornish couple, John Bree and his wife Mary Tredinnick, acquired a 400-acre property of dense bushland on the outskirts of Grass Valley, which they partly cleared to make an orchard. Bree was also one of the discoverers of the claim that became the rich Idaho-Maryland mine, though he sold his share before the property had developed its true worth. Samuel Blight arrived at Grass Valley at the age of 18, working in both deep hard-rock quartz mining and the environmentally destructive hydraulic extractive process which used high pressure water jets at surface to dislodge gold deposits. Frank Hooper, another Cousin Jack, became superintendent of the mill at the Empire Mine, eventually retiring to a 975-acre farm that he had acquired in Mendocino County. William Luke arrived in Grass Valley in 1863. His daughter married John James, born in Hayle in 1848, and after 15 years as a miner in Grass Valley James purchased 360 acres of land in nearby French Ravine.

As in Wisconsin, the Cornish miner-turned-farmer had become a familiar figure and other Cousin Jacks and Jennys settled into a variety of occupations. In

1884, for example, it was said of Grass Valley in the *West Briton* that 'The Cornishmen here are not engaged exclusively in mining. The signs over almost all stores bear Cornish names, and several of the businessmen hold responsible positions in the county and State.'[36] Henry Luke was an exemplar. Born at Carnhell Green in West Cornwall in 1849, he arrived in Grass Valley at the age of 16. He followed mining for all of 17 years but gave it up to join John Best in the shoe-selling business. Later, he disposed of this interest to become a purveyor of 'dry goods' in Grass Valley, later still opening the Empire Restaurant in the same town. Like many other Cornishmen, Luke was an enthusiastic freemason, a member of the grandly named Weimer Tribe of Red Men. When Luke died in 1902, it was the Red Men who made all the necessary arrangements for his funeral at Grass Valley's Congregational Church.[37]

But for all their success as farmers and as businessmen, it was as miners that the Cornish had established their reputation, especially as the individual prospecting ventures of the early gold rush days gave way to the intervention of outside capital from San Francisco and elsewhere, leading to the installation of mining machinery and the requirement for more sophisticated techniques. In 1861 the *Grass Valley National* declared Grass Valley 'the Cornwall of California', for 'mining is for the most part carried on by Cornishmen.'[38] By 1866, with improved overland communications to San Francisco, it was said that at Grass Valley 'the very best Cornish miners could be had for 3.50 dollars a day',[39] such was the attraction of the Californian gold-fields for the emigrant Cornish. A few years later, in 1871, the *Grass Valley Union* stated that:

> The Cornishman is probably the most skilful foreign miner that comes to our shores ... [he] is of quiet disposition, although very headstrong ... [Cornish miners] are mostly stalwart, good-look-ing fellows, dress better than any other class of miners and are very fond of women. They also appear more clannish than any other foreigners and a majority of them are very good singers. When they visit a saloon they generally arrange themselves around a table, call for a pot of ale or porter, and pass the time away in anecdote and song.[40]

Similar qualities and behaviour were observed in the churches and chapels. F.D. Calhoon's *Coolies, Kanakas, and Cousin Jacks* provides a popular but informative insight into the origins of ethnic stereotyping in Grass Valley and Nevada City. In a perhaps apocryphal but nonetheless telling story he emphasises the Cornish cultural dominance in Grass Valley. According to Calhoon, Daniel Collins, an Ulster Protestant born in Belfast in 1827 where he trained for the ministry, had left Ireland for America during the potato famine. Like many others, he made his way to California during the gold rush, where he engaged (unsuccessfully) in prospecting and in ministering (with greater success) to the spiritual needs of the diggers. Inevitably, in Grass Valley he came up against the Cornish, adopting as a result a sort of 'if you can't beat 'em, join 'em' strategy:

> The Cornishmen were strong Methodists, but Collins had very little quarrel with their theology. He could debate them as to the interpretation of some passages of the Bible, but he could not compete with their close-knit organization, nor with the financial backing of their own church ... shortly they had built him a fine building for his services, and a parsonage for his living quarters.[41]

Like Methodism, Cornish wrestling was an important badge of Cornish identity, with contests held at Grass Valley and elsewhere on the Fourth of July and other celebratory occasions. Joseph Taylor Williams, born in St Erth in 1830, was described in his obituary in the *Cornish Telegraph* as 'well known in wrestling circles throughout Cornwall, Devon and California', an opinion echoed in Grass Valley, 'At Cornish wrestling he had not an equal in his day at anywhere near his weight. He appeared in many tournaments here during the latter fifties and sixties, defeating all comers.'[42] And if prowess in the wrestling ring was an important signifier of Cornishness for Cousin Jack, then culinary expertise in Cornish fare was just as important for Cousin Jenny. In advanced old age in the 1980s, Loretta Henwood Trathen recalled with pride and nostalgia her grandmother's skill at preparing clotted cream in Grass Valley in the years before the First World War: 'If there was enough milk, Grandma would make Cornish Cream. The pan would be put on the back end of the stove, and it was there for hours. When it got to be glassy and wrinkly, Grandma knew it was done. She'd put the pan down in the cellar, and on the third day it was skimmed.'[43] As the populations of Grass Valley, Nevada City and environs grew, so such cultural signifiers became all the more important. Mann notes that 'The influx of Cornish miners ... contributed to another new phenomenon: the segregation of white ethnic groups. For the first time, in the late 1860s, two European-born groups, the Cornish and Irish, began to congregate in distinct areas',[44] forming recognisably 'Cornish' or 'Irish' precincts. As time went on:

> The white foreign-born, mostly Cornish, Irish, and German, still maintained separate identities in the two towns. Stereotypical ethnic images – sly Jews, brawling Irishmen, clannish Cornishmen – had not dimmed. And as the numbers and wealth of the foreign-born increased, distinct ethnic organisations began to function: B'nai B'rith for Jews, Wallace Monument Clubs for Scots, Gesangverein for Germans, Cornish wrestling meets and commemoration in 1859 of Burns and Schiller's centenaries shared newspaper space with accounts of High Holy Days, Chinese New Year, and St Patrick's Day.[45]

Such cultural differences, and the prejudices and fears that they sometimes engendered, could lead to violence – 'Irish and Americans shot it out over mining claims ... Irish fought pitched battles with both Cornish and Germans'[46] – but the several groups could also participate in and learn from each others customs, such as when the Irish, Germans and Americans all turned out to watch the Cornish wrestling bouts, or when the German Glee Club was invited to sing at civic events. Additionally, as Mann explains, 'the Cornish were of all the large foreign groups the most similar in appearance, values, and religion to the American-born ... the most accustomed to the emerging industrial mining life, and, because of their skills in hard-rock mining, the most vital to economic development, entered easily into town society.'[47] However, despite this ability to merge successfully in American society, the Cornish were especially sensitive about their reputation, the myth of Cousin Jack insisting that their superior skills be afforded due deference by others and that the competing claims of other ethnic groups, especially in the workplace, be resisted firmly. Ralph Mann again, 'Their prickly sense of self had helped involve the Cornish in ethnic brawls from the first days in the towns, and their pugnaciousness did not diminish as their numbers rose.'[48]

Such characteristics were in part behind the miners' strike at Grass Valley in 1869. Cornish prowess and self-pride were dependent to a degree on the skilful use of gunpowder in blasting and on 'double-jacking', the practice whereby one miner wielded a heavy sledge hammer while his 'pard' turned the drill bit. However, in the late 1860s, some Californian mines toyed with the possibility of introducing dynamite ('giant powder') and, because dynamite only required a small drill hole, of encouraging 'single-jacking' in which the miner worked on his own. Achieving greater economies lay behind both these innovations, as did a tougher approach in the same period towards the Cornish practice of 'high-grading', the habit of keeping some of the gold-bearing rock they had found for themselves, rather than handing it over to the company. Curiously, under Californian law this was not theft, merely trespass. Only when the rock had been broken down in the company's mill was the removal of gold considered theft. The normal practice was that, if the miner had uncovered a rich patch of ground, he would turn it all over to the company. But if the ground were poor and of relatively little consequence, he would keep it all for himself.[49] Although there is some debate as to just how widespread high-grading was among the Cornish, there is no doubt that it was a source of friction in the Californian mines, not least in the late 1860s as tension grew over dynamite and single-jacking.

For the Cornish, all this was a potential attack upon their status and privileges and the sanctity of their own practices. They protested that dynamite was a health hazard – its fumes, it was alleged, caused headaches – while single-jacking was, they insisted, inherently and inevitably inefficient. However, on 21 April 1869 the Star Spangled Banner mine at Grass Valley introduced both of these 'evils', an example followed shortly by the Empire and North Star mines. Aware, perhaps, of the strike action taken by their countrymen in recent years in both Cornwall and South Australia, and taking their cue from the successful formation of a Miners' League on the Comstock Lode in the neighbouring State of Nevada, the Cornish prepared to resist the innovations. Under the leadership of Captain Thomas Faull they formed a Grass Valley branch of the Comstock League, telegraphing Gold Hill (near Virginia City) for help. In the May the branch was reconstituted as the Miners' Union of Grass Valley, with another Cousin Jack, Philip Paynter, as President. On Monday 10 May the workers at the Empire Mine, 'probably the most predominantly Cornish-staffed one in the quartz region',[50] as John Rowe described it, went on strike. At the North Star the company locked-out all those who had joined the union. Anti-Cornish sentiment expressed by some newspapers fuelled the flame of conflict, arousing American indignation against a Cornish intransigence that was standing in the way of American progress. Editors mocked the Cornish belief that 'mining has been brought to perfection in Cornwall, and no improvement is possible on their systems',[51] and they made fun of the Cornish accent, accusing the Cousin Jacks of both ignorance and arrogance. Recognising that the Cousin Jack myth was about to backfire on them, the Cornish steered the debate away from the defence of traditional practices and towards health issues. They also demanded a flat rate of $3 a day for all underground workers, a device designed to secure the support (as indeed it did, albeit temporarily) of the Irish and other European groups. Pan-European solidarity was also encouraged by focusing discontent upon the Chinese, who were said to be keeping down wage rates.

For all the heat that had been generated, the strike ended quietly enough. Some miners, believing their own propaganda and fearing that the Chinese would take their jobs, drifted back to work. The mine companies, for their part, undertook not to use dynamite but reserved the right to experiment with new explosives, while the trade union conceded the companies' right to introduce single-jacking. Although only a partial victory, the Cornish considered that they had won. The Miners' Union secured its position in Grass Valley, with perhaps as many as 700 members employed in local mines.

However, by the early 1870s Grass Valley's boom times appeared to be over, with many Cornish miners moving on to the Comstock country. Elsewhere in California, where the Cornish had not been so strong, mine companies had introduced dynamite, the only sustained opposition being at Sutter's Creek where the Cornish were to be found in some numbers. And then in 1872 the Eureka Mine at Grass Valley introduced dynamite, precipitating a disastrous strike in which the Cornish and Irish failed to make common cause. Again, Americans expressed indignation that the Cornish had the audacity to stand in the way of progress, an attitude we detect as late as 1963 in Paul's history of the western mining frontier where he notes the 'nationalistic prejudice' of the Cornish and argues that it was the Sutter's Creek disturbances of 1871 and the Grass Valley strike of 1872 that alerted the American citizenship to what was going on: 'Only then did the public awake to the realization that Grass Valley had become a Cornish town and that Sutter's Creek was a mixture of Irish, Cornish, Austrians and Italians. At the workers' level, both communities were ruled as much by hereditary European attitudes as by American thinking.'[52]

In the years after 1872 the Cornish maintained their hold on employment opportunities in the Grass Valley mines in good times and bad but also, like the many Cornish who had already taken out American citizenship, they devised new strategies that would allow them to be both Cornish and American and thus avoid the objections of suspicious detractors. In many respects this plan was successful; for example, in the exploits of the Grass Valley Cornish Choir. Although Cornish carols had been sung at Grass Valley and elsewhere in California for many years, it was not until 1890 that the choir was formed formally. It met at the Methodist church and, although some tunes were committed to paper in fading pencil in a few notebooks, it was essentially an oral tradition, passed on from one individual to another and from one generation to the next. In this way, renditions of carols such as the famous 'Diadem' retained their essential Cornish characteristics but also developed local features, acquiring an American quality which both 'depoliticised' the Cornish content and won the attention and esteem of the nation as a whole. Under the committed leadership of Harold George, a second generation Cornish-American (his father was from St Austell), the choir emerged briefly as a national institution when in 1940 it broadcast Cornish carols across the United States (and Canada) from the 2000-foot level in the Idaho-Maryland Mine. So successful was this venture that it was repeated after the Second World War, with a record cut to preserve the carols for posterity and with the choir itself invited to perform in a variety of locations, from the State Capitol in Sacramento to Virginia City in Nevada and the Shattuck Avenue Methodist Church in Oakland.

Meanwhile, the sense of Cornish kinship had endured. On the eve of the First World War it was said of one visitor to Grass Valley that 'It then almost seemed that he had stepped into a foreign country. Fully three-quarters of the people were of Cornish birth or descent.'[53] Indeed, before and during the Second World War, and in the years leading up to the final closure of the Empire Mine in 1956, the local miners and their families retained a certain Cornish consciousness, 'proud that their grandfathers had been among the first of the "Cousin Jacks" brought to California from Cornwall.'[54] This identity was kept alive by the periodic infusion of newcomers from Cornwall itself, miners who had escaped the dreadful conditions of the inter-war years in the Old Country and who had been drawn to Grass Valley by the promise (by and large accurate) of preferential treatment for Cousin Jacks. Ed Farley, for example, had emigrated from St Just-in-Penwith to Flint, Michigan, to join his brother who was already out there. But the Depression hit in 1929 and, as Farley recalled, 'Thousands were lined up outside the Buick and Chevrolet factories, and people were eating out of garbage cans.'[55] His friend and colleague, John Hollow, also from St Just, had encountered identical conditions in Detroit but had gone on to Ely in northern Minnesota where he found work among the Cousin Jacks in the iron mines. Suitably encouraged by Hollow's success, in February 1930 – with the temperature at Ely 40 degrees below freezing – Ed Farley made his way to Minnesota, where he lodged with a Mr Pengelly who had been his Sunday School teacher back in Cornwall. From Ely, Hollow and Farley decided to try their luck in Grass Valley, arriving there in 1933 where – as Cousin Jacks – work was quickly found for them.

But for as long as such preferential treatment existed, critics of the Cousin Jacks would continue to make themselves heard. Calhoon complained that 'The Cousin Jacks were mostly Methodists of the extremely anti-Catholic variety', adding provocatively that, 'In fact, as late as 1928, crosses were burned on the hillsides of western Nevada County by members of the Ku Klux Klan. It took no intellectual genius to work out to which group the Klansmen belonged.'[56] Similarly, Calhoon recorded the story which accounted (to his satisfaction at least) for the otherwise inexplicable rendering of George McKnight, the discoverer of gold at Grass Valley in 1850, as George Knight on a commemorative monument erected in 1929. Knight is a common enough name in Cornwall and, according to Calhoon, '"Damn'e", said the Cousin Jack chairman of the committee which had the plaque cast, "we're not about to let a Pope lovin' Irishman get the credit for such a momentous event. Anyways, no one 'cept a good man from Cornwall wouldst 'av 'ad the sense to know gold in the rock when 'e sees it"'.[57]

Some years earlier, before the First World War, Frank Crampton, a young American hard-rock miner, had conspired to bring these opinionated Cornish down a peg or two. His friend, Jack Commerford, an experienced Irish shift boss:

> had drifted to Grass Valley where he worked for a time in the North Star. He told me of a couple of Cousin Jacks who thought they were good, and boasted that they were going to Butte [Montana] to drill in the contests to be held on Labor Day. They were second-raters, according to Jack. Would I team up with him, go to Grass Valley, get a job, and work up an argument with them so that they would challenge us?[58]

As Crampton went on to explain:

> Jack and I went to Grass Valley and got on at the North Star ... Those Cousin Jacks were a clannish lot, but broke down when they got to talking about their 'champion' double-jack team, and of how good they were. From the manner in which the virtue of the 'champions' was extolled, nothing to equal their prowess had ever appeared before. In reality the boastful 'champions' had never been in any contest to prove that they had been the best double-jack team in Grass Valley, but their

followers had been so enthusiastic that the other teams didn't dispute the claims.[59]

As Crampton had hoped, the Cousin Jacks were goaded into offering a challenge, with high monetary stakes to boot, and elaborate arrangements were made for the match, 'The contest was a gala event ... The confidence of the Cousin Jacks increased until the time for the contest drew near. How could a Cousin Jack team lose against an Irishman, and a kid still wet behind the ears?'[60] But lose they did:

> We had put our hole down forty-three and seven-eights inches, the champions forty-one and five eighths. To be beaten by over two inches was too much for those Cousin Jacks .... Those holes were measured, not once but several times, before the champions were satisfied they were beaten. Once I thought they were going to claim our hole as theirs .... It would take those Cousin Jacks, and their friends, months of work in the mines to get back what they had lost, even by combining pay with what they would pocket in high-grade. Our popularity had never been great, but it reached its lowest tide in Grass Valley that night ... We learned later that the Grass Valley "champions" decided not to go to Butte that year.[61]

By the early years of the 20th century, when Crampton and Commerford were standing up to the Cornish, the great days of Cornwall's mining pre-eminence had disappeared long since, the myth of Cousin Jack already living on borrowed time, Cornish claims to superior status seeming increasingly hollow. And just as the skills of individual Cornishmen were called into question, so too was the whole range of Cornish technology. In particular, the Cornish beam engine, lauded half-a-century or so before as the perfect application of high-pressure steam to the problems of deep mining, was now seen as a ponderous and out-dated monster ill-equipped for the demands of California. The insistence several decades before by a generation of Cornish mining captains throughout the Americas and Australia that mines could be made to pay only through the immediate installation of heavy Cornish pumping, winding and stamping machinery, had fuelled a certain scepticism, even cynicism, among the Cornishmen's detractors which was vented fully as new technologies came along to replace the old. Thus in 1908 the *Mining and Scientific Press* declared that 'it is inconceivable that the Cornish pump can successfully compete with the more modern steam or electric pumping plants',[62] an opinion expressed more forcibly by Otis E. Young Jr who observed that:

> Over the years the Cornish pump became ever more complicated but no whit more reliable ... it is as well to note that the claim that Cornish pumps were uncommonly economical to operate (nine cents per ton of water raised) was usually founded on an analysis of fuel consumption while disingenuously omitting such matters as capitalization and installation, maintenance, and general losses to the operation occasioned by down time for frequent overhaul and major repair.[63]

This assessment was echoed by Roger R. Lescohier in his discussion of *The Cornish Pump in the California Gold Mines*, who thought that 'The Cornish Pump was an outlandish device, huge, awkward, expensive to install, very complex and requiring constant inspection and maintenance. Its only redeeming virtue was its ability to remove substantial quantities of water from the deepest recesses of a mine.'[64] That said, Lescohier recognised that, despite their vast dimensions and the enormous expense of installation, the Cornish engines were the best technology available at the time. Moreover, in California they were expertly 'modified to suit local conditions by the American engineers.'[65] To avoid the difficulties and costs of moving massive machinery over difficult terrain, and of erecting it in giant purpose-built engine houses, 'The Californian shops redesigned the above-ground machinery ... They made the steam engines much smaller and faster running, and then provided a large flywheel ... Such steam engines were lower and required a building that was no more than a shelter from the weather.'[66] Approval for this 'Californian' version of the Cornish engine was mirrored in similar satisfaction with the 'Californian stamps' (used in the crushing of ore), developed locally from the familiar 'Cornish stamps', not least by the Sunnyvale firm of Joshua Hendy. Hendy, of course, is a Cornish name, and among the many who employed his stamping mills was Cornishman William Craddock who installed a set at his Hattie No.2 Mine (the 'Bug Mine') at Placerville around the turn of the century.[67]

This 'Americanisation' of Cornish technology was a metaphor for the wider convergence of Cornish and American culture in California – the inanimate, mechanical equivalent, perhaps, of the Grass Valley Cornish Choir. At any rate, Shirley Ewart concluded that, 'In the early days "Cousin Jack" evoked envy, jealousy and even hatred, for it seemed that every position in the mine was reserved for yet another "Cousin" from Cornwall.' And yet:

> In the end, they [the Cornish] found they had developed new roots in California and most Cornish eventually became American citizens. Especially they valued the opportunities that America provided for their children; they made sure that their children would get the education they themselves had never had, and when a son or daughter finished high school, or a grandchild went off to college, the Cornish family had realized its dream.[68]

Grass Valley, like Moonta in South Australia, was seen as the epitome of this Cornish experience. But in fact the Cousin Jacks and Jennys were to be found across California – not only in neighbouring Nevada City or in the larger Mother Lode towns such as Placerville but in a scattering of smaller settlements where they had also made their mark. In the northern Sierra Nevada county of Plumas, for example, was Johnsville, named after a Cornishman, one William Johns, who was – according to the *Illustrated History of Plumas County* of 1882 – 'a popular superintendent of the mines.'[69] The township grew up around the Sierra Buttes Company's gold-mine, the Plumas-Eureka, first started in 1876. Richard Smitheram, born in Breage in 1839, was one of Johnsville's Cousin Jacks. In 1861 he married Jennifer Richards, also of Breage, and their sons Richard Jr and William were born in 1862 and 1865 respectively. These were dark days for mining in Cornwall, and so in 1866 Richard Smitheram set out for Mexico, arriving eventually at Pachuca where – according to one of his letters – 'After a series of adverse conditions during our voyage, I rejoiced in reaching the mines where I found a Cousin Jack as the mine captain. I soon felt home along with the Cornish miners and their families.'[70] Richard saved hard but he soon realised that he would never have enough to bring his family out to Mexico. He decided to return to Cornwall and, travelling by mule to the Pacific port of Mazatian, joined a ship bound for San Pedro, California, on what was to be the first step on a long and circuitous journey home. On arrival in California he heard that miners were being recruited for the cinnabar workings near Santa Barbara, and he duly signed-up, earning additional funds to pay for the trip to Cornwall. Eventually, travelling by way of San Francisco and Panama, he reached Cornwall in July 1870 – only to find that many of his friends and relatives had left Breage for the iron mines at Millom in Cumberland. Richard and his family followed in their wake, and in Millom three more children were born – Thomas, Eliza, and Frank.

Then, in early 1884, enticed by encouraging letters from a Cornish friend in Plumas County, Richard Smitheram and his two eldest sons – Richard Jr and William – set out once more for California, bound this time for Johnsville. As Richard wrote on 1 June 1884:

> Arrived in Johnsville at noon thru high snow drifts along the road way. Very cold here. Met John Willoughby who owns a store; he said the snow pack was sixteen feet deep in front of his place in January. He and his brothers came here a few years ago from Cornwall. One brother has a meat house, the other runs a hotel, the Mountain House. We located the mine captain, William Hoskings, who seemed pleased to see us; he arranged for us to ride up the mountain side to Eureka Mills, where I have a promised job as timberman in the mine tunnels. Dick and Will were hired as miners.[71]

In August 1886 Jennifer and the younger children arrived from Cornwall, completing the settlement of the Smitheram family in California. Later, in 1896, Richard and Jennifer moved to Santa Barbara in the southern part of the state. Son William and his wife Florence also made the move south, arriving in the borax-mining district of Borate in the Calico Mountains north of the Mojave River in 1899 where William was to work as a mine captain. Florence kept a notebook in which she recorded aspects of life at Borate. She wrote that 'Many nationalities were represented over the years, all good workers for the most part: American, Cornish, English, Irish, Welsh, Greek, Dutch, German, French, Italian, Bohemian and Scandinavian', but her most detailed observations were reserved for the Cornish:

> the Cornish miners retained their speech mannerisms which were always amusing to me. They called tea leaves 'Brownshans' and coffee dregs 'Grishans'. There was no hard liquor available in Borate but sometimes the miners brought in their own ale. If one became tipsy he was said to be 'Tadly Odly'. If a man was helped into camp unable to walk straight, he was 'Prilled' .... We depended on many

home remedies for common ailments. I had no experience in relieving childhood colic and fever until an old Cornish miner advised that rhubarb brandy would cure the problem.[72]

Further north, in the Mother Lode gold country, the Cornish were also remembered for their distinctive habits, for example at Coulterville, lying to the west of Yosemite on the road north from Mariposa. Here, according to one contemporary report, 'many Cornish miners were employed who were highly skilled in the use of hammer and drill.' The inevitable Fourth of July contests put these attributes to the test, and 'Especially skilled were Joseph Broan and Edward Pope. These Cornishmen were exemplary citizens and powerful men',[73] and they were hailed as the champion drillers of Coulterville. In Soulsbyville, not far away in the district of Sonora, the Cornish in the period 1860–1890 constituted some 80 per cent of the local population, 'it was hard to find miners from any other ethnic group working there, and nearly all of them had family ties or cultural and religious backgrounds that welded them into a singularly homogenous group.'[74] Methodism guided the life of many, as it did in Cornwall, the *Tuolumne Independent* newspaper claiming in May 1877 that 'Soulsbyville is entitled to rank as the model mining camp of this county. Soulsbyville people are pious, and go to church regular. They are prosperous, hence their piety. Marriageable girls are no longer a curiosity there.'[75]

Behind the sometimes conflicting stereotypes of the Cornish – as model Americans or clannish obstructors of progress, as religious extremists or paragons of pious virtue – we see in California a coherent experience in which the Cornish emerged early as a significant ethnic group. Already in North America in large numbers, they had descended on the Californian gold-fields in the earliest days of the Rush, their ranks swollen further by arrivals from Cornwall as the emergence of deep, hard-rock quartz mining in the 1860s and 1870s increased Californian reliance on Cornish skills and Cornish technology. But although Cousin Jacks could expect to find preferential treatment at Grass Valley mines as late as the 1920s and 1930s, the emergence and application of new (non-Cornish) techniques and technologies, together with the rapid decline of Cornwall itself as the centre of mining prowess, made overt assertions of Cornishness somehow less convincing while further encouraging the process of Americanisation. In California, as in Wisconsin and on 'the Lakes', the Cornish retained an ethnic sense of self but found themselves conforming to – and profiting from – the demands of American citizenship.

# CHAPTER SEVEN

# GOLD!

# THE VICTORIAN RUSH

The Californian rush in 1848 precipitated a worldwide frenzy. International attention was focused suddenly on the possibilities of new gold discoveries in other frontier societies throughout the world. There was a spate of gold rushes across the globe – some minor, some more enduring – but the big one was in the Australian colony of Victoria in late 1851. In many ways, the Victorian rush looked like a re-run of the Californian bonanza. As in America, there were already substantial numbers of Cornish in Australia – especially in the neighbouring copper-mining colony of South Australia, a ready-made reservoir of expertise and experience from which the Victorian gold-fields might draw. Moreover, as Victorian gold-mining developed its own deep-quartz characteristics in the 1860s and, particularly the 1870s, so – as in California at the same time and in very similar conditions – Cornish skills and technologies became even more in demand. And while many of Victoria's Cousin Jacks came from Cornwall directly, or from neighbouring South Australia, there was also more than a sprinkling from California itself. As Geoffrey Blainey, Australia's foremost mining historian, put it – heaping praise on 'the bold Cornishmen and Californians, the innovators in Victorian mining' – it was 'Bendigo's great Cornish managers and miners [who] mastered easily the problems of deep-sinking.'[1]

And yet, in another comparison with California, gold had in fact been discovered in Australia in advance of the Victorian rush. As we saw in Chapter 2, there were Cornish folk among the free settlers enticed to New South Wales in the 1820s and 1830s, and they were to play an important part in the New South Wales gold rush of early 1851. As early as 1829 William Tom, born in Bodmin in 1791, and William Lane, both Cornish and related by marriage, had arrived in the colony. They took up land in an isolated valley some 28 miles west of Bathurst at a place they called 'Cornish Settlement'.[2] George Hawke, another Cornishman, travelled with them, and in 1830 John Glasson, also a Cousin

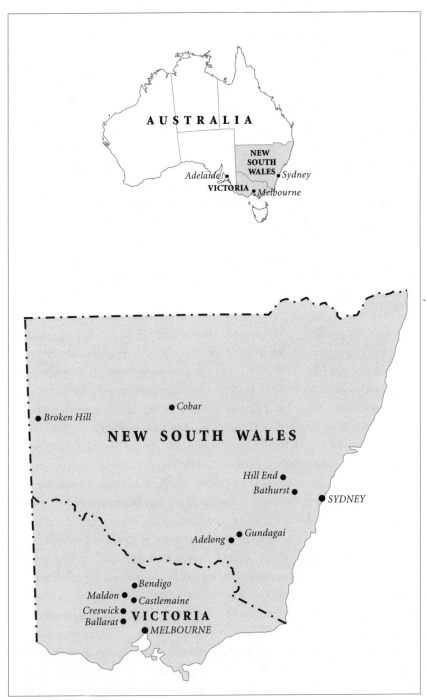

*Principal mining locations in Victoria and New South Wales*

Jack, arrived at Cornish Settlement with his family. Others from Cornwall included Richard Grenfell from St Just-in-Penwith, Robert Smith from St Keverne, Edmund Harvey from Camelford, Nicholas and Joanna Bray, Thomas and Mary Geake, John and Catherine Hawken, Walter and Mary Bryant, William and Dorothy Dale, Johanna and John Barrett, William Bishop, the Pearses, the Paulls, the Thomases, the Shorts, the Webbs, the Sloggetts and the Oateses. Farm names such as 'Pendarves', 'Godolphin', 'Rosemerrin', and 'Tremearne' were evidence of a strong Cornish impact at Cornish Settlement, as was the predominance of Wesleyan Methodism, reflected in the early construction there of a typically modest Cornish chapel. Years later, William Tom's grandson recalled that at Cornish Settlement, 'in my boyhood, I was taught to revere two things, John Wesley, and Cornwall .... All our relations and neighbours were Cornish, many being local preachers, Class leaders and Sunday School Teachers, good earnest men and women, some of them, I feel sure believed there was no place in heaven except for Wesleyans.'[3]

These families settled into a gentle pastoral life linked to the rhythms of the year and the passing of the seasons. But all this changed with the sudden discovery of copper at Cornish Settlement in 1849. Copper had already been found at Copper Hill (Molong) in 1845 and (together with some lead) in the neighbourhood of Bathurst in 1846. In 1848 Captain James Budge Clymo and 15 miners were brought out from Cornwall in the *Elphinstone* to work the Copper Hill deposits. Other Cornish miners were brought in from South Australia and by August 1850 John Glasson was able to describe the 'Cornish Mines' (as he called them) of New South Wales, 'I have now six miners employed, all tributors. Mr Lane has eleven. We have an engine house built for a five horse power engine and machinery all the way from Sydney, also a practical smelter to manage the smelting.'[4] Although the attempt at local smelting was a failure, the news of the copper discoveries at Cornish Settlement had expanded the population to several hundred strong, still predominantly Cornish in make up. It was decided to export the copper ore for smelting elsewhere, and in January 1851 a dray full of copper left Cornish Settlement, 'surmounted with a small banner bearing the Cornish coat of arms, with the motto "One and All" inscribed.'[5]

But in the very same month, Edward Hammond Hargraves, a veteran of the Californian rush, arrived in Australia in the neighbouring village of Guyong. He met up with William Tom Jr, to whom he taught the mysteries and techniques of gold seeking, and together with one William Lister and the other Tom brothers – James and Henry, they stumbled across payable gold deposits at Ophir, some 16 miles away. By May 1851, in the aftermath of the Hargraves/Tom discovery, a vigorous gold rush was sweeping the colony, putting such places as Ophir, Turon, Home Rule, Gundagai and Gulgong on to the map of New South Wales. News travelled fast, the *Sydney Morning Herald* declaring that at Bathurst 'A complete mental madness appears to have seized ... the community ... there has been a universal rush to the diggings.'[6] This assessment was echoed by the *Bathurst Free Press* which wrote that 'Men meet together, stare stupidly at each other, talk incoherent nonsense, and wonder what will happen next.'[7] The rush was underway!

In South Australia, these developments had been watched closely by the Burra Burra miners and several of the colony's Cousin Jacks decided to try their luck in New South Wales. The Alpha Mine at Hill End, for example, attracted a number of men from the Burra – as ever, they are distinguished by their tell-tale Cornish surnames – Lobb, Jeffree, Pasco, Clymo, Trevena, Hawke, Uren, Penhall, Nicholls, Roberts, Inch, Curnow, Blewett, Northey, Treglown, Bath, Carceek, Trestrail, Thomas and so on. The departure of these miners from the Burra had a visible effect on the size and activity of the local population, one James Jenkins writing home to Truro in Cornwall that 'A great number have left this place to go to the Sydney gold-fields.'[8] At Callington, in the Adelaide Hills, there was also a small-scale exodus, Absolom Tonkin, from St Blazey, among others heading off for Turon and Ophir. Later, Tonkin made his way to the Victorian gold-fields, eventually returning to South Australia where he opened a general store in Callington. That the Cornish were soon an integral and prominent part of the gold-fields communities is suggested in the 1850s folk-song 'Nine Miles from Gundagai', in which the principal character sports a Cornish name:

> As I was walking down the road
> I heard a lady say,
> 'Here's Joe Rule, the bullocky bloke,
> He's bound for Gundagai.[9]

In Sydney itself, the Cornish tended to cluster in identifiable communities within the main streets of the city – such as Castlereagh, Clarence, Dixon, Elizabeth, George, Gloucester, Goulbourn, Hunter, Kent, King, Liverpool, Macquarie, Market, Pitt, Princes, and Sussex – indicating perhaps an ethnic propensity to 'stick together' in the busy and sometimes bewildering urban and metropolitan environment. As the years passed, Sydney remained a magnet for Cornish people arriving in New South Wales. Among their number was John Garland Treseder, who as early as 1857 had been on the Victorian diggings, but who after a period back in Cornwall emigrated to New South Wales around 1870. A gardener by training, he founded his own nursery and set up a shop in Royal Arcade, Sydney. Among other things, he developed a new variety of camellia – *Camellia japonica thomas treseder* – and arranged for the red dracaena palms *Deacaena tresediana* and the exotic tree ferns *Dicksonia antarctica* to be exported to Cornwall. Here they helped stock the burgeoning semi-tropical gardens that were springing up in Cornish estates, testament to the scientific and artistic accomplishment of Cornwall but also a consequence of the Great Emigration.[10]

The Cornish were most especially 'visible', however, in the gold-mining communities that sprung up after the discoveries of early 1851. At Bathurst, situated on the western bank of the Macquarie River, the other side of the Blue Mountains from Sydney, the Cornish were already present as components of the district's farming communities. As copper and then gold were discovered at scattered locations throughout the area, so other Cornish folk were attracted. In Bathurst itself, the Cornish were also active in the town's business community. William Trezise and Edmund Webb were both storekeepers, while Samuel Bray was a tailor and draper. William Tremain and Frederick Crago ran (rival) flour mills. At the Cow Flat copper mines, south of Bathurst, names such as Crabbe, Eady, Hocking, Kissel, Tonkin, and Youren indicated a strong Cornish presence. At Orange the Cornish were involved in farming, orcharding and mining and there was a significant flow between these activities. There were mines at Cadia, where a fine Cornish engine house stands to this day,[11] and at Lucknow, Icely and Canobolas, the Cornish were to be found at each of these places. William Selwood, for example, arrived from Cornwall in 1860 and worked as a miner at Cornish Settlement, Lucknow, and Cadia before later taking up land at Springside. Josiah Holman, another Cousin Jack, was mine captain at Cadia until 1864. He was at the Icely mine in 1869 but by 1889 had turned his hand to farming, back at Cadia.

These mining communities were not exclusively Cornish and at Hill End there was the usual sectarian strife and ethnic competition between the Cornish and Irish. As non-conformists and freemasons, many Cornish were attracted to the ranks of the Orange Order (in those days by no means confined to Ulster and Lowland Scotland) and at Hill End:

Battles on a collective basis occurred fairly regularly between the Cornish and Irish miners ... Sectarianism as well as national rivalry formed the basis of this ceremonial warfare. The 12th of July procession of the Orangemen with white horse, brass band and vulgar parodies on the song 'The Boyne Water' infuriated the Irishmen, as no doubt they were intended to.[12]

Further afield, the Cornish also turned up in New South Wales gold-mining communities, notably at Adelong in the foothills of the south-eastern uplands of the colony. In the early 1850s alluvial deposits had been worked in the Adelong Creek but deep quartz mining commenced in 1857. By 1879 there were some 500 miners at Adelong, with one of its suburbs known as Cornishtown on account of the large numbers of Cornish settled there. Many of the Cousin Jacks and Jennys had come out from Cornwall directly, but there were others from across Australia and even from California. Typical of their number was Richard White who, at the time of his death in 1903, had 'lived in Adelong 43 years, chiefly engaged in mining.'[13] Much further north, at Armadale, gold had been found along the Rocky River in 1852, and the Cornish turned up there and in other areas of New England district of New South Wales, including Hillgrove where some years later there were also significant discoveries of tin. As Patricia Lay has indicated in her study, chain migration of families, friends and neighbours from particular parts of Cornwall accounted for the cohesive qualities of the communities that they created across the mining and farming districts of New South Wales, a 'clannishness' perpetuated and enhanced by the tendency to intermarry within these groups. For example, a total of 76 assisted emigrants arriving in the colony between 1837 and 1877 gave their place of origin as St Neot or one of its surrounding parishes, a mixed moorland farming and mining district whose own 'frontier' characteristics might have been expected to equip its inhabitants for the hardships and rigours of the interior of New South Wales.[14] So noticeable was this chain migration, intermarriage, and the creation of Cornish communities that in 1860 the Rev. John Dunmore Lang, a contemporary commentator on colonial settlement policy, proposed the creation of a new colony, to be called 'New Cornwall', in the northern rivers district between 30 degrees and the Queensland border.[15]

Be that as it may, within the Cornish communities of New South Wales there was the usual array of distinctive cultural activities that marked them out as 'Cornish'. In the gold-mining town of Nundle in 1871 there were 'many

Cornishmen with good singing voices'.[16] Brass bands were popular among the Cornish at Hill End, Bathurst and elsewhere, while William Thomas, who emigrated in 1849, was later remembered for his 'great love ... for Cornwall' and his hearty rendering of 'the old Cornish songs'.[17] As elsewhere, Cornish wrestling was also an important badge of identity and an opportunity for the Cousin Jacks to demonstrate their 'manliness' and physical prowess. William Oates from St Keverne, who arrived in New South Wales in 1853 to work as a blacksmith and wheelwright at Guyong and Orange, was a noted Cornish wrestler. At Bathurst in 1861 a grand Boxing Day match, to be held at the Miners' Arms at Rockley, was advertised. The contest was 'to be played in Cornish style' but 'In order to give fair play to each individual, one umpire will be from Cornwall, one from Devon, and the other Australian'.[18] Methodism, inevitably, was an important element of cultural identity, and Cornish preachers, laymen and ordained alike, played a significant evangelising and missionary role on the New South Wales gold-fields, 'As soon as a township began to appear, a Methodist emissary would be there. A stump, a mound or a convenient corner did service for a pulpit, from which the "local" held forth. Next a room would be hired and then a primitive chapel built of slabs would be the forerunner of the more stately church.'[19]

The Cornish also became involved prominently in a range of friendly societies and freemasonry activity, not only in the Rechabites (which had a strong Cornish following at home and overseas) but in the Sons of Temperence, Oddfellows, the Druids, the American Order, the Orange Order and other organisations. Some became trade unionists, not least in the mining industry, and many were involved in a variety of public and community activities, from local government through to participation in the New South Wales Legislative Assembly where more than a hint of the Cornish Liberal-Nonconformist radical tradition could be detected. Patricia Lay has argued that, in embracing public life in this way, the Cornish were not only aiming to achieve 'respectability' within colonial society but were balancing a desire to retain (and assert when necessary) their 'Cornishness' while also aspiring to become 'good citizens' of their adopted country. Lay considers that this strategy was largely successful, the convergence of colonial and Cornish cultures ensuring that, while the Cornish were indeed active in the institutions of their new land, their ethnic identity was durable and was 'permanently and publicly declared in the simple phrase "native of Cornwall" which was inscribed on so many of their tombstones in New South Wales, half a world away from their homeland.'[20]

All of this, however, was a far cry from the heady days of early 1851 when gold

234

had been found so dramatically at Ophir by that symbolically significant Californian/Cornish partnership of Hargraves and Tom. And paradoxically, while one of the consequences of this find and the subsequent rush was the creation of a strong long-term Cornish presence on the New South Wales gold-fields, the Ophir discovery and its aftermath had the effect of precipitating an almost immediate rush to the neighbouring colony of Victoria. In fact, gold had been located at Clunes in that colony as early as March 1850 but little excitement was generated until the discoveries at Mount Alexander in July 1851 and at Ballarat in the August. In several respects, the Victorian gold rush was a response to that of New South Wales, occasioned by the alarm at the drain of population to Ophir, Turon and elsewhere, and Victoria's worthy citizens were determined to make the most of their own colony's strikes. The Victorians need not have worried. Despite the excitement in New South Wales, fewer than half the diggers there were making a decent living and many found themselves working as labourers for the minority of successful men: wages being from 30s to 40s per week, with anything up to £3 for Cornish miners. These folk needed little inducement to try their luck anew on the Victorian gold-fields, while in South Australia reports of the Mount Alexander and Ballarat discoveries abruptly shifted attention from New South Wales to Victoria.

By October 1851 Adelaide newspapers were proclaiming 'Gold in Abundance' in the neighbouring colony and, with business in South Australia being generally slack at the time, many were inclined to join this new rush.[21] By December 1851 some 5000-7000 gold seekers had arrived in Victoria from South Australia and Van Diemen's Land. Hardships suffered by these early diggers were compounded by the drought conditions of 1852, but this had the effect of dispersing people to new districts and thus facilitating further gold discoveries. In this way, in the country around Mount Alexander new fields were opened up at Fryer's Creek, Sailor's Gully, Campbell's Creek, Forest Creek, Ranter's Gully and Cobbler's Gully. In February 1852 there were some 30,000 people in and around Mount Alexander, with perhaps as many as 40,000 at Bendigo by the June. The South Australians, for their part, seemed to prefer the northern diggings around Bendigo – at one time there were no fewer than 4000 of them at Mount Alexander.

At first many of the Cornish miners at the Burra Burra mine in South Australia were sceptical about the news from Victoria. However, they sent a deputation to the gold-fields to investigate. Excitement grew when these advance scouts returned to the Burra with positive news and the ensuing departure from the Burra caused a mass exodus from all the other South Australian mines as well. In December 1851 it was noted that 100 miners had arrived in Adelaide from the Burra to join ships bound for Victoria and they were followed by others during January and February of 1852. In September 1852 the Burra mine clerk, G.W Vivian, resigned his position to join the rush, leaving as his forwarding address the 'Post Office, Bendigo.'[22] A fortnight later Captain Matthew Bryant was granted two months leave so that he too might visit the diggings and by the beginning of September 1852 the Burra mine, by now seriously starved of labour, was virtually at a standstill. As the *Mining Journal* noted, 'the attractions of the gold diggings began to tell upon the great copper mine, wooing away its lusty Cornishmen to Forest Creek and Bendigo.'[23]

Among their number was John Treloar, born in Helston in 1832, who had worked in Cornwall at the Trewavas Head Mine and in Great Wheal Vor before emigrating to South Australia with his brother James in 1849. Treloar and his Cornish friends roamed across Victoria, working claims at Golden Point, Pennyweight Hill, Winter's Flat, Sulky Gully and Buninyong before moving on to New Zealand. His sojourn there was brief, however, and soon he was back in Victoria as captain of the Carrick Range Mine. William Gummow, originally from Padstow, also left the Burra mine to go to Victoria, prospecting at Pegleg, Ironbark Gully and Forest Creek before loyally returning to restart the whim engine on Peacock's shaft. William Worden, born in Cornwall in 1826, was absent in Victoria from his Burra job for 15 months, while James Bone, originally from Bosullow Mill, near Morvah, also spent some months at Forest Creek. Richard Snell, another Burra miner, had only just returned from the Californian rush when news of the Victorian finds broke in South Australia, and soon he was off to try his luck afresh. Among the many others who also decided to seek their fortunes in the neighbouring colony were Cousin Jacks like John Dunstan from Stithians, Henry Pinch from St Mabyn and William Richards, born in Cornwall in 1833, who spent seven years at Ballarat and Bendigo. There was John Phillips from Wendron, together with James Thomas from Ludgvan, Ralph Kestel from Portreath, William Sandow from Chacewater and Stephen Carthew from Redruth. Even prominent Burra Methodists such as James Blatchford and Thomas Ninnes succumbed to the temptation of gold.

For those who could afford it, the journey by sea from Port Adelaide to Port Philip (Melbourne) was quick and relatively comfortable, in contrast to the difficult three to four week overland trek across the wilderness. John Whitford, for example, left Burra with his brothers, James and William, during 1852. The proud owners of a bullock dray, they had at least some advantage over others who had no alternative but to walk. The Whitford brothers set out on 9 October, stopping at the small country town of Macclesfield to load up with flour and bacon before venturing into the unknown. As they progressed eastwards across arid country they were troubled by a lack of feed and water for their bullocks, and John complained bitterly about the mosquitoes. There was swampy country which was difficult to negotiate, and 'the short desert which is 18 miles'. John wrote that 'the mosquitoes and sandflies was tormenting the bullocks'. The poor animals bolted into the bush, and the Whitford brothers spent the best part of the weekend rounding them up. The arrived finally at the Daisy Hill Diggings on Wednesday 10 November 1852, where they found their first gold. Six days later they moved on towards Bendigo, camping on the way at Bullock Creek where they met two of their Burra colleagues – Thomas Philips, who 'has done very well', and William Begolhall (sic) who 'has done first rate'. They were told that 'almost all the Burra people are at Forest Creek; Nicholas Tambling ... William Trevena, George Roberts and all the rest of the party', while 'Captain Matthew Bryant is working at Forest Creek by himself'. The Whitfords lived frugally on potatoes and 'heavy current cake' (typical Cornish fare), with mutton on Sundays. They were moderately successful, concluding that 'we do not wish ourselves back to the Burra again.'[24]

The exodus from the Burra, Kapunda and other mining camps was mirrored in the widespread departure from Adelaide itself of people from all walks of life intent on trying their luck in Victoria. Fears for the future viability of South Australia were unfounded, not least because of incipient surge in the colony's agricultural production in response to the expanding demand from Victoria, though one alarmed colonist could complain in February 1852 that: 'The discovery of gold has turned our little world upside down .... In Adelaide windows are bricked up, and outside is written "Gone to the Diggings".'[25] Towards the end of 1852 these Australian diggers were joined in Victoria by a new wave of immigrants from Britain, Europe and even California. These newcomers gave the diggings a decidedly cosmopolitan flavour (soon to be heightened by an influx of Chinese) but among their ranks were many Cousin Jacks and Jennys from Cornwall – and California – who served to strengthen the already sizeable Cornish contingent on the Victorian gold-fields. Like the South Australian diggers before them, these Cornish immigrants displayed a preference for the northern gold-fields. They were responsible for the White Hill rush in that district and

Long Gully – where only the Cornish miners had the expertise to exploit the newly discovered deep lodes – became known as 'Bendigo's Little Cornwall'. Long Gully was also known as a Methodist stronghold and as the home of Cornish wrestling, Cornish carols, Cornish pasties and saffron cake.

In October 1852 there was the Oven River rush – there were some 20,000 diggers on the river by the following January – and in the November the Korong rush broke out. New gold deposits were proclaimed at Canadian Gully, Ballarat, in January 1853, and the spate of discoveries continued into 1854. In Cornwall, there was intense interest in all this activity, Victoria by now having replaced both South Australia and California as the current focus of attention. Letters written home to Cornwall from Victoria helped to popularise the diggings, especially when they were reprinted in newspapers such as the *West Briton*. 'Tell Mr Stephens of Troon that the best thing for his sons is to send them to Australia',[26] was the advice offered by one correspondent, while in July 1852 the *Royal Cornwall Gazette* published an enthusiastic letter from a woman in Port Phillip (Melbourne) to her sister in Gulval, 'There are plenty of Cornish here and they are doing well. Several from the parish of Gulval have saved £10, £100 and £200 per man in a few weeks.'[27] Considerable excitement was caused in Cornwall by Cousin Jacks landing at harbours such as Penzance and Falmouth with seemingly fabulous amounts of Victorian gold. In April of 1852 some 70,000 ounces of gold, worth £25,000, were said to have been landed at the former port, where a little over a year later one recently returned Captain Mathews was proudly displaying his five-pound Victorian nugget. Local syndicates – such as the Devon and Cornwall Gold Miners' Company – were formed to organise and equip prospecting parties in Victoria, and Cornish newspapers were full of advertisements for such enterprises. A prospectus for a Melbourne Gold General Mining Association appeared in the *West Briton* in February 1852, while in the April the same newspaper was able to announce not only the landing of £80,000 worth of Victorian gold at Falmouth but also the departure from that harbour of the Port Phillip Gold Mining Association's party of Cornish miners (selected by Captain W. Richards of Redruth) in the barque *Augusta Schneider*. 'Wanted immediately to proceed to the Gold Diggings a few active healthy young men of good character .... Apply W.N. Hosking, Falmouth',[28] announced one advertisement, with another calling for a party of ten to twelve miners to accompany 'a Cornishman and two friends'[29] to Victoria.

During 1853 a Victorian Goldfields display was exhibited in Truro and

Falmouth and in February 1854 it was reported that 50 people had left St Ives for the Australian diggings. In July it was further noted that 100 St Just men were at Liverpool, bound for the rush. At first it had been mainly miners who had responded to the call of Victoria but by now Cornish people of all classes and occupations were clamouring to become Australian diggers. From Newlyn, for example, a party of seven fishermen sailed their small boat, the *Mystery*, all the way to Port Phillip during 1854–55 so that they too might visit the rush. Others tried to emulate the success of their adventure but not all were so lucky, the St Ives fishing boat *Snowdrop* disappearing mysteriously in the huge expanses of the Pacific ocean after putting into the Galapagos Islands for water. Among the many unlikely individuals drawn to Victoria was one William Pomeroy Carlyon, the troublesome son of Colonel Angus Carlyon of Tregrehan, near St Austell. Colonel Carlyon took the view that a spell in the colonies would straighten out the way-ward ways of young William, and he corresponded with Captain Richard Rodda in South Australia and John Glasson in Cornish Settlement to identify potential destinations. Eventually, the Colonel contracted with William Goyne and John Hammer, a St Blazey miner, for them to take the incorrigible William to 'the gold-diggings of Australia' for the not inconsiderable amount of £50. Goyne and Hammer agreed to stay with William for at least 12 months after their arrival in Victoria, and by early 1853 they were at the Ballarat diggings. Soon William was writing home to his father, explaining that his hands were 'getting very stiff with work' (evidently a new experience) and expressing regret for his former lifestyle. Goyne and Hammer, for their part, promised to stick with William 'through the rough and the smooth' but the young Carlyon caught the dreaded 'colonial fever' (typhoid) and was dead by July. This death was made all the more ironic by the fact that the reformed William, with the help of Goyne and Hammer, had amassed some £1333 worth of gold during their short time in Victoria.[30]

For those Cornish who journeyed to the diggings by sea, whether from Port Adelaide or Plymouth, their first experience of Victoria was the booming city of Melbourne, in those days, as Geoffrey Blainey has described it, 'a second San Francisco'.[31] Many stayed a night or two in the Cornish Arms or the Great Western Hotel, the latter run by two Cornishmen and a regular advertiser in the *West Briton* where it hoped to catch the eyes of intending emigrants.[32] Peter Pascoe, a tailor from Helston, was in Melbourne during 1852. He wrote that 'Pecunary matters is good' and added that most people were 'Rich in a manner of speaking and as independent as Lords'. He had already encountered two friends from home, John Ellis and Edward Toy, and estimated that 'there is upwards of a Hundred with their families from Helston in Melbourne.'[33] The *West Briton* also noted Pascoe's success in Victoria, explaining to its readers that he had thrown a 'sumptuous dinner'[34] for 20 of his friends from Cornwall.

And if the Cornish tended to stick together in Melbourne, then this was even more so on the diggings themselves where, as in California (or New South Wales), ethnic, national and regional groups used separate identity to defend or extend their interests. In 1853 Peter Matthews, a Cornishman, wrote from Ballarat that 'The place in which we live is called Cornish Town, on account of the inhabitants being nearly all Cornish.'[35] Stephen Curnow, from Marazion, remarked that he 'fell in with [a] Cousin from Gulval', and from Friar's Creek in January 1853 he wrote tellingly that 'Cousin William Roach and his Mrs visited last Sunday has [sic] it was Ludgvan feast'. By the August he had encountered other 'Cousins', as he called them – 'John Lawry, Tom Polmear ... Joseph Williams ... [and] some new arrivals they where [sic] from St Ives, Lelant and St Hilary.' Curnow moved on to Spring Gully with Joseph and William Williams, two Cornishmen, and in September 1854 the party was strengthened by the arrival from Burra Burra of Thomas, John and William Roach. He came across 'many others from Ludgvan too numerous to mention', and in February 1855 noted that 'Cousins John and Thomas Roach left here a few days after Christmas for the Burra I think the[y] intend comming [sic] again as soon as winter sets in'.[36] Stephen Curnow returned to Cornwall during 1857 but a colleague, John Williams, wrote to him from the Reef Pleasant Creek diggings in March 1860 to let him know that 'thear is not manny cornish men cas it is a out of the way place .... Phillip Williams is still in Ballaratt [sic] keeping a otell I think he is getting on very well.'[37]

Henry Giles arrived in Victoria in 1854 with 30 other Cousin Jacks, 'principally from St Day and Chacewater and three from St Ives – Thomas Bennett, Matthew Thomas and William Daniel.' Among the 15 or so Cornish who accompanied him to the Creswick diggings were 'Richard Eddy from Treen and Matthew Thomas from Treen and David Eddy from Bosigran .... Matthew White .... Richard Eddy from Bosigran, John Hosking from Treveal .... and Arthur Chellew from Zennor Church Town.' To this close-knit group of relatives and friends, drawn from the countryside around Morvah and Zennor, were added 'two miners, one is from Sancreed called George Thomas, the other from St Day called Richard Harvey.' As Giles explained: 'George Thomas is my mate, he and me do belong on one pit we expect to Bottom next week which will be about 60 feet. John and Richard Harvey is together on another pit. Arthur Chellew is with William Wearne from St Just in another pit, so we shall all share alike on the gain.'[38]

In May 1855 Giles and his companions, together with 'a young man from Penryn', had gone to try their luck at the Daisy Hill diggings. Giles had injured his knee and while confined to his tent to recover somehow contracted dysentery, from which affliction he died on the morning of 16 May. A friend wrote to Giles' parents back in Cornwall, breaking the awful news but trying to console them in their sadness by assuring them that their son 'had a remarkably easy death, died without a struggle or a groan.' Moreover, 'the neighbouring people were very kind to him during his illness, there being many Cornish people near, especially Mary Ann Simmons from Madron Church Town.'[39]

Giles' death, like that of William Pomeroy Carlyon, was evidence that life on the Victorian gold-fields was never easy. Typhoid and dysentery were constant enemies, and so too were the violence and drunkenness that characterised many of the temporary camps that sprang up alongside the diggings. To survive the diggers had to be tough. As one arrival from South Australia recorded: 'We had to fight for our claim. It was nothing uncommon to find a big rough fellow working your hole and disputing your right to it. This, in the early days, had to be decided by a stand up fight, and I must say that it was a quick, if not just, way of arriving at a decision. The diggers would always see fair play.'[40] Such violence and rough justice was a theme returned to again and again by contemporary observers. As early as December 1851 the Adelaide *Register*, alarmed by the abrupt departure of many Cornish miners for Victoria, warned that 'life at the diggings must be a life of perfect wretchedness' with a need for 'incessant watchfulness ... [and] frequent resort to strong if not violent measures in self-defence.'[41] Likewise, in December 1852 the *West Briton* informed its readers of the cautionary tale of one John Semmens, from Ludgvan Leaze, murdered in Victoria for the 60 ounces of gold dust that he had won.[42]

Francis Treloar, from Penryn, catalogued in his diary the dangers of gold-fields life:

> <u>6th June 1852</u> last night a man was shot while stealing a bag of flour.
> <u>16th July 1852</u> Man killed in a hole at Wattle Flat.
> <u>12th August 1852</u> Mr Manchester, a storekeeper drowned while crossing Sawpit Gully, 8 miles from diggings.

15th August 1852 A man near us was shot.

17th August 1852 A woman fell in a water hole and was drowned. Supposed to be under drink.

9th November 1852 Man was killed today by cart upsetting on him.

11th November 1852 Man killed, going down hole. Windlass fell on him.

12th November 1852 Another man killed by hole falling in on him while working.[43]

Food shortages, and the attendant high prices, were a further source of hardship and conflict. Profiteering there certainly was and before his death Henry Giles had railed against the malpractices and shortcomings of many of his fellow diggers:

> This is a terrible place for sin and wickedness ... there is thousands here who don't pay any attention to Sundays no more than another day. They go shouting and cutting wood and spending the Sabbath in a most fearful way. Butchers do kill on Sundays the same as week days ... There is no respect of persons here, Jack is as good as is [sic] Master. There is no use for a man to come here unless he is steady and not given to drink. There is hundreds here who spend their money as soon as they get it. [44]

Disapproval of the moral climate on the Victorian gold-fields was also expressed by a delegation of Wesleyan ministers which visited the diggings on a fact-finding tour. Although 'Forest-creek and Bendigo diggings were successively visited; and many old friends, especially from Cornwall, gave the Deputation a cordial and hospitable welcome', the social conditions encountered were a cause for grave concern. Many of the diggers looked 'wretched and forlorn', while 'that eloquent peacemaker, the revolver ... has found a lodgement in every tent.' Moreover, 'Drunkeness appears to have latterly become common, and nearly all the breaches of social order and morality are traced ... to its accursed influence.'[45]

As in California, the rough justice of the gold-fields, together with a desire to see 'fair play' as well as to maintain order, drew upon the independent mining traditions of groups such as the Cornish. Again, the influence of the Cornish stannaries can be discerned, not only in the impromptu justice meted out by the diggers in remote spots beyond the law but in colonial legislation that was put in place for the colony of Victoria. Like neighbouring South Australia, Victoria developed its own mining law, with more than an echo of the Cornish experience, resulting in a quasi-separate legal system in which a warden was appointed to operate on the gold-fields.[46] However, the independent predisposition of the diggers did not always so easily influence the colonial administration, most notably in the Eureka Stockade rebellion of 1854 where – despite the preponderance of Irish and other ethnic groups – there was at least a sprinkling of Cornishmen in the ranks that withstood the Redcoats' bayonet charge. The Eureka episode has passed into Australian lore – part of the fabric of Australian national identity – but in 1854 it represented a serious challenge to the rule of law. The precipitating factor in the rebellion was the threat to double the cost of the miners' licence – already 30 shillings a month – a hated taxation which was enforced with authoritarian vigour by the police. Beneath it, however, was a democratic impulse which yearned for a better deal for the working man or woman in Australia and wished to shrug off the privileges and 'tyrannies' of the Old World. The unrest came to a head in Ballarat in November and December of 1854, the hard core of protesting miners constructing a makeshift stockade and raising the rebel flag – the Southern Cross in the form of a white cross on a dark blue background. It was a defiance that the British authorities could not allow to stand. In the ensuing attack on the stockade 14 diggers were killed and eight fatally wounded. Five soldiers also lost their lives. The miners were defeated. But the plan to increase the licence fee was dropped, while the colonial parliament promised new legislation to reform the administration of the gold-fields. In defeat there was a sense of victory:

> The wounded and the dying
> Lie silent in the sun
> But change will not be halted
> By any redcoat's gun.
> There's not a flag in Europe
> More moving to the will
> Than the flag of stars that flutters
> Above Eureka's hill.[47]

Be that as it may, much of the work in eradicating, or at least controlling, the worst excesses of the gold-fields was performed by the various Methodist denominations. Resorting to religious persuasion rather than to the law or to the gun, the Wesleyans, Bible Christians and others took the Word to the remotest spots, setting up tents as make-shift chapels on the diggings them-selves. Thus George Prout, a young lad from Camborne, was one of the first to attend the Wesleyan chapel at Forest Creek, while Peter Matthews wrote that at Cornish Town (near Ballarat) 'There is a large Tent erected for a place of Worship not far from us.'[48] When James Skewis arrived at Bendigo from California he was delighted to find three 'splendid good preachers' of the names of Stephens, Rowe, and Jeffrey. Skewis was a Cousin Jack and so too, from the evidence of their names, were these preachers. The latter was very probably James Jeffery, a local preacher who had emigrated from Illogan to work in the Burra Burra mine. Like many another Burra miner, he was drawn to the Victorian diggings in the 1850s, not returning South Australia until 1872 (he died in Moonta in 1877, aged 61). In their *Early Story of the Wesleyan Methodist Church in Victoria*, published in 1886, Blamires and Smith described James Jeffrey as the archetypal Cousin Jack: 'He was a short sturdy man with dark hair and features, twinkling eyes, and a pulpit and platform manner that was quiet and modest. His homely talk, quaint repartee, Cornish brogue, unexpected turns of speech and pertinent illustrations, conjoined with him a great power with the people in the mining districts.'[49] It is said that James Jeffery held the first-ever religious service on the Bendigo gold-fields. Certainly, his allegorical tales and telling allusions enchanted his Cornish audiences:

> You diggers mark out a claim and put down your pegs to a mount, say that it is Mount Alexander, or Mount Tarrengower, or the Wombat Hill, and you will go to work in the hope of finding the gold, and some of you come on a rich patch, and others sink 'schicer' holes; 'tis terribly uncertain about finding the gold; but I'll lay you on to the best place. Here, you diggers, come work out a claim by Mount Calvary.[50]

William Moyle was another Cornish preacher on the gold-fields. Like Jeffrey, he journeyed to Victoria from South Australia, and although he earned a reputation as a man of God his gold-seeking was dogged with ill-luck, it being observed that 'Good father Moyle was always richer in grace than gold.'[51] John

Trevellyan was also a local preacher, though thought by some 'a religious charlatan', an 'unreasoning Cornish miner' of doubtful background who had decided that gold-fields preaching might be a way to earn an easy living. At least this was the opinion of the contemporary writer John Sherer, who in *The Gold-Finder of Australia* of 1853 had several amusing stories to tell about Trevellyan. Sherer had first encountered Trevellyan at a funeral service at Forest Creek. Trevellyan had agreed to hold the service 'for a small consideration' and was in the middle of his address when he was recognised by a fellow Cornishman who knew him to be a unscrupulous operator. This Cousin Jack (identified by Sherer as 'Simon') called out to Trevellyan: 'How be the goats and kids to Stithians?'

Sherer recorded the subsequent exchange, a delightful cameo which, with its inimitable dry Cornish humour, exemplifies the Cousin Jack yarn:

> 'Oh Simon, Simon!' replied Jahn (sic), with well-feigned aston-ishment, and with a view to preserve the character in which he had appeared, 'be ye here, too, among the worshippers of Mammon?'
>
> 'Deed am I', said Simon, 'and how be ye here, if I should be so bould?'
>
> 'I came', said John, 'to call sinners to repentence.'
>
> 'Then you've come to a fruitful spot', returned Simon, 'for there's plenty of 'em here.'[52]

Simon later confided to Sherer that Trevellyan was a notorious back-slider who had had his name read out in chapel three times for drunkenness, twice for swindling and at least a dozen times for forging letters and 'evil speaking'. And yet, Simon admitted that Trevellyan was 'a good preacher ... and had been a great means of saving souls in Carnwall [sic]'. Even Sherer felt obliged to acknowledge that Trevellyan, "had the merit of courage, in placing himself (and preaching) in Friar's Creek, where ... the state of society was low in the extreme, and where the greatest insecurity of life and property existed. Bands of the blackest ruffians under the sun were well known to be continually haunting this spot, who every night, and sometimes even by day, committed the most impu-dent robberies."[53]

John Oliver, born in Ludgvan in 1830, emigrated to Victoria as a young man and made his way to the diggings township of Garibaldi where he was eager-ly accepted as local preacher:

When I arrived at Balarat [sic] I called on the Superintendent Wesleyan Minister, and presented him with a letter of introduction from the minister at home. My name and address were soon put on the plan, and I commenced to preach. My audiences were very much mixed being composed of Cornishmen, Yorkshiremen, Scotch, Irish, Welsh, and Danes. The Irish men and women were Roman Catholics. Their church being five miles away they often attended our little church at Garibaldi, and were very attentive hearers. For such a lot of different nationalities there existed a wonderful lot of equanimity: the little village appeared to be one happy family, but I must say here, that though they were members of the congregation they were not all members of the society, some of them were rough indeed.[54]

But behind this façade of ecumenical multiculturalism were deep-seated ethnic and religious suspicions which even in old age, as he penned his autobiography back in Cornwall, John Oliver could not forget. To begin with, there was the foul behaviour of the back-sliders and the unconverted at the mine in which he worked. 'During crib-time sometimes the conversation would be so filthy that I could not stay with them to finish my crib [snack]. It seemed to me that all they cared about was, talking about beer and women.' Far worse, however, was the influence of the Catholic priesthood:

A religious revival took place at our church, and several of the roughs were converted, and one of them was a Scotchman, he was the worse [sic] character of the lot guilty of almost every crime except murder, he was a cruel father and a dreadful husband. His wife, a nice little Irish woman, but a Roman Catholic, was delighted when she found her husband was so changed and had joined the little church. The Catholic Priest was in the habit of visiting his flock, and as his custom was he visited this little woman, and when he found that her husband was converted he concluded that the wife would not be long before she too would cease to be a Catholic. Such was the damning influence that that priest had over that wife that she never rested till she so tormented that man that he became as bad as ever. Thus to please the priest she turned her (for some time happy home) into as bad a hell as ever.[55]

However, before we rush to condemn Oliver for his intolerance, we must remember that the ecumenical ideas that he had espoused were advanced for his time. Elsewhere we see him struggling to temper his own thoughts and feelings with the teachings of his church, whether it was his belief that 'I cannot reconcile the Christian Hell-fire God with the sweet, loving, and forgiving Christ of the Gospels' or in his reaction to the suggestion by an attractive young woman that he should join her in the 'kissing ring' at a Ballarat festival: 'I refused saying what would people think of me in a kissing ring ... I must say, this was a great temptation; it was a struggle to resist it.'[56] Moreover, John Oliver's essential humanity, his keen sensitivity, is revealed in the description of his reunion at Ballarat with his brother Sampson after 16 long years of separation, a story that he chose to recall many years later in his autobiography. Intensely personal, it also stands for the experience of the many, an exemplar of the pain of emigration:

> One morning I had just returned from work, when I heard a knock at the door, I jumped out of bed and opened the door and a strange man stood before me, we stood looking at each other for a moment or two. I asked him what he wanted. Do you know me? he said, 'no' I said 'I do not'. 'I am Sampson, your brother', he said. Never! My brother is in South Australia. 'No' he said, 'he is here'. As I gazed at him I could see his curly locks and high forehead. I said Sampson, my dear brother, and fell on his neck and kissed him till we both wept with joy.[57]

It was men such as John Oliver, William Moyle, James Jeffrey, and even John Trevellyan, who performed a vital social and spiritual function in ministering to the needs of the diggers and their families. And yet the poor conditions that they sought to confront were the result not only of Godlessness, of drink and violence and disrespect, but of the plain fact that the majority of gold-seekers were ultimately unsuccessful in their quest to get rich. Of course, there were the lucky few, Cornish among them. Alfred Chenery, a Cousin Jack, was the first to prospect successfully on the Upper Goulbourn River in 1853, William Jewell and John Thomas discovered Fiery Creek in August 1854, Jack Bastian started Sailor's Gully, John Northey was responsible for the Stockyard Creek rush and so on – with Cornish names such as Richard Higgs, H.C.P. Pollard, John Roach, Thomas Kemp, W. Pawley, and W. Polkinghorne being prominent among the lists of other official gold discoverers. There were, too, startling cases of personal success. The Rowe brothers, for example, worked Ferron's Reef near Castlemaine for all of 13 years at an incredible profit of £400 per week, while both the world-famous 'Welcome Nugget' and 'Welcome Stranger' finds were made by parties of Cornishmen – in 1858 and 1869 respectively. News of the former was broken dramatically by the *West Briton* which had received word from Captain John Ivey of Camborne that an astonishing discovery had been made. Ivey had had a letter from his son in Victoria explaining that a huge nugget, weighing some 185 pounds, had been uncovered at Ballarat by a party of 22 Cornishmen – nine of whom were from Illogan, including William Jeffery (an early Californian digger) and his brother Richard.[58] Even more spectacular was the 'Welcome Stranger', at well over 200 pounds the largest nugget by far discovered in Australia. Its lucky finders were two Cornish miners, John Deason and Richard Oates, who came across the nugget only a few inches below the surface at Bulldog Gully on the central Victorian gold-fields.

Other success stories included that of John 'Cranky Jan' White, from Trewellard, near St Just, who made enough money at the diggings to retire in comfort to Cornwall, or William Mitchell, from St Agnes, who made his fortune as a carrier on the gold-fields and went into farming, his 'Trevellas' property being one of the largest in Victoria at the time. A Cornish party from the slate-quarrying town of Willunga in South Australia was also particularly successful, the *West Briton* noting that:

> A Cornishman, William Chenoweth, writes to his brother in the neighbourhood of Camelford, from the diggings. He says 'I am happy to inform you that I have been successful at the gold-diggings. I left here (Willunga) with Daniel Oliver, E Martin, Robert Sleep, and Richard Polkinhorn (from West Cornwall). We were wanting from here about nineteen weeks. We were ten weeks and four days at the diggings. We worked very hard for the first seven weeks, and made about $1^{1}/_{2}$ oz of gold each; the other three weeks and four days we made about £4,500, making £900 each. We are truly thankful for our success, we are one party out of a thousand to do so well.[59]

As Chenoweth admitted, however, he and his colleagues were among the lucky few. Many failed miserably and generally the only really successful diggers were those who were first on a particular gold-field, those who had the pickings of the most accessible and easily won deposits. In August 1853, in an attempt to entice

Cornish miners back to the Burra mine, the Adelaide *Register* drew what it considered a telling comparison between conditions at the Burra and in Victoria:

> Copper Digging v Gold Digging – a father and his three sons, tributers at the Burra Burra Mines, earned during the last 'take' – eight weeks – £24 5s 4d per week; and another party of men made nearly £4 per week during the same period – both men being employed in working 'fetches' in the shallow levels. Such wages as those, with comfortable houses and other advantages existing at Kooringa, will bear favourable comparison with the vicissitudes of the gold-fields in Victoria.[60]

Peter Matthews, writing home to Cornwall from Ballarat in July 1853, observed that 'Gold digging his [sic] Chance work, a person might make a fortune in the first pit he sinks or he might sink 20 and Get nothing',[61] while in the following year Stephen Curnow noted wryly that there were many 'wishing themselves Home if the[y] had been Transported for Life the[y] could not look more sad. Great numbers of Cornishmen lose all confidence as soon has [sic] the[y] loose [sic] sight of Engine houses and white jackets (i.e. mine captains)'.[62] Henry Giles, in February 1855, recognised that the easy days of gold-seeking were gone for good, and in a letter to his parents back in Cornwall emphasised that:

> I would not advise anyone at home to think they are sure of making their fortunes by coming to Australia. There is not the chance now that there was three or four years since. A man could not miss in them days. In fact the Diggins are still very rich but very likely there is fifty to one on the Diggins now to what there was four years since. However there is still a better chance for a careful industrious man here as what there is at home.[63]

As time went on, the chances of striking it rich on the Victorian gold-fields became more and more remote, Richard Hancock writing home to St Austell from Bell's Reef, near Tarrengower, in 1862 to explain that he was making only 'just enough to pay for meat'[64] and that, instead of digging on his own account, he was now working on 'tripped' (tribute) for someone else. By February 1867 conditions on the Victorian diggings, according to the *Wallaroo Times* newspaper, were what 'Cornish miners at home would call slavish'.[65] The Burra mine had already taken steps to woo the Cornish back to South Australia, a policy pursued in the 1860s by the Moonta and Wallaroo Mines, while attempts (largely unsuccessful) to open a gold-mining industry in South Australia itself – in places such as Echunga and Forest Range in the Adelaide Hills or Waukaringa and Tarcoola in the colony's Far North – were from time to time a temptation for wandering Cousin Jacks. However, many Cornish miners and their families were encouraged to remain in Victoria, with thousands of others enticed from Cornwall directly, by the shift from 'digging' to heavily capitalised, deep quartz mining – a transformation in which the Cornish, with their expertise as underground hard-rock miners, played a significant role.

Newly emergent mining companies at Ballarat and Bendigo adopted the Cornish tribute and tutwork system of employment, while the Victorian Parliament passed legislation both to create an independent legal structure for the gold-fields and to allow mining companies to be set up under the Cornish cost-book system. Some of the more enterprising Cornish diggers began to organise themselves into syndicates, using their savings to buy the necessary equipment and hire the requisite labour for deep mining. Peter Matthews, at Ballarat, joined a party of 22 other diggers (including John James, a mason from Polgooth) as early as 1855 to purchase a steam pump engine. Matthews observed that the mines were becoming 'deep and unpleasant' and that 'There are a great number of Horse Whims and Steam Engines now in operation at Ballarat'.[66] Some of these engines, indeed, were obtained from Cornish-owned foundries in Victoria, such as Abraham Roberts and Mitchell & Osborne, while others were imported directly from Cornwall. In 1860, for example, Holman's Tregeseal Foundry at St Just-in-Penwith constructed a 17-inch horizontal engine for the Ovens River diggings.

During the 1860s and 1870s Cornish emigrants continued to arrive in Victoria, especially during the late 1870s when immigration into South Australia was severely reduced and many were attracted to the deep Sandhurst mines where George Lansell, a local magnate, actively promoted their recruitment. He engaged men of the calibre of Richard Williams, who had already been out mining in America and who was so successful under Lansell's patronage that he was soon able to set up on his own account – founding the Williams United Mine. Other mine names, such as the Cornwall, the Duke of Cornwall[67] and the Cornish United, were also evidence of an intimate Cornish connection, while the minutes and records of gold town institutions attest to the presence of a great many Cousin Jacks and Jennys in Victoria long after the early rush days. The quarterly meeting reports of the Creswick Primitive Methodist Church in 1885–1888, for example, are full of obvious and typical Cornish surnames such as Grenfell, Jenkin, Rowe, Moyle, Rodda, Coad, Berriman, Tregloan, Langdon and Hawke.[68] In an echo of the experiences in California and on 'the Lakes', as the mines became more heavily capitalised, and as the division between workers and bosses became more apparent, so a trade union movement emerged. Although the link between Cornish ethnicity, Methodism and trade unionism that was to become so characteristic of the South Australian copper mining industry was never as apparent on the more cosmopolitan gold-fields of Victoria, there was nevertheless a strong Cornish involvement in the formation of the Bendigo Miners' Association in the summer of 1871–72 – a time when miners back home in Cornwall were experimenting with their own industrial organisations. The association campaigned successfully for an eight-hour day, for the exclusion of Chinese labour – socialism was often racist in those days – and for an input into the Regulation of Mines Act of 1874 which was to govern the new era of deep quartz mining. In 1874 the Amalgamated Miners' Association (AMA) was formed, growing out of the original Bendigo Miners' Association, an organisation which ultimately became the leading union for miners throughout the continent. A prominent Cornish trade unionist was John Sampson, the first president of the Creswick branch of the AMA, grandfather of Sir Robert Menzies – Prime Minister of Australia from 1939–41 and again from 1949–1966.

This Cornish involvement in trade unionism was mirrored in a Cornish contribution to the political life of Victoria, with Cornish politicians on the whole holding the liberal-non-conformist views that were familiar at home and abroad. In 1886, for example, two Victorian parliamentary candidates standing on a Methodist-Temperance ticket in Sandhurst secured 20 per cent of the vote, largely through the support of the Cornish community. Of particular note was John (later Sir John) Quick, a founding father of Australian Federation and a leading liberal statesman. Born near St Ives in 1852, probably in the tiny settlement of Trevessa, John Quick was christened in Towednack church and emigrated with his parents to Victoria two years later. The Quick family settled in Bendigo and, although John's father died shortly after their arrival, the decision was made to stay in Australia – the land of the future rather than the past. As an adult, John Quick became involved in local politics, entering the Victorian Legislative Assembly in 1880 and soon embracing the cause of federation – the visionary plan to bring together all the hitherto separate Australian colonies to create a united self-governing dominion within the British Empire. A devout Wesleyan,

Quick identified with all the great Liberal issues of the day. He became a member of the Federal House of Representatives (1901–1913), and was later a Federal judge – retiring in 1930 at the age of 78, two years before his death.[69]

As the works of Ruth Hopkins demonstrate in detail, both in Bendigo and in the wider expanses of Victoria the Cornish settled into a variety of occupations and made a wide-ranging social, economic, and cultural impact throughout the second half of the 19th century.[70] The Cornish were prominent as miners but also as foundry owners, as farmers, as artisans, as ministers of religion, their efforts forming an enduring cultural impact which – as well as throwing up statesmen of the stature of Sir John Quick – generated a enduring popular culture. Often naive but with a distinctive Cornish flavour, part of this popular culture was an earthy, self-mocking humour – such as the well-known 'pig or no pig' story:

> A Cornish miner attending a chapel ... repeatedly interrupts the sermon, as was the custom, with 'Amens' and 'Praise the Lords'. However he becomes such a nuisance that congregation members offer him a most valued prize of a pig if only he will be quiet. Nevertheless, the following Sunday, it all becomes too much for the miner and he stands up and hollers 'Pig or no pig, I'll praise the Lord'.[71]

If such humour seemed to have a wry, fatalistic tinge, then this was no surprise, reflecting as it did the rigours of colonial life in 19th-century Victoria, especially in the mining communities and, of course, down in the mines themselves. Charles Fahey has concluded that, despite the appearance of the Cornish across a range of different occupations, they in fact experienced relatively little occupational mobility and, in Bendigo at least, no fewer than a third of them worked as gold-miners. Indeed, in Bendigo in 1881, according to Fahey's research, an extraordinary 46.9 per cent of fathers and 41.4 percent of mothers were born in Cornwall. Almost one-in-four of Bendigo households was headed by a Cornishman, and at the census of 1881 the total Cornish population of the town stood at slightly more than 3000 souls. As Fahey concluded, 'Cornish householders probably outnumbered the combined total of Scottish and Irish householders'.[72] If Melbourne was a second San Francisco, then Bendigo was another Grass Valley.

However, in drawing attention to the relative poverty of many of these

Cornish, Fahey also comments that 'Although Bendigo's Cornishmen were prominent among miners and often managed the daily working of mines, few Cornishmen held real positions of power as miner owners, directors or large shareholders'. The career of Richard Pope, whose diaries form an invaluable commentary on the times, shows that for the ordinary Cornish miner life could be frustrating as well as tough. Born in Cornwall in 1834, Pope had mined – like many Cousin Jacks – in Ireland and the United States before landing in Victoria. He made his way to Ballarat and found work in the Daniel Webster Mine, only to be thrown out of employment almost immediately as the mine went bank-rupt. He took work where he could but by the late 1860s, as Ballarat's deep gold deposits appeared to be all but worked out, he went across to Bendigo where the quartz boom was beginning to get underway. Like many of the Cornish, he set-tled at Long Gully but by 1872 he was again out of work. He later found a job in the Old Chum Mine though by 1874 that venture too had failed. Employment in the New Chum was no more secure, Pope being laid off from there at the end of 1875 in response to various economic difficulties. The search for decent jobs took him off again across Victoria, moving from one hopeful venture to the next, until he decided to relocate to Broken Hill, where he died from 'miners' complaint' in 1900 aged 66.[73]

However frustrated (and maybe typical), Pope's unfulfilled career may have been, it cannot detract from the fact that Cornish miners were sought after as expert hardrock miners and employed throughout the Victorian industry as con-sultants, agents and captains of one sort or another. Leanne Lloyd has amassed the biographical details of no fewer than 700 Bendigo mine captains who were Cornish or of Cornish descent, an extraordinary catalogue of the managers of mines great and small which ranges from James Argall, born in St Agnes in 1826 and later captain of the Paddy Reef Tribute, to the noted Richard (Cap'n Dick) Williams – native of St Blazey – who in 1864 was engaged by Lansell to run his Cinderella Mine at California Gully. William Bolitho, from St Just-in-Penwith, was a shift boss at the Great Southern mine, near Bendigo, in 1893, while Robert Eddy, from Bugle, was manager of the Bendigo Amalgamated Goldfield's Londonderry Mine for many years until one month before his death in 1921. John Ennor, born in St Cleer, emigrated first of all to Moonta in South Australia but subsequently spent his mining career in Victoria, managing such mines as the Confidence Tribute, the Hercules and Energetic, and the Confidence Extended, before his death in 1933. William Robert, a son of St Austell, had been to South Africa and Tasmania before arriving in Victoria at the turn of the century to run mines such as the Phoenix Red, White and Blue, the South Confidence Tribute, and the Carshalton. The list of Victoria's Cornish captains seems endless – John Langdon from Calstock (who had mined in Peak Downs in Queensland before heading down to Victoria), James Nankervis from St Just (a veteran of Connecticut, New Mexico, Colorado and California), Wilfred Rickard from Helston (who had been to the lead mines of Wisconsin and the iron workings of Minnesota), and Joseph Trevean, born in Gwinear in 1839, who worked in the so-called Scottish and Cornish Mine in Ballarat before going on to Bendigo where he managed enterprises such as Pascoe's Tribute and the Golden Pyke.[74]

In her analysis of the Cornish in Victoria in the post-rush era, the years after 1865, Anne Colman notes the impact of this new wave of experienced Cornish immigrants upon the life and work of deep quartz settlements such as Maldon where, according to one observer in 1864, 'Many of the cottages belong to Cornish quartz-reefers, who are nearly all Wesleyan Methodists, and many staunch teetotallers.'[75] But while the Cornish helped develop this new era in Victorian mining, gold production in Victoria actually declined by half in the years 1865–1880, as did the number of gold-miners. People were increasingly employed in allied trades or in supporting service industries, and, notwith-standing Fahey's research findings, this was true for the Cornish as it was of other groups. Cornish artisans appear as bootmakers, saddlers, tailors, farriers, carpenters, joiners, stonemasons, brickmakers, iron founders, blacksmiths, wheelwrights and a variety of other occupations relevant to life on the colonial frontier. To take one example, Thomas Trease, a skilled blacksmith who emig-rated from Cornwall in 1864, worked first in the mining industry in Ballarat. In 1876 he moved to St Arnaud, this time setting up a shop to manufacture and market farm implements as well as to make iron 'lace-work' for verandahs for new housing with its distinctive 'colonial' style. Others became farmers such as William Yelland from Newlyn who made £1000 on the Ballarat diggings and in 1858 purchased 125 acres at a location called Spring Hill. Among a notable group of Cornish contractors and architects was Joseph Reed, from Constantine, who was responsible for a number of fine ecclesiastical and pub-lic buildings in Melbourne and elsewhere.

Throughout this period of development and change, the Cornish maintained separate identity in Victoria, not only in the various Methodist denominations but in what Anne Colman calls 'Cornish rituals and customs', practices and habits which were 'changed and adapted by Cornish immigrants to accom-modate their new environment'.[76] There were sports such as quoits, foot races, horse racing, ploughing matches, and the inevitable Cornish wrestling bouts, together with musical activities such as brass bands, Sankey hymns, and Cornish carols. In particular, argues Colman, 'The cultural inheritance of Cornishmen centred on the notion of solidarity, as exemplified in the Cornish motto "One and All"'.[77] This was reflected in the clannishness so often remarked upon by external observers, as well as explaining the great efforts made by Cornish communities in Victoria in 1867 and 1879 to respond with financial support to the crises back in Cornwall. But it was also a valuable element in Victorian colonial society for, in a convergence of Cornish and colonial culture similar to that noted by Patricia Lay in New South Wales, the Cornish developed a strong sense of community which led to their active participation in public life. This was a tradition which survived Federation, vibrant still in the years before and after the First World War. And just as the Cornish in California had responded positively to the pressing ideology of 'Americanisation', so the Cornish in Victoria had participated actively in the emergence of a new polity and its attendant identity – the Commonwealth of Australia, founded in 1901. In the complex legacy of the Californian and Victorian gold rushes, two features stand head and shoulders above the rest – the immeasurable boost given to the further development of the international mining economy and the energetic, catalytic impact of the rushes upon the rapid growth of the new nation-states of America and Australia. The Cornish had had a hand in both.

# CHAPTER EIGHT

# CRASHED COPPER,

# TUMBLED TIN

# & 'THE LARGEST

# CORNISH COMMUNITIES

# BEYOND LAND'S END'

The emergence of the international mining economy is one of the dominating themes in Cornwall's Great Emigration, as we have seen in previous chapters, with the Cornish providing much of the skilled labour force, expertise and – initially, at least – technology that made this development possible. Latin America, the United States, Australia and, to a degree, New Zealand had each contributed to the international production of important metals, notably copper and gold, and by the 1850s this global pattern of mineral exploitation had become clearly established. A decade later, however, change was in the air. For Cornwall, the mid and late 1860s were years of unrelieved tragedy which witnessed not only a quickening of the pace of emigration but also the onset of de-industrialisation – with the crash of Cornish copper, the faltering of Cornish tin, and the first signs of the long fall from grace of Cornish engineering – as Cornwall became one of the first European regions to move inexorably towards a 'post-industrial' economy.

Of course, the major Cornish copper mines were by now extremely deep. They were more difficult and more costly to manage than before. Some were almost worked out, their mineral reserves on the point of exhaustion, while others were confronted with the prospect of ore bodies of ever-decreasing richness and worth. In the Camborne-Redruth district some of these copper mines, notably the mighty Dolcoath, fortuitously struck tin at depth – lending them a much-needed new lease of life – and later in the Tamar Valley some copper workings (such as Devon Great Consols) were able to survive by turning their attention to the production of arsenic. However, the condition of the Cornish mines themselves was only part of the story, because the underlying cause of Cornwall's distress in the 1860s and beyond was the changing nature of the international mining industry, first – and most cataclysmically – in copper and later in tin.[1] From the late 1820s Swansea had become the focus for the international copper trade, not only monopolising the smelting of Cornish-produced ore but also encouraging and tapping the increasing supply from overseas. As the overseas producers of copper began to proliferate, so the Swansea interests tightened their oligopolistic control of the market. By the 1840s four Swansea companies accounted for the overwhelming bulk of international copper purchases, and in 1844 they came together in a 'secret' cartel – the Copper Trade Association – further to strengthen their position.

For Cornwall, the strenuous attempts by the Swansea smelting interests at first to promote and then (increasingly frantically) to control the world output of copper was evidence enough that the Cornish near-monopoly of production had been swiftly eroded. As we have seen already, the United States had opted for a policy of copper self-sufficiency, while Chilean production had trebled between 1851 and 1860, and was to treble again in the following decade. As early as 1830, Cuba was producing 20 per cent of the world's copper. The huge South Australian discoveries in the 1840s added to world production and in the same colony came the significant finds on Yorke Peninsula – at Wallaroo in 1859 and at Moonta in 1861. In the end, Swansea's bid to keep control of this rapidly expanding international trade was doomed to failure, indigenous smelting industries springing up sooner or later across the globe from America to Australia. And if Swansea's strategy had contained the seeds of its own destruction, then so too did Cornwall's, with the role played by Cornish capital and, most especially, Cornish labour, expertise and technology in facilitating this international expansion.

However, despite the long-term impact of these significant changes in the international copper market, the consequences were not felt in Cornwall immediately. Indeed, in August 1862 the *West Briton* could note that in Redruth there was actually a housing shortage, caused by 'the almost total cessation of emigration to our colonies, as well as the return of many persons from America and elsewhere.'[2] The outbreak of the American Civil War in 1861 had encouraged a number of Cornish on the Lakes and in other parts of the United States to return home, while also deterring those in Cornwall from seeking employment in the USA for as long as hostilities lasted. Moreover, the falling value of the dollar in the Civil War period (1861–65) was itself a further disincentive to emigration from Cornwall to America. At the same time, there was a temporary lull in emigration to that other by now traditional destination, South Australia, the result of internal political and socio-economic change in the colony that had resulted in a suspension of assisted passages. Additionally, the Spanish blockade of Chile in the early 1860s made emigration to that country more difficult – as well as providing for Cornwall a welcome respite in the export of Chilean copper – while the domestic upheaval in Cuba a few years later effectively ended Cornish movement there too.

And yet, this was only the lull before the storm. In South Australia there was much unease over the suspension of government-sponsored emigration to the colony, especially after the Yorke Peninsula copper discoveries at Wallaroo and Moonta in 1859 and 1861. Critics pointed to the central role played by the Cornish in developing the colony's mining industry and doubted the wisdom of closing the conduit between Cornwall and South Australia. Over 2000 Cornish people had emigrated to the colony in the late 1830s and early 1840s and between 1846 and 1850 some 6277 'government emigrants' had sailed from Cornwall to Australia as a whole. Of these, no fewer than 4775 had gone to South Australia. In other words, between 1846 and 1850 some 71 per cent of all Cornish emigrants to the Australian colonies had gone to South Australia, while 27 per cent of all government emigrants to the colony in that period were from Cornwall. Similarly, between 1851 and 1860 some 48,509 immigrants were recorded in the colony's shipping passenger lists, of whom 5177 (or 10.7 per cent) were from Cornwall.[3] Given the strength of the Cornish presence, it was no surprise when the Adelaide government was presented with a string of petitions demanding a resumption of immigration, one from the copper-mining town of Kapunda demanding the recruitment of a 'thousand miners'.[4] The bumper wheat harvest in the colony in 1861 also led to calls for renewed immigration and in 1862 the colonial government responded to these demands. At the end of the year the Waste Land Sales Act revived the policy of selling hitherto unimproved Crown lands to finance assisted immigration, with one-third of annual land-sales revenue allocated to the fund.

Against the background of the discovery of Wallaroo and Moonta, and with the false dawn of the early 1860s giving way to renewed pressure in Cornwall for emigration, the effect of this new policy in Cornwall was immediate. By October

1863 the *West Briton* was reporting that 'Large numbers of the mining popula-tion are emigrating to Australia, Chili, California, New Zealand, Queensland,'[5] many from the districts of St Just-in-Penwith, Camborne, St Agnes and St Blazey, where their wholesale departure was leading – it was alleged – to a scarci-ty of labour. The newspaper also acknowledged the importance of money sent home by these emigrants, an indication that Cornwall's 'dependency culture' was already in the making. The complexity and sophistication of Cornwall's by now well-developed 'emigration trade' and 'emigration culture' were also apparent in the diversity of responses to the changing conditions. Slate-quarrymen from the neighbourhood of Delabole, for example, were by now joining the ranks of skilled emigrants, taking their particular expertise to destinations such as the Pen Argyl slate district of Pennsylvania or the quarrying village of Willunga, near Adelaide, in South Australia. The Cornish had first arrived at Pen Argyl in the early 1850s – among them Robert and Joseph Kellow from Delabole – and by the mid-1860s there was a steady stream of quarrymen and their families moving from Cornwall – especially North Cornwall – to the Pennsylvania slate country. As ever, they are readily identified by their Cornish names – Bray, Davey, Gist, Hockin, Kellow, Lane, Parsons, Paul and Venning. As the *West Briton* reported in March 1864, 'there is great emigration going on among the labour-ing classes from the neighbourhood of the Delabole Slate Works. A Cornishman, who has been in the United States, and worked there very success-fully, having returned home with his wondrous stories, has so wrought upon the minds of the people that a large number of them are thinking of emigrating and about twenty families are now on their way to Liverpool for that purpose.'[6]

Rather different was the call in June 1863 by W. Wade, an emigration agent in Redruth, for applications for assisted passages to New Zealand from miners 'with grown-up daughters',[7] farm labourers, shepherds, smiths, masons and carpenters, a call echoed a few years later by B.J. Nott of St Austell who advertised assisted passages to Otago, New Zealand, for single female domestic servants, farm servants, labourers and shepherds. Wages in New Zealand were 'higher than in other provinces', he said, and skilled artisans could make between 10s and 15s a day.[8]

During 1864 and 1865 things moved from bad to worse in Cornwall, the *West Briton* noting in September 1865 that during the previous three months there had been a marked deterioration, 'Employment is more difficult to obtain, emigration is going on upon a scale hitherto unprecedented, many of the small [mining] undertakings are being wound up, and the large ones becoming unprofitable.'[9]

With South Australia once again a potential destination, much of the renewed rush of Cornish emigration from 1863–65 was to that colony. Indeed, 3651 'government emigrants' sailed from Cornwall to South Australia between 1860 and 1867, some 25 per cent of all emigrants to the colony in that period. In 1863 four shiploads of emigrants arrived at Port Adelaide, each with Cornish contingents, while in 1864 there were seven arrivals at Port Adelaide, each one from Plymouth and again each ship sporting a Cornish contingent. During 1865 there were no fewer than 14 arrivals from Plymouth, with a massive Cornish presence: 211 out of 315 passengers in the *Queen Bee*, 207 out of 383 in the *Clara*, 99 out of 295 in the *Coldstream*, 128 out of 422 in the *Electric*, 242 out of 388 in the *Gosforth*, and so on.[10] In 1864 over 16 per cent of all South Australian immigrants were from Cornwall, while in 1865 the figure rose to an extraordinary 42.5 per cent. For their part, the rapidly developing Wallaroo and Moonta mines actively sought Cornish miners for their workings, building upon the experiences of Kapunda and Burra Burra in their general adoption of Cornish methods, employment practices and technology. Although in 1874 the Moonta and Wallaroo directors thought briefly to obtain '200 Miners or Pitsinkers of other than Cornish nationality'[11] in order to break the ethnic solidarity of their workforce, the prevailing assumption in South Australian boardrooms was that the Cornish were unrivalled in the realms of mining expertise. In South Australia, the myth of Cousin Jack reigned supreme.

In acquiring their Cornish workforce, the Moonta and Wallaroo companies sought first of all to recruit from Kapunda, Burra Burra, the plethora of smaller South Australian mines and from the Victorian gold-fields. But none of these sources was large enough or sufficiently consistent to respond to this demand for labour and in 1864 the Moonta company was shocked when a brief but bitter strike revealed just how short was the supply of miners in South Australia. Accordingly, in April 1864 the Moonta Mining Company wrote to its London agents:

> You will learn from the Adelaide papers that the miners at Moonta and Wallaroo Mines are now out on strike – this circumstance coupled with the fact that considerable difficulty has been experienced hitherto in getting really good hands, has induced the Directors to send to Cornwall through you for fifty men to be brought out under the Assisted Passage Regulations of the Government.[12]

Not long after, on the advice of its general manager, Captain Henry Richard Hancock, the Moonta company requested an additional 200 Cornish miners. These men were duly recruited and dispatched, usually with their families and although not used as strike-breakers (the dispute was already settled) they were invaluable to the Moonta Mine in its formative years. At neighbouring Wallaroo, similar measures were taken. By the end of 1864 a party of men had arrived in the *Tarquin*, with a further body of smelters recruited from Swansea and Cornish miners preparing to come out under the direction of Captain Paul Roach, a mine manager recently engaged in Cornwall. Other Cousin Jacks earmarked for Wallaroo Mines arrived, along with their wives and children, in the *Queen Bee* in 1865.[13]

The ultimate year of reckoning for the Cornish copper mining industry was 1866. The problem was not a short-term cyclical fluctuation but rather a deep-seated structural change in the international copper market at a time when the global supply of copper was expanding despite falling prices. In the unprotected British market prices fell still further, with disastrous effects in Cornwall.[14] The end of the Civil War had signalled the full return of the United States as an international copper producer, while serious financial difficulties at home in Britain, not least the catastrophic collapse of the Overund-Guerney bank in 1866, added to the increasingly dangerous structural problems already threatening the Cornish copper industry. The crisis facing Cornwall was distilled in the falling prices realised at the Swansea 'ticketings' (sales) for what the Cornish termed ore copper – 'as much ore as will make a ton of fine copper.'[15] In January 1860 the price had stood at £102.18s. A year later it had fallen to £86.2s, while in 1862 it fell to £84.5s and in 1863 to £79.10s. In 1864 there was an encouraging if temporary rally, the price rising to £94.19s, but in 1865 there was a fall to £80.14s with the price rising only slightly to £80.18s in 1866. By January 1867 the price had slumped to a disastrous £71.16s, at which no Cornish mine could hope to make a profit, the *West Briton* lamenting that 'very large shipments are reported from Chili'.[16] Indeed, the awful truth was beginning to dawn that 'the price of 1860 will not be realised again, the production of Chili and Australia ... being now so very large that the decreasing yield of the Cornish mines makes very little difference to prices.'[17]

As the *West Briton* had intimated, the fall in copper prices had been accompanied by the diminishing output of the Cornish industry. The peak of Cornish production had been in 1855–56. But this was due largely to the output of the recently discovered East Cornwall and Tamar Valley mines, disguising the fact that many of the older workings of Gwennap, Redruth, Illogan, and Camborne were already failing. From the peak of 1855–56, Cornish copper production had fallen by as much as a third by June 1866 and between 1865 and 1870 production fell still further from 160,000 tons to 80,000 tons per annum. This was reflected in the wholesale closure of Cornish copper mines, first of all in the ancient and all but worked-out district of Gwennap but, after the crash of 1866, the shocking list of casualties also including hitherto illustrious names from all over Cornwall – Crenver and Wheal Abraham in Crowan, Perran Great St George at Perranporth, Fowey Consols. As noted above, some Camborne-Redruth copper mines – among them Dolcoath, South Crofty Tincroft, Cook's Kitchen, South Frances, Wheal Buller – were able to fight off the evil day by turning their attentions to tin production. However, tin prices had fallen from £71.11s per ton in 1860 to a mere £45 in 1866 and several Cornish tin mines were also abandoned in that fateful year. In July 1866 one observer in Cornwall recorded that 'a settled anxiety dwells upon the countenance of almost every decent person you meet; and the general conversation is upon the great question of mining'.[18] In January 1867 the *West Briton* reviewed the events of the preceding year in sombre mood:

> The year now ended is one of the most disastrous for the mining interests of Cornwall during the present century. Certain indirect prejudicial influences have tended to paralyse nearly all our industrial resources, such as the failure of banks and public companies, leading to panic, distrust, an absence of speculation, and leading further to high rates of discount which locked up money ... all the miseries and privations have fallen upon us which await crushed speculators, a partially employed working class, and a general languor and depression in trade.[19]

The unusually severe winter of 1866–67 caused further distress in Cornwall and at St Ives the difficulties arising from the closure of local mines were compounded by 'great distress among the fishermen's families, the late pilchard season having proved a failure.'[20] At the other end of Cornwall, in Callington, 'In consequence of the stoppage of mines ... there is great distress among the poor and labouring classes'.[21] In the Helston district, the closure of mines 'has thrown hundreds of men and children out of employment, producing a state of things which it is only possible to conceive on actual inspection', the nearby village of Ashton being 'a concentration of poverty'.[22] By early 1867 a 'Truro Coal, Bread and

Soap Fund' had been set up, with similar funds emerging in St Ives, Penzance, Helston, Falmouth, Penryn, Redruth, Camborne, Chacewater, St Austell, Tywardreath, St Blazey St Columb, Bodmin, Liskeard and Launceston. The need for other relief measures was recognised in districts as disparate and diverse as Breage and Sithney, Carharrack, Fowey, Looe, Lanreath, Lostwithiel and Boscastle. These individual efforts were co-ordinated into a 'Cornwall Distress Fund', with Queen Victoria sending a princely £10 to swell the coffers. Sir William Williams, the Scorrier mining magnate and investor in Latin American copper ventures, lent his support to propping-up the ailing Poldice mine (or St Day United, as it had become), and so through the 'liberal manner in which he dispenses his boundless wealth [he] ... prevented a large number of families being deprived of employment.'[23] Modest support came from other sources in Cornwall, such as the £4.3s.7d raised during an evening of 'musical entertainments and readings'[24] at Duloe, or the £5.7s.6d raised by the church choir at Pelynt. Mr Deeble Bolger of Wolsden, near Torpoint, donated £10 to the cause.

The overseas Cornish also rose to the challenge, an indication of the strength and self-consciousness that by now characterised the international Cornish identity, as well as providing a new dimension to the 'dependency culture' that was already emerging in Cornwall. In 1868 Cornish folk on the Oven River diggings in the Australian colony of Victoria – named after the Queen who had donated £10 – sent home £71 to support the relief fund, and later the Sandhurst district in the same colony raised £500 for the distressed in Cornwall. Later still, in 1880, it was reported that continuing efforts on behalf of Cornwall had raised some £3179 in Australia, £1050 in South Australia and the rest in Victoria. The year before, some £4000 had been sent home to Cornwall from South Australia, £300 from the town of Kapunda alone.[25]

However, despite this support, the Cornwall Distress Fund was hardly equal to its task. In January 1868 it was noted that the average earnings of 1000 people of all ages at Chacewater was only 1s.6d per week, the situation little better in St Agnes and St Just-in-Penwith. Penzance Union workhouse was brimming with its 312 inmates, the largest number 'for many years'.[26] At Helston £50 was voted to assist 197 families in Sithney, Breage, Germoe, Godolphin and Carnmenellis, and likewise £100 was voted for St Just-in-Penwith, £50 for Lelant, £50 for East Penwith (Camborne and Redruth), £60 for Tywardreath and £30 for Callington. But, welcome though it was, such relief did not begin to address the enormity of the situation. In an echo of the Hungry Forties, there were threats of civil disturbances and a return of the 'bread riots' of former days. In 1868 one provision dealer in St Austell was warned that 'You had better keep down your [flour] prices, or we are determined to burn you down. We are fifty .... We have Greek fire.'[27] As a precaution, 130 special constables were sworn in, an echo of events two years earlier when strikes in the East Cornwall and Tamar Valley mines had also prompted the mobilisation of the constabulary as half-forgotten fears of the 'lawless tinner' were once again rekindled.

Against the background of this continuing turmoil, the Cornwall Distress Fund (and the Cornwall Central Relief Committee which ran it) turned increasingly to emigration as the means of 'improvement', a close relationship developing between the Fund and the various emigration agents across Cornwall. As well as promoting the cause of emigration and helping the agents to publicise their work, the Fund was also on occasions prepared to pay the passage of deserving would-be emigrants, as in January 1868 when it arranged for several miners' families in the East Penwith and St Austell areas to join husbands overseas.[28] The 'emigration trade' itself responded vigorously to the new conditions, building upon half a century's experience to speed the Cornish towards a multiplicity of destinations.

Given the continuing strength of the South Australian mining industry, it was inevitable that many of the Cornish emigrants of 1866 and subsequent years should find their ways to the Antipodes. Arrivals at Port Adelaide during 1866 included sizeable Cornish contingents, such as the 103 in the *Trevelyan*, the 162 in the *Salamanca*, and the 51 in the *Atlanta*, page after page of the shipping passenger lists revealing tell-tale Cornish surnames – James Berryman (miner), Fanny Pascoe (servant), John Angove (copper miner), Samuel Williams (quarryman), William Roskelly (labourer), Joshua Treloar (labourer), William Trembath (miner). Although a more restrictive immigration policy between 1867 and 1871 served to prevent a mass exodus from Cornwall to South Australia, large numbers of individuals continued to find their ways to Wallaroo and Moonta. In 1872 immigration rules were again relaxed, precipitating a new wave from Cornwall, the directors of the Moonta Mine in September 1872 suggesting that 5000 miners be recruited from Cornwall at the expense of all the dividend-paying mines in the colony (a plan that was dropped when it was pointed out the expense would fall almost entirely on Wallaroo and Moonta).

An array of emigration strands was by now apparent, not only those which built upon existing contacts on the Lakes or in South Australia to smooth the paths to Keweenaw or to Moonta, but more modest chains which, for example, continued to facilitate movement within Cornwall from the declining mines of the West to the developing china-clay country around St Austell or the still active copper mines of the East. Plymouth, with its evermore important naval dock-yard, was increasingly a magnet for the Cornish – both skilled and unskilled, male and female – while the Royal Naval connection accounted for a strong Cornish presence in Portsmouth. Cornwall's other maritime activities also lay behind a string of migration linkages along the southern coast of Britain, from Devon and Dorset to Sussex and Kent.[29]

Further afield, there was movement to more far-flung parts of the United Kingdom, as in October 1865 when Samuel Abbott of Redruth advertised to the effect that he was acting as agent for the Esk Valley Iron Company which planned to recruit Cornish miners to work its ironstone deposits at Grosmont, Yorkshire. In August 1866 St Ives, St Just and Calstock men were noted mining in the South Wales coalfields, while in the November 300 Cornish miners were reported on their way to Scotland. During 1867 'several widows and their families'[30] in the neighbourhood of Camborne and Redruth were recruited for the cotton mills of Lancashire. In the 1860s and 1870s there was also a considerable exodus to the iron mines of Furness – 69 per cent of the 515 adult workers resident in the mining village of Roose in that district were Cornish-born according to the Census of 1881 – where they created Cornish communities with all the usual attributes from Methodism to music.[31] Cornish carols were popular in Furness and elsewhere in the North of England, a collection of 'northern' compositions – carols written by Cornish musicians in the North – finding their way to publication in Polperro (of all places) as late as 1927. Variations in words and tune of the familiar Cornish forms, they are instantly recognisable:

> He comes the tyrant's kingdom to destroy,
> To publish peace and universal joy;
> From pole to pole, o'er all the vast domain,
> The king of Salem shall for ever reign .[32]

Even in the 1840s Cornish miners had been recruited for the coal mines of Durham and Northumberland, sometimes as strike-breakers. The Cornish were also persuaded to play the role of 'scabs' in the Lancashire coalfields in December 1866, when 200 Cornishmen joined 300 other miners from Staffordshire and a further 500 locally recruited Lancashiremen to break systematically a county-wide strike .[33] Again, in 1873 900 men were enticed from Cornwall to Lancashire as strike-breakers to make 'Burnley a village of Cornish miners',[34] observers noting that 'The departures from St Cleer,

Pensilva, and Linkinhorne have been so numerous that there are scores of houses tenantless.'[35] Trade union representatives had visited Cornwall to try to deter the Cornish but had met with little success. Instead, the Lancashire men decided to adopt the same tactics as their opponents, the employers, by offering the Cornish liberal inducements to return home. A leaflet distributed among the Cornishmen explained the terms of the offer, concluding that 'As soon as you desire to go, we will at once make arrangements for your going back to Cornwall.'[36] In the Scottish coalfields the Cornish were recruited in times of labour shortages, as in 1866–67 when many Scots miners had emigrated to America and others were demanding an eight-hour day. In November 1866 the Cornish arrived in Lanarkshire in strength (some 300 had been contracted for Scottish coal and iron mines), a 'considerable number' finding employment at Gartsherrie and a 'large detachment' descending on a colliery in the Holytown district. In the same month, 79 hitherto unemployed Cornish miners commenced work in the pits in Kilwinning in Ayrshire for wages that were 2s.6d a day less than those which Scots miners in the district would entertain.[37] Bernard Deacon has warned against the uncritical embrace of the stereotypical depiction of the Cornish miner as strikebreaker. He has noted that a year after 428 Cousin Jacks and their families had been used in 1865 to break a strike at Cramlington, north of Newcastle, a public meeting of 400 miners in Liskeard had voted to 'stay at home until all differences were settled between the masters and men'[38] in the coalfields of Northern England and Scotland. That said, in October 1877 over 100 strikebreaking miners left Cornwall for the Sunderland coalfields.

The departure of Cornish folk for other parts of the British Isles in the aftermath of 1866 should not be underestimated. But the long-term focus of emigration remained overseas. In June 1866 the *West Briton* reported grimly 'The unprecedented exodus of the bone and sinew of the working population of our county',[39] adding in May 1867 that in the previous twelve months no fewer than 7380 miners had left Cornwall. Of these, it was said, 1155 had gone to the United States, 450 to California, 670 to Australia and New Zealand, and 1090 to Scotland and the North of England.[40] Some 1390 of these emigrants had come from Camborne-Redruth, 880 from Gwennap and environs, 1390 from Lelant and St Just, 80 from Wendron, 205 from St Agnes and Perranzabuloe, 220 from the St Austell area, and 1200 from around Liskeard and Callington. Six months later and the emigration of a further 4000–5000 miners was reported, the consequence of the closure of a further 300 mines in the previous half year. In January 1868 the *Royal Cornwall Gazette* recorded that 'Eight thousand miners have recently left Cornwall.'[41]

This exodus was perpetuated into the 1870s – so much so that a brief up-turn in the fortunes of the tin industry in the early 1870s revealed an acute shortage of skilled labour – the closure of the Clifford Amalgamated Mines in April 1870 marking the end of copper mining in its former Gwennap heart-land. In May 1871 'The tide of emigration has again set in the mining districts', while 'In the Redruth district, although tin is high, and times should be better, there appears to be a feeling of general depression among the labouring classes – a longing to be off somewhere, anywhere, in fact, to escape the grinding process now being brought to bear upon mine labour'.[42] And, the crash of cop-per having wrought destruction upon the social fabric of Cornwall, it was now the turn of tin. The Cornish were right to be wary about the apparent up-turn in the fortunes of tin mining in the early 1870s, for all the experience of the previous half century had taught them to beware the inexorable increase in overseas production and competition. As early as 1815 alluvial tin from the Malay States (the 'Straits') had started to make its impact felt upon the tin market, while Peel's abolition of duty on imported tin in 1845 had brought depression to the Cornish industry. A revival in tin prices after 1869, associat-ed in part with civil unrest in the Malay States, had brought happier times to Cornwall but soon the States were restored to full production, to be joined by the fabulous 'Mountain of Tin' discovered on Mount Bischoff in Tasmania. By 1873 tin prices were starting to fall, but 1874 was far worse. There was consternation in the ranks of mining investors, attempts at wage cuts and a return to the notorious 'five week month', and the inevitable closure of Cornish tin mines – 47 in 1874, 48 in 1875, and 37 in 1876. In April 1874, with the aban-donment of Balleswidden, Wheal Owles, North Roskear, and Wheal Seton, along with the partial closure of Botallack, 'there is quite a panic in the West Cornish mines'.[43] As the *West Briton* observed sadly in January 1875, 'In the history of mining in Cornwall it has known no such disastrous year as 1874 .... Australia, which has been made the home of many Cornishmen, threatened at one time to annihilate altogether tin mining in this country.'[44]

The 1870s, too, were a time of agricultural depression in Britain, with the emerging competition from North American produce being compounded by a series of bad harvests at home. There were epidemics of foot-and-mouth disease and swine fever and falling wheat prices contributed further to agrarian poverty all over the United Kingdom. Britain alone of all the major European powers, with its commitment to free trade and the economic philosophy of *laissez-faire*, was slow to protect its agricultural industry. Farm incomes fell and wages for agricultural labourers were reduced, resulting in a renewed emigration of young country-folk from Britain and Ireland to Canada, Australia, and New Zealand. A Royal Commission into the causes of agricultural depression found Cornwall less badly hit than other parts of the United Kingdom, this being due to changing agricultural patterns – less wheat was being grown in Cornwall and instead there had been a movement towards horticulture, dairying and stock farming. That said, Cornish farming was often already of a marginal nature – with many tiny, under-capitalised properties – and, coming on top of the crises in tin and copper, the effect of the agricultural depression was to provide yet another boost to Cornish emigration.

New Zealand, for example, was a recipient of both mining and agricultural labour from Cornwall during the 1870s. From the earliest days of the Wakefieldian settlements of the late 1830s and the exploitation of copper in the 1840s, there had been an important Cornish presence in New Zealand. During the 1850s Cornish emigrants had continued to turn up, such as John Grigg, from Liskeard, who arrived in Auckland in 1854. After farming for a decade in the Auckland area, he moved to Canterbury where between 1864 and 1871 he acquired some 32,000 acres of ostensibly swampy wasteland. With considerable patience and ingenuity, Grigg spent the rest of his life draining and improving the land, selling off parcels to would-be yeomen farmers and pioneering the development of the frozen meat and dairying industries. This Longbeach property was farmed on a massive scale. In 1889, for instance, it was reported that there were 7000 acres in crop, of which 4000 acres were of wheat, averaging 35 bushels to the acre. Some 300 men, 300 horses, 35 reapers, 60 drays and wagons and several traction engines and threshing machines, were required to handle such a harvest. When, in the 1870s, Cornish agriculturists began to arrive in New Zealand in significant numbers under the colony's new assisted passage scheme, many were attracted to the Longbeach area. Thomas Henry Brewer, for example, was born in St Columb Minor in 1856 and emigrated to Canterbury as a farm labourer in 1875. Working first as a railway navvy, he soon made his way to Longbeach where he worked for two years, acquiring the wherewithal, support and confidence to open a livery-stable in Gore: of which town he was later mayor. Equally successful, in its way, was the career of William Gluyas, a saddler from Helston. Like a number of Cornish people in the 1870s, he had spent some time in the English Midlands before emigrating to New Zealand with his wife and young daughter in 1877. Settling first in Christchurch, he later moved to Longbeach as saddler to John Grigg, later still taking advantage of the government's rural settlement scheme to acquire 193 acres of land leased to him in perpetuity.[45]

In the early 1870s, as New Zealand strove to build its rural infrastructure in the aftermath of the debilitating Maori wars, the New Zealand Colonial Treasurer, Julius Vogel, launched an ambitious scheme to finance the construction of railways and roads and to pay for a new assisted passage immigration scheme. Cornwall, with its reputation for emigration, was identified as a likely source of emigrants and in September 1871 the New Zealand emigration agent, Charles Carter, enlisted the services of Captain A. Antony of Hayle to assist in the selection of suitable applications. Results were disappointing, however, partly because potential emigrants were required to pay £5 in cash for each adult member of a family (and children of 12 and upwards were counted as adults), and partly because the rise (albeit temporary) in tin prices had for the moment distracted Cornish attention away from the cause of emigration. In the following year, 1872, the recruiting campaign met with greater success (not least because the financial qualifications were relaxed) and in the April 60 adults were selected from Falmouth and environs. They sailed that month in the *Schiehallion*, and among their number was one John Reynolds, from Shute Lane, Penryn, who had emigrated ahead of his family in anticipation of their joining him in the colony once he was established there, as indeed they did. Contemplating the opportunities that New Zealand had opened up before him, Reynolds opined that 'Any man is an enemy to himself to stay at home.'[46]

Thereafter, many others took advantage of the liberal schemes to emigrate to New Zealand, such as the 190 or so Cornish folk who departed in the *Chile* in September 1872. In all, some 5540 Cornish emigrants arrived in New Zealand during the 1870s, 10 per cent of all immigrants from Cornwall and England. As Rollo Arnold has argued in his study *The Farthest Promised Land - English Villagers, New Zealand Immigrants of the 1870s*, in New Zealand 'they joined a population already rich in Cornishmen ... Since Cornwall possessed a highly distinctive social and economic life, her contribution to the making of rural New Zealand is too significant to be ignored.'[47] And, citing the case of William Kittow, who claimed to have operated the very first cream separator in the colony and was an early user of shearing machines, Arnold has added that:

> New Zealand's agricultural technology seems to have benefit-
> ed from the rich experience of mechanical skills among Cornish
> immigrants .... It seems to have been common for Cornish
> immigrants to combine farming with contracting ... for the
> building of roads and bridges .... Cornish immigrants were also
> to be found in good numbers among the colony's artisans ....
> New Zealand would surely have been much the poorer if her
> immigration drive had not recruited in Cornwall.[48]

Many of the male emigrants from Cornwall to New Zealand in this period were listed as 'agricultural labourer and miner',[49] reflecting the blurred divisions between occupational categories (many miners rented smallholdings or had cleared waste land) and accounting for the particular blend of 'frontier skills' that made them so successful in pushing back the agricultural bounds of New Zealand (or Australia or America). They came predominantly from mid and West Cornwall. John Hebbett, for example, who sailed for New Zealand in the *Clarence* in September 1874 at the age of 21, came from St Keverne, the son of a coastguard. Thomas Lukers emigrated from nearby Gunwalloe in the *Rakaia* in 1879 and from Helston came 28-year-old James Rowe and his wife Elizabeth who sailed in the *Isles of the South* in November 1873. In the same ship were emigrants from the Penzance and St Just areas, notably the widow Mary Ellis, aged 52, with her six sons and daughters from the mining village of Boscaswell. In the follow-ing year, 1874, the *Tweed,* bound for Otago carried 22-year-old Philip Edwards from Fore Street, St Just-in-Penwith and Mary E. Bottrell, a 21-year-old servant, and her brother Henry, aged 16, from Pleasant Row in the same town. In the Camborne-Redruth district, emigrants included Thomas Moyle from Illogan who sailed for New Zealand in the *Charlotte Gladstone* in November 1871. Others were Samuel Prisk from Four Lanes, Paul Prisk of Porkellis and Stephen Trevela of Roskear Fields, Camborne. Still others were from St Agnes, such as John Whitford, navvy, aged 23, who sailed with his wife Mary Ann in the *Berar* in May 1873, or Thomas Fowler, a labourer aged 28, who set sail for New Zealand in the *Lady Jocelyn* in July 1872.

Further east, at St Columb Major, Thomas and William Giles, two brothers, decided to emigrate to New Zealand after the trauma of the great china clay workers' strike in mid-Cornwall in 1876–77. Robert Grigg, also from St Columb, decided upon New Zealand after sojourns on the Nevada and Australian silver and gold diggings in the 1860s and early 1870s. Like others from the mid-

Cornwall clay country, Grigg had also spent a brief spell on the New Zealand gold-fields, before later returning as a government emigrant in 1877. Nominations by colonists already established in New Zealand were part of the immigration strategy of the 1870s, and numerous nominations were received from the Otago gold-fields for prospective emigrants from the St Austell area. In May 1872, for example, Miriam Wedlake, 32, housemaid of Roche, together with her eight-year-old daughter Catherine, were nominated from Otago. So too were four other young people named Wedlake (Julia, 17; Fred, 14; John, 12; Lottie, 10), who were nominated by their kinsman, one F. Wedlake of Tuapeka, on the Otago gold-fields in September 1873.[50]

New Zealand's efforts to improve its rural infrastructure and expand its agricultural frontier in the 1870s were matched by a very similar policy in South Australia in the same decade. This was associated with James Penn Boucaut, born in Mylor in Cornwall in 1831, who as Premier of South Australia sought to build 13 new railways to penetrate the colony's farthest corners, at the same time stimulating emigration to populate the country thus opened up.[51] Although the Cornish had made their mark most visibly in mining, they had from the first played an important role in the creation of rural communities and the expansion of the colony's agricultural frontier. As in Wisconsin and other parts of the United States, the miner-turned-farmer became a familiar figure in 19th-century South Australia, especially in the so-called 'Mid-North' country around Burra and Kapunda and, a little later, on Yorke Peninsula. But others had come from Cornwall for the expressed purpose of farming rather than mining, while Cornish artisans – wheelwrights, builders, blacksmiths, masons, iron founders, millers – were often important figures in the foundation and construction of rural townships. Together, the farmers and the artisans who followed in their wake made South Australia the so-called 'granary of Australia', the upsurge in demand for wheat occasioned by the gold rush in neighbouring Victoria increasing South Australian wheat acreage from 41,807 in 1850 to 175,865 in 1857, the colony's production by then out-stripping all others in the continent.

One early settler on Adelaide's rural periphery who participated in this rapid expansion was Thomas King, from Landrake in East Cornwall, who had arrived in South Australia in 1845 in the *Isabella Watson*. He selected land outside the city in a district known as Morphett Vale and set about clearing the land and establishing a farm. Other settlers on the Adelaide plains included the extended James family from West Cornwall. Charles James from Porthleven had married Emma Trevenen Gundry of St Hilary and in 1865 they emigrated to South Australia where they established a market garden near Adelaide, rather grandly calling their property 'Lanhydrock' after the great house and estate of that name at home. Charles' cousin Thomas followed suit, establishing an orchard and vine-yard at a place called East Marden. Impressed by this success, other members of the family came out to join them, notably William Wearne James, from Gwithian, who, after a short spell in the coal mines in Ebbw Vale in South Wales, arrived on the Adelaide plains to grow citrus fruits, grapes, peaches, apricots and figs. Despite Methodist opposition to 'hard drink', this Cornish prominence in mar-ket gardening and horticulture was mirrored in their penetration of South Australia's developing wine industry, notably in the activities of William Thomas Angove (from Truro) and his wife Emma Carlyon who established the village of St Agnes, near Adelaide, where their celebrated 'Tregrehan Claret' was produced in honour of the Carlyon family of Tregrehan in Cornwall.

In the Adelaide Hills, running down the eastern side of the city, the Cornish were also among the early settlers. By 1840 there were already 2036 acres of land enclosed in the Mount Barker-Strathalbyn portion of the hills, and a visitor to the area at that time 'found only four persons settled where the town of Nairne now stands', one of whom was a Mr Hilman, 'a Cornish carpenter'.[52] Soon Hilman was joined by other Cornish folk – John Rundle, a Mr Rendell from Linkinhorne, George and Grace Venning from Altarnun, William Tonkin, Joseph Bull, Edward Hender, Peter Medlend from St Blazey. Rendell wrote home to his father in Cornwall explaining that 'William Tonkin has a farm to himself of 40 acres, and six good working oxen. Joseph Bull has a section of 80 acres and six working bul-locks .... William Tonkin has had this year about 400 bushels of wheat, and will have more next year.'[53] Reflecting the same sense of Cornish community, William Medlend added in another letter home that 'Mr Tonkin's son William, we hear is doing well, he has got forty acres of cultivated land in the district of Mount Barker, about thirty miles from the city, he lives near the old John Rundle, and has got 3 children and we believe are quite well.'[54] In the coastal district to the south-east of Adelaide, there was also a clutch of Cornish emigrants, especially around the slate-quarrying village of Willunga where the settlers included individuals such as John Pengelly, Abraham Pethick, who named his farm 'Bowithick' after his old home on Bodmin Moor, George Sara from Perranwell, John Orchard from Wendron, Honor Vellanoweth from St Ives and a group of specialist slate-workers from North Cornwall: James Kernick, W.B. Male, William Cobbledick, Thomas Polkinghorne, Simon Sibly, William Herring and Thomas Martin. The local pub was the 'Cornwall Inn', while in 1859 the congregation of the thriving

Bible Christian chapel was, from the evidence of its names, overwhelmingly Cornish – Trenaman, Male, Bastian, Sibley, Harris, Thomas, Williams, Sanders, Pearce, Polkinghorne, Osborne, Nicholls, Vanstone.

North of Adelaide, on the Gawler Plains and in the township of Gawler itself, the Cornish were also much in evidence, not least in the form of James Martin, from Stithians, who had arrived in the colony in 1848 and from that moment on had been a stout advocate of its charms and potential. As he wrote to his friends in Cornwall:

> allow me to say, as the Queen of Sheba did, the half was not told me. If ever you should come here I know you would like it ... you will find it full of wheat, barley, and oats, vines and figs, almonds, peaches ... a complete Paradise .... Behind the hills, there are tens of thousands of sheep and bullocks, grazing in the meadow land .... I very much regret not coming here before; remember me to my friends at Stythians. I thank God I was never better in my life.[55]

James Martin later became proprietor of what was to become a major foundry business which by 1900 was employing 700 hands and covered a site of some 18 acres. From bullock drays and farm implements, Martin's Foundry soon progressed to innovations such as the 'stump-jump plough' (so important in cultivating South Australia's mallee scrub country), later still building railway locomotives for the South Australian Railways and constructing mining machinery for Broken Hill, Western Australia, even South Africa. Further north still, around Kapunda and Burra Burra, townships and agricultural communities had sprung up in the wake of the copper discoveries. As elsewhere, the Victorian gold rush had been an important stimulus to wheat production and many Cornish miners came back from the diggings with enough money to purchase land in the Mid-North. William Trevena, for example, came back to Kapunda from Victoria with just enough finance to purchase 300 acres and John Curnow returned with funds enough to acquire a plot of land: he and his sons set to to clear the property by hand, preparing the soil for plantation by the painstaking (and backbreaking) turning of the earth with spades, the only implements that they could afford. At the Burra, the story was much the same. Henry Pinch, originally from St Mabyn, purchased his 784-acre 'Pencarrow' property after a particularly successful spell on the gold-fields, and William

Pryor, born in St Austell in 1830, returned wealthy enough to buy land at neighbouring Baldina. At Spring Farm, near Clare, to the south of the Burra, there developed a veritable Cornish community where the settlers became close-knit, inter-married, carved out large farms with names such as 'Trevenson' and 'Treview', and moulded their social life through the medium of the local Wesleyan chapel. Spring Farm earned something of a reputation in the colony as a Cornish-Methodist stronghold.[56]

It was Thomas Ninnes, one of the Spring Farm Wesleyans, who in 1862 was responsible for opening the important track linking the Burra with the newly emergent copper country of northern Yorke Peninsula. With the help of his colleagues from Clare, Ninnes blazed a trail through the Barunga Gap in the Hummocks range of hills, clearing the scrub to form a trail and linking the two communities. In the following year the first Hundreds of officially surveyed land on Yorke Peninsula were proclaimed, opening the way for agricultural settlement, and in 1867 the Adelaide government made available three million acres of frontier mallee scrubland across the colony for selection by farmers. This, in turn, was followed in 1868 by the so-called Strangways Act which allowed easy credit and low interest rates for purchasers of this new land who undertook to settle and improve it. In the wake of the Strangways Act, Yorke Peninsula was swiftly opened up for farming. Among the early miners-turned-farmers was John Phillips, originally from Wendron, who took land at Green's Plains. Others, like Joseph Rodda, were swift to follow his example, the Adelaide *Observer* noting in July 1870 that 'Green's Plains is gradually being occupied for agricultural purposes ... Farmers are struggling manfully to supplant mallee scrub with cornfields.'[57] In 1872 the Strangways Act was improved and updated and in May 1873 an editorial in the *Yorke's Peninsula Advertiser* called for greater agricultural expansion in the district. Twelve months later a petition from the Yorke Peninsula miners called on the government to make more land available in the area, emphasising that many of them had had experience of farming in Cornwall. By June 1876 the *Yorke's Peninsula Advertiser* could note that 'land in the vicinity is being taken up ... and cultivation is transforming that which was a desert and scrubby waste.'[58]

Although a drought in the summer of 1876–77 drove many off the land, an experience repeated again with greater ferocity in the parched decade of the 1880s, many Cornish had by now exchanged the pick for the plough, some even venturing into the more marginal country of the 'Far North'. A number of northern districts was opened up in the wake of the Strangways Act and during

1870 Edward Dunstan, a Wendron man, purchased 240 acres of virgin bush country in the neighbourhood of Belalie and Jamestown. A frontierman of considerable experience he had mined at Kapunda, Wheal Blinman and Yudnamutana in South Australia, as well as in Victoria, Queensland and New Zealand, before deciding to turn his hand to farming. As he explained, he and his brother-in-law rode up from Kapunda to examine the available land, sleeping rough as they traversed this remote country. They eventually selected blocks 'near the surveyed township of Jamestown for the convenience of obtaining water supply and education for our children.'[59] Then:

> Having become the owner of a piece of virgin unfenced land;
> our next problem was to get a piece ploughed up to be sown so
> that we would have seed for the next season. I managed to get six
> acres ploughed, put in a bag of wheat and reaped ten in return ...
> Then there was fencing to be done. There was no timber nearer
> than Wirrabarra, 25 miles distant. Often I worked for part of the
> day on the farm then put the horses in and went as far as the
> Rocky River that night, camped there, drove into the Forest next
> morning, loaded up with posts and out to the Rocky again that
> afternoon, rested and fed the horses and traveled during the
> night reaching home perhaps at daylight.[60]

To today's reader this seems a lonely story full of hardship and undue exertion but at the time it would have been told with pride and a sense of achievement, no doubt prompting others to take the plunge. Cornish miners in the colony were increasingly keen to turn to farming and back in Cornwall miners and agriculturalists alike were aware of the success that their countrymen had achieved on the land in South Australia. Indeed, between 1872 and 1879, approximately seven per cent of the 24,000 or so emigrants to South Australia recorded in the shipping passenger lists were from Cornwall, many of them miners drawn to Wallaroo and Moonta but others responding to Boucaut's call to push back the agricultural frontier. However, despite the achievements of South Australian agricultural expansion, the process had overstretched itself by the 1880s – the fearful drought of that decade demonstrating vividly the falseness of the vain hope that 'rain follows the plough' and returning many northern properties to semi-desert.

At the same time, the effects of the continuing downturn in copper prices had caught up with South Australia. Kapunda and Burra Burra had already gone to the wall, along with scores of smaller ventures, while even the mighty Wallaroo and Moonta Mines were forced to trim their operations. As early as 1873, with vacancies at the Yorke Peninsula mines becoming fewer and fewer, the miners began to express concern about the continuing high levels of immigration. And in May 1874 they were dismayed to learn that Mr Gowling, a newly appointed emigration agent, was being especially active in Cornwall. Many felt that their kinfolk back home were being given an unduly rosy picture of prospects in the colony. A highly satirical article in the *Yorke's Peninsula Advertiser*, purporting to be a 'Report of an Emigration meeting held in St Just, Cornwall near England, last evening, Sir John St Aubyn in the chair', made the point with wry humour designed to show both the gullibility of the Cornish and the unscrupulousness of the emigration agents. It was also, *inter alia*, an insight into the fears, prejudices and preoccupations of emigrants at the time:

> Mr TREVORROW would ask if there were any snakes there?
> Mr GOWLING would answer that there had been snakes in the colony, but the last one had committed suicide several years ago.
> Mr TREVASKIS would ask if there were any 'skeetas there?
> Mr GOWLING in reply said that the white man had, by means of his higher civilization, so trained the mosquitoes that they had been found a very useful ally in stinging the natives back into the interior, thereby transforming what might have been a great scourge into a great blessing.
> Mr GILES would ask if people stood on their heads out there?
> Mr GOWLING replied that that they did sometimes by reason of the earth being spherical. When it was twelve o'clock in St Just, the earth was upside down in Australia. But of course every honest man would be in bed at that time, so that it was all in favour of the colony, as rogues could not do much injury to lives or property if they had to do it on their heads.[61]

Similarly, in November 1876 one Edward Trewidden of Kadina, the township adjoining the Wallaroo Mines, wrote to the *Yorke's Peninsula Advertiser*, explaining how he and his wife had been deceived by the emigration agents. Apocryphal or not, the point was well made:

What sort of joke do you call this? I had just got back to Camborn [sic] from America where I had been working and picked up a few dollars to marry my little maid, and meaning to take her back to the Lakes, where I had done considerably well. Well, Grace said to me, says she, 'Isn't it very cold out there Ned?' 'Well, Grace', says I, 'it is tarnation cold I must say'. 'There was a man giving a lecture on going to South Australia, Adelaide', says Grace, 'and I thought he gave a pretty good account of it, and it is never cold out there, and I think I could bear the heat better than the cold of America. He said miners' wages was 45s to 50s a week, and that bread and beef, and mutton, and tea, and sugar, were very cheap, and everything else in proportion.'[62]

Swayed by Grace's enthusiasm, Edward decided that their destination would, after all, be South Australia, and they made their way to Kadina. However, on arrival on Yorke Peninsula Edward was dismayed when 'I went to a man that I knew home in Camborn and I asked he if he could point me out a job of work. 'You've come in a poor time, Ned', says he, 'they are sacking men here instead of putting them on'.'[63] Such an account was echoed in the comments of one 'New Chum' who arrived on Yorke Peninsula in 1877. Although he found Adelaide 'a fine little town, very little inferior to Truro at home', he was appalled by the drought conditions he encountered, 'this is one of the most barren places I have ever seen, and many of the poor cattle are dying of starvation ... Is this the beautiful country we heard so much about at home, the land flowing with milk and honey?'[64] The Cornish may have taken the more extravagant claims of emigration agents with a pinch of salt, but they relied upon the Cousin Jack network for accurate international information. When it let them down, they were outraged. The Rev. John Thorne, a Bible Christian minister, had been at Moonta during the heady days and had returned to Cornwall with wondrous stories of boundless opportunities. Things, though, had changed, and one correspondent in the *Yorke's Peninsula Advertiser* in 1877 had 'heard a new chum cursing that Bryanite preacher, called Thorne, as he had said there was plenty of work in South Australia for miners ... the Captains of the mines would come on board ship and put them straight to the mines'.[65] John Prisk, a leader of the increasingly organised and vocal Moonta Miners' Association, in September 1979 recommended that men ought 'to be writing home to Cornwall ... to give them a truthful account of how things are here ... it would keep others from coming out to swell the number of unemployed'.[66] The Association lobbied the Adelaide government, and it is significant that when, in 1879 and 1880, immigration was severely reduced, this was in direct response to public opinion.

A more liberal immigration policy was again instituted in 1881 and this coincided with an exciting, if rather exaggerated, upturn in the fortunes of the South Australian copper industry. Promising new lodes had been struck at Wallaroo Mines in the old Devon Consols sett, prompting the directors to decide in October 1882 that Captain Richard Piper should be sent home to Cornwall to recruit a new generation of Cornish miners. On arrival in Cornwall, Captain Piper inserted a discreet advertisement in the West Briton, 'Wanted immediately, Fifty good Miners, including steady young men, also married men with their families, to proceed to the Wallaroo Copper Mines, South Australia. For rates of wages and all particulars apply at once in person, to Mr Richard Piper, 3 Falmouth-road, Redruth.'[67] In April 1883 Piper was instructed to increase the number of recruits to 250. Back at Wallaroo Mines, the construction of new cottages was evidence that something was afoot and although the directors were unwilling to release details of Piper's mission, rumour and gossip were rife. As the curious enquired, 'Where is Captain Piper? And is he going to bring coolies or Cornishmen? And supposing the Dolcoath Mine stops working will he engage all the miners in a mass to come out here?'[68] The Moonta Mines, meanwhile, had also asked for 100 Cornish miners, and Captain Piper arrived finally in South Australia in August 1883 with 408 New Chums in the ships Oriana, Glen Osmond and Rounsdad. Most were accommodated at Wallaroo Mines, with 70 finding lodgings in Moonta Mines, and Captain Hancock addressed both groups of immigrants to help smooth their integration into the local communities. One New Chum, Hancock reported approvingly, had declared 'that he had eaten more meat in Australia in the short time he had been here than he would have eaten in a year in Cornwall.'[69]

Alas, it was not as simple as that, and many felt that Piper had exaggerated the attractions of northern Yorke Peninsula. One critic, rather tongue-in-cheek, complained that 'They were told that the Company had built them five-storied houses, such as adorn the streets of Plymouth, with gardens in which vine and fig-trees flourish exceedingly'.[70] The recruits themselves responded by voting with their feet, a number of them – John Kinsman, Samuel Curginben, William Annear, and 26 others – having disappeared from the district before their initial contracts had expired. News of this debacle, filtering back to Cornwall, would hardly have encouraged further emigration, and in any case in 1886 assisted emigration to South Australia came finally to an end, some 50 years after the colony was first proclaimed. By then, however, the mark of the Cornish was stamped indelibly upon South Australia. Northern Yorke Peninsula was already 'Australia's Little Cornwall', its townships of Moonta, Wallaroo and Kadina, in the words of Australian historian Geoffrey Blainey, 'possibly the largest Cornish communities beyond Land's End.'[71]

The twin mines of Moonta and Wallaroo came to dominate the area's copper production but there was any number of smaller ventures on Yorke Peninsula, many of which failed, some of which were incorporated into the two giants, and a handful that survived as independent operators. The Wandilta, the New Cornwall, the Karkarilla (later renamed the Hamley), the Matta Matta, the Paramatta, the Yelta, Wheal Hughes, the Poona, the Kurilla and Devon Consols, were all local mines of standing. More obscure were most of the 54 separate workings listed by the *Yorke's Peninsula Advertiser* on 16 May 1873, Wheal Burty, Wheal Prosper (known locally as Wheal Chips and Leather United), Wheal James, Wheal Stuart, Wheal Humby, Wheal Goyder, the Albion, the Agery, the Euko, the Mattapara, the Challa, the Copper Valley, the Old Cornwall, the New Moonta, the Derrington, the Goldsworthy and so on. Their managers bore the familiar, tell-tale Cornish names – Williams, Warren, Northey, Ellis, Bennetts, Mathews, Lean, Thomas, Snell, Gray, Pascoe, Trenouth, Edwards – and the local hamlet and suburb names such of Tuckingmill, Helston, Menadue, Portreath, even Jericho, were also a clue to heavy Cornish involvement from the earliest days. Men such as Francis Manuel from St Blazey and John Tamblyn from St Agnes made their way to Yorke Peninsula from the Burra during the 1860s. Others, like John Retallick, born in St Austell in 1815, arrived from Kapunda, while others such as William Pearn from Lezant and John Nancarrow from Redruth travelled across from the Victorian gold-fields. Many more, of course, came direct from Cornwall – Methuselah Tregoning from Wendron, John Noble from Penryn, Alice Williams from Constantine, Charles Harris from Tywardreath, Thomas Cowling from Baldhu, Richard Cowling from Gunnislake.

By 1875 it was estimated that there were some 20,000 to 25,000 people resident on northern Yorke Peninsula, mostly of Cornish birth or descent. They huddled together in the three main townships of Moonta, Wallaroo and Kadina, though many of the miners themselves lived in the tumbled array of cottages on the mineral leases at Moonta Mines and Wallaroo Mines. Although often squalid, and never entirely free of 'colonial fever' or 'black measles' (the typhoid which decimated the infant population in the period 1873–75), the mineral lease settlements were an extraordinary and strangely comforting sight, as one observer recorded in 1873:

> There is no attempt to form streets here, but houses have been built in every direction, each on its little plot of ground, with tank and fence .... To the stranger this all presents a novel and pleasing appearance. The noises of engines and gear, the clink of the blacksmith's hammers ... the hoarse rattle of chains and the escapement of steam, the sight of immense chimneys and tall engine houses, crushing machinery and pumping machinery ... all combine to impress the least observant of spectators ... and to see the cottages all round, with the trim house-wife waiting for her husband to come home after morning core [shift], the glimpses of snugness and comfort within, the chapels rising up above the other buildings as if it was a great city, forms a picture as beautiful to the artist as it must be gratifying to the lucky shareholder who is part of all around him.[72]

Despite the multiplicity of mineral claims in the area, it was the Moonta and Wallaroo Mines that provided the economic backbone of the district. Ultimately, through financial pressures and the search for economies of scale, the two mines were forced into amalgamation, but until 1889 they were independent concerns: albeit operating in close co-operation, their position strengthened by the construction of a large smelting works at Wallaroo. Wallaroo's most productive years were 1866–75 (the same period that saw the virtual extinction of copper mining in Cornwall), with 25,000 tons of ore being raised per annum. Moonta proved the more productive of the two mines in the years before amalgamation, production for the entire period 1862–89 averaging 19,000 tons per annum. Together, Wallaroo and Moonta acquired an air of quiet superiority – in South Australia but also on the world stage. The *Wallaroo Times* newspaper in August 1868 spoke of 'Cornish mines, poor and low as colonial miners regard them'[73] and in 1875 it was alleged in the *Yorke's Peninsula Advertiser* that the production of the Moonta alone had already outstripped that of the once-great Cornish copper mines. In the period 1861 to July 1875, Moonta had raised 236,160 tons of ore worth £4,000,000, while the Consolidated Mines (in Cornwall) had between 1815 and 1856 raised only 230,296 tons of ore worth £2,893,482, with Dolcoath, Fowey Consols and even mighty Devon Great Consols all similarly falling short of the Moonta perform-ance.[74] In 1873 Anthony Trollope, the novelist, wrote truly that 'when men talk of the mining wealth of South Australia they allude to Wallaroo and Moonta.'[75]

This position of pre-eminence and the ability to survive lean years when mines elsewhere were forced to close was due in part to a willingness to inno-vate. In the familiar Cornish manner, it had been argued in the early days that heavy capitalisation and the introduction of machinery for pumping, winding, stamping, ore-dressing and smelting would put the mines on a secure footing to help them weather the days when rich and easily accessible ores had been exhausted. By and large, the plan seemed to work. In July 1864 a 22-inch rotary beam-engine, together with crusher, crusher rolls, whim chain, brasses, kibbles and drawings for an engine house and crusher house were ordered from the Bedford Foundry in Tavistock by the Wallaroo Mines. Later, other materials – such as the kibbles and dialling (surveying) instruments ordered in 1866, or the six jigging machines procured in 1867, or the four Cornish boilers and 400 fath-oms of whim chain purchased in 1868 – were acquired from William West & Co. of St Blazey. For very large engines, the Wallaroo Mines relied on Harvey & Co. of Hayle, as in 1876 when Harvey's supplied a 60-inch pumping engine. In 1862 '100 Cornish shovels'[76] were imported direct from Cornwall, to be followed in 1864 by copies of *Penrose's Ore Tables*. In 1875 it was decided to purchase 'Pitwork from Cornwall'.[77] The Moonta Mines, like its Wallaroo counterpart, began the early import of machinery and materials. In 1862 a 60-inch pump engine was ordered from Harvey & Co., this being the celebrated Hughes' engine which unfailingly performed the bulk of the Moonta Mines' pumping duties until closure in 1923. Other machinery was acquired from the Bedford Foundry, while items such as rope, chain, rivets and pressure gauges were imported directly from Cornwall, with costly theodolites coming from the firm of W. Wilton of St Day.

If some of the credit for the successful development of Wallaroo and Moonta must be given to the Cornish foundries which produced their engines and machinery, then equal attention should be devoted to the fascinating managerial regime of Captain Henry Richard Hancock.[78] Hancock was born in Horrabridge in the western fringe of Devon that was effectively a Greater Cornwall in the days of copper mining. Not strictly speaking a Cousin Jack, he was thought 'near enough to one' by his Cornish workforce, though local trade unionists never for-got that 'the manager of the Moonta is a Devon Dumpling'.[79] Hancock arrived in South Australia in 1859, at the age of 23, to work at Wheal Ellen in the Adelaide

Hills. In 1862 he moved to Yorke Peninsula, working on short-term contracts as assayer and draughtsman for both the Yelta and Moonta Mines. His chance came in June 1864 when he was appointed Chief Captain at Moonta, to replace Captain James Warmington who had fallen from favour. He immediately took steps to recruit new miners from Victoria and Cornwall and appointed his own choice of Cornish captains – Malachi Deeble, William and James Datson, James Barkla, C. Mitchell – to key positions. Frederick May, from Perranporth, became chief engineer and Bennett Opie was made head carpenter. In the closing months of 1864, Hancock formulated a plan for rapid expansion – a bold, innovative programme which in the years ahead would bring him into conflict with the more cautious of his directors. Even in 1878 and 1879, when the Moonta directors were dismayed by the sudden loss of profitability, Hancock reacted by acquiring redundant plant from Wheal James and the Paramatta, and in the 1880s he purchased a diamond drill for exploratory work and arranged the import of durable Oregon timbers to secure the underground workings.

Hancock also became chief captain of the Wallaroo Mines, following a succession of unsatisfactory appointments there. Eneder Warmington, like his brother James at Moonta, had been dismissed in 1864, to be replaced by another Cornishman, Captain Edward Dunstan, who served until February 1869. Dunstan quarrelled with his second captain, Paul Roach, and was accused of laxity in his sampling of tributers' ore. Captain Dunstan was thus replaced in turn by Samuel Higgs, quite a coup for the Wallaroo Mines directors who had sought 'a person of Education, and scientific as well as practical knowledge'.[80] Higgs, a past Secretary of the Royal Geological Society of Cornwall and contributor to its learned *Transactions*, was the member of a well-known Penzance family that had made its money from its interests in Wheal Providence and Wheal Margery. By 1872 Higgs was on the fabulous salary of £850 per annum, a measure of the regard in which he was held by his employers, but as the decade wore on the Wallaroo directors were increasingly disturbed that their mine was being consistently out-performed by the neighbouring Moonta. The relative inferiority of the Wallaroo ores was part of the explanation but the directors eventually took the view that management and mining acumen must also be part of the equation. In April 1877, therefore, the unthinkable happened and Higgs was dismissed, the Wallaroo directors explaining to their astonished but erstwhile chief captain that they 'wish to try if under other management more successful results can be obtained'.[81]

The position of chief captain was then given to Hancock, who immediately undertook a review of the Wallaroo ore bodies and claimed that 'Higgs ripped out everything',[82] having 'picked the eyes' out of the mine by plundering its best reserves without consideration for a long-term ore conservation policy. Be that as it may, Hancock was himself unable to revitalise the Wallaroo Mines, at least in the short term, but he was able to steer Moonta and Wallaroo towards ever greater integration and eventual merger. He became general superintendent of the combined Wallaroo and Moonta Mining and Smelting Company in 1889, a position he was to hold until 1898 when – in the best traditions of Cornish nepotism – he handed over the reins to his son, H. Lipson Hancock. During his time on Yorke Peninsula, Henry Richard Hancock had acquired a formidable reputation – his legend spreading not only to distant Cornwall but to America and South Africa too – and, as well as being held in awe in mining circles, he was also the butt of the dry Cornish humour which insisted that in his private life he was 'a dreadful libertine'.[83] Yet one person who came to know him in later life saw a gentle, measured man of quiet but outstanding leadership. He was 'a benign, white bearded patriarch with an old-world courtesy, and I came to the conclusion that the numerous stories about him ... were myths. That he was a masterful man, there is no doubt.'[84]

The demise of Higgs was perhaps something of a blow to the myth of Cousin Jack and the suggestion of Cornish infallibility, giving fuel to the debate that, as on the Lakes in Upper Michigan, occasionally reared its head in South Australia – the extent to which the 'innate' skill of the Cornishman was outweighed by his 'conservative' temperament. Satirical articles in the press made fun of the superstitious and quaint habits of the Cornish, such as the belief in 'ore dowsing', with an article in the *South Australian Register* in 1864 taking the form of a humorous report on a 'Wheal Bald Hill John Mining Company' (the 'John' element being an allusion to 'Cousin John', a variant of Cousin Jack). The mine had been discovered through 'the miraculous interposition of Providence by a pious Cornishman, who walking up a Bald Hill by a night saw a dog tail-piped with a lantern, running from south to north, and, taking the sight as a splendid surface indication, he immediately took out the section'. The article satirised all the typically bland and hopelessly optimistic assessments that characterised mining reports in the colony. There were 'strong and unmistakable indications of this valuable section having once been part of a sheep-walk', while in the northern level, driven 2 feet 6 inches, the reporting captain had encountered 'metallic roots ... evidently leading to the bottom of a splendid tree'.[85] Other articles were similarly disarming, with their sharp and telling wit, and most carried – either implicitly or explicitly – a criticism of Cousin Jack. One piece in the *South Australian Register* in 1872, for example, was a prospectus for a 'Great Distended Bubble Company', its property said to be adjacent to 'the world renowned Wheal Barrow Mine', its glowing report furnished by a 'Captain Trepolpen'.[86]

Humour aside, some critics were more direct in their condemnation, such as the correspondent in the *Yorke's Peninsula Advertiser* in 1878 who dismissed 'the great mass of Cornish miners [as] ... just so many ore-producing machines. Their art is instinct, and they are about the last class of whom to expect any departure from the old beaten track that their grandfathers had trod.'[87] Correspondence raged in the newspaper's columns about the relative advantages and disadvantages of 'book-learned', 'scientific' miners as opposed to those of 'practical miners' (the Cornish), Captain Anthony recalling the wisdom of Captain Joe Odgers (a well-known Camborne personality) whose favourite saying insisted that, 'I have been a barrow-boy, kibble-filler, tutworkman, tributer, and cappen, forty years: and where there's ore there's ore, and where there's none there's none'.[88] Put another way, theoretical applications 'may sound very grand to men who never saw a mine. But to a man that has been bred in Cornwall it is all humbug.'[89] There were some observers prepared to object to the 'nonsensical twaddle against Cornish miners',[90] and others who, with qualified praise, might admit that 'with the exception of Germany, Cornwall produces the best copper miners in the world'[91] and that 'though we are apt sometimes to laugh at Cousin Jack we might occasionally gain some lessons from him'.[92] Even the Cornish were incensed by the activities of the inexperienced and the unscrupulous, such as the incompetent Captain Tremaine who reported incorrectly on the Almanda silver mine ('Who is Captain Tremaine? Cornwall does not acknowledge him, but hands him back to South Australian speculators as theirs'[93]) or the two Cousin Jacks – Penberthy and Williams – who perpetrated the Victoria Mine swindle in 1864.[94] However, as the Cornish well knew, whatever might be said of the Cousin Jacks by their detractors, South Australian mining companies – not least the mighty Moonta and Wallaroo under the firm guidance of Captain Hancock – were persuaded of the superiority of Cornish miners, together with their methods and technology.

As ever, the construction of visibly Cornish communities did much to foster the mystique of Cornish exclusivity, although in the early days there would have been little in the remote, arid expanses of northern Yorke Peninsula to remind the Cousin Jacks and Jennys of home. Captain Dunstan's wife refused to join him at Wallaroo Mines – 'a whim rope wouldn't be strong enough to draw her'[95] to the district – while another early arrival described the locality in distinctly unflattering terms: 'there's neither water, grass nor trees – only scrub, interminable, horrible, dwarf scrub ... parched, scanty, hard baked soil ... desert'.[96] Gradually, however, the Cornish mining families – and the artisans and farmers who followed in their wake – transformed northern Yorke Peninsula, not least in the physical creation of communities and the transplantation therein of familiar social and cultural patterns inherited from Cornwall. Peter Thomas recalled the feelings of uncertainty and doubt that he experienced as he travelled up by coach from Port Adelaide. But he need not have worried, for when the coach pulled up in Kadina 'someone called out, who's that – old Bill? [Thomas's father] – how is Redruth looking, meaning ... the place I came from in Cornwall, and then another called out is there anybody there from Camborne. Thus was my reception. As I soon found out, I was not the only one from Cornwall, and I replied asking how is the bal looking, meaning the mine, and the answer was, plenty, of ore.'[97]

But if Cornish folk were made to feel immediately at home, the experience of the 'foreigner' might be entirely the reverse. At the turn of the century, one newcomer observed, 'My first impression of Moonta Mines was – what had I let myself in for? It was soon made clear that I was a foreigner with habits and opinions to be viewed with suspicion'.[98] Physically remote from Adelaide, Yorke Peninsula was cut off from the rest of the colony by the Hummocks range of hills, more of psychological than physical barrier (but akin to the Tamar border at home), a delineated boundary which led to the Cornish threat to unwelcome intruders: 'I'll send 'ee over the Hummocks.'[99] In 1873 Anthony Trollope wrote that 'so many of the miners were Cornishmen as to give Moonta and Wallaroo the air of Cornish towns',[100] and when W.G. Spence visited the district in 1889 he found that the locals 'lived isolated from the rest of the colony, remaining more Cornish than Cornwall itself'.[101] This impression was echoed in the assessment of the Rev. John Thorne, a Bible Christian minister, who observed in 1874 that:

> He felt very much at home on the Peninsula, it was more like Cornwall, almost surrounded by sea and insulated in position, the miners preserved the same rugged characteristics that marked them in Cornwall, and preserved their independence. Wherever they went they never forgot themselves as Cornishmen; they carried their principles and convictions with them and never failed to give them expression and effect.[102]

Significantly, such assertions of Cornish identity were accepted, if not always understood, by the non-Cornish of South Australia, further heightening the sense of Cornish exclusivity and lending yet more fabric to the myth of Cousin Jack. In the 1890s, when many Cornish people travelled down to Adelaide from Yorke Peninsula to make their way to the Western Australian gold-fields, the *People's Weekly* newspaper carried an amusing but telling feature:

> Some of the Adelaide folk who had assembled to witness the arrival of the 'Port Munta' [Moonta] people appeared surprised that they were so much like ordinary beings. As the Cornish men and women alighted from the train and proceeded from the station, one young lady, who evidently had not been far outside the precincts of the city, remarked in astonishment to her mamma, upon whose arm she gracefully leaned: 'Are those people really Cousin Jacks? I thought they had long tails.'[103]

The phrase 'Cornwall near England',[104] used habitually in the South Australian press, enhanced the already pronounced sense of Cornish ethnic identity, and even if the Cornish did not look very different from other people, their speech certainly marked them out as distinctive. Cornish dialect words, some derived from the only recently defunct Celtic language of Cornwall, which had disappeared as a community language by the mid-18th century, though lingering on the lips of individuals until perhaps as late as the 1890s, peppered Cornish speech on Yorke Peninsula. To 'clunk' was to swallow, tree roots were 'motts', 'nuddick' was the nape of the neck, a 'zawn' was a chasm or precipitous pit, to 'scat' was to push, slap or break. Cornish idiomatic expressions were equally prevalent. An overstaffed yet unpromising mine was 'like Wheal Scat, where they've got two capns and a clerk looking after three men', a crying baby would be said to be 'screechin like Tregeagle' (the Cornish folk villain), while summer days might be hot enough to 'scrowl a pilcher' (boil a pilchard). Naughty children would be threatened with being 'took to Bodmin' (the gaol), while miners would claim that 'mundic rides a good horse' (the presence of pyrites indicates the existence of payable lodes). More philosophically: 'if wishes were horses, beggars would ride.'[105] Folk rhymes also survived:

There were three sailors of Mevagissey
Who took a boat and went to sea
But first with pork and leeky pasties
And a barrel of pilchards they loaded she.[106]

Robert Stephen Hawker's rousing ballad, 'The Song of the Western Men', or plain 'Trelawny' as it was known, was adopted as a national anthem by the Yorke Peninsula Cornish as surely as it was elsewhere in the world, paraphrased versions appearing from time to time as commentaries on local issues. Thus in 1875, when the Central Board of Health Inspectors decided to impose new sanitary conditions on the mineral lease settlements, one outraged resident 'invoked [the] spirit of the illustrious Trelawney':

And shall th' Inspector dare,
And will th' Inspector care
To brave a thousand Cornishmen
As good as anywhere?

And shall he touch our tanks
Despite our serried ranks?
Then all the rowdy Cornish boys
Will give him backhand thanks![107]

Later, in 1883, another incensed Cousin Jack objected to the manner in which non-Cornish folk were insinuating themselves into the community and taking positions of power and importance. 'And shall Trelawney die/ Then twenty thousand Cornishmen/ Will ask the reason why', he stormed. And elsewhere: 'Sir – So essentially Cornish are we that we would think not only our habits and national amusements would prevail, but that our Mayor, magistrates, and leading men would be chosen from among them.'[108]

Within the repertoire of 'essentially Cornish' activities that characterised the cultural life of the Yorke Peninsula, perhaps the most vivid was Cornish wrestling. Matches were held on the usual holidays, such as Easter and Christmas, but also on 24 June (Midsummer's Eve, 'as Cousin John still persists in calling it'[109]) when numerous bonfires were also lit across the peninsula. There was the dramatic occasion when John H. 'Dancing' or 'Dancer' Bray, the Moonta champion, defeated his Ballarat opponent in 1868, 'like a flash of lightning, he [Bray] brought off the "Flying Mare" trick. It was said that 20 captains who were there declared they had not seen anything like it in Cornwall .... Then followed a shout such as might have been heard when Sebastopol was captured'.[110] Equally Cornish were the sumptuous dinners held to christen the starting of new engines, such as when Captain East invited all the local captains to the starting of his new 80-inch engine at the New Cornwall mine in 1866, 'It was a good old Cornish custom to meet together on occasions like the present, and to show a friendly feeling, although engaged on different mines'.[111] Similarly, at the starting of the Paramatta engine in 1869, 'By the liberality of the Directors a plentiful dinner had been provided for every miner or other person in connection with the mine'.[112]

Also among Yorke Peninsula's 'habits and national amusements' were the numerous brass, silver, and fife and drum bands that at the slightest excuse would emerge to lead Sunday school parades, trade union marches, and other demonstrations and carnivals. There was Bargwanna's Band at Moonta, the Wallaroo Town Band, Mr Ricard's Kadina Brass Band, the Cross Roads Fife and Drum Band, and very many more. Choral activities were especially popular, not least the male voice choirs that emerged towards the end of the century. A leading vocalist was Lesley Davey, and in October 1907 people thronged to the East Moonta Literary Society to hear his rendition of 'Lead, Kindly Light' which, as A.K. Hamilton Jenkin once observed, was also for a time a Cornish national anthem.[113] Certainly, its words were uncannily appropriate for a people so given to emigration and to mining:

> Lead, Kindly Light, amid the encircling gloom,
> Lead Thou me on;
> The night is dark, and I am far from home;
> Lead Thou me on.
> Keep Thou my feet; I do not ask to see
> The distant scene – one step enough for me.

Jennie Opie, born at Kadina, was steeped in this choral tradition, and for a time emerged as South Australia's answer to Dame Fanny Moody Manners, the 'Cornish Nightingale', travelling throughout Australia at the turn of the 20th century and to Japan, India and China to sing to her enraptured audiences. More introspective, perhaps, were the composers and performers of Cornish carols, little-known outside Cornish communities at home and abroad but for the Cornish themselves important iconographers of the

Cornish international identity. Volumes of Cornish carols were published across the world and in 1893 The *Christmas Welcome: A Choice Collection of Cornish Carols* was published at Moonta. Arranged or composed locally by musicians such as J.H. 'Johnnie' Thomas and James 'Fiddler Jim' Richards (from Perranporth), these carols followed faithfully the Cornish form of frequent word repetitions and flowing bass:

> Calm on the list'ning ear of night,
> Came heaven's melodious strains,
> Where wide Judea stretches far,
> O'er silver mantled plains.[114]

Among James Richards' compositions was the funeral music 'Rapture', set to the words of the hymn 'Thee We Adore'. A ritual developed whereby the coffin was picked up by the bearers during two lines from the third stanza of the hymn – 'What e'er we do, where'er we be/We are travelling to the grave' – the haunting, moving strains of the tune drifting across the mineral lease settlements as the deceased was borne solemnly to his or her final resting place. The Rev. William Francis James, born in Truro in 1846 and ordained as a Bible Christian minister in 1876, recalled the memorable funerals he had known at home in Chacewater: 'The corpse was preceded by some twenty to thirty men, having good voices, with measured step and slow, singing a hymn to an appropriate tune. I have never heard anything like it, save at Moonta.'[115] Methodism itself, of course, was deeply ingrained in the social, cultural and spiritual life of the peninsula. The Rev. W.H. Hosken, a Cornish Bible Christian minister from neighbouring Victoria, visited Yorke Peninsula in January 1875 and was 'persuaded that I have never seen a finer field of labour anywhere in our Connexion.'[116] Years later, another Methodist activist recalled that:

> I came to Moonta in 1883 just after the famous Captain Piper
> had returned from Cornwall with his hundreds of immigrants
> and I am asked to give my impressions of Cornish revivals.
> What were the miners' characteristics? In things religious,
> fervid, strong in their feelings, love or hate, emotional in the
> extreme, passionate if you will ... Those were days when
> preachers spoke of hell with an absolute belief in it as the
> abode of damned souls.[117]

In the Great Revival that swept Yorke Peninsula in the aftermath of the Great Strike of 1874, the Rev. John G. Wright, formerly of Burra Burra, wrote in his diary that 'There is grand work doing in all the Chapels'. At Wallaroo Mines 'Many were shouting and weeping', and at Moonta there were 'Souls saved every night. At Cross Roads 30 souls in three nights. One woman 60 years of age while our people were singing "Come to Jesus" cried "Yes, I am coming", she came and fell on her knees, found peace .... How grand to see souls cast themselves on the altar'.[118] The Sunday school anniversaries were also rousing affairs, 'The children headed by a brass band and the school Superintendent marched around the streets in class order .... Upon returning to the school, each child received a large bun and a packet of lollies ... and the elders would have a sit-down meal of home-made eatables'.[119] The Yorke Peninsula Methodists, not least the Bible Christians, were especially active in their missionary work in the colony – bringing the Word to outlying rural districts on the Peninsula and, especially, in the far North. As early as 1873, the Bible Christians had seven ordained ministers at work in the far North (six Cornishmen, one Devonian), and in 1876 the Bible Christian Conference in Zion Chapel, St Austell, had no fewer than 297 vacancies to fill in Australia. The Rev. John Thorne was home to address the Conference, 'Br. John Thorne spoke with great ability on the claims of South Australia ... "But", said Mr Thorne, "some say you can't get anyone to go .... We don't want you to get anyone else, come yourselves".'[120]

As in Cornwall, this all-pervading Methodist influence helped mould the course of political development, though in Cornwall the early collapse of the mining industry and the mass emigration of potential leaders had retarded the growth of both the Labour Party and trade unionism, 'fossilising' the Liberals as the expression of Cornish nonconformist radicalism. On northern Yorke Peninsula, however, where the mines and mining communities remained intact during the period that witnessed the rise of organised labour, the story was somewhat different. As early as 1848 the Cornish miners had struck at the Burra Burra mine (see Chapter 5), and in 1864 there was a strike at the Moonta and Wallaroo Mines against the allegedly 'tyrannical' regimes of William and Eneder Warmington, two Cornish brothers who had been in America before taking up the positions on Yorke Peninsula (a third brother, James, had already been dismissed from Moonta Mines in 1862 for 'misconduct'[121]). The Warmingtons were forced to resign, thus settling the dispute and ushering in ten years of relatively harmonious developmental work at the mines. In 1874, however, the Great Strike disturbed this atmosphere (at a time when embryonic trade unionists back in

Cornwall had been flexing their muscles in opposition to the 'five-week month' pay period, and when the Cornish on the Lakes had also been on strike), creating a rift between employers and employees and laying the foundation for what was to become a vigorous trade union movement. An epic poem was written to commemorate the event, elevating its leaders to the status of martyrs and heroes, its melodramatic style adding to the mystique that grew up around the strike:

> And soon they met at Elder's Shaft;
> The 'Ring' was formed, the glor'ous ring,
> Where Cousin Jack stands like a king;
> And freely to each thought gives vent,
> As to his brain each thought is sent,
> In eloquence that's all his own,
> States his opinions quick and clear,
> Nor will he yield to force or fear
> Nor will he back from anything
> He states when standing in the 'Ring'.[122]

The precipitating cause of the strike was a general reduction in remuneration at the mines, announced on 2 April 1874. The miners' solidarity was almost entire, the remaining black-legs who had kept the pump engines going being swept (quite literally, with broomsticks) from their posts by the enraged Cousin Jennys: itself a fascinating event which has established itself in both local lore and the historiography of South Australia, one of the rare occasions when the all too invisible Cornish women have been allowed their place in the otherwise male-dominated narrative of the Great Emigration. As Roslyn Paterson has observed in her treatment of the Cousin Jennys of northern Yorke Peninsula, the women were for the most part the silent, compliant servants of their husbands' wills, 'Wherever you go, I will go, wherever you live, I will live.'[123] But behind this veneer of passive domestic duty and sexual obligation, with its continuous round of child-bearing, was the potential for spirited, independent action on the mining frontiers of the New World. This owed something to the tradition of the independent bal-maiden back in Cornwall but it was also Cousin Jenny's own 'myth' – the inherent toughness of Cornishwomen and their suitability for the harsh life of the frontier.

Faced with the unanimity of action displayed by the miners and their wives, together with the tacit support given to the strikers by the local business community, the employers backed down, agreeing to restore the former wage rate for a further two months and to give one month's notice of any future cuts. The Moonta Miners' and Mining Mechanics Association that had been launched as a friendly society in November 1872 had by now transformed itself into an embryonic trade union movement, rooted not merely in class but in ethnic identity too:

> We invite the young and old
> To join our miners' band;
> Come and have your names enrolled,
> And join us heart and hand.
>
> Cornwall was never conquered yet,
> By men of mighty powers; .
> And shall we in silence sit,
> And show ourselves like cowards?
>
> We have this motto 'one and all';
> This coat of arms is ours;
> Then let us rise both great and small
> To carry out our endeavours.[124]

A similar association was formed at Wallaroo, in practice a branch of the larger Moonta organisation. Among the early leaders were John Prisk, a Bible Christian local preacher, and the mining engineer John Visick (or Visack), from Kea, the son of a schoolmaster and 'A radical all his days.'[125] There was also Reuben Gill, 'The Billy Bray of South Australia' as he was known, a much-loved personality and a favourite speaker at miners' meetings. As one commentator noted, 'Mr Gill's style was extraordinary. Jumping upon the platform as though propelled there by a catapult, he would jerk his head from side to side, and instantly let loose his eloquence at a tremendous rate.'[126] Another remarked that, 'His rough eloquence would fall from his lips in a rapid stream, and apt metaphor and racy extemporaneous rhyme follow each other with almost lightning-like rapidity, while the attention of his audience would remain enchained throughout his speech.'[127] Together, Prisk, Visick and Gill set the tone for trade unionism on Yorke Peninsula, infusing it with a strong Cornish-Methodist appeal which spoke directly to the miners and established the Association's credibility and legitimacy in the community. Significantly, one of the first issues to be confronted by the Association was the 'five-week month', the very issue at the heart of recent industrial action in Cornwall. Taking their cue from miners recently, arrived from Cornwall, they demanded an end to the practice in South Australia. More significantly, however, they extended their criticism of the employment system itself, articulating with increasing vigour their concerns about tribute and tutwork contracting.

Although, with its entrepreneurial element and its recognition of the skill and enterprise of the supposedly 'independent' and 'individualistic' Cousin Jack, tribute and tutwork contracting had generally enjoyed the support of generations of Cornish miners at home and abroad, it increasingly fell into disrepute in the new industrial giants such as Calumet and Hecla or Moonta and Wallaroo. Here, as the divide between workers and managers grew, so contracting was seen increasingly as a device by which the bosses were able to retard wage rates. In September 1879, in response to agitation from the Association, the Moonta and Wallaroo Mines replaced the 'open bidding' for contracts by a confidential 'private tendering' in which groups ('pares') of miners seeking to work a particular piece of ground ('pitch') were required to submit their bids on slips of papers instead of shouting one another down. This alleviated the worst excesses of 'downward bidding', as competing pares struggled to win the contract for an especially attractive pitch, but one sceptic observed in April 1880 that 'Cornishmen are generally of an envious disposition ... and so with tendering. I have heard a remark passed when a miner has heard another is tendering for the same job. "Ef 'ee d'get un 'ell have taw tender some law", and hence they all tender low and labor is bought below a nominal fig-ure.'[128] That this was so was demonstrated in 1879 when tenders were invited for a tutwork contract for the sinking of four fathoms of a six foot wide shaft at the East Moonta Mine: T. Williams £26 per fathom (accepted); S. Stephens £28; J. Angove £28 5s; J. Rowe £28 2s; R. Hancock £29; W. Pengelly & Co. £34; R. Gill £35; J. Bray £37; H. Stephens £38; J. Murrin and S. Samson £44 15s; Samuel Richards £90 for the first two fathoms and £100 for the next two fathoms.[129] With a trade union structure now in existence, the growing opposition to contracting could be organ-ised and articulated. In 1884 there was a brief and partially successful strike over the abolition of 'subsist' (an advance on earnings) for long-term contracts, an issue which was again fought with some success in 1888. By then, as W.G. Spence observed in his 1909 history of the Australian labour movement, 'The Cornish miner is generally a man who can do his share of grumbling ... so when Unionism caught on they realised that many injustices might have been remedied years ago had they been organised and pulled together.'[130]

Tension at the mines continued during 1889 and 1890, and in September 1891 the Moonta Branch of the Amalgamated Miners' Association (an Australia-wide trade union which the Association had joined) declared a strike against the contracting system. The strike lasted a gruelling eighteen weeks and, despite the strike fund being swollen by some £8507 sent by sympathetic miners at Broken Hill, Bendigo and Charters Towers (Queensland), the action was broken finally by desperate workers (later vilified on the Peninsula and even as far away as the Western Australian gold-fields as 'Ninety-Twoers') going to the mines to beg for work. The Moonta and Wallaroo company, recognising that hostility to contracting was by now deeply ingrained, sought to create a more harmonious industrial atmosphere by introducing various adjustments to the system, most significantly in 1903 when 'captain's prices' (the mechanism that had determined the value of a particular pitch) was replaced by a 'sliding scale' related to the international price of copper in which the contractor participated directly in the company's profits.[131]

Unlike Calumet and Hecla and the other multi-ethnic mines on the Lakes in Upper Michigan, Moonta and Wallaroo had remained more homogeneously Cornish, the Cousin Jack imprint stamped firmly upon local trade unionism. The union itself survived the trauma of 1891, establishing itself even further as an integral part of peninsula life, while it played a major role in the development of the United Labor Party (ULP) in South Australia. In contrast to the Labor Party as it developed in the eastern colonies, with the influence of Irish Catholicism, the ULP was from the first nonconformist in flavour. According to Dean Jaensch, a leading authority on South Australia's political history, the ULP's politics were more '"democratic" rather than "socialism" .... From its beginnings, South Australian Labor was a moderate movement, practical rather than ideological in its outlook and essentially pragmatic in its activities.'[132] This reflected the impact of the Cornish. The colony's first Labor MP, elected to the Adelaide Parliament in 1891 as the Member for Wallaroo, was a Cornish Methodist trade unionist, one Richard Hooper, and South Australia's first Labor Premier, in 1910, was John Verran, another Cornish miner, Methodist and trade union activist from northern Yorke Peninsula. Verran articulated what he (and much of his party) saw as the fundamental link between religious belief and political action, 'Religion is citizenship, and the relationship between religion and politics is very close .... When we come to justice and righteousness and truth ... religion is not just a question of going to heaven. It is a question of living and making the world better for having been in it.'[133] Significantly, it was this religious/political nexus that increasingly defined 'Cornishness' in South Australia: the cartoonist's stock figure of a South Australian Labor politician even into the 1930s was a jovial, corpulent Cousin Jack, complete with Moonta billy-goat beard, and, as a closet socialist, with a red flag hidden behind his back.[134]

If this was a removal from – or at least a refinement of – the traditional myth of Cousin Jack, then so too was the changing focus of Cornish loyalty in South Australia in which Moonta and environs – rather than distant Cornwall – had become 'the Hub of the Universe'.[135] It was not just that 'Moonta, in its proximity to the sea, is able to carry the role of an outpost of the delectable Duchy',[136] but rather a question of – as George Jose of Illogan, a former Moonta miner, put it in 1923 – 'What do they know of Cornwall, Who only Cornwall know?'[137] As May Vivienne had already observed wryly in 1908 in her book *Sunny South Australia*, 'the majority of the miners in this district [Moonta] are Cornishmen ... the people living there have a very high opinion of themselves'.[138] But there was also reflective sensitivity behind this apparently arrogant loyalty to northern Yorke Peninsula, expressed, for example, in the verses of Thomas Burtt who penned the following on his return to Moonta after several months absence, the 'dirge-like sound and muffled reverberations' awakening in him subtle appreciation of the singular, rather awesome environment and atmosphere of Moonta Mines:

> Hark! Methinks I hear the echo!
> Of those solemn Moonta Mines;
> Sadly sounding distant far-off,
> Over flow'rets, trees and vines.
>
> Listen to the ceaseless throbbing,
> Of those engines measured slow;
> Telling many a weary spirit
> How it shares a world of woe.[139]

# CHAPTER NINE

# NEW FRONTIERS –

# AUSTRALIA

In the 50-year period between the end of the Napoleonic Wars in 1815 and the crash of Cornish copper in 1866, emigration had become firmly established as an integral part of Cornish life. Cornwall had emerged as a significant European emigration region, while the Cornish themselves had played a major role in the settlement and development of new lands, not least as skilled facilitators in the creation and expansion of the international mining economy. They had assisted the early penetration by British capital of Latin America, and by the 1840s were already a crucial element in the lead and copper mining industries of the United States and Australia. The discovery of gold in California in 1848 and in Australia a few years later added a new dimension to this international mining economy, so that by the fateful year of 1866 a sophisticated repertoire of mining destinations had been constructed for potential emigrants from Cornwall. To this was added a strong Cornish presence in the expansion of the agricultural frontiers of Canada, South Australia, New Zealand and parts of the United States, a reminder that not all Cornish emigrants were miners – even if agricultural expansion was often linked to the spread of mining, the Cornish miner-turned-farmer becoming a familiar figure in both America and Australia.

After 1866, as Cornwall entered upon its long, dark period of de-industrialisation, the Cornish were well-placed to respond to the new crises in which they found themselves. Existing conduits of emigration took them to Upper Michigan or Yorke Peninsula or to the agricultural frontiers of New Zealand and South Australia, while a vast new panorama of potential destinations was already unfolding – an extraordinary canvas which stretched from Nevada in the United States and British Columbia in Canada to Broken Hill in New South Wales and Kalgoorlie in Western Australia. The picture was soon to encompass the emerging world of South Africa while embracing yet more for far-flung spots such as India, Nigeria and the Gold Coast (modern Ghana). At first glance a bewildering and ad hoc flowering of opportunity, there was in fact a certain logic to this process, a progressive development of the international mining frontier in response to the trends that had already been established by the late 1850s and 1860s.

In Australia, for instance, the impact of the rushes to New South Wales and (especially) Victoria had, despite the resurgence of copper mining in South Australia in the early 1860s, alerted observers to the potential for further gold discoveries within the continent. Paradoxically, one effect was to lure gold seekers to the neighbouring islands of New Zealand, already a destination for Cornish folk – the Wakefieldian settlements of the 1840s, the copper mining on Kauwau island, the agricultural expansion of the 1870s – and now a magnet for Cousin Jacks in the heady days after the New South Wales and Victorian rushes. Gold discoveries in the 1860s drew Cornish miners to New Zealand from South Australia, notably Captain James Datson from Moonta who spent several months exploring the alluvial deposits of the Molyneux and Shotover Rivers, while in the 1870s a further rush to the Otago district attracted Cousin Jacks from both Cornwall and Australia.

A Cornish community grew up in the mining town of Hamiltons in Eastern Otago, and the surviving diary of one of its Cousin Jacks – Thomas Common from Stenalees, near St Austell – forms the basis of Audrey Paterson's illuminating study *A Cornish Goldminer at Hamiltons*.[1] Together with his friend Silas Hore, Common emigrated to New Zealand in 1871, visiting first the Waipori diggings, where there were numerous Cornish, before travelling on to Hamiltons itself. Hamiltons was then a lively town of some 4000 souls, a bewildering mixture of Chinese, Irishmen, Englishmen and other nationalities, but within this colonial melting pot Common found more than a smattering of Cousin Jacks and Jennys. There were miners with familiar Cornish surnames such as Thomas, Kitto, Nicholls, Pascoe, Kinsman, and Rosevear, while among the Wesleyan local preachers was a Cornishman called Henry Flamank. Cornish wrestling was popular, especially on Boxing Day and as part of the New Year festivities, and one contemporary observer noted with some amusement the protective Cousin Jack exclusivity with which the Cornish sought to guard their sport: 'It was amazing at New Year time to see the suspicion on the faces of those in authority, or those that the programme pleased, at the sight of a stranger, dreading he might spoil the fun of Cornish wrestling.'[2]

In 1878 Thomas Common was joined in New Zealand by his sweetheart from Stenalees, one Elizabeth Martyn, and in the same year they were married. Later, Common went into partnership with Thomas Roseveare (of the well-known Luxulyan family of that name) to open a store in the nearby township of Enfield. By then the Hamiltons mines were in decline, their major workings abandoned by 1888, although elsewhere in New Zealand alluvial gold-fields continued to attract Cornish miners, especially the unemployed from Moonta and Wallaroo during the difficult decades of the 1880s. Others were drawn to yet more far-flung parts of Australasia, in particular to the French colony of New Caledonia where there were several copper mines. Captain Isaac Killicoat, from Perranwell, visited the colony briefly during his time as superintendent of the smelting works at Burra Burra, while Captain John Warren later resigned his position at the Hamley Mine (at Moonta) to visit New Caledonia, taking with him Cousin Jacks such as William Bray from St Just-in-Penwith and William Stocker from Biscovey. Papua New Guinea also attracted Cornish adventurers, and as late as 1935 advertisements appeared in the Moonta *People's Weekly* for skilled hard-rock miners to go to the copper mines of Bougainville.[3]

Back in continental Australia, the success of South Australian copper and Victorian gold had encouraged men to search elsewhere in the country for these lucrative metals. Queensland, for example, had already attracted Cornish emigrants, miners among them, no fewer than 202 Cousin Jacks and Jennys having arrived in Moreton Bay (as Queensland was known before it was separated from New South Wales) in the decade 1849–59.[4] Individuals such as Joseph Eade, a Cornish miner who arrived in the *Phoebe Dunbar* in 1856, or Elizabeth Pascoe, a servant in the *Shackamaxon* in 1859, responded enthusiastically to offers of free or assisted passage to the colony. One such advertisement, placed in the Liskeard *Cornish Times* in March 1858 by the local emigration agent, John Philp, explained that emigrants paying their own way would receive a £30 Land Order (equivalent to 30 acres of land) on arrival in the colony, while free or assisted passages would be awarded to members of useful occupational groups such as wheelwrights, shepherds, miners, masons, carpenters, bricklayers, blacksmiths, shipwrights and female domestic servants 'of good character'.[5] That such folk would prospect for minerals in their new home was inevitable and in 1861 a rich copper deposit was located at Peak Downs in the remote expanses of central Queensland. A handful of professional copper miners from the Burra Burra mine was hired to commence operations at the site and in January 1868 an article in the Adelaide *Register* on 'the migratory tendencies of Cousin Jack'[6] noted the departure of several Moonta miners for

Peak Downs. In the same month the *Wallaroo Times* recorded the departure of some 70 to 80 men who, with their families, were travelling to Peak Downs under Captain Osborne.[7] Although a number of these miners wrote back to Yorke Peninsula complaining of fever and high prices this did not discourage Captain Tredinnick (originally from the North Downs Mine, Scorrier) from leaving Wallaroo Mines to try his luck in Queensland.

It was not until the copper price rises of 1872–73 that extractive work was undertaken at Peak Downs on any scale and in April 1872 the *West Briton* noted the departure of 200 miners from Cornwall for that district. In the spring of 1873 another 350 emigrants left Cornwall for Peak Downs, enticed by promises of wages from £15 to £30 per month. Among their number was Charles Simmons, from the lead mining village of Menheniot, near Liskeard, who worked at the mine until it was abandoned in the price downturn of 1876–77. Thereafter, he made his way down to Moonta, as did other Peak Downs miners, such as Philip Orchard, Thomas Cock from Redruth, and John Retallick from St Austell, with Peak Downs itself doomed to remain idle for ever. But many remained in Queensland, working in the colony's gold-mines or prospecting on their own account in the gold-fields in the hope of striking it rich. In 1867 extensive gold deposits had been found in Gympie in southern Queensland and, as was so often the case, the South Australian Cornish were at the forefront of its initial exploitation, Thomas Warn and Edward Dunstan travelling up from Kapunda as soon as news of the discovery had been made public. In the economic downturn of the 1880s, Cousin Jacks from Moonta and Wallaroo were still arriving at Gympie, although by that time attention had switched to other parts of Queensland. The Cornish played their part in the discovery and exploitation of gold at Charters Towers in 1871, at Palmer River in 1873, and later at Mount Morgan in the 1880s where Cornish metallurgists such as Captain G.A. Rickard and Henry Trenear helped realise the astonishing £7 million in dividends paid out by the Mount Morgan company by 1907.

The Palmer River rush, the result of a deliberate strategy to locate gold reserves in the almost impenetrable tropical vastness of the Cape York Peninsula of northern Queensland, fell victim to the appalling floods of 1874 when many of the hitherto enthusiastic diggers were marooned or even drowned. Others died of starvation, so complete was their isolation, while bands of panicky miners tried to force their way upon the Sydney-bound steamers at Cookstown on the east coast of the Peninsula. The *West Briton* recorded the eye-witness account of one Cousin Jack who had seen it first hand:

> Every steamer to Cook Town brings numbers of fine, strong, healthy-looking fellows, who are full of hope, and will listen to no tale of disaster, resolved upon going to the diggings to see for themselves how matters are. The same boat takes away South about the same number of men, pale, and thin, and glad to escape from the country, many of them with no money in their pockets, and few, indeed, with the gold they so eagerly seek.[8]

It was a familiar enough tale, one heard in various forms throughout the Australias and the Americas in this period but, as the *West Briton* account observed, diggers rarely seemed to learn their lesson:

> Still they come and still they go in hundreds from all parts of the colony, steamboat companies benefiting from the ill-wind that blows for so many. The chief thing that attracts men to the North is that it is a new country, a golden country too, and there is no knowing what riches may be found between Palmer and Cape York, a distance of about five hundred miles, where the white man has never trod – in fact, a terra incognita.[9]

For Cousin Jacks elsewhere in Queensland, the struggle for survival or to secure advantage was of a different nature. F.C.B. Vosper, from St Dominick, migrated from Cornwall to Queensland in 1883, making his way to the gold-mining district of Charters Towers. There he rapidly became involved in local politics and in journalism, two activities that would bring him fame (or notoriety) a decade later in Western Australia. He was soon appointed sub-editor of the Charters Towers *Northern Miner*, later forming his own labour weekly, the *Republican*. Through its pages he lent passionate and articulate support to the Queensland sheep-shearers' strike in 1890 and he led his own miners' strike in Charters Towers, the resultant rioting was a good excuse for the three-month prison sentence that he received subsequently. Thereafter, he worked briefly for newspapers in Sydney and Melbourne, before heading West in 1892. When not confronting the bosses, Queensland's European miners, not least the Cornish, were opposing the presence and influence of the Chinese. On the Palmer River the Chinese completely outnumbered the European miners (some 17,000 compared to only 1400 white men) and they were feared as aliens and also because, it was alleged, their presence had a generally depressing effect on conditions and wage rates.

The problem did have a lighter side, which John Langdon Bonython appreciated when he wrote that 'A storekeeper in Queensland with a good old Cornish name, John Tonkin, to wit, had to advertise that he hailed from Cornwall, and not from China',[10] but the predominant Cornish view was that articulated by one Cousin Jack in 1881, 'I would advise ... my countrymen, for I am a Cornishman, to scout [scat] these pests, and show them unmistakably that they are not welcome here.'[11] The neighbouring Northern Territory also had its 'Chinese question', the discovery of gold there in 1871 in hopelessly remote country (where the costs of extraction would inevitably be high) leading to demands for the employment of cheap labour – the Chinese. 'Coolies', as they were known in the pejorative language of their European detractors, flocked into the territory, especially after the Palmer River debacle, and by 1879 they outnumbered the Europeans by seven to one. As in Queensland, the territory's administrators acted against the 'yellow peril', as the Chinese 'threat' was known to the paranoid Europeans anxious to defend their status, with discriminatory measures (only partially successful) designed to make life difficult for the Asiatics, spurred on by assertions such as those of one Cousin Jack who insisted that 'there is no comparison between Chinese and such miners one finds at Moonta Mines'.[12]

Queensland's mix of copper and gold was mirrored in New South Wales. As we saw in Chapter 7, there had been early discoveries of copper at Cornish Settlement, while gold was found in the same general locality on the eve of the New South Wales gold rush in early 1851. Both copper and gold were also mined at Cobar, an arid, isolated spot some 400 miles from the coast in the midst of outback New South Wales between the Lachlan and Darling rivers. Copper was first identified at Cobar in 1870 by Sidwell Kruge, who in Cornwall had worked as a bal-maiden, when she was shown some unusual rocks encountered by two Danish well-sinkers. Captain James Varcoe was employed to open the resultant Cobar (later Great Cobar) mine but the real development work was left to Captain Thomas Lean, who arrived from Moonta in December 1871. Other Cousin Jacks accompanied him, including his son Thomas, together with Edward Tonkin, Peter Andrewartha, Thomas Prisk and Thomas Rogers. Further copper discoveries led to new mines, notably the C.S.A. – short for Cornishman, Scotchman and Australian – named in honour of its proprietors, Henry and Richard Nancarrow, George Gibb and John Connelly. Captain Morrish (or Morish), originally from Truro, travelled up from Ballarat to become underground captain of the Great Cobar, while Captain Dunstan came across with a further party from Moonta and Wallaroo, still other Cornish miners making the difficult journey down from Peak Downs. Some copper mines found gold at depth, and others, such as the New Occidental, were gold-mines from the start. But whatever the metal, these were very much Cornish mines. The labour force, terminology and technology were overwhelmingly Cornish, as were the working practices, with their tribute and tutwork system and 'club & doctor' funds. It was an appalling environment – one contemporary observer complained of the heat and water shortages and the dust 'which blinds the eyes', opining that 'A dust storm at Cobar is worse than anything of the kind experienced anywhere else in the colony'[13] – but by 1880 Cobar's population had risen to some 2000 souls – many living in the suburb of Cornish Town. Although some of Cobar's wandering Cousin Jacks were enticed away to Broken Hill during the 1880s, the mines continued to prosper. Indeed, there was a boom in 1906–07 and the district benefited from the relatively high copper prices during the First World War. But the dramatic slump in prices that accompanied the peace brought an abrupt end to Great Cobar, which closed in March 1919.[14]

Copper was associated with the Cornish at home and abroad, and gold, not least in California and Victoria, had also become a Cornishman's metal. Coal, by contrast, was beneath the dignity of Cousin Jack (or so it was said), notwithstanding the increasing willingness with which destitute Cornish miners made for the coalfields of South Wales, the North of England and Lowland Scotland in the years after 1866. Indeed, the Cornish had also found their way to the anthracite country of Scranton in Pennsylvania – some directly from Cornwall and others via South Wales – while in New South Wales in Australia the Cornish were attracted to the coal mines of Newcastle and the Hunter valley region. In the period 1860 to 1900 the overwhelming majority of Newcastle miners were from Wales, Scotland, the Midlands and North of England, and Cornwall – the traditional homes of British mining. Of the 'English' miners, 11 per cent were from Staffordshire, 41 per cent from Northumberland and Durham, and six per cent from Cornwall. A number of the Cornish had already acquired their coal mining credentials in England, such the Rundle family from Liskeard which had spent some 20 years in County Durham before emigrating to Newcastle in New South Wales in 1888. Others had mined in other parts of Australia, such as the party which arrived at Newcastle from Moonta in 1868.[15]

Tin mining, perhaps, was more to the Cornishman's liking. Tin had been found at Fisher's Gully in southern Queensland by four Cornishmen from South Australia, but originally from Redruth, in 1872, while in northern New South Wales places such as Stannum and Stannifer were for a time the focus of Cornish tin seekers. Earlier, in December 1871, tin had also been discovered in

Tasmania in the remote western highlands at Mount Bischoff. This was the celebrated 'Mountain of Tin' which, though playing an important role in the continuing saga of Australian mineral development, posed an overwhelming and almost fatal threat to Cornwall's own tin mining industry at the very moment when it seemed on the point of revival. In 1875 the *West Briton* lamented that 'In the history of mining in Cornwall it has known no such disastrous year as 1874 .... Australia, which has been made the home of many Cornishmen, threatened at one time to annihilate altogether tin mining in this country.'[16] Two years later, in June 1877, the *West Briton* could add that 'a very large number of our Cornish mines must cease working ... we Cornishmen have never had such a competition in the production of tin as we have at present in Australia'.[17] But Mount Bischoff did provide employment for emigrant Cousin Jacks, not least at the so-called Cornwall Tin Mine which was an early producer of note. Captain William White was brought out especially from the St Just United Mine in Cornwall to manage the West Bischoff mine, while Captain W. H. Wesley – from the same parish – went to another of the Bischoff workings. As ever, parties of eager adventurers turned up from Moonta and Wallaroo, while in 1914 one perhaps over-exuberant enthusiast could claim that those 'who know anything about Latchley or Chilsworthy in eastern Cornwall'[18] would find much in common between the Cornish and Tasmanian landscapes – despite the bitter blows that Tasmanian tin had rained upon the mining economy of Cornwall, the colony had nonetheless found a place in the iconography of Cornishness.

Amidst this proliferation of Australasian mining frontiers, two destinations stand out strongly as bastions of the Cornish – Broken Hill in the 1880s and beyond and the gold rush to Western Australia in the 1890s. South Australia's roving Cornish miners, so important in the development of mining elsewhere in the continent, were prominent in both and as early as 1867 they had explored the remote Barrier district of New South Wales in which the Broken Hill finds were later made. Far from existing centres of population and supply, with little shelter and water hopelessly scarce, the fearsome expanses of the Barrier Ranges – the strange pimple-like hills that marched across what were to European eyes an otherwise barren and featureless landscape – were one of the most hellish spots of inland, outback Australia. Tucked into the so-called 'corner country' of north-western New South Wales, with South Australia to the west and Queensland in the north, the Barrier was, to even the most unobservant of eyes, clearly mineralised country, with its tell-tale stainings and outcrops which hinted at lead, tin, copper, iron, silver, perhaps even gold. During 1867, as the international downturn in copper prices threatened the viability of the by now ailing Burra Burra, so the copper mine's anxious Cousin Jacks began to ponder pastures new. In February of that year the *Wallaroo Times* reported an alleged discovery of gold on the Barrier and anticipated that 'As the Burra mine will be knacked [closed] next month ... we would not wonder if some of the miners made tracks for that locality'.[19] It was said that at Kadina, on Yorke Peninsula, 'no subject was spoken of or talked over but the Barrier Ranges'.[20] Although the 'old hands' in South Australia's copper mines advised caution in attempting to penetrate the Barrier, the return to Burra Burra from there at the end of March by a Cousin Jack called Waters caused a sensation. He had no gold to show but he described the mineralised features of the Barrier in vivid detail, enthusing his friends and workmates. Soon groups of miners, on foot and carrying their provisions and tools on their backs, tramped off into the unknown. The result was a horrific debacle amidst the bewildering environment of the outback. The gold remained elusive and the harsh conditions took their toll. Less than a month later the survivors (for already several had become lost in the bush) were heading home, one furnishing the *Wallaroo Times* with grisly details of his discovery of a decomposing human body on the Barrier trail.[21]

The shock of 1867 was remembered for a very long time. Almost 30 years later J.B. Jaquet wrote that:

> The history of metalliferous mining on the Barrier ranges may be said to have commenced this year [1867] when a rush of men in search of gold took place from Burra Burra in South Australia, which was attended with many sad results. The prospectors, wandering in the almost waterless and sparsely settled country, endured terrible hardships, and not a few perished miserably of thirst.[22]

Later still, in 1904, Donald Clarke recalled that when:

> it was reported that gold had been found in the Barrier Ranges, miners from Burra Burra, in South Australia, rushed off to the new land of promise. The tale of the sufferings and privations of these unfortunate men will never be told ... many perished, while the survivors found no gold, and returned with such harrowing descriptions of the place that it was shunned as a land accursed.[23]

For almost a decade after 1867 the Barrier was avoided as a death-trap. But in 1876 there was a chance discovery of galena (silver-lead) at Thackeringa. The parcel of ore sent back to the Burra was forwarded to Britain for expert analysis but somehow it was lost in transit, the diggers then losing interest, with Thackeringa lying idle until the 1880s. But then, with the onset of hard times in South Australia, prospectors were drawn anew to the Barrier country, including some of the colony's most hardened and tenacious diggers, such as John Treloar from Helston and George Prout from Camborne. They pressed on through the Barrier to the impossibly remote Mount Browne district. This time there was at least some gold, but at a terrible price. As one old-timer recalled in 1938: 'It was never known how many perished on that track, but in my boyhood old settlers on the Barrier still told stories of the Mount Brown [sic] gold-rush and disaster … a man has to take his hat off to these old diggers for blazing a track across such a country – all right as long as rain came, but a death-trap when it failed.'[24]

The return from Mount Browne coincided with renewed activity on the Thackeringa silver-lead fields. A mine was opened at nearby Umberumberka and the township of Silverton sprang up around this new working in 1882 and 1883, its population overwhelmingly 'Cornishmen or sons of Cornishmen'.[25] In November 1885 Captain Luke, one such Cornishman, sent down to Moonta from Silverton for 20 miners and a blacksmith, 'and had no difficulty in securing the number'.[26] An Umberumberka Extended mine was soon in operation under the direction of Captain Phillips, yet another Cousin Jack, while Captain Williams was at the West Umberumberka. As ever, the Methodists saw it as their duty to minister to these newly emergent communities, the Revs Charles Tresise and John Thorne crossing the border from South Australia for the purpose. Thorne was a Devonian, from Shebbear, the intellectual and moral home of the Bible Christians, but Tresise was a Cornishman through and through – born in St Erth in 1843 and ordained as a Bible Christian minister 20 years later in 1863. It was not long before, as Geoffrey Blainey has written, one could hear 'the voices of Cornish men and women singing hymns and part-songs as they filed over the hill from the Bible Christian chapel to the Umberumberka mine.'[27]

Even more important than the rise of Silverton in precipitating an exodus of Cornish people from South Australia to the Barrier was the discovery of nearby Broken Hill in September 1883 by Charles Rasp ('German Charlie'), a boundary rider from Mount Gipps station. Along with Rasp on that fateful day – perhaps crucially, given the Cornish propensity for mineral-seeking – was James Poole from Kapunda, a Cousin Jack. Born in Cornwall in 1848, Poole had worked in the

South Australian copper-mining towns for many years before venturing to the Barrier. He was one of the original Syndicate of Seven which owned the shares in this newly discovered Broken Hill mine but he disposed of his interests in the venture before it had realised its true value. Another of the syndicate also missed out on a potential fortune, throwing it away in the celebrated 'game of euchre', euchre being essentially a Cornish card game, a kind of 'Cornish whist'. Following the Rasp/Poole find, developmental work at first was slow. Little work was done at Broken Hill until October 1884, when a Cousin Jack named Rosewarne began sinking Rasp's Shaft on the syndicate's claim. But before long other mines were springing up – Broken Hill North, Broken Hill South, the Victoria Cross, the Great Northern Junction – and shortly thereafter the whole 'line of the lode' was bristling with new silver-lead claims. Commercial, communication and family links were with South Australia rather than distant Sydney, and in 1884 one observer could note astutely that Broken Hill 'geographically belongs to New South Wales but commercially to South Australia'.[28]

Many remembered the earlier rushes to the Barrier and Mount Browne, and in October 1886 the *Yorke's Peninsula Advertiser* published a warning from 'Old Moonta Miner' about the dangers of lead-poisoning at Broken Hill, a misgiving strengthened by the opinion of one Cousin Jack at the Umberumberka who wrote that 'I would rather work in the old Moonta for 30s a week than here for £25.'[29] However, few heeded such concerns. At first it was the unemployed who left, but by 1895 H. Lipson Hancock, general superintendent of Moonta and Wallaroo, was bemoaning the shortage of good hard-rock miners due to 'men ... leaving the district for Broken Hill'.[30] The *Burra Record* newspaper reported many 'old Burra boys' at Broken Hill and as late as 1905 there were said to be 300 Burra men on the Barrier, raising the fear that 'We are gradually losing our population, the place of refuge being Broken Hill'.[31] By 1891 Broken Hill boasted a population of some 20,000 souls, crowded together in this 'Silver City' (as it was known), with streets names taken straight from a geology text-book – Argent, Sulphide, Oxide, Blende, Carbon, Crystal, even Slag Street. Among the Cousin Jacks were men like Joseph Kemp, from Redruth, who 'worked on about every mining field in the [Australian] Commonwealth, and went to several gold rushes',[32] together with Stephen Pellew Carthew, also from Redruth, who had toiled in half a dozen mines in South Australia and Victoria before settling at Broken Hill, and his namesake John Carthew who travelled across from Moonta. William Henry Matthews, another Cornishman, journeyed down from Darwin in the Northern Territory, where he had been prospecting for tin. Charles Pyatt, who had arrived in Wallaroo Mines from Cornwall in 1883, was soon at Broken Hill.

The Wesleyan Marriage Registers for Silverton and Broken Hill in the 1880s and 1890s reveal the usual plethora of Cornish names, as well as indicating that the Cornish tended to marry within their own kind, perpetuating on the Barrier their own sense of ethnic identity. The marriages themselves were solemnised by Cornish preachers – the Revs Henry Trewin, Thomas Trestrail, and John Grenfell Jenkin – while those joined in holy matrimony included couples such as John Hocking from St Blazey and Elizabeth Whitburn from St Cleer, William Scown from Moonta and Catherine Pergam from Scorrier, Alfred Chappel from Moonta and Catherine Harvey from Camborne.[33] Local business directories also reveal more than a smattering of Cornish names. At Thackeringa in 1891 there were miners such as Cornish, Davy, Edwards, Polkinghorne, Sampson and Williams. At the Pinnacles, some ten miles southwest of Broken Hill, there was a Britton, a Berryman, a Brokenshire, a Bennets, a Dunstan, several Hoares, a Martin, a Mitchell, a couple of Pearces, a Peters, a Rosewarne, a Richards, a Sibly, a Trembath, a number of Tremaines and a whole colony of Thomases. The Trembath was perhaps James Warren Trembath, born in St Just-in-Penwith in 1836, who had mined at Bendigo and at Wallaroo Mines before going to the Pinnacles in 1891. He died there in the mine in 1902, from heart failure.

As elsewhere in Australia and America, the Cornish on the Barrier were prominent as mine captains. In June 1886, for example, it was noted that the manager of the junction mine was Captain George Rogers, a man known for his 'experiences in Cornwall and his subsequent experience here [Moonta]',[34] Captain Matthews, another Cousin Jack, was at the Round Hill mine, while the celebrated Captain Richard Piper, formerly of Wallaroo Mines, was appointed underground captain of the Broken Hill Proprietary. Piper was later employed by both the North and South mines, while James Retallick was at the British, and John Warren, formerly captain of the Hamley Mine at Moonta, was manager of the Block 10 mine. His underground captain was Dick Thomas, another 'Moontaite'. The Victoria Cross was managed by yet another Cornishman, William Kerby, born in Liskeard in 1854. And in the front rank of these Cornish captains was William Henry Morrish, born in Truro in 1844. This was the same Captain Morrish who had already mined at Ballarat and Bendigo in Victoria and at the Great Cobar copper mine, his career as a wandering Cousin Jack having commenced many years before when at the age of 16 he went to the coal and iron mines of South Wales. In the early 1860s he emigrated to Wallaroo Mines, and from their began his great Australian journey which culminated in appointments in 1886 as captain of both the South and Central Mines. He was also a founding member of the Mining Managers' Association of Australia (the bosses' answer to the burgeoning trade union movement) and was a successful dabbler in mining shares, so much so that he was able to retire comfortably to his villa in the Adelaide suburb of Plympton.

Morrish's success was mirrored in the albeit more modest achievements of other Cornish folk on the Barrier. A Devon and Cornwall Syndicate was responsible for some useful prospecting work amidst the multiplicity of small silver-lead workings that sprang up in the shadow of the giants such as Broken Hill Proprietary or the Block 10. As ever, many of these smaller claims were worked or managed by Cousin Jacks and, as one observer noted in 1888, they 'renew on the Ranges friendships made in Cornwall and California, New Zealand, Tasmania, and other parts of Australasia'.[35] Captain T. Tregoweth, well-known in South Australia, ran the Rise and Shine mine, 15 miles northeast of Broken Hill, while Captain T. Rowe, from Yorke Peninsula, managed the Hidden Secret, near Silverton. Captain Trezise was at the optimistically named Bonanza property, while Captain Penberthy was at the Big Hill. Nearby was the Anaconda, managed by Captain Dunstan, another of Great Cobar's Cousin Jacks. Dunstan was also at the Rising Sun, while Captain Hawke was at the Lady Bevys and the Hidden Treasure, with Captain Stevens at the neighbouring New Mile claim and Captain Bennett at the Rockwell Paddock. In the Thackeringa district, Captain Polkingthorne was manager of the Gypsy Girl, while the Terrible Dick (named after its discoverer, one Richard Tonkin) was run by Captain Hocking. The Eagle Hawk was managed by Captain James Eddy, the Great Britain by Captain Hicks, the War Dance by Captain Ellis. Further north in the Euriowie tin-fields, some 50 miles from Broken Hill, the Cornish were also active in extending the Barrier mining district. First discovered c. 1888, the Euriowie claims were opened up by Cornishmen such as Captain William Oates, from St Just, a man with 'considerable experience in tin mining in Cornwall'[36] who was engaged to work the Victory Mine, and Captain William White (formerly of St Just United in Cornwall and West Bischoff in Tasmania) who was hired by a South Australian syndicate to prospect in the area. Intriguingly, local mine names such as Carn Brea, Botallick, Dalcooth, Tincroft, and Mount Tincroft, were more than an echo of the tin-mining districts at home in Cornwall.

Not surprisingly, the Cornish influence on the Barrier ran deeper than mining terminology and personnel and in the early days at least the Cornish technological impact was significant. May Brothers' Foundry in Gawler in South

Australia, set up in 1885 by Frederick and Alfred May, from Perranzabuloe, built machinery for the 'Cornwall Smelters' at the South Mine. They also constructed the concentrator and the crusher for the mill at the Umberumberka, and they manufactured a whim engine for the Britannia mine. Their greatest contribution was the development of machinery to deal with Broken Hill's so-called 'sulphide problem', the difficulty of extracting silver-lead ores from the sulphides in which they were increasingly found at depth. Together with Captain Richard Piper at the South Mine and Captain John Warren at the Block 10, the May brothers overcame the problems of mechanical separation and ensured the continuing viability of the industry. Other equipment came from Cornwall directly, such as the Holman pneumatic rock drills (manufactured in Camborne) which were in widespread use in Broken Hill in 1908. In the mines themselves, extractive work was according to the well-tried Cornish open stope type, employing either overhand or underhand stoping. However, the relative instability of the ground, in contrast to Cornwall or Moonta, together with a growing appreciation that North America rather than Cornwall was increasingly the source of best practice in mining matters, not least the winning of silver-lead ores, led to the adoption of the radical square-set timbering that had already been developed on the Comstock Lode in Nevada. Ironically, some of the go-ahead mining managers brought in from Nevada were of Cornish stock, notably one Captain Retallick whose resonantly Cornish name must have provoked wry smiles from the Barrier's Cousin Jacks.

Be that as it may, the Cornish had already established themselves as a visible and permanent component of the Broken Hill community. Much of the Barrier's commercial life, for example, was in the hands of Cornish families. Samuel Gray, born in Cornwall in 1849, ran a building firm (he constructed engine houses for the Central Mine and the Zinc Corporation), while James Burnard, born at Boscastle in 1837, was a local shopkeeper. So too was Sydney Trenomon, who arrived from Moonta to open a general store. Richard Warren, from St Just-in-Penwith, moved from Wallaroo Mines to set up a store in Oxide Street and other local firms such as Pellew & Moore, Penhall Roberts & Co. and J.W. Pengelly, were of obvious Cornish provenance. A suburb of south Broken Hill was known as Moonta Town, reflecting the strong connection with South Australia's Cornish communities, while public house names such as the 'South Australian' and the 'Duke of Cornwall' also spoke volumes about the locality's cultural roots.

But not all of Broken Hill's citizens were Cornish and out of the usual ethnic mix of Irish, English, Scots, Germans, Chinese, and others, arose the paradoxical estimations of the Cornish already familiar elsewhere in the world. Sought after eagerly by mining companies and extracting a sneaking regard from even their most persistent detractors, the Cornish were nevertheless disliked for their self-pride and for their tendency to stick together. William Harry – from the evidence of his name – was probably of Cornish descent. Nonetheless, he too had an ambivalent attitude towards the Cornish – even if they were his own countrymen – providing revealing evidence to government Commissioners investigating mine safety in 1897. Harry was asked about the operation of an underground ore-shute in his charge:

> Q. Is it called all sorts of names?
>
> A. Yes, 'Cousin Jack', 'Irishman', and such like, just according to what the navvy takes it into his head to call it. He generally names it after the man on whom he has the greatest set; and I suppose that is the reason why it has been named here 'Chinaman' ...
>
> Q. You want competent men, and you do not care what nationality or association they belong to?
>
> A. No; I would not care if they were Chinamen, but I bar 'Cousin Jacks' sometimes.
>
> Q. Very good; but would you ask them if they were 'Cousin Jacks'?
>
> A. No; I know them by sight.[37]

With a reputation for eccentricity, some of these Cousin Jacks were real 'characters', notably Richard Thomas, underground captain at the Block 10, who had the alarming habit of dismissing men for whistling. As he explained, 'No man can strike a drill into hard rock, and whistle and sing at the same time. It takes a man all his wind to fulfil his duty.'[38] Of similar reputation was Captain Richard Piper, the subject of numerous Cousin Jack yarns. According to one story, a miner approached Captain Piper, asking for a job. Piper replied by asking the applicant if his name was Oates. Somewhat startled, the man replied that it was and Piper explained his advance knowledge by pointing to the miner's stunted fingers. Piper then went on to recount, so the story goes, how in Cornwall 150 years before the Oates families had been notorious 'wreckers'. On one occasion, a ship had had the misfortune to come to grief on a Cornish shore and its sole survivor clambered to the top of the adjacent cliff. As he reached the top, however, a wrecker named Oates cut off his fingers, causing him to lose his grip and plunge to his death on the rocks below. Now there would be no survivors to witness the plundering. But then to his horror Oates found that the sailor he had just killed was his eldest and favourite son. Filled with remorse, he plunged into the raging sea and was drowned. Thereafter, the remaining three Oates brothers left the district, settling in Truro where they lived in quiet piety for the rest of their days. But ever since, according to Piper, male members of the Oates family had been born with stunted fingers on their right hand; a reminder in perpetuity of that terrible deed.[39]

Reminiscent of the Cornish folk-stories being collected at that time in Cornwall by antiquaries such as Robert Hunt and William Botterel, Piper's tale is a fascinating insight into the survival and deployment of Cornish lore overseas. Other cultural signifiers were brass and silver bands (the first at Broken Hill was formed by a Cousin Jack named Kendal) and Cornish wrestling. A celebrated local wrestling champion was Jacob Burrows, born in St Austell in 1838, who had arrived in Broken Hill from the Burra in 1887. The pervasive quality of the Cornish inheritance was demonstrated in 1901 when the *Barrier Truth* newspaper carried a short-story 'Union by Love' which, as well as playing upon a Christian socialist theme designed to be attractive to Cornish Methodist radicals, involved fictional characters such as Marion Tregellas – 'a Cornish Barrier lassie' – and a 'jovial young Cornishman, Charles Pentreath'.[40] It was also evident in the creation of the Cornish Association of Broken Hill in 1892, the *Burra Record* noting proudly that 'In a large mining field like Broken Hill, as with all other great mineral centres, it is not surprising to find the Cornish element is so predominant, for Cornishmen and mining are closely allied'.[41] The dry, fatalistic Cornish humour was evident in the Barrier's repertoire of Cornishness, not least in the tragicomic Cousin Jack yarn recorded by Geoffrey Blainey in which the colleague of a miner who had just been killed in an underground accident went to break the sad news to the dead man's wife. As the wife opened the door in response to heavy knocking, the colleague solemnly removed his hat and said 'Good afternoon, Widow Tregonning'. Somewhat shocked, she retorted 'I'm no widow. My husband's down there working'. 'Would you like', said the colleague, 'to take a bet on it?'[42] Of course, behind such a story was the fatalistic or risk-taking perspective of the Cornish miner, an attitude of mind encouraged by Methodism in which the Lord would lend his protection to those toiling underground, but if anyone was taken it was an expression of His will.

Needless to say, many of the Barrier Cornish were Methodists, the circuits as ever reliant upon the enthusiasm and commitment of the local preachers. James Bennets, from Camborne, helped found the Blende Street North Bible Christian chapel in the mid-1880s, while in 1887 Jacob Burrows, the wrestling champion, arrived in Broken Hill to open the Blende Street Primitive Methodist meeting place. It was said in 1888 that Burrows was 'an effective preacher to the Cornish miners'.[43] His ripple-iron chapel had seating for 150 people and among his congregation were Cornish folk such as Eliza Uren from Calstock, George Trenerry from Newlyn East, and John Bishop from Redruth. At the South Broken Hill Wesleyan chapel, the roll book for the years 1892 to 1912 shows that the Cornish were overwhelmingly in the majority there, with page after page of records dominated by Cornish surnames such as Prisk, Dunstone, Scown, Angove, Pascoe, Treloar, Bray, Rundle, Tremelling, Rowse, Goldsworthy, Trebilcock, Angwin, Nancarrow, Tredinnick, Sandow, Prideaux, Berriman, Nankivell, Sara, Tresize, Bastian, Penna, Lander, Tremberth, Moyses, and very many more.[44] There were the usual tea-treats, anniversaries and revivals, one observer in 1889 opining that 'the finest sight that catches one's eye of an evening in Broken Hill is the gas-lit Wesleyan Church that stands out with all the solemnity of an English cathedral – a lasting monument to the home training of our Cornish friends.'[45]

As Brian Kennedy has argued in his *Silver, Sin and Sixpenny Ale: A Social History of Broken Hill 1883–1921*, the Methodist influence could be detected in a number of Barrier institutions, not least the trade union movement that emerged in the mid 1880s where the Cornish-South Australian connection was prominent. One of the first union agitators, William Rowe, was a Wesleyan miner from Moonta, while Josiah Thomas, who became president of the Broken Hill branch of the Amalgamated Miners' Association of Australia (AMA) in 1892, was also a Cornish local preacher.[46] A branch of the AMA was formed at the Purnamoota mine as early as January 1886 and by May 1887 there were already signs of friction between the workers and the management in what was a rapidly capitalising industry. In echoes of the experiences at Calumet and Hecla, as well as Moonta and Wallaroo, there was concern that tribute-style contracting was being used by the bosses as a deliberate device to keep down wage rates. To this was added the fear of 'getting leaded', the frightening effect on the human frame of plumbism. The *Yorke's Peninsula Advertiser* reported that 'A number of old Moonta miners and others are having some difficulty with the management at the Broken Hill Mining Company. The difficulty there as here appears to be about the contracting system, which is not popular with the men up there any more than in Moonta Mines'.[47] The *Barrier Miner* newspaper, edited by a Cornishman from South Australia, one Samuel Prior, emerged as a strongly pro-worker voice, pointing to the evils of plumbism and periodic unemployment and complaining in March 1892 that trade union members were being victimised by the mine owners.[48] The *Burra Record*, meanwhile, had in 1891 informed its readers of the sad case of Samuel Curgenwin who had left the Burra to mine at Broken Hill but was now 'leaded' and confined permanently to bed. In the following year the same newspaper wrote that 'Big stalwart men who left the Burra and Moonta Mines just a year or two ago to toil in the silver mines of the Barrier, are now in many instances past recovery, and the rest of their days apparently must be spent in helpless misery'.[49] This was no exaggeration, a report in 1904 noting that 'In no town in Australia can one see so many men propped up against walls, or aimlessly walking about; the women age rapidly, and even the young children have old faces'. Indeed, 'Miners, working among the dust of carbonate ores, become leaded, and even now there are many human wrecks left as relics of the boom days of Broken Hill.' Even 'Fowls, which picked up the surface soil, and cats, who cleansed their fur, soon succumbed, while many children were leaded in this unhealthy town'.[50]

It was against the background of such conditions that labour relations deteriorated on the Barrier, leading to a major strike in 1892 (when Moonta and Wallaroo were already embroiled in industrial action) in which Cousin Jacks took a key role. E. Polkinghorne, John Bennett and other AMA leaders were arrested and gaoled for their role in the strike; the Cornish-born Labor politician, David Morley Charleston, travelled up from Adelaide to address strike meetings; and the Rev. R.J. Daddow, a Primitive Methodist minister, praised the 'martyrs' for their 'self-sacrifice, self-control and moral courage'.[51] Police troopers brought in from Sydney helped to break the strike, locking-up its ringleaders, while non-Cornish 'free labour' was brought in from outside. Contracting was confirmed as the principal method of employment in the Barrier mines and output doubled as a result. However, profits dipped in 1893, wages fell and hours were made longer. And although the AMA had been damaged badly by the experience of 1892, seeds of bitterness had been sown which would ensure that Broken Hill would become a bastion of trade unionism. There were strikes and lock-outs in 1909 and 1916, and in the famous strike of the 600 days in 1918–1919 the resurgent trade unionists won a 35-hour week, compensation for plumbism and a minimum wage.

Meanwhile, connections had been maintained with the Cornish communities in South Australia. In 1893 one report recorded that 'A frequent question just now among ex Peninsularites is "Har ee goin ome Xmas?"' It was thought that 'there is no other town in Australia from which there is a greater exodus of holiday-makers at this season than at Broken Hill, and on this occasion there is quite the usual number leaving for the well-remembered sights of Kadina, Moonta and Wallaroo'.[52] A further expression of these links was a poignant poem published in 1893, an account in verse of a romance between a Moonta girl and a Barrier miner boy who was working at Broken Hill in the Block 11 mine. The poem begins by recalling how they met and fell in love:

> When first I was courted by a Barrier miner boy,
> He called me his jewell, his heart's delight and joy,
> It was in this Silver City, our town of noted fame,
> Where this 11 Block mining lad accourting with me came.

The piece continues with a description of the many virtues of the miner boy and of the couple's happiness, but goes on at length to tell how the lad quit the district, deserting his Moonta girl and leaving her devastated. The final stanza tells its own dismal story and no doubt spoke directly and painfully to the many whose own relationships had foundered on the rocks of emigration and its inherent geographical mobility:

> And when I'm dead and gone, this one request I crave,
> You'll take my bones to Moonta and lay them in the grave.
> Some words write on my tombstone to tell the passer-by,
> I died all broken-hearted through that 11 Block miner boy.[53]

But sentimental though the links between the Barrier and South Australia's 'Little Cornwalls' had become, they were by no means the only intra-continental connections of note. By the 1890s, indeed, Western Australian had replaced Broken Hill as the principal focus of Cornish attention. The Cornish had been in Swan River Colony (as it was first known) in the early days, the *West Briton* in April 1852 carrying advertisements for emigration to the colony, including one entry that month that called for 'steady, active, young men having a thorough knowledge of copper mining'.[54] These recruits were for the modest copper workings (the Geraldine Mines) then being opened up on the coast between Geraldton and the Murchison River, some 300 miles north of the colonial capital of Perth. Lead was also discovered in the area and in 1867 Captain Samuel Mitchell arrived from Cornwall, where he had been born in 1839, to manage the Geraldine Lead Mine, near the small township of Northampton. Mitchell also became manager of the Badra lead workings, some seven miles from Northampton, and was responsible for opening Wheal Ellen, a silver-lead mine with a resoundingly Cornish name which yielded some £70,000 worth of metal during its relatively short life. Although never a major centre, the Murchison-Geraldton field offered intermittent employment for a number of years, as in 1874 when James Whitburn arrived from West Cornwall to work in the Old Geraldine copper mine. Later, Whitburn made his way across the continent to work at Great Cobar, later still moving on to Broken Hill and eventually returning to Western Australia during the 1890s rush. Over the same years, gold seekers who had made their way north-wards from Victoria and New South Wales into Queensland and the Northern Territory, had spilled across into the barren north of Western Australia, preparing the ground for the so-called Kimberley rush of 1886. Cousin Jacks travelled up from Moonta and from Victoria, the latter teaching the techniques of 'dry-blowing' a form of panning without water in which a pan of dirt was held aloft and tilted, the light sand blowing away while the heavier, mineralised material fell into another pan placed on the ground directly below. However, the rush fell victim to disease, heat and water shortages, not to mention the indifferent nature of the gold-fields themselves, and several diggers lost their lives in that unforgiving country – including the unfortunate Captain James Newton from St Just, a former underground manager of the Levant mine. Meanwhile, the survivors pressed south into the Pilbara region, still looking for gold. Although hardly successful, their efforts caught the attention of other experienced gold-seekers in the continent, drawing them to the virgin lands of the Far West. Captain Thomas Gilbert Pearce, for example, born near Marazion in 1842, had mined in Victoria and in New Zealand before being drawn in the 1880s to Marble Hill in the Pilbara. Later, Pearce became an important manager and entrepreneur on the Coolgardie gold-fields, the presence of Pearce and others like him being a significant factor in the scope and success of the Western Australian rush in the 1890s.

Meanwhile, the activities of other diggers had led to the discovery and exploitation of gold deposits at Southern Cross, some 200 miles east of Perth. Among their number was Captain William Oates, born in St Just in 1842, a former underground captain at Wheal Owles who had been persuaded to emigrate to Victoria in 1884 by George Lansell, the Bendigo 'quartz king'. But Oates was soon on the move, travelling first to Adelaide and from there to Southern Cross to become manager of the Fraser South Mine. It was said that Captain Oates was the first man in the West to smelt gold successfully and in May 1897 the *Kalgoorlie Western Argus* decided that 'Of all West Australian mining engineers, Captain Oates is the mining engineer par excellence.'[55] Certainly, taking heart from the success of Southern Cross, bands of eager diggers continued to press eastwards into the semi-desert. And in June 1892 came the spectacular discovery of rich gold deposits at Coolgardie, some 350 miles east of Perth, triggering a rush which was given further momentum by a second and equally significant find at neighbouring Kalgoorlie. A third important find, at nearby Boulder, was the result of prospecting by Samuel Pearce from Kapunda, along with his mate W.G. Brookman. Pearce had mined in California, Mexico and South Africa, but it was on Ivanhoe Hill at Boulder that he made a lasting name for himself. His Great Boulder claim turned out to be hugely rich, as did other workings in the area such as the Lake View, the Three Australias, the Iron Duke, the Royal Mint, Consols, and Associated.

In the wake of the discoveries at Coolgardie, Kalgoorlie and Boulder, thousands clamoured to become West Australian diggers. There was considerable immigration from other Australian colonies, 16,000 arriving in 1894, another 18,000 in 1895, and a massive 36,000 in 1896. Inevitably, many of these were from South Australia, not a few Cornish-born or of Cornish descent. In August 1894 the Moonta *People's Weekly* could report that 'the Western Australian Goldfields ... are attracting large numbers of miners and mechanics' from Wallaroo and Moonta, adding that 'the West is an outlet for miners, and more especially so for those of Yorke's Peninsula, who are preferred above any other miners in the colonies.'[56] Indeed, the transformation from individual or syndicate prospecting to deep, hard-rock mining by a heavily capitalised mining industry was remarkably swift in Western Australia and it was in this environment that the Cornish were especially in demand. Consequently, unemployed, under-employed or under-remunerated miners continued to leave Yorke Peninsula in a manner reminiscent of 'the palmy days of Broken Hill',[57] while one observer at Moonta thought that 'this exodus ... will prove as successful in taking away the surplus labor from this district as Broken Hill did'.[58] There were departures from Yorke Peninsula during 1896 and 1897, with a further wave in 1899. Some made their way by sea, travelling from Port Adelaide to Fremantle and thence inland to the gold-fields, but others chose the overland route from South Australia, traversing as it did the endless, arid expanses of the Nullarbor Plain. The series of letters written by Daniel and David Williams to their parents in Wallaroo afford many insights into the vicissitudes of the overland route.

The Williams brothers left Yorke Peninsula in the early part of April 1894 and by 30 May they had reached Eucla, the border between South and Western Australia. They were obliged to pay a crippling £8 10s 0d duty on their horses to pass from one colony to the next (hopes of inter-colonial free trade, let alone Federation, seemed a world away), writing that 'we had a pretty hard time of it (or rather the horses did) coming from the Bight here the last 3 days we couldn't get any water for them for there was teams in front of us and they took the lot but we got through all right.'[59] By mid-August the Williams brothers were nearing the gold-fields, writing that there were many Wallaroo men heading West and that 'there are a terrible lot of teams coming the overland trip and some of them are getting a rough time of it .... Waggons, vans, spring drays, pack horses, camels, and foot men. Some have come from Queensland, New South Wales and Victoria'.[60] Once on the gold-fields, Daniel and David found that the easy pickings were already taken long since, the chance of striking it rich by now remote. However reluctantly, Daniel found work as a miner in the large Bendigo Coolgardie venture, while David was fortunate enough to acquire a wheelwright's business in Coolgardie. This upturn in their fortunes led Daniel to believe that 'there's a grand future for WA. There's a lot of good mines in this country ... there's a lot of females getting here now, and the place is getting quite toffy, Dave and I are beginning to wish we brought out Sunday clothes with us.'[61] However, the arrival of extreme temperatures in November brought a change of mood, the prevalence of disease and the renewed shortage of water sending the Williams brothers scrambling in the direction of the comparative safety of Perth.

Unpleasant social conditions – heat, fever, periods of unemployment and so on – were a subject mentioned in almost every letter written home – whether to Camborne, Moonta, or Ballarat. Cornish miners spoke with their typical dry humour of 'Hotgardie', while in November 1894 the *Cornish Telegraph* published a most discouraging missive from one Cousin Jack on the gold-fields, 'Western Australia, taken all round is the most God-forsaken place a man can set foot in. It is an awfully rough life here. I have not slept in a bed for over three months, and only get a wash once a fortnight. The food is also bad; no fresh food of any description – all tinned; and now the weather is very hot it is all in a liquid state .... You can't buy water even in this great city of Coolgardie under nine-pence per gallon .... There is no sport here of any kind out here – not a living animal except flies, ants, and snakes.'[62]

It was not unusual for a death notice such as the following to appear in the *Kalgoorlie Western Argus*, 'A young man named John Cocking has died in the hospital from fever. He was a native of Cornwall'[63] – and the behaviour of the diggers only served to aggravate the deplorable conditions. In March 1895 three diggers from Kadina were under arrest for the 'wholesale murder of blacks',[64] while in March 1896 a Cousin Jack named Bluett was in trouble for shooting off his half-brother's finger. But it was disease rather than violence that claimed the most lives and caused the most misery, it being said of one Joseph Lathlean, a Cousin Jack from Moonta, that he 'went to Western Australia, where he was stricken with pneumonia which left a weakness which soon developed into consumption, and gradually he faded from us'.[65] Many of the Cornish congregated in the so-called 'Moonta Camp' at Boulder which, to judge from the following composition of December 1896, was a decidedly unattractive locality:

> Tis a number of camps of rising ground,
> And a few lateens scattered around
> Of the same style of architecture:
> They're built of poles and old chaff bags,
> Canvass, calico tents, and rags,
> All of different hues and texture.
>
> Tins and bones are lying round,
> Bags and other filth abound,
> And things of a similar stamp;
> And fever germs have a depot there,
> And a horrid perfume fills the air,
> In the Boulder Moonta Camp.
>
> The Moonta Camp looks old and scarred,
> The hill they're on looks strange and weird –
> It oppresses one with dread;
> And the costeen pit, where the lateens wave,
> Looks like a huge uncanny grave
> Awaiting for the dead.[66]

The terminology in the poem is revealing. A lateen – a maritime term (like so many others co-opted by Cornish mining) – was a sail erected over a mine working to improve its ventilation. Costeen was the familiar Cornish word for an exploratory trench. These terms were more than a clue to a Cornish presence, though one report considered that Moonta Camp 'represents only a small selection'[67] of Cousin Jacks on the gold-fields. It was certainly true that the Cornish could be found throughout the Coolgardie-Kalgoorlie-Boulder district and beyond. Stanley Whitford was on the gold-fields at the turn of the 20th century and 'was camped with a nest of Cousin Jacks from Moonta'.[68] There was Jack Pascoe, he said, together with Alf Northey, Jos Liddicoat, and Merts Trebilcock. He added that Bill Roberts and Jack Warwick, both Moonta men, were underground captains at the Australian and Great Boulder mines, while Tom Horton – then manager of the Malcolm Proprietary, was a former captain of the Yelta mine at Moonta. Indeed, many of the Western Australian gold-mines were run by Cornishmen, many of whom had arrived on the gold-fields from Yorke Peninsula or other mining districts in the continent. Thus in January 1895 it was reported that the Royal Mint, Lake View, Great Boulder, Australian, and Iron Duke mines were managed by men 'well known to Kadina and Broken Hillites', while the captain of the Ivanhoe was 'an old Moonta identity', and W. Rowe, manager of the Maritana and Napier claims, was 'late of Moonta'.[69]

Captain Nankivell was appointed chief captain of the Great Boulder in June 1895, while Tom Warren became manager of the Great Coolgardie. Other Cornish captains included W.E. Francis at the Adelaide Sovereign and the Kalgoorlie Reef, William Begelhole at Bayley's Reward, William Hambley at the Arrow Proprietary, Frederick Rodda at the Hit and Miss, Thomas Pascoe, vice-president of the Kalgoorlie Mine Managers' Institute in 1897, at the True Blue, and Captain Dunstan at the Hannan's Consols and Colonial Goldfields mines. Occasionally, these Cornish captains went on to even greater things, becoming significant investors and dabblers in mining shares. In 1895, for example, Captain Thomas Gilbert Pearce was behind the successful promotion of a string of Coolgardie gold-mines – the Richmond Gem, the Irish Lily, the Lady Loch, the Easter Gift – while John Treloar from Helston, who had mined at the Burra and in New Zealand, Victoria and the Barrier, made a small fortune as an entrepreneur. One contemporary account charted his progress:

> Captain John Treloar, well-known to most Australian mining
> men, has been on a visit to Cornwall – his birthplace – where he
> has been giving some attention to Cornish mining .... Captain
> Treloar, who has had 47 years' practical experience in Australia

and New Zealand, and who is associated with some of the best Westralia finds, notably McAuliff's Reward, Reefer's Eureka, and Hannan's Brown Hill, has done a certain amount of business here [London], but he thinks he might have done far better had he taken his Westralian properties to Adelaide. On arrival at Albany, Captain Treloar will proceed to Coolgardie to report progress. He will then return to Adelaide to rejoin his wife.[70]

The majority of Cornish, however, did little more than scratch a living, their Cornishness exhibited in a range of day-to-day activities from the ubiquitous Cornish wrestling matches to the singing of Cornish carols. At the Moonta Camp the men would pass the evenings playing euchre, while at Boulder the Australian Rules football team was known as the 'Amber-and-Blacks' on account of the traditional Cornish colours that it wore. As always, the Methodists were active in the saving of souls. The first wedding at Coolgardie, so it is said, was solemnised by the Rev. Thomas Trestrail, a Cornishman who had already laboured among his kith and kin at Broken Hill, while the Rev. G.E. Rowe, also Cornish, became the first president of the Western Australian Methodist Conference. The *Australian Christian Commonwealth* magazine, musing upon Rowe's many talents, thought him a man 'who can tell a Cornish story exceptionally well'.[71] At Boulder there were three Methodist chapels, each denomination with its committed advocates – 'many of them Cousin Jacks'[72] – 'while on 'The Twelfth' in July 1896 100 Orangemen marched through Kalgoorlie – 'several Moontaites being conspicuous'.[73] Rather like the Cornish Methodist sympathy for 'Free Trade' (smuggling) at home, 'high-grading' – to use the contemporary Californian term – was not seen as incompatible with Methodist ideals of honesty and integrity:

> The tradition of 'making a bit extra' has always been strong among Kalgoorlie's miners. It is said that [Captain] Tom Hewitson, a chapel man himself, was once inspecting a level after the face had been fired out. In a dark corner he came on a religious old Cousin Jack, seated on a heap of broken quartz. The Cornishman was practising a hymn for the church choir as he picked over the stone. 'Do Not Pass Me By', he sang, and softly the words echoed through the dark stope as he put aside what he looked on as his portion of gold.[74]

The tradition of 'making a bit extra' was sometimes a cause of conflict, however, as in March 1896 when William Berryman was charged by Captain Pollard with stealing over £15 worth of gold from Bayley's No.1 South Mine. This was, in turn, part of a wider contest between bosses and workers and which saw the Cornish wrestle with the Irish for control of the emerging gold-fields trade unions. The Kalgoorlie and Boulder Branch of the AMA was formed in August 1896 and from the first the Cornish Methodist influence was apparent. Moreover, the Labor Party that grew out of the AMA bore a Cornish stamp, several of Western Australia's prominent Labor politicians – including the Premiers Scadden, Hawke and Tonkin – being 'products of the Cornish-South Australian tradition'.[75] So too was George Pearce, 'A Protestant and of Cornish extraction' who was active as a pro-conscriptionist during the First World War.[76] Several decades earlier, the most colourful personality in the emerging gold-fields Labor movement had been Captain William Oates, from St Just-in-Penwith, the first man to have smelted gold in the West. He became mayor of Southern Cross in 1894 and in 1897 stood as the Labor candidate for the gold-fields seat in the Perth Parliament. A contemporary account reported that 'he has risen from the ranks, and he believes in men rising from the ranks .... He believes in a mutual ground of co-operation between employee and employer. He would like every employee to own a share in the mine in which he is working'.[77] An early advocate of what we would today call industrial democracy, he was also – like many Labor men of his day – a champion of the White Australia policy. In the unpleasant but typical racist language of one contemporary newspaper, 'William Oates has never employed a nigger in his life, and never will.'[78]

Oates won his seat in parliament and among his Labor colleagues elected in 1897 was Captain Samuel Mitchell (the Geraldton mine manager known for his 'liberal and progressive activity'[79]), together with F.C.B. Vosper – the 'liberal and democratic' politician born in St Dominick in 1867 who earlier had become embroiled in Queensland's industrial turmoil. Moving to Western Australia in 1892, he became editor of the *Coolgardie Miner* in which he displayed his 'hearty regard for the working people'.[80] A striking figure with jet-black hair, Vosper was infamous across the colony, but he died prematurely in his 30s before could really make his political mark. Vosper's successor at the *Coolgardie Miner* was Henry Kneebone, a Cousin Jack from Wallaroo Mines. He too was a Labor man, staying in the West until 1910 when he moved to Adelaide to join the staff of the Labor-sponsored *Daily Herald*. He became editor in 1911, and in later years entered both the Adelaide Parliament and the

Federal Senate as a Labor politician. But Labor politics and journalism aside, it was as expert hard-rock men that the Cornish miners in Western Australian were especially remembered. When Henry Richard Hancock resigned his position as general superintendent at Wallaroo and Moonta, he toured the mining districts of Australasia. In September 1901 he remarked that: 'He had heard a great deal about them [the Cornish] from those in authority over them, but in no single instance had he ever heard one word against them as miners, but on the other hand he had heard a great deal in their favour. In Kalgoorlie and other places in the West they were in the front rank as miners.'[81]

We might forgive Captain Hancock for the uncritical bias of his comments – for, as we know, the Cornish did have their detractors – but behind his enthusiastic embrace of the myth of Cousin Jack there was more than a hint of truth. By the turn of the 20th century, the Cornish had reached all corners of the Antipodes and where there was complex hard-rock mining to be done the Cousin Jacks were still sought after for their 'hands-on' skills and experience. Even in the technologically advanced mines of Bendigo, Broken Hill and Kalgoorlie, where new techniques and appliances had sometimes ousted Cornish ways, the Cornish miner remained an invaluable member of the workforce. It was the same the world over.

# CHAPTER TEN

# NEW FRONTIERS –
# NORTH AMERICA

T he Cornish had turned up in Australia wherever there were minerals to be had, even in the most remote places, while maintaining their distinctive habits and their identity as 'Cousin Jacks'. This behaviour was no less apparent in America, where the Cornish contrived to preserve their exclusivity in the workplace or in the community and were duly recognised as 'different' by other ethnic groups. As in Australia, even in the most far-flung localities in North America the Cornish asserted their distinctive identity, their 'difference' readily apparent to contemporary observers. Most famously, Robert Louis Stevenson wrote in 1879 of a railroad journey *Across The Plains*:

> There were no emigrants direct from Europe – save one German family and a knot of Cornish miners who kept grimly to themselves, one reading the New Testament all day long through steel spectacles, the rest discussing privately the secrets of their old-world, mysterious race. Lady Hestor Stanhope believed she could make something great of the Cornish; for my part, I can make nothing of them at all. A division of races, older and more original than Babel, keeps this close, esoteric family apart from neighbouring Englishmen. Not even a Red Indian seems more foreign in my eyes. This is one of the lessons of travel – that some of the strangest races dwell next door to you at home.[1]

In Australia, the cycle of mineral discoveries, and with it the migratory and settlement patterns of the Cornish, was, if we may generalise, essentially anti-clockwise – moving eastwards from South Australia in the early 1850s to New South Wales and Victoria, swinging northwards into Queensland, and then westwards across the Northern Territory and northern Western Australia, before sweeping southwards to Coolgardie and Kalgoorlie in the 1890s. In North America, there was also a pattern of mineral discovery. From modest beginnings in the Appalachians and elsewhere in the East, the hard-rock mining frontier had expanded westwards by the 1840s into Wisconsin, Illinois and the copper country of 'the Lakes' in Upper Michigan. From there, there was the giant leap to California, establishing an entirely new mining frontier in the Far West. Thereafter, the expansion was twofold. There continued to be movement westwards from the Missouri frontier – the 'greenhorns' and 'tenderfeet' of popular fancy who hesitantly ventured forth into 'Indian country' from the Mid-West or the South. At the same time the so-called 'yonsiders' or 'yondersiders' of California headed east and north with almost unseemly self-confidence into the virgin interior of the continent.

There was certainly more than a sprinkling of Cousin Jacks among the eastern 'greenhorns' who moved West. Although the emphasis here is on the miners, there was a parallel movement of farmers and artisans, not least on the so-called 'Oregon Trail' which even in the 1840s was bringing many hundreds to the Pacific Northwest by wagon train from the East and Mid-West. Samuel James, from St Keverne, one of the early Wisconsin settlers, made for Washington Territory (later State), believing that the climate west of the Rocky Mountains was more equable, its air healthier and the waters pure and clear. Moreover, there was land for the taking, and 'every man is his own lord, and, therefore, can do as he pleases with it'.[2] More especially, the eastern states acted as a reservoir of Cornish labour from which the expanding mining frontiers might draw. Both coal and hard-rock mining in the East had attracted Cornish attention, and there were sizeable groupings of Cornish in the anthracite (and slate-quarrying) districts of Pennsylvania. As early as 1848 Daniel Bullock had written home from Pennsylvania to his sister Naomi in St Columb Minor, enthusing about the 'American way', with its inherent democracy and egalitarianism:

> 'I like america first rate', he wrote, 'some of the rich folks [in Britain] will not speak to a poor man, now in america the rich be not so proud. the [sic] do not look upon riches here but little. the look more on industresousnefs honesty Sivility uprightnefs ... we can venture to Speak to a rich man hear when we meet him and he Stop his horse and waggon and talk with a poor man.'[3]

Bullock also noted that he was earning some 14 dollars a month in Pennsylvania, in contrast to the two pounds a month that he had received at home in Cornwall.

Moreover, the cost of his board, lodging and laundry was the equivalent of £2 16s per month, so now he was able to save for the future. For many like Bullock, the taste of American freedom and (relative) affluence was enough to tempt them into the unknown vastness of the Far West, with its beckoning promise of yet greater opportunities. Certainly, the Appalachians remained an important reservoir of Cornish labour into the 1880s and beyond, with a continual westward leaching of Cousin Jacks. Collamer M. Abbott has opined that 'it may be literally true that there was at some time a "Cousin Jack" in every copper mine in the Appalachian Range from Maine to Alabama', adding that 'At any rate, Cornish miners flocked to the Appalachian copper camps ... between 1850 and 1880, the heyday of copper mining in the eastern United States'.[4] During that period, the two most significant centres of mining – and thus Cornish concentration – were Orange County in Vermont and Polk County, Tennessee. In Vermont, the Ely mine was in production by 1860, with a staff of 27 Cornishmen and 29 Irish. By 1870 there were 81 Cornish and 43 Irish, and by 1880 the figures had leapt to 209 Cousin Jacks and 281 Irishmen. In the Duckworth region of Polk County, meanwhile, there were some 137 Cornish miners at work in 1860, though – with the dispersals caused by the Civil War and the drift to the new mining frontiers of the Far West – the number had fallen to 70 by 1870.

These Cornish miners included in their ranks individuals such as Thomas Pollard, born in Chacewater in 1815, who had mined in both Ireland and Wales before emigrating to Pennsylvania in 1842 to work in the coal mines. He then moved to Virginia in search of copper and gold, and in 1854 he was hired as a mine captain to work the Vermont Copper Mining Company's claim in Vershire, Vermont.Pollard later acted as inspector or overseer of a string of mines in Vermont, New Jersey, Massachusetts, Maine and Connecticut and – like many another Cousin Jack – also turned his hand to farming by purchasing a property in Vermont.[5] Like Pollard, many of these wandering Cornish were mobile in the extreme. John Trevithick of Tennessee, aged 27 in 1860, was the father of three children, one born in Cornwall, a second in Georgia, and the third in Tennessee itself. William Lydecoat, aged 30 in the same year, had children born in Tennessee, Virginia, and Pennsylvania. As ever, the Cornish were to be found in the skilled and supervisory jobs. As early as the 1830s William Chynoweth and William Gundry held key positions at the South Strafford copper mine in Vermont. Captain James Harvey ran the Wheatley mine in Pennsylvania in the 1850s. At Duckworth in Polk County were Cousin Jacks such as James Jory, John Tonkin, George Trenwith, T.A. Easterbrook, James Spargo, and William Tippett.

Thomas Pascoe was underground captain at the Ely mine in Orange County from the 1850s through into the 1880s, and at the nearby Pike Mine John Glanville, John Berryman and other Cousin Jacks were employed as captains. William Veague, from Truro, had arrived in the United States at the age of 17 and worked in mines in New Jersey, New York, Pennsylvania, Alabama, Vermont and Maine, as well as undertaking a fleeting foray into Montana in the Far West. Not surprisingly, the Cornish established their familiar tribute and tutwork system of employment in these Appalachian mines, along with other Cornish mining practices, technologies and terminology, and in the mining camps themselves cultural activities such as Methodism and Cornish wrestling were a mark of their impact. Always individualistic, it was not unusual to find 'the Cornish raising the Union Jack on our Fourth of July as some did at Duckworth in 1860, much to the dismay of the local native [sic] population which sometimes looked askance at the unfamiliar customs of the "Cousin Jacks"'.[6]

It was in the far West, however, that the Cornish impact was more clearly marked and is today so readily recalled. In 1858 reports of gold discoveries on the Fraser River in New Caledonia (British Columbia) precipitated a new rush from San Francisco. In the words of the contemporary ditty, 'Oh, I'm going to Caledonia – that's the place for me; I'm going to Fraser river, with a washbowl on my knee.'[7] The journey to Fraser River from California involved a long and dangerous trip northwards through Oregon and Washington, a vast and forbidding wilderness in which the disoriented might be lost forever and where hostile Native Americans were an ever present threat. More immediate and more accessible was the Comstock Lode in the neighbouring state of Nevada, first discovered in 1859. In 1860 attention shifted to the Humboldt district of Nevada and to Bodie (on the California-Nevada border), while in 1862–64 the focus was on Montana. In the mid-1860s the White Pine and Ruby Hill areas of central Nevada caught the attention of prospectors, as did South Pass in Wyoming. By 1868 Helena (Montana) was also firmly on the mining map of America, and 'Among the miners were many Cornishmen and Irishmen'.[8] Thereafter, the Stikine mines were opened in Alaska in 1874, the Black Hills of South Dakota were invaded in 1874–76, while Tombstone in Arizona grew up in the period 1878–79. In all this expansion, as Rodman Wilson Paul recognised in his classic history of mining on the Western frontier, 'Cornishmen were an important element ... In the Far West, the Cornishmen readily found work in the lode mining towns, such as Virginia City. Everywhere they were known by the nickname of "Cousin Jack" (and their women folk as "Cousin Jennie").'[9]

In Colorado, in particular, after a false start in 1859–61, huge silver-lead deposits (together with some zinc and copper) were discovered at Leadville and in Gilpin County in 1877. In 1917 Frederick L. Ransome could reflect that this was the all-important region 'where so much in mining and metallurgical technique had its beginnings ... a position analogous to that of Cornwall in Great Britain'.[10] As early as 1880 Leadville had sported a population of 14,820, while 'Irishmen, Cornishmen, Canadians, and Germans formed an important part of the labor force'.[11] Mark Wyman has noted that 'It was the Cornish who developed one of the best systems for spreading the word on Western job opportunities, the "Cornish grapevine"',[12] while Richard E. Lingenfelter in his masterly study *The Hardrock Miners: A History of the Mining Labor Movement in the American West 1863–1893*, considered that:

> Cornish and Irish made up the majority of the hardrock miners in, the larger camps. The Cornishman, or 'Cousin Jack', was raised in the trade ... he came to the western mines with few illusions. Higher wages, not dreams of quick fortunes, attracted him and he came to work. His greater skill gave him an obvious advantage in the competition for jobs – an advantage that occasionally sparked resentment among his American and Irish fellow workers. His clannishness ... heightened the antagonism.[13]

Indeed, Lingenfelter has argued that:

> This animosity between the skilled Cornish and the initially unskilled Irish and American miners was, in fact, the most explosive internal threat to the mining labor movement in the West: on the Comstock at the very start of the movement when Cornish were hired effectively as strike breakers; in Gilpin County, Colorado, where Irish and American miners refused to join a predominantly Cornish union; at Cherry Creek, Nevada, where a union was organized to 'counteract the manifest preference given by mine managers to Cornishmen', and at Butte where Cornish-Irish rivalry for control of the union reached proportions so grotesque that it ultimately split the union. Despite such deviations, however, the Cousin Jacks ... became the leaders of the mining labor movement in the West.[14]

The broad sweep of Lingenfelter's assessment reveals the extent to which the Cornish retained and deployed ethnic identity as they spread so comprehensively to the new mining frontiers of North America. A mere decade after the Californian gold rush had enticed so many Cornish from Wisconsin and elsewhere, in early 1858 news of the Fraser River finds reached the Cousin Jacks of the Sierra Nevada. By May 1858 the *Grass Valley Telegraph* was reporting that some 150 men had already left the town for Fraser River, an exodus that continued through into the summer months.[15] However, it was soon apparent that the reports of a new bonanza had been greatly exaggerated, the difficulties of finding gold exacerbated by the swollen nature of the treacherous Fraser River which had submerged many of the bars in which the metal was supposedly located. By the spring, disappointed diggers were already drifting back to California, although in October 1858 there was a substantial discovery of gold at a place called Cornish Bar. Encouraged by this success, others pushed on into the unknown of British Columbia in the hope of uncovering yet richer deposits. Eventually, their perseverance was rewarded, for at Cariboo there was a significant find. Among the lucky band of diggers who struck it rich was one Martin Raby, a Cornish miner and a veteran of the Californian and Australian rushes, whose letter in the *Mining Journal* in May 1864 explained that 'If a man should be fortunate enough to strike a lead, he is almost sure to make a fortune, and that is what we are all after in Cariboo'.[16] Billy Barker, a former seaman and also said to be Cornish, found and lost a fortune in Cariboo country, the frontier township of Barkerville named in his dubious honour. John Teague, born in Redruth in 1835, was another Cornishman in British Columbia at this time, settling in the embryonic city of Victoria in about 1860. As the western seaboard of Canada began to develop in the wake of the Fraser River and Cariboo rushes, so new trades were called for. Teague found work as a carpenter in the emerging Royal Naval Dockyard at Esquimalt (some three miles from Victoria) before later embarking on a successful career as an architect. Among his many triumphs was the City Hall in Victoria, the only 'monumental symbolic city hall'[17] built in British Columbia in the 19th century.

But for every Cousin Jack who had tried his luck in British Columbia there were perhaps at least half a dozen who, in the manner described by Lingenfelter, reckoned that they would be better placed competing for the high wages offered for steady, skilled employment in that other mining district which in 1859 and the early 1860s also attracted California's Cornish miners: the Comstock. Gold and silver which had been found together in the so-called 'Washoe' district of

Nevada in 1859, the area of Storey County which would shortly spawn the important settlements of Virginia City, Silver City and Gold Hill. By March 1860 men were passing through Placerville in California on their way to cross the high sierra to Washoe country at the rate of 75 a day. In the August one observer (presumably a Cousin Jack) at Gold Hill could insist that 'the experienced miners of Mexico, Chile, and Peru, the hardy gold-seekers from California and the sturdy copper miners from Cornwall, one and all agree that this region is without a rival in the richness and variety of its metallic deposits'.[18] In 1870, by which time the trail was already well trodden, Thomas Couch from Crowan described the journey by stage coach across the Sierra Nevada from Grass Valley to Virginia City. It was a steep, winding, nerve-wracking descent from the mountain peaks to the dusty base on the Washoe side but 'The driver's face occasionally wears a conquering smile, and he says, with a slight impatience at our timidity and in an assuring tone and manner, "Perfectly safe, boys, driven here a long time and no accident has happened; I guess you'll get down all right".'[19]

By 1870, according to John Rowe's estimates, there were at least 250 Cornish people living at Gold Hill and with well over 300 at neighbouring Virginia City, the heart of the Comstock Lode country.[20] Even Mark Twain, who for a time worked as a journalist on the Comstock, could claim Cornish connections, being a descendent of the Clemens family from Looe (his real name was Samuel Langhorne Clemens). Meanwhile, Cousin Jacks from California had been joined by a fresh wave from Cornwall, and by 1880 the Cornish population of Storey County had swollen to at least 1000. This was fewer than the 5000 or so Irish and Irish-Americans but it was a significant element of the district's overall 15,000 population. Indeed, in 1894 a visiting Cornishwoman reckoned that the Cornish constituted some 20 per cent of Virginia City's population of some 6000 souls.[21] Moreover, at least a third of the Comstock miners were Cornish, emphasising their economic importance and ensuring an ethnic visibility which the Cornish themselves went out of their way to enhance. Ronald M. James, the Nevada historian, considers that at Virginia City and elsewhere in the West, for the Cornish 'maintenance of ethnic identity was a matter of choice, encouraged by an economic environment ... white Protestant native speakers of English could have blended in without notice. Instead, they found it expedient to project themselves as ethnically distinct'.[22]

Demanding respect as 'superior miners' and actively encouraging preferential treatment for their kith and kin in the mines, the Cornish made a special niche for themselves as they had done so often before in the mining camps of America and Australia. James adds that the Cornish on the Comstock were generally younger than their English and Irish counterparts, and much more likely to find employment in the mines. Moreover:

> The Cornish were also prone to living in neighbourhoods set apart from the Irish and others. While the Irish dominated parts of Virginia City, many of the Cornish settled in Gold Hill to the south and in the area known as the Divide, separating the two communities. The tendency of the Cornish to live in their own neighbourhoods is repeated in the cemeteries. Both the Virginia City and Gold Hill burial grounds have sections where most or all of the tombstones discuss Cornwall as a place of birth or have surnames which appear to be of Cornish origin.[23]

John Rowe, too, has noted the Cornish headstones with their weathered legends 'Native of Cornwall', commenting that 'For the most part they lived out barely two of man's allotted span of three and a half score years'.[24] The trade-off for high wages and superior status was a shortened life-span, for the increasingly deep Comstock mines were notorious for the hot, dry, dusty atmosphere in which many soon succumbed to 'miners' complaint'. The mines were of course intrinsically dangerous places and accidents took their usual toll. John Henry Carter was killed underground on the Comstock in September 1859, leaving a widow and two children to mourn him back in St Agnes. James Prout, another St Agnes man, was killed in a mining accident three months later. Yet another St Agnes miner, Martin Tregellas, lost his life in an underground fire in the Gould and Curry mine in July 1887. When Adolph Sutro began his famous tunnel – an extraordinary engineering feat linking the Webber and Corral canyons – in 1865, it was the Cousin Jacks who showed how the job could be done with great skill and relative safety. But this did not prevent one of their number, Alfred Cox, from being crushed to the death in a run of ground in the Sutro Tunnel. Another, Jack Bluett, was dug out alive. In another accident, in the Yellow Jacket mine the cable attached to the skip in the decline shaft suddenly parted, sending the skip slamming into a group of miners. Four Cousin Jacks, Charles Bennet, Samuel and Thomas Odgers, and Francis Polkinghorne all suffered horrific injuries, and a fifth – Richard Pearce – was killed instantly as the back of his head was torn off. Outside of the mine, conditions could on occasions be just as hazardous, as in hard winters such as those of 1868, 1875 and 1916 when many were frozen to death or overtaken by avalanches. In January 1875, for example, it fell to Richard Gluyas to try to dig out three other Cousin Jacks whose cabin on the bleak mountainside had been wrecked by a snowslide. Thomas Champion was still alive when reached but Isaac Jewell and Moses Willey, both Helston men, were dead.

Eliot Lord, writing in 1883, painted a fearful pen-picture of the miner's lot on the Comstock Lode:

> View their work! Descending from the surface in shaft-cages, they enter narrow galleries where the air is scarce respirable. By the dim light of their lanterns a dingy rock surface, braced by rotting props, is visible. The stench of decaying vegetable matter, hot foul water, and human excrement intensify the effects of the heat. Only a light breech-cloth covers their hips, and thick-soled shoes protect their feet from the scorching rocks and steaming rills of water that trickle over the floor of the levels. Except for these coverings they toil naked, with heavy drops of sweat starting from every pore .... Yet, though naked, they can only work at some stopes for a few moments at a time, dipping their heads repeatedly under water-showers from conduit pipes, and frequently filling their lungs with fresh air at the open ends of the blower-tubes. Then they are forced to go back to stations where the ventilation is better and gain strength for the renewal of their labor.[25]

It was against the background of such conditions that trade unions emerged on the Comstock Lode. The early prosperity of the Comstock was based on half a dozen mines – the Ophir, the Gould and Curry, the Chollar-Potosi, the Original Gold Hill, the Yellow Jacket – and as these became more heavily capitalised, so (as at Calumet and Hecla or Moonta and Wallaroo) the miners were more inclined to organise. The demand for skilled labour had pushed wage rates up to an average of $4 a day and more in the early 1860s, more than generally could be obtained in California (let alone Cornwall), but by 1864 the initial boom period seemed to be over already. There were attempts at wage cuts, not least at the Uncle Sam mine in Gold Hill where the company decided to reduce remuneration to $3.50 a day. John Trembath, a Cornishman, was the newly appointed captain. It was his job to announce and implement the cut and when he did so the men pounced on him underground, tied him up, lashed him to the cable in the shaft and hoisted him to the surface bearing a label which read, 'Dump this pile of waste dirt from Cornwall.'[26] Trembath was sacked as a convenient scapegoat but the Uncle Sam went ahead with the wage cuts anyway. A strike ensued and led by their brass band the miners marched on Virginia City with the cry 'Four dollars a day!'[27] The bosses capitulated, leaving the newly formed Miners' League of Storey County to celebrate their victory in the first ever miners' strike in the West. However, the employers proceeded quietly to employ non-union labour, not least Cornishmen who – in the words of one contributor in the Gold Hill *Daily News* who criticised the Cornish habit of sending 'home pay' – 'are aliens and who come here only to carry them [wages] back to their native land'.[28]

Its position undermined, the league found itself powerless to enforce its demands for a closed shop in the Comstock mines and its credibility declined. However, by 1866 prosperity had begun to return to the Comstock mines. Some were again paying $4 a day and, suitably encouraged, the Gold Hill miners set about trying to secure $4 as the minimum wage throughout the district. This time the Cornish were in the forefront of the renewed trade union activity, helping to found the Miners' Union of the Town of Gold Hill in December 1866. The driving force was John G. White, a 47-year-old Cornishman who arrived in California in 1852 and had mined at both Mariposa and Grass Valley before moving to Nevada in 1860. White declared himself opposed to 'the tyrannical oppressive power of Capital', encouraging the miners 'to elevate our social condition and maintain a position in society'.[29] Before the end of December the new union had 158 members, and throughout 1867 it was successful in securing both union recognition and $4 a day at mines across the Comstock. John White helped form a sister union in Virginia City in July 1867, and it proved equally successful in its negotiations with the employers. However, in contrast to the almost revolutionary rhetoric of John White's early pronouncements, much of the union's work was aimed at improving the social conditions of the mining towns by enlisting the assistance of the employers in projects such as the formation of club and doctor funds. And, again reflecting the moderate and pragmatic Cornish Methodist self-help ethos which informed Comstock unionism, there was the all-important construction of union halls. These became the community centres of intellectual and social life and the foci of various mutual improvement activities, from annual picnics to the establishment of lending libraries. In February 1878 the *Territorial Enterprise* considered that 'Every book added to this library means a further and further withdrawal from saloons and places where men lose money at cards ... [it] means a lifting up of men's minds and a softening of their hearts, and is more needed in Virginia [City] than is either food or clothes.'[30]

The saloon culture criticised by the *Territorial Enterprise* was symptomatic of the rapidly expanding North American mining frontier, and – notwithstanding their reputation for piety and temperance – the Cornish were as likely as any other ethnic group to spend their leisure hours drinking and gambling. At Christmas in 1874, for example, four Cousin Jacks – Thomas Trembath, Joseph Hodges, Michael Roach, and John Skewes – were playing cards in the Washington House saloon on the Divide. At about midnight they were joined by 27-year-old Alfred Rule, a Camborne man, who suggested that they start playing for drinks. The alcohol made them quarrelsome and Rule accused Skewes of cheating. The *Territorial Enterprise* takes up the story: 'they became excited about the matter, when Rule called Skewes a liar. Skewes told him he must take that back. Rule said he would "take nothing back". Skewes then drew his six-shooter and said "If you do not take it back, I'll kill you." Rule declared that he would not take back what he had said, when Skewes fired on him. The bullet struck Rule just back of the left ear, passing into the head and producing an almost instant death'.[31]

Normally a mild man, Skewes was shocked by the enormity of his deed and immediately surrendered to the sheriff. His Cornish friends raised the $10,000 bail and at his subsequent trial for murder the jury failed to agree. A retrial was ordered but, with numerous departures for new mining destinations during 1875, many of Skewes' friends had left the district and he was unable to raise the $6,000 bail. He languished in gaol until the October of 1875 when a terrible fire destroyed much of Virginia City. He was hurriedly lodged in a mine tunnel for safety as the conflagration engulfed the town and thereafter, remarkably, he disappeared from public view – the newspaper-reading citizens no doubt by now far more eager to learn about plans to rebuild their smouldering precincts. Virginia City was rebuilt, including the saloons that had wrecked the lives of men such as Alfred Rule and John Skewes. Wells Drury, author of the amusing and colourful *An Editor on the Comstock Lode*, first published in 1936, recalled that back in 1876 there were 100 retail liquor dealers in Virginia City, 37 in Gold Hill and seven in Silver City – 'The Delta, the Silver Palace, El Dorado, Palace, Capitol, the Sawdust Corner – these were among the best-known of the places of refreshment in Virginia [City]'.[32] As Wells added, some of the saloons were well-conducted and others riotous and disorderly affairs, their reputations depending on the style of management and the clientele thus encouraged. Singing was always popular in the Comstock's bars, a pastime favourite among the Cornish: 'And with what zest they can sing their fellowship song, *One and All* and their old patriotic ballad, *Shall Trelawney Die*.'[33]

It was into this environment that young Richard Jose was plunged around 1878, following his father's death in Cornwall. Born in Lanner in June 1862, Richard Jose was the eldest child of a family of four and on the death of his father he was shipped across to America to join his uncle, Alfred Jose, in Virginia City. Alas, Uncle Alfred had disappeared and young Richard was forced to fend for himself, delivering bread for miners and lodging – like many Cousin Jacks – in one of Virginia City's boarding houses. In the evenings he visited the many saloons, where his exquisite rendering of sentimental ballads such as *The Lone Grave* and *Where is My Wandering Boy Tonight?* touched the hearts of countless miners far from home. Finding that he was Cornish, the Cousin Jacks made sure that the young Richard did not go short, keeping an eye on him as he made his way from one bar to the next. He also tried his luck in Carson City, some 25 miles distant, where again he was a firm favourite with the miners in the saloons and drinking dens:

> Youthful minstrel of the Comstock,
> Carson's barefoot ballad boy,
> Who filled saloons with Cornish tunes
> And miners hearts with leaping joy.[34]

It is said that the local Women's Temperance League intervened to save this young innocent from sin and corruption and he was dispatched to Reno where, quite by chance, he came across a relative, Bill Luke, the blacksmith. Richard Jose worked as a blacksmith in Reno for several years but his vocation lay elsewhere and in 1884 he joined a California minstrel troupe. Performances at Sacramento and San Francisco were followed by an invitation to Broadway and thereafter his career as a countertenor took off. Tours of South America and South Africa followed. In the latter, so it is said, Cecil Rhodes personally ordered the suspension of operations at the diamond mines so that his Cornish miners might have time off to listen to their countryman, Richard Jose. Jose also visited Cornwall to renew his acquaintance with Lanner and the places and people of his early youth. However, this did not prevent him from affecting an Hispanic identity as Juan Ricardo Jose and alleging that he was in fact of Spanish descent, a romantic conceit that appealed to his sentimental audiences.

Curiously enough, his pronounced Cornish accent survived all these attempts at re-invention. It can be heard clearly in the priceless recordings that were made just after the turn of the 20th century. Re-discovered and presented afresh in recent years by Joe Pengelly, the well-known BBC South West broadcaster, these recordings reveal to the contemporary ear from all those years ago the quality and style of Jose's performances:

> I cannot sing the old songs
> I sang long years ago,
> For heart and voice would fail me,
> And foolish tears would flow...,
> I cannot sing the old songs,
> Or dream, those dreams, again.[35]

Wells Drury, in his days at the *Territorial Enterprise*, knew Richard Jose, a friendship they took with them as each went his separate way:

> we loved to hear the sweet voice of Dick Jose, the big-hearted Cornish lad who left a Reno's blacksmith forge to go on the stage as a ballad-singer, beloved by all the world. Informality of the old days was Dick's. One night in Los Angeles I sat with a thousand others to hear him sing. Dick spied me in the audience – we hadn't seen each other for years – came to the footlights, and heedless of the rest waved his hand, calling in greeting, 'Why, hello, Wells!'. Then he sang *Belle Brandon*.[36]

Drury was in other respects too a keen observer of the Cornish miners and their habits. He knew that 'The Cornishmen loved wrestling, and fierce were the contests in which they struggled – wrestling in canvas jackets, in accordance with the usage of their native county'.[37] He also recognised Comstock's many Cornish surnames, noting that 'the payrolls of the mines bristled with names like Trevillion, Trelease, Trezona, Tregellis, Treglown, Trewhella, Trewartha, Trezise, Trevaskis, Tremayne, Treloar, Trevethan, Polmear, Pengilly, Penaluna and Penrose'.[38] He confessed that 'I was always on terms of good-fellowship with the hearty Cornish folk', adding that:

> Many Cornish miners ... have astonished people by their eloquence, and some have developed this talent as to become

pulpit ministers and even cabinet ministers, charming by their discourse. They possess a strain of religious fervour, and even in rough surroundings display a fondness for books, as witness their patronage of the well-stocked Miners' Library in Virginia City. Independence, thrift, geniality, excitability, contempt for familiar dangers – these are characteristic of them.[39]

Drury recalled with wry amusement when a visiting Irish patriot lectured to empty seats at Piper's Opera House as there was the rival attraction of a Cornish wrestling match at the Miners' Union Hall that night. The Cornish also had a reputation as prizefighters. Drury described 'the whole series of slashing fights'[40] between Jimmy Trevillion (Cornish) and Patsey Hogan (Irish), and wrote that 'As gory a battle as any I saw in Nevada was the mill ... in which Dublin Pete Lawlor beat Jack Askew (alias "Skewers"). It was Ireland against Cornwall, and the big crowd yelled itself hoarse throughout the 65 rounds.'[41] But the Cornish had their day in March 1897 when Bob Fitzsimmons, the Helston-born blacksmith known variously as Fighting Bob, Freckled Bob, Ruby Robert, or simply The Cornishman, defeated 'Gentleman Jim' Corbett (an American) in 14 rounds at Carson City and took the world heavyweight championship.

Although the Cornish remained prominent on the Comstock Lode for many years, by the mid-1870s many were already on the move. Drury noted that a number had gone to other parts of America, while 'some wandered to Australia and South Africa; others went back to Cornwall, and many are the pleasant messages I have had from old cronies, postmarked Redruth and Penzance'.[42] But many had simply shifted to other parts of Nevada; to the arid Humboldt Valley, to Pioche near the Utah border – where in 1873, according to the *West Briton*, 'many Cornishmen are here today who are bumming around the saloons for a drink, and are half-starved'[43] – and to White Pine where there were 30 Cornishmen working in the mines in 1870. Later, the Cornish were to be found in places such as Eureka and Tonopah and a string of other desert mining communities that today are, for the most part, little more than ghost towns. In June 1881 the *West Briton* estimated that there were as many as 600 Cornish people at Eureka, with the miners making up to seven times as much in wages than they would have done if they had remained at home.[44] As on the Comstock, the Eureka miners combined to try to secure $4 a day as a minimum wage, the Ruby Hill Miners' Union calling a brief strike over the issue in 1884. William J. Penrose, editor of the Ruby Hill *Mining News* and a former Cornish miner, also opposed the introduction of tributing, claiming that it was a device by which the employers sought to drive down wages to a mere $2 a day. The union, responding to Penrose's encouragement, sought to create a closed shop in the mines but the mine companies simply brought in non-union tributers from outside. The mines were tough places, as rival union and non-union workers confronted each other, and the townships too were as rough as any that could be found in Nevada. Men outnumbered women by at least two to one in Nevada and in consequence women were sought eagerly, not only for companionship but because of the 'civilising' influence they were imagined to have in such places. It was no surprise, then, when the young and innocent Lavinia Johns, a Cousin Jenny, found herself the centre of attention when she arrived in Eureka in 1888. Within no time at all she was being courted by William Spargo, from Stithians, and before long they were married. Years later they ended up running a restaurant in Helston, back in Cornwall.

From Eureka it was a relatively short step across the mountain ranges into Utah, where the Cornish had already made their presence felt, not least in Salt Lake City where John Rowe Moyle, a stonecutter born in Wendron in 1808, and Charles William Penrose, born in London of Cornish parents in 1832, became notable activists in the Mormon church. But the Mormons were reluctant to sanction the development of Utah's mineral wealth, fearing the deleterious impact of the sudden arrival of hundreds of unbelievers. There had been some limited placer mining in the Bingham Valley in the 1860s but it was not until 1871 that Captain James Nancarrow, a Cornishman who had already managed mines in Mexico, Chile and Spain, was sent out by British investment interests to survey the prospects in Utah. Silver was discovered in payable quantities in a canyon east of Salt Lake City in 1872, and hard-rock miners were brought in from Virginia City to develop what was to become the significant Ontario mine. It was said that the Cornish found conditions there 'almost identical to those they had known in Cornwall, with the difference that here they were paid a living wage'.[45] By now the copper deposits of Bingham Canyon were being exploited and in 1880 there were 450 American miners (including, no doubt, many second-generation Cousin Jacks), 170 British (overwhelmingly Cornish), 80 Scandinavians and 50 Irish in the canyon. Among the Cornish was Joseph James Rowse, from St Austell, who made his way to Utah via New Jersey and Grass Valley. Arriving in America in 1878, he made several trips home to Cornwall before sending for his family in 1886. Retiring from mining, he used his savings to start up a family grocery business in the township of Ogden.

Elsewhere, the Cornish also played their part in the opening up of the far West. They were prospecting in Idaho as early as the 1860s, as they were in Colorado. In 1877 there was a huge silver and lead boom at Leadville, Colorado, followed by the unexpected but equally spectacular discoveries of gold in the same state at Cripple Creek in 1891. The mines of Leadville and Cripple Creek quickly became very deep and heavily capitalised, conditions in which the hard-rock expertise of the Cousin Jacks was all important. As R.W. Paul has observed: 'at many mines highly professional Cornish or Irish miners took the place of American amateurs .... In Gilpin county the Cornishmen became an especially notable part of the life of the community. With their long experience in underground work, they contributed much to the improvement of mining techniques.'[46] Among these Cornish experts was Richard Pearce, born at Barrippa, near Camborne, in 1837. His father, a captain at Dolcoath, recognised his son's aptitude for the science of mining and by 1858 Richard was taking mining classes at various institutions in Cornwall. He later attended the Royal School of Mines in London and in 1865 he made a name for himself by assisting the Swansea smelters in dealing with the difficult refractory copper ores from Chile. In 1871 he was invited to Colorado to inspect minerals that had been located there and to advise on their treatment. So successful was his advice that Pearce rapidly became the guru of mineral processing in Colorado, not least at Leadville after 1877 where he was able to manage the efficient treatment of the rich but complicated silver-lead ores. It was probably also Pearce who first recognised the unusual tellurides of gold (and silver) at Cripple Creek, facilitating their extraction and treatment. Acutely aware of his Cornish credentials, Pearce went out of his way to assist other Cousin Jacks in Colorado, his home in Denver becoming 'open house' for passing Cornish folk, and he formed a close friendship with T.A. Rickard, the celebrated American mining engineer of Cornish descent. Significantly, perhaps, Pearce never did take out American citizenship, and he retired to his native Cornwall in 1902.[47]

In the 1880s Leadville and nearby Central City were 'full of Cornish',[48] as was neighbouring Nevadaville. As ever, it is the individual experiences of ordinary people which provide the most vivid insights into the conditions that obtained in such places. Take, for example, the story of Mary Wall, born at Carnyorth, near St Just, in 1841. She worked as a bal-maiden and it may have been at the mine that she met her future husband, Will Grenfell. Eventually, Will went to Nevadaville, Colorado, in search of work, leaving Mary in Cornwall with three young children. When he had saved a bit, Will sent home for his family. Alas, one of Mary's small daughters died of measles shortly after their arrival at New York but worse was to greet her in Colorado. She was met from the train at Denver by her brother Matthew, a miner who had been in America for some years, and it fell to him to break the news of her husband's recent death. Will Grenfell had died but a week before of so-called 'mountain fever' and was already in his grave, interred on Bald Mountain, Gilpin County, on 10 November 1879, aged just 38 years and 10 months. Further miseries were heaped upon poor Mary, for within a week her second daughter, Martha, had also succumbed to disease in this new land. A group of miners from St Just took pity on Mary, building her a shack on Bald Mountain where she settled down to a life of baking and laundry. As she used to say in later years, 'When I went to Bald Mountain I washed and baked from four in the morning to twelve at night.'[49] Her hard work paid off and in a few years she had saved enough to open a modest boarding house for Cornish miners. And then, in 1880 or thereabouts, she married her cousin Andrew Stevens, one of the many St Just miners in Nevadaville. The couple returned to Carnyorth in 1892 and a touching postscript to the tale tells us that one day Mary received an unexpected call from a Mrs Rowe who had walked the six miles or so from New Mill to express her gratitude for the way in which Mary had nursed her dying husband years before in her Nevadaville boarding house.

But if the Cornish stuck together in their hours of need, this sense of solidarity did not extend to the wider community. Despite the conditions in Colorado, trade unionism was retarded as a result of 'hostility toward the Cornish by Irish and American miners and the community at large'.[50] In 1873 a Central City Miners' Union had been formed with a Cornishman, Andrew Stevens (perhaps Mary Wall's cousin) as president. Other Cousin Jacks flocked to join the union but the Irish and Americans, sensing a Cornish plot to dominate the mines, refused to sign up. Undeterred, the Cornish union men toured local mines and neighbouring districts such as Black Hawk and Nevadaville, encouraging the Cousin Jacks to join their ranks. Rumours abounded that the Cornish were intent on the seizing the whole area for themselves. There were frantic calls to the state governor for military support to counter 'the Cornwall secessionist movement',[51] as it was called. Needless to say, Cornish ambitions were by no means as extravagant as their alarmist detractors alleged but that such fears seemed credible at the time speaks volumes for the ethnic solidarity of the Cornish and the suspicion that it could generate. In 1885 it was said that at Leadville 'over three-quarters of the miners in the Small Hopes [mines] were Cornish',[52] but thereafter their numerical strength, and cultural dominance, declined in Colorado with the increasing arrivals of Irish and Americans, and Austrians and Scandinavians.

Just as the Cornish had moved into Utah and Colorado, many moving east-wards from their concentrations in Nevada, so other Cousin Jacks had gone to South Dakota after the discovery of gold in the Black Hills in 1874–75. This was the infamous episode that led to the destruction on 25 June 1876 of Custer and his Seventh Cavalry at the Little Big Horn at the hands of the Sioux, Cheyenne and their allies. But the Cornish were used enough to the 'Indian wars' and the formidable military prowess of the Plains nations did not deter them from cash-ing in on the Black Hills bonanza. Among their number was Richard Bullock, from Ruthvose (or Ruthvers) on Goss Moor, the legendary 'Deadwood Dick' who rode shotgun on the Deadwood stagecoach. Another was Thomas White, from Pensilva, who arrived in Dakota from Nevada in 1877. James Gluyas arrived from Grass Valley in the summer of 1879 to manage the Caladonia Quartz Mine, and another of the region's mine names – the Caradon – carries more than a sugges-tion of Cornish involvement or influence.

However, despite later reports that tin might also be lurking in the Black Hills, Dakota was a relative sideshow compared to the other areas of Cornish influence. Rather more important was Arizona, where silver was discovered in 1874 at the Silver King Mine at Globe, east of Phoenix. Globe remained an important mag-net for the Cornish well into the 20th century and even on the eve of the Second World War it could still be asserted that, 'The three hills [district] – Noftgers, Pascoe, and School, are said to be Cornish territory. Pascoe Hill is separated from Noftgers Hill by a deep steep-sided canyon ... Noftgers and School Hills share the nickname of Cousin Jack Hill ... Pascoe Hill has been corrupted to Pasty Hill.'[53] Copper was discovered in Arizona in 1877 at Bisbee, leading to the early rise of two important claims – the Atlantic and the Copper Queen. The captain of the Atlanta was a Cornishman, one John Prout, and in the normal way he sought out Cousin Jacks to occupy the key positions at his mine. At Tombstone and Jerome the Cornish were also present in some numbers, and at Ray – to the east of Phoenix – Ernest Jenkin from Carn Grey (near St Austell) was recruited in 1907 to manage a large copper mine. By then Arizona had become the principal copper producer in the United States of America.

Tombstone, in particular, with its silver and gold mines, has a still-remem-bered place in the Cornish iconography of the West. To the general mystique of Wyatt Earp, the gunfight at the OK Corral, and the notorious Boot Hill – with its infamous cemetery full of the bones of gunslingers and ne'er-do-wells, was added a Cornish dimension in which Tombstone seemed to epitomise all the hardships and dangers faced by the Cousin Jacks and Jennies on the American frontier.

Mining accidents and disease – not least 'miner's complaint' in the hot, dusty atmosphere underground – took more than their usual toll, as in the autumn and winter of 1886–87 when Edward Richards from Breage, John Bennets of St Blazey Gate and Thomas Martin from Halsetown were all killed in the mines. The tale of Thomas Martin's demise had a particular twist, combining allegations of safety lapses with accusations of ethnic animosity. Martin had been killed by the sudden falling of a cage on him while he was at work in the shaft of the Silver Thread mine. The failure of a safety pin was said to have been the cause of the accident, and at the subsequent inquest the engineer, James Leggett, admitted that he knew the pin to be unsafe and that he had neglected to report this fact to the captain, one John Crago, a Cornishman. Moreover, it was said that Thomas Martin had lived in fear of Leggett, on the day of the accident expressing his anxiety that one way or another Leggett would kill him. Leggett denied that he had been out to 'get' Martin but one witness did testify that Leggett was 'particularly down on Cornishmen; that he had spoken disrespectfully of them as a class'.[54]

Ethnic antipathies were to reach even greater heights at Butte, Montana, as the Cornish competed with the Irish and other groups for both dominance in the mine workforce and for control of the trade unions. The first mineral discoveries – of gold – had in fact been made as early as the 1860s in places such as Last Chance Gulch, near Helena. The *West Briton* reported the finds in December 1865, and Cousin Jacks from elsewhere in the far and mid-West, from Wisconsin and Michigan, and from Cornwall itself were among the first on the gold-fields. The Irish were not far behind, along with Americans from both the West and Back East, with southern European emigrants arriving in later years. As Mark Wyman put it, 'The Butte cycle was described as Yankees, Cornishmen, Irishmen, Missourians, South Dakotans, and – by 1910 – Balkan immigrants.'[55] There were also Welsh, English, Scots, Finns, Swedes, Italians, Austrians, Germans, Mexicans, even Filipinos. Within this multicultural melting-pot the various ethnic groups retained their separate identities and attracted the usual stereotypical depictions:

> Half-clad miners chewing the rag,
> This one a thinker, that one a wag.
> A swarthy Hunk sits and grins
> As a shameless Cousin [Jack] talks about his sins.[56]

Although by the early 1870s the best days of the Montana gold-fields seemed to be over already, the discovery of silver later in the decade perpetuated Butte as a mining district long enough for 'the richest hill in the world'[57] to be uncovered. This time it was copper that caught the attention of the Cousin Jacks and other nationalities, and it was the exploitation of these huge deposits that led to the rapid transformation of Butte into a modern industrial centre based on heavily capitalised, technologically advanced, deep hard-rock mining. The Cornish came into their own, deploying their skills to facilitate this swift development, and using ethnic identity as a device to protect and enhance their position. Although never as homogeneously Cornish as Grass Valley or Moonta, Butte soon took its place in the Cornish imagination alongside Virginia City, Broken Hill and Kalgoorlie as a 'Cornish' town, or at least as a place where the Cornish were a visible and active ethnic group. There was, for example, William Dyer, born in St Austell in 1853, who had mined in New Jersey and Colorado before arriving in Butte in 1878. He invested his savings wisely, affording a visit home to his native Cornwall in 1884–85 before returning to Montana to resume his new but lucrative career as a mining speculator. Another success story was that of Captain Thomas Couch, born in Camborne in 1843. Like many a wandering Cousin Jack, he had emigrated, at the age of 20, to Upper Michigan, moving on shortly to Grass Valley and then venturing to Nevada where in 1868 he became manager of the Hidden Treasure mine at White Pine. From there it was on to Utah and then eventually to Butte in 1886 where he became captain of the Mountain View mine.

The Butte Carol Club, founded by Alfred Paynter about 1880, was the Montana equivalent of the Grass Valley Cornish Choir, and the Cornish were also prominent in the Butte Miners' Brass Band. Cousin Jacks travelled from all across the West to compete in Butte's famous Fourth of July drilling contests and Cornish wrestling matches were no less popular. It was said that bets of $1000 were common in drilling and wrestling contests. In 1900 Tony Harris was Butte's wrestling champion, 'acclaimed by every Cornishman on "the hill" as "the best man to ever wear a [wrestling] jacket"'.[58] There were the usual Cousin Jack yarns, with their dry, often self-mocking (even if racist and sexist) humour:

> On one occasion a squaw, with a solemn-faced papoose strapped to her back, attracted the attention of a woman travel-ing to Butte for the first time. The woman was interested in the baby, which appeared to be of lighter complexion than those most often seen in papooses. She addressed the mother on the subject, speaking patronisingly in what she supposed to be the

vernacular of the Indians. "Him full-blooded Injun?" she asked, pointing to the child. "No", the squaw answered after a moment, her eyes expressionless, "him part Injun, part Injuneer."[59]

There was also the melancholy (or happy?) tale of Molly Demurska, a girl of 'high heart and low morals' who won the affections of one Jack Jolly (a Cornish name). Jolly was a widower, so the story goes, having lost his wife and seven children in an influenza epidemic. But he found solace in the embraces of young Molly. Soon they were engaged to be married and at last the big day arrived:

> The officiating officer [judge] himself prepared the bride for the ceremony. The girls of the 'house', in decollete which left nothing to the imagination, lined the stairway. The guests were assembled below. Jolly and Molly descended the staircase .... The judge pronounced them man and wife. The bridesmaids stood on their heads with delight. Molly Jolly was an honest woman. Her last indiscretion had been with the judge. But fate was unkind. The bride and bridegroom set out for Alaska and Jack Jolly killed a man on the train in a gambling row. Shortly thereafter he himself was killed by Soapy Smith, one of the most notorious confidence men in the history of the West. Anyway, that is the judge's story, and what he says he sticks by.[60]

But behind the humour and tall stories was the reality of a tough and often short life in the unhealthy Montana mines. As the mines became deeper and more developed, so 'miners' complaint' was a more frequent, almost inevitable, accompaniment of Cornish endeavours. The disease accounted for a high proportion of the miners who died prematurely at Butte in their early 40s. In the autumn of 1899, quite unexpectedly, Joe Thomas of St Austell, aged 40, John Johns of Stoke Climsland, aged 41, and Samuel Rowe of Goldsithney, aged 43, all succumbed to 'miners' complaint'. With lungs already irrevocably damaged by many years' exposure to the searing dust, an even mild attack of influenza or pneumonia might prove fatal. Thus in the hard winter of 1908 we learn of the deaths of a string of Cornishmen: John Williams, aged 49, Thomas Edwards, aged 31, Edward Pollard, aged 42, William Eddy, aged 43, Thomas Magor, aged 62, Richard Trenerry, aged 37, James Waters, aged 44. Almost overnight, or so it seemed, the Butte copper mines had become extremely deep and decidedly unpleasant, the application of heavy and sophisticated mining machinery ushering in a new era in which, ironically, the Cornish were both much sought after and exposed to ever-greater risks.

This process of rapid development and industrialisation at Butte was associated especially with the deadly rivalry of two competing magnates, William Andrews Clark and Marcus Daly. Clark, a Pennsylvanian, was a book-learned mining professional who had already made a name for himself in smelting in Colorado. He transferred his energies with equal success to mining and smelting in Montana and went on to become a senator for Montana. Daly, by contrast, was an Irish working man who had made his way to Butte from California. He had considered that beneath the shallow silver deposits lay at depth vast reservoirs of copper, a hunch that proved spectacularly correct and had in no time propelled Daly into the limelight as controller of the mighty Anaconda mining empire.[61] Daly, hardly surprisingly, gave preferential treatment to the Irish, employing them wherever or whenever he could. Clark, on the other hand, preferred the Cornish and gave the skilled and supervisory positions in his mines to the Cousin Jacks. His Mountain View mine, for example, run by Captain Couch, was known colloquially as the 'Saffron Bun' on account of its overwhelmingly Cornish 'flavour'.

Ethnic conflict between the Cornish and the Irish became a proxy for industrial competition, the Cornish miners infiltrating the underground workings of rival claims (and causing endless lawsuits as a result), in a real territorial battle for control of the copper lodes. At times it looked like open warfare, the Cornish deploying high-pressure hoses on 'enemy' territory and even making impromptu hand grenades by stuffing empty cans full of dynamite. Politically, Daly was a Democrat and Clark a Republican and they encouraged their employees to take sides accordingly. Certainly, this competitiveness influenced political debate at every level. In early 1889, for instance, the Montana State legislature discussed the appointment of mine inspectors. Given the Cornish-Irish rivalry, some legislators felt that all foreign-born should be barred from holding such positions. As the Helena *Independent* explained, the problem was that: 'the miners employed at Anaconda were ... almost exclusively Irishmen and those at Granite almost exclusively Cornish. Would a man appointed to the office from either of these nationalities be likely to prove as impartial in the exercise of his duties as one who was not influenced by prejudices that these facts showed to exist?'[62]

Such prejudices were most readily apparent in the emerging trade union activity. By 1885 the Butte union boasted some 1800 members – higher than at

Virginia City in Nevada – but there was already 'bad blood between the Irish and Cornish miners ... [which] would slowly grow to a dispute of grotesque proportions'.[63] A stalwart of the Butte union was William J. Penrose, editor of the Butte *Mining Journal*. Born in Cornwall in 1856, Penrose had worked in the Cornish copper and tin mines from the age of seven. Later, he had emigrated to America, toiling first of all in the mines of Pennsylvania and Illinois, before moving on to Tuscarora and Ruby Hill in Nevada. Notwithstanding Clark's affiliations, Penrose was a radical Democrat, his sworn enemy – Irishman and trade unionist, Patrick E. Boland – a Republican. Confusing though these ideological inconsistencies might seem to the modern observer, they were hardly of weight in the Butte of the 1880s and 1890s when political allegiance was a function of ethnic identification. If Clark was a Republican, then the Cornish were right behind him. If Penrose was a Democrat, then he too could count on solid Cornish support. Penrose was duly elected to the state legislature and in 1891 a bill – drafted by Boland and other union officials, and calling for an eight-hour day – was introduced. Penrose appeared to support the bill, especially when Cornishman William Eddy, president of the Butte Miners' Union, went to the legislature to lobby on its behalf. In the end, however, Penrose changed his mind, arguing that the:

> passage of the bill would surely cause many mines to shut down and consequently cause the discharge of thousands of miners .... Montana as a mining center would sink to the level of the copper centers of Vermont and Michigan, the iron customs of New Jersey, the coal methods of Pennsylvania, the craving practices of the gold kings of California and the domineering rules of the moneyed kings of the Old World.[64]

The bill was defeated, ushering in a new period of hostility on the mines. Penrose was condemned as a 'Judas' by his opponents, and shortly before midnight on 9 June 1891 he was gunned down on a street corner in Butte. The police eventually arrested one Emma Turner, a young woman said to be insanely infatuated with Penrose, but the Cornish were not alone in imagining darkly that his assassin was more likely a member of some conspiratorial secret society, 'like the notorious Molly Maguires'.[65] Serious though it undoubtedly was, the feud between Penrose and Boland was but one episode in the wider conflict that continued to colour Cornish-Irish relations in Montana. In May 1893 delegates from the various

Western mining camps met in Butte and agreed to the foundation of a Western Federation of Miners. Inevitably, there were Cornishmen among the leaders of this vast, new combination, including figures such as John L. Williams, president of the Butte union, and the veteran James H. Rowe – former president of the Ruby Hill Miners' Union in Nevada. Branches were formed throughout the West but in the economic downturn of the mid-1890s when, despite union pressure, many mines suffered wage cuts, the federation found it difficult to make an impact. The federation was also 'handicapped by chronic Irish-Cornish feuding within the Butte union',[66] the Irish and other ethnic groups complaining that the Cornish saw themselves as a cut above other classes of worker and were thus disdainful of everyday labouring tasks. As one balladeer put it:

> He can take the eight penny strike
> And bend it in his hand –
> The strongest little Cousin Jack
> That ever struck the land.
> Though when it comes to loading rock
> He will not do it – nay
> He wouldn't load a cart of ore
> Not in a twelve-hour day.
> In wrestling down upon the mat
> This Cousin's the best bet
> But the fellow who can make him work
> Has not seen daylight yet.[67]

The relative weakness of the federation was still apparent in the early years of the 20th century, the habitual violence of a handful of extremists alienating many otherwise enthusiastic unionists as well as perpetuating the deep ethnic splits. In 1917 the International Workers of the World – the so-called Wobblies – tried to take over the labour movement in Montana. Despite their reputation for being 'pro-German' and 'anti-American', the Wobblies managed to set up a 'Committee on Grievances' at Butte. One by one an Irishman, a Finn, a German, an Austrian, a Bulgarian, a Russian, even a reluctant Italian, were appointed to the committee. But when it was suggested that a Cousin Jack be elected, a noisy group shouted down the proposal, 'We don't want any of them. We will let the Irish take care of them!'[68] The mood was serious enough for the Federal government to declare martial law at Butte, a state of affairs that was maintained until the end of the First

World War. By then, however, the relative importance of Butte as an industrial producer had already declined, the copper output of Arizona having been in front for more than a decade. Moreover, the disastrous Granite Mountain underground fire which had killed more than 150 miners (Cornish among them) had at a stroke reduced Butte's copper production by at least a quarter.

Montana was the last of the great North American mining frontiers in which the Cornish participated in strength, although in the still-depressed atmosphere of the 1890s some of Butte's Cousin Jacks set off for the newly discovered Klondike gold-fields in northwestern Canada. Other Cornish arrived on the Klondike from as far away as Moonta in South Australia, a party setting out for their distant destination in 1897, and some travelled directly from Cornwall itself. William Grigg, for example, left the family farm at Gweek in the late 1890s to try his luck on the Klondike. Like many others, however, he found to his cost that descriptions of Klondike wealth had been greatly exaggerated and he returned home to Cornwall not much richer than before. Moreover, by the 1890s North America had already been replaced in the forefront of Cornish attentions by South Africa, the land of diamonds and gold, which in the closing decades of the 19th century had emerged as the latest focus in the continuing development of the international mining economy.

# CHAPTER ELEVEN

# 'BUT A SUBURB OF CORNWALL' – SOUTH AFRICA

I n the crisis years of the mid-1860s, as we saw in Chapter 8, there was destitution and want on a grand scale in Cornwall. Emigration, however, was a safety valve. Cornwall's by now well-developed 'emigration culture' and 'emigration trade' smoothed the way for the speedy departure of thousands, while newly emergent agricultural and mining destinations overseas beckoned enticingly to the unfortunate of Redruth, St Austell or Callington. A decade later and things had not improved, a brief revival in the tin industry in the early 1870s proving a false dawn. And although the increasing multiplicity of overseas destinations continued to draw the Cornish abroad to new frontiers, poverty and even hunger remained the lot of many who stayed at home. Indeed, by 1879 Cornwall was facing a crisis comparable to that of the 1860s. Mining was again in decline and grave financial difficulties threatened the underlying fabric of the Cornish economy. The failure in early 1879 of the Cornish Bank, with its branches at Falmouth, Penzance, Redruth, and Truro, combined with the crash of the Union Bank in Helston in raining the heaviest of blows upon business confidence. Savings disappeared and the means of marshalling resources for new investments were lost.[1]

In February 1879, in an echo of the dreadful days more than a decade before, a Central Committee was set up to direct a newly formed Cornwall Distress Fund. At Redruth there was concern at the unemployment of children due to the abandonment of various tin streams, while in the March the *West Briton* reported sadly that in the parish of Gwennap, where only 25 years before the monthly wage bill was £33,000 per month, less than £100 a month was being spent on miners' wages. This was a district of 'oppressive death-like silence .... The grand granite engine-houses are roofless and desolate, the tall and graceful chimney

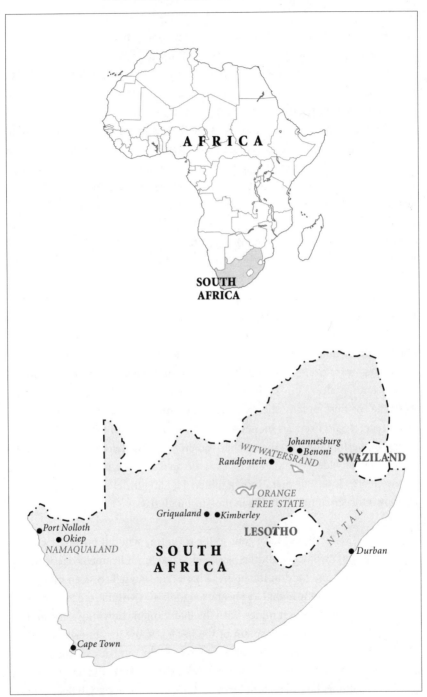

*Principal mining locations and cities in South Africa*

stacks smokeless and the swallows build their nests therein; they are but the monuments of colossal activities expired'.[2] Meanwhile, soup kitchens were again a familiar feature of Cornish life in towns and parishes such as Truro, Redruth, Camborne, St Agnes, Bodmin, Breage and Hayle. Cornish communities overseas, notably in South Australia and Victoria, responded liberally with financial assistance and individual émigrés continued to send their 'home pay' back to Cornwall. Such remittances were awaited anxiously in Cornwall, not least in those many families where the menfolk were toiling overseas, with mother or wife or sister left to run the home. As J. Henry Harris wrote at the turn of the 20th century, gone long since were the days when: 'The mine was the soul of the moor, and the pumps and stamps its music. The young men now are spread over South Africa and Australia, South America and the regions of Klondike; and the old people and young wives and children were left at home, dependent for daily bread upon the love of kindred whom they might never see again.'[3]

In 1871, for example, Jane Bray of Trefula Moor (between Redruth and St Day) had become head of the household when her husband had gone off to Peru in search of work. She had five daughters, of whom the eldest was only eight years old, but, according to the census enumerator of that year, she was in receipt of 'home pay' from South America. There were numerous such references in the census enumerators' books in Cornwall to 'husband abroad', 'husband in Australia', or 'husband in America', but not all women were as lucky as Jane Bray. Some received no overseas money at all, and many tried to make ends meet by taking in washing or working as charwomen.[4] Shortly before her death in the early 1920s, an elderly woman in Helston dictated a brief autobiographical note to one George Jose, a former Moonta miner, detailing the effect of her husband's disappearance in South Australia in those difficult days:

> Many times I have gone to the wash tray without breakfast, and my two dear children have had to stay until I came home without any food in the house. I have cried myself to sleep many a night. One night I lost heart, so I took my two children to a water shaft at Basset mines, with the intention of drowning them and myself; but the captain of the mine saw me just in time. I told him my trouble and he wrote to Captain Hancock in Australia, and found my husband was working there. He could not do anything, but asked him to write. Captain Hancock's daughter sent me £1. I often wished I could write; I would thank her so much.[5]

Indeed, as late as 1920 families in Cornwall were still trying to trace relatives who had disappeared overseas decades before. In that year the Moonta *People's Weekly* inquired after the whereabouts of William Gilbert Thomas, 'formerly a Miner, of Camborne, Cornwall ... who is believed to have arrived in Australia about 28 years ago',[6] while in Cornwall itself there were solicitors and others who specialised in the tracking-down of lost individuals overseas – a new dimension to the emigration trade. For those who had given up hope of finding errant husbands or lovers, despair led sometimes to abortion, or infanticide, or indeed suicide. In February 1880, for instance, the body of a newly born female child was found at the bottom of a well in Camborne, the second such discovery there in a fortnight.[7] More prosaically, the absence of menfolk overseas meant not only a declining population but also smaller 'nuclear' households and a sharp change in the rate of reproduction. Indeed, by the 1870s households in the mining districts, especially in West Cornwall, had begun, in the jargon of the sociologists, to 'huddle' or 'collapse' as multiple family households containing the remnants of two or more nuclear families were created. As Mark Brayshay has shown, many of these households contained women whose husbands had emigrated, and who, unable to afford their own accommodation, had moved in with parents or other relatives. Other women had no alternative but to throw themselves on the mercy of the not always sympathetic Boards of Guardians. Caroline Gay, such a woman, was one of the lucky ones when she persuaded the Redruth guardians to provide her and her five children with relief to the tune of five shillings and five loaves, her overseas husband having failed to send her any money.[8] By the 1881 census these socio-demographic changes were plain for all to see. The population of St Agnes parish, for example, had declined by 2346 compared with that of 1871, with St Ives down 1156 and Redruth falling by some 1350.[9]

Fortuitously, this renewed crisis in Cornish socio-economic life occurred alongside the rapid rise to pre-eminence of South Africa as a destination for Cornish mining expertise, a pre-eminence which allowed both the ready escape of skilled labour from depressed Cornwall and a steady stream of eagerly awaited funds flowing in the opposite direction. In this way, Cornwall was spared the worst ravages of mass unemployment in the late 19th century but developed an informal welfare system or 'dependency culture' of hitherto unparalleled proportions, in which the well-being of large sections of the community in places such as Redruth or St Just-in-Penwith was reliant upon the efforts of Cornish miners in South Africa. In September 1896, for example, the *West Briton* considered that:

> If our mining population centres in Cornwall are being depop-
> ulated ... it is satisfactory to know that large and continuous
> remittances are being received at home, especially in the
> neighbourhood of Redruth, from Cornish emigrants ... It is
> reckoned that every week a sum of money probably from £1000
> to £1300 is received in Redruth alone, and a like sum at
> Camborne, amounts in proportion being received at Lanner and
> other places where miners' families do congregate.'[10]

Two years later, the same newspaper was even more supportive of the process,
notwithstanding its jibe at the profit-making sensibilities of local shop owners:

> Saturday morning last saw the arrival of the African mail – the
> main delivery from Johannesburg, Kimberley, &c. The heavy
> mail was promptly dispatched from the post-office, and it was
> not long before the banks of the town [Redruth] were busy
> cashing drafts. With such an influx of money into the town a
> busy Saturday market was an assured thing .... People from
> Portreath, Illogan, Carnkie, Lanner, and, in fact, every village
> and hamlet for miles around came in, and shopkeepers ... had a
> busy market up to a late hour. So the money circulates, African
> gold eventually coming into the pockets of the larger shops, who
> occasionally build houses, and, when the opportunity serves,
> erect villas by the seaside![11]

By then, the flow of miners to South Africa seemed inexorable, the year 1885 having
witnessed the departure from Cornwall of no fewer than 2086, at least 1000 of these
from Camborne and Redruth alone. As J. Harry Johns explained to the Mining
Association and Institution of Cornwall in October 1895, 'Cornish people have got
to regard South Africa as Greater Cornwall ... the amount of money which at the
present moment is finding its way to the old county from the Transvaal for the support of the families of the miners is astounding'.[12] As C. Lewis Hind put it in his *Days
in Cornwall*, published at the turn of the 20th century, 'Johannesburg is but a suburb
of Cornwall.'[13] Or alternatively, as one commentator wrote in the early 1900s:

> South Africa is a sort of outlying farm for the mining division,
> and when things are brisk every mail brings twenty or thirty

thousand pounds sterling for wives and families and the old folks at home. Every market night is an object-lesson in political economy. When the Boer War was on, most of the shops were in mourning, and people went about with hunger in their eyes. Cousin Jack goes abroad to make money, and what he saves he sends home. On his return his delight is to get a wheelbarrow mine [smallholding], and come into Redruth market, and talk tin.[14]

Of course, as we saw in Chapter 2, Cornwall's earliest links with South Africa preceded by half a century and more the intimacy described above. There were Cornish families among the Cape colonists in the early 1820s and from 1836 onwards some Cornish took advantage of assisted passages to South Africa. Notable among these colonists were John and Mary Higgo, from Penzance, who emigrated with their six sons and four daughters in 1850. Together, they founded the quarry and settlement of Higgoville, just below Table Mountain, where they employed many Cornish in the provision of dressed granite for the grand public and commercial buildings of Cape Town. As Horst Rossler has shown, South Africa remained an important destination for Cornish granite quarrymen throughout the second half of the 19th century and into the early 1900s.[15] From the 1870s onwards, skilled Constantine stonemasons such as John Pascoe (1876), William Henry Pascoe (1876), William Symonds (1876), and John Henry Tremayne (1878), had left for South Africa, to be followed in later years by individuals such as Thomas Jenkin (1882), Thomas Williams (1882), John Jenkin (1890), and Thomas H. James (1891). Richard Grigg, a Constantine man and a member of the Constantine Lodge of the Operative Stonemasons' Society, died on the Kimberley diamond fields in South Africa in the late 1880s. A tragic death was that of 24-year-old George Trethowan, also from Constantine, who was pinned under the cowcatcher of a moving train at a level crossing near Cape Town in October 1912. Trethowan's injuries were horrific, 'terribly mutilated about the head. The flesh is torn along the spine and the back of the scalp is taken off. The doctor attending the accident gave Trethowan an hour to live'.[16] His funeral in Cape Town was attended by various Cornish friends and colleagues, including the Vague brothers from Constantine, J. Reynolds and N. Easom of Penryn, N. Pascoe of Stithians, and others from further afield in Cornwall, indicating as ever the Cornish tendency to stick together in good times and bad.

Samson Rickard Stuttaford, from Helston, was another of the early Cornish arrivals in South Africa, having turned up at the Cape in 1857 as a young man of 27 to open a haberdasher's shop. Successful from the first, Stuttafords grew over the years into one of South Africa's major department store groups. More overtly Cornish, perhaps, were the miners recruited in the early 1850s for the copper mines of Namaqualand in the Western Cape – men such as Thomas Rodda from St Just-in-Penwith, James Thomas from Gwennap, and John Wadge from Gunnislake. Centred on O'Okiep and operational from 1852 until 1919, the Namaqualand mines and their communities exhibited a range of Cornish features, from their typically Cornish engine houses (at least one 50-inch beam engine was acquired from Harvey's of Hayle) to Cornish wrestling and Cornish carols. Over the years the mines continued to recruit directly from Cornwall, as in April 1877 when the *West Briton* carried this advertisement, 'For the Cape Copper mine, Namaqualand, Ten good Miners, accustomed to work in shafts and winzes. Men from 30 to 40 preferred. Also a good Mine Carpenter and Two Platelayers. Apply, with testimonials, to Mr James Williams, Devoran, Cornwall.'[17] Mine names such as New Burra Burra and Wheal Julia were also more than a clue to Cornish influence. As Graham Dickason concluded, 'Peopled and staffed by Cornishmen from the very first days, Namaqualand's copper mining areas were to become virtually an exclusive Cornish preserve.'[18] Geographical remoteness helped to create this sense of exclusivity but, at more than 90 miles from the coast, O'Okiep's isolation was also something of a problem, the copper ore having to be taken laboriously by pack mule to Hondeklip Bay for shipment to Swansea. The solution was the construction of a railway from O'Okiep to Port Nolloth, an engineering feat conducted by Richard Thomas Hall, a former superintendent engineer of the Redruth and Chasewater [sic] Railway in Cornwall. Port Nolloth also became something of a Cornish community, the port of entry for the Namaqualand district, attracting folk such as Nicholas Edward Moffet from Tuckingmill, a devout Wesleyan who was for some 34 years Sunday school superintendent and organist at Port Nolloth chapel.[19]

The Cape, of course, was a British possession, and so too was neighbouring Natal. There were various emigration schemes to encourage settlement in this colony, those between 1849 and 1851 attracting Cornish folk such as Paul Henwood from Tideford and his brother John from neighbouring St Germans – Paul opened a hardware shop in Durban, John was an engineer, with grants of land in Natal for intending colonists being advertised in the *West Briton* in 1868.[20] No doubt the most famous Cornish settler in Natal in this period was

John William Colenso, from St Austell, who arrived in the colony in 1855 as its Anglican Bishop. His cousin, William Colenso, was, interestingly enough, a missionary in New Zealand who suffered an unhappy marriage and had a child with a Maori woman, an event which would have scandalised colonial society if news of it had leaked out at the time. A.L. Rowse has provided a sympathetic sketch of these two *Controversial Colensos*:

> John William Colenso (1814–1883), Bishop of Natal, and William Colenso of New Zealand (1811–1899), each made a distinctive and striking contribution to the age in which he lived. The bishop won world-wide fame – at the time notoriety, rather – as a foremost figure in Biblical criticism in the century, in England its leading exponent. He won a second fame – and again much unpopularity and vilification – as the friend and defender of the blacks in South Africa, particularly of Langa-libalele and King Cetshwayo of Zululand in their troubles. William Colenso was even more intimate with the Maoris, whose language he mastered – and spent years compiling a dictionary of it – as his cousin mastered Zulu and published both a grammar and a dictionary, besides many translations. Even more, William Colenso became the first of New Zealand naturalists, sending hundreds, if not thousands, of new plants and seeds to Kew and home to Cornwall.[21]

Among the blacks, especially the Zulus, Bishop Colenso was 'Sobantu', Father of the People, so complete was his defence of the civil rights, interests and sensibilities of the Africans. Even his friend, H. Rider Haggard, author of *King Solomon's Mines*, thought him too 'intemperate an advocate of the rights of the natives'.[22] The Zulu War, with the massacre of a British column at Isandlhwana (including the death of Lieutenant Adjutant Teignmouth Melvill of Lostwithiel who died trying to save the Queen's Colour of the 24th Regiment, an event commemorated in a window in St Winnow church) and the heroic defence of Rorke's Drift, was almost too much for Colenso to bear. He died on 20 June 1883, attacked by evangelical fundamentalists and Anglican conservatives alike for his critical interpretation of the Old Testament, condemned too for his role as champion of the Zulus. It was perhaps a mercy that he did not live long enough to see the destruction of Zulu power:

'Two or three weeks after our dear Lord [Bishop Colenso] left us',
Mrs Colenso wrote home, 'there came a dreadful account from
Zululand that Ulundi had been surprised in the night, the [Royal]
kraal burnt, the King killed and his family slaughtered. We looked
at each other and each thought, "This would have broken his
heart. Thank God for taking him to Himself".'[23]

Even more than the Zulu War, the first and second Anglo-Boer Wars would have
profound effects upon the Cornish in South Africa. The first Boer War, which culminated in the defeat of the British at the Battle of Majuba Hill in February 1881,
established the independence of the two Boer Republics, the Transvaal and the
Orange Free State. But, given the expansionist designs of British commercial and
imperial interests in southern Africa, the outcome was necessarily conditional
and, as we know with hindsight, temporary. In Cornwall, the first Boer War
aroused considerable passion and debate, a reflection of the place enjoyed
already by South Africa in the Cornish imagination, and a vocal 'pro-Boer' camp
had emerged around Leonard Courtney, Liberal MP for East Cornwall, who
argued strongly for the independence of the Transvaal. The Cornish stake in
South Africa had increased immeasurably with the discovery in 1866 and subsequent exploitation of extensive diamond deposits in the Kimberley region of
Griqualand West. Many Cousin Jacks rose to prominence at Kimberley, including
Josiah Angove, from Camborne, who ran the *Diamond Fields Herald* and
*Diamond Fields Times* newspapers, and Lewis Mitchell, the Cornish banker and
financier who underwrote a number of Cecil Rhodes' ambitious schemes. Best
remembered today, perhaps, is Francis Oats, born at Golant, near Fowey, in 1848,
who had risen to the rank of captain at the Botallack mine at St Just-in-Penwith
before going to Kimberley in October 1875 as a mining engineer and government
mine inspector.[24] By 1877 Oats was captain of the important Victoria Diamond
Mine, which in 1886 was taken over by Cecil Rhodes' De Beers company as part
of Rhodes' attempt to control the entire diamond fields. Oats was appointed a
director of De Beers, an important Cornish ally for Rhodes in his designs to
promote British imperial hegemony from Cape to Cairo.

Richard Dawe considered that, 'There was always a large contingent of
Cornish miners at Kimberley especially as the mines went deeper and the
demand for the skills of the Cornish hard rock miner increased'.[25] Thus, as at
Grass Valley in California or Bendigo in Victoria, it was the Cornish on the
Kimberley diamond fields who had the necessary skill, experience and self-

confidence to undertake deep mining in difficult conditions, and so in South Africa the myth of Cousin Jack was perpetuated – the Cornish asserting superior status and attempting wherever possible to promote or defend preferential treatment for their own kind. William James, for example, from St Just, had worked as a boy in the Levant mine before going on to the copper, iron and silver workings of Upper Michigan and Idaho. From the United States he was enticed to South Africa, where he lauded the qualities of the emigrant Cousin Jack and was himself so successful that he returned to Cornwall a well-off man as well as captain of the still-mighty Wheal Basset. Likewise, Thomas Collingwood Kitto had been in Brazil before turning up at Kimberley, and his contribution to the socio-economic evolution of the diamond fields was to press for the construction of large prison-like compounds and barracks for the migrant black labour force, such as he had witnessed in South America. Thomas Rogers, from Camborne, arrived on the diamond fields in 1896 to lecture at the new Kimberley School of Mines, an institution with strong Cornish links, not least because its first head was Professor Gunson Lawn, a former principal of the Camborne School of Mines. Technology as well as know-how was also exported from Cornwall to Kimberley, the *West Briton* in November 1876 noting the shipment from Harvey's of Hayle of machinery comprising one 22-inch pumping engine, two pairs of 14-inch winding engines, five tubular boilers, and winding gear.[26]

Dawe detected a particular relationship between Kimberley and the St Just-in-Penwith mining district at the far-western end of Cornwall. He suggested that this intimacy may have reflected the pivotal role played by Francis Oats in the development of the diamond fields but has also noted that it was in the 1880s – as Kimberley went from strength to strength – that one after another of the St Just tin mines was closed. As early as 1876 the *Mining Journal* had reported that emigration seemed now to be affecting St Just more than other districts (St Just being one of the areas that had survived the demise of Cornish copper by turning to tin), the monthly wage bill having declined from some £3500 seven years ago to a mere £800. Over the same period, the number of individuals employed in mining in St just had declined from 2700 to 1250, a drop of more than 50 per cent.[27] The once mighty Balleswidden tin mine was effectively abandoned by 1877 and was wound up in 1881. Wheal Cunning United, an attempt in the early 1870s to combine the remaining potential of Wheal Cunning, Bosweddan, Boscean and Wheal Castle, had failed by the late summer of 1876, while an attempted reworking of Wheal Castle in 1883 proved fruitless. Wheal Hermon raised a mere one ton of tin in 1880, while Wheal Drea was abandoned in 1884.

Even the extensive St Just Amalgamated, which had brought together St Just United and other important tin workings in the hope of benefitting from economies of scale, was closed in January 1889.[28] Mines such as Botallack and Levant soldiered on but the frequency with which St Just men appeared on the Kimberley diamond fields was reflected in the gruesome toll of the awful De Beers underground fire in July 1888. In this dreadful catastrophe some 178 Africans and 24 Europeans lost their lives, and among the latter was a number of Cornishmen, the St Just contingent being prominent. An urgent telegram was wired home from Kimberley, 'Postmaster, St Just, Cornwall, De Beers mine on fire. Maddern Leggo, Thomas Nankervis and Benjamin Thomas killed. All the rest of the men from St Just safe and well. Make this known publicly. John Vingoe.'[29] If disasters took their toll, then in the sporting life of the diamond fields too the St Just folk were also to the fore, notable Cornish wrestlers including 'Little Dick' of Pendeen and the so-called 'St Just Pug'.[30]

While the Kimberley region was reaching its apogee, the Transvaal was also beginning to develop its mining industry, although this time it was gold that was attracting prospectors and capitalists into the interior of Southern Africa. Mark Pascoe, from Crowan, had been digging for gold in the Transvaal as early as the 1870s, and before long he was joined by other Cousin Jacks. William Hosken, for example, had arrived in the Transvaal in 1874 to assess its potential, before moving on to Natal. Later, in 1889, he was back in the Transvaal, settling at Johannesburg where he became local director of the British South Africa Explosives Company Ltd. whose works at Modderfontein employed some 1200 people.[31] T.R. Parkyn, son of the well-known Captain Parkyn of Roche, had reported favourably on the Transvaal on his return to Cornwall in 1885 and a decade later the Cornish were responsible for some of the early gold diggings near Barberton, especially the Thomas Reef mine, run by the Thomas brothers from Gulval. As the *Cornishman* newspaper put it, 'The proprietors are brothers and Cousin Jackys (in fact we are all over the country)'.[32]

Thereafter, the development of the Witwatersrand gold-fields, or 'the Rand', as it was popularly known, was swift. Although communications were difficult in the early days, prospectors and investors alike soon turned their attention to this new district and before long the plethora of small, often individually owned diggings was swallowed up in the new industrial giants run by the so-called 'Randlords'. Cecil Rhodes was among this hungry band of capitalists but, in contrast to his Kimberley monopoly, his control was restricted to a handful of the really big mines such as Robinson Deep, Knights Deep, and the Witwatersrand

Deep. By 1899 there were nine major companies managing more than 100 mines. Even more than at Kimberley, and like the rapid transformation at Kalgoorlie and Coolgardie in Western Australia, the process of heavy capitalisation was speedy and impressive. As ever, this development favoured the Cornish, Richard Dawe observing that 'As the stamp batteries, crushing mills and cyanide tanks arrived so too did the highly skilled hard rock man – the Cornish miner'.[33] In perhaps as many as a third of the principal gold-mines almost all of the white employees were Cornish, with experienced Cousin Jack miners earning between £6 and £9 per week, a far cry from the £3 per month that was then the going rate in Cornwall. Careful to publicise their prowess, the Cornish made much of their 'innate' skills, a team of 19 miners (12 of whom were Cousin Jacks) creating a stir when at the Simmer and Jack mine in 1895 they broke the world record by sinking a 127-foot vertical shaft in just one month.[34]

As in earlier days at Burra Burra and Ballarat, Grass Valley or Mineral Point, the Cornish occupied key positions across the Rand. St Just men continued to be prominent. John Rowe was manager of the Central Langlaagte mine and Solomon James was captain of the George Goch. James Matthews, also from St Just, was at the Worcester, and Nicholas Williams ran the Knights Deep. Other Cornish captains included John Pope, from Breage, who was at the Glenhuis mine until 1895 when he transferred to the Barberton Estate Gold Mining Company. In 1905 Charles Pearce, from St Austell, became manager of the Van Ryn Apex and Kleinfontein group of mines, while James Donald, from Perranzabuloe, arrived from California to run the Nourse Deep. James Whitburn, another Cornish captain, came by way of Chile. Most famous of all, perhaps, was John Henry Johns ('J. Harry' to all who knew him), born in St Hilary in 1857, whose father had been in Cornwall a notable Dolcoath captain. In 1888 'J. Harry' was appointed captain of the prestigious Ferreira Deep in the Transvaal, home of many Cousin Jacks (including more than a few Dolcoath men), having spent the previous seven years as a miner in India.

Although often invisible in the history of Cornish emigration, the Indian sub-continent in fact played a role of some significance in the Cornish diaspora. As early as 1839, there had been Cornish miners at work in India,[35] and before that the Cornish had been present as soldiers and administrators. William Henry Sleeman, for example, born in Stratton in 1788, joined the East India Company and, rising to the rank of major general in the army, was responsible in the 1830s for the suppression of the cult of 'Thuggee' whose adherents, the 'Thugs', had practised sacrifice by strangling in honour of Kali, the goddess of destruction.

Among the miners were men such as Henry Blackwell, born in Scorrier in 1846. As a youth he had worked in mines at St Neot and near Liskeard in East Cornwall before returning to the west in the 1860s to find employment in the West Chiverton lead mine in the parish of Perranzabuloe. A brief period at Harvey's of Hayle was followed, some time before 1884, by a journey to India to install mining machinery and boilers, probably in one of the western provinces of the country where gold-mining was already in operation. In January 1887 the *West Briton* recorded the continuing attraction of India for itinerant Cornishmen:

> Cornish miners ... are always open to chances of 'bettering themselves' – to good employ at higher wages. One such opportunity offered a month since, when Mr St. Stephen, a mine speculator, visited Helston and, having taken Capt. N.W. James into his counsel, selected half-a-dozen skilled and steady men to go to Mysore and develop a gold-mine. The village of Ashton will lose its popular landlord, Mr W.G. Eustice, of the Lion and Lamb, who goes to India for two years as a carpenter .... We learn that this little colony of Cornishmen will work in a good gold-bearing locality. A few days since all met at Mr Eustice's and enjoyed a good meal and a convivial evening, in the course of which it was resolved, from departure to return (if God spares their lives), that it should be 'One and All'.[36]

*Thacker's Directory* of 1903 points to the continuing presence of the Cornish in the Indian mining industry into the 20th century, despite the pull that newly emergent South Africa had by then for men such as 'J. Harry' Johns. The Mysore Gold Mining Company, for example, had developed extensive mines at Marikuppam in the Kolar district of Mysore State. The chief captain was one J.P. Stapleton, from Illogan, and among his Cornish colleagues were individuals such as R. Hancock (superintendent), E.A. Hosking (chief engineer), H. Curnow and W. Kendall (assistant engineers), and Captain W Symons (assistant mine captain). Likewise, at the Ooregum Gold Mining Company's workings at Kolar were miners and engineers with Cornish names such as R.H.P. Bullen (superintendent), W.J. Harry and W.J. Harry Jnr. (assistant engineers), and C. Odgers and J. Thomas (mine captains). At the Nundydroog mines, also at Kolar, was an underground captain with the resoundingly Cornish name of W. Bawden Skewis and among the other employees was William J.H. Trethewey. Born in 1854 at

Brentor, near Tavistock, of Cornish parents, Trethewey was reckoned by the *Mining Journal* in 1903 to be 'one of the oldest hands on the [Kolar] field'.[37] He had arrived in India in 1885, working at the Ooreguum Mine as assistant captain until he moved to the Nundydroog mines as chief captain in 1896. He died, unexpectedly, of bronchitis (possibly a result of 'miners' complaint') at Madras in 1903. Collectively, the Kolar mines retained their Cornish flavour for many years to come. A pamphlet *The Kolar Gold Field*, published just after the Second World War in 1945, contains an array of Cornish mining terms – underhand stopes, back stopes, champion lodes, slimes – as well as more subtle influences such as a well-established club and doctor fund.[38] Tell-tale chimney stacks, built in the Cornish style, along with the tell-tale surnames, were also a clue to a long standing Cornish involvement in the gold mines of India.

Meanwhile, back in South Africa, the Cornish had continued to arrive in droves – perhaps as many as 10,000 all told[39] – many as itinerant individuals (often with wives and families back in Cornwall) but some as permanent settlers who, sooner or later, were joined by their loved ones from home. More than a few, as noted above, had already been overseas – folk such as John Whitford, born in Newlyn East in 1858, who had worked at the West Chiverton, Blue Hills and Wheal Coates mines before leaving for Brazil in 1881. By 1889 he was back in Cornwall but in the same year he left for South Africa, moving up the managerial scale as he went from mine to mine, rising to become captain of the Robinson Central Deep and, in 1908, manager of the City Deep. Charles Gluyas, born in Wendron in 1865, had worked in the tin mines of Wendron Moor and, later, at Phoenix United near Liskeard, before emigrating to South Africa with his brother Richard in 1887. Both became successful mine captains on the Rand, as did Ernest Thomas and his brother R. Arthur Thomas. These Thomas brothers were members of the celebrated Camborne family noted over several generations for its outstanding contribution to mining, education and public life in Cornwall and their father was none other than Captain Josiah Thomas, captain of Dolcoath, who had himself toured the Rand to judge its potential. Ernest became manager of the Worcester mine and in 1896 left for Western Australia to work as a consultant mining engineer, while R. Arthur was appointed captain of the City and Suburban mine. Later, when Josiah Thomas retired, R. Arthur returned to Cornwall to take over the reins of Dolcoath and much else in the Camborne district. As Richard Dawe rightly observed, the death of R. Arthur Thomas in 1949, aged 82, 'removed from Cornish public life one of its last remaining figures of a famous generation.'[40]

The centre of the Rand was Johannesburg – 'but a suburb of Cornwall', as

C. Lewis Hind had called it – and it was full of Cornish folk. Many stayed at the boarding house of Mrs Doney, who was a native of Penzance, in Frederick Street, where 'Very often 200 Cornish miners would sit down to a Sunday dinner of Cornish pasty'[41] and others would meet at the famous Cousin Jack Corner to renew friendships from Moonta or Kalgoorlie or Butte, to swap news from Cornwall, or to discuss job prospects. As ever, such networking was important, providing support for new arrivals as well as ensuring the accurate and speedy inter-flow of information between South Africa, Cornwall, and other Cornish communities across the globe. Graham Dickason's account catches the mood precisely:

> At the corner of Pritchard and Van Brandis [sic] [streets] was Heath's Hotel, a corner that was to become known as Cousin Jack Corner. It was here on Saturday night that Cornishmen and their womenfolk would gather to promenade down the length of the street and back, exchange news of friends and family at home in Cornwall or scattered all over the developing mining communities strung along the line of the reef. The men would recognise each other as Cornish by the Cornishman's hand-shake, the palm outwards, followed usually by 'where be'ee workin' or 'ows everbody 'ome?'[42]

Another essential component of the Cornish iconography of Johannesburg was Mounts Bay House, a draper's store on another corner of Pritchard Street, opened by Charles Chudleigh, a Scillonian who as a young man had worked for an outfitters' shop in Penzance. Equally symbolic were the 'Cornish Yarns' which appeared regularly in the *Standard and Transvaal Mining Chronicle*, while the visit of Fanny Moody-Manners, the so-called 'Cornish Nightingale' of operatic fame, to South Africa in 1896 proved an important catalyst for Cornish sentiment. Her tour culminated in what she later saw as the greatest night of her life: a concert for the Cornish in Johannesburg. As she recorded in her diary:

> When we arrived at the Park station a perfect mob of people appeared to be waiting for us. They gave a hearty cheer when they saw me, and they also presented me with an illuminated address of welcome. Amongst the people there were many I had known in my Redruth days, or who had at least known some

member of my family. Indeed, it seemed as if every Rand man who hailed from the rocky moorland, every Jack from Camborne or Redruth, every fisherman from Mount's Bay, and every reefman who claims the Duchy as his native heath, had made it his business to be on the platform that morning.[43]

That night she delivered her long-awaited concert. In return she was given a diamond tiara with the 15 bezants of the Cornish Arms picked out in Kimberley diamonds and with the motto 'One and All' in silver and jewels. As an encore, she sang her favourite Cornish songs, including an arrangement of 'Trelawny' that had been especially written for the tour. As one Johannesburg newspaper put it, 'And as she sang, these big men of Cornwall wept. They did not applaud, they hid their faces from each other and went quietly away when she had finished.'[44] This was not merely homesickness, the longing for family that no doubt affected many a Cornish heart, nor even a bitter-sweet expression of ethnic identity in a distant land, but was also the mourning of past glories, for an era that many sensed was passing already. Many, possibly the majority, of Cornish on the Rand at the end of the 19th century knew that the great days of Cornwall were unlikely to come again, and that South Africa, with its constant flow of money orders back home, was a vital lifeline for so many individuals, families, businesses and communities in the otherwise deadening paralysis of the de-industrialising duchy. As one observer of the Cornish on the Rand wrote in 1900: 'They looked prosperous but not happy.'[45]

This melancholy and yet vital relationship between Cornwall and South Africa goes a long way towards explaining Cornish attitudes and activities in the second Boer War and its aftermath. As noted already, the first Boer War had prompted the emergence of a vocal 'pro-Boer' camp in Cornwall, one which had been motivated by both a traditional Liberal-nonconformist sympathy for the self-determination of small nations and a desire to avoid prolonged conflict which might harm Cornish interests. These sentiments would again appear in the second Boer War, though made exceedingly more complicated by the vastly increased number of Cornish in South Africa, many of whom were the despised 'Uitlanders' of the Transvaal, as the Boers referred to foreigners, as well as through a division in Cornish opinion as to the relative merits of British imperialism. In contrast to those who continued to support Boer freedoms and to emphasise the necessary avoidance of upheaval, were others who now saw Cornish interests as tied inextricably to the expansion of the British commercial and political empire in Southern Africa.

For this latter reason, a number of Cornish was caught up in the vainglorious Jameson Raid – the foolhardy attempt in December 1895 to overthrow President Paul Kruger's government in the Transvaal. At least two Cornishmen, William Hosken and C.A.C. Tremeer of the Cape Frontier Police, were implicated as leaders in the abortive insurgence and were arrested by the Transvaal authorities, along with other members of this failed coup.

In Cornwall, news of the Jameson debacle was accompanied by extraordinary accusations that the Cousin Jacks of the Transvaal had displayed great cowardice in the moment of conflict. Although the Cornish on the Rand were a large proportion of the Uitlanders – the foreigners denied the vote and thus citizenship by the hostile Transvaal authorities – many were more interested in making money than achieving civil rights. One report insisted that 'There was scarcely a Cornishman agitating against the Boers – unless perhaps a shift boss or capitalist',[46] and that many Cornish had decided to avoid the clash altogether by leaving the Transvaal (even if temporarily) to return to Cornwall. However, the 'cowardice' accusation stuck, the *West Briton* reporting in January 1896 the story of the escape by train from Johannesburg: 'interest centered chiefly on the third class saloon, which was packed by a body of men, the Cornish element predominating. The sentiments which the public entertained towards the occupants were expressed in the words "Cowards' Van", which a wag had inscribed with chalk in large letters outside the carriage.'[47]

At Durban an angry mob was waiting to give a rough welcome to the 'deserting' Uitlanders, and the vans containing the Cornish were shunted quietly into a siding to avoid identification. News of the cowardice accusations spread quickly around the world, the Moonta *People's Weekly* responding firmly that such reports were 'resented locally by Cornishmen'.[48] Moreover, it was soon established that the Cornish who had left the Rand were small in number compared with those who remained, pro-Cornish elements pointing to the self-styled Cornish Brigade as an instrument to keep the peace and defend Cornish interests in Johannesburg. Numbering perhaps some 400 members, the brigade made its presence felt by parading through the city, forming up outside the offices of the Cornish Association and then marching to the Wemmer mine, the band all the while blasting out the strains of 'Trelawny'. Back in Britain, Arthur Quiller-Couch, Cornish scholar and public figure, insisted that he had 'not lost faith in Cornishmen and saw no reason why our miners in the Transvaal should rise against armed Government forces when a stock jobber waved a Union Jack in their faces'.[49] In Cornwall itself, the continuing decline of the mining industry meant that those who had fled the Rand were already thinking of returning, to be joined by many more who considered that being a disenfranchised Uitlander was a small price to pay for a chance to use their skills in well-paid employment. Indeed, it was estimated in October 1896 that since January of that year some 1000 miners had left Camborne and Redruth for South Africa.[50]

The failure of the Jameson Raid prompted the resignation of Cecil Rhodes as premier of Cape Colony and in the tense aftermath the British garrison in the Cape was reinforced. In the Transvaal the Boer authorities continued to make life difficult for the Uitlanders, Cornish among them, while the British demanded that the residence qualification for the franchise be relaxed. Kruger, having just been re-elected as president of the Transvaal for a fourth time, was in no mood to compromise. This renewed sense of confrontation stemmed the flow of miners from Cornwall and by 1899 the movement was again in the opposite direction – men deciding to quit the Rand before it was overtaken by a second Jameson Raid or worse. As Richard Dawe has shown, the impending war between Britain and the Boers was viewed with great alarm in Cornwall. The *Cornish Post* reminded its readers that the apparent commercial prosperity of Camborne and Redruth was built on South African money, 'The shops are larger, better and constantly being rebuilt, the result of those bad laws we hear about in the Transvaal.'[51] Anticipating a British annexation of the Boer Republics (the Transvaal and the Orange Free State), the newspaper warned that the economic consequences for Cornwall would be catastrophic, its editorial carefully dissociating itself from the distant and uncomprehending 'English' government across the Tamar in London. 'If the English take the country, what's going to become of we?', asked the paper, voicing the apprehension of many in Cornwall who knew that Cornish well-being was based on South African stability. As the paper added, emphasising and explaining what it saw as the difference in perspective between Cornwall and England, 'The Cornish miner still speaks of the English as another people living East of the Tamar.'[52]

That a distinct political perspective was being built around perceptions of ethnic and territorial identity is a telling clue to how the Cornish saw themselves at the close of the 19th century. The great days of domestic industrial prowess might already have passed from view but the Cousin Jacks (and Jennys) remained a people apart with interests of their own which, if necessary, Cornish ethnicity could be deployed to promote and defend. A developed sense of anti-metropolitanism was already apparent, the 'English' government seen as having interests and agendas which took no account of Cornwall's well-being.

Paradoxically, however, while there was genuine pro-Boer feeling in Cornwall, many of the Cornish Uitlanders had no particular love for the Boers who they saw as cruel and corrupt. Indeed, back in Cornwall the *Cornish Post* struck an imperialist note when, bristling with indignation, it shrilled that 'the Boers will learn by bitter experience that the citizens of a world power like Great Britain cannot be bled and defrauded of their rights, and that for their brutality to the black races they will have to pay with their blood.'[53]

Meanwhile, as the diplomatic climate deteriorated still further, British forces in Natal under the command of Major General Sir William Penn-Symons, a Cornishman, from Hatt, near Saltash, had moved close to the Transvaal border. A Boer ultimatum to withdraw was ignored and on 11 October 1899 the Boers declared war on the British empire. Peace did not return to South Africa until 31 May 1902 and although the Boers ultimately could not resist the might of the British empire, they fought a spirited and determined defence of their homeland, employing daring guerilla tactics which on not a few occasions made fools of the British and won international regard for their struggle. Penn-Symons himself was killed in the opening days of this second Boer War, at the battle of Talana Hill in Natal, and many other Cornish soldiers fought and suffered in the conflict. The Duke of Cornwall's Light Infantry saw action in the battle of Paardeberg, losing several of its number in that and other fights, while some Cornish, such as Thomas Ham from St Day, who lived to tell the tale, were at the slaughter of Spion Kop. Many Cousin Jacks fought in impromptu militias such as the Namaqualand Light Horse or the Kimberley Town Guard, the names of those who fell recorded carefully on the South African War Memorial in Truro's new cathedral.

Back in Cornwall, the economic plight caused by the war was every bit as bad as had been predicted, the situation made still worse by the return of many by now unemployed Cornish miners from South Africa. A few found work in Cornwall but at wages that were derisory when compared with Kimberley or the Rand and though they tried to put a brave face on things, their colonial bravado impressing the stay-at-home locals, many were in dire straits. A correspondent in the *West Briton* in December 1899 had this to say:

> As to the Afrikanders [returned Cornish], they seem to cross one's path at almost every turning. You can tell them by their gold rings, gold alberts, gold watches, and plenty of the don't care element mark them off. Some old friends who were thought to have been under the sod long ago turn up again, and are

easily recognized. There is a murmur with many of them because of their expulsion from this modern ophir ... from the varying angles of their outlook they blame Oom Paul [Kruger], or Joe Chamberlain [Liberal Unionist leader], or Mr Gladstone, or the millionaires, or anybody. I find but little employment at hand for them, and the wages are beggardly after Africa. Some of them are on 'the rocks' already, for they had not reaped a big harvest of gold, and now the pinch will be felt in many ways.[54]

The arrival back home of so many Cousin Jack 'Afrikanders' brought yet further influences to bear upon the Cornish political scene. Notwithstanding the by now deeply ingrained liberal nonconformist tradition, Joseph Chamberlain's Liberal Unionists – those who had split from Gladstone's Liberal Party as a result of their opposition to plans for Irish Home Rule – had been notably successful in Cornwall. In the 1886 general election, for example, the Liberal Unionists did especially well in 'Chamberlain's Duchy' (as Cornwall was dubbed), taking three of the six available seats, the others remaining in Gladstonian Liberal hands. Thereafter, the Liberal Unionists were a significant force in Cornish politics until the 1906 'Liberal Landslide' Election and, indeed, they resurfaced in 1910 as a force to be reckoned with. Support for the Liberal Unionists in Cornwall reflected widespread fears that Home Rule was 'Rome Rule', the Cornish expressing solidarity with their fellow nonconformists in Ulster. To this was added the concern that Cornish fishermen might be excluded from Irish waters by a self-governing Ireland, persuading the coastal communities to vote Liberal Unionist, despite the fact that 'The fishermen... were regarded as being strongly Radical'.[55]

Where the Liberals had resisted the Liberal Unionist onslaught, the resilience of traditional liberal values had been bolstered through the radical intervention of the overseas Cornish, most graphically in 1886 when the victory in the Camborne constituency of the Radical Liberal candidate, C.A.V. Conybeare, over his official Liberal rival, Pendarves Vivian, was assisted by the encouragement and moral support of Cornish miners in America.[56] However, in 1895 Conybeare lost his 'Mining Division' seat, for the reasons summarised by the historian Henry Pelling:

the acute depression of the tin and copper industries in the middle 1890s demoralised the miners. Many of them lost the vote owing to dependence on poor relief; others emigrated;

and still more were inclined to listen to the promises of a wealthy tin-merchant, A. Strauss, who, standing as a Liberal Unionist, advocated various nostrums including bimetallism, which would 'tend to raise the price of tin'. In an election which turned entirely on these local problems, Strauss secured victory in 1895.[57]

However, Strauss' rhetoric did not translate into practical policies and in the continuing crisis of the Cornish mining industry his credibility and thus local support dwindled quickly. More particularly, the second Boer War had emerged as a point of conflict in the Camborne constituency. There were, as has been observed already, those who feared that hostilities would dry up the all important flow of funds to Cornwall as well as wrecking the South African mining industry, while there was also a genuinely 'pro-Boer' faction. The Liberal Unionists, by way of contrast, argued for a vigorous imperial policy and condemned the Boer treatment of the Cornish Uitlanders. Remarkably, in the 1900 election the 'pro-Boer' radical, W.S. Caine, defeated Strauss in the Camborne constituency. As Dawe noted, 'On the political front Cornwall voted against the national tide when the Liberal Unionist lost to the Liberal Radical, who was a pro-Boer'.[58] Caine, like Conybeare before him, derived support from emigrant Cornishmen, claiming that 'out of 700 Cornish miners home from South Africa, at least 650 had voted for him'.[59] Caine was not alone in his pro-Boer sympathies. Leonard Courtney, the MP for Bodmin (ironically, now a Liberal Unionist), was a long-standing pro-Boer, and so too was the Cornish philanthropist, and former Liberal MP for Salisbury, J. Passmore Edwards. Cornish novelist, Silas K. Hocking, from St Stephen-in-Brannel, was another public figure of stature sympathetic to the Boer cause. He was chairman of the Stop The War Committee and, a staunch Methodist, opposed the war on religious and moral grounds. He was disillusioned when some of his Liberal friends in Cornwall appeared equivocal on the issue and in consequence he resigned as president of the Liberal Association. Indeed, there were those who were pleased to see him go, not least Liberal Unionists who in Cornwall continued to agitate against the pro-Boer faction. A.L. Rowse tells the story of a public meeting in Liskeard, organised by Courtney and chaired by Quiller-Couch, at which the youthful Lloyd George – radical liberal, Welsh nationalist, and pro-Boer – had been invited to speak: 'this was a risky thing to do. For this impassioned pro-Boer had been hounded off platforms, his life threatened. While Q. [Quiller-Couch] was speaking a note was passed to him that a man in the audience was out for Lloyd George with a revolver. The platform was stormed and the meeting broken up, though Lloyd George got away without harm.'[60]

From St Ive, near Liskeard, came Emily Hobhouse, daughter of the local vicar. She was a descendent of Sir Jonathan Trelawny, the Cornish folk-hero celebrated in the song 'Trelawny', and was the niece of Leonard Courtney. Working for the church, she had already been out in the far West of the United States of America, where she had met and observed many Cousin Jacks toiling on the mining frontier. Armed with this impressive array of Cornish credentials, she took a keen interest in the second Boer War, her humanitarian instincts siding her with the 'underdog' Boers, especially the women and children who suffered disproportionately as the conflict grew worse. In Britain she formed the South African Women and Children's Distress Fund, and in 1900 she visited South Africa to see conditions for herself. Travelling across the country, she witnessed first hand the fruits of Britain's scorched earth policy: the burnt-out Boer homesteads, the rotting carcasses of farm animals, and of course the so-called concentration camps in which many Boer women and children had been confined. Inevitably, disease had taken its toll in these appallingly unsanitary compounds and Hobhouse was horrified by what she found. Returning to Britain in May 1901, she instigated a vigorous public relations campaign to draw attention to the ills and miseries of the concentration camps and to criticise British policy in its dealings with non-combatants. In October of 1901 she attempted to go back to South Africa but was physically restrained from landing at Cape Town and forced to return home. The strain was by now beginning to tell and in the spring of 1902 she sought the peace and quiet of Switzerland, where she penned her testimony *The Brunt of the War*. Eventually, in May 1903, Emily Hobhouse did return to the now peaceful South Africa where she received a warm welcome: not only from the Boer women and children whose cause she had championed but from the Cousin Jack Afrikanders whose sympathy and regard she had also won.[61]

However, the end of the second Boer War did not mean the end of South African conflict in Cornish politics. With the achievement of peace, the restoration of the South African mining industry to full production was a priority. To this end, it was suggested that some 60,000 Chinese workers be brought into South Africa over the four years from February 1904. This would be an efficient and cost-effective method, it was argued, of swiftly bringing the mines' output up to pre-war levels. That said, European miners, not least the Cornish, were on the whole opposed to Chinese labour, fearing the sheer numbers of the Chinese as well as arguing that their presence had a generally depressing effects on wages and conditions. And yet, in Cornwall itself the reaction to the plan was at first ambivalent, for while Cornish miners shared in the general hostility to the Chinese, the Cornish economy relied almost entirely upon the speedy and successful restoration of South African mining. *The Mining Journal* expressed the situation succinctly: 'contrary to what might be generally have been expected in a county which, taken by and wide, is essentially Liberal not to say Radical, as regards its political opinions, the proposition to employ Chinese labour in the Transvaal, instead of being opposed, is receiving active support, not only from the local Press, but from mining men generally.'[62]

The actual arrival of the Chinese in South Africa galvanised Cornish opinion, however, the fear that Chinese workers would take Cornish jobs – and thus Cornish wages destined otherwise for Cornwall – proving irresistible. This hostility was given a Christian and radical edge through the effective deployment of arguments which held that these poor Chinese were to all intents and purposes the victims of an exploitive conspiracy designed to coerce them into 'slavery', unfair contracts forcing them to work for a pittance. This 'Chinese slavery' scare was taken up in Cornwall and beyond as a major political issue, the *Cornubian* newspaper demanding to know of its Cornish readership: 'Will you vote for a Government that has ruined South Africa for the Cornish miner? Will you vote for Chinese labour? If it be not a kind of slavery, what is it?'[63] In the end, the Liberal Party in Britain as a whole adopted opposition to 'Chinese slavery' as part of its political programme, not least in the 1906 'Liberal Landslide' general election when the Liberals won every seat in Cornwall. For many Cornish Methodists, opposition to 'Chinese slavery' in South Africa was but an extension of their longstanding commitment to the abolition of the slave trade (which accounted, it was said, for the Cornish reluctance to take sugar in tea), the reassertion of the Liberal-Methodist link proving crucial in achieving the 1906 election result. The *West Briton* thought that 'nearly every Nonconformist chapel in this [St Austell] constituency was used as a Liberal committee room'[64] in the 1906 election, while the *Western Morning News* noted that at Launceston 'The chapel, on the quiet roadside or in the secluded valley, is the governing factor in this division. It has been said that in these little Bethels, is preached the Radical shibboleth from January to December.'[65] In fact, the victorious Liberal government did indeed put a stop to 'Chinese slavery' and in the General Election of 1910 – when the Liberal Unionists regained many of the rural English seats they had lost in 1906 – Cornwall remained solidly Liberal.

If South Africa continued to provoke controversy in Cornwall after the peace of 1902, then the Cornish on the Rand itself continued to be embroiled in conflict of one sort or another. With the end of the war, Cornish miners were once again enticed to South Africa in considerable numbers, benefiting from the demand for skilled labour as the mines were returned to full production, the *Cornish Post* remarking in December 1906 that 'When the button is pressed in Africa, the bell rings in Cornwall ... a change in thought and action in South Africa affects the little western county which has contributed so much of the labour and enterprise to ... the land of gold and diamonds.'[66] However, in the years before the First World War there was growing disillusion with South Africa, partly due to the realisation of the frightening extent of the disabilities among Cornish miners caused by phthisis and partly because of growing industrial unrest on the Rand and by 1913 there was a steady stream of workers returning home to Cornwall. As in Australia and America, the Cornish in South Africa had emerged as important figures in the labour movement on the mines, striving to win and protect privileges in the face of both attempts by the bosses to restrain wage rates and the willingness of other ethnic groups to work for poorer wages in poorer conditions. Moreover, the embrace of trade unionism by the Cornish was a conscious attempt to alleviate the risks of mining by forcing employers to address health and safety issues, especially with regard to the introduction of new machinery and new working practices.

For the Cornish overseas, mining was always a gamble, the relatively high remuneration that their skills commanded to be balanced against the inherent dangers of their occupation – not only the all too familiar mining accidents but the widespread incidence of 'miner's complaint', that catch-all term for a variety of pulmonary and respiratory diseases ranging from pneumoconiosis (in the coal mines of Pennsylvania or New South Wales) to plumbism (at Broken Hill) and phthisis (in the quartz dust of South Africa). As A.K. Hamilton Jenkin wrote in 1927, when many of South Africa's Cousin Jacks had come home to endure a rasping, lingering but early death:

> The name 'South Africa' is cut deep in the heart of mining in Cornwall, not so much engraved with an instrument of steel as jagged and ghastly with the malignant quartz that hid the gold and filled the lungs of Cornish pioneers. Nevertheless, the allurements were strong. There was plenty of money, plenty of fun, plenty of 'life', and niggers to do the work on the Rand, even

though the dread scourge might be biding its time in the dust-filled stopes where the drills roared out unceasingly.[67]

As well as being unhealthy, the South African mines were deep and dangerous, newspapers on the Rand and at home in Cornwall carrying a depressing catalogue of obituaries and reports of accidents and funerals. In December 1898, for example, the *West Briton* wrote that:

> The South African mail on Christmas-eve brought the sad news of a mine accident in East Simmer and Jack Mine, whereby three Cornishmen, two from Gwennap and one from Camborne, lost their lives. The cage, consisting of two compartments, was being lowered with men, when something went amiss with the skip road, and a huge splinter of wood from one of the runners, or wooden rails, pierced through both compartments of the cage, and killed three of the occupants – William Francis, aged 38, from Tresamble, Gwennap, and Frederick Bowden, of St Day, and a miner from Camborne .... Both the [Gwennap] men have widowed mothers, with whom great sympathy is felt. Francis had only left home about three months ago.[68]

Acts of heroism were also frequent, as at an underground fire in the Wemmer Gold Mining Company's Salisbury Mine in June 1904 when 21 white miners saved the lives of a large number of black miners. Seventeen of the white miners were Cornishmen – Geo Matthews, T. Christophers, John Webb, James Moon, W.H. Sandoe, E. Dunstan, R. Lanyon, J.H. Axford, E.J. Craze, W. Bawden, S. Bennetts, John Moon, J.H. Pascoe, James Harris, J.H. Whitford, C. Angwin, W. Polgrean – the company secretary in a presentation address praising them for 'the noble manner in which you all behaved ... in rescuing many of our Native Labourers from what might have been a ghastly death', adding that the directors were 'genuinely pleased to find that they employ men courageous enough to help their fellow creatures.'[69] Each of the brave Cornishmen was further presented with a sum of money and an engraved silver watch, the latter a fitting memento by which the daring deeds might be remembered many years hence.

However, despite the fine words and the displays of gratitude and generosity on such occasions, mine owners tackled matters of safety and occupational health but slowly. But at least safety issues were recognised, albeit sometimes grudgingly. Phthisis, by contrast, was either ignored altogether or dismissed as that 'natural' phenomenon, 'miner's complaint', part of the inevitable cycle of growing old (or at least older) and the acquisition with the passing years of various aches and pains and ailments. It took the energy and courage of Captain Francis Oats, a director of De Beers, to force his colleagues to recognise the real nature of phthisis. Returning home to Cornwall as he did from time to time, Oats had been struck by the high incidence there of wheezing, coughing men old before their time, and had decided that their plight warranted investigation. Modern research has confirmed the extent of the phthisis problem identified by Captain Oats. Gillian Burke and Peter Richardson in their 'The Profits of Death: A Comparative Study of Miners' Phthisis in Cornwall and the Transvaal, 1876–1918' have provided a clear picture of the disease's extent and this in turn has been made accessible to the general reader by Richard Dawe in his excellent treatment of the subject.[70] Dawe noted, for example, that in 1902 the Chamber of Mines in Cornwall reported that of the miners who had returned from South Africa during the war, no fewer than 600 had died from phthisis.[71]

During Oats' time in Cornwall in 1902, he requested that the Redruth Medical Officer of Health investigate local deaths from phthisis. In March 1904 the officer reported that out of 21 deaths in the previous 12 months, 11 men had returned from South Africa and all bar one was under 37 years of age. Moreover, of 342 miners' deaths investigated in Redruth, Illogan and Camborne for the years 1900, 1901 and 1902, 216 of the individuals reported on had been overseas during their working lives. South Africa dominated the report, more than half of those who had been overseas having worked there, while others had been to North America (68), Central America (11), South America (15), the Mysore gold mines in India (19), Australia (6), West Africa, the Straits Settlement, Ceylon, Germany, Italy, Ireland, Wales, and the North of England. Many had worked in more than one overseas destination during their mining careers:

Case No58 age 58
   Condurrow (Cornwall) some years
   Durham 15 years
   Montana 2 years
   South Africa 5 years
Case No93 age 46
   Dolcoath some years

Peru 3 years
California 8 years
South Africa 1$^1$/$_2$ years
South Africa 4 years

Meanwhile, back in South Africa itself, Oats had been successful in pressing for a commission into phthisis. When it reported, one startling find was that the average lifespan of the miner in South Africa was a mere 35.5 years. An important result of these new insights into the disease was the increased interest in phthisis taken by inquests in Cornwall into early deaths. Time and again, inquests were told that deceased miners had mined for gold in the deep quartz of California or, more often, South Africa, with the modern pneumatic rock drills (the 'widowmakers', as the Americans rightly called them) identified increasingly as the major source of the lethal dust clouds underground. Evidence also emerged to suggest that the few rock drills which were fitted with water jets to damp down the dust, were appreciably safer than other types.

In South Africa, resultant unease at the use of rock drills was compounded when mining companies decided in 1907 that the number of drills supervised by individual white miners was to increase from two to three. This innovation was tried first at the Knights Deep mine in May 1907, where the men's reaction was to walk out on strike. The Cousin Jacks reasoned that if the effects of supervising two drills was to seriously shorten one's life, then to take responsibility for a third was almost suicidal. To this was added anxiety over the effective de-skilling that was threatening the status and privileges of the Cornish miner. With the introduction of rock drills, the role of the Cornish had become merely supervisory, with individuals managing their two drills and teams of about five black miners each who actually performed the mining task. Although this might look like 'promotion' for the Cornish miner, the danger was that – as the black miners became more accustomed to their work, and as the number of drills a Cousin Jack was expected to supervise increased – so the Cornish might eventually become redundant. Motivated by these twin concerns of occupational health and occupation status, the Cornish led the strike as it spread to more than 50 mines. The head of the strike committee was Tom Matthews, originally from Newlyn, who had mined in Upper Michigan and at Butte, at the latter becoming for a time president of the Miners' Union of Montana. He was thus no stranger to industrial action, or indeed to the use of trade unionism in the defence of Cornish rights and privileges, bringing to South Africa the Cousin Jack tradition of the far

West which stretched back to the days of the 'giant powder' and 'double-jacking' disputes at Grass Valley (see Chapter 7).

However, despite the widespread nature of the strike, support was not solid, and even Matthews could not persuade the Cornish miners at the Ferreira Deep to join the protest. Worse still, many of the mines simply sacked the Cornish and employed Boers in their stead. Despite their defeat in the war, the Boers by now held political power in the Transvaal colonial government (the Union of South Africa as a self-governing dominion of the British Empire was created later in 1910), with Premier Louis Botha pouring scorn on the Cornish and suggesting that their day had passed, 'It is time that South Africa began to raise her own skilled workers ... in this vast, amply rich country with its army of imported artisans, with its perpetual stream of postal orders flowing to Cornwall.'[72] It was a defining moment for the Cornish, the strike petering out amidst violence (including the murder of William Webb Richards, from Four Lanes, near Redruth) and acrimony. In July of 1907 the astute *Mining World* journal observed that in South Africa the Cornish 'monopoly exists no longer'.[73] Of course, there were still many Cornish at work on the Rand, including numerous captains who (like J. Harry Johns at Ferreira Deep) had vigorously opposed the strike. Matthews, meanwhile, focussed attention upon the phthisis question, petitioning the Transvaal colonial government in 1908, and paving the way for the controversial Miners' Phthisis Acts of 1911 and 1912 which were attacked by Cornish trade union leaders as too little and divisive. In 1913 there was more violence in Johannesburg and a brief strike, the news of which caused alarm in Cornwall where, after a brief but illusory spell of Edwardian prosperity based for the most part on South African money and the energy of returned migrants, there was again heavy reliance on those postal orders and bank drafts. Moreover, many Cornishmen were now sick of the Rand and were returning home, though with little prospect of employment in Cornwall.

Matthews died, ironically of phthisis, in 1915 aged only 48. In other respects too the Cornish influence, in the mines and in the trade union movement, had also dwindled by the early years of the First World War, and after 1918, as the price of gold fell and as production costs soared, there were fewer Cornish at work on the Rand than at any point hitherto. There was another bitter and violence-ridden strike in 1922 but this time the Cornish were hardly visible, the action led by the Boer militants who had replaced the Cornish as the 'labour aristocracy' in the South African mines. Indeed, by 1922 immigration of overseas miners into South Africa had virtually ceased, while Cornwall's own 'Great

Emigration' had by then almost run its course. 1922 was certainly a grim year for Cornwall, but those who were leaving were heading now for the automobile factories of Detroit or the gold-mines of Ontario. In Africa itself, many Cornish had already quit the Rand for other parts of the continent, not only the neighbouring Rhodesias – modern Zimbabwe and Zambia, where as early as 1880–81 two Cornish prospectors, James and William Job from Lanner, had trekked northwards from Kimberley and made contact with chief Lobengula of the Ndebele people – but more far-flung spots such as Nigeria and the Gold Coast (Ghana) in West Africa. These sported modest but important Cornish colonies in the inter-War period, including individuals such as Will Bosanko who, having fought in the First World War, went back to a Cornwall bereft of jobs. He travelled first to West Africa, working there in the mines during the 1920s, later moving on to Burma and eventually returning to Cornwall to run a pub at Park Bottom, near Redruth.[74] By 1933 a branch of Holman's of Camborne, the mining equipment manufacturers, had been opened at its 'Cornwall House' in Takoradi in the Gold Coast, handling the firm's trade with Nigeria, the Gold Coast, Sierra Leone and the Cameroons. Needless to say, many Cornish people had decided to stay in South Africa, settling into a variety of jobs, including engineering which, as well as supplying the mining industry, continued to enjoy close contact with Cornwall – especially Holman's of Camborne which had by 1933 completed the erection of the first stage of extensive works at Johannesburg, with Cornishmen brought out to run the business – 'another colony of "Cousin Jacks"'.[75]

The enduring Cornish legacy in South Africa was reflected in the activities of its several Cornish associations. As early as December 1889, Moses Roberts, from Truro, editor of the *Daily Independent*, organised a Cornish Association at Kimberley and held its inaugural annual dinner in Spargo's Gladstone Hotel, the occasion marked with the singing of 'Trelawny' and other affirmations of Cornish identity. A Cornish Association of the Rand (later Transvaal) had been formed not long after but it lapsed during the second Boer War, to be re-launched during 1905, its first annual dinner in Johannesburg attracting some 400 Cornish enthusiasts. So successful was this association, that soon it spawned supporting branches throughout the Witwatersrand, at Fordsburg, Germiston, Roodepoort, Krugersdorp, Randfontein, Benoni, Denver and Johannesburg itself. The Fordsburg branch was especially strong, drawing upon the nearby Ferreira Deep where at Christmas the miners formed themselves into a Cornish choir to regale Johannesburg with the stirring strains of 'Hark the Glad Sound!' and other Merritt compositions. Rugby football, soon to be as important to the South African identity as it was to the Cornish, also attracted Cousin Jacks on the Rand, the Randfontein Cornish Association Rugby Football Club playing in the traditional Cornish colours of black-and-gold.

As well as organising these cultural activities, the Cornish Association of the Rand also looked after new arrivals from Cornwall, helping them to find work and making social introductions as well as collecting relief for Cornish widows and other deserving cases in the Transvaal and in Cornwall. And although the Cornish Association was theoretically apolitical, in practice it drew the favourable attentions of the liberal Progressive Party and the trade unionists of the Labour Party, gently exhibiting opposition to the more extreme examples of conservative Boer nationalism as well as perpetuating the liberal nonconformist tradition imported from home. William Hosken, most notable of the Rand's Cornishmen, was a strong supporter of Gandhi during his South African sojourn, opposing the restrictions on citizenship imposed on Asians by the Boer-led Transvaal government and approving Gandhi's Satyagraha, the doctrine of peaceful resistance.[76]

By now, the experience of the Cornish overseas had come a remarkably long way from the dawn of the 'Great Emigration' in the years after 1815. As well as participating prominently in the creation and expansion of the international mining economy, its frontiers and its labour force, the Cornish had also played their part in agriculture, in politics, in religion, in culture, contributing to the construction of an international Cornish identity which had been for several decades at least of global significance. But after the First World War, this identity appeared to fade – in Moonta, at Grass Valley, on the Rand, to a degree even in Cornwall itself as it retreated into a culture of 'making do' – victim of the changing nature of the international mining economy and evidence of the powerful assimilatory agents at work in new countries such as the United States of America and Australia. Cornwall was no longer the international centre of mining expertise and technological excellence – the myth of Cousin Jack was but a shadow of its former self and Cornish miners were no longer sought above all others in the mining districts of the world.

# CHAPTER TWELVE

# 'ALL HAIL! OLD

# CORNWALL!

# MAY THY GLORY LAST' –

# THE END OF AN ERA

By the eve of the First World War, as we saw in Chapter 11, the 'Great Emigration' from Cornwall had all but run its course. Even South Africa, that last great home of the Cornish overseas, had ceased to be the ready recipient of countless Cornish that it had been less than a decade before. Australasia and North America no longer offered new, expanding frontiers to tempt the Cornish on the grand scale, while in Cornwall itself the Cornish could no longer project themselves as leading-edge miners and engineers. Indeed, the rump of Cornwall's tin mining industry had all but expired, its attendant engineering industry, with the notable exception of Holman's at Camborne, also in decline. Even 'home pay' was dwindling, with fewer Cousin Jacks overseas to send back money to folks at home. The gradual decline of this informal welfare system was a blow to the veneer of prosperity that had built fine new buildings and stocked the shelves of fancy stores in towns such as Redruth.

In such circumstances, the 'myth of Cousin Jack' that had galvanised admirers and enemies alike and had underpinned assertions of Cornish ethnicity the world over was no longer a dynamic or even credible force. As the Cornish economy slipped ever further into its 'great paralysis' – the period of social, economic and political inertia that characterised much of the first half of the 20th century – so the ordinary Cornish turned away from their hitherto confident, even aggressive trumpetings of industrial prowess and separate identity to embrace a new, fatalistic, inward-looking culture of 'making do'. Though still immersed in a world of Methodism, brass bands, Cornish carols, male voice choirs, rugby football, dialect stories, pasties and saffron cake – those icons of a disappearing industrial age – these ordinary Cornish were increasingly 'invisible' to outside observers who were taught to look now for new images of Cornwall – the romance and mysticism of the 'Cornish Riviera' and 'King Arthur's Land'. Even the Cornish, or at least some of them, were drawn to these new images, the more courageous of the new Cornish-Celtic revivalists acknowledging that their project – with its Anglo-Catholic sympathies and its desire to revive the Cornish language – was designed to create a new, post-industrial culture by looking back over the debris of the industrial period to the model of an older, more reassuringly 'Celtic' Cornwall.[1]

And yet, on the eve of the First World War, many of the cultural attributes that had accompanied the construction of an international Cornish identity were still in place, reflected, for example, in the literature of the period in which, to explain and explore the complexity and nature of modern Cornwall, the overseas dimension was necessarily and routinely invoked.[2] For writers such as W. Herbert Thomas, born in St Day in 1870, a journalist who had worked for two years on the *San Francisco Examiner*, the pain of emigration was a dominant theme:

> Stand back, you wives and sweethearts,
> Cease your kisses, sighs and tears.
> For the last 'Good-bye' and a weeping eye
> Are the worst of the miner's fears.
> He will face the blinding sun-glare
> And in the deep weird caverns dwell,
> But the anguish spent in parting,
> Means a moment spent in Hell.[3]

Stronger still was James Dryden Hosken's 'Farwell to Thee My Native Land', published after a visit to Australia in 1912 in a collection dedicated to Sir John Langdon Bonython (of Cornish descent, a luminary in the Cornish Association of South Australia) and two other prominent South Australians:

> Cast from the country of my heart,
> Where men denied me bread;
> From wife and children doomed to part,
> These lonely shores I tread:
> O world, of souls the blood-red mart,
> O God, that I were dead.[4]

Here the relationship with 'the country of my heart' – Cornwall – is as important as that with family, the distance from homeland as emotionally significant as the estrangement from kin, a sentiment echoed in another of Hosken's poems, the 'Chant of a Cornish Exile':

> Land of my heart, bourne of my dreams,
> Fount of my song art thou, Cornwall;
> Casket wherein my hopes
> And my memories are hidden forever.[5]

And yet, alongside this mourning of loss stood the celebration of triumph, that other dominant emotion of the 'Great Emigration'. W. Herbert Thomas, this time in expansive mood, in his poem 'All Hail! One and All!' articulated the Cousin Jack myth in imperialist tones, extolling the global achievements of the Cornish and demanding their proclamation:

> Join hands, ye Cornish lads, across the main!
> Let Asia clasp Colombia's outstretch'd hand!
> Come forth, Australia! Swell the glad refrain!
> And touch the fringe of Afric's golden strand!
> Swift o'er the boundless ocean rings the call!
> The mystic girdle round the world is cast!
> Shout now with thund'rous voices 'One and All'!
> All hail! Old Cornwall! May thy glory last![6]

Equally explicit in its ethnic assertion was Hosken's own 'One and All', his hymn of 'holy passion' and 'proper pride' penned for 'all the Cornish clan', defying those who would deny or belittle Cornwall's international identity:

> Ah, Cousin Jack, though half the earth
> Makes game of your unbounded mirth —
> You're nature's favourite from your birth.[7]

Mark Guy Pearse's 'The Miner in Foreign Parts', a poem arranged in three sections – 'California', 'Australia', 'Klondyke'[8] – dwells on the pain of separation but is (as one would expect from a Methodist writer) a work of religious and moral message. So too, to turn to prose, are many of the novels of the brothers Silas K. and Joseph

Hocking and emigration (an everyday theme with allegorical possibilities) is one of the literary devices used by them to develop an authentically Cornish plot. Thus in Joseph Hocking's classic tale *What Shall It Profit a Man?* the hero is the splendidly named Granville Poldhu, who has returned to Cornwall from South Africa where he had 'worked under one of the ablest mining engineers in that continent'.[9] Likewise, in Silas K. Hocking's *The Lost Lode*, it is Jasper Blake who returns to Cornwall, to the fictional village of his birth, Pengowan. With the £40 his father had given him, Blake had made his way to Quebec and from there across North America, taking some 11 years all told to reach the Yukon where at last he struck it rich.

But:

> To other fortunate ones gold had spelt Seattle, or 'Frisco, or Los Angeles, or the cities back east; Toronto, or Chicago, or Washington, or New York. To him it spelt Pengowan. There was only one thought in his mind, one desire in his heart — he must get back home. His Cornish hills called him across the ocean and mountain and plain; the lure of his native land was in his blood; it had never left him during all the years of his absence. Nothing would ever satisfy him until he had seen again the little grey town lying in the lap of the hills, it was a home-sickness that only the sight of home would cure.[10]

Jasper Blake does indeed return to Pengowan but he is not recognised in the local inn, where he is eyed as a stranger who has 'Been in furren parts, p'raps?', and feels depressed and disappointed:

> Till a few hours ago, Pengowan had been the paradise of his dreams, the climax of his ambitions, the sum of his desires; and yet an hour's ramble through its streets and lanes had convinced him that he had been entirely out in his reckoning. Pengowan was not an end in itself, it was only another stage on the journey. Once more he was up against the constantly recurring question, 'What next?'[11]

The theme of the returned emigrant who finds things much altered and who is unrecognised in his hitherto familiar environment, is a common one in Cornish literature of the period. J. Henry Harris' short story 'Cousin Jacky', published in 1901, for instance, tells the tale of a Cornish miner who had returned from Chile to a village near Redruth. He finds the village locked in desolation and despair, his father dead, his brothers in South Africa, and his sweetheart married to another and gone away, 'Now that he had returned with his welcome in his hand, there was no one to rejoice with him'. As he meanders with an increasingly heavy heart through the village, everyone he meets is a stranger, 'He wandered as one living with ghostly memories, and no one in the deserted village in which he was born to say "How are 'ee?". His dream of a joyous homecoming was thus wiped out and he went again into voluntary exile'.[12] The Hocking brothers and Harris were Cornishmen, indigenous authors, but their theme influenced other writers, notably D.H. Lawrence who spent a traumatic spell in Cornwall during the First World War.

An astute if ambivalent observer of the Cornish, Lawrence understood the often complicated relationship between Cornwall and the distant lands of its diaspora. In his short story 'Samson and Delilah', first published just after the First World War in 1922, Lawrence writes of a Cornish miner who has come home to St Just-in-Penwith from America, arriving late one night and making his way to the 'The Tinners' Rest', the local inn. The returned miner is instantly regarded by the landlady, Mrs Nankervis, 'She had noticed the man: a big fine fellow, well-dressed, a stranger. But he spoke with that Cornish-Yankee accent she accepted as the natural twang among the miners ... He was handsome, well coloured, with well-drawn Cornish eyebrows, and the usual dark, bright, mindless Cornish eyes.'[13] And yet she did not see that he was her husband, home from America after many years, and only a confrontation of violence and passion brings them together, in a strange, crude, indifferent intimacy born of separate lives: 'his hand insinuated itself between her breasts ... "And don't think I've come back here a-begging", he said, "I've more than one thousand pounds to my name, I have. And a bit of fight for a how-de-do pleases me, that it do. But that doesn't mean as you're going to deny as you're my Missis".'[14]

In much of this literature, produced around the turn of the 20th century – or in the years before, during and just after the First World War – there is a sense that the 'Great Emigration' has indeed run its course, that it is time to reflect and take stock but with the knowledge that things will not be the same again, that something in Cornwall has died and that the experience of emigration has altered irrevocably those who have gone overseas: and indeed those who have stayed at home. This literature also mirrors the changing nature of Cornish emigration itself, dwelling not on those families who had emigrated 'for good' in earlier decades now forgotten but featuring instead the wandering Cousin Jack of more recent years who had left loved-ones at home in the expectation that one day he would return. The mood is melancholy, introverted, a reflection of the 'making-do' culture of Cornwall in its 'great paralysis', a mourning for the passing of former glories as well as testament to the damage done to Cornish communities by the uprooting of so many people.

In Cornish fiction produced abroad, however, the mood is different. In Newton G. Thomas' *The Long Winter Ends*, as we saw in Chapter 4, the fatalistic acceptance that the Cornish miner is predestined to wander the globe in pursuit of his traditional occupation is replaced by a gradual awakening to the opportunities of America, of the overwhelming attractions of becoming American. The experience of Jim Holman, the hero, exemplifies this process. Initial thoughts of returning home some day are dropped when he brings his family over to Upper Michigan from Cornwall. A determination to cling to the ways of the Old Country is similarly modified and then abandoned altogether, as Jim rises to the challenge of becoming American: a challenge for which the Cornish turn out to be particularly well equipped.[15] In Phyllis Somerville's novel *Not Only In Stone*, the heroine, Polly Thomas, has more than her fair share of hardships and reversals on the arid mining frontier of South Australia's Yorke Peninsula but she triumphs over each one in turn, living to the ripe old age of 89, her energetic life a memorial to the 'spirit of endeavour'[16] that had made Australia.

Thus while much of the literature produced in Cornwall mirrored an increasingly introverted, fatalistic society resigned to the worst ravages of de-industrialisation, there was in the Cornish fiction of America and Australia a sense not only of survival but of accomplishment and achievement. This mood was echoed in the activities of the various Cornish Associations that sprang up around the globe in the years before the 19th century's close. Here the agenda was subtle, the creation of a Cornish Association presented as a contribution to the institutional growth of the particular host country, a mechanism of conformity rather than dissent, and yet a device by which separate identity might be articulated for whatever purpose whenever necessary. A Cornwall and Devon Society had been established in South Australia as early as the 1850s but it was essentially a pressure group, lobbying the colonial and British governments to maximise Cornish emigration to the colony as well as trying to win specific advantages for the Cornish (and Devon) settlers. The later Cornish Associations were more complex affairs, for while they too sought to defend and extend the interests and opportunities of newly arrived immigrants from Cornwall, they also wished to celebrate Cornish achievement: a process which gave institutional expression to the 'myth of Cousin Jack' but which increasingly sounded a romantic, nostalgic, even sentimental note. With long years having passed since a willing departure from the hungry Cornwall of the 1840s or the copper crash of the 1860s, those who had done well overseas – or those who were comfortably-off second or third generation Cousin Jacks and Jennies – could afford the luxury of viewing Cornwall through rose-tinted spectacles.

A Cornish Association had been formed in Kimberley, in South Africa, in December 1889 by Moses Roberts, editor of the local *Daily Independent*, who drew together Cornish folk from across the diamond fields to partake of a sumptuous dinner, the first of many in the Association's busy life. A few months later, in February 1890, another Cornish Association was formed, this time in Adelaide in South Australia, its inaugural banquet held in Adelaide Town Hall. Its example was followed in 1892 by the founding of a similar association at Broken Hill in New South Wales. Membership of the South Australian association was open to all who were 'Cornishmen by birth, descent or long residence', the aims being to: 'assist in forming and maintaining friendly intimacy and interest among those who are of Cornish birth or extraction, to keep alive Cornish customs; to encourage the settlement of that colony [sic] in this; and to disseminate information regarding South Australia in Cornwall; and to assist any who may be in difficulty or distress.'[17]

James Penn Boucaut, born in Mylor and brought up at Saltash, and a former premier of the colony, was the first chairman and president of the Cornish Association of South Australia, while John Langdon Bonython – born in London of Cornish parentage and by now a significant South Australian public figure (a newspaper magnate with Radical Liberal sympathies) – was vice-president. It was declared at the banquet 'that South Australians and Cornishmen were synonymous terms',[18] so inextricably entwined were the epic stories of Cornish emigration and Australian expansion, the Cornish Association insinuating itself swiftly as an indispensable and familiar component of the Adelaide establishment. Bonython, later knighted for his services to Australia as well as elected Bard of the Cornish Gorsedd and president of the Royal Institution of Cornwall, was troubled by what he saw as the contrast between the triumph of the Cornish overseas and the impending demise of the Cornish at home. While the Cornish had made a huge contribution to the development of Australia, he said, 'I felt that Cornwall was losing its character, its individuality; that the people were rapidly becoming like people elsewhere; it is not well for a race to lose its individuality'.[19] After the federation of the

Australian colonies to form the Commonwealth of Australia in 1901, Bonython was elected to serve as a member of the new House of Representatives. His electioneering took him to Moonta where, inevitably, he talked of things Cornish: 'Not a word was said about politics, but all the votes were caught'.[20]

Bonython's confidence in the Cornish identity in Australia rested to a considerable degree upon the continuing visibility of the Cornish radical tradition in politics. Indeed, between the turn of the century and the years leading up to the First World War, the evidence served to suggest the continuing rise of Cornish influence in the South Australian Labor Party. The greatest triumph, and, paradoxically, the greatest failure, of this Cornish hegemony was the premiership of 'Honest' John Verran in 1910–12. Born in Gwennap in 1856, as a youngster Verran had worked as a pickey-boy (ore sorter) at Kapunda before moving to Moonta Mines where he worked underground until his election to the Adelaide Parliament in 1901. By then the United Labor Party was already making its presence felt in South Australian politics, with the strong moral and organisational backing of the miners' trade union at Wallaroo and Moonta, and Verran joined a growing band of first and second-generation Cornish Labor and Radical Liberal members – notably Richard Hooper, Henry Adams, John George Bice, and the enigmatic David Morley Charleston, who had emigrated to Australia from St Erth by way of San Francisco. Charleston was a man who talked of the need 'To love, and be loved .... To dream of perpetual bliss, and feel the union of souls in the one great love for Nature'.[21]

A Methodist local preacher as well as president of Moonta branch of the Amalgamated Miners' Association of Australia, John Verran was a keen advocate of Christian socialist policies. He became leader of the United Labor Party just before the election of April 1910, an election in which he was swept to power in South Australia with a clear mandate for reform. Yorke Peninsula went wild with rejoicing:

> There could be no doubt as to the warmth of the welcome which the Cornish miners sought to give to their President on his being raised to place and power, and the gathering will mark an epoch in the history of Moonta. Bunting was flying all over the town, and all Moonta and his wife were out to take part in the gathering. At Kadina and at Wallaroo hundreds of workers joined the train, and the scene on arrival at Moonta was an animated one. The Wallaroo town band and the combined Moonta Common-

wealth and Model brass bands discoursed music as the train drew up at the platform'.[22]

However, the euphoria was illusory, for the Labor victory had the effect of galvanising hitherto disparate non-Labor factions into a new and strong opposition force. As T.H. Smeaton observed, writing in 1914, 'The path trodden by the Verran Government was not at any time a smooth one; beset as it was by snares skilfully laid by its enemies, as well as by obstacles which were heedlessly cast there by its friends'.[23] Strikes, an ill-conceived scheme to nationalise and revitalise moribund copper mines and a controversial budget, combined to provoke the state's conservative Upper House into action. As well as rejecting more than a dozen bills, the Upper House deferred the Budget Bill – tantamount to refusing the government's supply. Verran secretly, and unsuccessfully, appealed to Asquith for imperial intervention and in the end decided to go to the electorate. The ensuing election in February 1912 was a disaster for Labor, which was forced from office, and in the following year Verran resigned the leadership of the party. Even his friends began to desert him, the normally pro-Cornish *Australian Christian Commonwealth Methodist* magazine deciding that Verran and his colleagues were too 'prepared to take their orders from the more violent and revolutionary forces in their party ... efforts are being made to dominate the Labor Party by the Church of Rome'.[24]

With hindsight, we can see that Verran's fall from grace was the beginning of the end for the strong Cornish influence in South Australian politics (though its lingering presence could be readily detected even into the 1930s) but on the eve of the First World War it seemed but a temporary setback. After all, the Moonta and Wallaroo mines remained powerful elements of the state's economy, Wallaroo mines in particular having witnessed high levels of investment during the boom period of 1905–07, and later during 1911–18. This energetic development was associated with the regime of H. Lipson Hancock, son and heir of the celebrated Captain Henry Richard Hancock, who had taken over from his father as general superintendent of the mines in 1898. Born and bred on Yorke Peninsula and possessed of a distinct Cornish accent, H. Lipson Hancock was generally considered a Cousin Jack. One of his colleagues wrote that, 'Lipson Hancock had all the Cornish virtues and only one of the vices. He was warm-hearted, hospitable, and genuinely concerned for the welfare of those under him .... Lipson's one limitation – and he knew it – was that of suspiciousness, characteristic of Cornishmen.'[25]

And yet, H. Lipson Hancock was in many respects a different breed from the earlier generation of Cornish miners. To begin with, he was opposed to tradition for tradition's sake, sweeping away the long-cherished and much-prized title of 'captain' for a mine agent, foreman or superintendent, and abandoning Cornish technology in favour of new applications. Cornish engines were broken up and engine houses demolished as electricity replaced steam and as new power houses and giant head-frames came to dominate the landscape. He was, after all, a 'book-learned' mining engineer (he was a graduate of the Ballarat School of Mines), in contrast to those earlier Cornish miners who had gained their knowledge through experience, and he insisted everywhere on scientific method and order. This was reflected in his root-and-branch reform of the club and doctor fund which he transformed into the 'betterment principle', a code of action which covered everything from the provision of baths, changing-houses, libraries, recreation hall, musical instruments, rotunda, children's playgrounds, croquet pitch, tennis court, and even a tree-planting programme, to sophisticated medical care arrangements. All this was reported with awe by the *South Australian Department of Mines Mining Review*, impressed as it was by the widespread sense of 'tidiness, space, and light' at Wallaroo and Moonta.[26] If the 'betterment principle' was a model of clarity and order, then H. Lipson Hancock's 'rainbow system' of Sunday school organisation was little short of authoritarian rigidity. The Moonta Mines Primitive Methodist chapel, made redundant by Methodist Union in 1900, became the new Sunday school and the focus of the 'system'. Wooden huts were erected alongside the old chapel to accommodate the ten 'grades', which ranged from the 'Cradle Roll', for children from infancy to three years, to the 'Home Grade' for adults attached to the school who were too old or infirm to attend. A prescribed course of instruction commenced with 'Lesson 1: The Bible and How We Got It' and continued through to 'Lesson 100: The Call of China'.[27]

With a concern for precision and detail bordering on the obsessive and the eccentric, H. Lipson Hancock seems a singular character. And yet he exemplified what Gage McKinney has called 'a different kind of Cornishman',[28] a label that McKinney has applied to another 'book-learned' second-generation Cousin Jack (the noted T.A. Rickard) but which might be applied more generally to those human products, like Hancock and Rickard, or indeed Bonython, of the Cornish emigration process. Here, in the manner first detected by Bonython, was a group of dynamic, cosmopolitan, highly educated, cutting-edge professional men who were creations of the Cornish experience – and proud to be called Cornish – but who were now much removed in culture, outlook and circumstance from those in Cornwall itself on the eve of the First World War. Author of the well-known

*History of American Mining*, T.A. Rickard was born in Pertusola, Italy, of Cornish descent. His father, Thomas Rickard, was the eldest of five brothers, each of whom was a mining engineer, and his grandfather was Captain James Rickard, a Cornish miner who had gone to the Californian gold-fields in the summer of 1850 to report on prospects at Mariposa. T.A. Rickard's upbringing and education were extraordinary, taking him across Europe from the Urals and the Alps to Cornwall and London. His first language was German (his early formative years were spent in Switzerland) and he learned Russian before he had mastered English. He attended the Royal School of Mines in London, the prelude to a mining career that took him initially to Colorado and California in America and Broken Hill and Mount Morgan in Australia, eventually returning to the United States via London. In 1903 he became editor of the *Engineering and Mining Journal* in New York, and was later editor of the London *Mining Magazine* (1909–15) and *San Francisco Mining and Scientific Press* (1906–09 and 1915–22). He took up American citizenship (that all-pervasive desire 'to become American') but he was nervous about losing his British birthright, retiring eventually to British Columbia where he became again a British subject.

In all this he never forgot that he was Cornish, but always an international Cornishman whose sympathies were cosmopolitan:

> I am proud of my Cornish ancestry and of my descent from the mine-captains of the 'delectable Duchy'. Our people, like many of the Cornish, are of Breton origin, for Brittany is much closer to Cornwall than people realize, and many family names are common to St Malo and Penzance. This sentimental tie with France [sic] pleases me, for I love France .... As a boy, in my visits to Cornwall, I used to look from the cliffs at Newquay across the Atlantic with the fixed intention of going to America, of which I had heard much from my father .... Besides, I met many Americans at our home, and I liked their cheery ways and expansive manner. As soon as I graduated I came across.[29]

Back in Cornwall, of course, the names of Hancock and Rickard and others like them were hardly known outside the dwindling mining elite and the international links that were maintained by ordinary people were more intensely intimate; sometimes financial and always personal and emotional. Privately, almost secretly, amidst the culture of making do, individuals struggled to keep contacts going against the background of huge distances, constant mobility, and fast-changing circumstances. In August 1911, for example, Tilly Tripp of Tredor Farm on the Lizard wrote to her young grandson, Frank, in impossibly distant New Zealand, her brief and partially literate postcard message both concealing and conveying the sentiment that welled in her heart: 'My Dear grand sun [sic] thank you every [sic] so much for card Dear it is lovely with best love from your loving grand mother Tilly Tripp.'[30] Frank also heard from his Aunt: 'To Little Frank with very Best love and kisses: I hope he has spent a nice Christmas, and trust the "New Year" will bring Health and all that his little heart desire. Auntie Loveday.'[31] The younger generation, perhaps, was less inhibited – or had a better command of written English – when corresponding with relatives overseas. Amy Rogers, from Poltesco Farm, Ruan Minor, wrote to her Aunt Bess in New Zealand enclosing a photograph of herself and sister Lill outside their home in Cornwall:

> Dear Auntie Bess, I suppose dont know who these are but they are Lill and I dont you think we are getting big girls I am nearly 16 and Lill 15 years old perhaps you will wonder why Lill has got a pinefore on & I have not well I was on my way home from shop & I never had time to put a pinefore on & I had to take my hat off after we where [sic] out to the Garden & we had some people in to tea. Our Charlie is gone to America & Jack Carter what do you think of it, with love to Uncle baby & yourself from Amy.[32]

And then the First World War changed everything – for individuals, for empires, for humanity. As the Scots historian Niall Ferguson has written, 'the First World War remains the worst thing the people of my country have ever had to endure'.[33] For Cornwall, the First World War brought respite for the hard-pressed mining industry. Strategic metals were suddenly of concern to the government while the excess labour that in 1913 was no longer needed for the Rand was now swept up by the insatiable demands of the armed forces. Cornish engineers, for example, who in other circumstances might have found themselves in the Ferreira Deep or Simmer and Jack mines were now on the Western Front. The Cornwall Fortress Royal Engineers, a territorial unit, saw action in the trenches throughout the conflict. In 1915 its No.2 (Fowey) Company was mobilised as part of the British Expeditionary Force and on the eve of the second battle of Ypres in April was the victim of the enemy's first gas attacks in the area. In 1916 the Company was busy manufacturing mining timbers for the use of the tunnelling companies during the Battle of Messines, moving to heavy bridging tasks during 1917 and 1918. The No 3. (Penryn) Works Company was also involved from the first, the regimental history opining that 'the Penryn men had the luck to be in the thick of the fighting and they took full advantage of it to prove what Cornishmen – particularly Cornish engineers – were capable of doing'.[34] On 7 July 1916 the Company joined the Fourth Army to participate in the Battle of Somme, taking responsibility for running the strategic engineer dump on the Albert-Dernancourt road, and in 1917 it was engaged in heavy bridging operations in the Somme area. During the great German counter-attack of November 1917, the Penryn men were moved to forward positions to dig new trenches and erect wire in the face of the advancing enemy. Worse was to come, the Penryn Company working night and day to prepare defences for the impending German offensive of March 1918, an engagement in which they were to fight as infantry. Later, in the August, the Company was placed under the Australian Corps for the Battle of Amiens, sapping for the Australians as they attacked and took Mont St Quentin. In the closing months of the war, the Penryn men were engaged continuously on the Front, constructing bridges over canals and rivers as the Allies pressed home their advance.

Of course, there were Cornishmen in other units – or at sea in the Royal Navy – with a number of first and second generation Cousin Jacks serving in Imperial, and, later, American, forces. Charles Blackwell, for example, found himself fighting the Germans in South West Africa (modern Namibia). Born at Cost-Is-Lost in the parish of Perranzabuloe in 1872, Blackwell worked for Harvey's of Hayle until the closure of its world-renowned foundry in 1894, making his way then to South Africa where he became embroiled in the second Boer War, later returning to Cornwall briefly before becoming chief engineer of the Langlaagte Deep in the Transvaal in 1903. With the outbreak of the First World War, he joined the South African Motor Corps as an officer, playing a major role in the swift defeat of the Germans in South West Africa in 1914–15.[35] Tom Whetter, born in Gorran, left Cornwall in October 1914 with his Aunt Grace to start a new life in Canada. They already had relatives in Ontario, in townships such as Markham, Stouffville and Brechin, and were soon joined by Tom's father – Jacob Whetter – who travelled up from North Dakota to take up an appointment as a Methodist minister. In March 1916 Tom Whetter joined the Canadian Army, and he soon found himself back in Europe. He arrived in France in time to see action at the horrific battle for Vimy Ridge and later in other bloody engagements such as Arras, Passchendaele and

Cambrai. It was in France that Tom got to know Fred Whetter, from Lorneville in Ontario, whose family had come originally from Lostwithiel. They planned to visit Cornwall together during leave, so that Tom might show Fred the sights and perhaps try to find a relative or two in Lostwithiel. Alas, it was not to be, for Fred Whetter was one of the many thousands of Canadians who died taking Vimy Ridge.[36]

If the name Canada is forever tied to Vimy Ridge, then that of Anzac – the Australian and New Zealand Army Corps – is linked no less inextricably with Gallipoli, scene of the fateful adventure of 1915. Private William Brokenshire, killed at Gallipoli soon after the landings at Anzac Cove, was the first Moonta boy to be killed in the First World War – within nine months another 156 soldiers from the township had also fallen, an appallingly high casualty rate which deeply affected Moonta folk. It was hardly surprising when Private M. Petherick wrote home to Moonta from a training camp in Dorset, explaining that 'There is not much love between the Tommies and the Colonials here',[37] the Australians and New Zealanders showing a healthy disrespect for a British leadership that had already cost them dear, but – as in the case of Tom and Fred Whetter's desire to visit the Old Country – the proximity of Cornwall for those based in Europe had a curiously tantalising appeal. Of course, the First World War had the effect of making yet more complex the emergence of Australian national identity, notions of a 'Little Cornwall' secure in the relative isolation of South Australia's Yorke Peninsula to be weighed against the sometimes conflicting, sometimes complementary emotional pulls and claims to loyalty from the wider Australia, Britain and empire. In this kaleidoscopic identity, Cornwall itself had a place. When Albert Jacka, born in Bendigo in Victoria, was awarded the Victoria Cross in 1915 (he was the first Australian to receive it) the Moonta *People's Weekly* was quick to note in an article 'Heroic Sons of Cornwall' that Jacka was of Cornish descent.[38]

And, like the Whetters, there were those in Britain on leave or convalescence who felt the draw of Cornwall, Harry Pascoe in the 1920s recalling the war years 'when scores of Australian khaki clad soldiers sought out remote corners of the County to visit for the first and last time the homes of their fathers'.[39] Private Leigh Lennell, in a series of letters written to his parents in Moonta mines, described how he and Art Trenwith had left their nursing home at Putney – where Lennell had been fitted with an artificial arm – to go to Cornwall. They lodged at the Tywarnhaile Hotel in Perranporth, Lennell furnishing a captivating and deeply revealing account of their experiences:

> You will see by this address that I am down with the Cousin
> Jacks. It is perfectly lovely here, and just like home again. The
> people talk exactly like the Cornish at Moonta. The scenery and
> sights are simply beautiful, and as soon as people knew we were
> Australians and of Cornish descent, they crowded around us
> and talked for hours .... I feel sure some of them must have rela-
> tives in Moonta. Such names as Polkinghorne, Pengilly,
> Polgreen, Penberthy, are all folk here. Today we went to
> Bedruthan Caves and to St Agnes tin mines. I feel quite at home
> here. They all say, 'How art e gettin arn, ma son', and 'Es, boy, es'.
> They are all delighted here because we can understand them and
> can talk like them.[40]

When Private Lloyd Pollard, another second-generation Cousin Jack, was in
Cornwall in 1916 while on leave from France, he too wrote to his parents back on
Yorke Peninsula: 'At last I can write to you about my trip through dear old
Cornwall – the places you used to speak of when Roy and I were boys. Then we
used to hear dad and grandfather speak of the places I had the pleasure to see'.[41]
Pollard enthused about holding 'my first conversation with a Cornishman in his
native country .... It was grand to hear the Cornish dialect',[42] but all too soon it
was time to return to France. Shortly after his arrival back at the Front, Lloyd
Pollard was seriously injured while stretcher-bearing under fire, and he spent an
agonising 28 months incapacitated in bed before finally expiring. This uncomfortable contrast between the blissful respite of welcoming Cornwall and the
unspeakable terrors of trench warfare is, for the modern reader, ameliorated
somehow by knowledge of the cheerful insistence by Moonta boys at the Front
that Moonta itself was 'the hub of the universe'. Here Moonta and environs, with
their still booming copper mines and a home-grown Cousin Jack identity based
on a strong sense of place and a pride in Little Cornwall's own industrial prowess,
had effectively replaced Cornwall as the focus of Cornish ethnicity. Oswald Pryor
recorded the tale told by one veteran of the First World War:

> One evening I was drinking in an estaminet [or small café] in
> France with a cobber, Billy Bray from Moonta. He was small in
> size but big in heart, and Moonta was his theme song. Some
> liquid had been spilt on a table, and when the waitress came to
> take our order Billy said: 'Mamzelle you compree the world?' as

he drew a circle with a wet finger. She said that she did. 'Then', said Billy, dabbing a finger in the centre of the circle, 'there is where I come from – Moonta!'. To thousands of people like Billy Bray, Moonta was the hub of the universe.[43]

But if the First World War had changed everything, then the peace that followed was, for Cornwall, a retreat into the paralysis from which Cornish society and its economy had been lifted momentarily by the conflict. After the war the government lost interest in Cornish mining. As in other industries, there was an initial post-war boom but soon tin prices fell. Intense lobbying by mine owners and labour unions failed to win renewed government support for the Cornish industry and by the spring of 1919 many were predicting the final demise of Cornish mining.[44] The dreadful Levant mine disaster at St Just in October of that year, when 31 miners lost their lives, cast a further shadow of despair across the whole industry, a strangely symbolic event which – in the words of one Cornish newspaper of the time – sent 'a shudder ... like an earth-tremor to Johannesburg and Butte City, to Broken Hill and Pachuca to Grass Valley and Ballarat and many other abodes of Cornish exiles and their descendents'.[45] The closure of Wheal Grenville, near Camborne, in 1920 heralded a deepening crisis in Cornish tin mining, with news that Dolcoath too was abandoned being met by shocked disbelief. Tincroft and Cook's Kitchen closed during 1921 and other mines were at a virtual standstill. Hunger again stalked the streets of Gunnislake, Redruth, Camborne and St Just, with soup-kitchens reminiscent of 1866 and 1879 set up in the mining districts.

In December 1921 it was claimed that 'there were at Penzance children practically starving and men and women suffering in secret hunger and privation without murmuring',[46] while in the little villages of mid-Cornwall there was fearful hardship as a result of the depressed condition of the china clay industry. John Rowe recalled that:

> Harrowing tales have been told of the distress prevalent in Cornish mining districts during 1921 and 1922. Relief funds were organized, and associated with them was the organization of a Miners' Choir which after giving a number of concerts in the less fortunate towns and villages of the home county went up-country to London, Bournemouth, Taunton, Cardiff .... Further money for relief came back from Cornish emigrants in

Canada, Australia, the Transvaal, and the United States. Camborne police station was transformed into an emergency centre for clothing, and one estimate reckoned that 3800 folk had received clothes with a further four thousand still in need.[47]

The Redruth Guardians, besieged by the despairing unemployed seeking help, had no idea how to cope and, without imagination, suggested that the distressed should emigrate. Perhaps as many as a 1000 miners did find their way up-country or overseas during the 1920s but, as the Cornish well knew, the days of plentiful, highly paid mining jobs in South Africa or North America had gone for good. A number of Cornish miners went to the Hollinger gold-mines in Ontario, Canada, the British government paying two-thirds of the expenses for up to 100 of these emigrants, with smaller groups and individuals making their ways to the Calumet copper mines of upper Michigan, to Butte in Montana, and to the gold-mines of Grass Valley, California. The 'Cornish Arms Hotel' in New York City acted as an important landfall and conduit for Cornish emigrants in this period, run by one Sid Blake, who was himself a Cornishman, from the St Austell district. As well as providing accommodation in a friendly and welcoming 'Cornish' environment, the hotel made introductions and put people in contact with other Cornish emigrants and prospective employers. It also published its own newsletter – the *Cornish Arms Hotel Bulletin* – which gave details of the comings and goings of Cornish folk. Notable among the lists is the high incidence of women, evidence no doubt of wives and sweethearts following in the tracks of their roving men. Thus in October 1921, for example, we learn of the journey of Mrs K. Wyatt from Menheniot to Kansas City. Miss Amy Hingston is returning from Butte, Montana, to Sticker near St Austell, while Miss Frances Ellen Bray is coming home from Skidmore, Missouri, to Blisland near Bodmin. Even in 1921, Butte remained an important destination or point of return for many of the mobile Cornish. Garfield Nicholls, for example, was en route to Butte from Tregonnisey, near St Austell. So too were Mrs E. Rowe and Miss Penhalurick, both from St Austell, while Mrs Pope was returning from Butte to St Hilary. However, another destination that was increasingly apparent by this date was the automobile-manufacturing city of Detroit, already the home of many Cornish who had made their way across from the nearby copper and iron country of upper Michigan. In 1921 Miss V. Hore of St Austell was heading for Detroit, as were James Tonkin of Gwinear Road, Leonard Johns of Redruth, and Mrs Eva Wellington from St Just.[48]

Indeed, Detroit was the one overseas destination that in the 1920s offered the ordinary emigrant Cornish real hope of secure employment, although in the Great Depression of the 1930s even this lifeline disappeared. Car sales in the United States boomed to a high of almost 4.6 million vehicles in 1929 but had slumped to less than 1.6 million by 1933, with hundreds of automobile workers, Cornish among them, laid off or fired.[49] Harry Clarke, from near St Austell, was one of those who ended up in Detroit during the boom times of the 1920s. Years before, his parents had spent time in Butte, Montana, and America had always been a lively topic of conversation in the Clarke household in Cornwall. Indeed, Harry's older brother, Will, had joined the United States Army during the First World War and, having fought in France, went out to Butte before returning to Cornwall in 1925. Two other brothers went to New Zealand during the awful year of 1921. Harry, however, went first to British Columbia, travelling with three young men from the china clay village of Foxhole, before going on to Washington State, where many Cornish had found work in the aircraft factories of Seattle, and eventually arriving in Detroit. Harry claimed that in Detroit he met 'about forty [who] had attended Carclaze school', near St Austell, and that:

> I first went to Detroit in 1928, but I was told by some of the fellows from home that a few years before then, about 1923 or 1924, a large group of Cornishmen used to gather down on Detroit's main square, Cadillac Square, every Saturday evening, where they used to meet their friends, just the same as they used to meet in the towns and villages of Cornwall on Saturday nights. The crowd was finally broken up by the City Police. I suppose they wondered what kind of organization was gathering there. When we lived in Detroit we used to have several men from Tregonissey and Carclaze and their wives come to our house on Christmas Eve and sing many of the old Cornish carols. I'll mention a few who used to come – Passmore Edwards, Bill Trethewey, Jim and Jack Andrew, Clifford Hick from Charlestown, Dick Lagor from St Stephen's.[50]

Needless to say, the Cornish were but one ethnic group among many in Detroit, the Irish being present in great numbers. One third-generation Cornish- American who as boy moved from upper Michigan to Detroit remembered the 'cultural shock' of finding himself in a multi-ethnic community. The day before

St Patrick's Day, the boy's teacher asked each pupil in turn to relate his or her family's national origins: 'When my turn came I proudly stated "Cornish", to which the teacher replied, "You mean English!" I quickly responded, rather dismayed, "No, I'm not English, I'm Cornish" [and] ... they had me explain what Cornwall was.'[51] Often invisible in this melting pot, some of the Detroit Cornish drifted across to Grass Valley in California, where preferential treatment for skilled Cousin Jack hard-rock miners was known to exist. In the 1930s, especially, as the Depression threw hundreds out of work in the automobile industry, some of those who did not return to Cornwall headed west to Grass Valley where they hoped that their Cornish credentials would give them a head start over the many thousands of all nationalities from back East who were also on their way to California.

Several of the big Grass Valley mines, notably the Empire and the North Star, had combined in 1930 to form the 'Empire-Star Mines' which sought to achieve new economies of scale and attract new investment. In February 1934 President Franklin D. Roosevelt, elected to implement a 'New Deal' for America, raised the price of gold in the United States from the long-standing $20.67 to $35.00 an ounce. Wages rose almost overnight by 11 per cent, while production increased to reach an average of between 600 and 700 tons of ore per day during the 1930s. In 1939–40 underground development at the Empire-Star Mines totalled a record ten miles. As Lescohier put it, in his inimitable laconic style, 'Prospects for the company appeared excellent for many years to come. As it turned out, they would be excellent for but one more year.'[52] When the United States entered the Second World War in 1942, gold-mining was declared a non-essential activity and preferential treatment ceased, so that by 1946 the mines were at a virtual standstill. Under new peacetime conditions the Grass Valley mines struggled on for another decade but in 1956 all underground activity came to an end.

In Australia change was – like it or not – also in the air. On Peace Day in July 1919 every schoolchild in Moonta, Wallaroo and Kadina was presented with a Cornish pasty – perhaps a carefully chosen metaphor – an icon of community solidarity – that served to emphasise reassuring continuity in the face of bewildering change.[53] But metaphor or not, it was a forlorn gesture, for the ending of the First World War meant sudden death for the mighty copper mines of northern Yorke Peninsula. Despite the feverish activity of the war years, the demand for copper had slumped dramatically at the end of 1918, to be followed inexorably by tumbling copper prices. There were long periods of inactivity at Moonta and Wallaroo from March 1919 and in October 1923 the mines were abandoned for good. With almost indecent haste the infrastructure was broken up for scrap, the auction catalogue produced for the subsequent sale listing everything in minute detail from winding engines and railway locomotives to emery cloth and miners' helmets.[54]

In an echo of events in Cornwall itself, a miner's choir was formed to tour Adelaide and other spots to raise funds, while many of the younger people drifted off to try to find work elsewhere, leaving behind 'a high proportion of aged and infirm',[55] as one report put it. Despite a 'strong defeatist attitude', many 'clung on, eking out a bare living by casual labour on farms, docks and grain depots until entitled to age or incapacity pensions'.[56] This was hardly the climate in which a youthful, vigorous Cornish culture might be passed on to an eager new generation, although the *People's Weekly* put a brave face on things, reminding its readers periodically that 'The Celtic spirit is deep set in folk that hail from Cornwall ... and Moonta people are mostly Cornish'[57] or that 'Our community has been in every sense a bit of old Cornwall ... Moonta, in its proximity to the sea, is able to carry the role of an outpost of the delectable Duchy'.[58] But, as in Cornwall, such appeals to Celtic Revivalist sentiment seemed hardly relevant amongst the dereliction and depopulation of Yorke Peninsula and the Moonta people too resorted to a fatalistic, inward-looking culture of making do. Even the Cornish Association of South Australia found itself in swift decline, not least in its embarrassing inability now to respond to appeals for help from Cornwall, a request for financial assistance from the Camborne Town Band being turned down in 1930.[59] By now, of course, (and in contrast to South Africa or even Butte or Grass Valley) it was many decades since the last great Cornish influx in the 1880s, the Yorke Peninsula newspapers marked already by the endless obituary columns of the first-generation Cornish – William Abraham from Warleggan, John Pedlar from St Kew, Emma Curnow from Marazion, Richard Retallick from St Agnes, William Rowe from Hayle Copperhouse, Thomas Towan from Tuckingmill, Ann Rule from Crowan, Sarah Trewartha from Breage, James Martin from St Blazey, Grace Goldsworthy from St Buryan, and very many more.[60] One 'old timer' confided that he could 'still tell a few Cornish yarns' but more typical, perhaps, was the elderly Cousin Jack who in 1932 lamented that 'saffron cake is a thing of the past .... I am lost for a good Cornishman to have a bit of a chat with. They are all dead and buried.'[61]

In contrast to the Cornish literature of the pre-First World War years, with its habitual reference to the emigration experience, treatment of the 'Great Emigration' in the 1920s and beyond was increasingly retrospective, no longer the preserve of contemporary fiction but rather the stuff of historical writing. In short, the 'Great Emigration' was seen increasingly as a historical rather than contemporary phenomenon, something that had happened in the past, a subject to be incorporated in the writing of Cornish history – a task that in the 1920s fell principally to Harry Pascoe and A.K. Hamilton Jenkin. Pascoe contributed a chapter 'Cornishmen and Emigration' to the far-sighted *Cornwall Education Handbook*, published in 1927. His tone was wistful, almost melancholic, reflecting passively and with quiet regret on former days. Thus a:

> typical trio set out from the same village and journeyed in a sailing ship to Australia. No.1 married a colonial girl, lived steadily and soberly, and died in middle age. No.2 was lost sight of. No.3 came home and went again, came and went several times – gold digging in Australia, tin mining on Mt Bischoff, Tasmania – pump man on the Rand – copper mining on Lake Superior – and is now a quiet little elderly man who rarely steps from his small holding in the St Austell parish.[62]

A.K. Hamilton Jenkin drew heavily on Pascoe's material for the chapter 'The Exodus of the Seventies' in his book *The Cornish Miner*, also published in 1927, conveying the same wistful, heavy-hearted, sighing manner. There were similar stories of families and friendships split asunder – 'Jerry' who died in Butte, Montana, 'Martin' who was killed in New Zealand, 'Johnny' who died in Cornwall of African phthisis, 'Willie' who 'visited half the world, made a small fortune, and settled down alone'[63] – and an eerie, lonely tale that somehow encapsulated the frightening enormity of the emigration experience:

> A Cornishman, nicknamed 'Chippy', was a passenger in a train in Western America, and was showing considerable interest in the progress of the journey. 'Where are we to?' he bawled through the window, as the carriage drew up at a wayside station. 'Roche Rock', came from a window at the other end of the train. 'And wher av us got now?' he shouted at the next stop. 'Goss Moor', was the answer from the other end. 'And where's this to?' he called at the third halt. 'St Columb', came the same mysterious voice. At the first opportunity Chippy started to look through the train for his fellow countryman, but the other lay low and the mystery was never solved.[64]

By the time the Second World War erupted in Europe in 1939, the Great Emigration had ceased to be an integral part of Cornish life. Of course, many families still maintained close relationships with kinfolk overseas, while knowledge of Butte, Johannesburg, Detroit and other areas of Cornish settlement had by no means departed from popular consciousness. However, the 'emigration trade' and 'emigration culture' that had underpinned the process had on the whole disappeared, while the 'myth of Cousin Jack' had itself run its course.

In such circumstances, the Second World War could only serve to emphasise the sense of disjunction, fragmentation and scattering that many Cornish people had experienced already, though now without any specific Cornish dimension. To be sure, among the numerous Americans stationed in Cornwall prior to D-Day, were those with Cornish family connections who sought out hidden places and distant cousins, while on the wider canvas Cornish servicemen and women found themselves in all corners of the globe. But more important for the Cornish international identity was the aftermath of the Second World War, rather than the conflict itself. It was in the years after 1945 – as we shall see in Chapter 13 – that this international identity experienced an astonishing renaissance – slowly, imperceptibly at first in the 1960s and 1970s but gaining in momentum in subsequent decades and into the 21st century as the international Cornish emerged as one component of the new ethnic and multicultural reaction to the postmodern forces of 'globalisation'.

# CHAPTER THIRTEEN

# AN ENDURING

# IDENTITY?

## THE CORNISH IN A

## GLOBALISED WORLD

In the years after 1945, rather like the period after 1815 when Cornwall's 'Great Emigration' had first emerged, there was a fundamental restructuring of geopolitical power on the world stage. In addition to the continuing engagement of America with Europe through the North Atlantic Treaty Organisation (Nato) and the creation of the Soviet-dominated 'Eastern Bloc', European states such as Britain and France were confronted with both the rapid decline of their colonial empires and the first moves towards European unity.

Both these developments had implications for Cornwall. Although Cornish public opinion was often ambivalent in its attitude towards Europe, with European Union policies in the 1990s seemingly indifferent to the particular problems of Cornish farming and fishing, there were many Cornish activists drawn to the idea of a confederal Europe of the Regions, in which Cornwall might appeal over the head of the United Kingdom government to like-minded regions such as Brittany or indeed to Brussels and Strasbourg themselves.[1] Here the Cornish identity was seen as essentially European, its strengths and weaknesses, and its potential, to considered akin to and alongside those of similar regions and small nations such as Wales or Galicia – a view that was reinforced in 1999 when Cornwall was designated a 'European Region' and became the recipient of significant 'Objective 1' European Union funding on account of its relative poverty.

At the same time, Britain's divestment of empire after the Second World War meant a re-assessment of ties with former colonies and the so-called 'white' Dominions. Certainly, there was a smattering of Cornish folk amidst the flood of British emigrants after the war to Australia, New Zealand, Canada, and South Africa, more than a few from Cornwall hidden amidst the tide of assisted 'Ten Pound Poms' in the 1950s and 1960s. But although these folk were themselves indisputably Cornish there was nothing distinctively 'Cornish' about this emigration in the sense that there had been before in the erstwhile mass movement of Cornish miners across the globe. In South Africa, in particular, the 'Wind of Change' that blew through the African continent from the 1960s led to an estrangement of that country from Britain and the Commonwealth, in which notions of Cornish identity were bound to suffer. Government-led emphasis on 'white' cohesion did not encourage the Cornish in South Africa to deploy a different or dissenting identity – especially when historically the Cornish had been generally sympathetic to the predicament of the non-European population – while overt expressions of Cornishness in the context of racist Apartheid policies might lead to embarrassment in Cornwall itself. Occasionally, such expressions did find their way into Cornish magazines, where for many they made uncomfortable reading: 'How can Apartheid be condemned when South Africa is bringing to the Black people homelands, the place of their ancestors, where they can live and work, and be self governed, is this not what we want for our Kernow [Cornwall]?'[2]

Paradoxically, it was in South Africa that the Cornish institutions that had been inherited from the turn of the 20th century survived intact the longest, reflecting no doubt the relatively 'recent' nature of the emigration from Cornwall. As Cornish Associations elsewhere in the world disappeared or became moribund (even the Cornish Association of South Australia, which also survived, was at the nadir of its fortunes in the 1950s), the Cornish Association of the Transvaal soldiered on, continuing even to publish its newsletter, the *Cornubian*. Despite an admission in November 1949 that 'The Cornish Association is now but the pale ghost of what it once was',[3] the Association in the early 1950s still sported branches at Johannesburg, Roodepoort, Randfontein, and Springs, with a full calendar of events. By the 1960s, however, the Cornish Association had disappeared from view, and its successor – the Cornish Association of the Witwatersrand – did not appear until the late 1990s, by which time the political structure of South Africa had altered entirely. By then there had also been a flowering of Cornish associations on the wider international stage. One or two were legacies of the 19th century, having survived (at least on paper) through the bleak years, for them, of the 1950s and 1960s to experience a rekindling, slowly at first in the 1970s but with increasing energy in the 1980s and 1990s and into the new millennium. Many more, however, were new products of a growing enthusiasm for Cornishness, a phenomenon exhibited most strongly in the United States and in Australia but also evident in Canada and New Zealand, as well as in more unlikely places such as Cuba. By the early 1990s there were dozens of Cornish associations worldwide from California, Colorado, Michigan, Wisconsin, Texas, Toronto, and Vancouver, to Bendigo, New South Wales, Victoria, Western Australia, Queensland, and New Zealand, with confederal umbrella organisations in both North America and Australia. Publications abounded, such as the *Cornish Immigrant* (journal of the Cornish Society of Greater Milwaukee), the *Newsletter of the Cornish Association of New South Wales*, and *Kenderwi Kernewek (Cornish Cousins)*, the organ of the California Cornish.

At first glance this sudden reassertion of an international Cornish identity seemed inexplicable. Some 80 years since the end of the First World War and 50 since the end of the Second in 1945 – and many decades after the dwindling of the 'Great Emigration' and its supporting trade and culture – the Cornish had suddenly re-emerged as if from nowhere. Why? Part of the answer, of course, is that the overseas Cornish had never disappeared entirely, a residual identity keeping alive ties with the Old Country or links with family back in Cornwall, Cornish popular culture itself still remembering – or half-remembering – connections with far-flung places across the globe. Despite everything, Moonta had retained a sense of itself as 'Australia's Little Cornwall' and 'the Hub of the Universe'. On Michigan's Upper Peninsula the half-remembered origins of the pasty had led to rival Cornish, Finnish, Slav and Italian claims upon it, a confusion which nonetheless did much to boost the pasty as an icon of that peninsula's coalescing regional identity – one in which the Cornish inheritance had its place.[4] More clearly recalled but still 'residual' was the identity expressed by one woman in Wisconsin in the mid-1970s. When asked whether being of Cornish descent was important to her, she replied:

> Yes, it's important because it's our roots. It's where we come from and why we're here .... Of course, we're Americans, there's no question of that .... It's just that our heredity is Cornish. I think it's still the Cousin Jack feeling because there's a strong sense of family and cousinship among the Cornish in this area, and the fact that we're all related and share the same roots makes for a happy neighbourhood.[5]

In California the same was true. As the years passed, so the idea of a collective 'Cornishness' became important for former mining towns such as Grass Valley and Nevada City. Although, historically, the Cornish had claimed an exclusive ethnic identity, the myth of Cousin Jack asserting the superiority of the Cornish above all-comers, in practice the boundaries of Cornishness had been blurred from the earliest days of the gold rush. As the Cornish strove to establish their superiority as hard-rock miners, keeping potentially competing ethnic groups at bay, so others sought to gain or insinuate Cousin Jack status – to demonstrate one way or another a Cornish connection or sympathy. These were the 'galvanised Cousin Jacks' of Grass Valley and Nevada City – those who did not possess a full set of Cornish credentials but who were nonetheless able to present themselves plausibly as 'Cornish'. In the days of Cornwall's undisputed pre-eminence it had been relatively easy to maintain the boundaries of exclusivity. But as Cornwall's position was slowly but surely eroded as the 19th century drew on, so Cornish claims to superiority seemed less convincing, the 'galvanised Cousin Jacks' finding it increasingly easy to penetrate and indeed assimilate within the Cornish ranks. Moreover, as the gold-mines of Grass Valley and Nevada City themselves declined and many of the Cornish melted away, so the process of 'galvanisation' continued apace. As Gage McKinney explained in his major study *When Miners Sang, The Grass Valley Carol Choir*, as the Cornish identity of these Nevada County towns appeared to dwindle in the mid-20th century, so people from a variety of backgrounds came together to cherish, preserve and even assert the district's Cornishness, 'Whether they were Cornish or not, many Grass Valley residents drew some portion of their own identities from a familiarity with, or participation in, the Cornish culture that had once been so distinctive.'[6]

As McKinney argued:

> For people to appropriate a Cornish identity in Grass Valley was not entirely new. For some time, and for a variety of reasons, people had willingly identified with the Cousin Jacks and Jennies. When the Cornish were still a sizeable contingent some people did this to get along or to gain a commercial or personal advantage. Paradoxically, as the Cornish population declined, others emphasised their Cornish connections – no matter how tenuous – in order to identify with the 'old timers.'[7]

McKinney, an important voice for the contemporary overseas Cornish, considered that the appropriation of ethnic identity could in certain situations appear unsavoury, and it may be that in Nevada County at its zenith the Cornish did indeed resent others passing themselves off as Cousin Jacks in their pursuit of advantage or favour. However, he insists that at Grass Valley and Nevada City the process was on the whole positive:

> Many in Nevada County ... appropriated Cornishness in the right way. They built up loyalties, adopted Cornish customs, sang in the Carol Choir, or merely came to accept the Cornish by working alongside them during the week or worshipping beside them on Sunday. Their manner of appropriation validated Cornish culture as the [Nevada] county's unique heritage. As a result the expression 'galvanized Cousin Jack' became popular in Nevada County for those who had assumed, as it were, an electro-charged patina of Cornishness.[8]

Thus, for example:

> Harold Hansen, a miner of Norwegian and Irish descent, called himself a 'galvanized Cousin Jack'. He ran an underground railroad at the Brunswick Mine and joined the Grass Valley Carol Choir in 1938 .... Anyone with a Cornish wife, anyone who valued Cornish customers, and anyone who worked in the mines might be considered galvanized. Verlon McKinney, a wholesale lumber salesman from San Francisco, always let his Nevada County customers know he was 'galvanized'. His wife descended from a Redruth miner, and he was glad to feel accepted in the mining country.... The most obvious examples come from people of different races who had their own traditions, and yet managed to identify with the Cornish. One of these was bootblack Hibow Allen, an African-American who played clarinet in the Grass Valley Band. He had a business on Mill Street in the 1950s, and many remember Allen as one of the few blacks then in Grass Valley ... he felt possessive of his town and looked askance at the influx of newcomers. 'We don't want people coming in', he would tell his Cornish customers, 'and spoiling things for *us* Cousin Jacks'.[9]

In the great flowering of Cornish-American identity in the closing decades of the 20th century the process of 'galvanisation' seemed more dynamic than ever, increasingly ready to embrace and assimilate people from different backgrounds. For example, Eleanor Kenitzer, originally from North Carolina, arrived in Grass Valley in 1988 and was before long director of the Carol Choir. Ed and Alice Tinloy Yun, descendants of the district's 19th-century Chinese community, were leading lights of the annual Methodist Cornish Christmas Faire, for which Alice baked saffron cake. At the 1999 faire Ed and Alice both wore black-and-gold badges that proclaimed proudly – 'Cornish person.'[10]

Despite the apparent thread of continuity in this ever more inclusive 'galvanisation', there were new forces at work. The international Cornish identity that had re-emerged by the 1990s was no longer residual or half-remembered.[11] On the contrary, it had been determinedly 're-invented' on the basis of a new set of assumptions and aspirations. Moreover, this 're-invented' identity was increasingly clearly defined, its practitioners for the most part sure of their project and its components. On occasions this Cornishness could be expressed with remarkable clarity, as in the so-called 'ancestry question' in the 1986 Census in Australia where some 15,000 Australians were prepared to admit to Cornish descent or to claim Cornish ethnicity. Although in one sense the tip of the iceberg (Charles Price estimated that in 1992 between 245,000 and 290,000 Australians were of significant Cornish descent, with perhaps as many as 850,000 with some Cornish connection in their family trees),[12] the fact that 15,000 Australians considered it important to register their Cornish backgrounds was a telling indicator of a popular ethnic consciousness.

In the United States, similar identification was observable. As early as 1978, Richard White, an American of Cornish descent, could write about 'Growing up Cornish in a Mining Town in Michigan', re-assessing his 'Cornish' childhood in terms of the new multicultural perspectives of American society that were by then emerging, insisting that the Cornish were one of the constituent ethnic groups that went to make up the United States .[13] Another Cornish-American admitted that it was not until 1970 – with access to new ways of thinking about herself and her origins – that she had at last realised that she had been 'raised in a Cornish home'[14] in the mining town of Globe, Arizona. In Calumet in 1995 a third Cornish-American considered that: 'My generation is the first to have shown an interest in the Cornish ancestry .... I suppose the principal compulsion has been curiosity, perhaps mixed with a measure of pride in our rather distinctive origins – distinctive, that is, by comparison with much larger and less cohesive groups of people.'[15]

Such curiosity and pride had led, among other things, to a remarkable explosion in family history activity amongst people of Cornish descent overseas. There was a burning desire in many thousands of Australians, Americans, Canadians, New Zealanders and South Africans to know Cornwall, the land of their forebears. For many, family history was the fount of this enthusiasm, the starting point for an intensely personal quest that led them not only to research their family trees but also to visit Cornwall to experience for themselves the remote farms and cottages whose names they might not yet be able to pronounce but whose damp granite walls spoke eloquently of the former generations of ancestors who had lived there. For such people there was in Cornwall an emotional intensity of place – an environment to fire the imagination – genealogy no longer a crisp research exercise but a drive for understanding, for knowledge of oneself and one's location in the history of the world.

Roslyn Paterson, for example, another important voice for the contemporary overseas Cornish, has described her journey – spiritual as well as physical – from northern Yorke Peninsula, South Australia's 'Little Cornwall', to seek out the tiny cottage at Woon and the hamlet of Bokiddick, once the home of her farm labouring-cum-mining ancestor, Walter Phillips:

> The ... day was memorable as I retraced the steps of Walter Phillips .... We visited Lostwithiel and found [that] the chapel where Mary Ann and Walter had married was now a parking lot for an adjoining pub! But we were able to wander up a street called Bodmin Hill where Walter had lived at the time of his marriage. We then began to search for the cottage ... [and] we were directed ... to a small derelict cottage known as Woon. Finally, a short distance down the hedged road, I pushed back the blackberries and squeezed past an overgrown hedge. And there complete with rusting galvanised iron additions was Walter Phillips' birthplace.[16]

Likewise, Patricia Lay, another prominent Cornish-Australian, has explored the expanses of Bodmin Moor in search of family homesteads, and in her volume *Cornish Australian Heritage* she has included biographical sketches of her Cornish forebears, together with those of several hundred other mainly 19th-century emigrants from Cornwall, their stories lovingly drawn together and eagerly contributed by their descendents today. Plainly, with quiet humility and due deference, Patricia Lay has told the story of Mary Stephens, her great-great-grandmother:

Mary was the third of the twelve children of Richard Stephens and Charity Coombe. At the time of her baptism in Lewannick in 1828 her father was a farm labourer in the neighbouring parish of Altarnun, having moved from Lewannick after the baptism of Mary's older sister Elizabeth in 1826. The family lived on the isolated hill farm 'Trederras' on the edge of Bodmin Moor beyond Trewint. In 1846 they had moved to 'Cargelly' at the other end of the parish where Richard was a tenant farmer, but Mary was already working in service at 'Trevell' where she had been at least since the age of thirteen. By the time of her marriage to Jonathon Mullis in 1850 and their emigration to New South Wales the same year, her father had acquired his own property 'Coombe Farm' Lewannick where he remained until his death in 1881.[17]

This new curiosity and pride was also symptomatic of a wider phenomenon: the new assertions of ethnic identities in increasingly multicultural societies such as the United States and Australia in reaction to the forces of 'globalisation' that had emerged in the period since 1945. By the 1990s, when the European retreat from empire was all but complete, and when the geopolitical complexion of the world had been further changed by the collapse of the Soviet bloc, ethnicity had become a major determinant of social and political activity as individuals and communities sought to reconcile the local with the global. As people led increasingly homogeneous lives, particularly in Western societies – wearing similar clothes, consuming identical products and exposed to the same televisual and internet messages – so the cultural differences between communities had become correspondingly more important. This newly apparent diversity was seen variously as a welcome enrichment of otherwise mundanely uniform societies or as a dangerous threat to social cohesion.

In Western Europe in particular, the rise of ethnic and territorial politics began to threaten the integrity or at least constitutional structures of states such as Britain, Spain, Italy and Belgium, while in the eastern portion of the continent ethnic rivalries led to confrontation and bloodshed in countries such as Russia and the former Yugoslavia.[18] In Australia, notwithstanding the brief popularity of the reactionary 'One Nation Party', the tide of immigration from southern Europe and from Asia, together with the loosening of ties with Britain and a greater determination to reach a just accommodation with the Aborigines, had led to the emergence of an increasingly multicultural society. In New Zealand a similar accommodation had been effected between Europeans and Maoris, while in Canada the growth of nationalism in francophone Quebec had put issues of multiculturalism centre-stage. South Africa had emerged at last as a multicultural democracy, while in the United States an increasing acceptance, even celebration, of diversity – Hispanic Americans, Native Americans, African Americans, Irish Americans and so on – had replaced the apparent momentum towards an anglophone 'Wasp' (White Anglo-Saxon Protestant) conformity.

The implications of these developments for the Cornish identity were enormous. To begin with, in Cornwall itself rapid socio-economic change since 1945 had led to a heightened sense of Cornish ethnicity, one that existed against the background of the changing nature of 'Britishness' in which a supposedly homogeneous 'British' identity was replaced by its constituent national components (Scots, Welsh and so on), with the provision of devolution to Scotland, Wales and Northern Ireland radically reforming the nature of government in the United Kingdom. As part of this enhancement of Cornish ethnic identity, Cornish-Celtic revivalists had shown an increasing willingness to broaden their project to include consideration of contemporary Cornish socio-economic issues. This had led to the emergence of the nationalist political party Mebyon Kernow – The Party of Cornwall – but it also facilitated a new synthesis of Celtic revivalist and popular cultures in Cornwall. St Piran's flag, the Cornish national tartan (invented in 1948), the Cornish kilt, even the revived Cornish language (in its several versions), found new popular appeal as icons of contemporary identity, to be placed alongside rugby football, brass bands, Cornish carols and other symbols of working-class culture. As Cornish society moved at last from its 'making do' paralysis, beginning to voice and assert its heightened identity with increasing confidence, so the synthesis of Celtic revivalist and popular cultures came to dominate and characterise the Cornish identity of the early 21st century.[19]

In Australasia and North America, the 're-invented' identity of contemporary Cornwall became an important resource for those wishing to mobilise Cornish culture as part of the new mood of multiculturalism. An almost extravagant display of Cornish tartan and Cornish flags was observable at Cornish events in both continents, with trade stalls invariably doing brisk business in artefacts which ranged from Celtic jewellery to Cornish sporrans and tam-o'-shanters. The Cornish language was adopted as a legitimate expression of contemporary Cornish identity in Australia or America, even to the extent of importing heated debates as to which version of the revived language was to be preferred. The

Cornish Gorsedd (Gorseth Kernow), the most prestigious of Cornwall's Celtic revivalist institutions, drew the enthusiastic attention of Cornish-Americans, Canadians, Australians, New Zealanders, a number being elected to Bardship of the Gorsedd, with the Gorsedd Council (its ruling body) allowing shortened versions of the Gorsedd ceremony to be performed overseas at Cornish events.[20] A willingness to adopt a pan-Celtic identity was also a notable feature of this process, today's overseas Cornish enthusiasts expressing pan-Celtic sympathies in a manner that often eluded their 19th-century immigrant for-bears, not least with regard to the Irish. The most innovative aspect of this new pan-Celticism was the participation of Cornish associations in Australia in the construction at Glen Innes in New South Wales of a 'Celtic' stone circle, mim-icking the ancient stone circles that occur across the Celtic lands from Brittany to the northern Scottish Isles.[21]

And in a further echo of the experience in Cornwall, the new Cornish identi-ties in Australasia and North America also attempted a synthesis of Celtic revivalist and 'popular' culture, returning afresh to historic sites – engine houses, Methodist chapels, old cottages, mining landscapes – to co-opt them as icons of the new Cornishness. Thus Gorsedd ceremonies have been held amidst the ruined engine houses of Moonta Mines in Australia, while in the United States New Almaden has become a site of special pilgrimage for the California Cornish Cousins. This process has, in turn, been linked to Cornish 'gatherings', generally biennial get-togethers in North America and Australasia where Cornish enthusi-asts travel huge distances to participate over several days in a range of events (lectures, receptions, ceremonies, workshops, and so on) in places of Cornish connection such as Calumet in upper Michigan and Ely in Minnesota, or Moonta in South Australia and Bendigo in Victoria. In Australia in particular, such festi-vals have become linked to the burgeoning growth of heritage or cultural tourism. The Kernewek Lowender Cornish festival at Moonta, Wallaroo and Kadina, first instituted in 1973, has grown from a long-weekend to full-week event crammed with ambitious activities, attracting thousands of people – Cornish and non-Cornish – from across the continent and beyond.

In South Australia especially, the heritage 'tourist gaze' is now fixed firmly upon the striking Cornish mining landscapes of northern Yorke Peninsula, Burra Burra and other sites scattered across the state, an enlightened state government having assisted the careful restoration and interpretation of sites and artefacts. Here there is emphasis on Cornish people and Cornish culture in addition to a concern for industrial archaeology, encouraging a Cornish-Australian sense of ownership and further allowing the sites to be co-opted in the interests of the new Cornishness. Indeed, it was in South Australia that notions of an 'international Cornish mining landscape' first emerged, a perspective which emphasised the international significance of the Cornish mining impact in the 19th century and identified a peculiarly Cornish industrial landscape of engine houses, chimney stacks, Methodist chapels, miners' cottages and so on. Significantly, this recognition was manifest at official levels, the South Australian government emphasising not only the intrinsic worth of the state's Cornish mining landscape but also its economic regeneration potential in cultural or heritage tourism. It was no accident when in 1986 the Department of Mines and Energy in South Australia published *Cornish Mining Heritage*, a booklet by R.K. (Keith) Johns, then the Department's director-general who had recently completed a comparative study tour of Cornwall.

In his volume Keith Johns, himself of Cornish descent, acknowledged the profound Cornish influence in the development of South Australia, where Cornish technology had remained in ascendancy until the early 20th century. As he observed, the derelict engine houses and other remains in South Australia were more than redolent of Cornwall. But his interest went further than mere comparison. 'What is their significance?', he asked, and setting out to answer this question himself he went on to 'consider how [these] relevant archaeological relics might be recognised, interpreted and preserved for educational, historical and tourist purposes'.[22] Johns viewed the Cornish mining landscape as possibly the most distinctive physical feature of the South Australian historical heritage, so much so that he had already approved the work and helped secure the funding for the restoration of one of the remaining engine houses at the dramatic Burra Burra copper mine site. He explained, 'In the State's 150th year [1986] and in anticipation of the Australian bi-centenary [1988], concerted effort is being given to the restoration of Morphett's Engine-house and appurtenances at Burra in association with a local committee concerned with planning, development and funding'. Moreover, 'For its part the Department of Mines and Energy has endeavoured to foster awareness of South Australian mining heritage through publications, lectures and field activities, interpretation and identification of mining relics, conducting excursions for school parties and other interest groups ... [we are] on the right track with regard to catering for [the] tourist.'[23]

Despite his emphasis on technology and artefacts rather than people, Johns' efforts contributed significantly to the enhancement of the Australian dimension of the rapidly re-emerging international Cornish identity. As well as securing and drawing attention to its not inconsiderable memorials, Johns had conveyed the importance of the material aspects of that identity, not just in the past but for the present and the future. Historical validity was important but, for those anxious to assert a South Australian-Cornish dimension as part of a wider international Cornish identity, contemporary relevance was vital. So too was 'Cornishness' as cultural capital for the future, a means of demonstrating to South Australian society at large the worth of the Cornish inheritance and its economic potential in the years ahead. Indeed, in 2001 the Kernewek Lowender festival – the first of the new millennium – had done just that. Not only had it demonstrated its continuing success as a cultural/heritage tourism extravaganza in a hitherto economically lacklustre locality but it had also emphasised the importance of 'identity' in generating pride of place, socio-economic visibility and confidence in the ability of a region to face the future with optimism and energy. Additionally, the success of Kernewek Lowender as a prestigious South Australian event drew the attention of Federal politicians in distant Canberra who saw in its celebration of 'Cornishness' a welcome inclusivity which represented the multicultural imperative of contemporary Australia. To be 'Cornish' in South Australia was not to draw boundaries between peoples but rather to celebrate one aspect of a felicitous diversity.

At its most extreme, this process was evident at Kapunda in South Australia where, no engine house having survived, a huge seven-metre tall sculpture of a Cornish miner had been erected. Unveiled in June 1988 and costing over A$100,000, the statue was itself an interesting synthesis, for it was named not (as logic and historical sensitivity might have suggested) 'Cousin Jack' but rather 'Map Kernow', 'Son of Cornwall' in the Cornish language. Moreover, in the interests of multicultural diversity, Map Kernow was conceived as a memorial to 'all the people who are part of Kapunda's history – the Cornish, Irish, German and other nationalities'.[24] This synthesis was also detected in a new literature that had emerged overseas, notably in the United States in fiction such as *Thomasina and the Tommyknocker*, a children's novel by Juanita Kennedy Brown, and *Cousin Jack*, an epic blockbuster by Daniel Mason, where traditional images of Cornish mining life in 19th-century frontier America have been presented afresh against the backdrop of the new Cornishness.[25]

If the reconstruction of identity in contemporary Cornwall had profound effects upon North America and Australasia, then the emergence of new Cornish identities in those places was no less significant for Cornwall itself. Indeed, the very existence of those identities was enormously supportive of attempts in Cornwall to assert separate identity, the international flavour of contemporary Cornishness a firm rebuttal for those claiming to detect parochialism in Cornish perspectives. Moreover, in an increasingly creative symbiosis, Cornwall itself was soon to play an important role in the promotion of Cornish identities abroad. The *Journal of the Cornish Family History Society*, without an ideological axe to grind, created a community of thousands of like-minded Cornish enthusiasts across the globe. A more ethnically conscious magazine, *Cornish Worldwide*, published under the auspices of the London Cornish Association, also took the message around the globe, to be joined from June 1994 by the highly successful quarterly glossy magazine *Cornish World*, produced in Cornwall and edited initially by Phil Hosken who – alongside the almost evangelical efforts of Howard Curnow – played a major role in building lines of communication and understanding between the resurgent Cornish organisations overseas and Cornwall itself.

This new symbiosis was also observable in more serious Cornish literature, for example in Alan M. Kent's *Cousin Jack's Mouth Organ*, which is a Brysonesque journey across Cornish-America, published in 2004, in which Kent relates his adventures and experiences as he visits places with Cornish connections and meets folk of Cornish descent.[26] Earlier, D.M. Thomas – the distinguished Cornish poet and novelist – had recognised the significance of the 'Great Emigration' to the identity and life of modern Cornwall. He also saw that the contemporary search for 'roots' was not a one-way process, that in addition to those overseas Cornish who yearned to know more about Cornwall and their Cornish forbears, so there were those in Cornwall who were determined to seek out Cornish places abroad and to honour their own ancestors who had emigrated all those years ago. His poem 'A Cornish Graveyard at Keweenaw' appeared in the *Cornish Review* as early as 1973, reflecting upon a visit to Upper Michigan. This was the final resting place of:

> Rosewarne
> Opie. Paull. Rule.
> Trethewey.
> Berryman.
> Curnow.
> Mineral is their true root, and now their night.
> Rickard is turned to rickardite, to a tellurite
> Of copper immortalised, Pearce to pearcite.
> This graveyard
> at Eagle Harbour

> by Superior's groundroar
> Makes heavy weather quelling the continuous drama
> Of Celtic hands and features, dry humour,
> Cough and gob of spit, a quiet snicker,
>              and cannot quell
>        their deep and daring harmony.[27]

Emigration had loomed large in the personal experiences of D.M. Thomas, shaping his Cornish identity and informing his work as a writer. His own parents had been out in America for a time, and his novel *The Birthstone* – written as he mourned the death of his mother and published in 1980 – betrayed this emigrant influence. The 'birthstone' of the novel's title is the Men-an-Tol, the mysterious holed stone on the moors of West Penwith, an ancient monument reputed to possess healing powers. By passing through the hole three times against the sun, it is said, the afflicted may be cured of rickets and much else. This belief underpins *The Birthstone*, a Freudian fantasy tale in which Thomas assembles a trio of unusual characters – each 'sick' in one way or another – and has them crawl through the Men-an-Tol. Significantly, two of these characters, Lola and her son Hector, an academic, are Americans from Grass Valley, who are in Cornwall to trace their family roots. As Thomas explained, 'They come from Grass Valley, a Cornish community in California. Influenced by my parent's life in Los Angeles, I have always been moved and fascinated by the blend of survival and change which is a marked feature of Cornish mining communities in the world.'[28]

Indeed, D.M. Thomas' more distant forebears had been a part of this Cornish emigration in its 19th-century heyday. William Thomas, born in Carnkie, near Redruth, in the early 1800s or thereabouts was a mine carpenter and had already been out in Latin America before deciding to emigrate from Cornwall to South Australia. He sailed from Plymouth to Port Adelaide in the *Royal Admiral* in 1838, along with many other Cornish bound for the infant colony. More than a century later, D.M. Thomas, a schoolboy, followed in his Antipodean footsteps, not to Adelaide but to Melbourne in neighbouring Victoria, part of that immediate post-Second World War British emigration, his parents looking to start life afresh. But intense homesickness overcame them, and within a few years they were back at Carnkie. Yet it was an experience that added a new dimension to D.M. Thomas, reinforcing that sense of a greater Cornwall beyond the seas, knowledge of which was indispensable if one was to truly understand Cornwall today. Years later, he was in South Australia, a literary celebrity, and visited a school in the country town of

Truro, named after its Cornish namesake. Here, he said, 'Cornwall seemed close ... Cornish miners had come in droves in the last [19th] century, and played a large part in founding the State. A High School class to which I read and talked had three children with solidly Cornish names, who knew all about their ancestry.'[29] His sister Lois was likewise affected and ended up in California: 'from California to Cornwall to Melbourne to California ... Her voice was American, though an expert might have detected hints of Australia and Cornwall'.[30]

To this literary activity was wedded a wider academic endeavour, with Cornwall established as a major centre for the study of the international Cornish identity. At the Institute of Cornish Studies – part of the University of Exeter in Cornwall but part-funded by Cornwall County Council and in 2004 included in the new Combined Universities in Cornwall campus at Tremough, Penryn – emigration formed the central part of an ambitious research strategy that ranged from statistical analysis of the origins and destinations of 19th-century Cornish migrants to the oral history of overseas Cornish communities. At Murdoch House in Redruth, Moira Tangye founded the Cornish-American Connection, constructing a major database of Cornish emigrants to the United States, a project developed by Sharron Schwartz into the still more ambitious Global Migration Programme. Indeed, Schwartz and Parker's *Lanner, A Cornish Mining Parish* (with an entire chapter devoted to the theme of emigration), published at the end of 1998, was evidence not just of a welcome shift from the antiquarian approach that has so often in the past retarded analysis and comparative interpretation in the writing of Cornish local history, but also of the central place that emigration had come to enjoy within the study of modern Cornwall.[31] Likewise, Bernard Deacon's *The Cornish Family: The Roots of Our Future*, published in 2004, had a great deal to say about the 'Great Emigration' and was as eagerly sought after by readers overseas as it was in Cornwall.[32]

In keeping with the demands and opportunities of the electronic age, much of both academic and popular contact within Cornish emigration studies is through the internet. Individual Cornish enthusiasts across the globe are in almost constant contact through email communication, creating what is in effect a Cornish 'virtual community' in which the international identity has become 'deterritorialised[33] (to use Robin Cohen's term), bridging the gap between the global and the local. Here globalisation, not least the power of communication and information technology, may be seen as an asset in the further enhancement of a Cornish international identity (or identities). As Cornwall itself is confronted continually by threats to its own territorial integrity and identity, from moves to combine the Cornwall and Devon Fire Services to the creation of a South West Regional Development Agency and a

South West European Parliamentary Constituency, it may be that it is in the 'deter-ritorialised virtual community' of the newly re-emergent Cornish diaspora that the future of Cornish ethnicity rests. More controversially, it might also be argued, as it was by Bernard Deacon, Andrew George (now Liberal Democrat MP for St Ives), and Ronald Perry in 1988, that Cornwall has since the 1960s suffered 'ethnocide by default',[34] the flow of young Cornish across the Tamar in search of education and jobs continuing unabated but with the residual Cornish population overwhelmed by the in-migration of 'middle-class, middle-aged-and middle-brow' in-migrants who have effectively imposed their standards on local society.[35] If this were true, then assertions of Cornish ethnic identity might indeed be expected to come from outside, reflecting the dynamism of the international Cornish in the face of the dis-abilities endured by the indigenous Cornish at home.

Be that as it may, there can be no doubt that the opinions, activities, aspirations and resources of the international Cornish will impact upon the future of Cornwall. The manner in which this should be managed and the extent to which it should happen was by the 1990s a matter of debate within the international Cornish com-munity. For example, Chris Dunkerley, a leading figure in the Cornish Association of New South Wales, stated that 'The new Cornwall can draw on all the old and newer influences in Cornwall and from us – the Cornish cousins overseas'.[36] For Dunkerley, this relationship between Cornwall and Australia was a direct one, unhindered by notions of 'Britishness', reflecting the changing nature of Australia and its relationship with the United Kingdom. In sharp contrast, however, for Gage McKinney, a past president of the California Cornish Cousins, it was the 'British' dimension that underpinned the relationship between the United States and Cornwall. Explaining his ambivalent attitude towards the 1997 commemoration of Cornwall's 1497 An Gof rebellion, McKinney emphasised the significance for many Americans (Cornish among them) of the 'special relationship' with Great Britain. He felt uncomfortable, he said, in lending support to any activity that might be construed as a gratuitous intrusion into the internal politics of another sovereign state – the United Kingdom.

Moreover, McKinney argued that the Cornish in the United States had become part of America's 'culture of success', enjoying to the full the fruits of American pros-perity, freedom and self-confidence. It was this very success, he added, that some-times made it difficult for Cornish-Americans to identify with the sense of loss and 'victim' status that continued to haunt some dimensions of popular culture in Cornwall. In the end, struggling to reconcile the outlook of Cornish-Americans with that of those in Cornwall who lived still in the shadow of massive emigration and de-industrialisation, McKinney decided that in commemorating the rebellion of 1497, 'What our cousins are celebrating in Cornwall ... is the endurance of the Cornish identity, the courage of a people who have known victory, but who have also withstood defeat and humiliation, and so have earned a deeper and more resilient identity than one based on success alone. We Americans know how to succeed, but we have not yet been tested to know whether we can endure. The Cornish are enduring and will endure'.[37]

In the aftermath of the horrific attack on the Twin Towers in New York on 11 September 2001, Americans may have felt that now too their endurance was being tested. In Cornwall, the years after 1997 had shown what such endurance – a tenacity born of stubborn pride and increasing self-confidence – might achieve. The acquisition of European regional status – and with it substantial European Union Objective 1 funding to tackle Cornwall's deep-seated economic problems – was evidence that sustained political activity could win significant results for Cornwall. This lesson was not lost on those who early in the new millennium founded a Cornish Constitutional Convention designed to achieve for Cornwall a devolutionary assembly similar to those recently afforded Wales and Scotland. In a startling demonstration of political mobilisation as well as a remarkable exhibition of renewed Cornish self-confidence, the convention swiftly organised a petition of 50,000 signatures demanding such an assembly. It remained to be seen whether the convention would persuade the British government that Cornwall should have its own place within the constitutional restructuring of the United Kingdom. But it did show that a new mood of optimism and determination was abroad in Cornwall in the early 21st century. As the political commentator Tom Nairn put it, 'Beyond the familiar Scotland-Wales-Ireland triad there now lies the question of Cornwall.'[38]

The extent to which the wider world had taken notice of this new mood was revealed, perhaps, in the American cartoon show *The Simpsons* where – as *The Independent* newspaper put it – the 'Cornish ... movement has probably realised its best publicity coup to date with the news that the eight year-old pointy-haired schoolgirl Lisa Simpson has become enamoured with their cause'.[39] In a four-minute television special broadcast in the United Kingdom on Christmas Day 2004, Lisa was shown charging around the Simpsons' home town of Springfield, USA brandishing Cornish slogans and shouting in the Cornish language, 'Rydhsys rag Kernow lemmyn!' – Freedom for Cornwall now! – and 'Kernow bys Vyken' – Cornwall For Ever![40] The international Cornish identity had come of age – or at least had come full circle – the globalising force of American mass culture now a transnational vehicle for asserting Cornwall and the Cornish.

# NOTES AND REFERENCES

## Introduction

1. This is the opinion of Dudley Baines, *Migration in a Mature Economy: Emigration and Internal Migration in England and Wales, 1861-1900*, Cambridge University Press, Cambridge, 1985, pp.157-159.

2. A.L. Rowse, *The Cornish in America*, Macmillan, London, 1969, repub. Dyllansow Truran, Redruth, 1991, p.viii.

3. The historiography of the 'Great Emigration' is now considerable. Volumes especially worthy of note include: A.C. Todd, *The Cornish Miner in America*, Arthur H. Clark Co., Spokane (Washington), 2nd ed., 1995; A.C. Todd, *The Search for Silver: Cornish Miners in Mexico, 1824-1947*, Lodenek Press, Padstow, 1977; A.C. Todd and David James, *Ever Westward the Land*, University of Exeter Press, Exeter, 1986; John Rowe, *The Hard-Rock Men: Cornish Immigrants and the North American Mining Frontier*, Liverpool University Press, Liverpool, 1974; Oswald Pryor, *Australia's Little Cornwall*, Rigby, Adelaide, 1962, repub. Seal Books, Adelaide, 1973; Mandie Robinson, *Cap'n Ancock: Ruler of Australia's Little Cornwall*, Rigby, Adelaide, 1978; Roslyn Paterson, *Thankyou Walter Watson Hughes: Essays on Northern Yorke Peninsula*, Gould Books, Adelaide, 1993; Diana C.Hancock and Roslyn M. Paterson, *Cousin Jacks & Jennys: The Cornish in South Australia*, Cornish Association of South Australia, Adelaide, 1995; Ian Auhl, *Burra Sketchbook*, Rigby, Adelaide, 1969; Ian Auhl and Denis Marfleet, *Australia's Earliest Mining Era: South Australia 1841-1851*, Rigby, Adelaide, 1975, repub. Axiom, Adelaide, 1988; Ian Auhl, *Burra and District: A Pictorial Memoir*, Lynton Publications, Adelaide, 1975; Ian Auhl, *The Story of the Monster Mine: The Burra Burra Mine and Its Townships, 1845-1877*, Investigator Press, Adelaide 1986; Jim Faull, *Cornish Heritage: A Miner's Story*, Lutheran Publishing House, Adelaide, 1980; Jim Faull, *The Cornish in Australia*, AE Press, Melbourne, 1983; Anne Colman, 'Colonial Cornish: Cornish Immigrants in Victoria, 1865-1880'; unpub. MA thesis, University of Melbourne, 1985; Patricia Lay, 'One and All: The Cornish in Nineteenth-Century New South Wales', Heritage 2000 Plus, Qeanbeyan (NSW), 1998, also MA thesis, Australian National University, 1992; Gage McKinney, *A High and Holy Place: A Mining Camp Church at New Almaden*, New Almaden County Quicksilver Park Association, New Almaden, 1997; Richard Dawe, *Cornish Pioneers in South Africa*, Cornish Hillside Publications, St Austell, 1998; Philip Payton, 'The Cornish in South Australia: Their Influence and Experience from Immigration to Assimilation, 1836-1936', unpub. PhD thesis, University of Adelaide, 1978; Philip Payton, *Pictorial History of Australia's Little Cornwall*, Rigby, Adelaide, 1978; Philip Payton, *The Cornish Miner in Australia: Cousin Jack Down Under*, Dyllansow Truran, Redruth, 1984; Philip Payton, *Cornish Carols From Australia*, Dyllansow Truran, Redruth, 1984; Philip Payton, *The Cornish Farmer in Australia*, Dyllansow Truran, 1988. See also Ruth Hopkins, *Where Now Cousin Jack?*, Bendigo Bicentennial Committee, Bendigo, 1988; Ruth Hopkins, Cousin Jack, *Man for the Times: A History of the Cornish People in Victoria*, Hopkins, Bendigo, 1994; Sharron P. Schwartz, 'Cornish Migration to Latin America: A Global and Transnational Perspective', unpub. PhD thesis, University of Exeter, 2003.

4. From 'The Emigrant's Farewell' by Thomas Thorpe, 1836; I am indebted to Bill Jones for drawing this composition to my attention.

5. Dudley Baines, *Emigration from Europe 1815-1930*, Macmillan, London, 1991, pp.7-8.

6. Dai Smith, *Wales! Wales?*, George Allen & Unwin, London, 1984, p.17.

7. William D. Jones, *Wales in America: Scranton and the Welsh 1860-1920*, University of Wales Press, Cardiff, 1993; Bob Reece, 'The Welsh in Australian Historical Writing', *Australian Studies*, No.4, December 1990, p.96.

8. T.M. Devine, 'The Paradox of Scottish Emigration', in T.M. Devine (ed.), *Scottish Emigration and Scottish Society*, John Donald, Edinburgh, 1992, pp.1-15.

9. Patrick O'Farrell, *The Irish in Australia*, New South Wales University Press, Sydney, 1986, revised ed. 1993, p.1.

10. Bernard Deacon, 'Proto-industrialization and Potatoes: A Revised Narrative for Nineteenth-Century Cornwall', in Philip Payton (ed.), *Cornish Studies*: Five, University of Exeter Press, Exeter, 1997, p.80.

11. Christine Kineally, *This Great Calamity: The Irish Famine 1845-52*, Roberts Rinehart, Boulder (Colorado), 1995, p.344.

12. A.K.Hamilton Jenkin, *The Cornish Miner*, 1927, new ed. David & Charles, Newton Abbot, 1972, p.321.

13. Gill Burke, 'The Impact of Industrial Change on Working Class Family Life in the Mining Districts of Nineteenth-Century Cornwall', *Bulletin of the Society for the Study of Labour History*, 48, 1984, p.14.

14. Philip Payton, '"Reforming Thirties" and "Hungry Forties": The Genesis of Cornwall's Emigration Trade', in Philip Payton (ed.), *Cornish Studies: Four*, University of Exeter Press, Exeter, 1996.

15. Bernard Deacon, *Migration and the Mining Industry in East Cornwall in the Mid-Nineteenth Century*, University of Exeter, Exeter, 1985, pp.12-13.

16. *West Briton*, 24 March 1848; *Burra Record*, 25 March 1890.

17. M.G. Dickinson, 'Mining Activity and Cornish Migration at Mary Tavy', *Devon and Cornwall Notes and Queries*, 36, pp.5-8; Tom Greaves, 'Adventures with Fiery Dragons: The Cornish Tinner in Devon from the 15th to the 20th Century', *Journal of the Trevithick Society*, 19, 1992; A.K. Hamilton Jenkin, *The Mines of Devon: Vol. 1 - The Southern Area*, David & Charles, Newton Abbot, 1974.

18. W. Phelps, *History and Antiquities of Somersetshire*, 1836, Vol. 1, p.18.

19. *Gentleman's Magazine*, Pt. 1, 1794, p.400.

20. J.W. Gough, *The Mines of Mendip*, Clarendon, Oxford, 1930, p.188; Roger Burt, *The British Lead Mining Industry*, Dyllansow Truran, Redruth, 1984, p.195.

21. W.J. Lewis, *Lead Mining in Wales*, University of Wales Press, Cardiff, 1967, p.98, p.164, pp.176-177, p.214, p.248, pp.264-265.

22. Gill Burke, 'The Cornish Diaspora in the Nineteenth Century', in Shula Marks and Peter Richardson (eds.), *International Labour Migration: Historical Perspectives*, Temple Smith, London, 1984, p.59, citing R. Palmer, A Touch on the Times: Songs of Social Change 1770-1914, London, 1974, p.130.

23. Baines, 1985, pp.242-243.

24. Mark Brayshay, 'The Demography of Three West

Cornwall Mining Communities 1851-1871: A Society in Decline', unpub. PhD thesis, University of Exeter, 1977, p.250.

25. A.L. Rowse, *A Cornish Childhood*, Jonathan Cape, London, 1942, p.23.

26. Claude Berry, *Cornwall*, Robert Hale, London, 1949, pp.4-5.

27. Claude Berry, *Portrait of Cornwall*, Robert Hale, London, 1963, 2nd ed. 1971, p.17.

28. Burke, 'Cornish Diaspora', 1984, p.72.

29. Rowse, 1942, p.23

30. See Ronald M. James, 'Defining the Group: Nineteenth-Century Cornish on the North American Mining Frontier', in Philip Payton (ed.), *Cornish Studies: Two*, University of Exeter Press, Exeter, 1994.

31. Horst Rossler, 'Constantine Stonemasons in Search of Work Abroad, 1870-1900', in Payton (ed.), 1994, p.77.

32. Rossler, 1994, p.63.

33. *Granite Cutters' Journal*, December 1888.

34. *Yorke's Peninsula Advertiser*, 29 July 1873; *People's Weekly*, 24 June 1899; H.T. Burgess (ed.), *The Cyclopedia of South Australia*, 2 Vols., Alfred G. Selway, Adelaide, 1907, Vol.2, p.546; W. Frederick Morrison, *The Aldine History of South Australia*, Aldine Publishing Co., Sydney & Adelaide, 1890, p.641; *Australian Christian Commonwealth*, 27 September 1912; 17 June 1910.

35. Burgess, 1907, Vol. 1, pp.351-352; *People's Weekly*, 8 April 1905; 8 January 1910; 20 January 1912; 28 April 1917; 5 May 1923.

36. Greaves, 1992, pp.14-15.

37. *People's Weekly*, 9 June 1906.

38. *Yorke's Peninsula Advertiser*, 27 February 1883.

39. *People's Weekly*, 4 April 1908.

40. Sharron Schwartz and Roger H. Parker, *Lanner: A Cornish Mining Parish*, Halsgrove, Tiverton, 1998, p.152.

41. Schwartz and Parker, 1998, p.152.

42. *Tales of Hardrock Miners in the Northern Mines* (video), Empire Mine Park Association, nd c.1995.

43. *Minutes of Committee Meetings of the Cornish Association of South Australia*, 30 August 1930, 27 September 1930.

44. *Cornish World*, No.16, Mar-Apr-May 1998.

45. *West Briton*, 23 January 1879.

46. *Cornubian*, 31 January 1902.

47. Shyrle Pedlar Hacker, *A Gold Miner's Daughter:*

# NOTES AND REFERENCES

*Memoirs of a Mountain Childhood*, Johnson Books, Boulder (Colorado), 1996, p.7.

48. Hacker, 1996, p.28.

49. Phyllis Somerville, *Not Only In Stone*, 1942, repub. Seal Books, Adelaide, 1973, Dustcover Notes.

50. Lyn Bryant, 'The Cornish Family', in Philip Payton (ed.), *Cornwall Since The War: The Contemporary History of a European Region*, Dyllansow Truran/Institute of Cornish Studies, Redruth, 1992, p.186.

51. *Cornubian*, 2 September 1892.

52. Todd, 1967, p.19.

53. Bernard Deacon, 'Cornish Emigration', unpub. paper, 1993, p.5.

54. Baines, 1985, pp.157-159.

## Chapter 1: A Culture of Mobility

1. James Whetter, *Cornwall in the 17th Century: An Economic History of Kernow*, Lodenek Press, Padstow, 1974, p.175.

2. A. L. Rowse, *The Cornish in America*, Macmillan, London, 1969, repub. Dyllansow Truran, Redruth, 1991, p.38.

3. See Royal B.Hassrick, *The Colourful Story of North American Indians*, Octupus, Indians, London, 1975, p.33.

4. A. L. Rowse, *The Expansion of Elizabethan England*, Macmillan, London, 1955, repub. Cardinal, London, 1973, pp.232-236; see also A. L. Rowse, *Sir Richard Grenville of the Revenge*, Jonathan Cape, London, 1937, pp.238-243.

5. Rowse, 1955 & 1973, p.236.

6. Alistair Cooke, *Alistair Cooke's America*, BBC, London, 1973, pp.62-63.

7. Rowse, 1969 & 1991, p.41.

8. Barry E.Tracy, 'Maine and New Hampshire', *Cornish World*, No.15, Dec-Jan-Feb 1997-98.

9. See Philip Payton, *Cornwall*, Alexander Associates, Fowey, 1996, Chapter 7.

10. Anne Duffin, *Faction and Faith: Politics and Religion of the Cornish Gentry Before the Civil War*, University of Exeter Press, Exeter, 1996.

11. Rowse, 1969 & 1991, p.44

12. A. L. Rowse, *Four Caroline Portraits*, Duckworth, London, 1993, p.97.

13. John Keast, *The Story of Fowey*, 1950, repub. Dyllansow Truran, Redruth, 1983, p.58.

14. See R.P.Stearns, *The Strenuous Puritan: Hugh Peter 1598-1660*, University of Illinois Press, Chicago, 1954, p.98.

15. Stearns, 1954, p.162.

16. William Curnow, 'Cornwall... In Pennsylvania', *Cornish World*, No.8, Mar-Apr-May 1996.

17. Rowse, 1969 & 1991, p.101.

18. Rowse, 1969 & 1991, p.109.

19. Cited in Rowse, 1969 & 1991, p.104.

20. Linda Colley, *Britons: Forging the Nation: 1707-1837*, Pimlico, London, 1994.

21. June Palmer, *Cornwall, The Canaries and The Atlantic: The Letter Book of Valentine Enys 1704-1719*, Institute of Cornish Studies, Truro, 1998.

22. Lady Boscawen's phrase, cited in Nicholas Rodger, '"A Little Navy of Your Own Making": Admiral.Boscawen and the Cornish Connection in the Royal Navy', in Michael Duffy (ed.), *Parameters of British Naval Power, 1650-1850*, University of Exeter Press, Exeter, 1992, p.86.

23. For information on the Trevenen family, I am indebted to Ann Trevenen Jenkin, former Grand Bard of Cornwall.

24. Alan Moorehead, *The Fatal Impact: The Invasion of the South Pacific 1767-1840*, 1966, repub. Mead & Beckett, Sydney, 1987, pp.30-31.

25. Cited in Moorehead, 1966 & 1987, p.58

26. See William Bligh, *The Mutiny On Board HMS Bounty*, 1787, repub. Pageminster Press, Guildford, 1981.

27. Manning Clark, *A History of Australia, 1962-87*, repub. Chatto & Windus (abridged by Michael Cathcart), London, 1994, p.39.

28. Cited in Robert Hughes, *The Fatal Shore: A History of the Transportation of Convicts to Australia 1787-1868*, Pan, London, 1988, p.290.

29. Hughes, 1988, p.292.

30. Hughes, 1988, p.111.

31. Cited in Hughes, 1988, p.84.

32. I.D.Spreadbury, *Famous Men and Women of Cornish Birth: 100 Lives*, Kingston, Mevagissey, 1972, p.39.

33. Cited in Martyn Brown, *Australia Bound: The Story of West Country Connections 1688-1888*, Ex Libris Press, Bradford-on Avon, 1988, p.52.

34. Hughes, 1988, p.99.

35. Clark, 1962-87 & 1994, p.28.

36. Clark, 1962-87 & 1994, p.32.

37. Cited in Brown, 1988, p.74.

38. Cited in Hughes, 1988, pp.69-70, and in Brown, 1988, p.42.

39. Philip Payton, 'The Cornish', in James Jupp (ed.), *The Australian People: An Encyclopedia of The Nation, Its People and Their Origins*, Angus Robertson, Sydney, 1988, p.327.

40. Judith Cook, *To Brave Every Danger*, Dyllansow Truran, Redruth, 1994.

41. Hughes, 1988, p.205.

42. Cited in Hughes, 1988, p.207.

43. Cited in Hughes, 1988, p.207.

44. Cited in Hughes, 1988, p.209.

45. Hannah Elwin, 'James Ruse: Cornishman and Pioneer Farmer', *Cornish Banner*, No.53, August 1988.

46. Elwin, 1988, p.12.

47. W.A.Tench, *A Complete Account of Port Jackson in New South Wales*, London, 1793, pp.80-81.

48. Tench, 1793, p.81.

49. Hughes, 1988, p.107.

50. Hughes, 1988, p.106.

51. Cited in George Nadel, *Australia's Colonial Culture*, Cheshire, Melbourne, 1957, p.26.

52. Alison Adburgham, *A Radical Aristocrat*, Tabb House, Padstow, 1990.

53. Cited in Adburgham, 1990, p.54.

## Chapter 2: The Rage for Emigration

1. James Martin Hosking, *To America and Back with James Hosking, 1811*, Hosking, Penzance, 1970, p.3.

2. Douglas Selleck, *Another Cornish Bedside Book*, Dyllansow Truran, Redruth, 1992, p.83.

3. Selleck, 1992, p.84.

4. *Royal Cornwall Gazette*, 3 July 1819.

5. *Western Luminary*, 26 May 1818.

6. *Royal Cornwall Gazette*, 22 May 1819.

7. *West Briton*, 23 June 1820.

8. *West Briton*, 10 March 1837.

9. *West Briton*, 6 April 1832.

10. *West Briton*, 17 February 1843.

11. A.C. Todd and David James, *Ever Westward the Land*, University of Exeter Press, Exeter, 1986, p.9.

12. A. C. Todd, *The Cornish Miner in America*, Bradford Barton, Truro, 1967, 2nd ed. Arthur H. Clark, Spokane (Washington), 1995, p.37.

13. Margaret James-Korany, 'Blue Books as Sources for Cornish Emigration History', in Philip Payton (ed.), *Cornish Studies: One*, University of Exeter Press, Exeter, 1993, pp.34-36.

14. Piers Brendon, *Hawker of Morwenstow*, Anthony Mott, London, 1975, p.171.

15. Brendon, 1975, p.173.

16. John Betjeman (selected by Candida Lycett Green), *Coming Home: An Anthology of Prose*, Methuen, London, 1997, p.187.

17. A. L. Rowse, *A Cornish Anthology*, 1968, repub. Alison Hodge, Penzance, 1982, p.6.

18. Michael J.L. Wickes, *The Westcountry Preachers: A History of the Bible Christians 1815-1907*, Wickes, Bideford, 1987, p.52.

19. Donald Meek, 'The Fellowship of Kindred Minds: Some Religious Aspects of Kinship and Emigration from the Scottish Highlands in the 19th Century', in *Hands Across the Water: Emigration from Northern Scotland to North America - Proceedings of the 6th Annual Conference of the Scottish Family History Societies*, Aberdeen and North East Scotland Family History Society, Aberdeen, 1995, p.19.

20. A. L. Rowse, *The Cornish in America*, Macmillan, London, 1969, repub. Dyllansow Truran, Redruth, 1991, p.111.

21. Jean Saxe Jolliffe (ed.), *Our Back Pages: Obituaries of Cornish and North Devonshire Settlers of Jefferson, Walworth and Waukesha Counties*, Wisconsin, USA, Vol. 1, Jolliffe, Brookfield (Wis.), 1992.

22. George Davey, 'Diary of an Emigrant', 1850, transcribed by John M. Schoenknecht, *Landmark*, Vol.39., No.3,4, Autumn/Winter 1996.

23. Davey, 1850 & 1996, p.8.

24. Davey, 1850 & 1996, pp.4-5.

25. Richard Rundell, 'The 1850 Voyage of the Belle', 1850, *Landmark*, Vol.39., No.3,4, Autumn/Winter 1996.

26. Palmyra Enterprise (Wisconsin), 2 April 1908; 12 August 1909; 13 December 1917.

27. Todd, 1967 & 1995, p.37.

28. Keith Skues, *Cornish Heritage*, Werner Shaw, London, p.238.

29. *Royal Cornwall Gazette*, 20 July 1819.

30. Graham B. Dickason, *Cornish Immigrants to South Africa*, Balkema, Cape Town, 1978, pp.18-21; Richard D. Dawe, *Cornish Pioneers in South Africa: 'Gold and Diamonds, Copper and Blood'*, Cornish Hillside, St Austell, 1998, pp.1-2. 'Cornish Assisted Immigrants in New South Wales 1837-1877', in Philip Payton (ed.), *Cornish Studies: Three*, University of Exeter Press,

# NOTES AND REFERENCES

Exeter, 1995, pp.41-42.

31. *West Briton*, 1 September 1820.

32. *Cornish Post*, 8 September 1910; Dawe, 1998, p.1.

33. *Western Luminary*, June 1830, cited in Basil Greenhill and Ann Giffard, *Westcountrymen in Prince Edward's Isle: A Fragment of the Great Migration*, David & Charles, Newton Abbot, 1967, p.133.

34. Western Luminary, 21 July 1825.

35. *West Briton*, 5 April 1844.

36. *West Briton*, 7 April 1854.

37. See Greenhill & Giffard, 1967.

38. Greenhill & Giffard, 1967, p.188.

39. Greenhill & Giffard, 1967, p.103.

40. *Royal Gazette* (Charlottetown), 1 June 1830; Greenhill & Giffard, 1967, p.103.

41. *North Devon Journal*, 14 April 1831.

42. Greenhill & Giffard, pp.145-146.

43. James-Korany, 1993.

44. *West Briton*, 27 May 1842.

45. John Bartlett, *Ships of North Cornwall*, Tabb House, Padstow, 1996, p.84.

46. Bartlett, 1996, Chapter 12 'Emigrant Ships and Square Riggers', pp.84-90.

47. Cited in James-Korany, 1993, p.40.

48. Cited in Wickes, 1987, pp.57-58.

49. Wickes, 1987, p.59.

50. Wickes, 1987, p.59; Cedric Appleby, 'Thomas Greenway, Prime Minister; John Greenway, Bible Christian Minister', *Journal of the Cornish Methodist Historical Society*, Vol.9, No.6, 1996, pp.164-171.

51. *West Briton*, 10 February 1832.

52. Margaret James-Korany, 'One Camborne ... Two Cambornes', unpub. paper, May 1992.

53. *West Briton*, 12 April 1839.

54. Patricia Lay, 'Not What They Seemed? Cornish assisted Immigrants in New South Wales 1837-1877' in Philip Payton (ed.), *Cornish Studies: Three*, University of Exeter Press, Exeter, 1995, pp. 41-42

55. Lay, 1995, pp.53-56.

56. Archive Offices of New South Wales (AONSW) Shipping Lists 9/6212, 29 December 1856; cited in Lay, 1995, p.54.

57. AONSW 9/6212, 19 January 1857; cited in Lay, 1995, pp.54-55.

58. Lay, 1995.

59. *West Briton*, 12 May 1843; 28 July 1843.

60. James-Korany, 1993, ppp.40-41.

61. John Langton and R.J. Morris, *Atlas of Industrializing Britain 1780-1914*, Methuen, London, 1986, p.161.

62. Lay, 1995.

63. Lay, 1995, pp.43-48.

64. E. Gibbon Wakefield, *A View of the Art of Colonization*, 1849, repub. Kelley, New York, 1969.

65. Henry Cornish, *Under the Southern Cross*, Higginbotham, Madras, 1880, repub. Penguin, Melbourne, 1975, p.50; Douglas Pike, *Paradise of Dissent: South Australia 1829-1857*, Longmans, London, 1957.

66. South Australian [State] Archives (SAA) PRG 125, *Papers Relating to the Stephens Family*, Letter, Stephens to Risdale, 16 May 1949.

67. John Stephens, *The Land of Promise: Being an Authentic and Impartial History of the Rise and Progress of the New British Province of South Australia*, Smith Elder, London, 1839, p.i.

68. Stephens, 1839, p.46.

69. Stephens, 1839, p.85.

70. John Blackett, *History of South Australia: A Romantic and Successful Experiment in Colonization*, Hussey & Gillingham, Adelaide, 1911, p.448.

71. *West Briton*, 6 December 1839.

72. *West Briton*, 13 September 1839.

73. *West Briton*, 30 August 1839.

74. *West Briton*, 30 August 1839.

75. *West Briton*, 13 September 1839.

76. *South Australian Record*, 11 September 1839; 30 May 1840; *South Australian News*, September 1847.

77. SAA PRG 174, *George Fife Angas Papers*, S.A. Colonisation Commissioners, 666, Letter from Marmaduke Laurimer to his mother in Falmouth.

78. SAA PRG 174, 666.

79. *West Briton*, 29 April 1840.

80. *South Australian Record*, 11 July 1838.

81. *South Australian Record*, 10 October 1838.

82. *South Australian Record*, 2 December 1839.

83. *West Briton*, 20 September. 1.839.

84. SAA D4718L, *Journal of a Voyage to South Australia* by George Richards.

85. Emigration Poster cl839, Courtney Library, Royal Institution of Cornwall; D.B. Barton, *Essays in Cornish Mining History: Volume 1*, Bradford Barton, Truro, 1968, p.72.

86. SAA 1529, *Alphabetical Index to Applications for Free Passage from the United Kingdom to South Australia, 1836-40*.

87. SAA PRG 174, Letter from James Sawle to his Brother.

88. Alison Adburgham, *A Radical Aristocrat*, Tabb House, Padstow, 1990, pp.54-55.

89. I am indebted to Mr Ian Wilson of Auckland, New Zealand, for this information.

90. *West Briton*, 28 February 1840; 6 March 1840.

91. P.A.J. McNicholas, 'The "Cinderella" of New Zealand: Race and Class in New Plymouth 1840-1858', unpub. MA thesis, Victoria University of Wellington, 1996, p.164.

92. *West Briton*, 22 May 1857; see also John Rowe, 'William Woon: A Cornish Missionary in Early Nineteenth-Century New Zealand', *Cornish Banner*, No.63, February 1991, pp16-19.

93. *West Briton*, 20 August 1852.

94. 'Letter from New Zealand' (contributed by Sheila Lightbody), *Journal of the Cornwall Family History Society*, No.56, June 1990, p.31.

## Chapter 3: Bonanzas and Bugbears – Latin America

1. James Hodge, *Richard Trevithick*, Shire, London, 1995; see also James Hodge, 'Richard Trevithick: His Place in Engineering History', *Journal of the Trevithick Society*, No.1, 1973.

2. Rodman Wilson Paul, *Mining Frontiers of the Far West 1848-1880*, Holt, Rinehart & Winston, New York, 1963, p.19.

3. George Henwood (Roger Burt, ed.), *Cornwall's Mines and Miners*, Bradford Barton, Truro, 1972, p.118-121.

4. Sharron Schwartz and Roger Parker, *Lanner: A Cornish Mining Parish*, Halsgrove, Tiverton, p.159.

5. Henwood (Burt), 1972, p.163.

6. John Basset, *Observations on Cornish Mining*, Rodwell, London, 1842.

7. *Royal Cornwall Gazette*, 25 May 1849.

8. *South Australian Gazette and Colonial Register*, 20 September 1845.

9. John Rowe, *Cornwall in the Age of the Industrial Revolution*, Liverpool University Press, Liverpool, 1953, new ed. Cornish Hillside, St Austell, 1993, pp.145-146.

10. For a summary of Taylor's Mexican activities, see Roger Burt, *John Taylor: Mining Entrepreneur and Engineer, 1779-1863*, Moorland, Buxton, 1977, pp.39-47; for the only general account of the Cornish in Mexico, see A.C. Todd, *The Search for Silver: Cornish Miners in Mexico 1824-1948*, Lodenek Press, Padstow, 1977.

11. Todd, 1977, p.34.

12. *Western Luminary*, 18 January 1825.

13. *West Briton*, 23 March 1838; 25 September 1846.

14. *West Briton*, 26 March 1824.

15. *Western Luminary*, 22 February 1825.

16. *West Briton*, 1 April 1825.

17. Todd, 1977, p.44.

18. *West Briton*, 7 April 1826.

19. Todd, 1977, p.36.

20. Todd, 1977, p.42.

21. *West Briton*, 7 October 1825.

22. Todd. 1977, p.46.

23. *West Briton*, 7 April 1826.

24. *Western Luminary*, 14 February 1826.

25. Todd, 1977, p.46.

26. Todd, 1977, p.54.

27. Todd, 1977, p.62.

28. Todd, 1977, p.78.

29. Todd, 1977, pp.78-79.

30. Edwin W.J. Rich, 'A Mexican Tragedy', *Journal of the Cornwall Family History Society*, No.5, September 1977, p.7.

31. Todd, 1977, p.89.

32. Todd, 1977, p.109.

33. *Mining Journal*, 14 March 1868.

34. *Mining Journal*, 21 November 1874.

35. Bernard Holowood, *Cornish Engineers*, Holman, Camborne, 1951, p.38.

36. For details of John Williams Goldsworthy I am indebted to current members of the Goldsworthy family.

37. *Blackwell Papers*; 'List of Employees and dependents of the Real-del-Monte Mining Company in March 1859', from book *Correspondencia General*, Tomo 62 (Maro-1859) 4th Sept 1856-5th April 1865; 'List of Persons Working for the Real del Monte Mining Company on the Safety/identification Lists for the Year 1859'; Mineral Del Monte December 29 1866 - From *Journal 'E'27 January 1866 to 29 June 1869*, 'Pormenor del Saldo de Particulars Haber'.

38. S. T. Dudley, 'Inscriptions on Headstones of English Cemetery at Real del Monte', unpub. paper, 1987.

39. *Blackwell Papers*, List of Remittances, March 16th 1867', *Mineral Del Monte*.

40. Geoffrey Blainey, *The Tyranny of Distance*, Sun Books, Melbourne, 1966.

41. Cedric Oates, 'William John Oates, 1859-1935', *Journal of the Cornwall Family History Society*, No.38, December 1985.

42. Material from the diary of James Skewes informs an important element of the overseas sections in Keith Skues, *Cornish Heritage*, Werner Shaw, London, 1983.,

43. Skues, 1983, p.221.

44. Skues, 1983, p.226.

45. Skues, 1983, p.227.

46. Skues, 1983, p.228.

47. Skues, 1983, pp.230-231.

48. C.C. James, 'Cornwall and Mexico', *Old Cornwall*, No.IV, Vol.10, Winter 1949, pp.249-352.

49. Todd, 1977, p.5.

50. Remarkably, the only serious study of the Cornish in Cuba to date is Michael Tangye, 'Cornish Miners in Cuba 1836-1838', in Terry Knight (ed.), *Old Redruth: Original Studies of the Town's History*, Redruth Old Cornwall Society, Redruth, 1992. Additionally, there are some references to Cuba in J.R. Polglase, 'South American Demand Expressed in Cornwall 1810-1920', unpub. MS, 1986 (Cornish Studies Library, Redruth).

51. Royal Institution of Cornwall (RIC), *Alfred Jenkin Letter Books*, Out Letters HJ/1/17; see also Frank Michell, *Annals of an Ancient Cornish Town - Redruth*, 1978, repub. Dyllansow Truran, Redruth, 1985, p.109.

52. *West Briton*, 29 November 1839; 7 January 1842.

53. *Royal Cornwall Gazette*, 7 February 1851.

54. Tangye, 1992, p.22.

55. Tangye, 1992, p.24.

56. Tangye, 1992, p.24.

57. Tangye, 1992, p.26.

58. *West Briton*, 29 November 1839.

59. *Martin Papers*, Letter from William Toll to his Wife, 13 September 1849.

60. Philip McColl, 'Virgin Copper', *Cornish World*, No.15, Dec/Jan/Feb., 1997/98.

61. Rowe, 1953 & 1993, p.309.

62. William W. Culver and Comel J. Reinhart, 'The Decline of a Mining Region and Mining Policy: Chilean Copper in the Nineteenth Century', in Thomas Greaves and William Culver (eds.), *Miners and Mining in the Americas*, Manchester University Press, Manchester, 1985, p.70.

63. John Mayo, 'Commerce, Credit and Control in Chilean Copper Mining Before 1880', in Greaves & Culver, 1985, p.32.

64. Edmund Newell, '"Copperopolis": The Rise and Fall of the Copper Industry in the Swansea District, 1826-1921', *Business History*, Vol.32, No.3, July 1990.

65. Mayo, 1985, p.44.

66. *Chilean Times*, 1880, cited in Mayo, 1985, p.33.

67. *West Briton*, 4 February 1825.

68. *West Briton*, 22 July 1825.

69. *Western Luminary*, 7 February 1826.

70. Polglase, 1986.

71. *West Briton*, 15 March 1897.

72. Polglase, 1986, pp.44-45.

73. *West Briton*, 24 August 1893.

74. South Australian [State] Archives (SAA) PRG 96, *Oswald Pryor Papers*.

75. *Western Luminary*, 1 March 1825.

76. *West Briton*, 9 January 1852.

77. *West Briton*, 6 January 1826; 21 April 1826.

78. *West Briton*, 10 November 1826.

79. *Western Luminary*, 5 February 1827.

80. *West Briton*, 17 April 1827; *Western Luminary*, 22 April 1828.

81. Eakin Marshall C., 'The Role of British Capital in the Development of Brazilian Gold Mining', in Greaves & Culver (eds.), 1985, p.13.

82. C.C. James, 'Some Notes on Cornish Miners in Brazil', *Old Cornwall*, Vol.V, No.5, 1954.

83. *West Briton*, 13 October 1826.

84. *West Briton*, 2 November 1827; 6 June 1828.

85. *West Briton*, 25 July 1828.

86. *West Briton*, 23 September 1831; 19 June 1835; 5 February 1836.

87. *West Briton*, 23 August 1844.

88. Eakin, 1985, p.13.

89. James, 1954, p.23.

90. D.M. Jones, 'Morro Velho – A Cornish Community in Brazil', *Journal of the Cornwall Family History Society*, No.55, March 1990.

91. *West Briton*, 31 August 1922; see also Polglase, 1986, p.36.

92. I am indebted to Joy Brealy for details of the Trethewey family in Brazil; Polglase, p.18.

93. Claire Leith, 'A South American Adventure with Francis Oats and his son Francis Freathy Oats in 1901', *Journal of the Royal Institution of Cornwall*, new series II, Vol.ll, Part 3, 1996.

94. Sharron P. Schwartz, 'Cornish Migration to Latin America: A Global and Transnational Perspective', unpub. PhD thesis, University of Exeter, 2003.

### Chapter 4: From Famine to Frontier – The Hungry Forties and the First American Mining Boom

1. Philip Payton, 'Re-inventing Celtic Australia: Notions of Celtic identity from the Colonial Period to the Era of Multi-culturalism', *Australian Studies*, Vol. 12, No.2, Winter 1997, p.81.

2. Tanya Louise Creswell, Emigration from the Western Isles of Scotland and Cornwall in the Mid-Nineteenth Century: A Comparison', unpub. MA dissertation, University of Aberdeen, 1995, p.23.

3. For example, see TM. Devine, *The Great Highland Famine: Hunger, Emigration and the Scottish Highlands in the Nineteenth Century*, John Donald, Edinburgh, 1988; Christine Kineally, *This Great Calamity: The Irish Famine 1845-52*, Roberts Rinehart, Boulder (Colorado), 1995.

4. Todd Gray, *Harvest Failure in Cornwall and Devon: The Book of Orders and Corn Surveys of 1623 and 1630-1*, Institute of Cornish Studies, Redruth, 1992, p.xi.

5. Mark Overton, 'The 1801 Crop Returns for Cornwall', in Michael Havinden (ed.), *Husbandry and Marketing in the South West 1500-1800*, Exeter Papers in Economic History No.8, University of Exeter, Exeter, 1973, p.56.

6. John Rowe, *Cornwall in the Age of the Industrial Revolution*, Liverpool University Press, Liverpool, 1953, new ed. Cornish Hillside, St Austell, 1993, p.231.

7. *West Briton*, 17 July 1846.

8. *South Australian Register*, 20 March 1847.

9. *South Australian Register*, 20 March 1847.

10. J.R. Leifchild, *Cornwall: Its Mines and Miners*, 1857, repub. Frank Cass, London, 1968, p.270.

11. F. E. Halliday, *A History of Cornwall*, Duckworth, London, 1953, repub. 1963, p.289.

12. Piers Brendon, *Hawker of Morwenstow*, Anthony Mott, London, 1975, p.71.

13. George Henwood (Roger Burt, ed.), *Cornish Mines and Miners*, Bradford Barton, Truro, 1972, p.72.

14. *West Briton*, 25 February 1831.

15. *West Briton*, 21 May 1847.

16. Thomas Oliver, *Autobiography of a Cornish Miner*, Camborne Printing and Stationery Co., Camborne, 1914, pp.12-13.

17. Oliver, 1914, p.12.

18. A.C. Todd, *The Cornish Miner in America*, Bradford Barton, 1967, repub., Arthur H. Clark, Spokane (Washington), 1995; A.L. Rowse, *The Cornish in America*, Macmillan, London, 1969, repub. Dyllansow Truran, Redruth, 1991; John Rowe, *The Hard-Rock Men: Cornish Immigrants and the North American Mining Frontier*, Liverpool University Press, Liverpool, 1974.

19. Rowe, 1974, pp.38-39.

20. *Devon and Cornwall Notes and Queries*, July 1962, p.60.

21. Todd, 1967 & 1995; pp28-29; Rowse, 1969 & 1991, pp.201-202; Rowe, 1974, p.39.

22. L.A. Copeland, 'The Cornish in South-west Wisconsin', *Wisconsin Historical Collections*, Vol. XIV, 1898, pp.319-320.

23. Rowe, 1974, pp.43-44.

24. Mark H. Knipping and Korinne K. Oberle, *On the Shake Rag: Mineral Point's Pendarvis House, 1935-1970*, State Historical Society of Wisconsin, Mineral Point, 1990.

25. Jim Jewell, *Cornish in America: Linden, Wisconsin*, Cornish Miner Press, Linden, 1990, p.11.

26. Frank Ruhrmund, *About St Just-in-Penwith*, Bossiney, St Teath, 1979, p.5.

27. Rowse, 1969 & 1991, p.224.

28. Todd, 1967 & 1995, p.31.

29. Todd, 1967 & 1995, p.46.

30. Todd, 1967 & 1995, pp.48-49.

31. Rowse, 1969 & 1991, p.187.

32. Rowe, 1974, p.59.

33. Rowe, 1974, p.67.

34. *West Briton*, 15 September 1865.

35. Rowe, 1974, p.65.

36. James Fisher, 'Michigan's Cornish People', *Michigan History Magazine*, Vol.29, 1945, pp.377-385.

37. Angus Murdoch, *Boom Copper: The Story of the First U.S. Mining Boom*, 1943, repub. Drier and Koepel, Calumet, 1964, p.128.

38. Rowe, 1974, p.73.

39. Rowe, 1974, p.73.

40. Rowe, 1974, p.76.

41. Rowe, 1974, pp.83-84.

42. Rowe, 1974, pp.86-87.

43. Todd, 1967 & 1995, pp. 120-122.

44. James J. Jamieson, 'The Copper Rush of the 50s', *Michigan History Magazine*, Vol.XIX, 1935, p.383.

45. Rowe, 1974, p.80.

46. *Mining Journal*, 14 December 1861.

47. T.A. Rickard, *A History of American Mining*, New York, pp.246-248.

48. Rowe, 1974, p.81.

49. Rowse, 1969 & 1991, pp. 171-172.

50. Rowse, 1969 & 1991, pp. 172-176; Alvah L. Sawyer, *A History of the Northern Peninsula of Michigan*, Lewis Publishing, Chicago, 1911, pp.1306-1307; A.T. Andreas, *History of the Upper Peninsula of Michigan*, Western Historical Co., Chicago, 1883, p.314; *Lake Superior Mining Institute: Proceedings*, Ishpeming (Mich.), 1839-1939, Vol.XXXVII, 1929, p.320.

51. Rowse, 1969 & 1991, p.178-179.

52. Rowe, 1974, p.90.

53. *West Briton*, 22 June 1849.

54. Murdoch, 1943 & 1964, p.205.

55. Murdoch, 1943 & 1964, pp.202-303.

56. Murdoch, 1943 & 1964, p.203.

57. Murdoch, 1943 & 1964, pp.216-217.

58. Murdoch, 1943 & 1964, p.217.

59. Newton G. Thomas, *The Long Winter Ends*, Macmillan, London, 1941, Wayne University Press, Detroit, 1998.

60. Thomas, 1941 & 1998, p.43.

61. Thomas, 1941 & 1998, p.242.

62. William H. Mulligan, 'Introduction' to Thomas, 1998, p.vii.

63. Mulligan/Thomas, 1998, p.ix.

64. Alfred Nicholls, 'The Story of My Life', unpub. MS, 1931, pp.37-38. I am indebted to Mr Harry Tregilgas of St Austell for drawing my attention to this document, and for depositing a copy at the Institute of Cornish Studies.

65. Nicholls, 1931, p38.

66. Nicholls, 1931, pp.38-39.

67. Nicholls, 1931, pp.39-40.

68. Nicholls, 1931, pp.42-43.

69. Nicholls, 1931, pp.45.

70. Rowe, 1974, p.167.

71. Murdoch, 1941 & 1998, p.205.

72. *Atlantic Mine Letter Book*, 24 February 1881, cited in Sandra Hollingsworth, *The Atlantic: Copper and Community South of Portage Lake*, Forster, Houghton (Mich.), 1978, p.43.

73. *Atlantic Mine Letter Book*, 14 August 1880, cited in Hollingsworth, 1978, p.45.

74. *Atlantic Mine Letter Book*, 7 March 1883, cited in Hollingsworth, 1978, pp.57-58.

75. Rowse, 1969 & 1991, p.168.

76. Flora O'Hagan, 'Lost Cornish Cousins', *Cornish Worldwide*, No.21, Summer 1997.

77. Lee Brownell, *Pioneer Life in Ely*, Iron Range Historical Society, Ely, 1981, p.35.

78. Brownell, 1981, p.7.

79. Brownell, 1981, p.7.

80. John H. Forster, 'Life in the Copper Mines Of Lake Superior', *Historical Collections of the Pioneer Society of Michigan*, Lansing, Vol.Xl, 1887, p.183.

81. George Cocking, *From the Mines to the Pulpit, or Success Hammered Out of the Rock*, Cocking, Cinncinnati, 1901, p.177.

## Chapter 5: South Australia's Copper Kingdom

1. *South Australian News*, August 1841; *Adelaide Chronicle*, 24 March 1841.

2. Edwin Hodder, *The History of South Australia from its Foundation to the year of its Jubilee*, 2 Vols., Sampson, Marston & Co., London, 1893, p.187.

3. South Australian [State] Archives (SAA), D3196A, Oswald Pryor, 'The Glen Osmond Mines and the Presence of Cornish miners there', unpub. MS, 1953; Pryor cites an identified issue of the *South Australian* newspaper to indicate the employment of balmaidens at Glen Osmond.

4. *West Briton*, 16 June 1848.

5. *Wallaroo Times*, 14 March 1868.

6. Francis Dutton, *Australia and Its Mines*, Boone, London, 1846, p.267.

7. SAA At 118, reprinted in SAA 1384 *Pioneer Association of South Australia Publications*, No.9, A Holograph Memoir of Captain Charles Harvey Bagot of the 87th Regiment, pp.24-25.

8. Dutton, 1846, p.269.

9. W. Frederick Morrison, *The Aldine History of South Australia*, Aldine, Sydney & Adelaide, 1890, pp.514, 518, 519, 520, 578; H.T. Burgess, *The Cyclopedia of South Australia*, 2 Vols., Selway, Adelaide, 1907, pp.380, 386; *Australian Christian Commonwealth*, 15 May 1908; 13 December 1912.

10. *South Australian Register*, 20 April 1850.

11. *South Australian Register*, 18 January 1845; 5 December 1846; 19 April 1848; 24 August 1854; 19 November 1864; *Mining Journal*, 14 April 1847; 2 September 1848; *South Australian News*, October 1846; November 1848; *People's Weekly*, 11 November 1911; 3 August 1912; SAA GRG24/6/317/1847, *Report upon the Mining Districts by the Commissioner of Crown Lands*, 13 March 1847.

12. Dutton, 1846, p.281.

13. J. B. Austin, *The Mines of South Australia*, Rigby, Adelaide, 1863, p.22.

14. SAA BRG22/960, *South Australian Mining Association, Directors' Letter Books*, Ayers to mine superintendent, 24 September 1845.

15. Cited in Jean Fielding, 'For the Wind Passeth', unpub. MS, nd, p.230.

16. SAA 1509, *Butts of Orders for Wages and other Expenses, Burra Mines; Burra Burra Mines - Copper Ore Day Book 1860-61* (held at Burra National Trust Museum).

17. *South Australian Register*, 8 April 1846.

18. *South Australian Register*, 7 August 1847.

19. SAA BRG22/960, Ayers to Bibby, 9 August 1847.

20. SAA BRG22/960, Ayers to Bibby, 9August 1847.

21. SAA BRG22/960, Ayers to Hallett, 28 April 1849.

22. SAA BRG22/960, Ayers to Hallett, 25 August 1849.

23. SAA BRG22/960, Ayers to Hallett, 4 May 1850.

24. SAA BRG22/960, Ayers to Hallett, 24 March 1851.

25. SAA BRG22/960, Ayers to Hallett, 10 May 1851.

26. *South Australian Register*, 11 July 1850; 13 November 1851; 24 August 1854; 21 October 1858; 21 April 1859; 11 November 1859; 13 July 1872; *Mining Journal*, 5 June 1847; 17 October 1857; 17 July 1858; 14 August 1858; 13 October 1858, 13 July 1861; *South Australian Primitive Methodist*, January 1898.

27. *South Australian Register*, 30 April 1857.

28. *People's Weekly*, 7 June 1902.

29. J.B. Austin, 1863, p.86.

30. 'Old Colonist' writing in 1851, repub. in E.M. Yelland, *Colonists, Copper and Corn*, Hawthorn, Melbourne, 1970, p.136.

31. SAA BRG22/960, Ayers to Hector, 17 November 1852.

32. Dutton, 1846, p.302.

33. *South Australian Gazette and Colonial Register*, 19 July 1845.

34. *Perth Inquirer*, 18 February 1846.

35. *Devonport Telegraph and Plymouth Chronicle*, cited in *South Australian News*, January 1847.

36. SeymourTremenheere,'Notice Respecting the Lead and Copper ores of Glen Osmond Mines, three miles from Adelaide, South Australia', *Transactions of the Royal Geological Society of Cornwall*, Vol,VI, 1841–46, pp.348-349.

37. *South Australian Register*, 9 June 1847.

38. *Cornishman Broadsheet*, 1954, articles by John Rowe.

39. J.R. Leifchild, *Cornwall's Mines and Miners*, 1857, repub. Frank Cass, London,1968, p.246.

40. *Northern Star* (Kapunda), 20 July 1861.

41. *South Australian News*, July 1848.

42. *South Australian News*, January 1846.

43. *South Australian Gazette and Colonial Register*, 20 September 1845.

44. SAA 313, Passenger Lists.

45. *West Briton*, 15 October 1847.

46. *South Australian News*, December 1846.

47. *South Australian Register*, 17 November 1846.

48. SAA 94, Letters, Chiefly Commercial, to James and Robert Frew, Angas to Frew, 7 May 1846.

49. *South Australian News*, February 1847, citing Devonport Telegraph, 20 February 1847.

50. SAA 313.

51. SAA 313.

52. *South Australian News*, February 1847; *citing Plymouth, Devonport and Stonehouse Herald*, 23 January 1847.

53. Mitchell Library, Sydney (ML), A3809/2, *Carlyon Collection*, Carlyon to Rodda, c.1848.

54. *West Briton*, 3 December 1847.

55. *South Australian News*, December 1847.

56. *South Australian News*, January 1848.

57. *South Australian News*, September 1847.

58. *South Australian News*, January 1846.

59. *South Australian News*, July 1847.

60. *South Australian News*, December 1846.

61. SAA PRG 86, Thomas Burgess, Papers Relating to Immigration c.1843-48, Letter from Robert Dare to his parents c. 1846.

62. *South Australian News*, September 1849.

63. *South Australian Register*, 1 January 1851.

64. *South Australian Register*, 8 January 1851.

65. La Trobe Library, Melbourne, Despatch: Cornwall and Devon Society to Young, *Memorial as to Emigration of Cornish Miners*, Despatch No.19, 31 January 1851.

66. SAA BRG 22/960, Ayers to Immigration Agent, 26 March 1850; Ayers to Stakeman, 19 November 1850.

67. SAA BRG 22/960, Ayers to Wilcocks, 3 November 1852.

68. SAA BRG 22/960, Ayers to Wilcocks, 24 December 1852.

69. SAA BRG 22/957, South Australian Mining Association, Directors' Minutes April 1852-June 1914,

# NOTES AND REFERENCES

2 August 1854.

70. SAA BRG 22/960, Ayers to Wilcocks, 21 September 1854.

71. SAA BRG 22/960, Ayers to Colonial Secretary, 25 January 1854.

72. SAA BRG 22/960, Ayers to Wilcocks, 21 September 1854; Ayers to Wilcocks, 31 January 1855.

73. SAA BRG 22/960, Ayers to Colonial Secretary, 25 January 1854.

74. *South Australian Register*, 20 April 1850.

75. SAA BRG 22/960, Ayers to Wilcocks, 17 March 1856.

76. SAA GRG 35/43 (Acc.333), Department of Land Records (including those of the former Department of Crown Lands and Immigration), Immigration Agents, Incoming Correspondence 1849-1878, Wilcocks to Agents, 11 April 1856.

77. SAA GRG 35/43 (Acc.333), Ayers to Wilcocks, 6 November 1857.

78. *Burra Record*, 28 September 1877.

79. SAA BRG 22/961, South Australian Mining Association, Letters to Burra Mine Officials/Superintendents Letter Books, Ayers to Sanders, 23 December 1873; Ayers to Sanders, 2 January 1874.

80. *Northern Mail* (Burra), 14 July 1876.

81. Reminiscences of 'Senex' in *A Circle of Friends, Memories of Kapunda*, Kapunda Herald, Kapunda, 1929, p.9.

82. *Northern Star*, 10 January 1861.

83. *Northern Star*, 19 January 1861; 6 July 1861.

84. *Kapunda Herald*, 13 May 1879.

85. *Kapunda Herald*, 13 May 1879.

86. *South Australian Register*, 17 May 1862.

87. Reminiscences of 'Old Timer' in *A Circle of Friends*, 1929, p.108

88. Michael Davitt, *Life and Progress in Australasia*, Methuen, London, 1898, p.63.

89. *South Australian Register*, 24 August 1867.

90. *South Australian Register*, 14 July 1851.

91. *South Australian Register*, 14 July 1851.

92. *South Australian Register*, 4 March 1859.

93. Cousin Sylvia, *Homing*, Hassell Press, Adelaide, n.d.

94. Cousin Sylvia, n.d.

95. *South Australian*, 14 March 1848.

96. *South Australian Register*, 30 December 1859.

97. *South Australian Register*, 3 January 1863.

98. *South Australian*, 14 March 1848.

99. *South Australian Register*, 27 June 1863.

100. SAA D2632(L), *Anonymous Diary of a Tungkillo Miner*, 1 February 1850-12 February 1851.

101. SAA 842m, *Notes on the Burra Burra Mine: Diary of Johnson Frederick Haywood 1846-56*.

102. Dutton, 1846, pp.269-270.

103. *South Australian News*, April 1848.

104. *Australian Christian Commonwealth*, 3 October 1902.

105. SAA 842m.

106. 'Old Colonist'/Yelland, 1851 & 1970, p.151.

107. Anonymous contributor in *Back to Burra: Official Souvenir Programme*, Bond's, Burra (?), 1936, p.20.

108. SAA BRG22/80, *South Australian Mining Association, Miscellaneous Papers*, Thomson to Ayers, 28 June 1847.

109. *South Australian Register*, 11 May 1872.

110. *South Australian Register*, 3 October 1846.

111. SAA 842m.

112. *South Australian Register*, 1 August 1849.

113. *South Australian Register*, 1 August 1849.

114. *South Australian Register*, 22 September 1849.

115. *Burra Record*, 18 September 1901.

116. *Miscellaneous Annual Report of the Missionary Society Under the Direction of the Bible Christian Conference*, 1850, p.7.

117. F.W. Bourne, *The Bible Christians: Their Origins and History*, Bible Christian Book Room, London, 1905, p.307.

118. *Australian Christian Commonwealth*, 1 March 1912.

119. *Australian Christian Commonwealth*, 1 March 1912.

120. *Wesleyan Methodist Magazine*, combined volume, 1848, p.1043.

121. *Wesleyan Methodist Magazine*, combined volume, 1848, p.1371.

122. H. R. Taylor, *The History of Churches of Christ in South Australia*, 1846-1959, Churches of Christ, Adelaide, 1959, p.83.

123. *Primitive Methodist Quarterly Review*, 1890, p.264.

124. *Australian Christian Commonwealth*, 14 November 1902.

125. *Primitive Methodist Magazine*, combined volume, 1853, p.484.

126. *Wesleyan Methodist Magazine*, combined volume, 1853, pp.86-87.

127. *Australian Christian Commonwealth*, 14

November 1902.

128. *Miscellaneous Annual report of the Missionary Society Under the Direction of the Bible Christian Conference*, 1854, p.24.

129. *Wesleyan Methodist Magazine*, combined volume, 1854, p.568.

130. *Primitive Methodist Magazine*, combined volume, 1855, p.51.

131. SAA SRG4/103/1, *Diary of the Rev. John G. Wright 1856-1901*, Wednesday, 8 April 1856.

132. SAA SRG/103/1,24 July 1857.

133. Records of the Kooringa Bible Christian Sunday School, 1857-64, held (in 1976) at Redruth Methodist (ex-Wesleyan) Church, Burra, South Australia.

134. *Kapunda Herald*, 12 January 1900.

135. Mel Davies, 'Collective Action and the Cornish Miner in Australia: An Early Repudiation of the "Individualistic" Thesis', in Philip Payton (ed.), *Cornish Studies: Three*, Exeter, 1995, University of Exeter Press, Exeter, 1995.

136. SAA GRG 24, series 6, Colonial Office Correspondence, A (1848) 1432, 15/9/1848.

137. *South Australian*, 19 September 1848.

## Chapter 6: Gold! The Californian Rush

1. John Rowe, 'News of Cornishmen from the Golden West', *Cornish Banner*, No.52, May 1988, p.11.

2. *West Briton*, 13 February 1835.

3. *West Briton*, 3 March 1848.

4. Milton Lanyon and Laurence Bulmore, *Cinnabar Hills: The Quicksilver Days of New Almaden*, 1967, repub. New Almaden County Quicksilver Park Association, New Almaden, 1991, pp.2-7.

5. A.L. Rowse, *The Cornish in America*, Macmillan, London, 1969, repub. Dyllansow Truran, Redruth, 1991, p.267.

6. A.C. Todd, *The Cornish Miner in America*, Bradford Barton, Truro, 1967, repub. Arthur C. Clark, Spokane (Washington), 1995, pp.84-85.

7. Rowse, 1969 & 1991, p.267.

8. E.T. Sawyer, *History of Santa Clara County*, California, p.1680, cited in Rowse, 1969 & 1991, p.269.

9. Todd, 1967 & 1995, p.92.

10. Mary Halleck Foote, 'A California Mining Camp', *Scribner's Monthly*, Vol.XXXV, October 1865.

11. Arthur Lakes, 'The New Almaden Mines', *Mines and Minerals*, Vol.XIX, No.8, March 1899.

12. *San Jose Daily Mercury*, 15 June 1886.

13. Gage McKinney, *A High and Holy Place: A Mining Camp Church at New Almaden*, New Almaden Quicksilver Park Association, New Almaden, 1997, p.45.

14. Rodman Wilson Paul, *Mining Frontiers of the Far West 1848-1880*, Holt, Rinehart and Winston, New York, 1963, p.10.

15. J.D. Borthwick, *Three Years in the Goldfields*, London, 1857, cited in Todd, 1967 & 1995, p.59.

16. Keith Skues, *Cornish Heritage*, Werner Shaw, London, 1983, p.222.

17. Skues, 1983, p.222.

18. *West Briton*, 5 January 1849.

19. *West Briton*, 19 January 1849.

20. *West Briton*, 29 August 1851.

21. *Royal Cornwall Gazette*, 12 September 1851.

22. *Royal Cornwall Gazette*, 5 November 1852.

23. *West Briton*, 9 January 1852.

24. Paul, 1963, p.17.

25. *West Briton*, 1 March 1849.

26. *West Briton*, 20 June 1851.

27. *West Briton*, 9 January 1852.

28. Paul, 1963, p.25.

29. Paul, 1963, p.23.

30. Skues, 1983, p.224.

31. Skues, 1983, p.224.

32. Ralph Mann, *After the Gold Rush: Society in Grass Valley and Nevada City, California 1849-1870*, Stanford University Press, Stanford, 1982, p.142.

33. Mann, 1982, p.143.

34. *[Grass Valley] Names Index: Citations to Selected Articles from The Union Pertaining to People Connected with Mining and the Empire Mine*, Compiled by Research Group, Empire Mine Park Association, January 1990.

35. David Allan Comstock and Ardis Hatten Comstock, *Nevada County Vital Statistics 1850-1869: Nevada County Pioneers Series, Vol. 1*, Comstock Bonanza Press, Grass Valley, 1996, pp. 1, 14-16, 22, 28, 60-69, 71, 81, 89, 91.

36. *West Briton*, 13 September 1884.

37. Unidentified Grass Valley press cutting, 1902, courtesy of Doreen Valleau; see also 'Prominent Grass Valley Businessmen' in *Nevada County Mining Review*, Grass Valley, 1895.

38. Cited in Mann, 1983, pp.86-87.

39. B. Sillman, *Notes on the Quartz Mines of the Grass*

*Valley District*, Nevada City, 1867, p.9.

40. *Grass Valley Union*, 28 May 1871.

41. F.D. Calhoon, *Coolies, Kanakas and Cousin Jacks*, Cal-Con Publishers, Sacramento, 1986, p.185.

42. Unidentified Grass Valley press cutting, 1907, citing unidentified edition of the *Cornish Telegraph*, courtesy of Doreen Valleau.

43. Shirley Ewart, *Cornish Mining Families of Grass Valley, California*, AMS Press, New York, 1989, p.119.

44. Mann, 1983, p.146.

45. Mann, 1983, p.120.

46. Mann, 1983, p.120.

47. Mann, 1983, p.120.

48. Mann, 1983, p.179.

49. *Los Angeles Mining Review*, 16 March 1907.

50. John Rowe, *The Hard-Rock Men: Cornish Immigrants and the North American Mining Frontier*, Liverpool University Press, Liverpool, 1974, p.121.

51. Mann, 1983, p.187.

52. Paul, 1963, p.94.

53. Edward Kinyon, 'Cornish Migration to Grass Valley', *Nevada County Historical Society Bulletin*, Vol.3, No.7, December 1953, p.3.

54. Calhoon, 1986, p.295.

55. Ewart, 1989, p.135.

56. Calhoon, 1986, p.301.

57. Calhoon, 1986, p.302.

58. Frank A. Crampton, *Deep Enough*, 1956, repub. University of Oklahoma Press, Norman, 1982, p.61.

59. Crampton, 1956 & 1982, pp.61-62.

60. Crampton, 1956 & 1982, p.64.

61. Crampton, 1956 & 1982, p.65.

62. *Mining and Scientific Press* (San Francisco), 2 May 1908; 1 August 1908; 24 October 1908; see David Beesley, 'The Cornish Pump', *Nevada County Historical Society Bulletin*, Vol.33, No.2, April 1979, pp.7-16.

63. Otis E. Young Jr, *Western Mining*, University of Oklahoma Press, Norman, 1970, p.171.

64. Roger P. Lescohier, *The Cornish Pump in the California Gold Mines*, Lescohier, Grass Valley, 1992, p.7.

65. Lescohier, 1992, p.11.

66. Lescohier, 1992, p.17.

67. Jack Clough, *Joshua Hendy Stampmill at Hangtown's Gold Bug Park*, Hangtown's Gold Bug Park Development Committee, Placerville, 1995.

68. Ewart, 1989, p.149.

69. *Illustrated History of Plumas County*, San Francisco, 1882.

70. William H. Smitheram, 'The Smitheram Family in Eureka Mills and Johnsville', *Johnsville Histories: Johnsville Historical Society*, Vol.1, No.8, July 1992.

71. Smitheram, 1992.

72. William H. Smitheram, 'Memories of Old Borate', in Jennifer Reynolds (ed.), *Memories, Minerals, Fossils, and Dust: Proceedings of the 1997 Desert Research Symposium*, *San Bernardino County Museum Association Quarterly*, Vol.44, No.1, Winter 1997, p.3.

73. Newell D. Chamberlain, *The Call of Gold: True Tales on the Gold Road to Yosemite*, 1936, repub. Western Tanager Press, Santa Cruz, 1981, p.142.

74. Judith Marvin and Carlo DeFerrari, 'Soulsbyville: An Enclave of Cousin Jacks and Jinnies in a Hard-Rock Mining Town', unpub. MS, c.1994, p.3.

75. *Tuolumne Independent*, 5 May 1877.

## Chapter 7: Gold! The Victorian Rush

1. Geoffrey Blainey, *The Rush That Never Ended: A History of Australian Mining*, Melbourne University Press, Melbourne, 1963, pp.48 and 77.

2. Una R. Emanual, 'The History and Decline of the Mining Village of Byng', *Australian Geographer*, Vol.1, Pt.2, November 1929; W.R. Glasson, 'Early Western Glimpses', *Journal and Proceedings, The Australian Methodist Historical Society*, No.43, January 1945.

3. Patricia Lay, *One and All: The Cornish in New South Wales*, Heritage 2000 Plus, Queanbeyan (NSW), 1998, p.8, citing J.W. Tom, 'Cornish Settlement: Reminiscences', unpub. MS, 1941; see also Patricia Lay, 'One and All: The Cornish in New South Wales', MA thesis, Australian National University, 1992.

4. Lay, 1998, p.12, citing John Glasson, 'Letters 1828-1857', with introduction by his granddaughter, Mrs O. Phillips, unpub. MS, Bathurst Historical Society.

5. *Bathurst Free Press*, 11 January 1851; Lay, 1998, p.5.

6. John Reynolds, *Men and Mines: A History of Australian Mining 1788-1971*, Sun Books, Melbourne, 1974, p.25.

7. Reynolds, 1974, p.26.

8. *Burra Record*, 24 October 1890.

9. John Meredith and Hugh Anderson, *Folk Songs of Australia*, Ure Smith, Sydney, 1973, p.95.

10. Lay, pp.47-55; Suzanne Treseder, *A Passion for Plants: The Treseders of Truro*, Alison Hodge, Penzance, 2004, pp. 27-55.

11. J.P. McCarthy, *Cadia Conservation Study*, Australian Institute of Mining and Metallurgy, Adelaide, 1989.

12. H. Hodge, *The Hill End Story*, Book 1, 3rd ed., Hill End Publications, Tooraka (Victoria), 1986, p.140.

13. *The Methodist*, 12 September 1903; Lay, 1998, p.82.

14. Lay, 1998, p.102.

15. Lay, 1998, p.109.

16. E.G. Clancy, 'The Ranter's Church', unpub. MS, Uniting Church Archives (Australia), pp.443-444, cited in Lay, 1998, p.112.

17. B.W. Thomas, *The Thomas Family of Guyong: 1849-1929*, Thomas, Wahroonga (NSW), 1974, pp.79-80.

18. *Bathurst Free Press*, 7 December 1861; Lay, 1998, pp.112-113.

19. H. Charleston, T Moase and D.N. Morison, *Seventy Years of Newcastle Methodism 1834-1904*, Newcastle (NSW), 1904, p.10; Lay, 1988, p.125.

20. Lay, 1998, p.139.

21. *South Australian Register*, 13 October 1851.

22. South Australian [State] Archives (SAA) BRG22/960, South Australian Mining Association, Director's Letter Books, Ayers to Vivian, 11 September 1852.

23. *Mining Journal*, 28 October 1871.

24. SAA D5049(L), Letter from John Whitford, Kangaroo Flat, Victoria, to his father and family, 12 December 1852.

25. Letter by Mr Evans of Evandale, 25 February 1852, cited in Edwin Hodder, *The History of South Australia from its Foundation to the Year of its Jubilee*, Sampson Low, London, 1893, Vol.1, pp.260-261.

26. *West Briton*, 31 October 1851.

27. *Royal Cornwall Gazette*, 23 July 1852.

28. *West Briton*, 2 April 1852; 9 April 1852; 16 April 1852; Philip Payton, *The Cornish Miner in Australia: Cousin Jack Down Under*, Dyllansow Truran, Redruth, 1984, p.118.

29. Payton, 1984, p.118.

30. Mitchell Library (Sydney) A 3809 *Carlyon Collection*, Rodda to Carlyon, 2 May 1848; Glasson to Coode, 9 January 1850; 'Memorandum of Agreement between Edward Carlyon and John Hammer, miner, of St Blazey'; Hammer and Goyne to Carlyon, 26 July 1853; Haggard and Pixley to Carlyon, 6 August 1853; SAA D6029/1 91(L), *Letters written Home by Cornish folk who emigrated to Australia in the Nineteenth century*, collected by Dr J.M. Tregenza, William Pomeroy Carlyon to his parents Col, & Mrs Angus Carlyon, 20 February 1853.

31. Blainey, 1963, p.39.

32. *West Briton*, 15 February 1856.

33. SAA D6029/1 0(L), Peter Pascoe to George Cunnack, 1 October 1852.

34. *West Briton*, 31 December 1852.

35. SAA D6029/91 (L), Peter Matthews to relations, 15 January 1854.

36. SAA D6029/35/38/39/41 (L), Letters from Stephen Curnow, 14 November 1852, 29 January 1854, 6 August 1854, 7 February 1855.

37. SAA D6029/46(L), John T Williams to Stephen Curnow, 13 March 1860.

38. SAA D6029/68/69(L), Henry Giles to his Parents, 15 November 1854, 3 December 1854.

39. SAA D6029171 (L), J. Stephens to Henry Giles senior, 28 May 1855.

40. SAA PRG3 *Leaworthy Papers*, 'A Trip to the Victorian Diggings' by Malcolm Henry Leaworthy.

41. South Australian Register, 21 December 1851.

42. *West Briton*, 3 December 1852.

43. SAA D4800(L) *Abstract of Diary of the Late Francis Treloar of Watervale: Taken Out By His Son Frank*, 6 June 1852 to 12 November 1852.

44. SAA D6029/69(L), Henry Giles to his parents, 3 December 1854.

45. *Wesleyan Methodist Magazine*, combined volume, 1854, p.1037.

46. W.P. Morrell, *The Gold Rushes*, Adam & Black, London, 1948, 2nd ed. 1968, p.246.

47. Jim Faull, *The Cornish in Australia*, AE Press, Melbourne, 1983, p.57; Len Fox, *The Eureka Flag*, Fox, Potts Point (NSW), 1992, p.9.

48. SAA D6029/90(L), Peter Matthews to relatives, 27 July 1853.

49. W.L. Blamires and John B. Smith, *The Early Story of the Wesleyan Methodist Church in Victoria*, 1886, pp.189-190.

50. Blainey, 1963, p.41.

51. Blamires and Smith, 1886, p.211.

52. John Sherer, *The Gold-Finder of Australia*, 1853, repub. Penguin, Ringwood (Victoria), 1973, pp.154-155.

53. Sherer, 1853 & 1973, pp.159 and 226.

54. Thomas Oliver, *Autobiography of a Cornish Miner*, Camborne, 1914, pp.26-27.

55. Oliver, 1914, pp.31-32.

56. Oliver, 1914, pp.38 and 98.

57. Oliver, 1914, pp.39-40.

58. *West Briton*, 27 August 1858.

59. *West Briton*, 11 February 1853.

60. *South Australian Register*, 6 August 1853.

61. SAA D6029/90(L), Peter Matthews to relatives, 27 July 1853.

62. SAA D6029/39(L), Letter from Stephen Curnow, 6 July 1854.

63. SAA D6029/69(L), Henry Giles to his parents, 3 December 1854.

64. SAA D6029/4(L), Richard Hancock to his mother, 20 June 1862.

65. *Wallaroo Times*, 2 February 1867.

66. SAA D6029/92(L), Peter Matthews to Relatives, 18 October 1855.

67. See Lesley J. Morton, *The Duke of Cornwall Mine, Fryerstown, Victoria*, Morton, Melbourne, 1992.

68. University of Melbourne Archives, *Creswick Primitive Methodist Church, Quarterly Meetings Minute Books*, 1885–1902.

69. L.E. Fredman, 'Sir John Quick's Birthplace', *Victorian Historical Journal*, Vol.48, No.1, February 1977.

70. Ruth Hopkins, *Cousin Jack, Man for the Times: A History of the Cornish People in Victoria*, Hopkins, Bendigo, 1994; Ruth Hopkins, *Where Now Cousin Jacks?*, Bendigo Bicentennial Committee, Bendigo, 1988; Lillian Dell and Joy Menhennet, *Cornish Pioneers of Ballarat*, Ballarat Branch of the Cornish Association of Victoria, 1992.

71. Hopkins, 1994, p.213.

72. Charles Fahey, 'Cornish Miners in Bendigo: An Examination of their Standard of Living', unpub. paper, Department of History, Monash University, n.d. p.3.

73. James A. Lerk, *Bendigo's Mining History 1851-1954*, The Bendigo Trust, Bendigo, 1991, p.37.

74. I am indebted to Leanne Lloyd for access to her database of more than 700 Cornish mine captains in Victoria. The continuing incidence of Cornish surnames after the Great War is evident in James A. Lerk, *Bendigo's Gold Mining Revival, 1929–1954*, Lerk, Golden Square (Victoria), 1997.

75. Anne Colman, 'Colonial Cornish: Cornish Immigrants in Victoria, 1865-1880', unpub. MA thesis, University of Melbourne, 1985, p.85, citing Jonathon G Moon, *Tarrangower, Past and Present*, Maldon, 1864, p.125

76. Colman, 1985, p.188.

77. Colman, 1985, p.201.

## Chapter 8: Crashed Copper, Tumbled Tin & 'The Largest Cornish Communities Beyond Land's End'

1. Edmund Newell, '"Copperopolis": The Rise and Fall of the Copper Industry in the Swansea District, 1826-1921', *Business History*, Vol.32, No.3, July 1990.

2. *West Briton*, 8 August 1862.

3. See Philip Payton, 'Cornish Emigration in Response to Changes in the International Copper Market in the 1860s', in Philip Payton (ed.), *Cornish Studies: Three*, University of Exeter Press, Exeter, 1995.

4. *Northern Star* (Kapunda), 27 July 1861.

5. *West Briton*, 23 October 1863.

6. South Australian [State] Archives (SAA) D5633(T), Malcolm Vaughan, *The Development of Agriculture and the Slate Industry in the Willunga area in the nineteenth century*, Tony Lucas, *Willunga Profile*, Lantern Black, Sydney, 1972; Martin Dunstan, *Willunga:Town and District 1837-1900*, Lynton, Adelaide, 1977; Catherine Lorigan, '"The Far Famed and Celebrated Old Delabole Slate Quarry": The Industrial History of the Quarry and the Making of its Village Community, 1840-1920', unpub. PhD thesis, University of Exeter, 2004, pp. 254-299; *West Briton*, 18 March 1864.

7. *West Briton*, 19 June 1863.

8. *West Briton*, 4 January 1867.

9. *West Briton*, 22 September 1865.

10. SAA 313 Passenger Lists.

11. SAA BRG40/543 Moonta Mine Proprieters, Minute Books, 1861-91, 3 May 1875, 7 February 1876.

12. SAA BRG40/538 Moonta Mines Proprieters, Out-Letter Books, 1863-69, McCoull to A.L. Elders, 26 April 1864, McCoull to Young, 26 April 1864; SAA BRG40/543, 24 April 1864, 29 August 1864.

13. Philip Payton, 'The Cornish in South Australia: Their Influence and Experience from Immigration to Assimilation, 1836–1936', unpub. PhD thesis, University of Adelaide, 1978, pp. 117-118.

14. Newell, 1990.

15. *West Briton*, 25 January 1867.

16. *West Briton*, 25 January 1867.

17. *West Briton*, 25 January 1867.

18. *West Briton*, 20 July 1866.

19. *West Briton*, 4 January 1867.

20. *West Briton*, 25 January 1867.

21. *West Briton*, 25 January 1867.

22. *West Briton*, 1 March 1867.

23. *West Briton*, 2 January 1868.

24. *West Briton*, 2 January 1868.

25. *Kapunda Herald*, 24 June 1879; 11 July 1879.

26. *West Briton*, 2 January 1868.

27. *West Briton*, 30 January 1868.

28. *West Briton*, 23 January 1868.

29. See Bernard Deacon, 'A Forgotten Migration Stream: The Cornish Movement to England and Wales in the Nineteenth Century', in Philip Payton (ed.), *Cornish Studies: Six*, University of Exeter Press, Exeter, 1998.

30. *West Briton*, 6 October 1865; 31 August 1866; 25 January 1867.

31. Bryn Trescatheric, *Roose: A Cornish Village in Furness*, Barrow, 1983.

32. Ben Barnicoat, *Old Cornish Carols*, Polperro Press, Polperro, 1927, p.10.

33. Raymond Challinor, *The Lancashire and Cheshire Miners*, Frank Graham, Newcastle-upon-Tyne, 1972, p.73.

34. *West Briton*, 20 October 1873.

35. *West Briton*, 18 September 1873.

36. Challinor, 1972, p.121.

37. Alan B. Campbell, *The Lanarkshire Miners: A Social History of their Trade Unions 1775-1974*, John Donald, Edinburgh, 1979, p.269.

38. *West Briton*, 7 December 1866.

39. *West Briton*, 15 June 1866.

40. *West Briton*, 17 May 1867.

41. *Royal Cornwall Gazette*, 2 January 1868.

42. *West Briton*, 16 May 1871.

43. *West Briton*, 13 April 1874.

44. *West Briton*, 7 January 1875.

45. Rollo Arnold, *The Farthest Promised Land: English Villagers, New Zealand Immigrants of the 1870s*, Victoria University Press, Wellington, 1981, pp.211-235, 275-276, 288, 337.

46. Arnold, p.10.

47. Arnold, p.211.

48. Arnold, pp.337-338.

49. Arnold, p.217.

50. Arnold, p.230.

51. See Philip Payton, *The Cornish Farmer in Australia*, Dyllansow Truran, Redruth, 1987.

52. SAA RN201 *A Few Notes on The History of Nairne*.

53. *South Australian News*, April 1847.

54. *South Australian News*, January 1848.

55. *South Australian News*, February 1849.

56. Stanley G. Forth, *Methodism in the Clare District*, South Australian Methodist Historical Society, Adelaide, 1974.

57. *Observer* (Adelaide), 9 July 1870.

58. *Yorke's Peninsula Advertiser*, 2 May 1873; 22 May 1874; 13 June 1876.

59. Nancy Robinson, *Change on Change: A History of the Northern Highlands of South Australia*, Investigator Press, Adelaide, 1971, pp.105-106.

60. Robinson, 1971, pp.106.

61. *Yorke's Peninsula Advertiser*, 22 May 1874.

62. *Yorke's Peninsula Advertiser*, 7 November 1876.

63. *Yorke's Peninsula Advertiser*, 7 November 1876.

64. *Yorke's Peninsula Advertiser*, 9 February 1877.

65. *Yorke's Peninsula Advertiser*, 18 September 1877.

66. *Yorke's Peninsula Advertiser*, 9 September 1879.

67. *West Briton*, 22 January 1883.

68. *Yorke's Peninsula Advertiser*, 27 April 1883.

69. *Yorke's Peninsula Advertiser*, 6 July 1883; *South Australian Advertiser*, 15 August 1883.

70. *Yorke's Peninsula Advertiser*, 24 August 1883.

71. Geoffrey Blainey, *The Rush That Never Ended. A History of Australian Mining*, Melbourne University Press, Melbourne, 1963, p.119.

72. *South Australian Register*, 10 June 1973.

73. *Wallaroo Times*, 5 August 1868.

74. *Yorke's Peninsula Advertiser*, 6 August 1875.

75. Anthony Trollope, *Australia*, 1873, repub. University of Queensland Press (ed. PD. Edward and R.B. Joyce), St Lucia, 1967, p.685.

76. SAA BRG40/537 Wallaroo Mines Proprietors, Out-Letter Books 1860-70, Mair to Young, 25 November 1862.

77. SAA BRG40/539 Wallaroo Mines Proprietors, Out-Letters to Superintendent 1875-1882, Davidson to Higgs, 8 June 1875.

78. See Mandie Robinson, *Cap'n Ancock. Ruler of Australia's Little Cornwall*, Rigby, Adelaide, 1978.

79. *Yorke's Peninsula Advertiser*, 3 August 1877.

80. SAA BRG40/542 Wallaroo Mines Proprietors, Minute Books 1860-1891, 30 March 1869.

81. SAA BRG40/539, Mair to Higgs, 23 April 1877.

82. SAA BRG40/542, 16 May 1877.

83. Oswald Pryor, *Australia's Little Cornwall*, Rigby, Adelaide, 1962, p.44.

# NOTES AND REFERENCES

84. SAA D3627(L), Stanley Whitford, *An Autobiography*, addendum, 'Impressions of Moonta', by Sir Lennon Raws.

85. *South Australian Register*, 25 January 1864.

86. *South Australian Register*, 24 September 1872.

87. *Yorke's Peninsula Advertiser*, 9 July 1878.

88. *Yorke's Peninsula Advertiser*, 9 August 1878.

89. *Yorke's Peninsula Advertiser*, 17 September 1875.

90. *Wallaroo Times*, 24 September 1870.

91. *Yorke's Peninsula Advertiser*, 3 August 1877.

92. J.B. Austin, *The Mines of South Australia*, Rigby, Adelaide, 1863, p.103.

93. *Wallaroo Times*, 23 September 1868.

94. *South Australian Register*, 9 August 1864.

95. *Wallaroo Times*, 31 March 1866.

96. *Yorke's Peninsula Advertiser*, 29 September 1874.

97. SAA D5341 (T), Peter Thomas, *Scrapbook relating to Kapunda, Burra, Wallaroo and Moonta Mines*.

98. SAA D3627(L), Flaws addendum.

99. *Yorke's Peninsula Advertiser*, 1 July 1879; 26 August 1881.

100. Trollope, 1863 & 1967, p.684.

101. W.G. Spence, *Australia's Awakening: Thirty Years in the Life of an Australian Agitator*, Workers' Trustees, Sydney, 1909, p,27.

102. *Yorke's Peninsula Advertiser*, 10 April 1874.

103. *People's Weekly* (Moonta), 12 September 1896.

104. For example, see *Wallaroo Times*, 30 May 1868; *Yorke's Peninsula Advertiser*, 22 May 1874; 15 September 1876.

105. Jean Fielding and W.S. Ransom, 'The English of Australia's Little Cornwall', *Journal of the Australian Universities Language and Literature Association*, No.36, November 1971; *Yorke's Peninsula Advertiser*, 25 February 1876; 3 March 1876; 14 April 1876; 5 May 1876; 2 March 1877; 23 March 1877; 9 April 1878; 5 July 1878; 3 September 1878; 3 June 1887; *Wallaroo Times*, 13 March 1867; *South Australian Register*, 26 December 1867.

106. *Yorke's Peninsula Advertiser*, 9 January 1874.

107. *Yorke's Peninsula Advertiser*, 16 April 1875.

108. *Yorke's Peninsula Advertiser*, 2 November 1883.

109. *Wallaroo Times*, 29 June 1867.

110. 'Autobiography of Thomas Cowling', unpub. MS, Part II, p.1., private collection of Mr John Cowling, Adelaide, South Australia.

111. *Wallaroo Times*, 31 March 1861.

112. *Wallaroo Times*, 6 November 1869.

113. Philip Payton, *Cornish Carols From Australia*, Dyllansow Truran, Redruth, 1984, p.xi; A.K. Hamilton Jenkin, *The Cornish Miner*, 1927, repub. David and Charles, Newton Abbot, 1972, p.330.

114. J.H. Thomas, W. Holman, Jas. Richards, J. Coad, J. Hodge, T. Spargo and Others, *The Christmas Welcome: A Choice Collection of Cornish Carols*, Grummet, Moonta, 1893, p.8.

115. *Burra Record*, 13 August 1902.

116. *Bible Christian Magazine*, combined volume, 1876, p.37.

117. *Australian Christian Commonwealth*, 29 March 1935.

118. SAA SRG4/103/1 *Diary of the Rev John G. Wright 1856-1901*, 25 April 1875.

119. SAA D3627(L), p.69.

120. *Bible Christian Magazine*, combined volume, 1876, p.417.

121. SAA BRG40/543, 6 October 1862.

122. SAA D4876(Misc) *The Great Strike*, by W. Shelley

123. Roslyn Paterson, 'The Cornish Heritage in Northern Yorke Peninsula: The Cousin Jenny Contribution'. unpub. MS, c.1993.

124. *Yorke's Peninsula Advertiser*, 13 May 1873.

125. John Rowe, *Cornish Methodists and Emigrants*, Cornish Methodist Historical Association, Camborne, 1967, p.24.

126. SAA Dr Charles Davies, *Biographies and Obituaries*.

127. G.E. Loyau, *Notable South Australians and Colonists: Past and Present*, Adelaide, 1885, pp.61-62.

128. *Yorke's Peninsula Advertiser*, 24 April 1880.

129. *Yorke's Peninsula Advertiser*, 8 January 1878.

130. Spence, 1909, p.27.

131. *South Australian Department of Mines Mining Review*, Half-Year ended December 1919, p.12.

132. Dean H. Jaensch, 'Political Representation in Colonial South Australia', unpub. PhD thesis, University of Adelaide, 1973, p.597.

133. *People's Weekly*, 18 August 1917.

134. Donald J. Hopgood, 'A Psephological Examination of the South Australian Labor Party from World War One to the Depression', unpub. PhD thesis, Flinders University of South Australia, 1973, p.335.

135. Pryor, 1962, pp.148-149.

136. *People's Weekly*, 10 June 1933.

137. *People's Weekly*, 29 September 1923.

138. May Vivienne, *Sunny South Australia*, Hussey and

Gillingham, Adelaide, 1908, pp.254-255, 263.

139. Thomas Burtt, Moonta Musings in Rhythmic Rhyme, by a Moontaite, *Yorke's Peninsula Advertiser*, Moonta, 1885, p.2.


## Chapter 9: New Frontiers – Australia

1. Audrey Paterson, *A Cornish Goldminer at Hamiltons*, Otago Heritage Books, Dunedin, 1980.

2. Paterson, p.15.

3. *People's Weekly*, 25 May 1935.

4. Margaret Verran, *Irish and Cornish Immigration, Moreton Bay 1849-1859*, n.d.

5. *Cornish Times*, 24 March 1858.

6. *South Australian Register*, 17 January 1868.

7. *Wallaroo Times*, 29 January 1868.

8. *West Briton*, 17 May 1875.

9. *West Briton*, 17 May 1875.

10. Philip Payton, *The Cornish Miner in Australia: Cousin Jack Down Under*, Dyllansow Truran, Redruth, 1984, p.194.

11. Payton, 1984, p.194.

12. Payton, 1984, p.195.

13. Cited in Patricia Lay, *One and All: The Cornish in New South Wales*, Heritage 2000 Plus, Qeanbeyan (NSW), 1998, p.85.

14. Lay, 1998, pp.82-85; Payton, 1984, p.194.

15. Lay, 1998, pp.74-76.

16. *West Briton*, 7 January 1875.

17. *West Briton*, 14 June 1877.

18. Payton, 1984, p.190.

19. *Wallaroo Times*, 27 February 1867.

20. *Wallaroo Times*, 27 March 1867.

21. *Wallaroo Times*, 24 May 1867.

22. J.B. Jaquet, 'Early Days at the Barrier Ranges', *Geology of the Broken Hill Lode and Barrier Ranges Mineral Field, NSW*, Department of Mines, Sydney, 1894, Memoir No.5.

23. Donald Clark, *Australian Mining and Metallurgy*, Critchley Parker, London, 1904, p.337.

24. Fred Blakeley, *Hard Liberty: A Record of Experience*, Harrap, London, 1938, p.84.

25. Brian Kennedy, *Silver, Sin and Sixpenny Ale: A Social History of Broken Hill, 1883-1921*, Melbourne University Press, Melbourne, 1978, pp.16-17.

26. *Yorke's Peninsula Advertiser*, 27 November 1885.

27. Geoffrey Blainey, *The Rush That Never Ended: A History of Australian Mining*, Melbourne University Press, Melbourne, 1964, p.141.

28. Anon, *The Barrier Silver and Tin Fields in 1888*, 1888, repub. Libraries Board of SA, Adelaide, 1970, p.5.

29. *Yorke's Peninsula Advertiser*, 1 October 1886.

30. South Australian [State] Archives (SAA) BRG40/1034 Wallaroo and Moonta Mining and Smelting Company, Minute Books 1895-1923, 22 October 1895.

31. *Burra Record*, 28 February 1890; 1 February 1905.

32. *People's Weekly*, 11 May 1935.

33. Charles Rasp Library (Broken Hill) (CRL) Wesleyan Marriage Register for Silverton and Broken Hill, 1886-1893.

34. *Yorke's Peninsula Advertiser*, 1 June 1886.

35. Anon, 1888 & 1970, p.62.

36. Anon, 1888 & 1970, p.78.

37. Geoffrey Blainey, *The Rise of Broken Hill*, Macmillan, London, 1968; cited in Payton, 1984, pp. 148-148.

38. Payton, 1984, p.165.

39. W. R. Thomas, *In the Early Days: A Faithful Account of the Early Days of the Barrier Silver Field*, Barrier Miner, Broken Hill, 1889, pp.20-21.

40. Barrier Truth, 20 December 1901.

41. *Burra Record*, 23 March 1892.

42. Blainey, 1968, p.94.

43. Anon, 1888 & 1970, p.9.

44. CRL *Broken Hill South Church -Wesleyan Methodist Roll Book, 1892-1912*.

45. Thomas, 1889, p.20.

46. Kennedy, 1978, p.53.

47. *Yorke's Peninsula Advertiser*, 6 May 1887.

48. *Barrier Miner*, 28 March 1892.

49. *Burra Record*, 1 November 1891; 2 March 1892.

50. Clark, 1904, pp.342-344.

51. *Burra Record*, 21 September 1892.

52. *People's Weekly*, 16 December 1893.

53. *People's Weekly*, 17 June 1893.

54. *West Briton*, 23 April 1852.

55. *Kalgoorlie Western Argus*, 6 May 1897.

56. *People's Weekly*, 23 August 1894.

57. *People's Weekly*, 8 JOune 1895.

58. *People's Weekly*, 30 March 1895.

59. SAA PRG341 Letters written by Daniel and David Williams to their Parents while travelling Overland from Wallaroo to Perth through the Goldfields, 1894-96.

60. SAA PRG341.

# NOTES AND REFERENCES

61. SAA PRC341.

62. *Cornish Telegraph*, 15 November 1894.

63. *Kalgoorlie Western Argus*, 12 March 1896.

64. *People's Weekly*, 9 March 1895.

65. *South Australian Primitive Methodist*, July 1898.

66. *People's Weekly*, 6 December 1896.

67. *People's Weekly*, 6 December 1896.

68. SAA D3627(L), Stanley Whitford, *An Autobiography*, p.252.

69. *People's Weekly*, 12 January 1895.

70. *Kalgoorlie Western Argus*, 27 August 1896.

71. Payton, 1984, p.185.

72. Gavin Casey and Ted Mayman, *The Mile That Midas Touched*, Rigby, Adelaide, 1964, p.82.

73. *People's Weekly*, 1 August 1896.

74. Casey and Mayman, 1964, p.145.

75. I am indebted to Professor Geoffrey Bolton for this opinion.

76. Peter Heydon, *Quiet Decision: A Study of George Foster Pearce*, Melbourne University Press, Melbourne, 1965; cited in Payton, 1984, p.187.

77. *Kalgoorlie Western Argus*, 6 May 1897.

78. *Kalgoorlie Western Argus*, 6 May 1897.

79. W.B. Kimberley, *History of Western Australia*, Niven, Melbourne, 1897, p.177.

80. Kimberley, 1897, p.182.

81. Kimberley, 1897, p.181.

82. Joan Tiver, *Harry Kneebone: A Son of 'Little Cornwall'*, Adelaide, n.d. c.1990.

83. *People's Weekly*, 28 September 1901.

## Chapter 10: New Frontiers – North America

1. Robert Louis Stevenson, *Across the Plains*, 1876, cited in A.L. Rowse, *The Cornish in America*, Macmillan, London, 1969, repub. Dyllansow Truran, Redruth, 1991, pp.255-256.

2. Cited in John Rowe, *The Hard-Rock Men: Cornish Immigrants and the North American Mining Frontier*, Liverpool University Press, Liverpool, 1974, p.131; see also A.C. Todd and David James, *Ever Westward the Land: Samuel James and Cornish Family on the trail to Oregan and the Pacific North West 1842-52*, University of Exeter Press, Exeter, 1986.

3. *Pauline Harman Collection*, Letter from Daniel Bullock to his sister Naomi, 25 June 1848.

4. Collamer M. Abbott, 'Cornish Miners in Appalachian Copper Camps', *International Review of the History of Banking*, No.7, 1973, p.199.

5. Collamer M. Abbott, 'Thomas Pollard - Cornish Miner', *International Review of the History of Mining*, No.6, 1973.

6. Collamer, No.7, 1973, pp.218-219.

7. Rodman Wilson Paul, *Mining Frontiers of the Far West 1848-1880*, Holt, Rinehart and Winston, New York, 1963, p.38.

8. Paul, 1963, p.140.

9. Paul, 1963, p.69.

10. Cited in Paul, 1963, p.115.

11. Paul, 1963, p.128.

12. Mark Wyman, *Hard Rock Epic: Western Miners and the Industrial Revolution 1860-1910*, University of California Press, Berkeley, 1979, p.43.

13. Richard E. Lingenfelter, *The Hardrock Miners: A History of the Mining Labour Movement in the American West 1863-1893*, University of California Press, Berkeley, 1974, p.6.

14. Lingenfelter, 1974, p.6.

15. Cited in Rowe, 1974, pp. 136-136.

16. *Mining Journal*, 21 May 1864.

17. H. Kalman, *A History of Canadian Architecture*, Oxford University Press, Toronto, 1994, Vol. 1, p.398; Mark de Caraffe et al, *Towns of Canada: A Collection of Essays on Pre-1930 Town Hall Buildings*, National Historic Parks and Sites, Ottawa, 1987, p.233; Dorothy Mindenhall, '"Work and Win": John Teague (1835-1902), Cornish Architect and Migrant Adventurer in Victoria, British Columbia, Canada', unpub. PhD thesis, University of Exeter, 2002.

18. Cited in Rowe, 1974, p.187.

19. *West Briton*, 31 January 1871.

20. Rowe, 1974, p.183.

21. *West Briton*, 19 July 1894.

22. Ronald M. James, 'Defining the Group: Nineteenth-Century Cornish on the North American Mining Frontier', in Philip Payton (ed.), *Cornish Studies: Two*, University of Exeter Press, Exeter, 1994, p.32.

23. James, 1994, pp.38-39.

24. Rowe, 1974, p.180.

25. Eliot Lord, *Comstock Mining and Miners*, GPO, Washington, 1883, p.386.

26. *Daily News* (Gold Hill), 21 March 1864; *Territorial Enterprise* (Virginia City), 22 March 1864.

27. Lingenfelter, 1974, p.34.

28. *Daily News*, 16 September 1864; 29 September 1864.

29. Cited in Lingenfelter, 1974, p.43.

30. *Territorial Enterprise*, 3 February 1878.

31. *Territorial Enterprise*, 20 December 1874; see also *West Briton*, 28 January 1875; *Cornish Telegraph*, 3 February 1875; Keith Skues, *Cornish Heritage*, Werner Shaw, London, 1983, pp.273-274.

32. Wells Drury, *An Editor on the Comstock Lode*, 1936, repub. University of Nevada Press, Reno, 1984, p.122.

33. Drury, 1936 & 1984, p.71.

34. A.C. Todd, *The Cornish Miner in America*, Bradford Barton, Truro, 1967, repub. Arthur H. Clarke, Spokane (Washington), 1995, p.106.

35. Audio Tape of Ballads sung by Richard Jose, prepared by Joe Pengelly. I am extremely grateful to Mr Pengelly for putting his extensive collection of Jose material at my disposal.

36. Wells, 1936 & 1984, p.60.

37. Wells, 1936 & 1984, p.90.

38. Wells, 1936 & 1984, p.70.

39. Wells, 1936 & 1984, pp.70-71.

40. Wells, 1936 & 1984, p.88.

41. Wells, 1936 & 1984, p.89.

42. Wells, 1936 & 1884, p.71.

43. *West Briton*, 17 July 1873.

44. Rowe, 1974, p.191.

45. W.M. McPhee, 'Vignettes of Park City', *Utah Historical Quarterly*, XXXIII, p.289.

46. Paul, 1963, p.122.

47. Rowse, 1969 & 1991, pp.324-330.

48. Rowse, 1969 & 1991, p.331.

49. 'Mary Stevens, nee Wall', unpub. MS in the possession of Carleen Harry.

50. Lingenfelter, 1974, p.103.

51. Lingenfelter, 1974, p.104.

52. Cited in Wyman, 1979, p.42.

53. Rowse, 1969 & 1991, p.386.

54. Rowe, 1974, p.221.

55. Wyman, 1979, p.42.

56. Todd, 1967 & 1995, p.241.

57. Rowse, 1969 & 1991, p.352.

58. Rowse, 1969 & 1991, p.360.

59. C.B. Glassock, *The War of the Copper Kings*, 1932, repub. Grosset & Dunlap, New York, 1966, pp.77-78.

60. Glassock, 1932 & 1966, pp.96-97.

61. Rowse, 1969 & 1991, p.353.

62. *Independent* (Helena), 20 February 1889.

63. Lingenfelter, p.189.

64. Cited in Lingenfelter, 1974, pp.191-192.

65. Lingenfelter, p.193.

66. Lingenfelter, p.225.

67. Todd, 1967 & 1995, pp.241-242.

68. Rowe, 1974, p.247.

## Chapter 11: 'But a Suburb of Cornwall' – South Africa

1. *West Briton*, 6 February 1879. The Union Bank's assets were later aqcuired by Bolitho's Bank of Penzance, which in turn was swallowed up in the Barclays empire.

2. *West Briton*, 31 March 1879.

3. J. Henry Harris, *Cornish Saints and Sinners*, Bodley head, London, 1906, pp.225-226.

4. Mark Brayshay, 'Depopulation and Changing Household Structure in the Mining Communities of West Cornwall, 1851–71', in Dennis Mills and Kevin Schurer (eds.), *Local Communities in the Victorian Census Enumerators' Books*, Leopard's Head Press, Oxford, 1996.

5. *People's Weekly*, 24 May 1924.

6. *People's Weekly*, 21 August 1920.

7. *West Briton*, 9 February 1880.

8. Richard D. Dawe, *Cornish Pioneers in South Africa: Gold and Diamonds, Copper and Blood*, Cornish Hillside, St Austell, 1998, p.119. I am deeply grateful to the late Richard Dawe for his permission to draw upon his various published and unpublished works, and his collection of photographs.

9. Dawe, 1998, p.119.

10. *West Briton*, 24 September 1896.

11. *West Briton*, 1 September 1898.

12. *Cornishman*, 21 November 1895; Dawe, 1998, pp.122-123.

13. C. Lewis Hind, *Days in Cornwall*, 2nd ed., London, 1907, p.352.

14. Harris, 1906, pp.217-218.

15. Horst Rossler, 'Constantine Stonemasons in Search of Work Abroad, 1870-1900', in Philip Payton (ed.), *Cornish Studies: Two*, University of Exeter Press, Exeter, 1994.

16. *Cape Argus*, 30 November 1912; *West Briton*, 17 January 1887.

17. *West Briton*, 12 April 1877.

18. Graham B. Dickason, *Cornish Immigrants to South Africa: The Cousin Jacks' Contribution to the Development of Mining and Commerce, 1820-1920*,

# NOTES AND REFERENCES

Balkema, Cape Town, 1978, p.39.

19. Dawe, 1998, p.10.

20. *West Briton*, 23 January 1868.

21. A.L. Rowse, *The Controversial Colensos*, Dyllansow Truran, Redruth, 1989, p.3; The Cornish played an important role in the colonisation of New Zealand flora in the United Kingdom, see also Paul Star, 'John Enys: Cornish Patron of New Zealand Science', *Journal of the Royal Institution of Cornwall*, new series II, Vol.ll, Pt.3, 1996.

22. H. Rider Haggard, *Days of My Life*, London, 1926, p.66.

23. Rowse, 1989, p.86.

24. Dawe,1998, pp.54-57.

25. Dawe, 1998, p.62.

26. *West Briton*, 9 November 1876.

27. Cyril Noall, *The St Just Mining District*, Bradford Barton, Truro, 1973, p.14.

28. Noall, 1973.

29. *Cornishman*, 19 July 1888; Dawe, 1988, p.64.

30. Dawe, 1998, p.69.

31. L.V. Praagh (ed.), *The Transvaal and Its Mines: The Encyclopedic History of the Transvaal*, Praagh and Lloyd, London and Johannesburg, 1906, p.311.

32. *Cornishman*, 4 November 1896; Dawe, 1998, p.79.

33. Dawe, 1998, p.85.

34. Dawe, 1998, p.85.

35. *West Briton*, 6 December 1839.

36. Henry Cecil Blackwell, *From A Dark Stream: The Story of Cornwall's Amazing People and their Impact on the World*, Dyllansow Truran, Redruth, 1986, p.226.

37. *Mining Journal*, 1 August 1903.

38. *The Kolar Goldfield*, Kolar Goldfield Mining Board, Kolar (India), 1946.

39. Dawe, 1998, p.xv.

40. Dawe, 1998, p.90.

41. Dickason, 1978, p.62.

42. Dickason, 1978, p.62.

43. David Mudd, *Cornishmen and True*, Frank Graham, Newcastle-upon-Tyne, 1971, p.33.

44. Mudd, 1971, p.34.

45. *Cornishman*, 15 March 1900; Dawe, 1998, p.110.

46. *Cornish Post*, 30 January 1896; Dawe, 1998, p.138.

47. *West Briton*, 27 January 1896.

48. *People's Weekly*, 7 April 1900.

49. *Cornish Post*, 20 February 1896; Dawe, 1998, p.141.

50. Dawe, 1998, p.144.

51. *Cornish Post*, 12 October 1899.

52. *Cornish Post*, 12 October 1899.

53. *Cornish Post*, 11 January 1900; Dawe, 1998, p.150.

54. *West Briton*, 7 December 1899.

55. Henry Pelling, *The Social Geography of British Elections 1885-1910*, Macmillan, London, 1962, p.164.

56. John Rowe, *The Hard-Rock Men: Cornish Immigrants and the North American Mining Frontier*, Liverpool University Press, Liverpool, 1974, p.292.

57. Pelling, 1962, p.165.

58. Richard Dawe, 'The Role and Influence of the Cornish in South Africa 1886-1923', unpub. MA dissertation, Middlesex Polytechnic, 1986, p.48.

59. *Cornish Post*, 27 September 1900.

60. A. L. Rowse, *Quiller Couch: A Portrait of 'Q'*, Methuen, London, 1988, p.81.

61. Dawe, 1998, pp.177-183.

62. *Mining Journal*, 2 April 1904.

63. *Comubian*, 20 January 1906.

64. *West Briton*, 23 April 1906.

65. *Western Morning News*, 19 January 1906.

66. *Cornish Post*, 20 December 1906.

67. A.K. Hamilton Jenkin, *The Cornish Miner*, 1927, David & Charles, Newton Abbot, 1972, p.330.

68. *West Briton*, 29 December 1898.

69. Wemmer Gold Mining Co. Ltd, Presentation Address, 1 July 1904, in the possession of Mr Paddy Bradley of Redruth.

70. Gillian Burke and Peter Richardson, 'The Profits of Death: A Comparative Study of Miners' Phthisis in Cornwall and the Transvaal, 1876-1918', unpub. paper, November 1977; see also Gillian Burke, 'The Cornish Diaspora of the Nineteenth century', in Shula Marks and Peter Richardson (eds), *International Labour Migration; Historical Perspectives*, Temple Smith, London, 1984, p.63.

71. Dawe, 1998, p.225.

72. *Transvaal Leader*, 24 September 1907; Dawe, 1998, p.235.

73. Cited in *Cornish Post*, 11 July 1907.

74. I am grateful to Alison Shipwright for details regarding Will Bosanko.

75. Bernard Hollowood, *Cornish Engineers*, Holmans, Camborne, 1951, p.90.

76. Dawe, 1998, pp.298-302.

## Chapter 12: All Hail! Old Cornwall! May Thy Glory Last' – The End of an Era

1. See Philip Payton, *Cornwall*, Alexander Associates, Fowey, 1996, Chapter 9.

2. For a discussion of the dynamics of culture change in modern Cornwall, see Philip Payton, *The Making of Modern Cornwall. Historical Experience and the Persistence of 'Difference'*, Dyllansow Truran, Redruth, 1992.

3. Reprinted in *Cornish History Network Newsletter*, No.1,.Spring 1998; I am indebted to Sharron Schwartz for drawing my attention to this important poem.

4. James Dryden Hosken, *Shores of Lyonesse*, Dent, London, n.d., p.106.

5. Hosken, n.d., p.108.

6. W. Herbert Thomas, *Poems of Cornwall by Thirty Cornish Authors*, Rodda, Penzance, 1892, p.iv; I am indebted to Dr.Alan M. Kent for drawing my attention to this and other Cornish literary material.

7. J.D. Hosken, *Poems and Songs of Cornwall*, p.34.

8. Mark Guy Pearse, *West Country Songs*, Horace Marshall, London, n.d., pp.56-65.

9. Joseph Hocking, *What Shall It Profit a Man?*, Hodder and Stoughton, London, n.d., p.21.

10. Silas K. Hocking, *The Lost Lode*, Sampson Low, Maiston & Co., London, n.d., p.13.

11. Silas Hocking, n.d., pp. 14-15.

12. J. Henry Harris, *The Luck of Wheal Vor and Other Stories*, Pollard, Truro, 1901, pp.85-91.

13. D.H. Lawrence, 'Samson and Delilah', in *England, My England*, 1922, repub. Penguin, London, 1960, p.126.

14. Lawrence, 1922 & 1960, p.141.

15. Newton G. Thomas, *The Long Winter Ends*, 1941, repub. Wayne University Press, Detroit, 1998.

16. Phyllis Somerville, *Not Only in Stone*, 1942, repub. Rigby, Adelaide, 1973.

17. *People's Weekly*, 12 July 1890.

18. *Commercial, Shipping and General Advertiser for West Cornwall*, 5 April 1890.

19. John Langdon Bonython, *Cornwall. Interesting History and Romantic Stories, Talks at Meetings of the Cornish Association of South Australia*, Advertiser, Adelaide, 1932, p.17.

20. *People's Weekly*, 14 July 1923.

21. *Christian Weekly and Methodist Journal*, 5 September 1890; D.M. Charleston, *Universal Depression: Its Cause and Cure*, Adelaide, 1895; D.M. Charleston, *What is Sociology?*, Adelaide, n.d., D.M. Charleston, *New Unionism*, Adelaide, 1890.

22. *People's Weekly*, 25 June 1910.

23. T.H. Smeaton, *The People in Politics: A Short History of the Labor Movement in South Australia, 1891-1914*, Co-op Publishing, Adelaide, 1914, p.17.

24. *Australian Christian Commonwealth*, 1 November 1911.

25. South Australian [State] Archives (SAA) D3627(L), Stanley Whitford, *An Autobiography*, addendum by Sir Lennon Raws.

26. *South Australian Department of Mines Mining Review*, Half Year ended June 1919, p.53; see also H. Lipson Hancock, 'Welfare Work in the Mining Industry', *Australian Chemical Engineering and Mining Review*, October 1918.

27. H. Lipson Hancock, *Modern Methods in Sunday School Work*, Methodist Book Depot, Adelaide, 1916, pp.20; H. Lipson Hancock and William Shaw, *A Sunday School of Today*, Hussey and Gillingham, Adelaide, 1912, pp.21-22; H. Lipson Hancock and William R. Penhall, *The Missionary Sprint in Sunday School Work*, 1918.

28. Gage McKinney (ed.), *Four Mining Engineers at New Almaden* by T.A. Rickard, New Almaden Quicksilver County Park Association, New Almaden, 1995, p.51.

29. McKinney, pp.53-54.

30. Postcard in the possession of Valentine Tonkin; I am indebted to Valentine Tonkin for permission to draw from her collection of family photographs and postcards.

31. Postcard in the possession of Valentine Tonkin.

32. Photograph and postcard in the possession of Valentine Tonkin.

33. Niall Ferguson, *The Pity of War*, Allen Lane, London, 1998, p.xxi. A quarter of all Scots who fought in the Great War were killed. What proportion of Cornish sailors, soldiers and airmen died, one wonders?

34. C.J.H. Mead, *Cornwall's Royal Engineers*, Underhill, Plymouth, n.d., c.1947, pp. 176-177.

35. Henry Cecil Blackwell, *From A Dark Stream: The Story of Cornwall's Amazing People and their Impact on the World*, Dyllansow Truran, Redruth, 1986, pp.147–158.

36. Tom Wesley Hicks Whetter, 'Canadian Pioneer',

*Cornish Banner*, Vol.2., No.8, September 1979.

37. *People's Weekly*, 11 August 1916.

38. *People's Weekly*, 28 August 1915.

39. Harry Pascoe, 'Cornishmen and Emigration: The Adventurous Cornish Miner', in *Cornwall Education Handbook*, Cornwall County Council, Truro, 1927, p.145.

40. *People's Weekly*, 15 March 1916.

41. *People's Weekly*, 6 January 1917.

42. *People's Weekly*, 6 January 1917.

43. Oswald Pryor, *Australia's Little Cornwall*, Rigby, Adelaide, 1962, pp.148-149.

44. John Rowe, 'The Declining Years of Cornish Tin Mining', in Jeffrey Porter (ed.), Education and Labour in the South West, *Exeter Papers in Economic History*, No. 10, University of Exeter, Exeter, 1975, p.67.

45. *Cornish Post*, 29 October 1919.

46. Cited in Bernard Deacon, 'The Inter-War Years: Making it Work, 1920-28' in Gordon McCallum (ed.), *A Story of Adult Education in Cornwall: 70 years of the WEA*, Weavers Press, Zennor, n.d c.1991, p.25.

47. John Rowe, 'Cornish Mining Crisis in the 1920s', *Cornish Banner*, August 1986.

48. *Cornish Arms Hotel Bulletin*, No. 14, 5 October 1921.

49. Harold Evans, *The American Century*, Jonathan Cape, London, 1998, p.220.

50. A.L. Rowse, *The Cornish in America*, Macmillan, London, 1969, repub. Dyllansow Truran, redruth, 1991, p.422.

51. Richard White, 'Growing Up Cornish in Michigan', *Cornish Banner*, Vol.2, No.5, December 1978.

52. Roger Lescohier, *Gold Giants of Grass Valley: History of the Empire and North Star Mines, 1850-1956*, Empire Mine Park Association, Grass Valley, 1995, p.102.

53. *People's Weekly*, 19 July 1919.

54. Wallaroo & Moonta Mining & Smelting Co. Ltd. (in Liquidation): *Catalogue of Machinery, Plant & Stores for Sale*, copy held by Kadina Branch of the National Trust for South Australia.

55. K.W. Thomson, 'The Changes in Function of Former Mining Settlements: The Wallaroo Copper Belt', in *Proceedings of the Royal Geological Society of Australia*, South Australian Branch, 56:47-58, 1955, p.57.

56. Thomson, 1955, p.57.

57. *People's Weekly*, 15 September 1927.

58. *People's Weekly*, 10 June 1933.

59. *Minutes of Committee Meetings of the Cornish Association of South Australia*, 30 August 1930.

60. *People's Weekly*, 15 May 1909 to 24 December 1910 inclusive.

61. SAA PRG96, *Oswald Pryor Papers*, Correspondence, Phillips to Pryor, 22 December 1932.

62. SAA PRG96, Thomas to Pryor, c.1930.

63. A.K. Hamilton Jenkin, *The Cornish Miner*, 1927, repub. David & Charles, Newton Abbot, 1972, p.328.

64. Hamilton Jenkin, p.329.

## Chapter 13: An Enduring Identity? The Cornish in a Globalised World

1. Philip Payton, *The Making of Modern Cornwall*, Dyllansow Truran, Redruth, 1992, pp.202, 213-217 and 231.

2. Vic Lawry, 'Apartheid: The Other Side of the Coin', *Cornish Banner*, No.35, February 1984, p.9.

3. *Cornubian Newsletter*, November 1949.

4. Yvonne R. Lockwood and William G. Lockwood, 'Pasties in Michigan's Upper Peninsula: Foodways, Interethnic relations, and Regionalism', in Stephen Stern and John Allan Cicala, eds., *Creative Ethnicity: Symbols and Strategies of Contemporary Ethnic Life*, Utah State University Press, Logan (Utah), 1991, pp.3-20.

5. Maldwyn A. Jones, *Destination America*, Weidenfeld and Nicholson, London, 1976, p.247.

6. Gage McKinney, *When Miners Sang: The Grass Valley Carol Choir*, Comstock, Grass Valley, 2001, p.239.

7. McKinney, 2001, p.239.

8. McKinney, 2001, p.240.

9. McKinney, 2001, pp.240-242.

10. McKinney, 2001, p.243.

11. See Philip Payton, 'Re-inventing Celtic Australia: Notions of Celtic Identity from the Colonial Period to the Era of Multiculturalism', *Australian Studies*, Vol. 12, No.2, Winter 1997.

12. Charles Price, 'The Cornish of Australia: An Invisible Minority with Distinctive Surnames', in Andrea McRobbie, *Arrivals, Departures, Achievements: Essays in Honour of James Jupp*, Australian National University, Canberra, 1992, pp.38–42.

13. White, 1978.

14. Violet A. Thomas, 'A Cornish Home in America', *Cornish Banner*, No.34., November 1983.

15. Anita Van Adelsbergen, 'Cousin Jack's Utopia:

Cornish-Americans in the USA', unpub. doctoral dissertation, University of Utrecht, 1997, p.27.

16. Roslyn M. Paterson, *Thankyou Walter Watson Hughes: Essays on Northern Yorke Peninsula*, Cornish Association of South Australia, Adelaide, 1993, pp.105-106.

17. Patricia Lay (ed.), *Cornish-Australian Heritage: A Biographical Register of Cornish-Australians, 1788–1998*, Volume 1, Heritage 2000, Qeanbeyan (NSW) 1999, pp.315-316.

18. See Philip Payton and Victoria Syme, 'Eastern Europe: Economic Transition and Ethnic Tension', in Michael Pugh (ed.), *European Security: Toward 2000*, Manchester University Press, Manchester, 1992; Philip Payton, 'Ethnicity in Western Europe Today', in Karl Cordell (ed.), *Ethnicity and Democratisation in the New Europe*, Routledge, London, 1998.

19. Bernard Deacon and Philip Payton, 'Re-inventing Cornwall: Culture Change on the European Periphery', in Philip Payton (ed.), *Cornish Studies: One*, University of Exeter Press, Exeter, 1993.

20. For example, see Gage McKinney, 'Culture Bearers: Cornish Bards in North America', in *Keltic Fringe*, Vol.XII, No. 1, Spring 1997; Vol.Xll, No.2, Summer 1997.

21. *Western Morning News*, 16 September 1997.

22. R.K. Johns, *Cornish Mining Heritage*, South Australian Government *Department of Mines and Energy*, Adelaide, 1986. p5.

23. Johns, 1986, p.48.

24. *Map Kernow Leaflet*, District Council of Kapunda, c. 1989; see also Philip Payton, 'Re-inventing Celtic Australia', in Amy Hale and Philip Payton (eds.), *New Directions in Celtic Studies*, University of Exeter Press, Exeter, 2000, pp.122-123.

25. Juanita Kennedy Browne, *Thomasina and the Tommyknocker*, Browne Books, San Diego, 1993; Daniel Mason, *Cousin Jack*, Alexander Associates, Fowey, 1996.

26. Alan M. Kent, *Cousin Jack's Mouth Organ: Travels in Cornish America*, Cornish Hillside, St Austell, 2004.

27. D.M. Thomas, 'A Cornish Graveyard at Keeweenaw', *Cornish Review*, 24, Summer 1973, pp.63-64.

28. D.M. Thomas, *Memories and Hallucinations*, Macmillan, London, 1988, p19.

29. Thomas, 1988, p.115.

30. Thomas, 1988, p.192.

31. Sharron Schwartz and Roger Parker, *Lanner: A Cornish Mining Parish*, Halgrove, Tiverton, 1998; see also Philip Payton, 'The New Cornish Historiography', in Philip Payton (ed.), *Cornish Studies: Five*, University of Exeter Press, Exeter, 1997.

32. Bernard Deacon, *The Cornish Family: The Roots of Our Future*, Cornwall Editions, Fowey, 2005.

33. Robin Cohen, *Global Diasporas: An Introduction*, UCL Press, London, 1997, pp.173–175.

34. Bernard Deacon, Andrew George, Ronald Perry, *Cornwall at the Crossroads? Living Communities or Leisure Zone?*, Cornish Social and Economic Research Group, Redruth, 1988, p.157.

35. Deacon, George, Perry, 1988, p.159; see also Ronald Perry et al, *Counterurbanisation: Inter-National Case Studies of Socio-Economic Change in Rural Areas*, Geo Books, Norwich, 1988.

36. Chris Dunkerley, 'The Cornish in Australia, with a Celtic Perspective', unpub. paper presented at the Conference on Cornwall, Perranporth, May 1992.

37. Gage McKinney, 'Cornwall's Enduring Identity', unpub. paper, 1998.

38. Tom Nairn, *After Britain: New Labour and the Return of Scotland*, Granta Books, London, 2000, p.14.

39. *The Independent*, 6 July 2004.

40. *The Independent*, 6 July 2004.

# INDEX

Note: Page references in *italics* refer to maps.

## A

Abbott, Collamer M. 325

Abbott, Samuel 265

Abraham, William 397

Adams family 88, 385

Adburgham, Alison 52

agriculture 90; Australia 49–52, 77, 85, 164, 175, 184, 232, 237, 248, 254, 258, 271–5, 300; Britain 267–8; Canada 66, 68, 71, 72; Cornwall 56, 268; New Zealand 44, 268, 269–70; South Africa 65; United States 61, 63–4, 111, 112, 137–8, 147, 209, 215, 325

Alaska 326

Alberta 39

*Alchemyst* (ship) 66, 70

alcoholism 115, 126, 144, 158, 190, 226, 241, 242, 333

Allen, Hibow 404

Allen family 97, 132, 138

Altarnun 76, 85, 272, 407

Amadas, Captain 30

Amalgamated Miners' Association (AMA, Australia) 251, 294, 312, 313, 321, 385

American Civil War 138, 143, 154, 257–8

An Gof rebellion 415–16

Andrew family 115, 395

Andrewartha family 168, 196, 301

Angas, George Fife 172, 176

Angier, Sampson 33

Anglesey 18, 95

Angove family 214, 264, 272, 293, 312, 356

Angwin family 312, 372

Annear family 121, 278

Antony, Captain A. 269, 284

*Arethusa* (ship) 39

Argall family 214, 253

Argentina 39

Arizona 326, 340–1, 347, 405

Arnold, Rollo 269–70

Artha, Henry and Richard 103

Arundell family 30, 32

Asbury family 37

*Ascendant* (ship) 181

Askew, Jack 'Skewers' 336

*Asp* (whaler) 92

*Atlanta* (ship) 264

*Atlantic* (convict ship) 47

*Augusta Schneider* (barque) 238

*Auriga* (ship) 120

Australia *162, 229*; Aborigines 41, 43, 45, 46, 82, 318, 407; Botany Bay 41, 42, 43; emigration to 76, 266, 268, 401; ethnicity 321, 405, 407–9, 411; exploration 40–1; penal colony 42–4, 45–52, 73; politics 197, 251–2, 255, 290, 294–5, 321–2; settlement 52–3, 73, 323; voyages to 73–5, 83–4, 86, 258 *see also states by name*

*Australian Christian Commonwealth* magazine 320, 386

Austrian miners 339, 341, 346

Axford, J.H. 372

Ayers, Henry 169–70, 173, 181–3, 186, 190, 198, 199

## B

Bagot, Charles 164

Baines, Dudley 11, 19, 28

Banks, Sir Joseph 41, 44

Barker family 72, 328

Barkla family 86, 282

Barratt, Captain 104

Barrett family 86, 230

*Barrier Miner* 313

*Barrier Truth* 311

Barton, D.B. 197

Basset, John 95–6

Bastian family 165, 247, 273, 312

Batavia 48

Bath family 166, 171, 231

# INDEX

123–7; Montana 341; N. Territory, Australia 301; Nevada 328–9, 331–2; New South Wales 228, 231, 233, 234–5, 301–2, 304–5; New Zealand 23, 271, 297, 298; Queensland 299–300; South Africa 358–9, 371, 372; South Australia 250; South Dakota 146, 326, 340; Victoria 23, 117, 173, 174, 182, 183, 194, 200, 228, 235–9, 247–8, 254; Virginia 201, 203, 325; Western Australia 121, 315–17, 319

Goldsworthy family 64, 87, 107, 167, 183, 214, 312, 397

*Gosforth* (ship) 260

Gowling family 276

Goyne, William 239

granite 21, 22, 23, 353 *see also* stonemasons

*Grass Valley National* 216

*Grass Valley Telegraph* 327

*Grass Valley Union* 214, 216

Gray family 279, 309

Great Emigration 9–10, 15, 16–17, 19–20, 26, 28–9, 56, 57, 93, 96, 127, 397–9, 414

Great Reform Act (1832) 10, 57

Greenhill, Basil 68

Greenway, Thomas 71

Gregor family 22, 126–7, 167

Grenfell family 84, 97, 230, 251, 338, 339

Grenville, Sir Richard 30–1, 38

Gribble family 115, 215

Grigg family 181, 268, 269, 270–1, 347, 353

Grose family 23–4, 103, 104, 107, 155, 157

Growden family 35

Grubb family 36

Grylls family 88, 133, 168

Gulval 240, 358

Gummow, William 165–6, 236

Gundry family 106, 165, 180, 271–2, 325

Gunnislake 279, 354, 393

Gurney family 120

Gweek 56, 347

Gwennap 125, 348, 350; emigrants 77, 85, 113, 114, 121, 266, 354, 372, 385; mining 97, 101, 140, 262, 267

Gwinear 96, 394

**H**

H. Sims, Scorrier 114

Hacker, Shyrle Pedlar 27

Haggard, H. Rider 355

Hall family 145, 354

Hallam, Judge Oscar 137

Halse family 120, 191, 192

Ham family 61, 366

Hambley, William 319

Hambly, Loveday 35, 36

Hambly Harris family 124

Hamilton Jenkin, A.K. 16, 18, 197, 288, 371–2, 398

Hammer, John 239

Hampton, Jeremiah 115

Hancock, Captain Henry Richard 261, 278, 281–3, 322, 350, 386

Hancock, H. Lipson 283, 306, 386–7

Hancock family 139, 196, 249, 293, 360

Hansen, Harold 404

*Harbinger* (ship) 77

Hargreaves, Edward Hammon 230–1

Harmer, James 84

Harper, Richard Bailey 204

Harris, J. Henry 350, 352–3, 381–2

Harris family 32, 143, 145, 165, 167, 181, 273, 279, 342, 372

Harry family 115, 196, 205, 206–7, 215, 310, 360

Harvard College 34–5

Harvey & Co., Hayle 99, 105, 106, 121, 169, 171, 281, 354, 357, 360, 390

Harvey family 230, 240, 241, 307, 325

Hawaii 39

Hawke family 73, 196, 228, 231, 251, 308, 321

Hawken, John and Catherine 230

Hawker, Rev. Robert Stephen 58–9, 132, 287

Hawkin, Richard 196

Hayes family 193

Hayle 66, 85, 96, 104, 114, 138, 215, 269, 350, 397

Haywood, Johnson Frederick 189, 190

health and disease: Australia 23, 64–5, 84, 189–90, 239, 241, 279, 306, 312, 313, 318; Latin America 100, 103, 115; South Africa 371, 373–4, 375;

# INDEX

# INDEX

# INDEX

## R

Rabling family 110, 111

Raby family 126, 328

*Rajah* (ship) 176

*Rakaia* (ship) 270

Raleigh, Sir Walter 30

Ransome, Frederick L. 327

Rapson family 107

Rasp, Charles 'German Charlie' 305

Rawle family 35–6

*Red Admiral* (ship) 85

Redruth 109, 133, 351, 414; agents 114, 120, 238, 259, 265; depression 263, 348, 350, 351–2, 393, 394; emigrants 57, 64, 77, 85, 86, 96, 107, 113, 114, 127, 136, 140, 146, 151, 163, 165, 167, 171, 172, 204, 257, 264, 266, 270, 279, 299, 302, 306, 312, 328, 350, 352, 354, 362, 365, 375, 394; mining 256–7, 262, 267

Redruth Institution 116

Reed, Joseph 254

*Register* (Adelaide) 241, 249, 298–9

Reinhart, Comel J. 119

religion 14, 45, 57, 58, 193–4, 246, 294–5, 337, 355 *see also* Bible Christians; Civil War; Methodism; Non-conformism; Primitive Methodists

*Rembang* (East Indiaman) 48

Remfrey family 139

remittances 26, 94, 109, 115, 126, 259, 332, 350, 351–3, 365, 375, 378

Rendell family 272

*Republican* (Queensland) 300

Rescarrick family 35

Reseigh, George 205

*Resolution* (ship) 39, 41

Retallack family 113

Retallick family 24, 279, 299, 307, 309, 397

Reynolds family 120, 269, 353

Rhodes, Cecil 334, 356, 358–9, 365

Rhodesia 376

Rich, Captain Thomas 103

Richard Hallett & Sons, London 169, 170

Richards, James 'Fiddler Jim' 289

Richards family 65, 84, 87, 107, 108, 120, 139, 166, 183, 191, 192, 214, 225, 226, 236, 238, 293, 307, 341, 375

Richardson, Peter 373

Rickard, Donald S. 139

Rickard, T.A. 144–5, 338, 387–8

Rickard family 214, 254, 299, 388, 412

Roach family 122, 167, 169, 170, 180, 184, 190, 240, 247, 261, 282, 333

Robartes, Captain 99

Robert, William 253–4

Roberts family 166, 199, 208–9, 210, 214, 231, 237, 309, 319, 376, 384

Robins family 165, 179, 199

Roche 62, 121, 199, 271, 358

Rodda family 19, 172, 176, 177, 214, 239, 251, 274, 319, 354

Roe, Richard 183

Rogers family 199, 301, 307, 357, 389

Roosevelt, Franklin D. 396

Roscarrock, William 32

Rosevear(e) family 72, 107, 297, 298

Rosewarne family 306, 307, 412

Roskelly, William 264

Rossler, Horst 21, 22, 353

*Rounsdad* (ship) 278

Rous/Rous/Rowse family 30, 312, 337

Rowe, John 9, 135, 136, 139, 142, 147, 174, 219, 329, 330, 393–4

Rowe, Rev. James 189, 192–3, 194, 195, 196–7

Rowe family 62, 73–4, 102, 139, 172, 186, 196, 205, 215, 244, 247–8, 251, 270, 293, 308, 312, 319, 320, 339, 343, 346, 359, 394, 397

Rowett family 185, 214

Rowse, A.L. 9, 20–1, 32, 135, 137, 146–7, 156, 203, 355, 368–9

*Royal Admiral* (ship) 413

*Royal Cornwall Gazette* 55–6, 59, 65, 66, 96, 114, 210, 238, 267

*Royal Gazette* (Charlottetown) 68

Royal Geological Society of Cornwall 105, 174, 282

Royal Navy 37, 38–9, 43, 390